VOL. XVII

# INSURRECTIONS, WARS, AND
# THE EASTERN CRISIS IN THE 1870s

## BELA K. KIRALY AND GALE STOKES
## EDITORS

SOCIAL SCIENCE MONOGRAPHS, BOULDER
DISTRIBUTED BY COLUMBIA UNIVERSITY PRESS , NEW YORK

1985

ATLANTIC STUDIES
BROOKLYN COLLEGE STUDIES ON SOCIETY AND CHANGE
No. 36

# TABLE OF CONTENTS

# III.
## Insurrections and Wars in the Balkans

## IV
## Peacemaking

## V
## Repercussions of the Insurrections and Wars on Armed Forces

## VI
## Conclusions

# Acknowledgments

The Program on Society in Change conducts research, organizes conferences, and publishes scholarly books. It has been encouraged, and supported by Brooklyn College. The National Endowment for the Humanities awarded it a research grant for 1978–81 and renewed it for another three-year term (1981–84). Without this substantial and much appreciated support, the Program would not exist. Additional contributions helped us in completing the research, holding conferences, and covering the costs of preparation of the manuscript for publication. Financial aid was granted by the International Research and Exchanges Board and the American Council of Learned Societies.

The copy-editing was done by Barbara Metzger and the preparation of the manuscript for publication by Dorothy Meyerson, Jonathan A. Chanis, and Maurice Leibenstern of the Brooklyn College Program on Society in Change. The maps were drafted by Robert Garitta.

Most of the essays contained in this book were read at the XIIIth Brooklyn College Conference on Society in Change held at Varna, Bulgaria, September 20–23, 1983. The host of this conference was the Institute of Balkan Studies of the Bulgarian Academy of Sciences. The Institute was a generous host, establishing the most pleasant atmosphere possible for this international, interdisciplinary conference. The organization of the conference and its administration were the work of Nikolai Todorov, Pantaley Shterev, and Simeon Damianov.

To all these institutions and personalities, I wish to express my most sincere appreciation and thanks.

Highland Lakes, New Jersey  
March 15, 1985

Béla K. Király  
Professor Emeritus of History  
Editor-in-Chief

# Preface to the Series

The present volume is the seventeenth in a series that, when completed, will constitute a comprehensive survey of the many aspects of war and society in East Central Europe. The chapters of this and forthcoming volumes have been selected from papers presented at a series of international, interdisciplinary scholarly conferences conducted by the Brooklyn College Program on Society in Change in cooperation with other institutions of higher learning.

These volumes deal with the peoples whose homelands lie between the Germans to the west, the Russians to the east and north, and the Mediterranean and Adriatic Seas to the south. They constitute a particular civilization, one that is an integral part of Europe, yet substantially different from the West. The area is characterized by rich variety in language, religion, and government, and, not surprisingly, a similar variety can also be observed in concepts of national defense, in the nature of armed forces, and in ways of waging war. The study of this complex subject demands a multidisciplinary approach, and, accordingly, our contributors represent several academic disciplines. They have been drawn from universities and other scholarly institutions in the United States, Canada, and Western Europe as well as in the East Central European socialist countries.

Our comparative investigation of military behavior and organization attempts to ascertain what is peculiar to particular nations and ethnic groups, what has been socially and culturally determined, and what has resulted from the exigencies of the moment. We try to define different patterns of military behavior, including decision-making processes, attitudes and actions of diverse social classes, and the degree of restraint (or lack thereof) typically shown in war. We endeavor to present considerable material that can help us to understand how the process of social, economic, political, and technological change as well as changes in the sciences and in international relations influenced the development of doctrines of national defense and altered actual practice in such areas as military organization, command, strategy, and tactics. We also present data on the social origins and mobility of the officer corps and the rank and file, on the differences between the officer corps of the various services, and, above all, on civil-military relations and the origins of the East Central European brand of militarism. The studies will, we hope, deepen our understanding of the societies, governments, and politics of East Central Europe.

Our methodology takes into account the changes in the study of war and national defense systems which have occurred in the last three decades.

During that period, the study of war and national defense systems has moved away from a narrow focus on battles, campaigns, and leaders and now views a country's military history in the context of the evolution of the entire society. In fact, historians, political scientists, sociologists, philosophers, and other students of war and national defense have come to recognize the interdependence of changes in society and changes in warfare; they accept the proposition that military institutions closely reflect the character of the society of which they are a part. Recognition of this fact is a keystone of our approach to the subject.

Works in Western languages now provide adequate coverage of the diplomatic, political, intellectual, social, and economic histories of the peoples of East Central Europe. In contrast, few substantial studies of their national defense systems have yet appeared in Western languages. Similarly, though some comprehensive accounts of the nonmilitary aspects of the history of the entire region have been published in the West, there is as yet no comprehensive account of the area's national defense systems in any Western language. Nor is there any study of the mutual effects of the concepts and practices of national defense in East Central Europe. Thus, this comprehensive study of war and society in East Central Europe is a pioneering work.

This volume concentrates upon the era of insurrections and wars of national liberation in the 1870s. For all these nations these were the crucial years of nation building, a process in which their armed forces played an important role.

As Editor-in-Chief, of course, I cheerfully take full responsibility for the comprehensiveness, cohesion, internal balance, and scholarly quality of the series I have launched. I intend this work to be neither a justification nor a condemnation of the policies, attitudes, and activities of any of the nations involved. At the same time, because the contributors represent so many different disciplines, languages, interpretations, and schools of thought, our policy in this, as in past and future volumes, is to present their contributions without modification. In this sense, the volume is a sampling of the schools of thought and the standards of scholarship in the many countries to which our contributors belong.

Highland Lakes, New Jersey
March 15, 1985

Béla K. Király
Editor-in-Chief

Gale Stokes

# Introduction

The papers in this volume were written in response to an invitation from the Director of the Brooklyn College Program on Society in Change, Professor Emeritus Béla K. Király, for selected scholars to gather in Varna, Bulgaria, in the fall of 1983 to discuss the great Eastern crisis of 1875–78. Taking advantage of the generous hospitality of the Institute of Balkan Studies of the Bulgarian Academy of Science, which with Brooklyn College was the co-sponsor of the meeting, approximately fifty scholars and guests from eleven countries gathered at the Frederic J. Curie House of Scientists at Druzhba, Varna, from September 18 through September 24. The presence of three Soviet scholars, including A. D. Narochnitski, as well as several members of the Bulgarian Academy of Sciences, a strong delegation from Romania, and a number of North America's most distinguished scholars of East Central Europe offered the opportunity for unusually frank and extensive discussions, an opportunity enhanced by the cordiality and organizational skills of the Bulgarian hosts.

The Eastern crisis of 1875–78 makes an unusually good subject for an international conference because at least two fundamental points of view can be taken concerning it. In the non-Balkan countries, the primary concern of both participants in the events and historians has been to elucidate the international implications of the crisis, the roles of the Great Powers, their gains and losses, the shuffling of positions in the European power game. For the Balkan participants, the primary interest in the crisis has been the establishment of national independence in sometimes heroic and always bloody struggles that ever since have been called wars of national liberation. A full understanding of the crisis requires not only that both viewpoints receive their due but that scholars who approach the crisis from different national and scholarly traditions present their particular facets of the problem fully. The term "facet" is a good one. If we were to become "hedgehogs," as Isaiah Berlin called them, and ask what one big thing we can learn from a scholarly gathering such as this one, it would be that the Eastern crisis, like all human realities, has no single "correct" interpretation. Like an immense jewel crafted over the decades by dozens of master jewelers, some of whom have made major cuts, others of whom have polished minor faces, the Eastern crisis provides differing sparkles of insight and changing views of its internal structure with each angular rotation along each of its various axes.

In this collection both Balkan and non-Balkan scholars address the international aspects of the crisis. For example, in answering the question why Austria did not accelerate the process of national liberation in the Balkans despite its early penetration into the peninsula, Tofik Islamov suggests that dynastic interests in the north and west distracted it and the danger posed by its minorities restrained it. Becoming expansionist by the middle of the nineteenth century, Austria succeeded in using the crisis of 1875–78 to occupy Bosnia and Hercegovina, only to find that in the long run this success caused it as many problems as Alsace and Lorraine caused Germany. Islamov's Soviet colleague V. N. Vinogradov, writing about the Berlin Congress, believes that Austria acted as a surrogate for Britain in attempting to maintain the status quo in the Balkans, whereas Russia, despite Gorchakov's interest in compromise solutions, turned out to favor change, which it achieved through support of the national liberation movements. The Berlin Treaty, usually interpreted as a defeat for the Russians, actually fatally undermined Britain's ability to pursue a status quo policy by recognizing the establishment of the Balkan states, including a Bulgaria that obviously would soon reunite. Thus, Vinogradov writes, whereas Russian policy did not achieve its full aims, it was not unprogressive in its results. Simeon Damianov s detailed article narrows the focus of attention in these matters to the diplomatic events of 1875–78 but also stresses the fact that only the Russians held out hope to the Bulgarians of achieving their liberation. True, it took the force of events generated by the Bulgarians themselves, such as the April Uprising, to force Gorchakov from his position of reserve, but once Alexander II chose war Russia adhered to its well-defined policy of no annexation in the Balkans and statehood for Bulgaria. None of these three authors denies that Russia had selfish aims of the normal Great Power variety or that it sought to advance its sphere of influence and enhance its prestige, but they stress that of all the Great Powers, only Russia was willing and able, eventually, to force a change in the Balkan situation.

Austria, on the other hand, as both Peter F. Sugár and Zoltán Szász point out, was in no position militarily to effect a change, even though Foreign Minister Gyula Andrássy, reflecting anti-Russian Hungarian opinion, hoped to find a way to thwart the Russians. In contrast to the Soviet analysts, Sugár sees Austria not as pursuing a well-conceived policy either of annexation or preservation of the status quo during the crisis but as constantly finding ingenious improvisations that in the end gave the appearance of successful policy. Not that Andrássy did not have goals; he did. They included satisfying his military, which wanted Bosnia and Hercegovina for defensive purposes, delaying the dissolution of the weak Ottoman state so as to prevent a vacuum susceptible to being filled by Russia, and thwarting Russian efforts to create a large Slavic state in the Balkans. But Sugár shows how in every instance Andrássy and the Austrians were forced to improvise a solution to a problem, never achieving a consistent policy line. Whether in the end it can be said that Austria was pursuing a policy of annexation, seeking to preserve the status quo, or simply improvising is a question each reader may ponder for himself.

Another thread running through these discussions of Great Power politics is the question of how much internal opinion affected policy. The effect of Gladstone's brochure on the Bulgarian Horrors is well known, even though it had little lasting effect on Britain's Turcophile policy. The lack of democratic forms in both Russia and Austria makes it all the more remarkable that in both countries public opinion actually influenced policy significantly. In Austria Andrássy's early efforts to devise an anti-Russian coalition reflected Hungarian popular antipathy toward Russia, while in Russia the activities of the Pan-Slavist committees, as well as other public outcries, were a crucial element in deciding the tsar's government on war. Several of the articles in Part II discuss public opinion directly but give less attention to its impact on policy, emphasizing instead how the peoples of East Central Europe showed their interest in and solidarity with the uprisings. Hungarians, Romanians Czechs, and Poles all followed the crisis with sympathy.

The second major approach to the Eastern crisis is the internal one, focusing on the actual prosecution of the wars from the viewpoint of the participants. Since the overall objective of the project on War and Society in East Central Europe, described by Király in his preface, is to investigate the manifold interactions between military affairs and society, the bulk of this book is devoted to the military affairs of the individual nations, from organizational preparations to formal campaigns, including volunteer and insurrectionary activities. The articles of Part III find that at least three types of military action characterized the crisis, the first of which was spontaneous uprising. National patriots in areas under Turkish domination had an almost anarchistic faith that the peasant masses would rally to the cause of national liberation once they had struck the spark of revolution, but in fact only in Bosnia and Hercegovina was insurrection sustained for very long, and there the uprisings were truly spontaneous rather than planned by the nationalists. Two established governments, Serbia and Greece, sought to harness this anticipated propensity to rebellion, the first by spreading arms to the south, the second by creating revolutionary committees, but both were disappointed. Indeed, one of the significant results of the crisis was the demonstration that the day of successful peasant uprisings along the lines of the First Serbian Uprising or the Greek Revolution was over.

The second sort of military action, of course, was the use of regular armies. Since Bulgaria and Albania were not yet independent, they were denied this option, although the Bulgarians provided volunteer forces for the Serbian army and assisted the Russians as well. The Albanians used the crisis to form their own national committee, but they also fought with determination on the side of the Ottomans when the Serbian army began to advance into Kosovo in the early winter of 1878. Serbia and Romania conducted formal military operations with their armies, the first independently, the second in coordination with the Russians. The articles in this collection thoroughly discuss this aspect of the crisis, showing in Serbia's case the problems a small and economically weak state confronted in conceiving and creating a viable army and in Romania's how successfully the Romanians participated in the war of 1877—78 from a military, political, and popular point of view.

Romania provides a good example of the third type of Balkan military campaign during the crisis, joint operations with the Russian army. The Russian declaration of war was almost as much a diplomatic problem for the Romanians as a military one, but they managed to use the Russian entry into the war creatively to fashion their own declaration of independence. When actual operations began, Prince Carol succeeded in maintaining the autonomy of the Romanian forces, enhancing both his own prestige and Romanian claims to independence.

All of the Balkan countries that became independent in 1878 can rightfully claim that their achievements were in good measure due to their own efforts and choices, but they also found that their military success depended on Russian arms and therefore in the end on Russian diplomacy. For this reason, Part IV takes up the question of the peace settlement. Hristo Hristov discusses the Treaty of San Stefano as a logical outcome not contrary to the interests of the other Balkan states. Britain and Austria, however, did not so interpret it. The Congress of Berlin adjudicated the issues to the temporary dissatisfaction of the Russians and the permanent dissatisfaction of the Bulgarians. Still, Vinogradov holds that the pluses of the crisis for the Balkan peoples far outweighed the minuses.

Imanuel Geiss, in his wide-ranging analysis, concurs that the consequences of the Berlin Congress were momentous, but he emphasizes the deleterious effects. Agreeing that the occupation of Bosnia and Hercegovina proved more and more dangerous to Austro—Hungarian survival as time went by, Geiss points out that the creation of new Balkan states on the nationality principle was analogous to the organization of Western Europe into competing Great Powers. The scale was smaller, but the antagonistic principles that tore Europe (and the Balkans) apart in 1914 were the same. Just as the unification of Germany and Italy permitted the new states to operate autonomously, thus disrupting the Concert of Europe, so the creation of the Balkan states permitted each small new country to pursue its narrow aims, thus seriously complicating the international game board and creating serious new possibilities for instability. The alliance system and protective tariffs that resulted from the political and military crisis of 1875–78, as well as from the economic crisis of 1873, to which it was related, led in a direct line, according to Geiss, to the conflicts that marked the first fifty years of the twentieth century.

Geiss's analysis shows how in Balkan history, as well as in the dialectical process of life itself, every event holds within itself contradictory elements. One of the most ironic such contradictions, implied but not discussed explicitly in this volume, is the contrast between the enthusiasms of the Balkan peoples, or at least of their elites, both then and now, for liberation in 1878 in the form of national independence and the actual lack of autonomy in international affairs enjoyed by the Balkan states. There is no question that independence in the framework of the European state system, in which only "state nations" had the right to participate, wrought a transformation in self-consciousness, autonomy, and esteem for Balkan peoples. On the other hand, the more or less successful efforts of Austria–Hungary to ensnare Romania and Serbia into its sphere of influence, the domination of Greek politics and economics by Britain, and the friendly relationship that Russia was able to maintain, albeit with fluctuations, with Bulgaria all indicate that national liberation was not as complete as nineteenth-century enthusiasts would have preferred.

In considering these paradoxes, it would be wrong to assert that any given interpretation of the Eastern crisis most accurately reflects the structure of the whole. The struggle of the Balkan peoples for national unification and recognition was successful both because of the initiative, courage, and tenacity of the Balkan peoples themselves and because outside forces imposed solutions on the peninsula; national liberation was a positive and progressive event in the achievement of selfhood at the same time as it introduced narrow and destructive principles of self-interest; the Balkan peoples became free and independent for the first time just at the moment that they were being integrated into larger economic and political structures; Russian policies could aim at changing the status quo and yet not be annexationist, while Austria could improvise policy and acquire territory. The crisis of 1875–78 can be understood as a moment when individual peoples sought and achieved self-determination, as an aspect of international politics in which certain Great Powers supported, disregarded, or even tried to suppress the national movements, or in terms of the reactions of individuals, groups, and peoples to the excitements of the actual events. All of these points of view reflect the same reality; indeed, together they constitute that reality as we know it.

# CONTRIBUTORS

Constantin Căsănişteanu, Professor of History, Military History Institute, Bucharest, Romania

Ilie Ceauşescu, Major General, Vice-Minister of Defense, Professor of History, Military History Institute, Bucharest, Romania

Florin Constantiniu, Professor of History, Nicolae Iorga Institute of History, Bucharest, Romania

Simeon Damianov, Director, Institute of Balkan Studies, Bulgarian Academy of Sciences, Sofia, Bulgaria

Strašimir Dimitrov, Professor of History, Institute of Balkan Studies, Bulgarian Academy of Sciences, Sofia, Bulgaria

Richard L. DiNardo, Ph.D. Candidate, Graduate School and University Center, City University of New York

Dimitrije Djordjevic, Professor of History, University of California, Santa Barbara

Doino Doinov, Professor of History, Institute of Balkan Studies, Bulgarian Academy of Sciences, Sofia, Bulgaria

Robert J. Donia, Professor of History, Ohio State University, Lima, Ohio

Alesandru Duţu, Professor of History, Nicolae Iorga Institute of History, Bucharest, Romania

Milorad Ekmečić, Professor of History, Faculty of Philosophy, University of Sarajevo, Sarajevo, Yugoslavia

Stephen Fischer—Galati, Distinguished University Professor of History, University of Colorado

Radu R. Florescu, Professor of History, Boston College

Anna Garlicka, Doctor of History, Polish Academy, Institute of History, Warsaw, Poland

Imanuel Geiss, Professor of History, University of Bremen, Bremen, Federal Republic of Germany

Hristo Hristov, Professor of History, Institute of Balkan Studies, Bulgarian Academy of Sciences, Sofia, Bulgaria

Ilia Iliev, Professor of History, Institute of Balkan Studies, Bulgarian Academy of Sciences, Sofia, Bulgaria

Mihail E. Ionescu, Major, Professor of History, Center for Military History, Bucharest, Romania

Momtchil Ionov, Professor of History, Institute of Balkan Studies, Bulgarian Academy of Sciences, Sofia, Bulgaria

Béla K. Király, Professor Emeritus of History, Brooklyn College and the Graduate School and University Center, City University of New York

Evangelos Kofos, Doctor of History, Greek Ministry of Foreign Affairs, Athens, Greece

Mircea Muşat, Doctor of History, Center for Military History, Bucharest, Romania

Gale Stokes, Professor of History, Rice University, Houston, Texas

Peter F. Sugár, Professor of History, University of Washington

Zoltán Szász, Professor of History, Historical Institute of the Hungarian Academy of Sciences, Budapest, Hungary

Miroslav Tejchman, Doctor of History, Czechoslovak–Soviet Institute, Czechoslovak Academy of Sciences, Prague, Czechoslovakia

Nikolai Todorov, Professor of History, Institute of Balkan Studies, Bulgarian Academy of Sciences, Sofia, Bulgaria

Tofik Islamov, Professor of History, Institute for Slavic and Balkan Studies, Academy of Sciences of the U. S. S. R., Moscow, U. S. S. R.

Vesselin Traikov, Professor of History, Institute of Balkan Studies, Bulgarian Academy of Sciences, Sofia, Bulgaria

Florian Tuča, Professor of History, Center for Military History, Bucharest, Romania

Vladien N. Vinogradov, Professor of History, Institute for Slavic and Balkan Studies, Academy of Sciences of the U. S. S. R., Moscow, U. S. S. R.

ATLANTIC STUDIES
Brooklyn College Studies on Society in Change
Distributed by Columbia University Press (except No. 5)
Editor-in-Chief: Béla K. Király

No. 1
*Tolerance and Movements of Religious Dissent in Eastern Europe.* Edited by
B. K. Király, 1975. Second Printing, 1977.

No. 2
*The Habsburg Empire in World War I.* Edited by R. A. Kann, B. K. Király,
P. S. Fichtner, 1976. Second Printing, 1978.

No. 3
*The Mutual Effects of the Islamic and Judeo-Christian Worlds: The East
European Pattern.* Edited by A. Ascher, T. Halasi–Kun, B. K. Király, 1979.

No. 4
*Before Watergate: Problems of Corruption in American Society.* Edited by
A. S. Eisenstadt, A. Hoogenboom, H. L. Trefousse, 1978.

No. 5
*East Central European Perceptions of Early America.* Edited by B. K. Király
and G. Bárány. Lisse, The Netherlands: Peter de Ridder Press, 1977. Distributed by Humanities Press, Atlantic Highlands, N. J.

No. 6
*The Hungarian Revolution of 1956 in Retrospect.* Edited by B. K. Király
and P. Jónás, 1978. Second Printing, 1980.

No. 7
*Brooklyn U. S. A.: Fourth Largest City in America.* Edited by R. S. Miller,
1979.

No. 8
János Decsy. *Prime Minister Gyula Andrássy's Influence on Habsburg Foreign
Policy during the Franco–German War of 1870–1871,* 1979.

No. 9
Robert F. Horowitz. *The Great Impeacher: A Political Biography of James
M. Ashley,* 1979.

\* \* \*

Nos. 10–19
Subseries: War and Society in East Central Europe (see Nos. 30–40 also)

No. 10 – Vol. I
*Special Topics and Generalizations on the Eighteenth and Nineteenth Cen-
turies.* Edited by B. K. Király and G. E. Rothenberg, 1979.

No. 11 – Vol. II
*East Central European Society and War in the Pre-Revolutionary Eighteenth Century.* Edited by G. E. Rothenberg, B. K. Király, and P. Sugár, 1982.

No. 12 – Vol. III
*From Hunyadi to Rákóczi: War and Society in Late Medieval and Early Modern Hungary.* Edited by J. M. Bak and B. K. Király, 1982.

No. 13 – Vol. IV
*East Central European Society and War in the Era of Revolutions, 1775–1856.* Edited by B. K. Király, forthcoming.

No. 14 – Vol. V
*Essays on World War I: Origins and Prisoners of War.* Edited by P. Pastor and S. R. Williamson, Jr., 1982.

No. 15 – Vol. VI
*Essays on World War I: Total War and Peacemaking, A Case Study on Trianon,* Edited by B. K. Király, P. Pastor, and I. Sanders, 1983.

No. 16 – Vol. VII
Thomas M. Barker. *Army, Aristocracy, Monarchy: Essays on War, Society, and Government in Austria, 1618–1780,* 1982.

No. 17 – Vol. VIII
*The First Serbian Uprising, 1804–1813.* Edited by Wayne S. Vucinich, 1983.

No. 18 – Vol. IX
Kálmán Janics. *Czechoslovak Policy and the Hungarian Minority, 1945–1948,* 1982.

No. 19 – Vol. X
*At the Brink of War and Peace: The Tito–Stalin Split in Historic Perspective.* Edited by Wayne S. Vucinich, 1983.

\* \* \*

No. 20
*Inflation Through the Ages: Economic, Social, Psychological, and Historical Aspects.* Edited by N. Schmukler and E. Marcus, 1982.

No. 21
*Germany and America: Essays on Problems of International Relations and Immigration.* Edited by H. L. Trefousse, 1980.

No. 22
Murray M. Horowitz. *Brooklyn College: The First Half Century,* 1982.

No. 23
Jason Berger. *A New Deal for the World: Eleanor Roosevelt and American Foreign Policy*, 1981.

No. 24
*The Legacy of Jewish Migration: 1881 and Its Impact.* Edited by D. Berger, 1983.

No. 25
Pierre Oberling. *The Road to Bellapais: Cypriot Exodus to Northern Cyprus,* 1982.

No. 26
*New Hungarian Peasants: An East Central European Experiment with Collectivization.* Edited by Marida Hollós and Béla Maday, 1983.

No. 27
*Germans in America: Aspects of German–American Relations in the 19th Century.* Edited by E. Allen McCormick, 1983.

No. 28
Linda and Marsha Frey. *A Question of Empire: Leopold I and the War of the Spanish Succession, 1701–1705,* 1983.

No. 29
Szczepan K. Zimmer. *The Beginning of Cyrillic Printing–Cracow, 1491: From the Orthodox Past in Poland.* Edited by Ludwik Krzyzanowski and Irene Nagurski, 1983.

\* \* \*

Nos. 30–40
Subseries: War and Society in East Central Europe (continued; see also Nos. 10–19)

No. 30 – Vol. XI
*The First War Between Socialist States: The Hungarian Revolution of 1956 and Its Impact.* Edited by Béla K. Király, Barbara Lotze, and Nándor Dreisziger, 1983.

No. 31 – Vol. XII
István I. Mócsy. *The Effects of World War I: The Uprooted: Hungarian Refugees and Their Impact on Hungarian Domestic Politics, 1918–1921,* 1983.

No. 32 – Vol. XIII
*The Effects of World War I: The Class War after the Great War: The Rise of Communist Parties in East Central Europe, 1918–1921.* Edited by Ivo Banac, 1983.

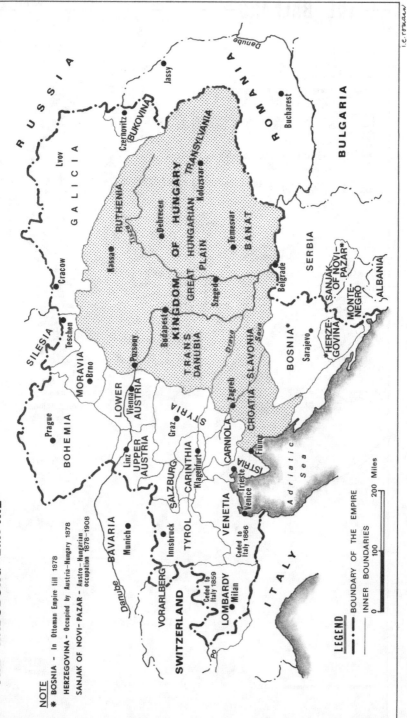

Map 1

# THE HABSBURG EMPIRE

NOTE

\* BOSNIA – In Ottoman Empire till 1878

HERZEGOVINA – Occupied by Austria–Hungary 1878

SANJAK OF NOVI-PAZAR – Austro–Hungarian occupation 1878–1908

LEGEND

—·—·— BOUNDARY OF THE EMPIRE

——— INNER BOUNDARIES

0        100        200 Miles

RUSSIA

GALICIA

Lvov

Cracow

SILESIA

Teschen

MORAVIA

Brno

BOHEMIA

Prague

BAVARIA

Munich

Danube

SWITZERLAND

VORARLBERG

TYROL

Innsbruck

SALZBURG

Linz

UPPER AUSTRIA

LOWER AUSTRIA

Vienna

Pozsony

CARINTHIA

Klagenfurt

STYRIA

Graz

CARNIOLA

ISTRIA

Trieste

Venice

Ceded to Italy 1866

VENETIA

LOMBARDY

Milan

Ceded to Italy 1859

Po

ITALY

Adriatic Sea

Fiume

CROATIA - SLAVONIA

Zagreb

Drava

Sava

TRANS DANUBIA

Budapest

KINGDOM OF HUNGARY

GREAT HUNGARIAN PLAIN

Tisza

Szeged

Kassa

RUTHENIA

Debrecen

Kolozsvar

TRANSYLVANIA

BANAT

Temesvar

Belgrade

Czernovitz

BUKOVINA

Jassy

ROMANIA

Danube

Bucharest

BULGARIA

SERBIA

BOSNIA*

Sarajevo

* HERZE- GOVINA

SANJAK OF NOVI- PAZAR *

MONTE- NEGRO

ALBANIA

I.E. FENWICK

Map 2

# THE BALKANS

## LEGEND

- ·—·— BOUNDARIES OF 1913
- 1878    YEAR OF INDEPENDENCE AND/OR YEAR OF AQUISITION FROM THE OTTOMAN EMPIRE
- ▨    TERRITORY LOST BY TURKEY AS A RESULT OF THE BALKAN WARS, 1912–13
- ▨    BESSARABIA
- ▨    SOUTHERN BESSARABIA FROM RUSSIA TO ROMANIA, 1856; FROM ROMANIA TO RUSSIA, 1878
- ▨    SOUTHERN DOBRUDJA FROM BULGARIA TO ROMANIA, 1913

RUSSIA

BESSARABIA

MOLDAVIA
Autonomous 1822

ROMANIA
1878

BOSNIA
Sarajevo

Belgrade
1830

●Bucharest

WALLACHIA
Autonomous 1822

DOBRUDJA
1878

S
E
R
B
I
A

●Nish
1878

1878

1913

1878

Black
Sea

Sofia

MONTE-
NEGRO
Independent
since 1389

1913

BULGARIA
1885

ALBANIA

1913

Ochrid

MACEDONIA

●Adrianople

Constantinople●

1913

Salonika●

1913

CORFU
English 1814-63
Greek 1863

G
R
E
E
C
E

1881

Aegean
Sea

TURKEY
●Smyrna

●Athens

1830

Mediterranean   Sea

0  50  100  150  200
Miles

DODECANESE
Italian 1912

CRETE
Greek 1913

i.e. romana

# POLAND (1815-1918)

Map 3

## LEGEND

- –··–··– BOUNDARY OF POLISH REPUBLIC, 1821
- "CONGRESS KINGDOM"
- REPUBLIC OF CRACOW (1815-46)

Miles
0    50    100    150    200

Baltic Sea

LITHUANIA

Minsk

Vilna

R U S S I A

Brest-Litovsk

EAST PRUSSIA

Danzig

Warsaw

CONGRESS KINGDOM OF POLAND

Lublin

Lvov

Cracow

GALICIA

POZNANIA

Poznan

Breslau

Berlin

P R U S S I A

Praga

A U S T R I A

I
Overview

Nikolai Todorov

# COMMON FEATURES OF THE NINETEENTH-CENTURY BALKAN NATIONAL LIBERATION STRUGGLES

It was characteristic of the liberation struggles of the Balkan peoples until almost the end of the eighteenth century that armed uprisings were connected with and depended on wars between European states and the Ottoman Empire. During the nineteenth century, major uprisings occurred without declared war against the Ottoman Empire, but they eventually succeeded only after Russian victories in anti-Turkish wars. These wars, along with certain other events of Europe-wide significance, played a positive role in raising the self-confidence of the Balkan peoples and drawing them together.

An important period in the maturing of the Balkan peoples was the revolutionary and Napoleonic era, when France's diplomatic and military activity extended into the Balkans and such statesmen as Prince Peter I of Montenegro, Ali Pasha of Janina, Osman Pazvanoglu, and others became linked with France. It was at this time that Rigas Velestinlis made the first serious attempt in Greek revolutionary thinking to give meaning to the ideas and example of the French Revolution in the context of Balkan reality. It should not be forgotten that the very term "revolution" came into use and gained acceptance only with the French Revolution. At the beginning of the events in Paris in 1789, La Rochefoucauld said to Louis XVI, "this is no longer a revolt, it is a revolution." To some this may seem merely a play upon words — *revolte, revolution* — but contemporaries knew what qualified a particular phenomenon as revolutionary. They began to contrast the "bloody" political revolution in France with the "peaceful" industrial revolution in England and, under the impact of the events in the Balkans at the beginning of the nineteenth century, with "national revolution."

What characterized the nineteenth-century Balkan national revolutions was that they were initiated by the Balkan peoples themselves and that their scope was conditioned by the degree of preparation for them. Another important feature was that unity of the Balkan peoples was regarded as a guarantee of success and an essential element in the strategy and tactics of armed action. The factors that turned the national aims of particular peoples into all-Balkan ones and led to the rallying of forces had their roots in the common historical fate of the Balkan peoples. Their economic and cultural links, which in the epoch of national revival acquired still greater strength and significance, also helped draw them together. As a result, the national liberation struggles of the Balkan peoples were similar in objectives and in character.

The different degrees of socioeconomic development of the Balkan peoples prevented them from achieving a general uprising against foreign domination, since the basic stages in the national liberation movements of the individual peoples did not fully coincide in time. Complete unity of action was not attained either in the period of the wars of liberation at the beginning of the nineteenth century or after the establishment of the young Balkan states. Attempts at uprisings showed how difficult it was to synchronize revolts against a powerful enemy in a generally backward time and in the absence of a class or an interested and authoritative elite to coordinate efforts. Circumstances hampered the full realization of the goals of the national liberation movements.

The Serbian Uprising of 1804 opened a new page in the history of the armed struggle for liberation of the Balkan peoples. Though to a certain extent stimulated by the general political situation in the Balkans and in Europe, this uprising broke out as a protest against specific conditions of national and social oppression, irrespective of any external factor. Representatives of all strata of Serbian society were involved. What was qualitatively new about the uprising was that it gave expression to an all-Balkan solidarity of unprecedented scope and depth. The Serbian leaders of the uprising, in seeking material and moral support for it, especially from Napoleon, asserted that "their brothers in Bosnia, Hercegovina, and the Kingdom of Hungary, and the Bulgarians as well" would follow their example.[1] "The neighboring Bulgarians" were mentioned as a reliable ally in several reports to the French, and there was talk about a secret Serb—Bulgarian agreement. For their part, the enslaved Balkan peoples understood that the Serbian Uprising was a genuine people's liberation war of a small nation against the enslaver.

A telling example of the way the Serbian Uprising was evaluated from the standpoint of Balkan revolutionary strategy is given by a book in Greek published in Italy in 1806. Greece was at that time the country with the most advanced political ideas in the Balkans and the eastern Mediterranean, but the complexity of its social structure predisposed the Greeks to sharp social and political collisions. Two questions that animated the Greek public were how the liberation of Greece was to be attained and for what kind of free Greece the Greek people were to fight. The unknown author of this book considered the Serbian Uprising an example for the Greeks to follow. He possessed the political insight to rise above the general admiration for Napoleon, who for the enslaved peoples continued to symbolize the omnipotent liberating French Revolution, and  raise a voice of warning: "Why, my brothers, should we replace a ruler when we can free ourselves? Do you think that the yoke of an alien dynasty is lighter? Do you not think that it is still a yoke?"[2] The rejection of outside assistance as involving the danger of replacing one slavery with another was a new phenomenon in the development of the Greek liberation movement.

There is ample evidence of the participation of Bulgarians in the Serbian Uprising. They joined the insurgent forces and were recognized and appreciated by the Serbian leaders. The beginning of military operations between Russia and Turkey led to the formation of volunteer units of Bulgarians, Greeks, and Romanians. A "Bulgarian territorial army" consisting of Greeks and Bulgarians from southern Russia was set up under the command of the Greek captain N. Pangalos. In a proclamation addressed "Brothers, brave and firm Bulgarians,"[3] Pangalos called upon Greeks, Bulgarians, Romanians, and Albanians to declare a general uprising. This was perhaps the earliest call for joint armed operations by someone personally prepared to seek Balkan unity through armed struggle.

This qualitatively new stage of the nineteenth-century national liberation struggle in the Balkans was linked to the establishment of the Greek Philiki Etaireia in Odessa in 1814. A secret revolutionary organization in the full sense of the word, the Etaireia had a fixed program and objectives based on the rich European revolutionary experience. The society's organizational network covered the entire peninsula and the Greek colonies scattered throughout Europe and the Near East and included representatives of other Balkan peoples as well. Its plan of revolutionary operations envisaged the participation of all the Balkan peoples in the struggle to throw off Ottoman rule. The activity of Philiki Etaireia as a conspiratorial organization that suffered not a single betrayal in seven years and succeeded in preparing and proclaiming an uprising became a model for clandestine activity and plans for revolts of the enslaved Balkan peoples throughout the nineteenth century.

The numerous documents and studies on the events of 1821 reveal the direct participation of the best representatives of revolutionary thinking and action from all the Balkan countries in the preparations for and progress of the Greek Uprising. Their efforts placed southeastern Europe in the front ranks of nineteenth-century revolutionary practice.[4] In Bulgaria's history these events occupy a special place. Heroic participation of Bulgarians in all the major battles was noted in numerous documents and recognized by the Greeks. Bulgarian volunteers joined the Greek People's Liberation Army and took part in its struggles even after it had shifted its operations fully to Greek territory, there confronting forces many times superior to its own, and the impossibility of raising a revolt outside Greece had become evident. On the other hand, though it is undeservedly overlooked by Bulgarian historiography, when the Bulgarians joined the preparations for the uprising they expected to bring about the immediate liberation of Bulgaria through a general armed campaign. It was no accident that the leader of the Bulgarian volunteers in Ypsilantis's army, A. N. Pavlović, was styled "prince" by the other captains, including the Bulgarian ones, even though he had no formal title. The title was given him because through him several score of Bulgarian commanders and illustrious voivodes hoped to draw even with their neighbors and gain the prerogative of rule in a liberated Bulgaria. Along with the Serbs Karadjordjević and Miloš Obrenović and the Romanian Tudor Vladimirescu, who emerged as leaders and received their prince's titles in the course of the armed struggle, the Bulgarians also put forward their prince.

The first wave of the national liberation revolution in the Balkans ended, thanks to the Russo—Turkish wars, with the establishment of an autonomous Serbia and an independent Greece and the elimination of the practical dependence of the Danubian principalities on the Ottoman Empire.

The revolutionary movements between the thirties and the fifties were brought about by social factors. Complicated land relations, the result of changes in the Ottoman military-feudal system in the epoch of the Tanzimat, gave rise to peasants' movements centered in northwestern Bulgaria and movements of large landowners and feudal lords in Bosnia and Albania. Despite their antipodal social character, these movements were transformed, although not at the same time, into a link between the struggles for national consolidation and liberation of Bulgarians, Serbs, Albanians, and Bosnians.

The revolts of Pirot and Berkovitsa in the thirties, the Niš revolt of 1841, and that of Vidin of 1850 enjoyed the support of the Serbian public. At the same time, revolutionaries were engaged in brisk activity everywhere in the Balkans. Clandestine and semilegal organizations emerged in Greece, Serbia, and Wallachia. A common feature of these organizations was that they were under the leadership of bourgeois circles who wanted to realize their national aspirations by directly linking their work with the policies of the governments of the Balkan states. The events in Brăila in 1841—43 were a clear example of this and another instance of cooperation among Bulgarians, Serbs, and Greeks. These movements, however, like the other rebel plots and attempts during the second quarter of the nineteenth century, cannot be called nationwide uprisings. Grounds for including them as examples are provided not so much by their popularity as by the character of their objectives.

The revolution of 1848—49, dictated by strivings for social transformation, occupied a special place in the series of revolutionary events. Under the influence of the specific national conditions in the Balkans, the events in some cases passed into their opposite – they assumed a counterrevolutionary character, especially in the areas under Habsburg control, where the movements of Serbs and Croats clashed with the revolutions in Austria and Hungary and contributed to their suppression. This is yet another example of the fact that in the historical process there is no simple accumulation of contradictions and that the force of public reaction cannot be measured by the mechanical sum of national and social factors. The revolutionary wave found particularly favorable soil in the Danubian principalities, which in 1848 became the arena of bitter class struggles. The same happened on Cephalonia.

The second revolutionary wave, which once again put the Eastern Question on the agenda and thoroughly shook the Ottoman Empire, began with the July 1875 uprisings in Bosnia and Hercegovina and the April 1876 Bulgarian uprising. Long planned by revolutionary organizations, they broke out, as did those at the beginning of the century, in a period in which the international situation did not favor military operations against Ottoman domination in the Balkans and expanded with great force. An important precondition for the new upsurge of the liberation movement was the existence of an ideological base that permitted close collaboration of the revolutionary leaders. Once again, as at the turn of the century, the revolutionary ideology in the Balkans in the sixties and seventies constituted a stage in European revolutionary thinking. The ideas of a democratic republic as a form of state structure and of broad international cooperation in the armed struggle, at the beginning of the century raised only as a distant hope, were now enriched with new social content and incorporated into the program of the national revolutionary movement.

In order to grasp the evolution of the Balkan national revolutionary ideas and the character of the liberation movements, it is necessary to take into account the role of the already independent Balkan states – of their bourgeoisies and monarchies and their national programs. On the one hand, the establishment of independent Balkan states had a revolutionizing effect on the peoples remaining under Ottoman rule by setting them an example. On the other hand, instead of a realistic national policy seeking the liberation by common action of the population still under Turkish rule, the governing circles came up with programs that clashed with the national demands of other peoples. The national programs of the Serbian and Greek bourgeoisies from the middle of the nineteenth century on boiled down to striving to attain the territorial boundaries of their medieval states at their most powerful. Thanks to their state organization, army, propaganda apparatus, diplomatic activity, and financial means, the young Balkan states had for a time a strong influence on the national independence movements of their enslaved compatriots. The same thing happened with the Bulgarians after the liberation of Bulgaria. The interference of the great European states, which according to their economic and political interests encouraged or limited the political activity of the Balkan states, also had its effects.

Gradually the national revolutionary movements sought to free themselves of the influence of government policy that might divert them from the only road to liberation: a decisive armed struggle prepared for with intensive organizational and ideological work among the people. It was in the second half of the nineteenth century that two lines became clear in activities for liberation on the Balkan Peninsula: a state-governmental line, controlled by the ruling bourgeoisie, which set the peoples against each other and led to disunity in the forces of those fighting for freedom and independence, and a democratic-revolutionary line, which led to a drawing together of the liberation movements and of the Balkan peoples. In certain cases, of course, these two directions did not remain completely isolated from each other. Thus, every initiative for establishing Balkans-wide unity of action against the Ottoman Empire enjoyed the support of the revolutionary forces.

I shall not dwell on the well-known cooperation between the revolutionaries and movements of the Balkan peoples or on the initiative for setting up a system of agreements and treaties among the Balkan states.

I should like only to quote the words of the most prominent Bulgarian of the preliberation period, Vasil Levski: "On our banner shall be written 'Sacred and Pure Republic.' I wish our Serbian, Montenegrin, Romanian, etc.. brothers the same, that they may not lag behind us. It is time to win with a single effort what the French brothers sought and are seeking, that is to say, a new France, a new Russia, etc."[5]

What is the meaning of these words? Did Levski not recognize the difference between the position of the Bulgarians, who were still facing a blood-drenched and selfless struggle for liberation, and that of the Serbs, Montenegrins, Romanians, and Greeks, who had had their free states for some time? The words quoted can mean only one thing — that with national liberation Levski wanted to solve the social problems that faced not only the Bulgarians but all of the Balkan states. He had in mind the problems that social development had already raised in states such as France and Russia. which were free from foreign domination but in which sharp social contradictions nonetheless gave rise to such dramatic revolutionary events as the first proletarian revolution and the Paris Commune and to the powerful revolutionary movements in Russia.

The April Uprising — the culmination of the national liberation movement of the Bulgarians — was at the same time an expression of the profound sense of solidarity of the South Slavic peoples. The news of the uprising in

Bosnia and Hercegovina served as a signal to the Bulgarians, who despite insufficient time for preparation did not hesitate to join the liberation struggle. The April Uprising ended in failure, just as did the Serbo—Turkish and, a little later, the Greco—Turkish War.

Without it, however, the conditions would not have been established for Russia's decisive diplomatic action and, after the failure of this action, for the Russo—Turkish War of liberation, which increased the liberated area of the Balkans by yet another independent country — Bulgaria.

## NOTES

1. N. Todorov, "The Bulgarian National Revolution and the Revolutionary Movements in the Balkans." — *Etudes balkaniques*, 1977, no. 2, pp. 36—37.
2. Anonymou tou ellinos. *Elliniki Nomarchia, iti logos peri elefterias* ("en Italia," 1806), p. 199.
3. E. Vîrtosu, "Despre corpul de voluntari eleni creat la Bucureşti în 1807." *Studii şi materiale de istorie Medie*, 5 (1962): 550.
4. N. Todorov and V. Trajkov, *Bălgari — učastnici v borbata za osvoboždenieto na Gărcia.* (Sofia, 1971); N. Todorov, *I Valkaniki diastasi tis epanastasis tou 1821. (I periptosi ton Voulgaron).* (Athens, 1982); Sp. Loukatos, *Shesis Ellinon meta Servon ke Mavrovounion kata tin Ellinikin epanastasin. 1823—1826* (Thessaloniki, 1970); "Les relations des révolutionnaires Grecs et des Bulgares volontaires à la lutte pour l'indépendance Hellenique," in I Ellino-voulgariko symposio, *Pnevmatikes ke politistikes shesis Ellinon ke Voulgaron apo ta mesa tou 15 eos ta mesa tou 19 eona.* (Thessaloniki, 1980), pp. 199—209; *Documente privind istoria Rominici. Rascoala din 1821,* 5 vols. (Bucharest, 1959—1962); *Revolutions nationales des peuples balkaniques. 1804—1814* (Belgrade, 1965).
5. Vasil Levski, *Svjata i čista republika. Pisma i dokumenti.* Săst. I. Undžiev i N. Kondarev. (Sofia, 1971), p. 34.

Béla K. Király


# EAST CENTRAL EUROPEAN SOCIETY, ARMED FORCES, AND WARFARE ON THE EVE OF THE MACHINE AGE


The era discussed in this volume was a momentous stage in European history. Domestic, international, military, and cultural institutions, schools of thought, and patterns of action underwent profound changes. At the bottom of all these changes lay the Industrial Revolution, with its effects on technology and production, life-styles, and social relationships. By the 1870s — the era of this study — Western Europe had seen the completion of the formation of nation-states with the unification of Italy and Germany. Enormous industrial potentials had been built up. Western Europe was ready for an unprecedented expansion into areas of the world not yet under the white man's control. At the same time, the decline of the powerful empires of the East — Ottoman, Mogul, Chinese, and Persian — invited Western Europe and later the United States to move into the power vacuum, and Western Europe took up the challenge: modern imperialism set in. The opening up of opportunities in the Far East reduced the importance of the Ottoman Empire for Britain and France. Consequently, the interest of these leading imperialist powers in protecting the "sick man of Europe" diminished. This offered the nations of southeastern Europe the chance to achieve national liberation without the traditional hostility of the West. Ideologies to justify the changes and/or to respond to the new requirements emerged — imperialism, nationalism, modern democracy, scientific socialism, and, in the sphere of national defense, the idea of the nation in arms.

East Central Europe lagged behind in most of these developments. Democracy and socialism were still far off, nationalism being the predominant school of thought and motivation. The aim was either the liberation of subject nations or the unification of nations partitioned under the rule of foreign powers. The Russo—Turkish War and the Balkan revolutions of the 1870s were the battlefield of East Central European nationalism. In this respect the region was not far behind Western Europe, for the unification of the Italians had taken place just a decade and that of the Germans just a few years earlier. The Balkan upheaval of the 1870s created a new map of East Central Europe that remained in force until the end of the Balkan Wars and was reshaped once again only as the result of World War I.

Under the label "East Central Europe" we include the peoples whose homelands lie between the Germans to the west, the Russians to the east and north, and the Mediterranean and Adriatic Seas to the south. They constitute a particular civilization, an integral part of Europe yet substantially different from both East and West. Within the area there are intriguing variations in language, religion, and government and differences in concepts of national defense, characteristics of the armed forces, and ways of waging war.

Our investigation focuses on a comparative survey of military organization and behavior in these various nations and ethnic groups. We examine the effects of social, economic, political, and technological changes and changes in the sciences and in international relations on the development of doctrines of national defense and on practices in military organization, command, strategy, and tactics. We shall also present data on the social origins and mobility of the officer corps and the rank and file, differences between the officer corps of the various services, and the civil-military relationship and the origins of the East Central European brand of militarism. The studies will, we hope, result in a better understanding of the societies, governments, and politics of East Central Europe.

Our methodology takes into account the fact that in the last three decades the study of war and national defense systems has moved away from narrow concerns with battles, campaigns, and leaders and come to concern itself with the evolution of the society as a whole. The interdependence of changes in society and changes in warfare and the proposition that military institutions closely reflect the character of the society of which they are a part have come to be accepted by historians, political scientists, sociologists, philosophers, and other students of war and national defense. Recognition of this fact is the keystone of our approach to the subject.

While works in Western languages adequately cover the diplomatic, political, intellectual, social, and economic histories of the peoples of this area, few substantial studies of their national defense systems have yet appeared in the West. Similarly, though some substantial, comprehensive accounts of the nonmilitary aspects of the history of the region have been published in the West, nothing has appeared in any Western language about the national defense systems of the area as a whole. Our publications in the recent past have begun to break the ice. This volume is another contribution to closing the enormous gap in English-language historiography.

The Balkan revolutions of the 1870s and the Russo—Turkish War were significant events in the evolution of East Central European warfare and in the interrelated social, political, economic, and international developments in the area. During the eighteenth century the northern part of the area witnessed major armed struggles waged mostly by the Poles and the Hungarians in defense of their independence and national identity. The First Serbian Uprising inspired similar wars of independence elsewhere in the Balkans, a series of struggles that reached its climaxes in the war of 1877–78, the theme of this volume, and the Balkan Wars of 1912–13, the subject of the forthcoming volume XVIII. The complete liberation of the subject peoples was accomplished only in World War I, the subject of volume XIX. These insurrectionary wars played an important role in consolidating national consciousness all over East Central Europe. A synthesis of all these will be presented in volume XXII.

This, then is, the theme and the era. To place them in proper historical perspective it is necessary to focus attention upon three spheres of change: the East Central European cycle of revolutionary warfare, the Industrial Revolution, and the trend toward ultimate violence and total war.

## The Cycle of East Central European Revolutionary Wars

The American Revolution initiated a transformation in warfare by reviving the classic concept of the citizen soldier. This concept was expanded by the French Revolution, which first established the principle of the nation in arms, in which every citizen regardless of race, sex, or age serves a function in the defense of his country. Modern military science, which emerged in the post-Napoleonic era, and the modern Prussian type of general staff – copied all over the world – provided theoretical and institutional leadership for these ever growing masses in arms. The concomitant spread of the Industrial Revolution gave real meaning to the *levée en masse* introduced by the French Revolution. Universal compulsory military service became technologically feasible, and popularly elected constitutional governments were capable of exacting such sacrifices. (Universal military service and universal manhood suffrage have more than their initials in common.) The political and economic changes of the late eighteenth and early nineteenth centuries thus made possible the dawn of modern warfare: war fought by very large, highly motivated citizens' armies whose weapons, transport, and food supplies depended on mature, productive industrial economies.

The Civil War in America and the Franco–Sardinian–Austrian, Bismarckian, and Russo–Turkish Wars in Europe were the first wars fought under these modern conditions. Two centuries of transformation in national defense and war, on the one hand, and of political, social, and economic change, on the other, had produced four basic shifts: (1) from a relatively peaceful age to an age of violence; (2) from the standing armies of eighteenth-century absolute kings to the nation in arms; (3) from limited to modern warfare in the late nineteenth century and to total war in the twentieth; and (4) from the balance-of-power system to the twentieth-century balance of terror.

What is the difference, if any, between Western and East Central Europe with regard to the evolution of warfare? For an answer, we must turn our attention to the nature of East Central European wars over the past two centuries.

The pivotal contrast between Western and East Central European warfare in this period is that in the West, with the substantial exceptions of the American and French Revolutions, the Napoleonic wars, and the American Civil War, wars were limited in goals, in scope, and in results, while in East Central Europe they were often ideological, more violent, broader in their goals, and therefore more consequential. These tendencies, in turn, had their roots in the previous centuries, when many of the wars waged in East Central Europe were between alien cultures rather than, as in the West, between members of the same one. East Central Europe was the frontier on which the Christian societies fought their centuries-long struggle with Islamic Ottoman power. Even when the great powers of the opposing camps were at peace, much of East Central Europe remained involved in protracted, violent, unconventional small wars between people who belonged to different civilizations.

East Central Europeans fought their small wars alone and served as auxiliaries in the armies of the major powers – often on both sides – during major wars, in both cases generally through irregular warfare. The knowledge of and skill in this kind of warfare that East Central Europeans had amassed over the centuries was utilized for their own purposes first by the Ottomans, then by the Habsburgs and the Romanovs. Russia and Austria gradually incorporated East Central European contingents into their military establishments.

East Central Europeans in the service of the Great Powers remained most effective when they were permitted to retain their traditional command and organizational structure, their internal autonomy, and their unconventional tactics. When the two Great Powers attempted to regulate their military behavior and incorporate them into standing armies, their efficiency declined. Circumstances rather than internal strength preserved the troops of the Habsburg Military Frontier into the late nineteenth century and the Cossack military structure in Russia until the end of World War I.

East Central European military formations and their command structure and tactics were alien to Western European military doctrine and practice.

Yet it was not these military considerations that distinguished East Central European warfare from war in Western Europe but ideology, politico-social concepts, goals, and expectations, as well as experience and tradition. No less an expert than A. H. Jacques de Guibert reminded his Western readers that success in such warfare was possible only for those who had the corresponding military tradition.

An earlier observer of East Central European irregular warfare, Lieutenant General Antoine M. P. Feuquieres (1648–1711), analyzed the Hungarian insurrection of the 1670s and 1680s, a response to the execution of the leaders of the Wesselényi Conspiracy (April 30–December 1, 1671), the occupation of Hungary by German troops, and the suppression of the Hungarian constitutional government. The rapidly spreading insurrection secured French cooperation and brought into Hungary a French–Polish force two thousand strong commissioned by Louis XIV. Hence the intimate French experience with this war.[1] Feuquieres recognized the precondition of this protracted insurrection as the precondition of any war of liberation: a high degree of motivation among a large number of warriors, motivation growing out of sociopolitical doctrines, interests, and goals. Feuquieres emphasized that the Hungarians were fighting for the constitutional prerogatives of their country, which the Habsburg rulers were trying to suppress by 'Poison, Dagger, and Murder of the [Hungarian] Grandees...."[2] He asserted that the Hungarian cause was just because the Habsburg rulers had violated their obligations as sovereigns.[3]

Feuquieres's observations were not isolated. Guibert, Chevalier Duteil, Francis Wimpfen, and the ambitious and diligent translator and interpreter of late eighteenth-century French military works Lieutenant Colonel John MacDonald also wrote about the East Central European military experience. The French officers who participated in the late seventeenth-century Hungarian insurgent wars either as combatants or as military advisors were much impressed by the performance of the Hungarian light horse and brought several *huszárokat* (hussars, light cavalrymen) back to France. This inspired Marshal Luxembourg to raise in 1692 the first French hussar regiment (called *mortagni*).[4] The French adaptation of the Hungarian military experience was then copied all over Europe.

Guibert describes the Hungarian light horse as basically dragoons. They did not wear boots or spurs. They fought as infantry, tying their horses together two by two and leaving them behind the firing line. Guibert explains that the Hungarian estates had made their peace with the Habsburg dynasty early in the eighteenth century.[5] Thus Maria Theresa was able to incorporate into her armed forces numerous Hungarian hussar regiments, which, like the Croat infantry, used irregular tactics. The first Hungarian troops fighting for the dynasty appeared in Flanders during the War of the Austrian Succession.

The French invaders of Bohemia, Guibert claims, were defeated primarily by Croat and Hungarian light troops.[6] Guibert was aware that light troops and unconventional warfare had sociopolitical prerequisites. Such warfare, he wrote, required "a vigorous undaunted people superior to others in point of government and courage." Referring to the Hungarian example, he identified the proper uses of light troops as reconnaissance and harassing the enemy, especially at night.[7]

MacDonald claimed that the future belonged to the light cavalry, which would replace heavy cavalry and be the dominant mobile service in all armies.[8] The light horse system on the Hungarian pattern was introduced in Britain with the establishment of the first British dragoon regiment as early as 1681.[9] In sum, then, East Central European methods of warfare had a considerable influence on the West during the eighteenth century.

All these late eighteenth-century military theorists were fascinated by the contrast between Western and East Central European warfare. Most of them restricted their remarks to the professional military aspects of the issue; others, like Guibert, understood that political, social, and ideological factors lay at the foundation of the contrast. Indeed, the typical soldier in the standing army of a Western absolute king had no vested interest in the war aims of his master; hence he had little motivation to fight better. Only brutal discipline kept him in the ranks. A Western soldier could either fight the "enemy" and hope to survive or try to desert and be killed if caught. In contrast, whether East Central Europeans fought the Ottomans or the neighboring Christian Great Powers, even when the struggle began as banditry, in the final analysis they were fighting for ideals that could mobilize a great portion of the population. East Central European wars were therefore more intense than balance-of-power wars in the West. A cycle of East Central European revolutionary wars commenced in the late seventeenth century and continued with ever increasing intensity throughout the following two centuries. The eighteenth- and nineteenth-century history of East Central Europe is the history of wars for national independence.

A typical East Central European revolutionary war opened the eighteenth century: the Hungarian Insurrection of Ferenc Rákóczi II (1703–11). A similar conflict, the Polish War for Independence (the Kościuszko Insurrection), almost closed the century. The Rákóczi war lasted as long as the American Revolution, more than eight years; Kościuszko's struggle began March 24, 1794, and ended with the capitulation of Warsaw on November 5, seven and a half months later. These Polish and Hungarian wars for independence were diametrically opposite to contemporary warfare in Western Europe. In many respects, the former resembled the American and French Revolutions, as did the Polish November and January Insurrections and the Balkan wars of liberation that started with the First Serbian Uprising

(1804–13). The mid-nineteenth century witnessed the revolutions of 1848–
49, a series of upheavals all over East Central Europe. In the military sense,
the most intense of these was Hungary's War for Independence. It took the
combined forces of the two reactionary dynasties, the Habsburgs and the
Romanovs, to subdue the army of Lajos Kossuth.

What began in Serbia in 1804 continued all over the Balkans throughout
the nineteenth century. One nation after another took up arms to free itself
from the Ottoman yoke. The trend culminated, of course, in the Balkan
revolutions of the 1870s and the Russo–Turkish War. By the Treaty of
Berlin (1878), all the Balkan nations except Albania were acknowledged as
sovereign nation-states (Greece had been independent since 1830), although
the liberation of all their national territories had to wait until the end of
World War I. With the Balkan Wars of 1912–13 the cycle of revolutionary
wars of liberation came to a close.


## The Industrial Revolution and East Central Europe

In the study of the Balkan revolutions of the 1870s and the Russo–Turkish
War, the effects of the Industrial Revolution emerge as one of the major
characteristics of the age. The technological effect of the Industrial Revolution on national defense and warfare was, of course, most intense in the
industrialized countries. East Central Europe in the 1870s was still on the
threshold of industrial development, but the experience of this upheaval
showed that countries that had not yet established their own industrial base
could adopt modern technology by importation.

The Industrial Revolution had a more far-reaching effect on society and
warfare than any other event in recorded history.[10] The most profound
effect was social. The ever increasing size and self-consciousness of the two
competing classes of modern society, the bourgeoisie and the proletariat,
gave birth to modern ideologies that sought either revolutionary or evolu-
tionary change in the political-economic-social environment. This change
of course profoundly affected the evolution of military doctrines and national defense practices.

As a consequence of the Industrial Revolution, world coal production
increased more than a hundred times between 1785 and 1914. "The world
output of the iron and steel for which the gods of war were thirsty increased
at least four hundred fold. As it poured from blast furnaces, the flood of
liquid metal came to rival the rising waters of ancient Israel which led Noah
to take to the ark."[11] Production on this scale enabled national economies
to feed, clothe, transport, arm, and supply most of the able-bodied men
of a nation at war. This capability made the levy en masse meaningful for

the first time. Prior to the Industrial Revolution, it had been a matter of principle rather than practice, since it was beyond the capacity of any nation's economy to equip all its young men. In consequence, the size of armies increased by leaps and bounds. Whereas Europe's population quadrupled between the eighteenth and the twentieth century, the strength of its peacetime armies increased by eight times.[12] Perhaps of even greater significance was the fact that the Industrial Revolution made it possible to mobilize reservists and deploy them in potential war zones with far greater dispatch than ever before.

A second profound economic change brought about by the Industrial Revolution was the creation of the capacity to "feed" war out of current production. In earlier wars all the matériel needed had had to be stored in military magazines in advance of the hostilities. In Russia Napoleon had not the slightest chance of resupplying himself out of current production: he launched his campaign in 1812 in the knowledge that he would have to win or lose with the matériel he had at the outset. In the era of the Industrial Revolution, the railroads became efficient transmission belts between the factories and the front line, supplying combat units with everything they required. This was already so in the wars of 1859, 1866, and 1870–71, as well as partially in 1877–78.

The final major change wrought by the Industrial Revolution was an enormous increase in the efficiency of armaments. Between Napoleon's time and 1914, for instance, infantry firepower increased from three rounds a minute to sixteen; the accurate range of artillery went from 1,000 yards to 6,000.[13] The profound change in firepower was dramatized in the Battle of Plevna.

The unprecedented growth in the industrial states' war potential was accompanied by two paradoxical developments. The comparative loss of life in battles dropped dramatically, and the duration of nineteenth-century wars was noticeably less than in the two previous centuries.

In the eighteenth century, Habsburg armies lost a greater proportion of their effectives in a single day than in any of the bloody battles of World War I. Prince Eugene of Savoy, for instance, lost 20 percent of his effective strength during the siege of Belgrade from June through August 1717. Even such an uncontested military campaign as the occupation of the Romanian principalities during the Crimean War cost the Austrian army 13 percent of its effectives. Thereafter, as the effect of the Industrial Revolution began to be felt, the relative casualty figures dropped considerably. In the Seven Weeks' War of 1866 losses were only 6 percent, and in the whole of World War I the Austro–Hungarian armies lost 15.3 percent of their manpower, less than the proportion lost by Prince Eugene in a single day's battle in 1709.[14] While relative losses went down, however, actual head counts went up enormously because of the huge increase in the number of men in combat as well as because, starting with World War I, wars tended once again to become protracted affairs. The Habsburg armies lost 12,500 men in 1859, 20,000 in 1866, and 2,000,000 in World War I.

The greater proportion of casualties in seventeenth- and eighteenth-century battles was due to the nature of combat. Hand-to-hand fighting, whenever the combat was pressed that far, ended in gory carnage in which no quarter was given. As a general rule in this period, a victor would lose about 10 percent of his men and the vanquished about 40 percent in a single battle. The ratio of the victor's losses to those of his adversary was about 11 percent to 23 percent in the early eighteenth century and about 11 percent to 17 percent during Frederick the Great's wars.[15] There was a further decrease to 9 percent to 16 percent during the French Revolutionary wars followed by a rise to 15 percent to 20 percent under Napoleon.

One reason for the decline in the proportion of casualties from the middle of the nineteenth century on was directly related to the Industrial Revolution: the advances in medical science in general and the development of military medical services in particular. Before this time armies lost far more men to disease, infection, lack of medicines, and the want of proper surgery and hygiene than to actual fighting. The improvement in medical knowledge and the treatment of the wounded reduced losses dramatically. The ratio between those killed in battle, including those who later died of wounds received in battle, and those who died of disease during the Crimean War was 1:1 in the Russian and 1:2.5 in the British army. In the Habsburg army it was 1:2 during the occupation of Bosnia and Hercegovina in 1878, 1:2.5 (compared with 1:2 for the Prussians) during the Seven Weeks' War of 1866, 1:3 (compared with 1:7.5 for the British) during the French Revolutionary and Napoleonic wars, and 1:3 during the Seven Years' War.[16] Despite the increase in firepower, a soldier in the second half of the nineteenth century stood a much greater chance of survival than his counterparts in earlier times.

At the same time, while the number of wars in a span of time was increasing, the length of wars was decreasing.[17] Both France and the Habsburg Empire spent fewer years in peace than at war during the eighteenth century: the Habsburg Empire enjoyed only forty-one years of peace and France forty-eight. In the following century the situation was reversed: the Habsburg Empire was at peace for seventy-five years and France for sixty-eight. While wars were supposed to be limited in the eighteenth century, it was hardly a peaceful era, nor were all the battles comparatively bloodless. The results of many engagements were Pyrrhic, both the victor and the defeated losing too much with nothing settled by the outcome. Wars often dragged on for years after the goriest encounters of the century had taken place, as was the case after Blenheim (1704), Malplaquet (1709), Fontenoy (1745), and Rossbach (1757).[18] In this respect there was a noticeable change after Napoleon in that, though battles were still sanguinary, at least they had immediate results. Peace negotiations began in earnest after the Battles of Marengo (1800), Austerlitz (1805), Jena and Auerstadt (1806), Solferino (1859), and Königgrätz (1866), within three months of the fall of Metz (1870), and within two weeks of Senova (1878), the Crimean War having been an odd exception.

The development of a modern economy in East Central Europe was hindered by the protracted existence of serfdom and partial (Hungary and Romania) or full (Poland, Serbia, Bulgaria) foreign domination. The elimination of both was a prerequisite for substantial economic progress.[19]

Emancipation of the serfs was partially accomplished by Napoleon in the Grand Duchy of Warsaw but fully achieved first in Hungary. The April Laws of 1848, enacted by the elected representatives of the last feudal diet, put an end to feudalism and serfdom. The emancipation could not even be reversed by the neo-absolutist Habsburg rule imposed upon Hungary after its defeat by the armed forces of Habsburg Austria and tsarist Russia. While the emancipation of the serfs was an important step toward modernity, the inequitable distribution of landed property remained unchanged even after the Compromise of 1867. In 1861 Russia followed suit with the emancipation of its serfs during the era of Great Reforms, benefiting the serfs in the Kingdom of Poland as well as in Russia's western provinces.

The rest of East Central Europe, the Balkan nations in particular, lagged behind. Continued Ottoman rule remained the greatest obstacle to social emancipation and national liberation, which had to evolve jointly. In Romania the agrarian reforms of 1863 and 1864 eliminated servile labor, and some distribution of land among the peasantry took place. Nationalization of the lands of the Greek Orthodox church and other social reforms in Romania contributed to the gradual modernization of society. Partial reforms in Bulgaria in 1853 and the complete elimination of Turkish landownership that followed transferred landownership to the peasants, but not before 1880–85. In Serbia a similar transformation started as early as 1830–33.

The major contrast between Western and East Central European evolution was that in the West industrialization started immediately after the elimination of feudalism. In East Central Europe, the introduction of capitalism into agriculture rather than industrialization was the essence of the transformation. Western urbanization and population growth created good markets for East Central European food products, and this provided the incentive for the modernization of agriculture. Cheap servile labor and low domestic consumption contributed to the creation of a food surplus for export. The wage labor that replaced servile labor, the mechanization of agriculture, and capitalist production methods caused an immense increase in agrarian production. During the last three decades of the nineteenth century the agricultural production of Romania and of Prussian Poland doubled, while food production in Hungary doubled in two decades.[20] The advance of East Central European Industrial Revolution was, however, extremely slow and far from uniform, the Northern Tier, Hungary, and the Congress Kingdom taking the lead and the Balkans lagging behind.

The first nine steam engines in Hungary were in operation before the revolution of 1848. Up to the 1860s, the increase in their number was sporadic. By 1863 there were 480, producing 8,134 horsepower, compared with 2,325 producing 35,837 horsepower in the Western provinces of the Habsburg Monarchy. The Hungarian Industrial Revolution began in earnest only after the Compromise of 1867. By 1884 the number of steam engines was 63,869, an eightfold increase since 1863. Per capita pig-iron production in 1882 was 11 kg in Hungary, 18 kg in Austria, and 55 kg in Germany. In 1898 the combined output rating of Hungarian industrial machinery was 262,070 horsepower, and by the eve of World War I it was 930,000.[21] The social effect of the Industrial Revolution was substantial. The industrial proletariat increased to 563,000, the basis of a substantial social class whose effect on society was forcefully demonstrated during and at the end of the war.[22]

A similar evolution occurred in the Congress Kingdom. The number of factories was 8,349 in 1877 and nearly 13,000 in 1895. By the outbreak of World War I the proletariat in that country amounted to 206,000 industrial laborers. Between 1877 and 1895 the value of industraial products rose from 274,000,000 to 739,000,000 francs, and by 1910 it was 2,279,000,000.[23]

The industrial development of the Balkan states was much slower. In Romania up to 1860 consumer needs were fulfilled by local agrarian-oriented industries. At the end of the 1870s, there were only 33 small local flour mills, 2 sugar factories, and 2 distilleries. The emergence of large industries began in 1876 with the establishment of the first large flour mill capable of producing for export. By 1902, there were 625 factories producing 45,200 horsepower. The emerging proletariat amounted to 39,700 laborers.[24] In Bulgaria, 20 factories were established between 1830 and 1879. By 1887 there were 36 factories in operation, of which 26 were flour mills, breweries, or distilleries, and by 1907 there were 206. The proletariat amounted to 12,000 men.[25]

The Balkan nations' industrial systems remained very weak until World War I. Their role in the national economy was small, and heavy industry was not predominant. In the Balkans the Industrial Revolution was still in the making at the outbreak of World War I, and industry remained largely agrarian-oriented. For example, the ratio between food and textile industries was 44 percent to 5 percent in Hungary, 55 percent to 10 percent in Romania, 58 percent to 18 percent in Bulgaria, and 55 percent to 8 percent in Serbia.[26] All over East Central Europe, the Industrial Revolution started with the mechanization of food industry, and the textile industry lagged far behind. This was because of the availability of raw materials, the nature of the domestic and international markets, and the competition of Western industries in the open market.

The technological advances that had the most effect on military operations were the railroad and the steamship. In Poland, Hungary, and Romania, the primary incentive for massive railroad building was the need to connect the agrarian areas with their natural Western markets or with the nearest seaport. In Serbia and Bulgaria, the incentive was strategic, and while for the first group Western investment was important, for these two countries it was predominant.[27] The first railroads were built in Hungary in the early 1840s, and all three parts of partitioned Poland followed in 1847. Romania began building railroads in 1869 and Bulgaria in the 1860s; the first railroad was built in Serbia immediately after the Berlin Congress in 1878.[28]

The density of nineteenth-century European railroad systems is shown in table 1, at the end of this chapter. By 1896–97 Hungary's system equaled and in certain respects even surpassed those of the Western provinces of the Habsburg Empire. At the outbreak of World War I all the countries of East Central Europe had well-developed railroad systems.

Modern industrial development and even agrarian revolution heavily depend on an organized credit and banking system, a pivotal element of the capitalist transformation of the economy. The banking system of East Central Europe was consolidated during the second half of the nineteenth century but remained predominantly agrarian-oriented.[29]

In partitioned Poland, land mortgage institutions were established immediately after the Napoleonic era, and by the 1870s all three parts possessed adequate banking systems. In the Kingdom at the outbreak of World War I there were 38 banks.[30] Chronologically Hungary came second, the first banks having been established in the 1830s. The financial system was much more developed in Hungary than in any other East Central European country and more like Western systems than those of its neighbors. In 1848, 36, in 1860, 60, and in 1873, 637 banks were operating in Hungary. Some of them, such as the General Credit Bank controlled by Rothschild interests, were huge financial enterprises. The capital of Hungarian banks increased between 1848 and the end of the century by 11,384 percent, a true financial revolution.[31] Romania established its first bank in 1857. At the outbreak of World War I there were 110 banks in Romania, again a financial revolution. In Bulgaria in 1887, there were 5 banks; by 1895 the number had increased to 36.[32] In Serbia the first bank was established in 1869, and by the end of the century there were 80.[33]

While the Western capital investments in Poland, Hungary, and Romania were predominantly commercial, in Serbia and Bulgaria they were predominantly military. Immediately after they achieved national independence, the Balkan countries received rather substantial Western credits to build up their armed forces. In 1900 Serbia owed 200,000,000 francs, and by 1914 its debt had increased to 850,000,000.[34] Most of these credits were advanced as state loans for the establishment of new governmental institutions and the modernization of the army. A substantial portion of these loans was designated for the construction of strategic railroads. The Serbian section of the Vienna–Istanbul railroad line was initiated with Austrian and French capital. In Bulgaria, railroad building began, with Turkish–British funds, well before the Russo–Turkish War. After the Berlin Congress, the existing railroad system was amalgamated, and the Vienna–Istanbul line was completed by 1888. The nearly 1,700-km railroad line was henceforth controlled by German technological personnel and financial interests. By the end of the century Bulgaria and Serbia were devoting 30 percent of their annual incomes to the payment of interest on foreign loans. One by one the Balkan states declared bankruptcy and were placed under foreign financial control, Serbia in 1895 and Bulgaria in 1902.[35]

All over East Central Europe the state played an important role in economic development. State intervention was, however, restricted to the insurance of interest payments for foreign investors, intended to provide an incentive to investment.

The nations of East Central Europe entered the 1870s in a backward state. The region was still excluded from the main network of world commerce; urbanization had not yet begun in earnest; capital accumulation was in its infancy; and foreign rule kept the economy stagnant. East Central Europe was agrarian even in the second half of the nineteenth century; the urban population of the Danubian principalities was still only 9 percent, that of Bulgaria 6 percent, and that of Hungary 17 percent. While the Northern Tier entered the twentieth century with the rudiments of the Industrial Revolution, in the Balkans it was still embryonic. Yet the Balkan revolutions and the Russo–Turkish War were fought with all the means the Industrial Revolution could offer. This was a modern war. How could an agrarian society wage such a war? The answer, of course, is through imports.

That war technology produced by a developed society can be operated by soldiers of a less developed one is clear from the examples of the Korean War, the Vietnam War, and many other twentieth-century wars of national liberation. In the 1870s, however, it was less so. The Balkan revolutions of the 1870s and the Russo–Turkish War were wars in which undeveloped societies' soldiers operated war technology far above their own developmental level. In an industrialized society, turning a factory mechanic into an artillery engineer is a simple matter. These wars proved that, though it may take time, an oxcart driver can be trained as a mechanic, and an effective one. In that respect, the East Central European experience in the 1870s broke new ground.

## Toward Ultimate Violence: Total War

The trend toward decisive campaigns and conclusive battles followed immediately by peace talks that typified the wars of the nineteenth century in Europe was absent in North America, where the United States Civil War was drawn out from 1861 to 1865. World War I was like the Civil War rather than those of the European war cycle of 1859–78. The similarity between the Civil War and World War I is not limited to their length, for the latter was the product of two factors present in both wars, one technical and economic and the other ideological and political. The technical and economic factor, of course, was the Industrial Revolution and the sophisticated arms that it produced, enormously improving their ballistics, range, and accuracy. The increase in firepower radically altered tactics. The defensive became the stronger battle stance; as long as a unit had the will to fight, selected and organized an adequate defensive position, and was supplied with enough ammunition, it could repel an attacking force two or three times its size, as was demonstrated by the troops of Osman Pasha at Plevna. This situation reached its peak in World War I and was the reason for the four years of deadlock and slaughter. Michael Howard's assertion that "so long as railways kept the armies supplied with blood and treasure of the nations, the armies could not be defeated until the nations themselves were exhausted and begging for peace"[36] was equally applicable to World War I and to the Civil War. It reflects both the material effect of the Industrial Revolution and the ideological and political nature of total war.

In total war entire nations, not just their armed forces, take part. Unless the population has the stomach to pursue such a war to its successful conclusion, the number of men under arms and the tonnage of supplies do not matter. Total war is waged not merely against the foe's armed forces, which are expected to surrender unconditionally, but equally against the civilian population, which is expected to beg for peace or rise up against its own rulers. During the Civil War, General William T. Sherman's march to the sea was a war against the populace. He wrote to General Henry W. Halleck, chief of staff in Washington, D. C.: "If the people raise a howl against my barbarity and cruelty, I will answer that war is war. ...If they want peace, they and their relatives must stop the war."[37] The same assessment was aired two generations later by Raymond Aron: "In absolute war, in which extreme violence leads to the disarmament or the destruction of one of the adversaries... bring into conflict collectivities which are united in expressing one will. In this regard, they are all psychological wars."[38] The elements of total war were emerging.

Total war is a contest involving men, ideas, and material, all of which were accumulating in abundance in the century or so preceding World War I. "What a change from 1785 to 1824," Stendhal had exclaimed. "In the two thousand years of recorded world history so sharp a revolution in customs, ideas, and beliefs has perhaps never occurred before."[39] The pace of change did not slacken up to the 1870s and beyond. The material changes caused by the Industrial Revolution can be measured in tons and miles per hour and kilowatts, and it is not much more difficult to measure its social, intellectual, and political impact. Nef has noted new cultural values that made old ones obsolete and a growing disparity of cultural and intellectual experiences and discord between nations that stimulated nationalism, the predominant ideology of the upheaval we are concerned with here. The working classes were growing faster than those of the power holders and reaching out for a share of wealth and authority. Thus, the Industrial Revolution brought heightened social and international disharmony and violence.[40] Both the limited wars of the balance-of-power era and the increasingly vicious confrontations of the era of modern warfare were, however, consistent with Clausewitz's dictum that "war is an act of violence intended to compel our opponent to fulfill our will."[41] Interestingly, wars waged among civilized peoples are not necessarily less violent than wars waged by less civilized peoples, for the basic cause of war is the hostile intent, not the sentiment of hostility. In general, given the hostile intent on both sides, passion and hatred soon animated the belligerents, but in theory a major war without hatred is conceivable. The most one can say apropos of civilized peoples is that "intelligence exercises greater influence on their mode of carrying on war, and has taught them more effectual means of applying force than these rude acts of mere instincts."[42] The fact remains that the desire to destroy the enemy, inherent in the concept of war, has not been diminished or repressed by the progress of civilization.

The drift of Western man toward violence has occupied the minds of all sorts of intellectuals, philosophers, publicists, men of letters, and psychological and scientific analysts. In various ways Marx, Engels, Freud, Nietzsche, Dostoyevsky, Proust, Proudhon, Sorel, and many lesser lights have pointed to the dawn of an age of violence. From the pages of their works the satanic face of power leers at a Western society luxuriating in unparalleled prosperity and influence and intoxicated by the speed of the social and political changes generated by the mature Industrial Revolution. Proudhon and Nietzsche saw war as an ennobling necessity for society and the individual and accorded the highest honor to its practitioners. From a proletarian viewpoint, Sorel ridiculed peaceful relations between human beings and denied the barbarity of violence, thus contributing handsomely to the eventual doctrine of total war. These intellectuals, whether advocates or critics of war, did not create the violence of the turn of the century but rather reflected the masses' state of mind. The mass mentality of violence was the psychological root of total war and did the most to lead doctrines and systems of national defense away from limitation. The "cult of violence is actually no substitute for material gains, nor is it equivalent to redemption. ...Violence is a substitute for redemption in the sense Hell is a substitute for heaven."[43]

The American and French Revolutions and the Napoleonic wars rattled the foundations of limitation. The American Revolution was in part a civil war between loyalists and patriots, and like all civil wars it was fought with a passion that defied reason and moderation. It was also an international war in which the stakes were independence, on the one hand, and the continuation of royal sovereignty, on the other: the former could be achieved only by complete elimination of the latter — another factor militating against limitation. "The American Revolution," as Higginbotham has observed, "was an upheaval of profound significance. It was a people's war for political independence, the first successful struggle to sever an imperial relationship in modern times. In one way or another it helped shake human society to its foundations, first in Europe, then in Latin America, and eventually in Africa and Asia, where the impact continues even today."[44] The American Revolution was the turning point in fact from the age of limitation to a new age of increased violence. The French Revolution pushed the trend farther. After the Convention's proclamation of November 19, 1792, offering assistance to any people that wished to overthrow its government and social system, limitation made little sense in the revolutionary and Napoleonic wars.

The revolutionary and ideological wars were the only Western European wars that were in intimate kinship with those of East Central Europe, since the typical war in the latter region was a profound flood of events whose intense violence served progress. Wars of liberation against foreign oppression — which the East Central European wars were — must be considered the truly just wars of modern times. "According to the profound and perhaps prophetic view of Immanuel Kant, humanity must travel through bloody roads of war to have access one day to peace. It is through history that the repression of natural violence is achieved: the education of man to reason"[45] and, one might add, the end of the suppression of men by men and/or nation by nation.

## TABLE 1

### DENSITY OF RAILROADS IN KILOMETERS IN VARIOUS EUROPEAN COUNTRIES, 1850 AND 1896–97

|  | 1850 | | 1896–97 | |
|---|---|---|---|---|
|  | Per 100,000 inhabitants | Per 100 km$^2$ | Per 100,000 inhabitants | Per 100 km$^2$ |
| Germany | 16.6 | 1.1 | 91.0 | 8.8 |
| France | 8.5 | 0.6 | 106.0 | 7.6 |
| Austria | 7.8 | 0.5 | 70.0 | 5.8 |
| Hungary | 1.7 | 0.1 | 86.6 | 4.8 |
| Polish Kingdom | – – – | – – – | 29.3 | 2.9 |
| Romania | – – – | – – – | 46.3 | 2.2 |
| Bulgaria | – – – | – – – | 29.0 | 1.0 |
| Serbia | – – – | – – – | 25.0 | 1.2 |

**Source:**    Sándor Matlekovits, *Das Königreich Ungarn*, 2:665.

## NOTES

1.  Count Imre Thököly (1657–1705), Prince of Transylvania and Upper Hungary, was allied with the Turks from 1682 on and exiled in Turkey after 1699.
2.  Antoine Manasses Pas, Marquis de Feuquieres, *Memoirs Historical and Military*, 2 vols. (London, 1736), 1:225.
3.  Feuquieres, *Memoirs*, 1:224–25.
4.  A. H. Jacques, Count de Guibert, *A General Essay on Tactics with an Introductory Discourse upon the Present State of Politics and the Military Science in Europe to which is Prefixed a Plan of a Work Entitled The Political and Military System of France*, trans. an officer (London, 1781), pp. 300–301.
5.  He refers, of course, to the 1711 Peace of Szatmár.
6.  Guibert, *Essay on Tactics*, p. 303.
7.  Ibid., p. 309.
8.  John MacDonald, trans. "Introduction," in Chevalier Dutel, *The Formation and Maneuvers of Infantry, Calculated for the Effectual Resistance of Cavalry and for Attacking them Successfully: On New Principles of Tactics* (London, 1810), p. i.
9.  Francis Wimpfen (de Borneborg), *The Experienced Officer, or, Instructions*, trans. John MacDonald (London, 1804), p. 98.
10.  On the impact of the Industrial Revolution on warfare, see John U. Nef, *War and Human Progress: An Essay on the Rise of Industrial Civilization* (Cambridge, Mass., 1950); John F. C. Fuller, *The Conduct of War, 1789–1961: A Study of the Impact of the French, Industrial, and Russian Revolutions on War and Its Conduct* (New York, 1968); Alfred Vagts, *A History of Militarism: Civilian and Military*, rev. ed. (New York, 1959); Bernard Brodie and M. Fawn, *From Crossbow to H-Bomb: The Evolution of the Weapons and Tactics of Warfare*, rev. and enl. ed. (Bloomington, 1974); Morton Fried

et al., *War: The Anthropology of Armed Conflict and Aggression* (Garden City, N. Y., 1968); and J. David Singer and Melvin Small, *The Wages of War, 1816–1965: A Statistical Handbook* (New York, 1972).

11.  Nef, *War and Human Progress*, p. 292.

12.  Ibid., p. 369.

13.  Ibid., p. 366.

14.  These calculations are derived from basic data in Samuel Dumas and K. O. Vedel–Petersen, *Losses of Life Caused by War* (Oxford, 1923); Singer and Small, *The Wages of War*; and Lewis F. Richardson, *Statistics of Deadly Quarrels* (Pittsburgh, 1960). In the war of 1859 the Habsburg armies lost 15.2 percent of their men. Though this was an industrial-age war, casualties were high mostly because the French artillery had more advanced rifled firearms and the Habsburg forces did not yet have modern medical services.

Habsburg casualty rates in selected single engagements were as follows: Luzzara (August 15, 1702), 13.5 percent; Blenheim (August 13, 1704), 26.0 percent; Malplaquet (September 11, 1709), 27.0 percent; Siege of Belgrade (June–August 1717), 20.0 percent; Mollwitz (April 10, 1741), 18.7 percent; Cuneo (September 30, 1744), 14.4 percent; Hohenfriedeberg (Dobromierz) (June 4, 1745), 12.8 percent; Kolin (June 18, 1757), 12.0 percent; Prague (May 6, 1757), 15.1 percent; Leuthen (Lutynia) (December 5, 1757), 15.4 percent; Kunersdorf (Kunowice) (August 15, 1760), 12.0 percent; Liegnitz (Legnica) (August 15, 1760), 13.4 percent; Torgau (November 3, 1760), 13.6 percent.

Habsburg casualty rates over the duration of hostilities were as follows: Crimean War (Austrian Army of Observation), 12.4 percent; Italian War of 1859, 15.2 percent; Seven Weeks' War of 1866, 6.1 percent; Occupation of Bosnia–Hercegovina in 1878, 1.7 percent; World War I, 15.3 percent.

15.  During the first four years of the Seven Years' War 33 generals, including two field marshals, were killed in action. In October 1756 Frederick the Great had 5,500 officers at his command. Half of them were casualties of the first three years of war; 1,328 more fell in 1759 and another 771 in 1760. A few recovered from their wounds and returned to service, but 4,000 were lost permanently, including 1,500 killed (Christopher Duffy, *The Army of Frederick the Great* [New York, 1974], p. 190).

16.  All calculations are based on Dumas and Vedel–Petersen, *Losses of Life,* and Singer and Small, *The Wages of War.*

17.  The figures are based on data in Dumas and Vedel–Petersen, *Losses of Life.* The wars include all armed conflicts, domestic and foreign, in which substantial use was made of firearms. Thus in the case of the Habsburg armies the nineteenth-century wars include such actions as the invasion of various Italian states during the revolutions of 1820–21, 1831, and 1848 and the quixotic naval expedition to Syria and the Levant in 1840 during the war against Muhammad Ali of Egypt. For this last, see Artur von Khuepach and Heinrich von Bayer, *Geschichte der k.-k. Kriegsmarine während der Jahre 1814–1847* (Graz, 1966), pp. 243–67.

18.  David Chandler, *Marlborough as a Military Commander* (New York, 1973), pp. 240–72.

19.  Iván T. Berend and György Ránki, "Az ipari forradalom kérdéséhez Kelet-Délkelet-Európában," *Századok* 102 (1968): 35–76; Emil Niederhauser, *Jobbágyfelszabadítás Kelet-Európában* (Budapest, 1962); László Katus, "A kelet-európai iparosodás és az önálló tőkés fejlődés kérdéséhez," *Történelmi Szemle,* 1967, no. 1, pp. 38–52.

20.  Niederhauser, *Jobbágyfelszabadítás,* pp. 67–81.

21.  Mihály Fute, *A magyar gyáripar története,* Special Bulletin of the Hungarian Institute of Economic Research 26 (Budapest, 1944), p. 301.

22.  Vilmos Sándor, *Nagyipari fejlődés Magyarországon* (Budapest, 1954).

23.  E. Piltz, *Poland* (London, 1909), pp. 159–60.

24.  N. N. Constantineşcu, *Contributii la istoria capatalului strain in România*

(Bucharest, 1960), p. 31; G. D. Cioriceanu, *La Roumanie économique* (Paris, 1928), p. 108.

25. Berend and Ránki, "Az ipari," pp. 74–75.

26. Jovan Kirkner, *Die Industrie und Industriepolitik Serbiens* (Halle, 1913), p. 154; Iván T. Berend and György Ránki, "Nemzeti jövedelem és tőkefelhalmozás Magyarországon, 1867–1914," *Történelmi Szemle,* 1966, no. 2; R. Aranitovic, *Les resources de la Jougoslavie* (Paris, 1930), p. 137.

27. Cioriceanu, *La Roumanie économique,* p. 126; Piltz, *Poland,* p. 195; Alexander Matlekovits, *Das Königreich Ungarn,* 2 vols. (Leipzig, 1905), 2:664–65; Lubomir Lestoff, *Die Staatsschulden und Reparationen Bulgariens, 1878–1927* (Leipzig, 1928), p. 120.

28. H. Feis, *Europe the World Banker, 1870–1914* (New York, 1964), pp. 294–96.

29. A Gerschenkorn, *Economic Backwardness in Historical Perspective: A Book of Essays* (Cambridge, 1962).

30. Piltz, *Poland,* p. 200.

31. *Magyar Statisztikai Közlemények,* no. 35 (Budapest, 1913).

32. Kiril Lambrev, *Polozsenyeto na rabotnyicseszkata klasza v. Balgarija ot oszvobodzsdanyieto do nacsaloto na XX vek* (Sofia, 1954), p. 49.

33. C. Colocotronis, *L'organisation bancaire des pays balcaniques et les capitaux étrangers* (Paris, 1934), p. 159; P. Douglas, "Capital in the United Kingdom," *Journal of Economic Business History* 35 (1929–30): 67.

34. Lestoff, *Die Staatsschulden,* p. 20; Milan Simitch, *La dette publique de la Serbie de l'origine a la guerre de 1914* (Paris, 1925), p. 74.

35. Feis, *Europe the World Banker,* p. 262.

36. Michael Howard, *Studies in War and Peace* (New York, 1972), p. 107.

37. William T. Sherman, *Memoirs of General W. T. Sherman,* 2 vols. (New York, 1891), 2:374.

38. Raymond Aron, *Peace and War: A Theory of International Relations* (Garden City, N. Y., 1973), p. 27.

39. Stendhal (pseudonym of Marie-Henri Beyle), *Racine et Shakespeare,* 2 vols. (Paris, 1925), 1:91.

40. Nef, *War and Human Progress,* pp. 290–96.

41. Karl von Clausewitz, *On War* (New York, 1956), Book 1, chap. 1, p. 2.

42. Ibid., pp. 19–20.

43. Ibid., p. 410.

44. Don Higginbotham, *The War of American Independence: Military Attitudes, Policies, and Practice, 1763–1789* (New York, 1976).

45. Aron, *Peace and War,* p. 16.

## II
## The Balkan Crisis and East Central Europe

Tofik Islamov


# THE BALKAN POLICY OF THE HABSBURG MONARCHY AND AUSTRO–RUSSIAN RELATIONS


When at the end of the seventeenth century the armies of Leopold I reached Vidin in Bulgaria and Prizren in Albania, it became clear that a new claimant to the Balkan heritage of the Ottoman Empire, already under pressure in the northeast from Peter's Russia, had emerged. Complex relations characterized by alternating cooperation and rivalry and at times even parallel development began between Russia and Austria over their common Balkan interests. In view of the European complications over the Spanish succession and the priority of European interests in the policy of the Vienna court, Austria was not then in a position to entrench itself in the Balkans, although at the beginning of the eighteenth century its southeastern frontiers had on the whole been stabilized. Owing to its possession of the Hungarian crown, including the Triune Kingdom (Croatia, Slavonia, and Dalmatia), Austria remained to a certain extent a Balkan power, but its position did not develop beyond that. Properly speaking, this was the end of the Austrian Habsburgs' "historical mission" in the East, of which so much had been written that it had become a virtually inalienable attribute of Austria's self-image. The wars waged by the Habsburgs against the Ottoman Empire in the seventeenth and eighteenth centuries undoubtedly weakened the Turkish war machine, unsettled its Balkan position, and diverted its forces and attention from other theaters of military operations, thereby contributing to the creation of favorable conditions for the liberation of the peoples of the peninsula. Because of its geopolitical position as a counterweight to Ottoman power, the monarchy could have played a decisive role in accelerating the historical process of disintegration of Ottoman domination over southeastern Europe. But this did not happen.

One reason for this was that in the course of the more than a century and a half following its first major successes in the anti-Turkish wars, the foreign policy of the Habsburg Empire was shaped by dynastic interests, the foci of which were the age-old struggle with France for European hegemony and, after the War of the Austrian Succession, the conflict with Brandenburg–Prussia for hegemony in Germany. Another reason had to do with the attitude of the enslaved peoples of the Balkan Peninsula toward the Habsburg Empire and its role in the affairs of southeastern Europe. To free themselves from the Porte's yoke, these peoples needed strong allies who could prevail over the Ottoman Empire. Austria and Russia were obvious choices for such allies, but Austria never became one. The Austro–Turkish wars of the late seventeenth century revealed one substantial feature that subsequently became a significant factor in Austro–Balkan relations and a constant concomitant of the Habsburg efforts to gain a strong position on the Balkan subcontinent: that the Christian peoples of the Balkans were inclined to accept Habsburg patronage only with serious reservations. They did not want to exchange Ottoman Muslim oppression for a Habsburg Catholic yoke. The Christians of Albania and Bosnia–Hercegovina did not respond as expected to the appeal of Ludwig of Baden, the Austrian commander in chief. As Austrian historians themselves write, "the Orthodox Christians of the Balkan countries were afraid of Catholic propaganda and the Germans, and therefore they turned to Russia."[1] In the course of time this fear and distrust intensified. This is the reason that, despite the numerous wars with the Porte, the Austrian advance into the interior of the peninsula stopped at the southeastern boundaries of the Kingdom of Hungary.

In the nineteenth century, the period of the triumph of capitalism, the Eastern Question, the question of the dissolution of Ottoman domination in southeastern Europe and the liberation of the Balkans, became an important component of the new system of international relations and of Austria's Balkan policy.[2] At the same time, Austro–Russian relations underwent substantial evolution, acquiring a number of qualitatively new features. The basis of the Danubian monarchy's desire to expand into the Balkans was no longer predominantly dynastic but increasingly bourgeois-capitalistic, as the Vienna court had more and more to reckon with the increasing economic power of the bourgeoisie. Robert A. Kann is incorrect in arguing that even in the 1870s dynastic interests lay at the basis of the Dual Monarchy's Balkan policy, the occupation of Bosnia and Hercegovina having merely the aim of compensating for the loss of strong positions in Italy and Germany.[3] Another new feature of Austria's Balkan policy was connected with the exhaustion of possibilities for territorial acquisition in the West and the weakening of Austria's position in Germany, making southeastern Europe the main direction of eventual expansion. But Kann refuses to see any signs of expansionism in the occupation of Bosnia and Hercegovina and, what is most inexplicable, in Austria's Eastern policy in general. This is all the more strange because earlier he asserted the opposite, namely, that Vienna regarded the occupation of the provinces not as an end in itself but as "a means of an ambitious foreign policy aimed at advancing into the Balkans and gaining an outlet to the Aegean Sea."[4]

These two features of Austrian policy in the Balkans — its conditioning by bourgeois pressure and the lessening of prospects for expansion to the north — conditioned a third, the inevitable deterioration of relations between the two continental empires.[5] The events of the first two decades of the nineteenth century in the Danubian principalities and in Serbia showed that Russia had become the external force that could destroy Habsburg chances of establishing their domination (or precedence) in these two areas of the Ottoman Empire. The consolidation of its rival in Wallachia and Moldavia meant for Vienna an end to the long-cherished dream of monopoly of the Danube from its upper reaches to its mouth, shattering the hope of an outlet to the Black Sea. Vienna also closely watched the rapprochement between Russia and Serbia, which was regarded as a "legitimate" sphere of Austrian interest.

Habsburg objectives were clearly revealed at each stage of the deepening of the Eastern crisis, in particular in 1854 and 1876–78. Especially indicative was Austria's conduct in the former case, for its anti-Russian actions seemed quite at odds with the cooperation of the two conservative monarchies since the Vienna Congress and came only five years after tsarist Russia had helped to remove a threat to the very existence of the Habsburg throne. The ultimatum presented to an ally cornered by the Anglo–French coalition and the occupation of Wallachia and Moldavia by Austrian troops opened the first breach in Metternich's carefully balanced system, which had as a major component joint action with the Romanovs to preserve the status quo in the Balkans. The Austrian emperor decided upon this risky step, which had far-reaching consequences first of all for the Habsburg Empire itself, not because of any pressure from the Tuileries or from the Court of St. James but in pursuit of its own Great Power aims, among them realizing its long-standing intention of establishing German control over the Danube from Ulm to the Black Sea. This design was a part of the more extensive project of creating a *Mitteleuropa* that had originated in Germany in the 1840s.[6] Count K. F. Buol, foreign minister of the Vienna court, dreamed of "grand conquests" in the Balkans; according to the conservative Austrian historian Hugh Hantsch, he "found the moment suitable for completing the work of Prince Eugene [of Savoy] and extending Austrian domination to the neighboring Balkans, thus contributing to the collapse of the Ottoman Empire in Europe and making some capital of it."[7]

Already in the Crimean stage of the Eastern crisis, Austrian generals headed by Field Marshal Joseph Radetzky indicated as direct targets of

Austrian expansion not only Bosnia and Hercegovina, but also Albania, Serbia, and western Macedonia. In January 1854, at a ministerial conference, the generals and the emperor himself advocated an immediate occupation of the provinces as soon as the Russian army crossed the Danube. At the meetings which followed in Vienna on March 22 and 25, 1854, Buol painted a prospect of easy "war fame" and "rich booty." A "reward" for coming out against Russia, he emphasized, would be "the preservation and increase of our weight and influence in the East and the security of our important commercial and industrial interests there." In insisting on taking possession of Moldavia, Wallachia, and the Danube (Germany's lifeline), Buol offered as justification the notion that Russia's policy created the threat of war and "revolutionary movements," as he called the national liberation movements of the Balkan peoples.[8]

Even though Buol initiated a break with the old policy and introduced the idea of a "protectorate" over the Danubian principalities and Serbia, Paul Schroeder is inclined to question the expansionist nature of the aims of Austrian diplomacy during the Crimean campaign, characterizing this policy as "conservative and defensive."[9] Austria's policy can be so regarded, however, only in the sense that nothing struck more fear into the hearts of the rulers of the monarchy than the likelihood of active participation of the peoples of the Balkans themselves in the resolution of the Eastern Question. Russia's policy, according to Buol's report to the emperor, created the threat of an outburst of "revolutionary movements in the East" against the Ottoman yoke, Balkan national liberation movements that could easily involve the oppressed peoples of the monarchy itself. Hence the conservatism of Vienna's Balkan policy; hence its desire to maintain the status quo in the Balkans as long as possible; hence its unwillingness to bring nearer the hour of the collapse of Ottoman domination in Europe. In the long run, this policy proved shortsighted and unproductive. Its positive results were paltry and its negative ones catastrophic. True, Francis Joseph managed to compel Nicholas I to withdraw Russian troops from the Danubian principalities and to occupy them with his own, but not for long. Soon after the Paris conference, Austria, disappointed in its hopes for the gratitude of the Western allies, had to vacate the Danubian principalities. At the same conference signs appeared of a rapprochement between Russia and France, which did not augur well for the Vienna court. During the wars of 1859 and 1866, which had a decisive impact on the destiny of the monarchy, Austria found itself completely isolated.

But the lesson was lost, except for the necessity of showing more circumspection in the choice of aims and in the means of attaining them. In view of the impracticability of a policy of large-scale acquisitions in the Balkans in the absence of strong allies and the benign neutrality or tacit approval of at least one Great Power directly interested in Balkan affairs, Austria gradually

concentrated its efforts on a single object — Bosnia–Hercegovina.
From the standpoint of Austria's strategic interests, these two Slavic
provinces, which provided protection for Dalmatia, were not only of great
defensive importance but also constituted a splendid beachhead for active
offensive operations in the direction of Salonika. This side of the matter is
often forgotten. Some modern writers, basing their conclusions wholly on
the defensive significance of the provinces in providing protection for the
maritime provinces, repeat the well-known thesis of Austrian (and, later,
Austro–Hungarian) diplomacy that Bosnia and Hercegovina were Dalmatia's "natural hinterland." Furthermore, until recently not enough attention
was given to the fact that the industrial bourgeoisie, which, though still
outside of the conduct of foreign policy, was carrying more and more weight
in the political sphere, viewed the neighboring Ottoman provinces, with
their rich forest and mineral resources, as a possible internal colony. This
lacuna is now being filled by the efforts of historians from Bulgaria and
Yugoslavia, who have recently published a number of interesting studies on
the economic expansion of the Danubian monarchy into southeastern
Europe.[10] Lastly, we should not forget that the possession of the provinces
gave the monarchy a powerful lever on the principalities of Montenegro and
Serbia, a lever which could be used if necessary to keep these Slavic lands in
check.

The consummation of the unification of Germany and of Italy at the
turn of the 1870s and the parallel dualistic reorganization of the Habsburg
Empire called for a corresponding reorientation of the foreign policy of the
monarchy. This reorientation began under Friedrich Beust, during the conclusion of the Austro–Hungarian agreement, and was completed under Gyula
Andrássy, foreign minister of the new Austria–Hungary. Its basic historical
meaning consisted of the adaptation of foreign policy to the new international situation, with due regard for the new alignment of forces produced
by the conversion of the integral empire into a two-centered monarchy.
More specifically, it meant that from now on Vienna had to coordinate
every foreign-policy step with Hungary inside the country and with
Bismarck's Germany abroad.

Contrary to expectations, new departures in Austria's policy were
associated with the name of Beust, whose appointment was meant to emphasize the determination of the court to continue the old dynastic course. But
times had changed, and hopes for revenge for Königgrätz could not be
entertained even by Beust, who had to pay more and more heed to the
advice and recommendations of a Berlin court vitally interested in the
establishment of tolerable relations between Vienna and St. Petersburg.
Conciliatory notes began to sound in the speeches Francis Joseph and Beust
addressed to Alexander II and Gorchakov, and the tsar, for his part, became

prepared to forget the Crimean wound. Proper adjustments were also introduced into Vienna's course in the Balkans.

Advancing the slogan of satisfying the "legitimate interests" of the Balkan countries and rendering diplomatic support to Serbia's efforts to rid itself of Ottoman control, Beust imparted flexibility to the traditional Austrian policy of preserving the integrity of the Ottoman Empire and containing the popular anti-Ottoman movements in the Balkans. While vying with Russia, with some success, for the sympathies of the Balkan countries, Austria nonetheless did not lose sight of the concrete aim of establishing its domination over Bosnia and Hercegovina. Guided by these considerations, in late 1866 and early 1867, when the talks on the Austro–Hungarian agreement were drawing to a successful conclusion, Austrian diplomacy, seeking to take advantage of the favorable situation created by the Cretan uprising, made an attempt to solve the problem of the provinces in its favor through an amicable agreement with the St. Petersburg court. The Austrian ambassador in Russia, Count Rewertera, in a talk with Gorchakov in December 1866 suddenly raised the matter of his government's views on Hercegovina. During the next meeting, in January 1867, he also mentioned Bosnia. In exchange the Vienna court expressed readiness to give its partner a free hand in the Danube's estuary. Gorchakov rejected the idea, and Austria had to disavow its diplomat.[11]

Austria's initiative also found no support in Hungary, where anti-Russian and pro-Turkish feeling had been running high since 1849. Besides, Hungary's ruling circles had more reason to seek control over Serbia than to seize Bosnia and Hercegovina. Guided by these considerations, Andrássy, the head of the Hungarian cabinet in 1867–68, came forward with the sudden proposal of turning the provinces over to Serbia; not to give offense to the friendly Porte, he stipulated that Belgrade was to govern them on behalf of the sultan.[12] Andrássy hoped thereby to prevent a Serbian–Russian rapprochement, believing that Serbia, grateful for this "gift," would no longer need Russia's patronage, and, more important, by tying the principality firmly to the chariot of the Dual Monarchy, to deprive the national movement among Hungary's Serbian population of its potential support. Moreover, the incorporation of the provinces into Serbia would have driven a wedge between Serbia and Croatia–Slavonia, whose dominant classes would have preferred to see these provinces, with their considerable Croatian minority, incorporated into Austria–Hungary.

Andrássy's proposal, actively supported by the Austro–Hungarian consul-general in Serbia B. Kállay, ended in dismal failure. Neither Beust nor the Austrian generals would consider any "ceding" of the provinces to anyone, especially Serbia. Viennese diplomatic circles got the impression in 1868 that the Danubian monarchy was prepared to sacrifice its last soldier and its last gulden to prevent the transfer of Bosnia and Hercegovina to the Serbian principality.

The new conception of Austria–Hungary's foreign policy formulated by Beust in May 1871, under the immediate influence of the Franco–Prussian War, viewed the acquisition of the provinces as a priority objective of Austro–Hungarian diplomacy in the Balkans. "Since in the future Austria's expansion is to all appearances possible only in the East, it would be desirable precisely in this direction to consolidate our possession of Dalmatia [by acquiring] a corresponding hinterland... ."[13] Anxious to prove his point to the opponents of annexation in Austria and Hungary, who saw the consequent increase of the Slavic population of the monarchy as a threat to dualism, Beust introduced two new arguments: without such expansion the peoples of the provinces would be disappointed in the hopes they had placed in Austria and, though "more and more turning away from Russia in recent years, would be thrust again into its embrace."[14]

Taking note of a new, strong and unified Germany in the Concert of Europe, Beust recommended seeking an agreement with Russia with German help. In August 1871, during Beust's meeting with Bismarck in Gastein, the chancellor expressed full support for Austria–Hungary's Eastern policy, emphasizing in connection with the question of the eventual disintegration of Turkey that "the concept of a great power makes its capacity for expansion a condition of life for that power."[15] Bismarck's words accorded with his steadfast and persistent policy of redirecting Austria's interests and efforts from the West to the East.

The changing of the guard on the Ballhausplatz and Andrássy's appointment as foreign minister signified that anti-Russian tendencies had moved to the forefront of Austro–Hungarian foreign policy. The hostility of that policy toward Russia and the Slavic world in general was stimulated by the ruling Hungarian oligarchy. "As is known, among Hungarians," writes the modern Hungarian historian István Diószegi, a specialist on the foreign-policy history of the Dual Monarchy, "hostility toward Russia was the initial position on which all the rest depended."[16]

Once he had become Hungarian premier, Andrássy offered Bismarck an alliance against Russia and of course met with refusal. No sooner had he assumed office than he instructed his predecessor, now appointed ambassador to London, to seek British guarantees in the event of a conflict with Russia over the Near East, promising in exchange support for Britain in the event of a threat to India on the part of Russia.[17] When Andrássy's dangerous designs were met with the same coldness on the Thames as on the Spree, the circle of possible allies narrowed. Only Germany remained, but alliance with it was incompatible with Andrássy's warlike intentions toward his northern neighbor. Nonetheless, despite the fact that Vienna had to seek rapprochement with Berlin on conditions that suited Bismarck, Andrássy never abandoned his attempts to hurl Russia back behind its "natural frontiers." "To extend a hand to Germany and show a fist to Russia!" is the way the Hungarian aristocrat formulated his foreign-policy conception.

In February 1872, the Austro–Hungarian ministers met in Vienna under the chairmanship of Francis Joseph to outline the monarchy's foreign policy. (The minutes of these meetings were published by the Austrian historian H. Lutz in 1974.) Explaining the strategic objectives and military-political tasks of the empire in the light of the new international situation, the foreign minister focused on the question of Austria–Hungary's attitude toward Russia. His conception boiled down to creating favorable internal and external conditions for a war against Russia before the Russians tried to use the "principle of nationalities in the East" to their advantage. Andrássy calculated that an Austro–Russian armed conflict might flare up within two years. In the meantime, he argued, it was necessary to ensure the benign neutrality of the German Empire and to lead the Russians into a trap by offering to let them occupy the Danubian principalities, thus drawing them into a war with the Ottoman Empire. Austria–Hungary itself was to enter the conflict against Russia only after the tsarist empire had launched its military operations against Turkey.

Touching on the problem of Bosnia and Hercegovina, Andrássy declared himself in favor of their annexation in principle but emphasized that the "way in which we have aimed to acquire them up to now is incorrect." He considered direct invasion of the provinces likely to precipitate a joint campaign against the monarchy by Serbia, Montenegro, Turkey, and Russia. He suggested that if Serbia were to enter the war on Russia's side it should immediately be occupied jointly with the Turkish army.

The idea of a war against Russia did not evoke any particular enthusiasm among the military, who recognized perfectly the hopelessness of such a war without Germany's participation. The latter could be counted on only if the monarchy agreed to guarantee the annexation of Alsace–Lorraine, and this was a very high price. The emperor himself leaned toward this view but eventually declared himself in favor of military preparations and large-scale maneuvers with an eye to a coming war.[18]

Andrássy did not deviate from his anti-Russian course even after the formation of the Three Emperors' League, in which only its architect, Bismarck, felt more or less comfortable. However tenuous this strange alliance may have been, for some time it removed the tension between the courts of Vienna and St. Petersburg. Taking heart, Andrássy did not speak again of concluding an anti-Russian alliance with Berlin until after the war alarm of 1875, which began an obvious cooling of relations between Gorchakov and Bismarck. But the latter did not succumb to the persuasions of the Austro-Hungarian minister.

The new intensification of the Eastern Question with the heroic rising of Hercegovina marked the beginning of complex diplomatic activities. In the initial stage of the crisis, relations between Vienna and St. Petersburg were more cooperative than confrontive. In the end, Austria–Hungary was able to occupy the provinces in 1878. The Austrian generals and the emperor himself insisted on an immediate invasion of Bosnia in the spring of 1875. At that time Andrássy was able to rein in the advocates of immediate action and to dampen the warlike mood of his monarch. At the same time, contrary to his initial intentions, he had to grant the wishes of the war party and launch diplomatic preparations for the annexation of Bosnia and Herce-govina. The landmarks of this policy were Reichstadt, the Budapest Conven-tion, and the Berlin Congress. These aspects of the Eastern crisis have been well covered in the literature, including Soviet studies. Throughout the crisis, Andrássy's main preoccupation was the attainment of the same anti-Russian and anti-Slavic aim – to prevent the formation of one or several large Slavic states in the Balkans under Russia's protection. The occupation of Bosnia and Hercegovina and the moving of troops into the strategically crucial Sanjak of Novi Pazar was not just a "preventive" measure undertaken ex-clusively for the purpose of ensuring the security of the monarchy, as some researchers believe.[19] Here is a passage from Andrássy's letter to the Prince of Württemberg in which he rather frankly set forth the true aims and inten-tions of the monarchy and the motives that guided it in 1875–78: "One of the main goals of this action from the Austro–Hungarian standpoint was the opening of the East for us politically and materially. . . ."[20]

Andrássy's diplomatic victory at the Berlin Congress ultimately created serious problems for Austria–Hungary in retaining its Great Power interests and position. In time the provinces turned into a dangerous source of inter-national and internal complications, playing approximately the same role as Alsace and Lorraine did for Germany. If in the middle of the nineteenth century the Habsburg Empire was the main external obstacle to the unifica-tion of the Germans and the Italians, in the thirty-five years that followed the occupation of Bosnia and Hercegovina it became the main obstacle to the national liberation of the Balkan and Austro–Hungarian Slavs.

## NOTES

1. "Aber die Ortodoxen Christen der Balkanländer fürchteten die katholische Propaganda und die Deutschen, sie wandten sich daher an Russland" (F. M. Mayer, R. Kaindl, and H. Pirchegger, *Geschichte und Kulturleben Österreichs*, vol. 2 [Vienna–Stuttgart, 1960], p. 206).

2. Soviet historians pay attention to this problem. See, for example: S. D. Skazkin, *Konetz avstro–russko–germanskogo sojuza.* (Moscow, 1974, 2nd edition);

N. S. Kinjapina, *Vneshnjaja politika Rossiji vtoroj polovini XIX veka* (Moscow, 1974); A. L. Narochnitzkij, "Balkanskij krizis 1875–1878 i velikije derzavi," *Novaja i novejshaja istorija*, 1976, no. 11; *Istorija diplomatiji*, vol. 2 (Moscow, 1962); K. B. Vinogradov, "Osnovnije napravlenija vneshnej politiki Angliji, Avstro–Vengriji i Germaniji v period Vostochnogo krizisa 1875–1878" in *100 let osvobozsdenija balkanskih narodov ot osmanskogo iga.* (Moscow, 1979).

3.   Robert A. Kann, "The Dynasty and the Imperial Idea," in *Austrian History Yearbook,* vol. 3, 1967, pt. 1 (Houston, 1967), p. 17.

4.   "Im Grunde wurde die Okkupation Bosniens und der Herzegowina im Jahre 1878 in weiten Kreisen nicht als Ziel an sich, sondern als Basis für eine ehrgeizige Aussenpolitik angesehen, die darauf abzielte, in den Balkan einzudringen um den Zugang zum Ägäischen Meer zu erringen" (Robert A. Kann, *Das Nationalitätenproblem der Habsburgermonarchie* [Graz–Köln, 1964], p. 185).

5.   The possibility and even inevitability of a collision of the interests of the two powers were foreseen by nationalistically minded German liberals at the beginning of the nineteenth century: see Paul A. Pfizer, *Briefwechsel zweier Deutscher* (Stuttgart–Tübing, 1832), p. 220, quoted in *Die Habsburgermonarchie 1848–1918,* ed. A. Wandruschka and P. Urbanitsch, vol. 3, pt. 2 (Vienna, 1980), p. 174: "Der Flug des habsburgischen Adlers, müsse, wolle er nicht stürzen, immer entschiedener der Richtung nach Osten nehmen."

6.   G. Otruba, "Der Deutsche Zollverein und Österreich," in *Österreich in Geschichte und Literatur,* vol. 3 (Vienna, 1971).

7.   "Graf Buol–Schauenstein... hielt die Gelegenheit für gekommen das Werk des Prinzen Eugen zu vollenden und die Herrschaft Österreichs über den benachbarten Balkan auszudehnen, an dem Untergang des osmanischen Reiches in Europa mitzuarbeiten und mitzuverdienen" (Hugo Hantsch, *Die Geschichte Österreichs,* vol. 2 [Graz–Köln, 1962], p. 358). A similar standpoint is taken by Heinrich Friedjung, *Österreich von 1848 bis 1860,* vol. 2 (Stuttgart, 1962), pp. 230–32.

8.   P. W. Schroeder, "A Turning Point in Austrian Policy in the Crimean War: The Conference of March 1854, Appendix 1, Buol's Speech of March 21, 1854," in *Austrian History Yearbook,* vols. 4–5, *1968–1969* (Houston, 1969), pp. 176–88.

Buol was firmly convinced that "noch keine Epoche dem Hause Österreichs eine günstigere Chance geboten hat, der orientalischen Verwicklung, die stets wie das Schwert des Damokles über den Geschicken Österreichs schwebte, eine vollgültige Lösung zu geben..." (p. 182), and, as a reward for Austrian sacrifices, "hätten wir die Erhaltung und Vermehrung unseres Einflusses im Oriente, unserer politischen Consideration, die Wahrung unserer dortigen wichtigen militärischen, commerciellen und industriellen Interessen..." (p. 181).

9.   P. W. Schroeder, "Austria and the Danubian Principalities, 1853–1856," *Central European History* 2 (September 1969): 216–36. The same opinion is expressed by Solomon Wank, "Foreign Policy and Nationality Problem in Austro–Hungary, 1867–1914," in *Austrian History Yearbook,* vol. 3, *1967,* pt. 3, p. 47: "After 1867, [the Monarchy] strove to prevent a nationalist solution for the Balkan question. In this sense, Austro–Hungarian imperialism had a defensive, one might even say a conservative, character in the Balkan peninsula."

Similarly, Enno E. Kraehe differs with Friedjung (*Österreich von 1848 bis 1860,* pp. 236–37) and A. J. Taylor *(The Struggle for Mastery in Europe* [Oxford, 1954], p. 64) concerning the expansionist nature of Buol's policy. "It is not necessary," Kraehe wrotes, "to charge Buol with aggressive intentions towards the Danubian Principalities to demonstrate the risks he ran in defending traditional Austrian interests in the Balkans against the power that had saved the Monarchy in 1849... . In his defense let it be said that the dangers of the Russian actions were real enough. Francis Joseph feared that 'the democratic tendencies of the South Slavs' would be stirred up by the presence of Russian armies in Moldavia and Walachia... ." ("Foreign Policy and the Nationality Problem in the Habsburg Monarchy, 1800–1867," *Austrian History Yearbook,* vol. 3, pt. 3 (1967), pp. 28–29). Let me say to this assertion that it is more than astonishing not to see the obvious aggressivity of Austria in the light of the fact of Austrian occupation of the Principalities. The fear of democratic movements in the Balkans and everywhere else was characteristic not only of the emperor of Austria but also of the Russian emperor, and the uncompromising struggle against democracy was perhaps the single common interest of the two rival powers.

10. V. Skarić, O. Nuri–Hadžić, and N. Stojanović, "Bosnia i Hercegovina pod Austro–ugarskom upravom," *Srpski narod u XIX veku* 15; Dž. Juzbasič, *Izgradnja željeznica u Bosni i Hercegovini u svjetlu austro–ugarske politike od okupacije do kraja Kállayeve ere* (Sarajevo, 1978); *Nemski izvori za bylgarskata istoriya*, vol. 1, ed. V. Paskalev and K. Kosev (Sofia, 1973); V. Paskaleva, *Za ikonomicheskoto vliyaniye na Avstro–Ungariya v bylgarskite zemi po vreme na Rusko–turskata voina (1877–1878)*, Izvestiya na Instituta za istoria, 1960, no. 8; E. Palotás, "Ziele und geschichtliche Realität: Wirtschaftsbestrebungen Österreich–Ungarns auf dem Balkan zur Zeit des Berliner Kongresses im Jahre 1878," *Studia Historica* (Budapest), 157 (1980).

11. "Kayserling an Bismarck, 30. I. 1867," in *Auswärtige Politik Preussens*, vol. 8, p. 348 (Oldenburg, 1933); E. Kovács, "Der österreichisch–ungarische Ausgleich vom Jahre 1867 und die europäischen Grossmächte," in *Der österreichisch–ungarische Ausgleich 1867*, ed. L. Holotik (Bratislava, 1971), p. 124.

12. Ede Wertheimer, *Graf Julius Andrássy: Sein Leben, seine Zeit*, vol. 1 (Stuttgart, 1910), p. 460; Th. v. Sosnosky, *Die Balkanpolitik Österreich–Ungarns seit 1866*, vol. 1 (Stuttgart–Berlin, 1913), p. 138; A. Radenić, "Die Balkanländer in der Strategie Österreich–Ungarns," *Balcanica* (Belgrade) 1 (1970): 147–63.

13. "Da eine Vergrösserung Österreichs zukünftig aller Voraussicht nach nur im Oriente stattfinden kann und eine solche namentlich in der Richtung (Ostens) wünschenswert wäre, unseren Besitz in Dalmatien durch ein entsprechendes Hinterland zu kräftigen... ." Beust an Kaiser Franz Joseph, 18. Mai 1871. Vortrag. Haushof- und Staatsarchiv, Min. des Ausser. Polit. Archiv, 40, Interna, fasc. 54, quoted in István Diószegi, *Österreich–Ungarn und der französisch–preussische Krieg 1870–1871* (Budapest, 1974) p. 276.

14. Ibid. Buol emphasized that Austrian policy, "welche ohne am staatlichen Bestande der Türkei zu rütteln, doch den Umstand nie aus dem Augen verliert, dass an unseren dortigen Grenzen stammverwandte Nationen leben, die in dem Kampfe um Verbesserung ihrer Existenz Hoffnungen in uns setzen, welche wir nicht täuschen könnten, ohne diese Völker, die sich im Laufe der letzten Jahre mehr und mehr von Russland abgewendet haben, gleichsam mit Gewalt wieder in die Arme der letzteren zu treiben."

15. Fr. F. Beust, *Aus drei Viertel-Jahrhunderten* (Stuttgart, 1887), p. 488.

16. "Bei den Ungarn war, wie wir wissen, die Feindschaft gegen Russland der Ausgangspunkt, alles andere hing nur davon ab" (Diószegi, *Österreich–Ungarn*, p. 283.

17. H. Wolter, "Die Anfänge des Dreikaiserverhältnisse," in *Die grosspreussisch-militärische Reichsgründung 1871: Voraussetzungen und Folgen*, vol. 2 (Berlin, 1971), pp. 29–37.

18. H. Lutz, "Politik und militärische Planung in Österreich–Ungarn zu Beginn der Ära Andrássy: Das Protokoll der Wiener Geheimkonferenzen vom 17. bis 19. Februar 1872," in *Geschichte und Gesellschaft: Festschrift für Karl R. Stadler* (Vienna, 1974), pp. 29–37.

19. Arthur J. May, *The Habsburg Monarchy, 1867–1914* (New York, 1968), pp. 113–29; Barbara Jelavich, *The Habsburg Empire in European Affairs, 1814–1918* (Chicago, 1969), p. 117.

20. Hantsch, *Die Geschichte Österreichs*, pp. 407–8. For evidence and some new viewpoints about Berlin's attitude, see Heinrich Lutz, *Österreich–Ungarn und die Gründung des Deutschen Reiches* (Frankfurt am Main–Vienna, 1979) and K. D. Kosev, "Bismarcks Orientpolitik und die Befreiung Bulgariens," *Südosteuropa Mitteilungen*, 1978, no. 1.

Simeon Damianov

# EUROPEAN DIPLOMACY AND THE EASTERN CRISIS
# UP TO THE BEGINNING OF THE RUSSO—TURKISH WAR

The Russo—Turkish War of 1877—78 was the direct upshot of the national liberation struggle of the South Slavs against Ottoman domination that reached its climax in the middle 1870s. The political crisis in the Balkans that erupted in the summer of 1875 as a result of the rebellions in Herce-govina and Bosnia reached its culmination during the April 1876 uprising in Bulgaria. These dramatic events once again put the notorious Eastern Ques-tion on the Great Powers' agenda and directly engaged their attention. One of the most acute conflicts of the second half of the last century had broken out in southeastern Europe, and its disentanglement was to prove beyond the capacity of the old diplomacy.

The inexorable logic of history compelled Russia to intervene actively in the armed struggle between the sultan and his Christian subjects. Its political interests in the Balkans made it take to heart the fate of the enslaved South Slavs, the Bulgarians in particular. Russia played a leading political role in every stage of the Eastern crisis. In the majority of cases, the international diplomatic actions for a peaceful solution to the crisis in 1875—76 were the fruit of its vigorous initiatives. But its interest in the Balkan question as well as the powerful pressure of the general public eventually persuaded St. Petersburg that peace efforts were to no purpose and that war was the sole means of rescuing the South Slavs from the Ottoman authorities. Thus Russia proved to be the only power prepared to undertake military operations for the liberation of the people south of the Danube.[1]

The true worth of the Russian decision to declare war on Turkey can only be appreciated in the light of Russia's difficult international and domestic position on the eve of and during the Eastern crisis. The decision came after painful struggles over the general direction of Russian foreign policy. The difficulties for Russia stemmed above all from the reluctance of the other states of the Concert of Europe to disturb the status quo in European Turkey.

The prospect of war with Turkey made it urgent for the Russian government to protect itself against the possible formation of a hostile coalition of Western states. Only after exhausting all peaceful possibilities were the efforts of tsarist diplomacy directed to creating the political-strategic prerequisites for the localization of a war with Turkey.

When the governments of the Great Powers learned of the rebellion in Hercegovina, this complication of the political situation in European Turkey seemed to them extremely ill-timed. No one wanted to believe that something serious, different from what had so often alarmed European cabinets, had begun in the Balkans. The European newpapers displayed rare unanimity in striving to minimize the event: "The revolt in Hercegovina has no political character," one paper confidently claimed; "this is but a protest against the oppressions and malpractices suffered by the raya during the collection of taxes."[2]

Other, far from disinterested considerations underlay this distortion of the character of the rebellion. The sultan's Western European protectors did not wish to allow any partition of the territories under his rule, since this threatened their own political and material interests in the entire East. "The European Powers have decided not to allow the appearance of a center of rebellion either in Romania, in Serbia, or in any of Turkey's provinces. If it becomes necessary, they will interfere in the affairs of the East and will maintain order and the political status quo in the country," declared the authoritative publication *Mémorial diplomatique.*[3]

The surprise caused by the rebellion was considerable in Russia as well. For nearly twenty years Russia, healing from the wounds of the Crimean War (1853–56), had had no forward-moving foreign policy. During the revolutionary crisis of the late fifties and early sixties the moderate liberals among Russian politicians, headed by Chancellor Prince Aleksandr Mikhailovich Gorchakov, had undertaken extensive domestic reforms designed to overcome economic backwardness and create the conditions necessary for normal economic activity and, in turn, for an increase in its military power. This called for the pursuit of a cautious foreign policy excluding any complications with the Western states. Russia's policy faced the task "of achieving a change in the system of alliances and in the equilibrium of the European Powers which are directed against us under the Treaty of 1856," Gorchakov declared in one of his secret reports to the emperor.[4]

This orientation of the Russian government also influenced its attitude toward the Eastern Question, long regarded with good reason as the most sensitive point in its foreign policy. Without giving up its fundamental traditional policy of further partitioning of the Ottoman Empire and of helping the liberation movements in the Balkans, St. Petersburg preferred acting by peaceful means within the framework of diplomacy. Soberly assessing its financial and military weakness and the amount of time it needed to complete the administrative and military reforms in progress, Russia sought to forestall the emergence of crises in European Turkey that could involve it against its will in a premature conflict with unforeseen consequences. In order not to lose its influence over the Balkan peoples under Turkish rule, it actively interceded with the Sublime Porte for such reforms as would ease their position and even ensure them national autonomy.[5]

In attempting to limit the revolutionary struggle of the Balkan peoples and keep them under control, the Russian government hoped through the Orthodox church, through cultural and other links, and through the Russophile circles of the liberation movements to preserve intact its centuries-old reputation as their ally, defender, and protector. Gorchakov believed it was in Russia's interest to wait for the natural outcome of the process of decay in the Ottoman Empire rather than risking a hasty unilateral military intervention that could set Russia once more against a united front of European states. "Russia has no intention whatever of fomenting rebellions in Turkey," he declared before the Prussian ambassador in St. Petersburg. "But this new course of Russia's policy toward Turkey can be realized only with great difficulty because it is at variance with our centuries-old traditional policy. Our blood relationship and common religion with the Slavs in Turkey oblige us to support them. In spite of everything, therefore, we shall assist them in the future, but only to ease their plight, to obtain reforms and autonomy within the framework of Turkey."[6]

Gorchakov, moreover, believed that any Russian diplomatic intervention in the Balkan question should be effected in the context of the Concert of Europe, i. e., with the consent of all the other Great Powers (Britain, France, Austria–Hungary, Germany, and Italy) that under the Paris Treaty of 1856 were the guarantors of the integrity of the Ottoman Empire. In order to overcome the resistance of Britain, which had emerged as the most zealous supporter of the status quo in European Turkey, Russia maneuvered – sometimes very skillfully – closer either to France, to Prussia (Germany), or to Austria–Hungary. Subjecting its Balkan policy to considerations of a broader all-European character, Russia pursued its main goal of overcoming its political isolation and restoring its political prestige by consistent efforts to sow discord among the other states and destroy their Crimean coalition. In the final analysis, its efforts were directed toward annulling the restrictions imposed on it by the Treaty of Paris – particularly in connection with the prohibition against keeping a navy in the Black Sea.[7]

The possibility for such a move did in fact arise. The collapse of Napoleon III, the one-time "arbiter of Europe," as a result of Prussia's military victories in 1870 removed France from the ranks of Russia's active enemies. Gorchakov immediately availed himself of the favorable situation and repudiated the clauses of the Treaty of Paris which restricted Russia's freedom of action in the Black Sea area. From this moment on Russian diplomacy grew more confident and independent. The beginning of the restoration of the Russian Black Sea navy made it possible to activate its Balkan policy. It was, however, bound by the Dreikaiserbund, or Three Emperors' League, which formally restrained Russia, Prussia, and Austria–Hungary from interfering in Balkan affairs.[8] Consequently, Russia's Balkan policy remained cautious.

It was just at this point, however, in the mid-seventies, that the national liberation movement of the South Slavs entered its decisive stage. The rebellion which broke out in Hercegovina and was at first met with disparagement by European diplomats soon spread to other parts of the Balkan Peninsula. In August 1875, the peasants of Bosnia also rose in revolt. The first attempts of the Porte to crush the rebels ended in failure. Those who had hastened to predict a speedy end to the uprising learned with surprise that the forces of revolution were gaining ground.

The Bulgarian revolutionary emigration in Romania was also stirring. Hristo Botev asked, "What South Slav heart will not beat faster at this signal of the revolution? What young hero will not twist his moustache and reach for his rusty yataghan? What patriot will not reflect and ask himself: 'What should we do?'[9] The great rebel insisted, "The only way out of this grim situation for the people is revolution, and popular revolution, immediate and desperate, at that, a revolution that will purge the Balkan Peninsula... of all that might hinder our genuine strivings for complete and absolute human freedom."[10]

The leader of the Bulgarian national revolution thought that revolt would be a worthy response for "Young Bulgaria" to the armed struggle of the raya that had already started in the westernmost Ottoman possessions of the Balkan Peninsula. "Now is the time to rouse the people to an uprising and by splitting the forces of the common enemy help ourselves and our brothers!... The idea of freedom is omnipotent, and love of it can do anything. ...Now is the time to show that we too are men and not beasts."[11] In his plans for rallying the Balkan people, an important place was occupied by the hope that Serbia and Montenegro would also rise and the European Turcophile diplomats who incessantly plotted against the freedom of the South Slavs would be faced with a fait accompli.

Russia's diplomatic corps learned with alarm in August 1875 that the Bulgarian Revolutionary Central Committee, headed by Hristo Botev, had decided to organize an uprising in Bulgaria as well.[12] At the end of September rebel detachments were formed in the Stara Zagora, Ruse, and Shumen areas. Bloody clashes occurred between the insurgents and the Turkish armed units sent against them.[13] Although the uprising was hastily prepared, its declaration indicated that the Bulgarian people had no intention of passively watching the development of events and waiting for others to offer them freedom without themselves making any effort. They wanted to be active participants in the life-and-death struggle that had begun. Their desire for liberation from alien political rule was irresistible.

The Stara Zagora uprising ended in failure, but the danger it posed was immediately grasped by the Ottomans. The uprising broke out in the heart of their European possessions, not far from the capital. They were therefore much more disturbed by it than by the rebel movements in the peripheral western parts of the peninsula. The Turkish government was aware that from a political and military-strategic standpoint it was immeasurably more important for it not to allow any revolutionary unrest in the Bulgarian lands. The strong forces the Porte threw against the small number of rebels, the mass detentions, and the rapid suppression of the rebellion bore witness to its realization that it must extinguish the fire beneath its feet as soon as possible.

Diplomats followed the development of the revolutionary process in the Bulgarian lands with close attention. Everybody knew that if a better-organized rebellion were to break out in Bulgaria, the Eastern crisis would be complicated still further. On October 4, 1875, the Russian in Ruse, I. P. Krilov, reported to Count Nikolay Pavlovich Ignatyev, the ambassador in Constantinople: "The cause of the youths who are sacrificing themselves is regarded as a sacred and popular one. [The Bulgarians] are sorry for their fate, but they are glad that by their sufferings they are awakening and strengthening the popular feeling. The time, it seems to me, is not far when the whole of Bulgaria will rise."[14] Gaillard de Ferry, the French vice-consul in Plovdiv, informed the minister of foreign affairs in Paris, Duc de Decazes, that new armed clashes between the population and the authorities could be expected in Bulgaria in the very near future. His assertion was based on the utter disorder that reigned in Bulgaria as a result of the outrages of the bashi-bazouks and the Circassians. The vice-consul pointed out that the Bulgarians, along with the rest of the rayas, had every legitimate reason for discontent, since they saw that the results of the Porte's reforms were insignificant and that no credence whatsoever could be given to the sultan's promises. In this respect, the Stara Zagora uprising in September 1875 was symptomatic. It showed that the Bulgarians were determined not to tolerate the Turkish outrages any longer. "The existence of the Turkish regime here is a question of days," Gaillard de Ferry assured his government with perfect knowledge of the facts. "It is quite possible that the Bulgarians, who have ultimately nothing more to lose, may act like the Greeks, Cretans, and Hercegovinans."[15]

In these circumstances the Eastern Question again occupied a central place in Russia's foreign policy. The course of events compelled the Russian government to abandon the reserve hitherto imposed on it. This was to a large extent a response to the demands of the Russian merchants and capitalists who after the reforms of Alexander II and the emancipation of the serfs more than ever before needed a free outlet to the Mediterranean. The question of the Black Sea straits had assumed primary importance for the development of Russian maritime commerce and for the whole economy of southern Russia.

The Russian government used the rebellion in Hercegovina and Bosnia to prove the correctness of its constant assertion of the need for radical reforms in European Turkey. It was, however, seriously alarmed by the attitude of Austria–Hungary toward the events in the Balkans. After the unification of Germany under the aegis of Prussia, the Habsburg Monarchy, having lost the battle for hegemony in the German world, had turned its attention to the south. It sought not only to make up for its territorial losses in Italy and its loss of influence in Germany by seizing new Slavic lands but also to prevent any revolutionary unrest in the neighboring regions that might galvanize its dependent Slavic peoples. For obvious reasons, Bismarck encouraged this policy; it both diverted the monarchy from the problems of Central Europe, which became a German monopoly, and placed it in confrontation with Russia.[16] The governments of Britain and France also took a markedly hostile attitude toward the rebellion in Bosnia and Hercegovina.[17]

These reactions put Russian policy to the test. The difficulties were increased by the lack of unanimity in St. Petersburg concerning the extent of Russia's involvement in Balkan affairs. At least two currents were discernible.

The aristocratic-bourgeois current of the Slavophiles headed by Ivan Sergeyevich Aksakov advocated speedier realization of Russia's liberating mission in the Balkans. They hoped to rally the young Slavic states created there with Russia's help as a means of consolidating the domestic and international positions of autocracy. The Slavophiles relied on Ignatyev, whose activity in favor of the autonomy of the Balkan peoples was widely known.[18]

The moderate liberal movement, expressing the interests of those connected with foreign capital and with expanded railway and industrial construction, declared itself in favor of the preservation of peace and against independent action by Russia in the Balkans. Without denying the need for intervention in the Balkan events, the adherents of this current believed that the Russian government should act in accord with the other Great Powers and that it should try to preserve peace as a prerequisite for the success of the ambitious economic undertakings of the Russian capitalists.

Alexander II and Gorchakov supported this second line of conduct. They believed that Russia could help the South Slavs and increase its prestige

among them without going to war by acting with Germany and Austria—
Hungary within the framework of the Dreikaiserbund and by respecting the
opinions of the other states in the Concert of Europe.[19] For this purpose
a center for coordinating action on the Balkan question among the Russian,
German, and Austro—Hungarian courts was set up in Vienna by agreement
with Count Gyula Andrássy.[20] At that point the Russian government was
obviously not yet aware of the duplicity of Austria—Hungary, which claimed
interest in the immediate pacification of the regions in revolt but in fact
was pursuing the annexation of Bosnia and Hercegovina, counting on the
pro-Austrian sentiments of some of the rebels, mainly the Bosnian Catholics.

The differences among the Great Powers, however, and particularly
Britain's resistance to any intervention in the internal affairs of the Ottoman
Empire, for a long time prevented any coordinated action before the Sublime
Porte in favor of the Balkan peoples. Russia's position of seeking compromise
did not contribute anything to the quicker settlement of the Eastern crisis.
Under these conditions Ignatyev found it expedient to avail himself of his
personal influence on the grand vizier Mahmud Nedim Pasha and unilaterally
convinced him of the need for some reforms that would partially meet the
demands of the rebels. Pretending that it was listening to this advice, in the
autumn of 1875 the Sublime Porte published a number of regulations
designed to convince both the insurgents and the European public of "its
sincere desire" to improve the position of its Christian subjects.[21]

On September 1, 1875, the Porte issued a *ferman* which provided for the
establishment of "impartial" justice. On October 2, the sultan promised to
lower taxes for the agricultural population, abolish the system of tax farming,
and grant municipalities the right to send representatives to the local
administrative councils. A further *ferman* was published on December 12
promising complete freedom of religion and equality of Christians before
the law.[22] Besides this, the Porte accepted Russia's proposal, supported by
Austria—Hungary, Germany, France, and Italy (without Britain), that its
negotiations with the rebels be mediated by the European consuls.[23]

The rebels in Hercegovina and Bosnia did not accept any of the proposals
of the Turkish government, nor did they believe its promises. Encouraged
by the sympathy and support of the European democratic public and the
news of the revolutionary unrest in Bulgaria, they agreed to conclude an
armistice, but they refused to lay down their arms and return to their
peaceful occupations prior to the withdrawal of the Turkish troops or to
abandon their goal of autonomy for the two provinces. The intermediary
mission of the consuls failed for the same reason. The reforms were
insufficient to justify hope that the rebels would accept them. The promises
of religious freedom, abolition of tax farming, use of part of the taxes

collected for local needs, etc., were not accompanied by any guarantees of their fulfillment.[24]

The failure of the consular efforts at reconciliation did not put an end to Russia's pursuit of a peaceful settlement. St. Petersburg was well aware that in order to help the rebels it had to achieve substantial unity with Austria—Hungary. Meanwhile, a serious change had taken place in the attitude of the Austro—Hungarian government toward the struggle of the South Slavs. Since its intention of annexing Bosnia and Hercegovina was frustrated by the striving of the insurgents for unification with Serbia and Montenegro, Vienna decided to proceed toward the "pacification" of the two regions by restoration of the rule of the sultan and to await a more propitious moment for their incorporation into the Habsburg Empire.[25] In the course of the negotiations between Andrássy and E. P. Novikov, the Russian ambassador in Vienna, the Austro—Hungarian government therefore adopted a negative attitude toward the Russian idea of more effective assistance to the rebels. Andrássy agreed to act jointly with Russia only under two conditions: (1) that the rebels be told categorically that they would not receive any outside help and (2) that Serbia and Montenegro be cautioned against supporting the rebellion.[26] It becomes clear from this that Austria—Hungary was trying to create a situation that would accelerate the crushing of the South Slavic uprising by the Turks.

To this Russia could not agree. Although restraining Serbia and Montenegro from energetic action to aid the insurgents,[27] Russia declared that it did "not regard it as possible to adhere to the principle of nonintervention" in the event that the Christians were beaten or subjected to repressions by the Turks. Gorchakov warned that intervention by the Great Powers to forestall bloodshed would become inevitable and intimated that Russia would not be the last in fulfilling this humane duty.[28] The Russian chancellor endeavored to convince Austria—Hungary of the need for such reforms in European Turkey as would ensure the rebellious provinces an autonomy close to independence (similar to the Romanian).[29] At this point, Russian policy left the period of restraint and compromises and entered a new stage characterized by enterprise and diplomatic initiative.

Russia's firm stand compelled Austro—Hungarian diplomacy to become more active. Andrássy himself conceded that it was necessary to bring more energetic pressure to bear on the Sublime Porte for "effective reforms." The essence of these "effective reforms," however, was not completely clear, because Andrássy did not accept Gorchakov's idea that the western provinces of Turkey should be autonomous. He regarded the establishment of a new Slavic state in the Balkans as dangerous for the Dual Monarchy in view of the natural ties it would establish with Serbia and Montenegro and its great attraction for the Austrian Slavs.[30] Andrássy's note to the Great Powers of

December 30, 1875, provided not for autonomy but for "improvement" of the status quo under the control of the powers. Although the Russian government did not consider Andrássy's note an effective means of resolving the crisis,[31] it had every reason to regard it as a victory for its initiatives. The control mentioned in Andrássy's note meant, according to the Russian government, recognition of the principle of intervention by the powers in the domestic affairs of the Ottoman Empire with a view to guaranteeing the Christian regions some self-government.[32]

None of these steps of the European diplomats contributed anything to the pacification of the provinces in rebellion. The insurgents were well informed about the differences among the powers and remained firm on the question of autonomy. They rejected with indignation Britain's insistent requests that they lay down their arms.[33]

It is not difficult to see that Russia proved the most zealous defender of the rebels' cause. Although Gorchakov continued to pursue a peaceful settlement of the crisis, he never stopped pointing out that this could be achieved solely by meeting the demands of the insurgents. Without giving up the main task — preparing the conditions for independent development of the Balkan peoples — the Russian government proceeded flexibly, emphasizing that the Eastern Question was an all-European issue which should be resolved by the accord of all the Great Powers. It assured the European cabinets that it had no desire to dictate its own solution and that it was striving to coordinate its actions with theirs and above all with those of its "allies" Austria–Hungary and Germany.[34]

This tactic was imposed on it by the bitter awareness of the country's financial and military impotence and by the prospect of thorough ruination before the completion of its intended sweeping reforms, especially the reorganization of the army initiated by War Minister Dmitry Alekseyevich Milyutin. It was on account of this that the Russian government sought roundabout ways of helping the liberation struggle of the South Slavs without entering into conflict with Turkey and the Western states. It tacitly supported the volunteer movement in aid of the rebels in Bosnia and Hercegovina while at the same time refuting their assertions that the "intrigues" of the "Moscow Pan-Slavic committees" were the principal cause of the rebellions.

The powerful explosion of the national liberation movement in Bulgaria in April 1876 and the war of Serbia and Montenegro with Turkey that began shortly afterwards marked the beginning of the next stage in the Eastern crisis and gave Russia grounds for still more energetic steps to rally the European states around its program for granting autonomy to the Balkan peoples. The Russian initiatives were facilitated by the circumstance that before any details about the April Uprising became known, the Ottoman authorities had committed crimes which directly affected the political interests and honor of some of the Great Powers. On May 6, in Salonika, a fanatical Muslim crowd killed the French consul Moulin and the German consul Abbott, who were attempting to defend a Bulgarian girl whom the Turks wanted forcibly to convert to Islam.[35] A little later it was learned that in the Rhodope Mountains bashi-bazouks had killed the French merchants Gouzon and Allard and their interpreter Sly[36] and that outrages had been perpetrated on the foreigners working on the construction of the Sofia—Belovo railway line.[37]

Meanwhile the Turkish capital had become the arena of bloody palace strife. Mahmud Nedim Pasha, accused of being a Russophile, was removed from power and the Anglophile Midhat Pasha installed in his place. Shortly afterwards, Sultan Abdülaziz was dethroned and assassinated. Several former ministers were also murdered. The complete anarchy and the inability of the ruling circles to impose order on the empire undermined Turkey's international prestige.[38]

St. Petersburg considered that these events, above all the murder of the consuls, gave European diplomacy sufficient grounds for swift intervention in Turkey's affairs. On the initiative of the Russian government, Germany, Austria—Hungary, and Russia reached agreement on May 14, 1876, on the text of the Berlin Memorandum, which proposed that the European states that had signed the Paris Treaty of 1856 send ships to Salonika for the protection of their subjects. France and Italy immediately endorsed the proposal.[39] However, when Britain refused to join the collective demarche of the powers because it contained the danger of "injuring the prestige of the sultan," the Berlin Memorandum failed.[40]

Immediately after that, the attention of European diplomacy became focused on the Bulgarian question. The main credit for this must go to the democratic public of Russia, Britain, France, Italy, and other countries, which sympathized with the Bulgarians and reacted vigorously to the unprecedented atrocities committed by the Turkish authorities in suppressing the April Uprising. The Great Powers were compelled by public opinion to take up the Bulgarian question. This was principal success of the organizers of the uprising, but even in this case the concrete initiative belonged to Russia.[41]

The international movement in defense of the Bulgarian people after the collapse of the April Uprising coincided, of course, with the measures taken by the Great Powers to forestall the defeat of Serbia and Montenegro. Both for the public and for the governments, the Eastern Question was connected not only with Bosnia and Hercegovina but also with the problem of the Turkish Slavs in general. The events in Bulgaria formed the focus of the Eastern crisis, and all new demarches of the powers before the Sublime Porte were connected with them. The spontaneous manifestations all over

Europe in favor of the liberation of the Bulgarians were the best proof of the great role the April Uprising played in creating the political and psychological atmosphere which ultimately led to the declaration of the Russo—Turkish War.[42]

More than a hundred flourishing Bulgarian towns and villages were destroyed, burned, and looted in the course of the "Bulgarian Horrors," and more than thirty thousand Bulgarians were killed. All unprejudiced politicians spoke without hesitation in favor of resolving the Bulgarian question by granting the Bulgarians political independence forthwith.[43] The "Bulgarian Horrors" inflicted a fatal blow on the international prestige of the Sublime Porte. Even its most zealous defenders, such as British Prime Minister Disraeli, were helpless to do anything to preserve the status quo. In these circumstances Russia's policy evolved rapidly from caution to more decisive action.

As early as the end of June 1876, when Serbia and Montenegro started military operations against Turkey, it was perfectly clear to the Russian government that in the event of a defeat of the weak Serbian—Montenegrin forces its active intervention to prevent the collapse of these two small South Slavic states and to resolve the Bulgarian question would become inevitable. In order to free its hand for more decisive steps, Russia found it necessary to coordinate its action with Vienna, which did not want a victory for the South Slavs.[44] On July 8, Alexander II met Francis Joseph in Reichstadt (Bohemia). During that meeting, Austria—Hungary and Russia undertook to act by mutual accord in the event of an unfavorable outcome of the war with Turkey for Serbia and Montenegro.[45]

At the Reichstadt meeting of the two monarchs the Bulgarian question was discussed for the first time. The agreement reached provided for the establishment of the principalities of Romania and Albania independent of the Porte and for the formation of an independent Bulgarian state.[46] The price Russia had to pay to neutralize Austria—Hungary in the case of a clash with Turkey was its consent to the occupation of Bosnia and Hercegovina by Austria—Hungary. "Russia has never cherished illusions about the political position of Austria and Andrássy," Gorchakov noted with regret in his report to the emperor on the occasion of the concessions.[47]

Serbian and Montenegrin military failures made the need for preparations for war with Turkey ever more obvious. The heartrending pleas of the Bulgarians to the Russian government also contained an ardent appeal for Russia's immediate military intervention in the Balkans. When the Bulgarian exarch Antim I sent his well-known letter of August 11, 1876, to Isidor, the metropolitan of St. Petersburg, containing a plea for protection of Bulgaria by Russia in order to prevent mass forced conversions of Bulgarians to Islam and raising the danger of the "eternal destruction of Christendom in

Bulgaria," Alexander II felt compelled to write on the message in his own hand: "Liberate Bulgaria!"[48]

While making every possible effort to preserve the unity of the Concert of Europe and exert stronger collective pressure on Turkey, the Russian government at the same time deemed it expedient to take some prompt military measures. The most important decisions were taken in conferences with the emperor in Livadia at the beginning of October 1876 with the participation of the heir to the throne, Gorchakov, Milyutin, Finance Minister M. H. Reitern, Ignatyev, and other senior statesmen. The view that war with Turkey was imminent was probably already prevalent.[49] The first important result of these deliberations was the Russian ultimatum to the Sublime Porte of October 31 to stop military operations against Serbia, which was threatened with complete collapse after the defeat at Kruševac on October 29. Meanwhile, in reply to Disraeli's threats, Alexander II declared on October 29 in a remarkable speech before the Moscow nobility that in the event that it became impossible to reach general agreement to grant autonomy to the Balkan peoples by peaceful means, Russia was firmly resolved "to act on her own initiative."[50]

The diplomacy of the Bulgarian liberation movement became active at that moment. The revolutionary emigration in Romania, concentrated around the Bulgarian Revolutionary Central Committee (renamed, for tactical reasons, the Bulgarian Central Charity Society), did a great deal to make the Bulgarian question the most discussed issue in European politics during the summer and autumn of 1876. Credit must go also to the patriotic circles of the Constantinople Russophile bourgeoisie grouped around Exarch Antim I. While the Central Charity Society in Bucharest organized the forwarding of numerous petitions from all parts of Bulgaria to the European governments, the Bulgarian municipality in Constantinople decided to send two delegates to the European capitals to acquaint the governments of the Great Powers with the national demands of the Bulgarians by submitting a specially prepared memorandum.

The Bulgarian delegates, Dragan Tsankov and Marko Balabanov, skillfully availed themselves of the favorable situation created in Europe as a result of the anti-Turkish campaign and, with the support of influential politicians and public figures convinced of the fairness of the Bulgarian demands, successfully fulfilled their mission. In England they were received even by the state secretary for foreign affairs, Lord Derby, and in this way were recognized as official representatives of the Bulgarian nation. With certain promises that "things would take a turn for the better," they were met also by the French foreign minister and by the German chancellor Otto von Bismarck.[51]

It was in Russia that Tsankov and Balabanov were received the most cordially. "Your cause has won here, so you will have no need to defend it either before us or before anybody else in Russia," declared Gorchakov. The emperor was categorical: "I do not know what the others are thinking of doing if Turkey does not voluntarily accept what is proposed to her, but I shall not be satisfied this time with hollow words and hollow promises. If the affair does not end peacefully, as I wish with all my heart, and if the others are satisfied with hollow words only, we shall move forward and shall do our duty."[52]

A partial mobilization of the Russian army, involving twenty infantry and nine cavalry divisions, began on November 1, 1876.[53] At the same time, a Bulgarian volunteer force was formed. The Grand Duke Nikolay Nikolayevich, commander in chief of the Balkan army, assumed the post of head of civil affairs, whose task was to get ready to organize the administration of the independent Bulgarian state.[54] These measures, which were aimed at strengthening Russia's position in the forthcoming negotiations with Turkey on the question of autonomy for the Balkan peoples, showed that the "party of action," influential adherents of which were the heir to the throne and the empress, had gained the upper hand in St. Petersburg.

The calling of the Conference of Constantinople (December 1876 – January 1877) was Russia's last major attempt to resolve the Eastern crisis by peaceful means. The main problem that had to be solved in Constantinople was that of the destiny of the sultan's Christian subjects in European Turkey. It became clear later, however, that Disraeli's giving way to public opinion on the question of the conference was a tactical maneuver. His actual intention was to torpedo the decisions of the representatives of the Great Powers assembled in Constantinople by encouraging the Sublime Porte to reject them.[55] Fully in tune with this intention were the words of Queen Victoria that no one in Britain would consent to sacrifice his honor and interests because of the Bulgarian atrocities.[56]

The balance of the military power of Russia and Turkey was such, however, that Disraeli foresaw a very rapid military defeat for the Turkish army. His principal objective, therefore, was to forestall the war and avoid the Russian occupation of the Balkan Peninsula. Before the departure of the Marquess of Salisbury, British delegate to the Constantinople Conference, Disraeli told him that any peace that did not lead to foreign occupation would be a triumph for Britain.[57] Salisbury himself became convinced of that during his visits to the European capitals before arriving in Constantinople. In Berlin, Bismarck told him frankly that Germany would support Russia.[58] In Paris, Decazes was still more outspoken: "I want to impede war, I am indifferent to everything else." Decazes's reasons were perfectly clear: he was ready to sacrifice Turkey's integrity so as to avoid the involvement of Russia and Britain in further complications in the East that could free Germany's hands for fresh aggression against France.[59] In his turn, Andrássy in Vienna declared that he made common cause with Bismarck.[60]

Salisbury wrote that during his travels in Europe he could not find a friend of Turkey anywhere. There existed no such friend. Practically all were of the opinion that Turkey's hour had struck. Not at all prepared for such a consensus,[61] Salisbury began to take a pessimistic view of Disraeli's policy of unconditionally preserving Turkey's integrity. The British representative arrived in Constantinople strongly shaken as to the correctness of the view propounded by the British government.[62]

The accord of the representatives of the Great Powers in Constantinople was facilitated by the Russian government's inclination to make serious concessions to avoid war. The Russian representative, Ignatyev, appeared at the conference with proposals in two versions, maximum and minimum: (1) autonomy for Bosnia, Hercegovina, and Bulgaria with occupation of Bosnia and Hercegovina by Austria–Hungary and of Bulgaria by Russia and (2) autonomy for the regions of European Turkey just mentioned without occupation but with specification of guarantees for its conscientious implementation. Gorchakov's instructions to Ignatyev spoke most eloquently about the willingness of the Russian government to make concessions in the name of a speedier agreement with Britain and the other powers: "If only our minimum is accepted, this will be a great result that will save us the military campaign, which is always a hazardous thing both politically and militarily and is particularly burdensome in its effect on our financial position. If this can be avoided while preserving the honor and dignity of the emperor unharmed, I will applaud with enthusiasm and our country will gain."[63]

As a result of Russia's conciliatory approach, Salisbury and Ignatyev reached, during the preliminary negotiations started in Constantinople on December 11, 1876, an accord proposing to the Porte that it adopt the principle of granting autonomy to the Slavic regions of European Turkey without their occupation by Russia and Austria–Hungary. "Russia has no intention of imposing on the other powers her previous plan for occupation, nor does she consider that this is the only way of achieving the result desired. Russia is ready to join in any other effective means of guarantee that may be proposed," the Russian government declared.[64]

The representatives of all the other powers accepted the "autonomy without occupation" formula. Irrespective of this conciliatory conduct, however, nobody doubted that in the event that Turkey refused to accept its "minimum," Russia was firmly resolved to wage war to impose it. The fear that this war could prove fatal for the Ottoman Empire explained the willingness of the Great Powers to rally around the proposal of Ignatyev and Salisbury.

The most important question discussed at the preliminary meetings in Constantinople was the question of the boundaries of autonomous Bulgaria. Ignatyev's proposal that the Bulgarian region comprise the lands included in the Bulgarian Exarchate met with no objection. The numerous preliminary studies on the ethnic structure of European Turkey carried out by the consuls on the ambassadors' instructions on the eve of the conference unambiguously revealed the numerical predominance of the Bulgarian element in the lands guided ecclesiastically by the Exarchate. The data collected were so categorical that none of the powers' representatives questioned them.[65]

In spite of this, because of fears that after the establishment of a major Bulgaria its independence of the Ottoman Empire would remain a fiction, it was decided to divide the Bulgarian lands into two autonomous regions. The initiators of this partition were Britain and Austria–Hungary. While the Dual Monarchy was afraid of the formation of a major Slavic state south of the Danube that by its very existence might "infect" the South Slavs under Habsburg rule, Britain was doing everything possible to limit the Russian influence in the Balkans. It also opposed Bulgaria's outlet to the Aegean because that could harm its commercial interests in the Balkans. In this way, the purely Bulgarian areas of Voden, Kukush, and Doiran were severed from Bulgaria.[66]

Bulgaria was divided along the meridian into eastern and western parts with Turnovo and Sofia as their capitals. The coordinated project of the powers included provisions for the appointment of chief governors of the two regions, the composition of the regional assemblies, reforms of the financial system, justice system, and gendarmerie, and specifications of the powers of the international commission that was to control the execution of the reforms.[67]

Proposals on other questions were also coordinated. It was suggested the Porte restore the status quo ante bellum with respect to Serbia, cede a small territory to Montenegro in southern Hercegovina and northern Albania (with the fortress Niksic, Zabljak, and Spuz), and consent to the unification of Bosnia and Hercegovina into an autonomous region under a special governor-general.[68] Owing to the readiness with which Russia took into consideration the most important objections of Britain and the other powers, agreement was reached and the preliminary conference of the ambassadors concluded successfully. But this did not complete the work of the Constantinople Conference. The most important task was still ahead: submitting the project to the Sublime Porte during the conference proper and convincing its representatives of the necessity of accepting it.

It turned out that this was not easy. During the summer and autumn of 1876 important governmental changes had taken place in Constantinople.

In August the throne had been occupied by Abdülhamid II, known for his extremely reactionary views. The grand vizier Midhat Pasha adhered to a firm nationalist course. In order to ward off the efforts of the Great Powers at intervention in its internal affairs, the Ottoman Empire had begun preparations for the introduction of constitutional rule. Moreover, enjoying the support of the British ambassador Henry Elliott, who had been personally instructed by Disraeli to distance himself from Salisbury, the Porte ignored the warning of the latter that if it refused to accept the proposals it ran the risk of a decisive battle that would probably mean the expulsion of the Turks from Europe.[69]

At the first official meeting of the conference (December 23, 1876) the Turkish minister of foreign affairs Safvet Pasha set forth in detail the reasons the Porte could not accept the reforms proposed by the Great Powers. With extraordinary insolence and cynicism he declared that it was not the difficult position of the Christians but "foreign propaganda" that had caused the rebellions in European Turkey and that the Turkish government had acted in full "conformity with the Law" by taking measures for their harsh suppression. Along with this, however, allegedly displaying foresight and a desire for complete pacification of the empire, the Porte decided to introduce constitutional rule guaranteeing civil and political equality to all subjects irrespective of nationality and religion and ensuring protection of their life, property, and honor. The booming of the guns at that moment, marking the proclamation of the constitution, meant, in the words of the Turkish minister, that the Porte alone would see to the implementation of the necessary reforms,[70] i. e., that the conference was pointless.

Turkey's refusal to accept the project proposed to it was accompanied by noisy nationalist demonstrations and calls for war with Russia.[71] For almost a month the representatives of the Great Powers made every effort to convince the Porte of the need for a more sober assessment of the situation, threatening that in the event of a refusal they would immediately leave the Turkish capital. Their efforts proved to be in vain. On January 18, 1877, the specially convened grand divan announced the final rejection of the proposals. Two days later the minister of foreign affairs informed the conference of the decision of the divan,[72] and shortly afterwards the ambassadors of the Great Powers left Constantinople.

Thus the efforts of Russia and the other European states at a peaceful settlement of the conflict between the sultan and his Christian subjects ended in failure. The main cause for this was the two-faced policy of Britain, which aimed at placating public opinion by sending Salisbury to Constantinople but at the same time through Elliott encouraged the Porte's resistance. The line to which Salisbury adhered also gave the Turkish government grounds for recalcitrance. Although advising the Turkish ministers to accept the project of the conference, Salisbury explicitly stated that Britain would not go along with any attempts at compulsion. This was more than enough to convince the Turks that in the decisive hour Britain would not leave them in the lurch.

Another reason for the failure of the conference was Bismarck's policy of exacerbating Russo–Turkish tensions. Exactly at the time of the conference, the German chancellor directed bellicose appeals to the tsar to rely on the help of Germany to neutralize Austria–Hungary and to "dispose" once and for all of the Turkish inheritance.[73] It was no accident that Reitern wrote:

> Prince Bismarck is obviously trying to involve us in war. His words to our ambassador are such as may compete with the most fervent Russophiles'. These words of his are aimed at arousing chauvinist passions and are most aptly calculated and consistent with the tsar's character. Bismarck speaks about Russia's honor, about the lowering of the army's morale in the event of demobilization, and about the harm of a peaceful outcome to the monarchist principle, and all these things have an effect on the tsar. ...The way I explain Bismarck's behavior to myself is as follows: he purely and simply wants to involve us to the very end in the insoluble Eastern Question so that we may no longer interfere in his European plans against France.[74]

These words of the Russian minister fully coincided with the French assessment. In reply to the provocative behavior of Baron Werther, the German ambassador in Constantinople, Decazes instructed the French delegates to the conference "to open Ignatyev's eyes" to the fact that "Germany is pushing Russia toward a catastrophe."[75]

With the failure of the Constantinople Conference, the Russian government became fully convinced of the inevitability of war with Turkey. The illusions of Gorchakov and the "peaceful" party about the possibility of effective steps by the guarantor powers burst like soap bubbles. In St. Petersburg there was feverish work in two directions: putting the army in complete combat readiness and establishing a sound diplomatic base for the war. The latter task involved ensuring that there would be no repetition of the Crimean situation and preventing the formation of an anti-Russian European coalition.

Alarming news reached St. Petersburg about attempts behind the scenes by Britain to reach an anti-Russian accord with Austria–Hungary. The Russian government decided to anticipate the "British intrigues" by achieving a quick understanding with Vienna. After prolonged negotiations conducted in the form of an exchange of letters between Alexander II and Francis Joseph, on January 15, 1877, in Budapest the two powers signed a secret military convention that secured for Russia the benevolent neutrality of Austria–Hungary in the event of a war against Turkey. By this convention Austria–Hungary obtained Russia's consent to occupy Bosnia and Hercegovina provided it did not move its troops into Romania, Serbia, Montenegro, or Bulgaria. In exchange Russia obtained the right to take up arms against

Turkey on Bulgarian territory, calling up for the purpose Romanian, Serbian, and Montenegrin troops.[76]

On March 18, 1877, the two states signed an additional agreement which specified the terms of Austro–Hungarian neutrality. Russia made concessions not only on the issue of Bosnia and Hercegovina; it was compelled also to confirm that it was not seeking to establish a major Slavic state in the Balkans. The agreement provided for the realization of the project worked out at the Constantinople Conference for the partition of Bulgaria into two autonomous regions. Vienna insisted that the western Bulgarian region, which embodied the Vardar Valley, should be a zone of Austro–Hungarian influence. This was a major sacrifice on Gorchakov's part that was poorly compensated for by the recognition of the Russian rights in Bessarabia.[77] The Russian government agreed to this compromise aware that it was dictated not only by the need to avoid political isolation but also by strategic considerations. When Russian troops penetrated into the Balkans, the Austro–Hungarian army might otherwise strike at their right flank as it did at the time of the Crimean War.

In February 1877, concerned about its lack of allies, St. Petersburg made a fresh attempt at coordinating the efforts of the Great Powers behind a diplomatic solution to the crisis. Ignatyev was entrusted with the mission of visiting Berlin, Vienna, and London with a view to negotiating joint action with the governments of the Western countries in the spirit of the decisions of the Constantinople Conference.[78] His talks with the German chancellor proved of special importance for Russia. Bismarck was trying to keep the "eastern ulcer" open longer, to involve Russia in a serious conflict with Turkey and consequently with Britain, so that he could, undisturbed, once again defeat France. He therefore suggested to Ignatyev that the Russo–Turkish crisis could be solved only by war and that the international conditions were entirely favorable for Russia. "Perhaps never again will Russia find such propitious circumstances as now and a cordon of friends securing her frontiers from any attack," the chancellor argued. In his view, Russia would lose its prestige if it renounced war. In order to prove his friendly attitude toward it, he expressed willingness to grant it a loan in the event of war, making use of his personal ties with the banking house of Bleichroder.[79]

The price of this willingness was well known to the Russian government. It responded with restraint to the chancellor's "generosity" and refused to sacrifice France in the name of the still unclear advantages of a war against Turkey that it would have to wage alone. According to Gorchakov's foreign-policy conception, Russia needed a strong France to act as a counterpoise to German aspirations for hegemony in Europe.[80] Ignatyev's efforts were therefore directed to London. The British looked with alarm on Bismarck's open sympathy for Russia. In order to prevent a further rapprochement between Berlin and St. Petersburg, the British cabinet decided to come to an agreement with the Russian government.

In February 1877, Disraeli and Derby unexpectedly expressed willingness to negotiate with the Russian government in working out a plan for joint demarches in Constantinople. Derby several times met Count Shuvalov, the Russian ambassador in London. The upshot of these meetings was the decision to propose to Turkey the implementation of the reforms mentioned at the time of the Constantinople Conference, giving it guarantees that the Great Powers would respect the "dignity" of the sultan and would not insist on any control. Disraeli hoped, not without reason, that because the Russian government seemed to be seeking an honorable way out of the crisis it would be satisfied even with insignificant concessions on the part of the Sublime Porte.[81]

After Ignatyev's arrival in London, the negotiations entered their concluding stage. In order to bring the British government around, Ignatyev was authorized to say that Russia would give up the thought of war and demobilize if Turkey did the same. Disraeli and Derby understood that this was a retreat, although an honorable one. Under these conditions an accord was reached with Britain without any particular difficulty. On March 31, 1877, the ambassadors of the Great Powers in London signed the protocol drafted by Derby and Shuvalov, which represented a mutilated version of the project put forward by the powers during the Constantinople Conference. In spite of Derby's statement that if Turkey rejected the protocol, Britain would regard it as *non avenu* (null and void), Russia doubtless scored a diplomatic victory. Turkey found itself isolated, and Russia emerged as a mandatory of Europe in the further negotiations with the Porte. As was noted in the London Protocol,[82] it had the right to take whatever measures were necessary "to ensure the welfare of the Christian population and general peace."

On April 9, however, the Sublime Porte rejected the Protocol. Nationalist circles in Constantinople, confident of Britain's support, qualified it as interference "contrary to the dignity of the Turkish state" in its internal affairs. It became clear to everybody that after the Porte had rejected this last appeal of the powers for prudence, the crisis could only be resolved by war.[83] Although Russia had no allies and no formal consent from the European governments to make war against Turkey, it had obtained the moral right to act without them. All the Great Powers had in principle recognized the pressing need for reforms in Turkey. The London Protocol in fact recognized Russia's right to fight Turkey in the name of humanity and justice.[84]

The simple truth that Russia had no alternative to war at last became an axiom for the Russian ruling circles as well. At the crown council with the tsar on April 11, Milyutin, who until then had been considered one of the most determined enemies of war, dealt a devastating blow to Gorchakov's illusions of peace. In his report "Our Political Position at Present," which was discussed at the council, he admitted that war would be "a great calamity" in impeding internal reforms and broad plans for economic reorganization but went on to say that in the international situation created by the Porte's refusal to accept the London Protocol war against Turkey was unavoidable and further vacillation by Russia contained the danger of still greater complications. After pointing out that the outcome of the Constantinople Conference had revealed the utter groundlessness of hopes of "European influence on Turkey," Milyutin warned that Russian inaction would result in new Turkish outrages in the Balkans that would still further undermine Russia's political prestige and material interests:

> The other states may hesitate but we cannot. We are committed to Russia, to the Christians in Turkey, and to the whole of Europe by the words of our emperor. We have mobilized our army, which in the eyes of the whole world has raised a sword to defend our honor. ...If we now disband this army without an honorable and fully satisfactory peace, it will undermine confidence in it both at home and before the world. Such a demobilization without any results would mean a second Crimean War, which would have the most serious consequences for us. ...Both history and recent events unconditionally show that we are called upon to play a principal role in resolving the Eastern Question. And we will pay dearly if we abandon the fulfillment of our mission. ...We need peace, but not peace at any price, an honorable peace even if we must achieve it by war. If we allow ourselves to seek peace at any cost and if we give our enemies the slightest occasion to suspect us of weakness, then in a few months' time we will certainly find ourselves involved in war but in totally different, immeasurably more difficult circumstances.[85]

Milyutin's arguments carried the day, and the Russian government took its historic decision to declare war on Turkey. The last diplomatic act connected with the preparations for war was aimed at ensuring free passage of Russian troops across Romania's territory. This was achieved by signing a treaty with the Romanian government on April 16, 1877.[86] On April 23 Russia officially announced that it was breaking off diplomatic relations with Turkey, and on April 24 in Kishinev, where the army headquarters was established, Alexander II signed the manifesto for the declaration of war.[87]

The Eastern crisis, which had started with the rebellions in Hercegovina and Bosnia in 1875 and deepened with the bestial suppression of the April Uprising in Bulgaria, now entered a new stage — the stage of its resolution through the intervention of Russia's armed forces.[88]

Study of European diplomacy during the period of the Eastern crisis up to the declaration of the Russo–Turkish War reveals a strong polarization of the political and strategic interests of the powers in the Balkans and the Near East. This polarization explains the drama and the unexpected collisions in the course of the diplomatic struggle to resolve the crisis. The difficulty and length of this struggle are to a considerable extent explained by certain weaknesses of Russia's diplomacy.

It is true that Russia had no direct aggressive intentions in the Balkans. The war was actually imposed on it by a mass popular movement in defense of the South Slavs and therefore had the character of a selfless liberation struggle in the name of an objectively progressive goal. The war was late, however, and failed to play its liberating role fully with respect to all the territories with a predominantly Bulgarian population. Gorchakov's excessive fear of the formation of an all-European coalition against Russia produced sluggishness, a rash willingness to make concessions, and diplomatic obstacles for politicians and officers who recommended more timely and independent action. The commitment to Austria–Hungary, the far-reaching and soothing declarations to the British, and the desire to preserve France as a counterbalance to Bismarck all tied Russia's hands and later adversely affected its efforts to consolidate diplomatically the brilliant results of the victorious war.

Nonetheless, it cannot be denied that Russian diplomacy achieved certain successes. Although at the cost of great sacrifices, it succeeded in neutralizing its most dangerous rival in the Balkans, Austria–Hungary. Britain, which in the course of the crisis declared itself most resolutely in defense of Turkey, was also neutralized to a high degree by the London Protocol of March 31, 1877. The sincere efforts made during the Constantinople Conference to find a diplomatic way out of the complicated situation convinced the European public of the peaceful intentions of the Russian government. The Ottoman Empire was politically discredited and isolated. All this had an extremely favorable effect at the beginning of the war and ensured the necessary conditions for the victorious advance of the Russian army.

## NOTES

1. V. M. Hvostov, *Istoriya diplomatii*, vol. 2, *Diplomatiya v novoe vremya (1871–1914 gg.)* (Moscow, 1964), p. 106.

2. Hr. Botev, *Izbrani proizvedeniya*, ed. P. Dinekov (Sofia, 1969), p. 426.

3. Ibid., p. 427.

4. Arhiv vneshnei politiki Rossii (hereafter AVPR), Otchet MID o 1866 g., 11:88–89.

5. P. A. Chihachov, *Velikie derzhavi i Vostochnii vopros* (Moscow, 1970), pp. 184 ff.; see also N. V. Zueva and E. M. Shatohina, "Ruskite proekti za reformi v Evropeiska Turtsiya ot 1867 g.," in *Sb. V chest na akad. Hristo A. Hristov* (Sofia, 1976), pp. 129–39.

6. "Die Auswärtige Politik Preussens (1858–1871)," in *Diplomatische Aktenstücke*, vol. 8 (1866–1867) (Oldenburg, 1934). p. 691.

7. L. Thouvenel, *Trois années de la question d'Orient, 1856–1859* (Paris, 1897); Ed. Driault, *La question d'Orient depuis ses origines jusqu'à nos jours*, 4th ed. (Paris, 1905); J. Ancel, *Manuel historique de la question d'Orient (1792–1923)* (Paris, 1923); J. A. Marriott, *The Eastern Question: An Historical Study in European Diplomacy*, (Oxford, 1963).

8. *Sbornik dogovorov Rossii s drugimi gosudarstvami 1856–1917 gg.* (Moscow, 1952), pp. 124 ff.

9. Botev, *Izbrani proizvedeniya*, p. 260.

10. Ibid.

11. Ibid., p. 430.

12. K. Kosev, N. Zhechev, and D. Doinov, *Istoriya na Aprilskoto vustanie 1876* (Sofia, 1976), p. 173.

13. Ibid., pp. 191 ff.

14. *Osvobozhdenie Bolgarii ot turetskogo iga: Dokumenti v treh tomah*, vol. 1, *Osvoboditelnaya borba yuzhnih slavyan i Rossiya (1875–1877 gg.)*, ed. S. A. Nikitina, V. D. Konobeeva, Al. Burmova, and N. Todorova (Moscow, 1961), p. 129.

15. Archives du Ministère des Affaires Etrangères de France (hereafter AMAE), Turquie, Correspondance politique des consuls, Philippopolis, vol. 1 (1857–1877), pp. 284 ff.

16. Hvostov, *Istoriya diplomatii*, pp. 88 ff.

17. C. Lowe, *Salisbury and the Mediterranean* (London–Toronto, 1965), pp. 19 ff.; *Documents diplomatiques français relatifs aux origines de la Guerre de 1914*, 1st series (1871–1900), vol. 2 (1875–1879) (Paris, 1930), p. 5.

18. "Zapiski grafa N. P. Ignatieva 1875–1877 gg.," *Istoricheskii vestnik* 135 (1914): 50, 53, 63.

19. Hr. Hristov, *Osvobozhdenieto na Bulgaria i politikata na zapadnite durzhavi 1876–1878* (Sofia, 1968), pp. 49 ff.

20. *Osvobozhdenie Bolgarii ot turetskogo iga*, pp. 34 ff.

21. "Zapiski grafa N. P. Ignatieva, p. 454.

22. *Affaires d'Orient (1875–1877)*, pt. 1 (Paris, 1877), pp. 104–5, 106–9.

23. Ibid., pp. 76, 97–98, 100. For more detail see V. Čubrilović, *Bosanski ustanak 1875–1878*, Posebna izdanja SAN 83 (Belgrade, 1930); M. Ekmečić, *Ustanak u Bosni 1875–1878* (Sarajevo, 1960).

24. "Zapiski grafa N. P. Ignatieva," p. 454.

25. *Osvobozhdeni Bolgarii ot turetskogo iga*, p. 38.

26. AVPR, f. Kantselyariya, 1875, d. 112, 11:454, 461–62.

27. *Osvobozhdenie Bolgarii ot turetskogo iga*, pp. 119–22.

28. Ibid., p. 63.

29. *Dnevnik D. A. Miliutina*, ed. and trans. P. A. Zayonchkovskogo, vol. 1 (Moscow, 1947), p. 225.

30. S. A. Nikitin, *Ocherki po istorii yuzhnih slavyan i russko–bolgarskiy svyazei v 50–70-e gody XIX v.* (Moscow, 1970), p. 174.

31. AVPR, f. Kantselyariya, 1875, d. 114, 1:173 cl.

32. R. Jacquemyns, *Le droit international et la question d'Orient* (Paris, 1877), p. 62.

33. AVPR, f. Kantselyariya, i. 126, 11:331–33.

34. Nikitin, *Ocherki*, p. 175.

35. L. Lamouche, *Histoire de la Turquie* (Paris, 1934), p. 312.

36. AMAE, Turquie, Correspondance politique des consuls, Philippopolis, vol. 2 (1857–1877), pp. 308, 455 ff.

37. Ibid., Correspondance consulaire et commerciale, Sofia, vol. 1 (1875–1885), p. 31; Correspondance politique des consuls, Sofia, vol. 1 (1876–1878), p. 12.

38. Yu. A. Petrosyan, *"Novie osmany" i borba za konstitutsiu v 1876 g. 1 Turtsii* (Moscow, 1958), pp. 86 ff.

39. *Documents diplomatiques français*, p. 113; see also Hvostov, *Istoriya*

*diplomatii,* pp. 93 ff.; N. S. Kinyapina, *Vneshnaya politika Rossii vtoroi poloviny XIX v.* (Moscow, 1974), pp. 148 ff.

40. F. Martens, *Vostochnaya voina i Bryusselskaya konferentsiya, 1874–1878 gg.* (St. Petersburg, 1879), p. 189; R. W. Seton–Watson, *Disraeli, Gladstone, and the Eastern Question* (London, 1935), pp. 22 ff.; Iv. Panayotov, "Osvobozhdenieto na Bulgaria i evropeiskata diplomatsiya," in *Sb. Osvobozhdenieto na Bulgaria ot Tursko igo 1878–1958* (Sofia, 1958), p. 87.

41. Yono Mitev, *Otrazhenie na Aprilskoto vustanie v chuzhbina* (Sofia, 1976), pp. 98 ff.

42. I will not dwell here on the repercussions of the April Uprising abroad, since this question has been comparatively well studied. Besides Mitev's book, indicated above, see Kosev, Zhechev, and Doinov, *Istoriya na Aprilskoto vustanie 1876,* pp. 481 ff.

43. Ibid., p. 524.

44. Nikitin, *Ocherki,* p. 176.

45. Kinyapina, *Vneshnaya politika,* pp. 152–53.

46. I. V. Kozmenko, "Bolgarskii vopros v mezhdunarodnih otnosheniyah 1876–1878 gg.," *Kratkie soobshcheniya Instituta slavyanovedeniya AN SSSR* 10, no. 964, p. 61.

47. AVPR, f. Kantselyariya, Otchet ministra inostrannyh del za 1876 g., 1:61.

48. *Osvobozhdenie Bolgarii ot turetskogo iga,* pp. 336–37; see also Iv. Ormandjiev, *Antim I, bulgarski ekzarh* (Sofia, 1928), p. 66; Kiril, patriarh bulgarski, *Ekzarh Antim I (1816–1888)* (Sofia, 1956), p. 728.

49. *Dnevnik D. A. Miliutina,* vol. 2 (Moscow, 1949), pp. 93 ff.

50. "Opisanie Russko–turetskoi voiny 1877–1878 gg. na Balkanskom poluostrove," *Osoboe pribavlenie* 1 (1899): 32.

51. M. D. Balabanov, *Stranitsa ot politicheskoto ni vuzrazhdane* (Sofia, 1904), pp. 155 ff., 302–5, 357–58.

52. Ibid., p. 372.

53. *Osvobozhdenie Bolgarii ot turetskogo iga,* p. 484.

54. AVPR, f. Kantselyariya, 1877, d. 123, 1:26; see also Hristov, *Osvobozhdenieto na Bulgaria,* pp. 57–58.

55. Ibid., pp. 59–60.

56. C. E. Buckle, *The Letters of Queen Victoria,* vol. 3 (London, 1930), p. 501.

57. C. E. Buckle and W. F. Moneypenny, *The Life of Benjamin Disraeli,* vol. 6 (London, 1920), p. 103.

58. AVPR, f. Kantselyariya, Posolstvo v Berline, 1876, d. 19, 1:3967.

59. Ch. Hohenlohe–Schillingsfürst, *Denkwürdigkeiten,* vol. 2 (Stuttgart–Leipzig, 1907), p. 205.

60. Iv. Panayotov, "Kum diplomaticheskata istoriya na Tsarigradskata konferentsiya," in *Izvestiya na Instituta po bulgarska istoriya,* vol. 6 (Sofia, 1956), p. 71.

61. Ibid.

62. Dr. Busch, *Die Botschafterkonferenz in Konstantinopel und russisch–türkische Krieg 1877–1878* (Berlin, 1909), p. 22.

63. *Osvobozhdenie Bolgarii ot turetskogo iga,* p. 511.

64. Panayotov, "Kum diplomaticheskata istoriya," p. 72.

65. For details concerning the consular and other information about the ethnic composition of European Turkey, see Hristov, *Osvobozhdenieto,* pp. 66–73.

66. Ibid., p. 86.

67. Gabriel effendi Noradounghian, *Recueil d'actes internationaux de l'Empire ottoman,* vol. 3, *1856–1878* (Paris, 1902), pp. 412–16.

68. Ibid., pp. 409–11.

69. AVPR, f. Kantselyariya, 1876, d. 33, 11:459–60.

70. Ibid., 1:458.

71. Petrosyan, *"Novie osmany,"* p. 117.

72. Hristov, *Osvobozhdenieto,* p. 92.

73. AVPR, f. Kantelyariya, 1876, d. 19, 1:548 ff.

74. M. H. Reitern, "Zapiski," *Russkaya starina,* July 1910, p. 49.

75. *Documents diplomatiques français,* p. 133.

76. S. S. Tatishchev, *Imperator Aleksandr II, ego zhizn i tsarstvovanie,* vol. 2 (St. Petersburg, 1903), p. 359.

77. C. de Grunwald, *Trois siècles de diplomatie russe* (Paris, 1945), p. 215.

78. *Dnevnik D. A. Miliutina,* vol. 2, p. 143.

79. AVPR, f. Kantselyariya, 1877, d. 19, 11:3, 19–24, 27–28, 31–32, 39–41 ff.; see also "Poezdka grafa N. P. Ignatieva po evropeiskim stolitsam pered voinoi 1877–1878 gg.," *Russkaya starina,* March 1914, p. 507.

80. *Dnevnik D. A. Miliutina,* vol. 2, p. 144.

81. Panayotov, *Osvobozhdenieto na Bulgaria,* p. 97.

82. Hvostov, *Istoriya diplomatii,* p. 123.

83. Even the British foreign secretary, Lord Derby, admitted: "Turkey's answer testified that she had already decided to go to war. ...Any intervention of diplomacy would be superfluous. ...Nothing more could be done. ...If Russia did not want war, she failed to avoid it; if she wanted it and aimed at putting all the responsibility for it on Turkey, she succeeded thoroughly" (*Documents diplomatiques français,* p. 158).

84. De Grunwald, *Trois siècles de diplomatie russe,* p. 127.

85. M. Gazenkampf, *Moi dnevnik na voine 1877–1878* (St. Petersburg, 1908), suppl. 2.

86. AVPR, f. Glavnyi arhiv V–A, 1876–1878, d. 1, 1:15, 23.

87. For details see P. K. Fortunatov, *Voina 1877–1878 gg. i Osvobozhdenie Bolgarii* (Moscow, 1950); Hristov, *Osvobozhdenieto,* pp. 102 ff.

88. V. Kolarov, "Dvata faktora, koito suzdadoha Bulgaria kato svobodna i progresivna durzhava," *Izbrani proizvedeniya* 3 (1956): 387.

Peter F. Sugár

# AUSTRIA–HUNGARY AND THE BALKAN CRISIS:
## AN INGENIOUS IMPROVISATION

Although the recurrent crises in the Balkans during the nineteenth century evoked great concern in the foreign ministries of the European powers, historians, except those of the Balkan states, have paid surprisingly little attention to them. The crisis of 1875–78, ending with the Congress of Berlin, June 13–July 13, 1878, is the exception. The literature dealing with it is voluminous,[1] and even textbooks discuss it.[2] It is, therefore, superfluous to recount the series of events that began at the end of 1874 with disturbances in Hercegovina and ended with the signing of the Berlin Protocol.[3] During these years the position of Austria–Hungary changed repeatedly in response to the constantly changing situations in the Balkans and on the international diplomatic scene. If the Ballhausplatz emerged from the Congress of Berlin as one of the victors (Great Britain being the other), it owed its success to the clever improvisation of the imperial and royal minister of foreign affairs, Count Gyula Andrássy.[4] This paper will explore the reasons for the various shifts in Austro–Hungarian attitudes in searching for a solution for the Balkan crisis of 1875–78.

Writing about another Balkan crisis, Roger V. Paxton has remarked,

> Diplomatic histories of "Great Powers" often reveal that... [they] fail to design foreign policies which can easily adjust to substantive changes: ...Instead of devising several contingency strategies... these governments frequently vacillate. ...This decision-making process becomes complicated when the problem under consideration is entangled in a web of revolutions, wars and diplomatic intrigues.[5]

The crisis of 1875–78 had all these elements — revolutions, wars, and diplomatic intrigues — and the Great Power to which these pages are devoted, Austria–Hungary, certainly vacillated. While the lack of a clear foreign-policy line and the absence of contingency plans are in most cases signs of poor diplomacy, in the case of Austria–Hungary they simply reflected the complicated and confusing domestic situation, which made a clear-cut foreign policy practically impossible. This situation must be understood by anyone who attempts to analyze the various diplomatic positions taken by Austria–Hungary during the years under consideration.

After the *Ausgleich* of 1867 that created Austria–Hungary, this new empire had three ministries: an Austrian ministry responsible to the Austrian parliament, a Hungarian ministry responsible to the Hungarian parliament, and a common ministry with three portfolios responsible to the emperor-king. The common ministries of foreign affairs, national defense, and finance could not function without the budgets annually allotted to them by the two parliaments, to which they owed only the nominal duty of reporting through the peculiar institution of the delegations.[6] That the two parliaments wanted the common ministers to act in conformity with their wishes goes without saying. The Hungarian position was stronger in this respect than the Austrian because the Hungarian prime minister had the right to be consulted on foreign affairs while the Austrian did not. Furthermore, the position of the Hungarian prime minister, who always dealt with a parliament in which he had a large majority backing him and practically no minority representation, was much stronger than that of his Austrian colleague, who more often than not was the leader of a coalition government facing a lower house in which minorities, especially Czechs and Poles, held numerous seats.

While it is hard to identify a clearly defined Austrian approach to foreign affairs in the second half of the 1870s, the Austrian government had to pay close attention to public opinion, at least as it was expressed by minority deputies, all of whom were pro-Slav and, with the exception of the Poles, often pro-Russian. Hungarian views were much clearer although by no means without contradiction. Andrássy and his colleagues were liberal nationalists and therefore sympathized with the national liberation movements in the Balkans. This attitude contradicted two other considerations. The more important was fear of Russia, which the Hungarians considered the greatest danger to their country's future because of its expansionism and its Pan-Slavism. They tended to see Russia's sinister maneuvering behind most manifestations of Slavic nationalism. Russia was the enemy and had to be thwarted, while other Slavs were to be handled accordingly. The second consideration was limited to the Balkans, where the Hungarians were interested in maintaining the status quo. They did not see any danger to themselves in the weak Ottoman Empire, which, if it disappeared, would, in their view, be replaced by the Russians or Russian-dominated states. On the contrary, they regarded it as extremely useful. Andrássy summarized this attitude concisely at the Crown Council of January 29, 1875: "Turkey is of almost providential usefulness for Austria. Her existence is in our best-understood interest. She maintains the status quo of the small states and denies, to our advantage, their aspirations. If Turkey did not exist this troublesome task would become ours."[7] The resulting Hungarian approach to the Balkans was, therefore, one which relied on improvisation depending on Balkan developments and the role Russia played in them. The continued existence of the Ottoman Empire, the bulwark against Russian expansion, had to be supported as long as possible. If the Ottoman Empire were to dissolve, Austria–Hungary would have to gain the loyalty of the Balkan people, detaching them from Russia and attaching them to herself.[8] This was not only in her own but in Europe's interest.[9] Only if the disintegration of the Ottoman Empire and the expansion of the Balkan states created the threat of Russian domination of the Balkans would Austria–Hungary have to act to secure for herself the territories on which her safety depended. In 1875 this alternative appeared to be developing: Andrássy expressed his fears at the already mentioned Crown Council when he argued for a strong policy: "Should Serbia and Montenegro acquire Bosnia and Hercegovina, creating a new state complex that we do not or cannot oppose, then we would be relinquishing our own existence and assuming the role of 'the sick man.' "[10]

Whatever Andrássy's views, and however much they were in accord with Hungarian wishes, he had to fit them into a foreign policy that took into account the opinions of the emperor-king and the military. These differed sharply from his own. Court circles were conservative, looked at foreign affairs as a prerogative of the crown, and even after 1870 were expansionist, although they recognized the altered European situation and were ready to change tactics. In contradiction to Andrássy's views, the court preferred agreement with Russia, possibly even an alliance, and considered partitioning the Balkans with the great Eastern power.[11] The military circles, dominated by Archduke Albert, the ruler's uncle, and Feldmarshalleutenant Beck, were also conservative, pro-Russian forces influencing foreign policy.[12] The military's influence was in part the result of the realization that *Realpolitik* was the only method possible in an age dominated by Bismarck. Francis Joseph himself made this clear when he informed those present at the Crown Council of February 17, 1872, that when "Andrássy accepted his portfolio he agreed to the principle that the conduct of foreign affairs must be in harmony with military interests."[13] The foreign minister made this even clearer on the same occasion by explaining that "the result of the last war is that might comes before right; consequently, no state can be certain today to maintain its rightful position unless it makes it a basic principle in all its calculations that it has to be capable of securing with arms the goals it strives to achieve by peaceful means."[14]

While *Realpolitik* gave the army a say in foreign affairs, the military had its own interests that it wanted pursued, especially in the Balkans. After the

Napoleonic wars the Habsburgs had acquired Dalmatia, a thin strip of land on the eastern shore of the Adriatic. In spite of its great strategic value, this new province was militarily indefensible because of its location and shape. From the military's point of view, Dalmatia had to be not only retained but also secured by acquiring a supporting landmass. Two years before his death, Field Marshal Joseph Radetzky had proposed the occupation of Bosnia–Hercegovina. Ten years later, Admiral Baron Wilhelm Tegetthoff had made the same request, and Beck reiterated it repeatedly between 1869 and 1875.[15] After 1867 this demand was further complicated by a basic constitutional question: if and when Bosnia–Hercegovina was annexed, who would conduct the annexation? The Dual Monarchy consisted of two equal states each of which could gain territory and population by annexing a new region, thus upsetting the balance between them. Neither half was willing to let the other grow without compensation, while at the same time both were loath to accept additional Slavs. Before 1875 this problem was not acute. Yet, whatever the situation, the army was never in a position to pursue its own goals or give the diplomats the backing that Andrássy considered necessary.

Whereas the armed forces had been fully reorganized by 1875, they were still extremely weak in comparison with other forces. Austria–Hungary, the second largest state in Europe, was economically a second-rate power. Her agricultural production was excellent, but only 15 percent of her population worked in industry, and consequently her iron and steel production, so crucial for the military, was even lower than that of Belgium. Road and railroad networks were inadequate.[16] Furthermore,

the parliamentary bodies... controlled the military expenditure of the Monarchy. The eternal parsimony of the Austrian and Hungarian governments and their parliaments was an important cause of the weakness of the military forces. ...From 1890 until 1912 the Monarchy fell steadily behind the other Great Powers in military potential. By 1913 Franz Joseph's subjects were spending more than three times as much money on beer, wine and tobacco than on the entire armed forces of the Dual Monarchy.[17]

The stinginess of the legislatures predated the period of this statement. Dominated by antimilitaristic liberals in the years under consideration, they never gave the military the financial means it needed. After the beginning of the economic recession in 1873 the armed forces fared very badly. Some figures illustrate this weakness (table 1).

The cumulative effect of this budgetary policy emerges clearly from figures that compare total military expenditures between 1867 and 1892 as calculated by the Austro–Hungarian chief of staff's office. The expenditures are given in French francs (no figures for Great Britain are given):[18] France,

23,154,480,000; Russia, 22,426,371,000; Germany, 14,208,000,000; Italy, 6,822,411,000; Austria–Hungary, 7,004,511,000. No wonder, then, that by 1875 "some observers doubted that Austria–Hungary could sustain a major war without foreign subsidy" and that in 1877 the monarchy negotiated for such help with Britain.[19] Military men not only were conscious of the disparity in power between their country and Russia but also realized that the various political orientations of the different ethnic groups living in Austria–Hungary deprived them of issues behind which the population could be united enough to support a war. Even Archduke Albert admitted that public opinion was against war and that the army could consider only defensive action.[20]

Finally, all those involved in framing Austria–Hungary's foreign policy were bound, at least to some extent, by the provisions of the Three Emperors' League in force since the spring of 1873, which stipulated that the rulers of Germany, Russia, and Austria–Hungary must consult one another on issues of common interest. Vague as this agreement was, it was taken seriously and produced, between 1875 and 1878, a voluminous correspondence between Francis Joseph and Tsar Alexander II. The problem was that in the Balkans the interests of these two rulers were not common but contradictory.

When in 1875 a series of events began to unfold in the Balkans involving "revolutions, wars, and diplomatic intrigues," those involved in directing Austro–Hungarian foreign policy had to reconcile their wish for maintenance of the status quo in the Balkans and the continued existence of the Ottoman Empire with the desirability for internal politics of a benevolent attitude toward the Balkan Christians and their cause. In deference to the sympathies of the large Slavic population of their own state, they had to reconcile their determination not to permit the creation of a major Slavic state south of the Danube–Sava line that might act as a magnet for conationals living north of it with a friendly attitude toward the cause of the revolutionaries. They had to cooperate with Russia because the weakness of the military did not permit opposing her, yet they had to make certain that the tsarist empire did not achieve its goals in southeastern Europe. In spite of constitutional difficulties and their abhorrence of including more Slavs in Austria–Hungary, they had to make plans for intervention and even territorial acquisitions should this be the only alternative to Russian domination of the Balkans. Practically any course of action open to the Ballhausplatz was certain to alienate important segments of public opinion and require funds that the parliaments, reacting to public opinion, were unlikely to make available. Under these circumstances it was impossible to formulate a clear policy line. It is not surprising that the first decision taken was simply to wait and see how events unfolded. After all, uprisings against Ottoman rule were nothing new in the

Balkans, had not involved the Great Powers directly since the end of the revolution in Bucharest in 1848, and usually ended with the Ottomans reestablishing order. The last uprising in Hercegovina, in 1858–62, had been put down by fifty thousand Ottoman soldiers. Yet this time the situation was different. Serbia and Montenegro were deeply interested, and the Ottoman government appeared to be neglecting its duty as pacifier of a region that bordered on Dalmatia.[21] Therefore, Austria–Hungary had to attempt to produce by diplomatic means some solution that would calm the insurgents, be acceptable to the Ottomans, Serbs, and Montenegrins, and make the Dual Monarchy appear a friend of the Slavs. Any diplomatic campaign with these goals in mind could succeed only if it involved Russia.

The interests and prestige of both states were involved. Both realized that if a peaceful solution were not found they would face greater difficulties. Therefore, they agreed to put pressure on the Ottomans and force them to institute reforms that would satisfy the insurgents and end the revolt. They approached the Porte jointly with this suggestion, but what they proposed, in rather vague terms, was rejected by the revolutionaries as not going far enough and by the Ottoman government as excessive.[22] Andrássy's hopes of maintaining the political status quo in the Balkans while gaining the gratitude of its Christian inhabitants had been disappointed. In August of 1875, Prince Aleksandr Gorchakov submitted a proposal to Vienna suggesting that the two powers demand that the Ottoman Empire give Bosnia and Hercegovina autonomous regimes similar to that enjoyed by Romania.[23] Prior to Serbia's and Montenegro's declaration of war and the Bulgarian uprising this proposal made some sense, but in Andrássy's opinion it showed clearly that Russia was pursuing her own goals and totally disregarding the interests of the Dual Monarchy. He described Gorchakov's plan as "purest nonsense," pointing out that "autonomy might be practicable for an entirely Christian region, such as Bulgaria; but such a weak system of government would never be able to maintain order in Bosnia, with its warring Moslem, Catholic, and Orthodox populations."[24] The result could only be annexation by Serbia and/or Montenegro, something that was totally unacceptable to Austria–Hungary. Anything was better than this solution, even the incorporation of these provinces into his own country. Only the Ottomans or the Austro–Hungarians could be masters of these provinces. In 1875 Andrássy wrote in an aide-mémoire: "It is not permissible to push Turkey out of the two provinces. On the contrary, she must be supported as long as possible with advice and by urging reforms on her. Nevertheless, at a given moment we must step into her place whenever she proves incapable of protecting the provinces."[25]

Since Gorchakov's proposal excluded both the Ottoman Empire and the Habsburg Monarchy from Bosnia–Hercegovina, Andrássy was forced to make counterproposals. His first move was unrealistic. He still clung to the illusion that the status quo in the Balkans could be maintained, thus sparing Austria–Hungary the need to give preference to some of her contradictory aims over the others. He hoped that if Russo–Austro–Hungarian pressure on the Porte could be increased by associating the other Great Powers with it, the Ottomans would yield. This is what he proposed to the various governments of Europe in the so-called Andrássy Note of December 30, 1875. This approach had no chance of success. No action was taken either by the two states most closely interested in Balkan development or by the other powers.

Intervention became much more likely after the Bulgarian uprising of April 1876, which finally produced Ottoman intervention and the "Bulgarian Horrors" that shocked European public opinion. On May 12, 1876, Andrássy, Gorchakov, and Bismarck met in Berlin. The Russian chancellor submitted a plan that basically consisted of military intervention in Bosnia–Hercegovina and a demand for a congress of the Great Powers to resolve the Eastern Question. To the Austro–Hungarian minister this solution was totally unacceptable. Military intervention on the part of his country without lengthy preparation of various kinds was impossible, whereas Russian intervention was anathema. A conference of the Great Powers, also calling for careful and lengthy preparation, might possibly bring results favorable to the Balkan Christians, but in this case they would owe gratitude to all those who attended it, thus diminishing the influence of Austria–Hungary in southeastern Europe.

What exactly happened in Berlin on that day is not clear. Obviously very tense negotiations took place that ended in the total retreat of the Russians.[26] Late in the evening the Berlin Memorandum was issued. A victory for Andrássy, the document called for a return to his policy of pressure on the Ottoman Empire, which was now requested to grant the various insurgents a two-month armistice and to use this time period for reforms and pacification. To show that the powers meant business, Andrássy agreed to Gorchakov's demand to send warships to the straits, but in exchange Gorchakov agreed to drop the plan for a Great Power conference. This was the last time that Andrássy was able to avoid painful decisions. Once the Bulgarians had joined the Hercegovinians and Bosnians in revolt and the Ottoman army had intervened, the chances of a peaceful settlement were practically nonexistent and public opinion in Serbia and Montenegro made intervention by these two states a foregone conclusion.

Six weeks after the Berlin meeting, Serbia declared war on the Ottoman Empire, and Montenegro followed two weeks later. The war created a new situation, and the two powers most closely involved had to ask themselves a simple question: What position do we take if the war is won by the Ottomans, and how do we deal with the small states should they emerge victorious? It was obvious that should they be unable to find an answer to this question satisfying to both of them a very serious crisis would emerge. This was the situation for which the Three Emperors' League had been created.

Russia and Austria–Hungary acted promptly. Within a week of Montenegro's declaration of war, Francis Joseph, Alexander II, and their major policy makers got together at Reichstadt (today Zákupy) in Bohemia. The result of these talks, known as the Reichstadt Agreement, was simply a gentlemen's agreement between rulers in keeping with the provisions of the Three Emperors' League. The document to which historians refer emerged as the *Résumé des pourparlers secrets de Reichstadt du 8 juillet 1876,* dictated by Andrássy on that day to the Russian ambassador in Vienna.[27] It was, as its title indicates, a secret agreement.[28]

In the event of an Ottoman victory, according to the *Résumé,* the two powers were to make certain that Christians under Ottoman rule were not harmed. Serbia and Montenegro were to retain their present borders, and no Ottoman troops were to be reintroduced into Serbia. Serbia was not to be allowed to declare her full independence, although Montenegro was to be recognized as a sovereign state. The Porte was to be asked to introduce the reforms in Bosnia–Hercegovina that her inhabitants had demanded when they revolted.

At first sight this solution appears to be in line with the policy pursued up to then by the Ballhausplatz: no military intervention and the reestablishment of the status quo ante. It is intriguing to speculate what prompted the Russians to retreat from their position as rapidly as they did in Berlin in May and to accept Andrássy's line in July, but this question would lead too far away from the topic of this paper. Actually, the Russians gained quite a lot by this agreement. Montenegro, then their favorite, was to gain full independence in spite of her defeat, Serbia was to owe her continuing existence at least in part to Russia, and in the arrangements that were to protect the Balkan Christians (Bulgaria, Rumelia, and Bosnia–Hercegovina) Russia was to play a decisive role. These developments certainly did not please those in Vienna, Andrássy included, whose primary goal was to keep the Russians away from the Balkans. Concessions were made by both sides in order to retain the chance of cooperation and to exclude the other powers from a region they considered in their sphere of influence.

It was much more difficult to reach an agreement on what to do in the event of an Ottoman defeat. At Reichstadt certain basic lines of action were outlined, but the need for further consultations was recognized. The two states agreed that for the security of Dalmatia the region between Dalmatia and Croatia (basically Bosnia) must be kept out of Serbian hands. Yet, the victors could not be expected to be satisfied with nothing, and should they be forced to return home empty-handed they would blame Russia and Austria–Hungary. This was something both powers wanted to avoid. In the case of the Dual Monarchy the reaction of its Slavic population would also have created serious internal problems. Therefore, Serbia was to receive some territory in Bosnia and the Sanjak of Novi Pazar, while Montenegro was to get some Hercegovinian territory and a port on the Adriatic. "The remaining territory of Bosnia and Hercegovina can be annexed by Austria–Hungary," stated the *Résumé*. The borders dividing the two provinces were not defined. Russia was to regain Bessarabia (lost in 1856) and enough territory in Asia — once again without defined borders — to equal her partner's territorial gains. Greece was to receive Thessaly and Crete, while Albania, Bulgaria, and Rumelia were to gain autonomy. The borders of these states also remained unclear. No major state was to be created in the Balkans. Should the Ottoman Empire collapse completely, Constantinople and some territory around it were to be declared a free city.[29]

Andrássy clearly would have had to abandon, in the event of an Ottoman defeat, his favorite solution, but the outcome would still have been acceptable. Montenegro and Serbia would still have owed some of their gains in part to Austria–Hungary's intervention; while the Dual Monarchy would have been forced to face the constitutional problem of annexation and the unwanted increase of her Slavic population, this action could have been sold to the governments and parliaments as the lesser of two evils, since the creation of a major Slavic state on the empire's southern borders was ruled out; Russia would have been excluded at least from the western Balkans; the breakup of the Three Emperors' League and military intervention by Russia would have been avoided; and Andrássy could have hoped to be able to match Russian influence in the newly autonomous states. This was a new policy, dictated by events over which Austria–Hungary had no control, and it was the first of many improvisations.

The Ottoman armies rather easily defeated the Serbs and Montenegrins, who were forced on October 31, 1876, to ask for an armistice. The victors refused to settle the war on the conditions stipulated by the Reichstadt Agreement and granted the armistice only after they had received an ultimatum from Russia. The possibility of an Ottoman–Russian war alarmed Britain. On her initiative, the ambassadors of the Great Powers prepared new peace proposals at the Constantinople Conference. These demanded even more from the Ottomans than had Russia and Austria–Hungary at Reichstadt. The Ottomans responded with a surprise: they transformed the empire into a constitutional monarchy, submitted the powers' proposals to an ad hoc conference of Muslim and Christian notables, and on their recommendation rejected the European demands.

It was obvious that Russia, having delivered an ultimatum to the Ottomans, would have to act. Austria–Hungary was not unprepared. Already during the summer of 1875, as soon as Serbia had declared war, Francis Joseph had instructed the general commanding in Croatia, Baron Anton Mollinary, to prepare plans for intervention in Bosnia–Hercegovina.[30] The army was, therefore, ready for at least limited action. Even before the Constantinople Conference broke up, Andrássy, predicting Russian military intervention, sent an aide-mémoire to his ambassador in St. Petersburg explaining that Austria–Hungary could not permit Russian troops to enter Serbia or any region in the western Balkans because

> when Russia begins to fight Turkey and to lead the forces of these countries [Serbia and Montenegro] the struggle acquires a completely different complexion. Cooperation with Serbia and Montenegro will transform a European action into a Slavic movement, the Christian-humanitarian approach will change into a one-sided Orthodox one, and the war will take on the features of a revolution. ...If Russian action brings under one roof all the, until now, isolated Slavic aspirations and thus turns into a propaganda campaign addressed to all Orthodox Slavs, then public opinion among our most important people, the Germans and Hungarians, will judge the existence of the Monarchy endangered by Russian action and will not permit the governments to remain passive observers.[31]

It would appear from this statement that Andrássy, seeing in Russia the greatest danger to his country, was ready to move against her under certain circumstances. While the general staff prepared contingency plans for a campaign against Russia in 1876, Archduke Albert and Beck made it clear that such a war would be too expensive for Austria–Hungary, would drag on forever, and could not be won; it was simply out of the question.[32] Andrássy's choices were limited by the position taken by the military leaders. Fortunately, the Russians were also eager to avoid a confrontation, leaving the door open for further negotiations and improvisations.

The Russians first approached Vienna with a plan that amounted to the virtual partition of the Balkans between the two states. "This proposal conformed with certain traditions of Austrian and Russian foreign policy. There were several individuals in the imperial capital who would have accepted it gladly, but Andrássy rejected it."[33] After receiving the Ballhausplatz's answer the Russians tried without success to get assurances from Germany that in the event of a war between two emperors in the Balkans, the third would remain neutral.[34] Andrássy too turned to Bismarck, who told him that balance-of-power considerations and the Polish situation would leave Germany no choice but to come to the aid of the apparent loser.[35] Under these circumstances Vienna and St. Petersburg had to get together and hold the additional consultations indicated by the Reichstadt Agreement.

Negotiations conducted by Andrássy and Novikov produced the Budapest Convention.[36] When the first, military part of the convention was signed the Constantinople Conference was still sitting, but the Russians were already thinking of war and wanted to secure Austria–Hungary's neutrality. Andrássy was convinced that Russia would take military action, and he knew that neither the military nor public opinion would permit the use of Austro–Hungarian military forces; events in the eastern Balkans, where the hostilities would occur, were too far from the monarchy's borders to permit calling military intervention there a "defensive war." He had to retreat to the minimal position of keeping Russia away from Serbia and Montenegro. He was, in fact, in a very weak bargaining position. Should St. Petersburg have gone to war, even without an agreement with Vienna, he could not have done anything to prevent it. Fortunately for him, the Russians were eager to secure their flanks before starting hostilities. The military part of the convention was the result of these mutual desiderata. It stipulated that in case of a Russo–Ottoman war, Serbia, Montenegro, and the Sanjak of Novi Pazar would be considered neutral territory by the Russians, who would not send troops into them. In exchange, Austria–Hungary promised to remain neutral and to prevent diplomatic intervention by the concert of the Great Powers. In the event of a Russian victory, Bulgaria was to receive practically full autonomy. Bosnia–Hercegovina might either receive limited autonomy or fall to Austria–Hungary in accordance with the Reichstadt Agreement; this question was left open for further negotiations.[37] Tsar Alexander II was at first outraged, saying "all these conditions are unacceptable, and I cannot understand how Novikov could have agreed to them," but finally even he accepted them.[38]

The additional convention is of greater interest not only because it is much more specific but also because it was open to contradictory interpretations that soon became a bone of contention. While Gorchakov excluded from this document any consideration of possible territorial gains by Russia in Asia, his country's right to annex Bessarabia in accordance with the Reichstadt Agreement was reiterated. Austria–Hungary received the right to annex Bosnia–Hercegovina, and Serbia and Montenegro were to gain additional territory in the Lim region and the Sanjak of Novi Pazar, with Montenegro also receiving the port of Bar (Antivari) on the Adriatic. Andrássy clearly made the agreement concerning Serbia and Montenegro reluctantly. By dividing the territories in question the two states would acquire a common border, and merger at a later date could create a "major Slavic state" on Austria–Hungary's southern border. To prevent this from happening, Austria–Hungary reserved to herself the right to take special measures in the Sanjak to safeguard her commercial interests in the Balkans. Crucial for Andrássy, and the source of future disagreements, was the third paragraph of the additional convention, which stated "that in case of either a territorial reorganization or the dissolution of the Ottoman Empire the establishment of a large, compact Slavic state is forbidden; in exchange Bulgaria, Albania, and what is left of Rumelia [basically present-day Macedonia] could become independent states."[39] Having the creation of a major Slavic state excluded from the possibilities and instead establishing three relatively small ones were critical for Andrássy. The problem this paragraph created stemmed from the possible dissolution of the Ottoman Empire and was eventually to become important in Austro–Hungarian–Russian relations, as will be shown below.

The Budapest Convention, concluded under the shadow of an approaching war, represented a serious retreat by Andrássy on several fronts and the abandonment of considerations previously presumed to be important. The idea of securing Serbia's friendship had been given up, and, consequently, the danger of creating serious opposition among the monarchy's Slavs had increased. The annexation of Bosnia–Hercegovina raised military and financial questions that required answers from the army and the two parliaments and presented the first serious constitutional complications since 1867. The liberal approach to nationalism was forgotten. Andrássy had fallen back on the cornerstone of his foreign policy, anti-Russianism, and even in this respect he had had to make concessions that only two or three years earlier he would have rejected out of hand. What he secured was a Russian-free western Balkans and a southeastern Europe in which no large state took the place of the Ottoman Empire, whose support he also had to jettison. Under these circumstances, it is hard to speak of a foreign policy; it makes more sense to see in Austria–Hungary's position a defensive stand dictated by circumstances. Diószegi points out, correctly, that Austria–Hungary took a grave risk in signing the Budapest Convention. If the Dual Monarchy could not prevent Russian military action prior to the outbreak of the war, what measures could she take against a victorious Russian army stationed in the Balkans should St. Petersburg, under the influence of victory, decide to disregard this agreement and reorganize the peninsula in accordance with its own wishes?[40] It was only about a year before Andrássy had to find an answer to this question.

On April 24, 1877, Russia declared war on the Ottoman Empire, and her armies began to move south through Romania, with which she had concluded an agreement making this possible. On May 11 Bucharest also declared war on the Ottoman Empire.[41] At first the hostilities went as expected. On June 26–27 the Russian–Romanian forces crossed the Danube, and by July 19 they had managed to cross the Shipka Pass, reaching the valley of the Tundzha River. One more mountain range had to be crossed before the advancing forces reached the Maritsa River basin, an easy highway to Edirne (Adrianople) and Constantinople. The fortifications around Plevna proved to be a serious obstacle, and the advance was halted there later in July. This somewhat calmed Europe's fears,[42] and it also cooled Russian enthusiasm. "On 26 July the tsar assured Franz Joseph that he had no intention of permanently occupying Bulgaria, or of introducing any 'democratic' elements there; that the Powers could assert their interests in the final peace settlement, and that Russia, for her part, would hold scrupulously to the Reichstadt agreement."[43] This was reassuring, and Andrássy played a very cautious game. When Great Britain suggested a military alliance, the Ballhausplatz refused it and confined itself to agreeing with the Foreign Office only on the limits of Russian territorial gains.[44]

The situation changed drastically when, on December 10, 1877, Plevna fell. This victory decided the war, and the Russian forces advanced rapidly to the outskirts of Constantinople, halting only at San Stefano (Yesilköy). Beginning in the middle of December, several notes were exchanged between Francis Joseph and Tsar Alexander II and their leading ministers. What emerged clearly from this exchange of ideas was that the positions of the two powers now diverged drastically. According to the Russians, the Ottoman Empire was in dissolution, creating an altogether new situation that made previous agreements obsolete. This was St. Petersburg's interpretation of the third paragraph of the additional convention. Andrássy's view was completely different. He did not recognize a lost war as a cause for dissolution and had for years opposed accelerating the process of dissolution of the Ottoman Empire by outside intervention.[45] Dissolution, according to him, had to be the result of a long process in which "internal gestation" brought about a gradual disintegration.[46] He once expressed himself on this subject humorously but clearly when he stated that "the situation with it [dissolution] is the same as it is with becoming bald. When does the process begin and when does it end?"[47] The new Russian position, which, among other provisions, ceded parts of Bosnia–Hercegovina to Serbia and Montenegro, created the major Slavic state of Bulgaria, in which Russian troops were to remain for two years, and gave Russia practically a free hand in Asia, was totally unacceptable to the Austro–Hungarian minister. Andrássy did not object to the creation of a Bulgarian state, because "Russia, once she has accomplished her mission, can easily leave Bulgaria again without endangering her interests. This country possesses all the prerequisites for an independent existence. After her reorganization she will remain Bulgaria."[48] What Andrássy had in mind was that while Russia had a legitimate interest in Bulgaria and was the power that could help her, Bulgaria was strong enough to be truly independent. What he objected to was only Bulgaria's proposed borders and the length of the Russian occupation. Russia was clearly violating the Reichstadt and Budapest agreements. Gorchakov admitted this but explained that *force majeure* made it inevitable.[49] In spite of numerous

Austro–Hungarian protests, Russia did not change her position; her single-handed reorganization of the Balkans was the basis of the preliminary Peace of Edirne of January 31, 1878, mainly the work of Count Nikolay Ignatyev.[50]

From the Austro–Hungarian point of view, the worst of all possibilities had to be considered. Cooperation with Russia had become impossible; Turkey might, indeed, withdraw from Europe; Serbia and Montenegro would owe all their gratitude to Russia, whose influence in the western Balkans would become supreme; and a major Slavic state, occupied by Russian troops, was emerging in the eastern and central Balkans.

Yet, Andrássy's position was not hopeless. Russia's behavior had seriously alarmed Britain and violated the Paris Treaty of 1856. He could now return to Gorchakov's idea, which he had rejected only a little time earlier, of a conference of the Great Powers. Bismarck was cool, in February 1878 still recommending direct Austro–Hungarian–Russian negotiations. Great Britain, on the other hand, now became very active. Russia held back, waiting to see how the European situation developed. It was encouraged by Bismarck's position but leery of Britain. Andrássy obtained assurances from London that in the event of common action by the two states Austria–Hungary would receive a subsidy making mobilization possible. He was no longer bound by the Three Emperors' League and hoped that under the circumstances the various forces influencing foreign policy would unite behind a clear plan of action.

The British not only offered military subsidies to the Dual Monarchy, but, on February 15, 1878, ordered their fleet to cross the Dardanelles and anchor at Constantinople. London was ready to go to war if Austria–Hungary joined her. The crucial decision was made in Vienna on February 24, 1878. Under the emperor's presidency, the ministers of both governments and the military leaders discussed the monarchy's next move. At this meeting Andrássy recommended war with Russia in alliance with Britain and demanded first 600, then 200 million gulden in credit for this purpose. He pointed out that this was possibly the last chance for Austria–Hungary to settle her Slavic problem with the help of Europe. His position was somewhat weakened by Bismarck's "honest broker" speech (made on February 19 in the hope of calming the British), which opened the door to a possible last effort to find a peaceful solution. If Andrássy really wanted war, he was disappointed. Only the Hungarian prime minister, Kálmán Tisza, backed his proposal.[51] The Austrian representatives made it clear that among the Slavs only the Poles would welcome a war with Russia and that the Germans of Austria were anything but enthusiastic. Finally, the army-court circles led by Archduke Albert continued to cling to their conservative and pro-Russian views. Thus "the absence of a unified foreign policy paralyzed the multinational Monarchy in spite of the favorable turns in the international situation. Although English financial backing was available, no Austro–Hungarian mobilization occurred. Because of Austro–Hungarian passivity the guns of the British ships also remained silent."[52] All that Andrássy salvaged from this meeting was the permission to ask the two parliaments for a credit of 60 million gulden to strengthen the forces on the southern border. When this issue was debated in the legislatures, he made it clear that the money would not be used to enter Bosnia–Hercegovina. That Bosnia–Hercegovina was later occupied became one of the reasons for Andrássy's fall.[53]

While the Russians did not know what had happened in Vienna on February 24, they saw clearly that Austria–Hungary was not mobilizing and that the British fleet remained inactive. Encouraged, they dictated the Peace of San Stefano to the Ottomans on March 3, 1878. Kars and Batum, in Asia, became Russian, as did Bessarabia; Romania, Montenegro, and Serbia became fully independent states; and a Greater Bulgaria, including Rumelia, with nearly 5 million inhabitants came into being. This state cut off Bosnia–Hercegovina and Albania from what remained of European Turkey. Fortunately for the Ottomans, not only Austria–Hungary but Britain found this solution unacceptable. From March to June the various European governments prepared themselves for the Congress of Berlin. The story of this congress is, as I have said, too well known to demand repetition. Austria–Hungary emerged from this meeting very well. Greater Bulgaria was dismantled and the major Slavic Orthodox state in the Balkans disappeared; Serbia and Montenegro were denied a common border; Russian prestige in the Balkans and in Romania diminished considerably; the right of Russia to station troops in the new Bulgaria was limited to nine months and in the new Ottoman province of Eastern Rumelia to three months;[54] the Ottoman Empire did not cease to exist in Europe and still stretched to the shores of the Adriatic in Albania; and Bosnia–Hercegovina was occupied, not yet annexed, by Austria–Hungary on the request of the powers assembled in Berlin.

It would appear that Andrássy, after twisting and turning for three years, achieved his goals. His country gained the territory for which its military leaders had clamored for many years, the western Balkans were under Austro–Hungarian influence, the Russian danger was, once again, averted, and the Ottomans were still the neighbors of Austria–Hungary. All he had to give up of his numerous original desiderata was the friendship of the Balkan Slavs. Yet he and his country did not gain all these advantages as a result of a clear-cut, consciously and determinedly followed foreign policy. No such policy existed. All the decisions the Ballhausplatz made during these crucial years were retreats forced upon it by events. Only during the February–July 1878 period, when Vienna was certain of Britain's full support and, increasingly, of Bismarck's diplomatic help, did Austria—Hungary follow a clear line in her demands and actions in preparing for and during the sitting of the Berlin Congress. Diószegi is right in saying that the successes of the Dual Monarchy at Berlin were the result "primarily of favorable turns in international relations"[55] and to a much lesser extent of her own ability to act. Austria—Hungary was a "great power" with vital interests in the Balkans, but given the complications created by the *Ausgleich*, her economic and military weaknesses, the multinationality of her population, and the diversity of views of her policy makers, she was unable to formulate and pursue a consistent foreign policy even when major events occurred on her border that could affect her very existence.

## TABLE 1

### DEFENSE ESTIMATES AND EXPENDITURES BY COUNTRY, 1870 AND 1880

|  | Estimates (in million Pounds Sterling) | | Per capita Expenditures | |
|---|---|---|---|---|
|  | 1870 | 1880 | 1870 | 1880 |
| Germany | 10.8 | 20.4 | 5s. 4d. | 9s. |
| Austria—Hungary | 8.2 | 13.2 | 4s. 6d. | 7s. 1d. |
| France | 22.0 | 31.4 | 12s. 2d. | 16s. 9d. |
| Great Britain | 23.4 | 25.2 | 14s. 9d. | 14s. 5d. |
| Italy | 7.8 | 10.0 | 5s. 9d. | 7s. 3d. |
| Russia | 22.0 | 29.6 | 5s. 4d. | 6s. 3d. |

**Source:**  A. J. P. Taylor, *The Struggle for Mastery in Europe, 1848–1918* (Oxford, 1954), p. xxviii.

## NOTES

1.   Among the numerous monographs dealing with the 1875–78 crisis are the following: Karl O. Frhr. von Aretin, ed., *Bismarcks Aussenpolitik und der Berliner Kongress* (Wiesbaden, 1978); Bertrand Bareilles, ed., *Le rapport secret sur le Congrès de Berlin adressé à la S. Porte par Karathéodory Pasha* (Paris, 1919); Vasco Čubrilović, *Bosanski Ustanak 1875–1878* (Belgrade, 1930); Milorad Ekmečić, *Ustanak u Bosni*

*1875–1878* (Sarajevo, 1950), also available in German translation, *Der Aufstand in Bosnien, 1875–1878* (Graz, 1974); P. K. Fortunatov, *Vojna 1877–1878 gg. i osvobož-denie Bolgarii* (Moscow, 1950); Sergei M. Gorianov, *Le question d'Orient à la veille du traité de Berlin (1870–1876) d'après les archives russes* (Paris, 1948); Imanuel Geiss, *Der Berliner Kongress, 1878: Protokolle und Materialien* (Boppard am Rhein, 1978); David Harris, *A Diplomatic History of the Balkan Crisis of 1875–1878: The First Year* (Stanford, 1936); Gisela Hünigen, *Nikolaj Pavlovic Ignat'ev und die russische Balkan-politik, 1875–1878* (Göttingen–Zürich–Frankfurt, 1968); Barbara Jelavich, *The Habsburg Empire in European Affairs, 1814–1918* (Chicago 1969); David MacKenzie, *The Serbs and Russian Panslavism, 1875–1878* (Ithaca, 1967); William N. Medlicott, *The Congress of Berlin and After,* 2d ed. (Hamden, Conn., 1963); Ralph Melville and Hans-Jürgen Schröder, eds., *Der Berliner Kongress von 1878* (Wiesbaden, 1982); Alexander Novotny, *Quellen und Studien zur Geschichte des Berliner Kongresses, 1878,* 2 vols. (Graz, 1957); Alfred F. Pribram, *The Secret Treaties of Austria–Hungary,* 2 vols. (Cambridge, Mass., 1920–21); Franz Ronneberger, *Bismarck und Südosteuropa* (Berlin, 1941); Georg H. Rupp, *A Wavering Friendship: Russia and Austria, 1876–1878* (Cambridge, Mass., 1941); Theodor von Sosnosky, *Die Balkanpolitik Österreich–Ungarns seit 1866,* 2 vols. (Stuttgart, 1913–14); Mihailo D. Stojanović, *The Great Powers and the Balkans, 1875–1878* (Cambridge, 1939); Benedict H. Sumner, *Russia and the Balkans, 1870–1880* (Oxford, 1937); Bruce Waller, *Bismarck at the Crossroads: The Reorientation of German Foreign Policy after the Congress of Berlin, 1878–80* (London, 1974); Walter G. Wirthwein, *Britain and the Balkan Crisis, 1875–1878* (New York, 1935).

2.  See, for example, Gordon A. Craig, *Europe since 1815* (New York–Chicago–San Francisco–Toronto–London, 1961), pp. 276–81; Carlton J. H. Hayes, *A Generation of Materialism* (New York–London, 1941), pp. 25–34; H. Hearder, *Europe in the Nineteenth Century* (New York, 1966), pp. 160–63; Charles and Barbara Jelavich, *The Establishment of the Balkan National States, 1804–1920* (Seattle–London, 1977), pp. 141–57; Alan Palmer, *The Lands Between* (New York, 1970), pp. 83–87; Robert R. Palmer and Joel Cotton, *A History of the Modern World,*4th ed. (New York, 1978), pp. 615–19; Norman Rich, *The Age of Nationalism and Reform, 1850–1890,* 2d ed. (New York, 1977), pp. 230–33; Leften S. Stavrianos, *The Balkans since 1453* (New York–Chicago–San Francisco–Toronto–London, 1958), pp. 393–412; Ferdinand Schevill, *The History of the Balkan Peninsula* (New York, 1922), pp. 393–406; F. Roy Willis, *World Civilizations,* vol. 2 (Lexington, Mass.–Toronto, 1982), pp. 1228–29; Robert Lee Wolff, *The Balkans in Our Time,*rev. ed. (New York, 1974), pp. 69–71, 82–85.

3.  The major turning points of the crisis prior to the Berlin Congress were as follows: Disturbances began in Hercegovina at the end of 1874. By the summer of 1875, this province was in full revolt, and in July the Bosnians joined the uprising. April 1876 brought insurrection in Bulgaria. On June 23 Serbia, on July 2 Montenegro declared war on the Ottoman Empire. Both requested an armistice on October 31. The Constantinople Conference was held December 12, 1876, to January 18, 1877. On April 24, 1877, Russia declared war on the Ottoman Empire. December 10, 1877, saw the fall of Plevna. On December 14 Serbia reentered the war. The Armistice of Edirne was declared on January 31, 1878. The San Stefano Treaty was signed on March 3, 1878.

4.  Count Gyula Andrássy von *Csík-Szentkirály* and Kraszna Horka (1823–90) was Hungarian prime minister 1867–71 and imperial and royal minister of foreign affairs 1871–79.

5.  Roger V. Paxton, "Russian Foreign Policy and the First Serbian Uprising; Alliances, Apprehensions, and Autonomy, 1804–1807," in Wayne Vucinich, ed., *The First Serbian Uprising, 1804–1813* (Boulder, 1982), p. 41.

6.  The Austrian and Hungarian delegations consisted of twenty members of the upper and forty of the lower houses of the two parliaments, elected by their colleagues. They met at least once a year. The common ministers' reports to them in practice

consisted of accounts of the events of the previous year, demands for funds, and vague statements about the future.

7. Horst Haselsteiner, "Zur Haltung der Donaumonarchie in der Orientalischen Frage," in Melville and Schröder, *Der Berliner Kongress,* p. 237, n. 33.

8. István Diószegi, "Die Anfänge der Orientalpolitik Andrássys," in Melville and Schröder, *Der Berliner Kongress,* p. 252. Diószegi also indicates that in 1868, while Andrássy was Hungarian prime minister, he even suggested to the then imperial and royal foreign minister, Baron Friedrich Ferdinand Beust (1809–86), that the monarchy should persuade the Ottomans to hand over Bosnia–Hercegovina to the Serbs because they constituted the cornerstone of its Balkan policy.

9. Ibid.

10. Haselsteiner, "Zur Haltung der Donaumonarchie," p. 230, n. 7.

11. See Gunther E. Rothenberg, *The Army of Francis Joseph* (West Lafayette, 1976), p. 91, and István Diószegi, "Az Osztrák–Magyar Monarchia külpolitikája a ki-egyezés után" (hereafter "Foreign Policy"), in *Magyarország Története tíz kötetben,* vol. 6, ed. Endre Kovács and László Katus (Budapest, 1976–), pt. 2, p. 903.

12. Archduke Albert (1817–95), grandson of the emperor Leopold II, became inspector general of the imperial and royal army in 1869 and held this post until his death. Friedrich von (after 1906 Count)Beck–Rzilkowski (1830–1920)was head of the emperor's military chancellery (1867–81) and then chief of staff (1881–1906).

13. Haselsteiner, "Zur Haltung der Donaumonarchie," p. 228, n. 4.

14. Ibid., p. 229, n. 6.

15. F. R. Bridge, *From Sadowa to Sarajevo: The Foreign Policy of Austria–Hungary, 1866–1914* (London–Boston, 1972), pp. 71–72. Radetzky (1766–1858) was Austria's military hero in 1848–49 and from 1849 to 1857 governor of Lombardy. Tegetthoff (1827–71) commanded the Austrian navy in 1866 and subsequently became its commander in chief.

16. Diószegi, "Foreign Policy," p. 898.

17. Bridge, *From Sadowa to Sarajevo,* p. 23.

18. The figures for total military spending are in Rothenberg, *The Army of Francis Joseph,* p. 106. The conversion rates of major currencies in the 1870s, according to the 9th edition (1878) of the *Encyclopaedia Britannica,* were as follows: 1 Austro–Hungarian gulden = 2.27 French francs, 2.00 German marks, 0.62 rubles, and 11 ½ d sterling.

19. Rothenberg, *The Army of Francis Joseph,* p. 78.

20. Haselsteiner, "Zur Haltung der Donaumonarchie," pp. 230–31.

21. The Ottomans did not send their army into the Balkans prior to the April Uprising in Bulgaria in 1876.

22. István Diószegi, "A keleti kérdés és az osztrák–magyar külpolitika" (hereafter "Eastern Question"), in Kovács and Katus, *Magyarország Története,* pp. 1181–82.

23. I was not able to find the exact date of the Gorchakov note. Prince Aleksandr Mikhailovich Gorchakov (1798–1883) held various important positions in Russia. Between 1856 and 1882 he was the tsar's chancellor. The content of the note is described in Bridge, *From Sadowa to Sarajevo,* p. 74.

24. Ibid.

25. Ede Wertheimer von Monor, *Gróf Andrássy Gyula élete és kora,* 3 vols. (Budapest, 1910), 2: 329. A German version, *Graf Julius Andrássy, sein Leben und seine Zeit,* 3 vols. (Stuttgart, 1913), also exists. Wertheimer considered this statement so crucial that he italicized it in his work.

26. Bridge publishes as his Documents 6 and 7 two telegrams, both dated May 12, 1876, sent from Berlin to Francis Joseph by Andrássy. The first was sent at 2:36 P. M. and the second at 10:35 P. M. In the afternoon the minister reported to his ruler on Gorchakov's unacceptable proposal, but by evening he was able to communicate the satisfactory conclusion of the day's work (Bridge, *From Sadowa to Sarajevo,* pp. 394–96).

27. Wertheimer, *Gróf Andrássy Gyula*, vol. 1, p. 406.

28. Besides the two emperors, Gorchakov, and Andrássy, the only persons promptly informed of the *Résumé's* contents were Eugene Petrovich Novikov (1826–1903), Russian ambassador in Vienna, 1870–80; Count Alois Károlyi von Nagy-Károly (1825–89), Austro–Hungarian ambassador in Berlin, 1871–78; and Baron Ferdinand von Langenau (1818–81), Austro–Hungarian ambassador in St. Petersburg, 1871–80. Even Bismarck was not told about the agreement until later (Wertheimer, *Gróf Andrássy Gyula*, vol. 2, pp. 409–10).

29. For details of the Reichstadt Agreement, see the relevant sections of the works cited in n. 1 and Bridge, *From Sadowa to Sarajevo*, pp. 77–78; Diószegi, "Eastern Question," pp. 1183–84; Wertheimer, *Gróf Andrássy Gyula*, vol. 2, pp. 408–10.

30. The order was given on June 30, 1875, to Lieutenant Field Marshal Baron Anton Mollinary von Monte Pastello (1820–1904) (Rothenberg, *The Army of Francis Joseph*, p. 93).

31. Wertheimer, *Gróf Andrássy Gyula*, vol. 2, pp. 487–88. The note was dated December 16, 1876.

32. Rothenberg, *The Army of Francis Joseph*, p. 94.

33. Ibid., p. 101.

34. Diószegi, "Eastern Question," p. 1183.

35. Ibid., p. 1184.

36. The Budapest Convention consisted, in fact, of two conventions. The first, a military agreement, was concluded on January 15, 1877, and the additional convention, predated to the same date, on March 18, 1877. They were considered interrelated, and unless both were observed neither was valid.

37. For details, see Bridge, *From Sadowa to Sarajevo*, pp. 81 ff., and Wertheimer, *Gróf Andrássy Gyula*, vol. 2, pp. 492 ff.

38. Wertheimer, *Gróf Andrássy Gyula*, vol. 2, p. 492.

39. Reprinted in the original French in Wertheimer, *Gróf Andrássy Gyula*, vol. 3, p. 112, n. 1.

40. Diószegi, "Eastern Question," p. 1184.

41. For details on Russo–Romanian negotiations and Romania's entry into the war, see the first half of Dan Berindei, "The Romanian War of Independence (1877–1878)," in Ştefan Pascu and Ştefan Ştefanescu, eds., *Pages from the History of the Romanian Army* (Bucharest, 1975), pp. 133–43.

42. On July 1877, the British cabinet decided to declare war on Russia should its forces occupy Constantinople and not evacuate the city promptly.

43. Bridge, *From Sadowa to Sarajevo*, p. 83.

44. Diószegi, "Eastern Question," p. 1185, and Bridge, *From Sadowa to Sarajevo*, p. 84.

45. For his views as early as 1871, see Diószegi, "Foreign Policy," p. 909.

46. For this interpretation of dissolution, see the statement made by Andrássy on January 29, 1875, in Haselsteiner, "Zur Haltung der Donaumonarchie," p. 232.

47. Wertheimer, *Gróf Andrássy Gyula*, vol. 2, p. 494.

48. Ibid.

49. The *force majeure* explanation was used by Gorchakov on February 12, 1878 (Bridge, *From Sadowa to Sarajevo*, p. 85).

50. Count Nikolay Pavlovich Ignatyev (1832–1908), a leading Russian Pan-Slavist, was his country's ambassador in Constantinople 1864–77. During the war he was the foreign policy adviser and, therefore, the leading diplomat on the spot of the commander in chief of the Russian armies, the brother of the tsar, Grand Duke Nikolay Nikolayevich (1856–1929). To what extent Ignatyev was following his own inclinations or orders from St. Petersburg at Edirne and later at San Stefano is not clear. Bridge believes that he was never informed of the Budapest Convention (*From Sadowa to Sarajevo*, p. 85).

51. Kálmán Tisza von Borosjenő and Szeged (1830–1902), like Andrássy a revolu-

tionary in 1848–49, was the leader of the Hungarian Liberal party and prime minister from 1875 to 1890.

52. Diószegi, "Eastern Question," p. 1187.

53. Peter F. Sugár, *Industrialization of Bosnia–Hercegovina, 1878–1918* (Seattle, 1963), p. 24. Wertheimer and other admirers of Andrássy claim that he resigned for reasons of health. The fact remains that the process of his resignation began when the delegations drew up a list of accusations against him in December 1878, including the charge that he had misused the 60 million gulden.

54. After Berlin, Bulgarian territory was limited to the region between the Balkans in the south and the Danube in the north. Eastern Rumelia lay between the Balkan and Rhodope ranges. The territory south of the Rhodope remained Ottoman.

55. Diószegi, "Eastern Question," p. 1190.

Zoltán Szász


# THE BALKAN POLICIES OF THE HABSBURG EMPIRE IN THE 1870s


Although the Balkans were always important for the Danubian monarchy, historically they were secondary to Central and Western Europe. The "German mission" — the acquisition and maintenance of German hegemony — was the monarchy's main task over the centuries. Advocates of an expansionist Balkan policy started gaining ground as early as the beginning of the nineteenth century. That "the Balkans are our India" was a widespread view around 1850. The Habsburgs occupied the Romanian principalities as early as 1854, but only after their expulsion from the German Federation and the events of 1870–71 did they begin to show a deeper interest in the Balkans. The traditional dynastic expansionist ideology was complemented by economic considerations after the great economic crisis of 1873 as certain branches of Austrian industry became interested in safeguarding the Balkan market against competition from cheap British and Belgian goods.

During the 1870s and the Russo–Turkish War, neither the governments nor the publics of Austria and Hungary favored the occupation of Balkan territories by the Habsburg Monarchy. From 1875 on, however, the official Habsburg foreign policy was expansionist. The monarchy first concealed this position and then made intentionally vague statements employing the formula that it was occupying Bosnia and Hercegovina at the request of the Great Powers. This formula reflected not only European power relations but also differences of opinion within the monarchy. Two case studies will make this clear. First we will look at the views held by the Habsburg military leaders and then at Hungarian public opinion.

The influence of the military on the Balkan policy of Austria–Hungary is not unknown to historiography, although a comprehensive presentation of the theme is lacking. In a narrow sense, the annexation of Bosnia was militarily motivated by the desire to protect the narrow coastal strip of Dalmatia. In 1872 the emperor, Foreign Minister Gyula Andrássy, and the military understood that the monarchy would have to give up its so-called policy of abstinence. The military justified a policy of expansion as necessary to protect Austro–Hungarian trade and to prevent the formation of a common border between Serbia and Montenegro, but Andrássy decisively rejected both these arguments. In November 1876, in a military policy conference, this time without Andrássy, occupation of the Sanjak of Novi Pazar as the gateway to the Aegean was discussed. At the end of that year, as the new research of István Diószegi and Emil Palotás has revealed,[1] Major General Beck also proposed the occupation of all of Albania and part of Macedonia including Salonika, now with the argument that it was essential for an Austro–Hungarian presence on the world's seas. Archduke Albert thought that it would be hard to win over public opinion for the acquisition of Bosnia but much easier for the acquisition of ports on the Aegean.

At the beginning of 1878 the official foreign policy of the monarchy, which wanted to participate with Russia in a division of the booty, experienced an unexpected blow with the Russian cease-fire. In a military policy conference held on January 15, 1878, planners considered turning their diplomacy to a new strategy of war with Russia, or at least of threatening war. But the military shrank from this possibility with horror and were not prepared to concentrate their troops or even to make any sort of unfriendly gesture. Instead, along with Bosnia and Hercegovina, they now wanted to occupy the Sanjak and northern Albania.

Two secret conferences held in April 1878 embodied, as Palotás writes,[2] a rare historical moment – the unity of the military and foreign-policy leadership on the tasks of the monarchy in the Balkans. Andrássy persuaded the military to take security precautions against Russia and separated the question of Bosnia from that issue. As compensation, he declared himself – perhaps, however, only as a tactical maneuver – prepared for a later Austro–Hungarian expansion into Albania and Macedonia.

After the bitter experiences of the Bosnian campaign, the Austro–Hungarian military leaders took a serious step backward. Field Commander Phillipovich wrote the Military Chancellery on August 28 that "in a practical sense the right to occupy the Sanjak is as costly as it is of doubtful value."[3] From the military side Phillipovich and then Beck began to revise the Sanjak's role as a gateway to the South. In September they repeated their earlier opinion in the discussion of the railroad question. The chief of the general staff, General Anton von Schönfeld, wrote, "it is to be doubted whether a railroad through Sarajevo, Novibazar, and Mitrovica would be the shortest route to Salonika. ...This leaves no ground for adventurism there."[4] Schönfeld went even farther: "As the decay of Turkey continues, Serbia and Montenegro will turn toward the monarchy because they will be able to pursue common goals. The trade route to Salonika will go just as well, or even much more comfortably, through an allied Serbia that is loyal to the monarchy than through the narrow throat of Novibazar."[5] At this point a new sort of behavior toward the small states in the Balkans appeared in military circles, and in 1879 the military gave up its idea of a great expedition toward Salonika.

Turning now to the question of Hungarian public opinion, if we accept the press of the age as representing public opinion we may say that Hungarian society in the 1870s did not support the expansionist policy of the Habsburg Monarchy but instead vigorously opposed the occupation of Bosnia and Hercegovina. At the same time, Hungarians did not give any active assistance to the Balkan liberation movements either, though they were not neutral with regard to the great transformations taking place. The most conspicuous signs one finds are the great number of pro-Turkish articles in the press, some street demonstrations expressing pro-Turkish sympathy, and some political speeches.[6] Hungarian papers sympathized with the small nations of the Balkans, but this does not alter the fact that on the whole Hungarian public opinion was pro-Turkish.

What accounts for Hungarian support of the despotic and anachronistic Ottoman Empire when Hungarians were sensitive to liberalism and national independence, had lived through 150 years of Turkish rule, and were once regarded as a bastion against the Turkish threat? The answer lies not only in the Balkan situation after 1875 but also in the special position of Hungary within the Habsburg Monarchy and in the peculiarities of the Hungarian national consciousness.

The attitude of the masses of Hungarian society was determined by the liberal nationalism that had prevailed since 1848. While Hungarians definitely took the offensive toward the nationalities in Hungary, their outward attitude was undoubtedly defensive. In the eyes of contemporaries, the independence of the Hungarian state, suppressed by Austria and Russia in 1849 and achieved only with great effort through the compromises of 1867, was threatened not only by external powers, as in the case of most small or middle-sized countries, but also by an internal enemy, Austria. With the Compromise of 1867, hostility toward Austria only gradually dwindled to distrust and jealous rivalry. In the 1860s and 1870s anti-Prussian feelings lived on primarily because of the antipathy toward the political system of Bismarck, who was feared as well as respected. Aversion toward the Russians had imbued the bourgeois masses since the Russian intervention of 1849. They not only saw tsarism as a potential ally of the Slavic peoples in Hungary (Serbs, Slovaks, Ruthenians) but also regarded it, in line with the general conception of progressive Europeans, as the main aggressive power of European reaction. Hungarian social thought also contained some sympathy for the democracy of the United States and especially for England, which was regarded as the model of the liberal state. England's traditional but modernized constitutional system was thought to be related to the Hungarian, and Hungarians found in England's economic growth a peerless example. All these factors are characteristic of the modern bourgeois nationalism of a small nation.

But Hungarian nationalism was not the attitude of a small nation. In 1862, when in connection with an Italian action aimed at closer relations among the Balkan peoples Lajos Kossuth elaborated a plan of Danube confederation calling for a close alliance of Croatians, Serbs, Romanians, and Hungarians and offering them a kind of collective Great Power status, the Hungarian political public rigidly and unanimously rejected the plan. "I would rather go to the Germans in Vienna than to the Serbs in Belgrade,"[7] a leading figure of the anti-Austrian movement wrote in his diary. The nationalism of a Great Power, proclaiming superiority to the national minorities and the neighboring small nations, became the dominant Hungarian national consciousness. Because of Hungary's relative weakness and its multinational character, this ideology had to be expressed within another hierarchy, the Habsburg Monarchy, which was regarded as a separate body from the nation. Nonetheless, Hungarians projected onto it Great Power expectations.

The 1870s were a transitional period for the Hungarian national consciousness. The masses accepted the Compromise of 1867 but were discontented with it, demanding a greater degree of independence. They wanted Great Power status without its consequences, the development of the army and territorial expansion. They remained on the defensive, longing for peaceful decades in which to establish and strengthen the Hungarian nation-state.

The repugnance to expansion had several causes, some of which coincided with the interests of Austrian liberals. Expansion would fortify the dynasty, which they did not desire; it would also strengthen the army, which they feared because for them the army was the main enemy of the dualist system. They looked upon the addition of new Slavic territories as the source of tremendous dangers. It would weaken the dualism in which the Germans and Hungarians exercised hegemony, increase the already large number of Slavic elements in the state, and revive the national movements within the empire. It would also create a new common undertaking between Austria and Hungary when the Hungarian government and the opposition were both striving to reduce the number of common elements. The debate over the question to which state the new territories should belong, Austria or Hungary, would raise endless complications.

The interests of the Hungarian economy did not demand an expansionist policy. Hungarian industry did not have serious market problems in the 1860s, nor was agriculture endangered by the importation of produce and animals from the Balkans. For Hungary, which was a center of grain milling, the importation of grain was advantageous. Overexpansion of livestock imports was prevented by the frequent outbreak of eastern cattle plague, and it could be limited when desired by closing the frontier. Hungary did not give up the principle of free trade until it was forced to do so by Germany at the very end of the decade.[8] The Hungarian conception differed from the Austrian even on the construction of railway lines in the Balkans. The Hungarians urged the construction of a Budapest–Belgrade–Istanbul railway line as early as 1869 in opposition to the Austrian plan, backed by the military leaders of the monarchy, to create a passage to Salonika through Bosnia. Foreign Minister Friedrich Ferdinand Beust even suggested that Turkey voluntarily cede the territories the railway would need.

The attitude of Ferenc Pulszky was typical of Hungarian Balkan policy. In a confidential talk with Beust, Pulszky said that if Austria gave up the idea of regaining German hegemony, Hungary would renounce the annexation of the Turkish provinces ("jedwede Annexion turkischer Nachbarprovinzen zu verzichten"). Beust replied, laughing, that this would not be a sacrifice on the part of the Hungarians, since Hungary had no interest in conquest. In 1868 Prime Minister Andrássy even contemplated giving Bosnia and Hercegovina to Serbia.

Hungary may not have had any claims on the Balkans, but it did not consistently support the national liberation movements either, even though a Balkan Peninsula consisting of small states would have fitted into the foreign-policy conceptions of Hungarian liberalism.

Russia's active anti-Turkish policy also influenced public opinion in Hungary. Hungarians feared that if their state contained several Slavic nationalities it might end up as a Russian vassal. The opposition regarded Andrássy's limited Austro–Hungarian–Russian cooperation as a pro-Russian policy, overlooking the rivalry between the two powers and their deepening conflict. While for the people of the Balkans Turkey meant oppression, Hungarians saw the Ottomans only as a counterbalance against Russia. Adopting the attitude of England, their "liberal model state," they were content with reforming the empire of the sultan. The picture of Turkey that took shape in the Hungarian mind after the reform attempts of 1876 was completely false. It appeared to Hungarians that a modernizing parliamentary state was emerging, especially militarily. The Ottoman army contained hundreds of English officers, and it built the fortresses in Bulgaria under German leadership. Later the legendary Hungarian general from 1848, György Klapka, advised the sultan as well. When in the spring of 1877 a Turkish professional youth delegation visited Budapest, the Hungarian capital used it as a symbol to celebrate "Turkish constitutionalism." And in such a sentimental age it also meant a lot that for nearly two centuries

Turkey had given refuge to many leaders of Hungarian liberation movements.

It was at that time that the last romantic plot of Hungarian history took place. Some representatives of the opposition in Transylvania led by Gábor Ugron undertook secretly to recruit an irregular band of some one hundred soldiers in the Székely region. With arms probably bought with English money, they planned to break into Moldavia, interdict the Russian reserves by blowing up a bridge on the River Seret, and stir up an armed uprising in Russian Poland. Of course, the government sent out gendarmes to seize the recruiters and confiscate their weapons.[9]

After the surrender at Plevna at the end of 1877, the Hungarian parliamentary opposition became especially active. At a general meeting leaders of the opposition announced that Hungary should defend the Turks if Germany, England, France, and Italy could not do so because of their other Great Power interests. They also called upon the government to start an armed action against Russia. Kossuth also demanded war against Russia, while other émigrés discussed setting up a Hungarian and a Polish legion in Turkey.[10]

The general public was unaware that the Budapest government had considered war against Russia but in the light of international power relations had dropped the idea. Nor did the masses believe that the government was against the occupation of Bosnia, even when Minister of Finance Kálmán Széll resigned and it filtered out that at the crown council he had told the emperor: "you can make money in peace and war alike, but not in an adventure like marching into Turkish territory."[11]

Sympathy for the Turks did not mean hostility toward the Balkan peoples, as press reports concerning the Bulgarians and Romanians demonstrate. Sztojan Radev has devoted nearly a hundred pages to the positive reactions in Hungary to the April Uprising, the heroic attempt of Botev, and the sufferings and struggle of the Bulgarian people.[12] Although Hungarian opinion saw some danger in the Romanian principality in the long run because of Transylvania, it had accepted Romania as an independent state even before 1877 and had admired the results of its development. Then in 1877, when the Romanian principality entered the war against Turkey, Hungarians heavily reproached the Romanians for their Russian alliance, all the more because they thought that Romania should not seek formal independence, which would come in any event. On the other hand, when Romania became involved in conflicts with Russia the general atmosphere became pro-Romanian again, as if to prove that all matters were seen from the aspect of averting the danger of Russian enclosure.[13]

The intentions and the conception of the government party and those of the opposition as regards Balkan policy were the same, but they acted completely differently. The government party — referring to "the strain of power realities" — served the interests of the empire's foreign policy even though it wanted just the opposite. In the 1870s the opposition was against conquest in the Balkans because it did not yet believe that the monarchy needed to act as an adjusting power over the Balkan peoples. The national indignation that followed the occupation of Bosnia nearly swept away the government in the general elections of the summer of 1878, but in scarcely a decade the views of the opposition had come closer to the government's. Fearing that the power vacuum that followed the weakening of Turkey would be filled by tsarist Russia, the opposition began to demand that it be filled by the monarchy. Thus it began to support the court and the military circles on basic foreign-policy questions, and at last the government and the opposition alike, that is, the whole official society of the age, turned against the national endeavors of the Balkan peoples, something that originally no one in Hungary had wished for. It was not the first or the last instance in Hungarian history of a wide gap between intentions, acts, and results.

## NOTES

1. István Diószegi, "A keleti kérdés és az osztrák–magyar külpolitika," in *Magyarország története 1848–1890,* ed. Endre Kovács and László Katus, (Budapest, 1979), pp. 1181–92; Emil Palotás, "Heeresleitung und Balkanpläne in Österreich–Ungarn in den Kriesenjahren 1875–1878," *Annales Universitatis Scientiarum Budapestiensis, Sectio Historica* 21 (1981): 187–204.
2. Palotás, "Heeresleitung," pp. 196–97.
3. Ibid., p. 199.
4. Ibid., pp. 200–201.
5. Ibid.
6. Zoltán Szász, "Bosznia és Hercegovina okkupációjának hatása Magyarországon," in *Magyarország Története 1848–1890,* pp. 1193–96.
7. Frigyes Podmaniczky, *Naplótöredékek,* vol. 3 (Budapest, 1888), pp. 143–44; Zoltán Szász, "Donaukonföderation oder Donaumonarchie: Eine Alternative zur ungarischen Politik im 19. Jahrhundert," in *Anzeiger der phil.-hist. Klasse der Österreichischen Akademie der Wissenschaften* 116, no. 15 (1979): 222–35.
8. Emil Palotás, "Ziele und geschichtliche Realität: Wirtschaftsbestrebungen Österreich–Ungarns auf dem Balkan zur Zeit der Berliner Kongresses im Jahre 1878," *Studia Historica, Academiae Scientiarum Hungaricae* 157 (1980): 10.
9. Szász, "Bosznia és Hercegovina," pp. 1194–95.
10. Dezső Szilágyi, *Beszédei,* vol. 1 (Budapest, 1906); Lajos Szádeczky Kardoss, *A székely puccs 1877-ben* (Budapest, 1920).
11. Archiv des Auswertigen Amtes, Bonn Konsularbericht 7.3.1878 IAA C58.
12. Sztojan Radev, *Bulgárok és magyarok* (Budapest, 1977), pp. 166–254.
13. Dan Berindei and István Csucsuja, *A függetlenségi háború és Erdély* (Bucharest, 1977), pp. 136–83; Emil Niederhauser and Zoltán Szász, "Románia függetlenségéről," *Századok* 111 (1977): 215–29.

Radu R. Florescu

# THE RUSSO—TURKISH WAR OF 1877—78: DIPLOMATIC AND MILITARY PREPARATIONS

The outbreak of the Russo—Turkish war that most European statesmen expected with the progressive disruption of the Crimean war establishment proved the correctness of John Bright's view that British Near Eastern policy had been based on false premises and that the Crimean War had not really resolved the Eastern Question.[1]

Among the diplomatic antecedents of the war were the wrong signals Britain sent to Constantinople encouraging the Turks to believe that the Crimean War coalition had survived to 1877. Without clearly defined aims beyond the desire of pulling off "a great coup" that would permanently disrupt the Dreikaiserbund, the government of Benjamin Disraeli wished to ensure the safety of the straits and British rights in eastern Mediterranean waters. Disraeli had little sympathy and less understanding for the nationalities of the Ottoman Empire, describing the massacres of Christians a "coffee-table babble."[2] A particularly provocative role consistent with this attitude was played by two successive British ambassadors to Constantinople: Sir Henry Elliott and, from April 1877 onwards, Sir Austin Henry Layard, the most Turcophile British ambassador ever sent to the Turkish capital.[3] In spite of Robert W. Seton—Watson's exhaustive studies, definitive analysis of their respective roles still awaits a historian, but I suspect that their contribution to starting the war was greater than that of Stratford Canning twenty years earlier. Canning, an abler diplomat, set a precedent in Constantinople of defying the instructions of his own government.[4]

Equally irritating to Tsar Alexander II, who was particularly sensitive to the views of crowned heads, was the impact of Disraeli's Turcophilism on Queen Victoria, whom he "lectured" on the Eastern Question through repeated audiences and personal correspondence. The queen's irrational Russophobia is reflected in her undiplomatic anti-Russian utterances and is also revealed in her voluminous letters as well as the unpublished diaries and sketches available at the Windsor Palace Library.[5]

In spite of opposition from the "three Lords" in the British cabinet, the Earl of Derby, Lord Carnavon, and the Marquess of Salisbury, all of them good "Europeanists" who believed in preserving the peace, it is conceivable that Disraeli's "brinkmanship" could have involved England in war even in the absence of allies by sending the fleet to the Dardanelles or dispatching an expeditionary force through Afganistan, options to which the prime minister occasionally alluded.[6] However, one of the most remarkable revolutions of public opinion in the annals of English democracy prevented such an extreme course of action. William Ewart Gladstone's reaction to the Bulgarian massacres became public in the pages of the *Daily News* on June 23, just over a month after the events, a fact made possible through the miracle of telegraphy.[7] As the reports of Walter Baring placed the appalling catalogue of Turkish horrors beyond dispute, the liberal leader Gladstone, who had been in semiretirement, made an extraordinary comeback with a publicity campaign centering upon the problem of Balkan nationalism. His *Bulgarian Horrors and the Eastern Question* (June 1876) became a best-seller overnight, with forty thousand copies sold within a span of four months. It contained the oft-quoted sentence that the Turks should clear out "bag and baggage," if not from Europe, then at least from Bulgaria.[8]

Through his philippics Gladstone succeeded in permanently undermining the Russophobia that had been built up over the years by skillful pamphleteers such as David Urquhart, nationalist diplomats such as Lord Palmerston, and inveterate Turcophiles such as Stratford Canning.[9] Most notable was his conversion of all the leading historians of the day — Thomas Carlyle, John A. Froude, E. A. Freeman, Lord John Acton, Bishop William Stubbs, and John Richard Green — as well as other leading members of the British intelligentsia, including many journalists.[10] The net result of this publicity campaign was to divide British public opinion so deeply that even Disraeli (who was angry at being misinformed by his ambassador Elliott about the real state of events) acknowledged that any further intervention against Russia was impractical.[11] One should bear in mind that cabinet divisions and the tergiversations of public opinion were very accurately reported to the tsar by the Russian ambassador in London, Peter Shuvalov, acting in concert with the Europeanists through Lady Derby.[12]

In the fall of 1876, Alexander II finally decided that he must abandon Prince Aleksandr M. Gorchakov's policy aimed at reaching an understanding with Turkey and instead support the South Slavic nationalities in the Balkans. In making this decision he was certainly deeply influenced by the limited but nonetheless very effective public opinion at home, which was disturbed by the Turkish victories over the Serbs. The Pan-Slavists had no program beyond vague sentimental appeals to a common race and a mystical Orthodox inheritance, but ultimately they identified Russia's national interests with grandiose schemes for a united Slavic empire under the tsar's hegemony.[13]

Irked by Disraeli's expressions of British militancy, Alexander II was in the mood for a change of policy when he reached Livadia in the Crimea in October 1876. Well-intentioned and only too conscious of the sufferings war entailed, this weak sentimentalist of average intelligence finally succumbed to the will of the strong personalities in his immediate entourage who supported the Pan-Slavist ideology. Here in the remote Crimea, far removed from the moderating influence of St. Petersburg, the war party headed by Nikolay Pavlovich Ignatyev, Russia's ambassador at Constantinople, proved more than a match for the vacillating octogenarian Gorchakov or the war minister Count Dmitry Milyutin, who initially thought Russia could not afford a war. Capturing the unusual atmosphere prevailing at Livadia, Tsarevich Alexander, the future Tsar Alexander III, wrote to his closest advisor and confidant, Constantine P. Pobedonostsev, complaining of the Europeanists' indecisiveness. He concluded his letter with the statement: "Fortunately, we have in our midst Ignatyev, who has opened everyone's eyes. He has nagged his opponents so much that they have been obliged to adopt his line of conduct... The emperor now believes that we shall obtain nothing without a war. He has decided for it and wishes for a rapid denouement. But it is not easy, for diplomacy has so confused things that we cannot declare war on Turkey without a sound reason."[14] Deliberately choosing Moscow rather than St. Petersburg as the place to make his conversion to the views of the war party officially known, Alexander ended his sensational November 11 speech with awesome words about his intentions to compel the Great Powers to respect Russia's dignity.[15]

It was now incumbent upon the diplomats to rationalize the declaration of war, since there were no clear objectives. Indeed, not even the war itself succeeded in producing them. Turkish intransigence at the Conference of Constantinople provided one pretext. Instead of negotiating, Midhat Pasha, the new grand vizier, who was an inveterate admirer of the British constitution, staged a coup de theatre. Encouraged by Sir Henry Elliott, Midhat crowned the reforming efforts of the Tanzimat by declaring Turkey a constitutional state and rejecting the intervention of the Great Powers. The word "fiasco" was used in all the correspondence of European diplomats to describe this event, because they realized that by it the war party in Russia had won the day.[16] The crowning blow to peace, spurred by the unusual chauvinism displayed by the new Turkish parliament, was Edhem Pasha's rejection of the terms of the London Protocol and his decision to renew hostilities with the Serbs and the Montenegrins.

Ideally, the tsar desired to obtain an international mandate from the

Concert of Europe or at least the moral support of the Great Powers. He felt it was essential to neutralize potential enemies, isolate England, and, at all costs, prevent the revival of the dangerous coalition of the Crimean War. Bismarck owed Russia a substantial debt of gratitutde for Russian neutrality in 1866 and 1870. But, sad to say, gratitutde is not a characteristic of the politics of the major powers, and Russia never obtained German commitment to neutralize its principal partner, Austria, by a threat of war.[17]

Equally unsuccessful were Russian overtures to France, still reeling under the impact of the defeat of 1870. Louis Decazes decided to sit the crisis out, realizing that in the long run a Russo–Turkish war would redound to the advantage of the Third Republic and weaken the Dreikaiserbund. Far more successful were negotiations between Gorchakov and Count Gyula Andrássy, the Austrian foreign minister, who could have "neutralized" the Romanian bottleneck and thus prevented a Russian attack on Turkey.

Andrássy, an Old World diplomat of the Vienna school and a good Europeanist, thought essentially as a Hungarian. Should the Ottoman Empire collapse, he was determined not to allow any nation other than Hungary to dominate the Danubian basin. Therefore, the Serbs must be brought under the influence of the empire, if possible without the war that militarists such as Archduke Albert and some members of the general staff (including many Croatian officers) were proposing.[18] The Austro–Hungarian foreign minister drove a very hard bargain indeed when he and Gorchakov signed the military part of the Budapest Convention on January 15.[19] Russia bought Austria's benevolent neutrality at a considerable price. Should Russia defeat Turkey, as most diplomats expected, Austria–Hungary would acquire Bosnia–Hercegovina; Serbia and Montenegro would form neutral buffer states between Russia and Austria–Hungary, while Russia would not support the formation of a large, compact Slavic state. In effect Russia, which had never been really interested in the Serbs, was secretly abandoning them to Habsburg patronage.

The final problem that faced Russian diplomacy concerned Romanian neutrality. What would be the attitude of the Romanian government toward the violation of its frontiers? Russian diplomats were concerned because of the neutralist attitude of the conservative government, which persisted in sheltering itself behind the guarantee of the signatories of the Treaty of 1856.[20] However, by the time Ion I. C. Brătianu was sent to discuss this problem with the tsar's representatives at Livadia, Prince Carol had made up his mind against the wishes of the majority of his politicians, of his father Prince Karl Anton, and of his diplomatic representatives in the major capitals of Europe, all of whom counseled prudence and neutrality.[21] His Hohenzollern pride injured at being a vassal of the sultan, Prince Carol was also anxious to prove the worth of the new Romanian army that had been built up during the last eighteen years by Ion Emanoil Florescu, chief military advisor to both Prince Alexandru Ion Cuza and his successor.[22] He would never accept independence as a gift of the powers but rather wished to earn it on the field of battle. There were, however, two conditions to be fulfilled before the Romanian army would enter the war. The tsar must respect the integrity of Romania's frontiers, and the Romanian army must fight as a separate unit under its own command. Neither, of course, was acceptable to the tsar, whose pride had been hurt by the cession of southern Bessarabia in 1856. Gorchakov, who professed not to need Romanian collaboration, would only agree to its army's fighting at its own risk under Russian command. Harsh words were exchanged, but in the end the Romanian foreign minister departed with the soothing advice that "in the event of war we shall know how to understand one another."[23]

When the Russo—Romanian Convention was finally worked out in great secrecy at Bucharest, it provided for *de jure* recognition of the presence of the Russian army on Romanian soil and a rough-and-ready system of collaboration between the local authorities and the military government of Grand Duke Nikolay, including the use of the Romanian railroads by the Russian army.[24] None of the basic issues raised by Ion Brătianu at Livadia had really been resolved, and formal approval of the Russo—Romanian Convention by the Romanian parliament was granted only after the arrival of the Russians on Romanian soil. Given the fact that the Western powers refused to guarantee Romania's neutrality, there was little Prince Carol could do beyond mobilizing the Romanian army to defend the line of the Danube in case of Turkish attack while maintaining an attitude sufficiently flexible to be able to take what advantage he could of the fortunes of war.

It is a truism to assert that in the last analysis diplomacy depends upon a nation's ability to wage war and that until our age of advanced military technology God always seems to have been on the side of the larger battalions. Since in 1877 all nations relied on conscription, military strength closely corresponded with population figures. This fact gave Russia an enormous psychological advantage, because in theory it could muster an army of over a million men.[25] In addition the Slavophiles counted on the collaboration of the Balkan peasant masses, who were supposed to revolt at the first signal, as well as on the untried Romanian army, which was organized on the traditional concept of the nation in arms.[26]

Exaggerated statistics also helped inflame the warmongering spirit of the Turks. "In the event of war," stated an editorial in the Constantinople newspaper *Bassiret,* we could easily find 1,000,000 soldiers in our land. Outside the 800,000 territorials and another 400,000 volunteers who are simply awaiting the orders of the sultan to descend upon the Russians, we have the Muslims of Rumelia, Anatolia, Arabia, Egypt, Tunis, and Central

Asia, who at the first signal will move en masse."[27] This was not counting
the British and the Austro—Hungarians, who, the Turks were convinced,
would move to their side once war was declared. Grand Vizier Edhem Pasha
even harbored the illusion that the Romanian army would honor its commit-
ments under the terms of the Capitulations and declare war on Russia.[28]
Talk of this kind undoubtedly helped churn up war hysteria on both sides,
though in practice neither the Russian nor the Turkish high command had
a very precise idea of how many men could be raised for either the Balkan
or the Caucasus theater of war.

It has been estimated that the Russian army destined for the Balkan front
had a rough total of 260,000 men comprising six army corps (the Seventh
through Twelfth) reinforced by three corps of reservists dispatched in May
1877 (the Fourth, Thirteenth, and Fourteenth. In addition, the Bulgarian
volunteers (formed in April) numbered 6,000 men (three brigades), and the
Romanian operational army that served after Plevna comprised 58,700
officers and men.[29] The Romanian army had value for the Russians even
*before* the beginning of hostilities, as was noted by a correspondent of the
London *Times* (May 17, 1877): "the Roumanian army is concentrated on the
Oltenitza and Kalafat positions. A heavy corps of Russian Cavalry with Horse
Artillery is already between these Roumanian Corps d'Armees extending
along the Giurgevo and Turnu Magurele line, so that the Russian and Roumanian Armies are already as it were interlaced with each other."[30] According
to Romanian estimates, the Turkish armies disposed of 412,000 men (not
counting the militia of 300,000), though they were dispersed over a wide
area and in fortress towns where they were needed to keep an eye on an
unfriendly population.[31]

Had the sultan's plan for a preemptive spring offensive through Romania
been adopted by the war council, it is conceivable that the course of the
war would have been different. However, because of opposition, instinctive
fear of fighting on unfamiliar terrain, and the imponderable presented by
Romania's attitude, more prudent counsel prevailed. The sultan Abdülhamid
II in the end expressed the traditional defensive philosophy deeply ingrained
in the Turkish mentality since the eighteenth century. The Russian forces
must be drawn into the heart of the Balkan range and defeated there. In the
event of victory, the Turkish army would pursue the enemy to the Pruth;
in the event of defeat it would regroup south of the Balkans, defend the
Quadrilateral forts of eastern Bulgaria and Vidin, and prevent the enemy
from extending its conquest.[32]

In contrast, the Russian plan of campaign was based on a rapid offensive
using friendly Romania as a base and the Romanian railroads in accordance
with the terms of the Russo—Romanian Convention.[33] The objective was to
be in a position to attack along the line of the Maritza toward Adrianople

but not necessarily to occupy Constantinople. The plan of the campaign had first been submitted at Livadia by General N. N. Obruchev in his *Considerations concerning the War* and then further elaborated and refined in March.[34] It called for a campaign ending before winter set in. The Russian army would cross the Danube from Zimnicea to Sistov, where the river was most fordable. The troops would be deployed south, cross the central Balkans through one of the passes, and defeat the Turks to the east between Vidin and the Quadrilateral fortresses.[35] There the Russians could make best use of their military superiority and would not have to use siege apparatus, with which they were poorly equipped. To produce this rapid denouement the high command  counted on  the aggressive spirit of the Russian infantry, the spectacular bravery of the officer corps in frontal attack, and the extraordinary mobility of the regular and irregular cavalry. In a word, the general staff reckoned on a soldier's war in which numbers and courage would ultimately prevail rather than on elaborate tactics and strategy.

But the Russians were outmaneuvered by a veteran of the Crimean War who commanded the Turkish forces at Vidin and who had already distinguished himself in defeating the Serbs. Like Henri Philippe Petain at Verdun in World War I, Osman Nuri Pasha, perhaps the only outstanding military figure that the war produced, blockaded himself before an obscure fortress called Plevna and simply held on against overwhelming odds through an elaborate system of fortifications and by concentrating his firepower. He impressed the world with his skillful tactics and genius in the art of defense. For a time he thwarted the Russian plan and once again changed public opinion in England, where Turkey benefited from the Englishman's traditional love for the underdog.[36]

In predicting a rapid summer campaign, most military analysts who accompanied the Russian army were overawed by the numbers psychology. They had forgotten that the Turkish armed forces had been radically modernized during the period of the Tanzimat and that the reforms of 1869 had been financed by the British while the officers and troops had been trained mostly by British officers and other volunteers from Western armies.[37] The Turks were certainly much better prepared than Russian intelligence would avow. Although still deficient in their junior officer cadres, the Turkish regular and irregular soldiers were praised by some of their foreign officers for their amazing tenacity and endurance. Comparing weaponry, the experts agreed that the Turkish Henry Martini rifle (range 1,200 meters) adopted by the British infantry in 1872 not only could outshoot the Russian Krnka and even the superior Berdan rifle but had a more rapid loading capacity. Although the Turkish cavalry was equipped with the American Winchester carbine imported from New Haven, Connecticut, it was very effective when it charged with the lance, the sword, and the revolver for hand-to-hand combat (the Russian infantry was similarly effective with the bayonet).[38]

Most telling, however, was the quantitative and qualitative superiority of the Turkish artillery. The Russians had a wide variety of pieces for field, mountain, and siege operations, and these need diverse types of ammunition: percussion fuse shells, shrapnel, and incendiaries. Nonetheless, much of the Russian artillery was outdated, and the gunners' firing was inaccurate. The inequality of firepower and the lower technical quality of the Russian artillery were to prove decisive handicaps at Plevna. The majority of the Turkish cannons were of the latest Krupp breech-loading design that had worked such wonders at Sedan. In their battle instructions the Turks made excellent use of their artillery in offensives coordinated with the infantry and the cavalry.

At a time when it was increasingly fashionable to speak of sea power, the Turks had the formidable advantage of possessing one of the most powerful navies in Europe under the command of the Englishman Hobart Pasha. In contrast, Russia had not had the time to rebuild its fleet after the clauses of the Treaty of Paris relating to it were scrapped in 1871.[39] Since Russia was not a riparian state, it had no Danubian flotilla. Only after the war broke out did the general staff transport some gunboats to the Danube by land. At the outset of the war five iron-plated Turkish cruisers, four monitors, and twelve torpedo boats were kept in check by four Romanian gunboats and their auxiliaries.[40] In the Black Sea, where Turkey had twenty-two iron-plated battleships (seven of the latest vintage with twelve heavy-caliber guns each), and in the Sea of Marmara, where it had fifteen cruisers together with numerous auxiliary vessels (the navy had a total complement of fifty thousand sailors), the Ottomans ruled supreme. The constant threat this navy posed of landing an expeditionary force behind the Russian lines led the general staff to mobilize some eighty thousand men to report on its movements.

These may have been some of the factors, in addition to serious economic deficiencies, which underscored the Russian desire to win a rapid victory at a time when new concepts such as naval power and industrial capacity rather than manpower were increasingly becoming the trademark of a Great Power.

In outlining the military and diplomatic antecedents of the war of 1877–78 two significant facts emerge that give these events a certain contemporaneity. The first refers to what we might consider a truism in our electronic age of instant satellite communications: no responsible politician can in this age ignore the impact of the media upon public opinion. In this respect the crisis of 1877–78 set a precedent in that the principal statesmen, who shared backgrounds with each other more than with substantial sections of their public at home, were compelled to listen to articulate domestic pressure groups drawn from all sections of their societies. In the case of England, opinion moved by Gladstone's rhetoric in the name of liberty turned against the aggressive nationalism of Disraeli and forced him temporarily to give up his policy of brinkmanship, thus working for the preservation of peace. In the case of Russia, the Pan-Slavists, who had canvassed all strata of Russian society over a lengthy period with a formidable propaganda campaign, gained so many converts that even the autocratic tsar, good Europeanist that he was, could not afford to ignore them. Sultan Abdülhamid II himself could not remain indifferent to the chauvinist clamors of the short-lived Turkish parliament, influenced by the masses, and a jingoist, sensation-seeking press that exaggerated the alleged triumphs of Turkish armies and was indignant at the threat to the nation's sovereignty implied by the demands of the Great Powers.

The second fact of interest to us still today is related to the causes of war. Although there had been so-called wars of national liberation since the French Revolution, leading statesmen usually paid lip service to nationalism in the Balkans, actually using *raisons d'état* as their justification for action. The war of 1877 was different in that respect: in it the hands of the diplomats were forced by the desire of the Serbs, the Montenegrins, the Bulgarians, and the Romanians to seek their independence from Turkish control. It was quite natural for jingoist politicians and militarists, always interested in war, to have exploited their patriotism, but this was not a war started by diplomats or soldiers: I believe that 1877—78 was the first war in southeastern Europe that was *caused* and not merely *occasioned* by the desire of the Balkan people to be free.

## NOTES

1. Bright's hatred of war in general and the Crimean War in particular is quite explicit in the wartime entries in his diary, though they had little impact on public opinion. See R.A.J. Walling, ed., *John Bright's Diaries* (New York, 1931), p. 217 n. 4. A good study on British public opinion at the time is B. Kingsley Martin, *The Triumph of Lord Palmerston* (London, 1924).

2. Disraeli's pro-Turkish views can be accounted for in part in terms of his Jewish ancestry and his contacts with the heads of the Jewish community in Europe. The flippant "coffee-table babble" remark was contained in his answer to a question in the House of Commons about the accuracy of the *Daily News* reports concerning the Bulgarian atrocities (R. W. Seton—Watson, *Britain in Europe 1789—1914: A Survey of Foreign Policy* [Cambridge, 1938] p. 519).

3. Only Elliott published his memoirs (Sir Henry Elliott, *Some Revolutions and Diplomatic Reminiscences* [London, 1922]), and they hardly reveal the full story.

4. Seton—Watson had access to both Public Record Office material and some important private papers; his *Gladstone, Disraeli, and the Eastern Question* (London, 1936) examines the problem from a British viewpoint. For Canning's role during the Crimean War the standard work is still Stanley Lane Poole, *The Life of Stratford Canning, Lord Stratford de Redcliffe*, 2 vols. (London, 1888).

5. The queen's letters for the 1837–78 period are covered by G. E. Buckle, ed., *Letters of Queen Victoria,* 2d series, 2 vols. (London, 1926), though these volumes contain only a fraction of the queen's correspondence. Her diaries remain unpublished.

6. In his Guildhall speech of November 9, Disraeli was quite belligerent: "There was no country so well prepared for war as our own... her resouces are, I feel, inexhaustible. She is not a country that, when she enters into a campaign, has to ask herself whether she can support a second or third campaign" (Seton–Watson, *Britain in Europe,* p. 521). Nevertheless, it should be pointed out that at Constantinople Britain attempted to persuade the Turks to grant an armistice to the Serbs.

7. Telegraphy was introduced just prior to the Crimean War. On October 18, 1853, Lord Clarendon had written to Lord John Russell, "these telegraphic dispatches are the very devil. Formerly cabinets used to deliberate on a fact and a proposition from foreign governments; now we have only the fact" (Sir Henry Maxwell, *Life of the Fourth Earl of Clarendon,* vol. 2 [London, 1913], p. 27). The *Daily News* got its information from the Turkish correspondent Sir Edwin Pears and the Irish–American journalist Januarius Aloysius MacGahan.

8. I do not believe that Gladstone implied, as has been generally assumed, that the Turks should clear out of all the European territories they possessed. He was obviously referring to Bulgaria alone.

9. I have investigated the impact of the anti-Russian activities of Lord Palmerston, David Urquhart, and Stratford Canning in my study *The Struggle against Russia in the Roumanian Principalities 1821–1854,* Societas Academica Daco–Romana 2 (Munich, 1962), pp. 21, 175–76 (based mostly on Public Record Office material). All told, two hundred thousand copies of the *Bulgarian Horrors* were sold.

10. See *Letters of John Richard Green* (London, 1901), p. 446. Among other notable converts were John Thadeus Delane (who retired as editor of the London *Times* in 1877), Alfred Lord Tennyson, Charles Darwin, John Ruskin, and Sir Edward Burne–Jones (Lord John Morley, *Life of Gladstone,* vol. 3, book 7 [London, 1903], chap. 4).

11. Disraeli realized only too well that the impression produced in England by events in Bulgaria rendered British intervention against a Russian declaration of war "practically impossible" (Letter of Elliott, August 29, 1876, cited by R. C. K. Ensor, *England 1870–1914* [Oxford, 1960], p. 44).

12. For the next nine months (from May 1876 on) an intimate working alliance between the ambassador and the foreign secretary in which Lady Derby also played an active part was one of the decisive factors in saving the situation (Seton–Watson, *Britain in Europe,* p. 525).

13. One of the most objective works on Russian foreign policy in the Eastern crisis of 1877–78 is B. H. Sumner, *Russia and the Balkans 1870–1880* (London, 1937).

14. Ion I. C. Brătianu, "România și chestiunea orientului, reflecțiuni, considerațiuni și amintiri," in *Războiul neatărnării conferințe ținute la Ateneul Român* (Bucharest, 1927) p. 70.

15. Brătianu, "România și chestiunea orientului," p. 90.

16. Brătianu, "România și chestiunea orientului," p. 72.

17. "It would affect the interests of Germany... if the Austrian monarchy were so endangered in its position as European power or in its independence that one of the factors with which we have to reckon in the European balance of power threatened to fall out in the future" (Bülow to Schweinitz, October 23, 1876, vol. 2, no. 251, cited by A. Mendelsohn–Bartholdy, I. Lepsius, and F. Thimme, *Die Grosse Politik der europäische Kabinette* [Berlin, 1922–26]). For French diplomatic correspondence see *Documents diplomatiques français, 1871–1914,* 1st series, vol. 2 (Paris, 1929).

18. In November, however, Archduke Albert concluded that a war against Russia was neither practicable nor desirable (G. H. Rupp, *A Wavering Friendship: Russia and Austria* [Cambridge, 1941], p. 234).

19. The political convention that made the military convention operative was signed only on March 17.

20. Conservative opinion and a good section of informed opinion were aware that if Russia were to be victorious, the tsar would demand the retrocession of Bessarabia. On January 10/22, the newspaper *Românul* mentioned that fact and concluded that if Prince Carol accepted that possibility he would, in fact, be signing his own abdication.

21. "Precipitate action would be a great mistake, and could not be excused, even were the peace of the country at stake" (Letter from Prince Karl Anton, dated December 1875, in *Reminiscences of the King of Roumania*, ed. Sidney Whitman [New York, 1899],p. 226). Also see N. Iorga, ed., *Correspondance diplomatique roumaine sous le roi Charles I-er (1866–1880)*, 2d ed. (Bucharest, 1938). The opposition to the war of Karl Anton remained steadfast throughout the crisis, and the reports of most of Romania's representatives abroad remained cautious. See Frédérick Damé, *Histoire de la Roumanie contemporaine* (Paris, 1900), pp. 278 ff. For Prince Carol's official attitude, see Constantin C. Giurescu, ed., *Cuvântările Regelui Carol I 1866–1886*, vol. 2 (Bucharest, 1939), pp. 213 ff. Only Constantin A. Rosetti, Ion I. C. Brătianu, and to a lesser extent, Mihail Kogălniceanu counseled action, largely to revitalize the waning fortunes of the liberal party.

22. For the role of Florescu in the creation of the modern Romanian army, see Radu Rosetti, "Un uitat: Generalul Ioan Emanoil Florescu," in *Academia Romãña*, Memoriile sectiunii istorice (Bucharest, 1926).

23. "Russia, 'stated Gorchakov to Brătianu', does not need the assistance of the Romanian army" (*Aus dem Leben König Karl's von Rumänien*, vol. 2 [Stuttgart, 1894], p. 167).

24. The Romanian railroad system was placed entirely at the disposal of the Russian troops, which enjoyed privileges equal to those granted to the Romanian army, namely, a 40 percent tariff reduction (Art. 6 of the Russo–Romanian Convention). For maximum speed of transportation, military trains had priority over all others except those ensuring postal communications. Articles 7, 9, 10–12, and 16 of the convention all dealt with rail communications. For the complete convention, see Demetre A. Sturdza, ed., *Charles I Roi de Roumanie, croniques–actes–documents*, vol. 2 (Bucharest, 1904), pp. 551–58.

25. In 1877, the Russian Empire in Europe had a total population of 74,000,000. According to official Russian statistics this meant a levy of 1,465,706 men (25,000 officers) (Ferdinand Lecomte, *Guerre d'orient en 1876–77: Esquisses des événements militaires et politiques*, vol. 1 [Paris, 1877], p. 55).

26. The Romanian term for the "nation in arms" is *gloatele*. See C. Soare, ed., *Istoria Gîndirii militare Românești* (Bucharest, 1974), pp. 88 ff.

27. Vicomte A. de la Jonquière, *Histoire de l'Empire Ottoman depuis les origines jusqu' au Traité de Berlin* (Paris, 1897), p. 590.

28. On April 11/23, the grand vizier telegraphed Prince Charles to invite him in the name of the sultan to take joint military action for the defense of the Romanian frontiers. Kogălniceanu answered that he would have to refer the request to the Romanian parliament. A day later the Russian armies crossed the Pruth. In fact, a Turco–Romanian alliance had never been seriously entertained.

29. Constantin Căzănișteanu and Mihail E. Ionescu, *Războiul neatîrnării României, împrejurări diplomatice și operații militare 1877–1878* (Bucharest, 1977), p. 123.

30. *Times* (London, May 17, 1877), p. 5.

31. The Turkish regular army (nizam) numbered 210,000 (of whom 150,000 were in active service and 60,000 on leave), the reserves (redif) 192,000, and the militia 300,000 (Ion Coman, ed., *România în Războiul de Independentă 1877–78* [Bucharest, 1977], pp. 81–82).

32. A good study on Turkish strategy is Izzet-Pacha, *Les occasions perdues... étude stratégique et critique sur la campagne turco–russe de 1877–78* (Paris, 1910).

33. In the Caucasus, where the Russians had posted 50,000 men, the plan of the campaign called for the capture of Kars and Batum (A. Barbasov, "Noviie jacti o planirovanii russko–turetkoi voini 1877–78," *Voenno-istoričeskii jurnal*, 1976, no. 2, pp. 100–101).

34. I. Gărdescu, trans., *Comisiunea istorică a Marelui stat major rus, Rasboiul ruso–turc din 1877–78 in Peninsula Balcanica,* vol. 2 (Bucharest, 1902), p. 7. A refined version of the project was presented to the War Ministry on March 29, 1877, under the title *Considerations concerning the Case of a War with Turkey in the Spring of the Year 1877.*

35. The Quadrilateral fortresses were Ruse, Sumla, Silistra, and Varna.

36. Even the American newspapers, inspired by the British, indulged in Osman Pasha hero worship. At the time of the fall of Plevna, the *New York Tribune* (November 29, 1877) devoted a whole page to Osman Pasha, "the heroic Turkish commander who was forced to surrender only because of lack of provisions." According to the *Louisville Courier,* Osman Pasha was of American origin; the *New York Times* (September 5, 1877) reveal his "original name," Crawford. See also William V. Herbert, *The Defense of Plevno 1877 Written by One Who Took Part in It* (London, 1895).

37. A good study of early British efforts to support Tanzimat Turkey is Frank Edgar Bailey, *British Policy and the Turkish Reform Movement: A Study in Anglo–Turkish Relations 1826–1853* (Cambridge, 1942).

38. An optimistic account of the state of Turkish military preparadness is I. Halil Sedes, *1877–78 Osmanli-Rus ve Romen Savasi* (Istanbul, 1935).

39. Hobart Pasha (Augustus Hobart–Hampden) (1822–86) entered the British navy in 1835, distinguished himself in the Crimean War, became a blockade runner during the American Civil War, and entered Turkish service as a naval advisor in 1867. He completely reorganized and commanded the Turkish navy during the 1877–78 war and in 1881 was appointed Marshal of the Empire. He wrote a romanticized autobiography, *Sketches of My Life* (London, 1887).

40. Of course, the Turkish navy retained its superiority on paper because it was never involved in major action. The four Romanian Danube gunboats, *România, Ştefan cel Mare, Fulgerul,* and *Rîndunica,* consistently did well against Turkish Danubian gunboats and destroyed many of them.

Alesandru Duţu

# ROMANIAN SOLIDARITY WITH THE NATIONAL LIBERATION STRUGGLES OF SOUTHEASTERN EUROPE, 1875–78

When the Eastern Question once again became critical with the outbreak of the anti-Ottoman uprising in Hercegovina and Bosnia, achieving freedom from Ottoman suzerainty and declaring their independence were the primary focus of attention for Romania, Montenegro, and Serbia. National liberation was also a goal for the provinces of the Balkan Peninsula directly under the control of the Ottoman Empire. Animated by common ideals and aims, the peoples of this part of Europe manifested solidarity in the struggle against foreign domination.[1]

Shortly after the outbreak of the uprising in Hercegovina in the summer of 1875, the rebels began to receive assistance in men and weapons from Serbia, which in its turn, along with Montenegro, openly made preparations for participation in the anti-Ottoman struggle. Within this framework, an uprising broke out in Bosnia as well, and despite all the efforts of the Otto-man authorities it could not be put down. As the Romanian historian Nicolae Iorga has said, while the imperial army "was scoring a victory in one place, the rebels made their appearance in another; the whole population was discontented, and what victories the Turkish army was able to gain were of no importance."[2] After a lull of some months, hostilities resumed in the spring of 1876.

Romania, surrounded by great empires in contention for supremacy in the Balkans and hoping both to avoid foreign domination and to negotiate its full independence with the assistance of the guarantor powers, at first declared its neutrality. Romanian Foreign Minister Vasile Boerescu asserted on August 9, 1875: "We are maintaining an attitude of reserve, and we shall watch and listen intently to everything in order to avoid any action that might compromise our neutrality." At the same time, he stressed that the Romanian nation sympathized with the nations on the right bank of the

Danube.[3] Their traditional relations and history of common struggle against foreign domination were important in making the declaration of neutrality no obstacle to the Romanian authorities in supporting the liberation struggles of the Balkan peoples.

The Romanians strongly sympathized with the events south of the Danube and the heroism of the insurgents. "It was natural," wrote T. C. Văcărescu at the time, "for Romania to set her heart on peoples of the same faith aspiring to a happier fate."[4] Boerescu reminded Romania's diplomatic representatives of the sympathy of the state for the Balkan nations and its friendly ties with Serbia and Montenegro.[5] Along the same lines, the newspaper *Românul*, which from the very beginning had sided with the insurgents, wrote with satisfaction in the autumn of 1875 about the new successes of the "heroic people of Hercegovina." "The advantage is huge," it asserted, "because out of bloodshed in a just cause from the wounds of a martyr springs the vigorous tree of truth and justice."[6] Added to these declarations of sympathy, as we know from the reports of the Serbian representative in Bucharest, were the requests of Romanians volunteering to go to Hercegovina.[7] Russian documents mention a Romanian officer who was preparing to lead an armed detachment across the Danube to help the rebels in Bosnia and Hercegovina.[8] For their part, the Bulgarian revolutionaries in Romania wrote in Hristo Botev's newspaper *Znanie* of their wish to "lend a helping hand to their brothers... in Hercegovina."[9]

The aspirations of the insurgent population, the continuation of Ottoman oppression, and the intense Ottoman preparation for the suppression of the uprising prefigured a generalization of the struggle of the subject Balkan peoples against foreign domination. The spirit of insurrection strongly affected the other peoples under Ottoman rule. The Bulgarian uprising of September 1875, organized by the Bulgarian Revolutionary Central Committee, headquartered in Bucharest, was quickly suppressed by Turkish troops. But the Bulgarian émigrés, with the tacit consent of the Romanian authorities, ardently continued their preparations for a major uprising south of the Danube in the spring of 1876. The Bulgarian rebellion broke out in April 1876 between the Balkans and the Danube. Hristo Botev organized a detachment of more than two thousand Bulgarian revolutionaries that on May 17, 1876, with the consent of Romanian Foreign Minister Mihail Kogălniceanu and the public's active support, crossed the Danube near Vidin and spread out over northern Bulgaria. Botev fell in action on June 2 in the mountains of the Vraţa area.

The April Uprising found a consistent defender in the Romanian people. The whole Romanian press strongly supported the rebels, publishing ample information on the development of the uprising and the heroism of the Bulgarians, who "had not only enough weapons, ammunition, and money, but also valiant and capable leaders."[10] Numerous publications deplored the atrocities committed by the Ottoman troops against the Bulgarian population. After the bloody suppression of the insurrection, the Bulgarians resident in Romania, with the assistance of the local authorities, set up many committees to assist the refugees. During the autumn a major meeting of Bulgarian leaders, termed by the revolutionary poet Ivan Vazov "the first unofficial parliament of Bulgaria," took place in Bucharest, and there the decision was made to continue the struggle.[11]

The former president of the Bulgarian National Assembly, Zahari Stoianov, brought Romania's assistance to the Bulgarian people into sharp relief in a letter to the Romanian socialist Arbore Zamfir in 1886:

No more or less cultivated or patriotic Bulgarian who has ever set foot on the free land of Romania has failed to experience the brotherly hospitality of the Romanians. For half a century, a horrible dark epoch for us, the eyes of the Bulgarian people have been fixed upon the left bank of the Danube. Everything great and honest, everything that mattered, everything that could not live and breathe in subjugated Bulgaria was alive and at work in holy Romania. For me and my friends, the words Romania, Bucharest, Giurgiu, Ploieşti, Brăila, Galaţi were like words in the Holy Scriptures. When one of our patriots, cruelly persecuted by the Ottoman government, succeeded in snatching himself at last from the jaws of the merciless foreigner, he took shelter in one of Romania's towns. Your country was for us the bright beacon of liberty, the hope for a better life.[12]

Serbia's and Montenegro's declaration of war on Turkey in June 1876 was met with great satisfaction in Romania because its traditional friendly relations with the two neighboring countries had been sanctioned by a treaty in 1868. Although the Romanian government did not officially join them, it backed them in various ways, allowing the activity of the Serbian committees in Romania and permitting transshipment of volunteers, weapons, and ammunition, particularly from Russia. Of special importance for the neighboring state was Romania's request, approved by the Great Powers, that the Danube between Negotin and Vîrciorova be declared a neutral zone, thus preventing Turkey from transporting weapons and troops on the river.[13] Romania's firm action evoked a wide international echo. Noteworthy for emphasizing the Romanian people's solidarity with the emancipation efforts of the subject peoples of the Balkans was Kogălniceanu's memorandum to the country's diplomatic representatives of July 20, 1876, in which he pointed out that the Romanians could not remain indifferent to the "cries of woe on the right bank of the Danube," that "popular unrest was daily increasing," and that "the Romanian army was chafing under the yoke of discipline and eager to take part in the struggle."[14]

In mid-1876, in the light of the failure of the negotiations aimed at diplomatic recognition of its independence and the evolution of the international situation, Romania made a diplomatic approach to Russia.[15] The Russo—Romanian Convention, concluded on April 4, 1877, brought Romania officially into the military operations in the Balkans. On May 9, 1877, the Chamber of Deputies proclaimed Romania's independence and broke off all ties with the Porte. This news was received with gratification by Serbia, Greece, and Montenegro, as well as by the Bulgarians and the other peoples of the Balkans.

In response to the request of Grand Duke Nikolay, the Romanian army crossed the Danube with fifty thousand men, to take part alongside the Russian army in the most important theater of combat. The blood shed by Romanians in the battles of Pleven, Rahova, Smîrdan, and Vidin sanctioned the historic proclamation of independence and contributed to the liberation of Bulgaria. Referring to Romanian assistance to the Bulgarian liberation movement, the Bulgarian historian Nikolai Ječev wrote: "The Romanian soldiers were received as brothers, as liberators by the Bulgarian people... It can rightly be said that in 1877—78 the Romanian people took an active and praiseworthy part in defeating the Ottoman Empire and undermining the sultan's domination in the Balkans, in winning Bulgaria's independence and asserting its own."[16]

The victories  scored on the battlefields in Bulgaria in 1877 were an impulse for the Serbs and Montenegrins to resume their own struggle, which they had been obliged to abandon in 1876 under strong Ottoman pressure. The emancipation movements of the Balkan peoples, the Romanian War of Independence, and the successes of Russian troops south of the Danube forced the Ottoman Empire, in the Treaties of San Stefano and Berlin, to grant independence to Romania, Serbia, and Montenegro and autonomy to the newly created Bulgarian state. Thus ended an important stage of the struggle of the peoples of southeastern Europe for independent national states. As Nicolae Ceauşescu, president of the Socialist Republic of Romania, said on the occasion of the centennial of Romania's independence, "These powerful tokens of solidarity and brotherhood in struggle are an eloquent illustration of the close relations of friendship, good neighbourliness, collaboration, and solidarity which have existed between the Balkan peoples for centuries in the fight against oppression, for liberty and a dignified life."[17]

## NOTES

1.   For details, see N. Ciachir, *România în sud-estul Europei (1848—1886)* (Bucharest, 1968); C. Velichi, *Istoria modernă a Bulgariei* (Bucharest, 1975); N. Ciachir, *Istoria modernă a Serbiei* (Bucharest, 1974); and *Istoria modernă a Albaniei* (Bucharest, 1974).

2.   N. Iorga, *Politica externă a regelui Carol I,* 2d ed. (Bucharest, 1923), p. 110.

3. *Documente privind independenţa României: Războiul pentru independentă,* vol. 1, pt. 2 (Bucharest, 1954), p. 12.

4. T. C. Văcărescu, *Luptele românilor în războiul din 1877–1878* (Bucharest, 1888), p. 2.

5. *Documente,* p. 8.

6. Ibid., pp. 22–23.

7. N. Ciachir, "Rolul României în lupta de eliberare a popoarelor din sud-estul Europei în anii 1875–1878," *Anale de istorie* 27, no. 3 (1981): 97.

8. Ibid.

9. *Documente,* pp. 19–20.

10. *Albina,* May 8, 1876.

11. V. Sişmanov, *Ivan Vazov* (Sofia, 1930), p. 48.

12. C. N. Velichi, *La contribution de l'émigration bulgare de la Valachie a renaissance politique et culturel du peuple bulgare (1762–1850)* (Bucharest, 1970), p. 7.

13. *Documente,* pp. 242, 244, 252–53, and 255.

14. Ibid., p. 292.

15. N. Ciachir, *Războiul pentru independenţa României în cotextul european (1875–1878)* (Bucharest, 1977), pp. 158–61.

16. Nikolai Ječev, "România si războiul ruso–turc din anii 1877–1878," *Voenno-istoriceski sbornik,* 1977, no. 2, pp. 94 and 106.

17. Nicolae Ceauşescu, *Romania on the Way of Building Up the Multilaterally Developed Socialist Society,* vol. 14 (Bucharest, 1978), p. 302.

Miroslav Tejchman

## THE CZECH PUBLIC AND THE EASTERN CRISIS

The response of the Czech public to the anti-Turkish revolt of the South Slavs in 1875–76 and to the subsequent Russo–Turkish War proved that Slavic sympathies were general in that nation. In its breadth and influence, the Czech response to the events in the Balkans during the second half of the 1870s was second only to the Russian, which was important in pressing the tsarist government to act more effectively in favor of the Turkish Slavs. News about the events in Hercegovina, Bosnia, and Bulgaria interested practically everyone in Bohemia. Analysis of the contemporary press, memoirs of those involved, and even police reports allows us to construct an approximate picture of the scope of the response.[1]

The main source of information concerning the events in the Balkans during the years 1875–76 is of course the press, which even before that time had devoted a great deal of attention to the fate of the South Slavs. When the revolt in Hercegovina broke out in 1875, news of it filled the first foreign-news pages of Czech newspapers. What is significant is not only the extent of the reporting but also its content; Czech newspapers of all political leanings unanimously described the rebels as heroes and the Turks as cruel barbarians and oppressors. They printed news of the events in the Balkans not only as the most important foreign news on the front pages but also in special regular columns, and all anticipated a victory for the rebels.

Most news items were reprinted from the foreign press, especially the Croat and Slovene. The important Czech newspapers sent their own correspondents to the Balkans, and several of these actually visited rebel territory. The leading reporter of the Old Czech paper *Politik* was A. Penecke, who settled in Cetinje and later in Belgrade. The same paper also published letters from special correspondents in Bucharest, Sofia, and Zagreb. The Young Czech *Národní listy* printed contributions from correspondents in Belgrade, Zagreb, Bucharest, and Ruse about the Bulgarian uprising. It sent special correspondents J. Holeček and Bohumil Havlas to the rebels in Hercegovina and Josef J. Toužimský to Serbia. *Národní listy* had for some time been receiving information from Jan Vaclík, who held an important diplomatic post in Montenegro. Valuable news items concerning the Bulgarian uprising came from reports of eyewitnesses and articles written by volunteers about their experiences in the south. Some Czechs, mostly engineers who had helped to build the railroad in southern Bulgaria, experienced the April Uprising and were therefore competent informants for the Czech press. The Czech public was particularly interested in the heroic deeds and fate of Hristo Botev. The entire Czech press followed in detail the fate of his regiment after its arrival on Bulgarian soil. Interesting information on the Balkans was published in *Politik* by Konstantin Jireček, then a student in Prague University's department of philosophy. A new wave of Slavic enthusiasm developed in May with the first news of the uprising in Bulgaria and reached one peak at the end of June, in connection with the Serbo–Turkish War, and another a year later, in connection with the Russo–Turkish conflict. Here again, the Czech press informed its readers fully, mostly through special correspondents and by reprinting reports from the press of neighboring countries.

Of course, the reporting varied in quality and was not 100 percent reliable. Quality varied especially in the reporting on the revolts in Bosnia–Hercegovina and Bulgaria and on the Serbo–Turkish War. It was much easier to collect information from the war fronts than from the rebel territories, and thus in the years 1876–77 the Czech press was flooded with information. Czech readers were well informed about all the important events of the Serbo–Turkish War, which the press correctly placed in the context of the Eastern crisis as a whole, the solution to which it unambiguously saw in the liberation of all Slavic nations from the Ottoman yoke. Information about this "Slavo–Turkish War," as the Czech press sometimes called the events of the years 1875–76, was augmented by various publications, pamphlets, and leaflets, for instance, the thirty-page pamphlet *Válka slovansko–turecká roku 1876* (The Slavo–Turkish War of the Year 1876), published in Czech and in German. Maps of the South Slavic battlefields were issued in a great number of copies.

This many-sided interest in the struggle of the Slavs in the Ottoman Empire for national liberation did not end with an expression of academic interest or abstract sympathy. On the contrary, it led to concrete efforts to help the rebels and later the Serbian and Russian armies. The various auxiliary actions, neither small nor insignificant, included collections of money, clothing, and medical supplies for the rebels and even the direct help of armed volunteers. Finally, there were efforts to help the South Slavs politically.

Soon after the revolt broke out in Hercegovina, a great collection to help the "brethren in the south" was undertaken. It was connected with the actions of auxiliary committees in Dalmatia, Slovenia, and Croatia, and its leading organizers were Czech and Moravian dailies. Organizationally it was aided by high-school and college students and women's organizations. This kind of activity intensified after the outbreak of the Serbo—Turkish War in 1876, when special committees for the organization of collections were set up. Most of the donors were artisans and intellectuals. Often, however, although the poor had been affected by the economic crisis of 1873, even factory workers pitched in. The data on these collections are fragmentary, but according to some incomplete information from October 1876 one may estimate a total contribution of 65,000 guldens. Hundreds of kilograms of clothing and medical supplies were sent south, primarily to Dalmatia, whence they were transported either to rebel territory or to Serbia. It is impossible at this point to ascertain whether anything was sent to Bulgaria or to the Bulgarian auxiliary committee operating out of Bucharest. The Austrian authorities tolerated these collections, although they tried to impede them by various official measures. The character of these collections is the best evidence of the positive response of the Czech public to the 1875—76 events in the Balkans.

A concrete step in the direction of helping the South Slavic rebels in their struggle against Turkey was the dispatch of volunteers. The Czech press printed the names of a number of Czech volunteers who left for Herce-govina and Bosnia in 1875 to take part in the fighting. Among the best-known was Havlas, who fought with the rebels in Hercegovina and informed the readers of the major Czech newspapers about his experiences. His comrade-in-arms František Klapka sent regular contributions to *Pražský denník*. Among the volunteers in Bosnia and Hercegovina were a number of Czech physicians and medical students, and others were active in neighboring Montenegro. After the outbreak of the Serbo—Turkish War there were news items about Czech volunteers on Serbian battlefields. A number of un-employed workers were among the students and officers who joined the Serbian army as volunteers. Most of these Czechs were part of the volunteer Infantry Legion of Princess Natalia. A number of Czech volunteer officers were decorated, among them a Captain Tešar, another Czech whom we know only as Srb, who commanded an artillery battery, Max Švagrovský, aide-de-camp to the British Cavalry Commander Colonel MacIrer, and General František Zach, commander of the southern Serbian army. Zach had taken part in the Polish uprising of 1830 and in the revolutionary events in Prague in 1848. Later he had been active in Serbia, where he had founded the artillery school and in 1875 had became aide-de-camp to the ruler. Czech volunteers evidently took part in the Bulgarian April Uprising of 1876, although concrete data are missing. The same is true of the cooperation of other Czechs with the secret Bulgarian revolutionary organization. At the time of the April Uprising a number of Bulgarians who were studying in Bohemia decided to return home and take part in the struggle against the Turks. Collections organized by their Czech friends financed their trip home and their acquisition of weapons.

Mass meetings and public gatherings focused on "the South Slavic brethren" were organized by Czech political parties in an effort both to influence Austrian foreign policy in a direction favorable to the rebels and to improve the position of the Slavs within the monarchy. Announcements of intentions to hold such gatherings first appeared in July 1876, but such meetings were forbidden and not one of them ever took place. Gatherings were planned for Prague and Roudnice and later for almost twenty other places in Bohemia and in Moravia. In some places the rising Social Democratic party took part in the preparations. The Austrian authorities refused to permit such gatherings on the ground that they might "agitate the public."

Czech political circles also did all they could to assist anti-Turkish efforts during the Russo–Turkish War of 1877–78. Ladislav Rieger, the leader of the Old Czech party, proposed organizing meetings at which support for Russia could be expressed. As early as the end of May solemn church services in Prague celebrated Russian victories. Greetings were sent from Prague and other towns to Moscow. A number of Czechs took part as volunteers on the Russian side. Czech specialists working in Bulgaria, for instance, railroad engineers and railroad employees, actively helped the Russian soldiers, and many of them joined Russian units. The Czech public as a whole celebrated the ultimate Russian victory.

The leading representatives of Czech cultural life reacted to the reports of the Balkan events through their work. The most immediate response was recorded by Jan Neruda in his feuilletons. Other writers – Alois Jirásek, Josef Holeček, Karel Mattuš, Josef Thomayer – noted the event primarily in their memoirs. The poet Eliška Krásnohorská devoted a collection of verses to the Balkan events; the poet Svatopluk Čech criticized the British coolness toward the Balkan Slavs. We find responses also in the poems of Jaroslav Vrchlický, Josef V. Sládek, and Karolina Světlá and in the works of the writers Jirásek, Neruda, Adolf Heyduk, and others. Important also was the work of Czech graphic artists working for the press.

The Eastern crisis was also reflected in Czech politics. So far as the main problem was concerned, Czech political parties and group were united as to the necessity of liberating the South Slavs from the Ottoman yoke. Most of them also envisioned an independent Serbian, Montenegrin, or Bulgarian state. Differences and contradictions, however, appeared with reference to relations with Vienna. In the Old Czech party, Rieger's group pursued a policy of rapprochement with Vienna while Jan S. Skrejšovský's group advocated an independent Czech policy. The Old Czechs had ties to some liberal Serbian leaders and organized concrete pro-Serbian actions according to their wishes. The Young Czechs viewed the Eastern crisis in a very utilitarian way and tried to exploit it for their own political ends (besides organizing aid, which they took for granted). They cooperated with the South Slavic revolutionary movement, but most of their actions had the character of a struggle to gain voters at home.

In sum, one may say that the Czech public was intensely interested in the events taking place in the Balkans, which it saw as a struggle for national liberation of the South Slavs from Turkey, and tried to help in any way it could. At the same time, the Balkan events influenced political developments in Bohemia and Moravia.

## NOTES

1. See, for examples, *Dějiny Bulharska* (Prague, 1980); *Dějiny Jugoslávie* (Prague, 1970); *Češi a Jihoslované v minullosti* (Prague, 1975); *Československo–bulharské vztahy* (Prague, 1981); Č. Amort, "Ohlas dubnového povstání v české a slovenské veřejnosti," *Sborník parcí filozofické fakulty Brněnské university* 23–24 (1976–77): 157–66; Č. Amort, "Ohlas rusko–turecké války v letech 1877–1878 v české a slovenské veřejnosti," *Slovanský přehled,* 1977, no. 6, pp. 495–509; R. Havránková, "Česká veřojnost na pomoc protitureckým povstáním jižnich slovanů v letech 1875–1877," *Slovanské historické studie* 6 (1966): 5–53. J. Kolejka, "Jižní Slované a Vvelká východní krize 1875 až 1878," *Slovanský přehled,* 1976, no. 2, pp. 111–27.

Anna Garlicka


# POLISH SOCIETY AND THE EASTERN CRISIS OF 1875–78


The decline of the Ottoman Empire and the territorial and qualitative expansion of national independence movements in the nineteenth century confronted European diplomacy with the problem of Turkish rule in the Balkans. Throughout the nineteenth century the Great Powers were actively engaged in this issue. It also aroused wide interest among the populations of Europe. The armed resistance of the oppressed nations made the future of the Porte's European possessions a permanent topic in both newspapers and cabinet meetings. The press of many European states carried extensive reports on the struggle of the Balkan nations, vividly depicting the persecutions and massacres. Expressions of anti-Turkish feeling by the Balkan nations, reflecting their dissatisfaction and efforts to change the status quo, drew the understanding and sympathy of the peoples of Europe. Religious sympathy played a considerable role in creating support for nations little known in political geography. The sense of religious solidarity with the Christian subjects of the sultan was stressed by the press both in Russia and in the countries of Western Europe.

The philhellenic movement of the 1820s was the most powerful and widespread European reaction to events on the Balkan Peninsula, but interest in the Balkans persisted in the years that followed. Expressions of sympathy were not infrequent, nor were demonstrations of solidarity with the Balkan nations fighting for independence. Even in the mid-nineteenth century, however, the European public had only a vague idea of the ethnic mosaic of the peninsula, although the problems of the Balkans' future or the fate of Christians there were the subject of many discussions, arguments, pamphlets, and books. It was the political activity of the Balkan nations that called the attention of Europe to the existence of an unsolved problem. It was reports in the press about the struggle in Bosnia and Hercegovina, Bulgaria, Montenegro, and Serbia that made Europeans aware of the maturing efforts of the Balkan nations to construct a framework for their own statehood.

The Eastern crisis of 1875—78 refocused Europe's attention on the Balkan Peninsula. In the years of crisis the Balkans became a central issue for governments and for public opinion. The manifesto to Europe issued by the Bosnian insurgents in 1875, asking for support and protection against Turkish oppression and declaring the insurgents' intention of fighting to the last drop of blood, did not fail to elicit a response. Progressive European opinion demanded energetic steps in favor of the South Slavic nations. In Europe anti-Turkish feeling ran high. The bloodshed on the peninsula, which was extensively covered by the Russian and thereafter by the Western European press, produced protests and support for the just demands of the oppressed nations. This fact is worth stressing, since in the not-so-distant past, the opinion persisted in the European press that the nations of the peninsula were incapable of building their own nation-states, either as separate organisms or in the framework of a federation.[1]

Public opinion was particularly stirred by the news of the massacre at Bataku, where on May 4, 1876, the Turks murdered some four thousand people and where two days later the German and French consuls were assassinated. Fyodor Dostoyevsky and Ivan Turgenev were among those who protested and demanded an end to the bloody repression, calling for the punishment of the guilty and the fulfillment of the demands of the Bulgarian insurgents. Leading Western European writers such as Victor Hugo and Oscar Wilde also took up the Bulgarians' cause. The outcry of the writers aroused the support of Giuseppe Garibaldi, the famous fighter for the freedom and unification of Italy. Many politicians also joined in and issued declarations. William Gladstone, the leader of the English liberals, on learning about the massacres, published a pamphlet in which he called on the European states to efface this disgrace. He also expressed the opinion that it would be a lesser evil for Bosnia, Hercegovina, and Bulgaria to be taken over by the Russians than for the populations of those states to continue to endure the bloody Turkish oppression. Gladstone also called on Parliament to grant autonomy to Bulgaria.[2] It should be remembered, however, that whatever his personal views, he was using the "Bulgarian Horrors" as an argument in his political battle against the pro-Turkish Tories.

Public opinion generally had little influence on the policies of governments. Often there were differences between the sympathies of the public and the decisions of the politicians. Only in Russia, where there was strong Pan-Slavic agitation and Slavophile propaganda, did the government secure wide popular support. In Hungary, in contrast, the uprising in Hercegovina and later the Serbo—Turkish War provoked demonstrations of sympathy for Turkey.

In Poland, too the attitude of the population toward the parties engaged in the conflict was not uniform. Politicians differed as to the feasibility of using the Eastern crisis to further the Polish cause, although generally they adopted positions calculated to be the least favorable to the tsarist regime. In the Austrian and Prussian sectors of partitioned Poland, not only did antitsarist feeling run high but also there were frequent expressions of sympathy for Turkey because of its traditionally friendly stance toward the Polish cause. It should be stressed, however, that irrespective of its political sympathies the Polish population was in solidarity with the struggle for freedom of the South Slavic states. While the Christian nations of the peninsula perceived Russia as the mother of Slavism and their potential liberator, Poles had precisely the opposite attitude, viewing the tsar as a sinister invader. The Polish political movement wanted to use the Eastern issue to reconstruct the Polish state, and this is also what directed the interest of Polish émigrés toward Balkan problems. Thus whereas the South Slavs had traditionally sought support in Russia, the Poles had initially looked to Turkey and its protector England. The hopes of early figures such as Adam Jerzy Czartoryski had, however, proven baseless. As early as the end of the Crimean War the policy of looking to England had drawn criticism from Polish democratic émigrés. After the failure of the January Insurrection of 1863 in Russian Poland, Galicia (under Austrian rule) had become the center of the struggle for Polish independence. Galician Poles hoped to offset the close anti-Polish cooperation between Prussia and Russia by seeking the support of Austria. Thus in the post-1863 situation the policy of relying on Turkey and the Western powers found few advocates.[3]

The recurrence of the Eastern Question in the years 1875–78, especially the outbreak of the Russo–Turkish War in 1877, reawakened earlier expectations and plans. Polish politicians began considering how to create an international configuration that would bring forward the issue of Poland. They hoped to bring Austria into the war on the side of England and Turkey against Russia. If the Russo–Turkish War were to lead to a conflict between Russia and Austria, this would make the Polish cause timely again as an international issue.

The attitude of the Polish people toward the Eastern war was expressed only to a limited extent in the military and political activities so characteristic of earlier years. The possibilities for action by Polish politicians in this period were limited. Neither in Vienna nor in London did they have sufficient influence to inspire diplomatic activity. Also, since the January insurrection the Polish national independence movement had become increasingly weak, and the social mood had shifted toward reconciliation with the foreign rulers.

In 1877, a detachment of Polish volunteers was formed in Turkey, along with Cossack and Polish dragoon regiments. Intended to constitute the nucleus of a Polish legion in Turkey,[4] it remained a small detachment without any real significance because no noted politician could be found to

sponsor it. The, British agent Butler—Johnston also encouraged Poles to form
military detachments, but once again no one with political influence would
support this activity. There were even suggestions from some Polish quarters
that a Polish army corps be formed in Turkey consisting of émigrés, deserters,
and volunteers. In return the sultan was supposed to state publicly the
Turkish position with respect to the issue of Poland and arm the detachments. The Turkish government had, however, no intention of becoming
involved in the Polish issue, all the more so since it could not find a political
leader who would provide momentum for this political and military action.
There is no doubt that after the experience of the January Insurrection no
one in Poland could secure the necessary support for a call to arms.

The victorious Russian campaign in the Balkans activated British
diplomacy, which attempted to play its Polish card. On the initiative of the
British, a meeting of noted Polish politicians took place in Vienna at the end
of July 1877. On July 26, a national government was established that included Adam Sapieha and Artur Gołuchowski. The scope of action of this
government was limited, and by December it had already dissolved. It is
worth noting, however, that the aim of this ephemeral formation was not in
the least to prepare a national uprising in Poland but rather to avert new
initiatives that could bring the catastrophic results of the 1863 Insurrection.

One of the major conspiratorial actions was the attempt to form Székely
detachments. This joint Polish—Hungarian undertaking sought to take advantage of the bellicose mood of the local population by sabotaging the rear of
the Russian army from Transylvania. It was thought that such actions would
lead to war between Russia and Austria. Sapieha became actively engaged
in the preparation of this action. The Székely expedition was easily thwarted
by the Austrian police, to whom the Hungaro—Polish plans were no secret.[5]

At the same time, action that could lead to diplomatic talks on the Polish
issue in an international forum was not neglected. In London and Vienna
Poles submitted memorials calling on England and Austria to take up the
Polish issue. However, these documents received no response.

In their turn, Polish members of the Galician parliament attempted to pass
a resolution in the summer of 1877 concerning the current Russo—Turkish
War. However, the speaker of parliament and the group of Cracow conservatives who supported him blocked passage of the anti-Russian proclamation,
not wishing to hinder the policy of the government in Vienna. In many
regions such tactics were criticized by the electorate, which demanded more
energetic action from the deputies. Several deputies resigned from the Polish
club of the Reichsrat in Vienna both as a form of protest and in order to gain
freedom of expression. In this parliament Ludwik Wolski and Otton Hausner
criticized diplomatic scheming and called for the defense of the interests of
the oppressed nations. This same Hausner at the end of 1879 severely con-

demned the Berlin Treaty.[6] Other Polish deputies to the Reichsrat submitted questions concerning two issues: (1) Was the government aware of the fact that the Russian army murdered prisoners of Polish descent? (2) Did the government intend to raise, during the future international conference on the issue of Christians who were Turkish subjects, the problem of the fate of partitioned Poles living in Russia? Both those questions received a negative reply.[7]

The next attempt to focus attention on the Polish issue in an international context was undertaken through diplomatic channels during the Berlin Congress. Several memoranda were submitted to the Congress, but they were not discussed, serving solely to enrich its internal documentation. The diplomats did not forget the Polish issue, but clearly it did not play any important role in the Eastern crisis of 1875–78.

Polish public opinion watched the course of events in the Balkans with attention. The newspapers published in Polish territories carried relatively extensive reports about the development of events on the peninsula. The Polish population, divided by the three partitioning powers, showed sympathy for the Balkan nations fighting for independence. The accounts of the noted Slavist Jan Grzegorzewski are interesting in this context. During the Eastern crisis Grzegorzewski stayed in the Balkans as a correspondent of *Gazeta Narodowa,* published in L'vov. His reports and books bear witness to the fact that even people with little sympathy for progressive ideals and for tsarist policy in the Balkans expressed solidarity with the fight of the South Slavs for national independence. His accounts of discussions with the leaders of the Bulgarian national independence movement reveal important differences among them in political views, but it is symptomatic that they all end with a toast to the victory of nations that are fighting for freedom.[8]

The brutal suppression by Turkey of the Bulgarian April Uprising was received with indignation in Polish territories, as it was in the majority of European countries. The sharpest protests against the bloody repressions were voiced by the Warsaw newspapers. Even the press in the Prussian and Austrian parts of Poland, which represented differing political views, did not pass silently over these facts. Thus, for example, *Przegląd Lwowski* carried an extensive account of the April Uprising and its many casualties. Stressing sympathy for the fate of "our Slav brothers," it condemned the atrocities of the Muslim forces.[9] The press in Russian Poland expressed solidarity with the nations fighting against the Turkish yoke much more lucidly and explicitly. In the Warsaw *Przegląd Tygodniowy* there were even comments critical of the Galician politicians for their indifference toward the actions of the Turks on Bulgarian and Serbian soil.[10] The press of Russian Poland not only carried extensive accounts of the events but made an effort to acquaint its readers with the history of the nations of the Balkan Peninsula, although the reports tried to avoid statements on matters of nationality. Burzyński, in an article entitled "South Slavism" published in *Niwa*, pointed out among other things that "among the Balkan Slavs the Bulgarians have the greatest predisposition to become independent in the future." Separate articles devoted to Bulgaria appeared in *Przegląd Tygodniowy* and in *Biblioteka Warszawska*.[12] In comparison with the Bulgarian problems the press gave even wider coverage to the uprising in Hercegovina and to the Serbo–Turkish War. The greatest interest was of course aroused by the Russo–Turkish War. Full and comprehensive data on the military operations were published in the *Gazeta Warszawska* and *Przegląd Tygodniowy*. The international context of the crisis and the attitude of Britain, Austria–Hungary, and Germany toward the Eastern crisis were widely discussed. There was criticism of the policy of the Western powers, whose pro-Turkish position and tactics hindered Russia in fulfilling its mission of freeing the South Slavic nations from the Turkish yoke. The press in Russian Poland also considered the Berlin Congress unfair in its decisions concerning the Bulgarian nation. During most of the period press commentaries characteristically consisted of discussions of Russia's role in the crisis. The efforts and aspirations of the Balkan states and nations were not infrequently left in the background.[13]

In analyzing the attitude of the press in Russian Poland one should remember that it cannot be identified with the opinions prevalent in the population at large. It was subject to strict censorship and subordination to the Russian authorities. On the other hand, many Polish politicians and journalists succumbed to the influence of the democratic alliance of Slavs and urged sympathy with the fighting Balkan nations and with Russia.[14] Typical in this respect are the articles of two leading journalists, Aleksander Świętochowski and Adam Wislicki, in *Przegląd Tygodniowy*. Wislicki questioned the creation of both a Bulgaria and an Eastern Rumelia, which would lead to an artificial division of the Bulgarian nation. He accused the Western powers of manipulating the fate of nations in the interest of their own political goals.

Prussian and Austrian Poland followed the Eastern crisis with more restraint. Since Poles had been deprived of their statehood, they understood perfectly the aspirations for independence of the Balkan nations. However, the tone that dominated in the press of Galicia and of the Poznań region was one of distrust of the role of Russia in the Eastern crisis and especially of its mission of liberating Slavs. Still, the Polish press was far from enthusiastic about the temporary victories of the Turkish forces in the Balkans. *Przegląd Lwowski* pointed out, for example, that Poles serving in the Russian army were being killed.[15]

An important part of Polish public opinion, especially from Galicia and Prussian Poland, was particularly interested in the influence of the Eastern crisis on the future of the Polish question. Newspaper reports were accompanied by political booklets and pamphlets. For example, a pamphlet bearing the title *Voice from Warsaw: Comments on the Eastern Issue with Consideration Given to the Polish Interests and Addressed to All Polish Patriots in Galicia and the Poznań Region* endeavored to persuade its readers that the best political solution for Poland would be cooperation with Russia.[16]

During the preparations for the Berlin Congress, a series of leading articles appeared in *Czas,* the organ of the Cracow conservatives, under the title "Pan-Slavism, Poland, and the Treaty of San Stefano."[17] These articles carried a warning against the dangers of Pan-Slavism and treated the tsarist policy in the Balkans with distrust. Nonetheless, this same newspaper criticized the Berlin Treaty some months later. In one of the articles the author asked, "What has happened to the national principle that seemed to be so close to the heart of Europe, and why does Europe strive to create a new source of political troubles which could perhaps erupt in the near future?"[18] *Dziennik Poznański* adopted a similar tone, stressing the artificial nature of the newly established territorial divisions and thus their transitory character. Criticism was aroused above all by the creation of a Turkish-dominated Eastern Rumelia. At the same time, expectations were revived for the establishment of a multinational federative state in the Balkans. Various rumors about this possibility appeared in *Czas* as well as in *Lech* (published in Poznań).[19]

In describing the attitude of the Polish society toward the Eastern crisis one cannot omit the active participation of Poles in the struggle for national independence of the Balkan nations. Many Poles fought in units of the Russian army; their number is estimated at fifty thousand. Thus Poles as well as Russians made an important contribution to the liberation of the Bulgarian nation.[20]

## NOTES

1. E. Wagemann, *Der Neue Balkan* (Hamburg, 1939), p. 20.
2. Robert W. Seton–Watson, *Disraeli, Gladstone, and the Eastern Question* (London, 1935), p. 183.
3. Jerzy Skowronek, *Polityka Bałkańska Hotelu Lamber, 1833–1856* (Warsaw, 1976); J. W. Borejsza, *Emigracja polska po powstaniu styczniowym* (Warsaw, 1966).
4. S. Kieniewicz, *Adam Sapieha* (L'vov, 1939); S. T. Gasztowff, *Turcja a Polska* (Paris, 1913), p. 10.
5. H. Wereszycki, *Walka o pokój europejski 1872–1878* (Warsaw, 1971), pp. 370–71.
6. Otton Hausner, *Ostatnie lata dziejów powszechnych od 1848 roku do dni dzisiejszych* (L'vov, 1881).

7. Wereszycki, *Walke o pokój europejski*, pp. 375–76.

8. Jan Grzegorzewski, *Współczesna Bułgaria*, vol. 1, *Przed i podczas wojny 1877/78* (Cracow, 1883), p. 32.

9. *Przegląd Lwowski*, 1876, p. 312.

10. *Przegląd Tygodniowy*, 1876, no. 41.

11. *Niwa*, 1876, no. 2, p. 181.

12. F. Jezierski, "Bułgarowie naddunajscy," *Biblioteka Warszawska* 3 (1876): 446.

13. For more details, see K. Wierzbicka, "Prasa Królestwa Polskiego wobec wyzwolenia Bułgarii 1876–1878," *Pamiętnik Słowiański* 24 (1974): 35–46.

14. M. Tanty, "Opinia polska wobec walki Bułgarów o wyzwolenie i zjednoczenie narodowe (1876–1914)," *Przegląd Humanistyczny*, 1978, no. 5, pp. 84 and 86.

15. J. Magnuszewski, *Otnoszenieto na polskato obszestwo k oswoboditelnite borbi na Byłgarita, oswobozdenito na Byłgarita i literazurata* (Sofia, 1878), p. 218.

16. *Głos z Warszawy: Uwagi w sprawie Wschodniej z uwzględnieniem interesów polskich poświęcone rozwadze patryotów polskich w Galicji i w Poznańskiem* (L'vov, 1876), p. 18.

17. These articles also appeared as a pamphlet, *Artykuły wstępne Czasu podczas Kongresu Berlińskiego: Panslawizm, Polska i traktat w San Stefano* (Cracow, 1878).

18. *Czas*, July 2, 1878; "Rumelia Wschodnia," *Dziennik Poznański*, 1879, no. 86.

19. *Czas*, June 6 and 27, 1878; *Lech*, 1879, no. 12.

20. S. Petrow, "Polacy w walkach o wyzwolenie Bułgarii," and A. Koseski, "Społeczeństwo polskie wobec wyzwolenia Bułgarii w latach 1877–1878," in Ivanov, ed. *Braterstwo-przyjaźń: Szkice z dziejów przyjaźni polsko–bułgarskiej* (Warsaw, 1970), pp. 53–55, 56–59.

# III
## Insurrections and Wars in the Balkans

Richard L. DiNardo

# RUSSIAN MILITARY OPERATIONS IN 1877–78

From the early eighteenth century through World War I, no two empires had been more consistent enemies than tsarist Russia and Ottoman Turkey, warring nearly a dozen times. During the nineteenth century they fought four times; in 1806–12, in 1828, in the Crimean War of 1854, and finally in 1877.

The immediate origins of the war of 1877 went back to 1875.[1] In that year a revolt broke out in the province of Bosnia, spreading to Bulgaria in the following year. Turkish attempts to crush the rebellion drew Europe's attention. Numerous atrocities were committed by both sides, but clever Bulgarian propaganda placed the Turks in the position of the villain. This greatly affected the Russian government, which was increasingly under Pan-Slavist pressure.[2] Feeling compelled to act after Turkey's rejection of a protocol proposed by the European powers, Tsar Alexander II declared war on April 24, 1877.

Moral support throughout Europe generally went to Russia, especially in England after Gladstone made an impassioned speech (called by Disraeli "the worst of the Bulgarian horrors") in Parliament. However, neither Bismarck nor Disraeli would countenance the destruction of the Ottoman Empire.

Militarily, both sides anticipated benefits from the war. For the Russians it would be the first opportunity to test the newly reorganized army since the major reforms of 1874. For the Turks it would be a chance to regain some of the martial respect they had lost over the previous century.

## The Balkan Campaign

Russian strategic options for the campaign were limited. Although in 1871 they had repudiated the articles of the 1856 Treaty of Paris prohibiting

Russian naval power in the Black Sea, the Russians had not yet created serious naval forces there. This vitiated the logical strategy, a seaborne leap-frog down the coast to Varna, followed by a march on Edirne using the Black Sea ports as bases. Given these circumstances, the Russian commander, Tsar Alexander's brother the Grand Duke Nikolay, deployed his 200,000 men (three corps plus auxiliary troops and Cossacks) as follows: the right wing, consisting of the Eighth and Twelfth Cavalry Divisions, plus three Cossack regiments, would cross the frontier at Ungheni and advance on the Iaşi–Ploieşti–Bucharest axis, with the Eighth Division going for the key town of Nikopol. The center, under Nikolay himself, with the Twelfth Corps, the Fifth Infantry Division of the Ninth Corps, and a Cossack regiment, would move parallel to the right wing to Bucharest. To carry out the most important part of the plan, the left wing was given a large force divided into three parts. The advance guard, composed of Cossacks, a rifle brigade, and some mountain artillery under Mikhail Dmitryevich Skobelev, had to take the railway bridge over the Seret at Galaţi to secure the Romanian rail system. The Eleventh Cavalry Division would move on Ruse. Finally, the Eighth Corps would move on Bucharest. These operations would be screened by the Eleventh Corps. Having advanced across the Wallachian plain, the army would then cross the Danube and fight its way over the Balkans to Edirne, opening the way to Constantinople. Since the army would have to pass through Romanian territory, permission was secured from Prince Carol of Romania to allow transit for the Russians.[3]

If there is one criticism that can be leveled at the Russians, it is of their paucity of numbers. Given the extended line of communication that had to be maintained, along with detachments and casualties, it was highly unlikely that the army could make it to Constantinople without reinforcement and replacements.[4]

The initial advance went without a hitch, beginning the day war was declared (see Map I). By May 24 the army was concentrated as follows: Niko-lay was at Bucharest with the Eighth, Twelfth, and half of the Eleventh Corps, the other half being at Olteniţa. The Ninth Corps was at Slatina, and the Rus-sians had a line of pickets from Nikopol to Silistra. Nikolay wanted to cross the Danube at Nikopol on June 6, but the wet spring (the Danube was 15 ft. above normal) and the railway bottleneck at Iaşi due to the difference between Russian and Romanian gauges severely hurt the Russian supply situation, forcing him to delay the crossing until the end of June.[5]

After being reinforced by another 72,000 troops in the Fourteenth, Fourth, and Thirteenth Corps, Nikolay planned his crossing, hoping to start after the small Russian navy had cleared the Danube of any Turkish presence. He wanted to cross at Ruse, but the delays, combined with the concentration at Bucharest, had tipped off the Turks, who fortified the

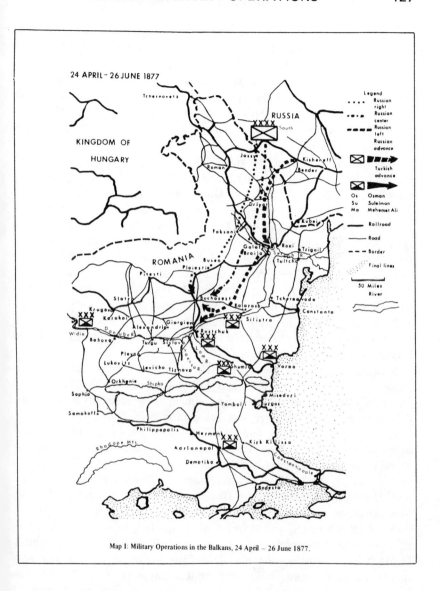

Map I: Military Operations in the Balkans, 24 April – 26 June 1877.

area. The grand duke therefore changed his plan. The real crossing would be made at Sistov by Fedor Fedorovich Radetzky's Eighth Corps, while diversions would be made at Nikopol, Flămînda, and Ruse.

The operation began at 1 A. M. on June 26, executed by the Fourteenth Infantry Division and the Fourth Rifle Brigade, supported by forty guns. By 3 P. M. the Russians had secured Sistov and were followed by the rest of the Eighth Corps (see Map II). The engineers then went to work, completing the bridge by July 3.

The bridgehead secured, the grand duke now organized an advance guard, a scratch force of 5,800 infantry, 5,000 cavalry, and thirty-two guns under General Count Ossip Vladimirovich Gurko, one of the ablest of the Russian commanders.[6] This force surged out of the bridgehead and captured the key road center of Tîrnova on July 7. Gurko was followed by the left wing (Twelfth and Thirteenth Corps) under the tsarevich (the future Alexander III). This force would screen the army's left flank and cover the Quadrilateral fortresses of Ruse, Silistra, Varna, and Shumen on one side. This was done by an advance up to the Lom by August 1. The fortresses were covered to the east by the Fourteenth Corps, advancing through the Dobruja to Trajan's Wall in July. The right wing, General Baron Nicholas Krudener's Ninth Corps, crossed the Danube on July 10 to attack Nikopol. The Eleventh and Fourth Corps were held in reserve.[7]

Meanwhile, what of the Turks? Theoretically, their strategic position looked very good. At the outset they had 50,000 troops in the Quadrilateral fortresses, 40,000 men at Vidin, and numerous detachments guarding the Balkan passes. Another force was being formed at Edirne. The Ottoman soldier was a good, brave, and steadfast fighter equipped with the latest weapons. The artillery, though weak numerically, was especially noted for its skill. Since the Russians had to maintain a long line of communication back to Russia, the Turks should have been able to mount heavy attacks on both their flanks. However, the Ottoman war effort was hindered by its own command system. Three field commands were created under Osman Pasha, Suleiman Pasha, and Mehmed Ali Pasha. Independent of each other, all took orders from a war council in Constantinople. The sultan, Abdül-hamid II, had originally wanted to defend the line of the Danube, but more timid counsels prevailed, thus letting the Russians cross easily. The Ottoman command system guaranteed a total lack of coordination among the field armies.[8]

After the completion of the crossing, things initially went well for the Russians. Having captured Tîrnova, Gurko planned to capture Shipka Pass, thus gaining a gateway to Edirne. Setting out on July 10, he took the advance guard through Elena Pass and was over the Balkans by the 16th, but he was a day behind schedule. As a result, on the 17th the Eighth Corps made an

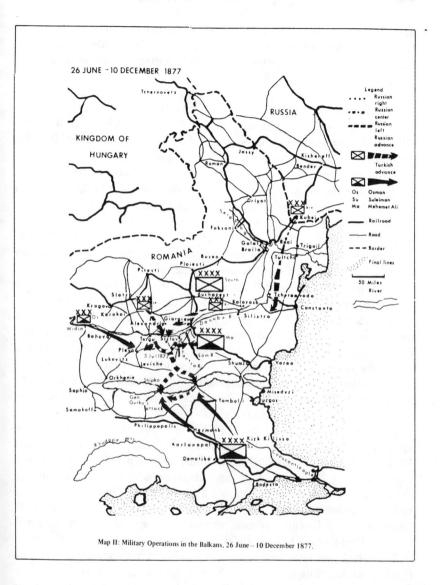

Map II: Military Operations in the Balkans, 26 June – 10 December 1877.

uncoordinated attack only to fail, and Gurko did the same the next day. However, on the 19th a coordinated attack was made and the Turkish forces surrendered, with the Russians taking 7,000 prisoners. Russian losses were light.[9]

It was on the right, however, that the main action of the campaign took place. After setting out from Sistov on July 10, Krudener, with the Ninth Corps and a Cossack brigade, advanced on Nikopol, which fell on the 16th. Nikolay then ordered Krudener to occupy Plevna, a key road center. Both Nikolay and Krudener ignored reports from prisoners that Osman Pasha, the ablest of the Ottoman commanders, was marching on Plevna with a large force.

Osman's army of 40,000 was at Vidin when the war broke out. From April to July it stayed at Vidin because the Ottoman war council feared a Romanian or Serbian attack. The Danube crossing, however, spurred Osman to action. He realized that possession of Plevna would threaten the flank of any Russian advance across the Balkans. Starting out on July 13, he reached Plevna by July 20 with his 15,000-man advance guard.[10]

Krudener sent Lieutenant General Schilder–Schuldner with a mixed force of 6,500 men out on the 18th to secure Plevna. That commander compounded Krudener's mistake by having his cavalry march in the rear of the column. The column thus maneuvered blindly into the Turkish position. On the 20th, Schilder–Schuldner attacked off the march with his column to attain the key position of Grivitsa, which overlooked the town. The column, still blind because of the misplacement of the cavalry, wandered straight into entrenched Turkish infantry. The attack was a disaster, with the Russians losing some 50 percent of their force.[11]

Krudener had come up by the 25th and was now reinforced by an independent brigade and elements of the Eleventh and Fourth Corps to about 30,000 men and 176 guns. Osman's force was in position at Plevna and Lovech with 24,000 men and 63 guns. Under pressure from Nikolay to take the town, Krudener decided to mount a second attack on July 30. This was to be a two-pronged effort, with the main attack being made by the Ninth Corps upon the Grivitsa redoubt, supported by elements of the Eleventh Corps and the Cossack brigade under Skobelev.

The attack was launched early on the 30th. After several hours of hard fighting the Russians were thrown back, suffering 7,300 casualties. Turkish losses amounted to about 5,000.[12] The attack was a fiasco for several reasons. First, Krudener committed his regiments one at a time, thus never really concentrating his force. Also, the broken and hilly nature of the terrain made the coordination of attacks difficult. Finally, the Turks, combining withering fire with an active defense, almost succeeded in collapsing the Russian left flank and were stopped only by Skobelev's brilliant leadership and hard fighting by the Cossacks.

Repulsed a second time at Plevna, Russian operations came to a halt. Osman was well entrenched and was soon reinforced to 50,000 men and Seventy-two guns. Any Russian move south would be threatened from Plevna. Given this situation, the grand duke had two choices. He could reconcentrate quickly and try to storm Plevna, or he could await reinforcements. With his army deployed in an ellipse from Nikopol to Shipka to Ruse and with Suleiman launching attacks at Shipka, Nikolay feared that any redeployment could cost him his foothold in the Balkans. Therefore he decided to await reinforcements. To aid his brother, Tsar Alexander sent the powerful Imperial Guard, along with the Grenadier Corps, four infantry divisions, and a cavalry division, all together 120,000 men and 460 guns. These arrived at the front only gradually, from August to October. The tsar also appealed to Prince Carol, who responded by putting a corps in the field amounting initially to 32,000 infantry, 5,000 cavalry, and 84 guns.[13] Back in Russia, to take over garrison duty 188,000 militia were mobilized.

Since the reinforcements would arrive little by little, the Russian army had to remain relatively immobile throughout August. The only real action on its part was the capture of Lovech, thus cutting Plevna off from the south.[14] On the Turkish side, Osman strengthened his position at Plevna, although for obscure reasons he launched a sortie on August 31 that accomplished nothing aside from the loss of 3,000 men. Suleiman launched a number of attacks on the Russians at Shipka, but many of these were pressed halfheartedly.[15] Mehmed Ali, with 65,000 men, made a strong attack on the Russian left in August, forcing the tsarevich back across the Lom and the Yantra. However, Mehmed Ali then withdrew and was back in his original positions by the end of September, having lost 4,000 men. He was relieved of command on October 2.[16]

Having strengthened their position and been reinforced, the Russians decided to make a full-scale assault on Plevna. Prince Carol commanded, with a Russian as chief of staff, the attacking force of 74,000 infantry, 10,000 cavalry, and 442 guns, which was to make a general assault on September 11. The Romanians (30,000 men and 126 guns) were to take the Grivitsa position in an enveloping attack. Redoubt # 10, the support of the Grivitsa position, was to be assaulted by the Fourth Corps. Krudener's Ninth Corps was to hold the left flank. Opposing them was Osman with 56,000 troops and 72 guns.

The assault began early on September 11 with a heavy artillery barrage. This did very little, as the Russians fired at the embankments instead of over them. The attacking units suffered heavily from accurate rifle and artillery fire. The Romanians took the Grivitsa position, but the assault on Redoubt # 10 failed. Once again Osman almost rolled up the Russian left flank with a strong attack across the Lovech road but was stopped by hard fighting. Turkish losses were anywhere from 12,000 to 15,000. The allied army lost 18,000 men, roughly 25 percent of its infantry strength.[17]

After the September 11 battle both sides were reinforced. Osman received 17,000 men, five guns, and rations from Sofia. In October the Russian Imperial Guard and Grenadier Corps finally arrived. After Gurko had cleared the Sofia–Plevna road on October 24, Nikolay decided on a siege. Count Franz Ivanovich Totleben, the hero of Sevastopol in 1856, was brought in to direct it.[18]

After learning of the siege of Plevna, Mehmed Ali, tranferred from the Lom, began planning a relief operation from Sofia. To break this up, Nikolay mounted a preemptive attack, sending Gurko with two divisions of the Guard, one Guard cavalry division, and some Cossacks, about 36,000 men in all, to attack the Turks. On November 15 Gurko surprised Mehmed Ali at Orkhanie, scattering the relief force and capturing the supplies earmarked for Plevna.

With 46,000 men left and lacking supplies, Osman's situation was desperate. Realizing that Plevna was now untenable, Osman decided to attempt a breakout. Launched on December 10, the attempt failed as determined Turkish assaults foundered on the resistance of the Grenadier Corps. The attack collapsed with 6,000 casualties, Osman himself being wounded in the foot.[19] Seeing his situation as hopeless, he surrendered. Plevna had cost the Russians five months and 40,000 casualties. Turkish losses were 30,000 casualties plus the 40,000 men taken prisoner on December 10.

Although Osman and his officers were treated with the utmost courtesy and respect, the lot of the soldiers captured at Plevna was a hard one. The prisoners were marched to Russia overland during the harsh winter. Many died of simple neglect. Of the 40,000 men captured at Plevna, only 12,000 ever saw home again.[20]

The fall of Plevna released 110,000 Russian and 25,000 Romanian troops for mobile operations. In addition, Serbia now put 25,000 men in the field. At this point, however, Nikolay faced a major decision. He could either wait for the spring in Bulgaria or attempt a crossing of the rugged Balkan Range in winter. Totleben advised the more cautious course, but the grand duke, supported by Gurko and Skobelev, decided on the latter (see Map III).[21]

Firmly committed to the winter campaign, he now reorganized his army into several groups, putting each force under one of his better commanders. Gurko, with the Guard and the Ninth Corps (65,000 infantry, 6,000 cavalry, and 280 guns), was to cross the Sofia–Araba–Konah pass and advance on the Sofia–Philippopolis–Edirne axis. Radetzky, with the Eighth and Fourth Corps (56,000 infantry, 2,000 cavalry, and 252 guns), was to break out from Shipka Pass and meet Gurko at Edirne. The tsarevich, with the Twelfth and Thirteenth Corps (54,000 infantry, 6,500 cavalry, and 324 guns), was to guard communications and besiege Ruse, with Totleben directing that effort. The Fourteenth Corps was to continue to observe the line of Trajan's Wall. The Black Sea coast was to be guarded by the Seventh and Tenth Corps. The Grenadier Corps and Eleventh Corps were to be held in reserve. Serbian troops were to assume positions along the Russian line of communication while the Romanians besieged Vidin to gain a political bargaining chip.[22]

After the fall of Plevna, the Turks had 100,000 men in the Quadrilateral fortresses, 30,000 at Shipka, 20,000 at Sofia, and 15,000 at Constantinople. Suleiman Pasha, entrusted with the defense of the Balkans, had two possible approaches to the problem at hand. He could concentrate at Edirne and thus be in a position to attack any Russian force as it debouched from the passes. This would entail risks, but it would give the Turks the advantage of concentration. The other option was to attempt to hold the passes by reinforcing their separate garrisons. This would give the Ottomans strength in any local action, but if the Russians broke through at any point there would be no strategic reserve to plug the gap. Suleiman chose the second option and made dispositions accordingly. Shipka and the Sofia area were reinforced to 40,000 men each. Some 10,000 were at Edirne, and 75,000 were left in the Quadrilateral.

Subsequent events showed Suleiman's forward deployment to have been disastrous. Setting out on December 23, Gurko used the Ninth Corps as a holding force while sending the Guard over the mountains around the Turkish left. This called for the utmost exertions from the troops, who had to struggle through snowdrifts sometimes 10 ft. deep. Nonetheless, the move took the Turks by surprise, and they abandoned the position. Gurko entered Sofia on January 4. Any supply problems that might have arisen were alleviated by captured stocks in Sofia and the timely arrival of a Russian supply train. Turkish losses were about 5,000, including three generals. After allowing his troops several days of rest, Gurko set off for Philippopolis on January 9.

Radetzky attacked Shipka on January 5 with a three-pronged assault. The center column was used as a holding force. The other two columns, led by Prince Mirsky and the indefatigable Skobelev, crossed the mountains and attacked from the left and right respectively. Once again the Russian soldier persevered in his struggle against the elements. Although taking heavy losses, Mirsky and Skobelev joined hands on the 9th, thus sealing off the garrison, which surrendered immediately. Russian losses were about 5,500 men. Although the Turks suffered only 6,000 casualties, the Russians took 30,000 prisoners at Shipka.[23]

Upon hearing of the Sofia disaster, Suleiman drew 20,000 more men from the Quadrilateral and sent them out past Philippopolis, along with other reinforcements. The force numbered somewhere between 40,000 and 45,000

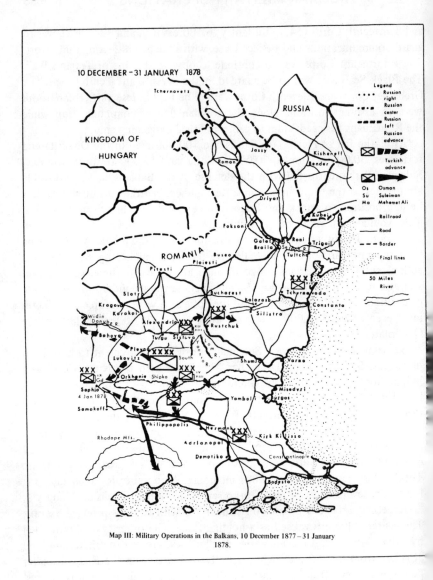

Map III: Military Operations in the Balkans, 10 December 1877 – 31 January 1878.

men in all. Suleiman felt that he could still fight a successful action against Gurko, as the terrain between Sofia and Philippopolis favored the defense. When Radetzky's capture of Shipka made this impossible, Suleiman retreated down the Philippopolis–Edirne road, with 20,000 men under Fuad Pasha conducting a skillful rearguard action.

On January 16, Gurko was able to get behind Suleiman and cut the Philippopolis–Edirne road. The Turks lost 15,000 men, including Fuad and much of the rear guard. The rest of the troops, Suleiman among them, had to retreat over the rugged Rhodope Mountains to the Aegean coast, where they were picked up by the Turkish navy and taken to Constantinople. Suleiman was court-martialed and sentenced to fifteen years in a fortress, although he was eventually pardoned.[24] The disasters at Shipka and Edirne ended effective resistance. Nikolay marched on Constantinople only to stop at its gates because of England's threat to declare war if the Russians entered. From this position, the Russians quickly forced the Treaty of San Stefano on the Turks.

### On the Blue Danube

When the Russians reached the Danube in May 1877, they were faced with a problem that European armies rarely had to deal with — waging riverine warfare.

In order for the Russians to make an uninterrupted crossing, the Danube had to be cleared of any Turkish presence. On the Danube below Brăila the Turks had eight ironclads mounting thirty guns. Between Vidin and Hirşova there were seven ironclads and eighteen wooden ships manned by 1,000 men and mounting sixty guns. All Ottoman naval forces on the Danube were commanded by Augustus Charles Hobart Pasha, a former British naval officer in the Turkish service.[25] The Russian flotilla on the Danube was commanded by a Commander Novikov. The Russian force was something of an improvisation, being composed of about twenty-five steam launches armed with torpedoes.

Novikov realized that the first step for the Russians should be to keep the Turkish forces separated. Thus it was decided to isolate the ironclads at Brăila by laying minefields at Brăila and Reni. These consisted mainly of lines of torpedoes strung across the river. The torpedoes could be detonated either automatically or electrically from the shore. The Turks attempted to counter this move on May 6 by having the ironclads shell Brăila. However, the Russian shore batteries got the better of the duel, sinking an ironclad.

The next major action took place on May 25. The Turks had begun concentrating their ships in small groups. One such group, in the Măcin channel, consisted of two ironclads and one wooden ship. One Lieutenant Fedor Vasilevich Dubasov launched an attack on this force on the night of May 25, using four steam launches carrying torpedoes. Surprising the Turks, Dubasov was able to hit the Turkish ironclad *Seife* with two torpedoes. It went down with all hands in a few minutes. So effective was the Russian surprise that Dubasov was able to withdraw his force without the loss of a single man.[26]

Meanwhile, Novikov continued to hem in the Ottoman forces by the use of mine barrages. This policy was brought to a successful conclusion at the end of June when the last navigable tributary of the Danube was cut. The remaining Turkish ships were confined to Ruse. After this there was no more action on the Danube. Of the remaining Turkish ships, one was sunk after hitting a torpedo. The rest eventually surrendered to Russian ground forces.[27]

## The Other Front

While events at Plevna held Europe's undivided attention, the Russians and the Turks were also waging a campaign in their traditional war zone, the Caucasus. Here this campaign was to depend, as had all the previous campaigns there, on possession of the two fortresses in the area, Kars and Erzerum.

Russian command in the area passed to another of the tsar's relatives, the able Grand Duke Michael. Though he had only 65,000 men, this gave him sufficient numerical superiority to allow him the initiative. For their part, the Turks, under Ghazi Ahmed Moukhtar Pasha, confined their efforts to the prudent policy of holding Kars and Erzerum.

The grand duke's first move was to try to take the more heavily fortified town of Erzerum by a surprise attack. This would allow the Russians to bypass Kars and dominate the Black Sea coast. However, as insufficient forces had been allotted to the operation, it was easily repulsed by the Turkish garrison. The grand duke was able to recoup his fortunes by routing the small Ottoman field army at Aladja Dagh.[28]

Michael, having cleared the Turks from the field, now realized that a more conventional siege operation would be necessary to take Kars. But with autumn coming on, he knew that he had to take Kars soon or his troops would be sitting outside it throughout the harsh winter. Further, it was clear that Kars would not fall quickly to a siege, as Russian intelligence (performing properly for once) informed Michael that the town's 24,500-man garrison had enough supplies for at least six months. With a conventional siege ruled out, Michael decided to take the town by storm in a surprise attack. The attack would be made at two points in the fortifications to ensure maximum concentration. To gain surprise, it would be mounted at night, without the benefit of a preattack artillery barrage.[29]

On November 17, 1877, the assault columns moved forward at 8:30 P. M. by the light of the moon. Quickly overrunning the Turkish pickets, they penetrated the fort. A vicious hand-to-hand fight between the attackers and the garrison ensued, and by morning the town and the garrison were in Russian hands. With the successful storming of Kars the campaign came to an end.

## Conclusions

For the Russians, the war showed that their new military system worked fairly well. The Russian soldier again proved a tough warrior inured to hardship. The standard small-arm, the Berdan rifle, had proved a fine weapon. The artillery, however, normally a strong suit for the Russians, had shown itself to be inferior in both equipment and technique.

In terms of leadership, Russian generalship was mixed. Grand Duke Nikolay had made a good showing.[30] Certainly his decision to mount a winter campaign after Plevna's fall shortened the war. He showed vision in the use of his commanders; for example, Gurko was a cavalry division commander in the Guard, but for the winter campaign he was given the command of two corps. Finally, he showed political astuteness by not taking Constantinople and inviting a general European war. The same cannot be said, however, of the subordinate commanders. With three notable exceptions – Gurko, Skobelev, and Radetzky – the ability of Russian general officers ranged from mediocrity to incompetence.[31] This was best exemplified by the amateurish maneuverings of Krudener and Schilder–Schuldner at Plevna.[32]

For the Turks, the war once again demonstrated the bravery of the Turkish soldier. Although his rifle was not quite as good as the Berdan, the Turkish artillery, equipped with Krupp guns, more than lived up to its reputation, doing especially good service at Plevna.

However, if the Russian commanders can be accused of mediocrity or incompetence, much worse can be said of the Turkish commanders. Undoubtedly the best of the group was Osman Pasha. His dauntless defense of Plevna turned what could have been an easy victory into a hard and costly struggle. Aside from Osman and Fuad's gallant rearguard actions against Gurko, however, Ottoman leadership was for the most part miserable. The command system of the empire guaranteed a lack of coordination between the field forces and was plagued by rivalry and intrigue, especially between Suleiman and Mehmed Ali.[33] In the field, the latter threw away a good chance for victory when he inexplicably withdrew after forcing the tsarevich back across the Yantra in August. After this fiasco he went to Sofia, where he was surprised by Gurko at Orkhanie, thus losing any chance of relieving Osman at Plevna. As for Suleiman, he failed to press his attacks at Shipka in August when the Russians were vulnerable. Later, his deployment of forces to hold the Balkans invited the catastrophe which ultimately befell him. The Ottoman war council was also responsible for several poor decisions, the two most important being not to defend the line of the Danube and to defend Plevna to the last man even after the Russians had begun siege operations.

Militarily the war again demonstrated the fact that defense had become the stronger form of war. The combination of infantry armed with modern weapons and field fortifications supported by artillery had proven almost invulnerable to direct assaults. This was convincingly demonstrated by Osman three times at Plevna. The Russians showed the best way to use cavalry during the war — as mounted infantry. The cavalry used its horses for mobility, but in combat it dismounted. Every trooper had a shortened cavalry version of the Berdan for this purpose. This extended to all cavalry units, from the Cossacks to the Guard Cuirassier Division. Their worth in combat was demonstrated by Skobelev at Plevna and in Gurko's operations in the Balkans.

The Russo—Turkish War of 1877 contained many valuable lessons for the military establishments of Europe. That they were soon forgotten is made more remarkable by the fact that several military officers from various military establishments in Europe wrote studies of the war with a number of shrewd observations. Nicholas Kuropatkin noted the importance of reconnaissance, citing the absence of it as one of the main reasons for Schilder—Schuldner's failure at Plevna.[34] Yet when Kuropatkin himself commanded the Russian army in Manchuria during the Russo—Japanese War, the Russians showed no great improvement in this area over their performance in 1877. The French military writer General H. Langlois wrote as late as 1909 that the war had shown the ineffectiveness of artillery against field fortifications.[35] Yet only five years later the British and French would find themselves hammering at complex field fortifications with artillery and frontal assaults, resulting in predictably disastrous defeats. The mistakes of 1877 were repeated in the Russo—Japanese War of 1904 and again in 1914. Perhaps that was the greatest tragedy of the Russo—Turkish War.

## NOTES

1. For the diplomatic background to the war, see A. J. P. Taylor, *The Struggle for Mastery in Europe 1848–1918* (Oxford, 1954), or B. H. Sumner, *Russia and the Balkans 1870–1880* (Oxford, 1937).

2. For a discussion of this question, see George F. Kennan, *The Decline of Bismarck's European Order* (Princeton, 1979), pp. 27–39.

3. Francis Vinton Greene, *The Russian Army and Its Campaigns in Turkey* (New York, 1879), p. 150.

4. William McElwee, *The Art of War: Waterloo to Mons* (Bloomington, 1974), p. 191.

5. Greene, *The Russian Army*, p. 151.

6. Nikolai Yepanchin, *Operations of General Gurko's Advance Guard in 1877* (London, 1900), p. 4.

7. Frederick Maurice (*The Russo–Turkish War of 1877* [London, 1905], p. 73) is very critical of this deployment on the grounds that it constituted a dispersal of forces on Nikolay's part.

8. Valentine Baker Pasha, *War in Bulgaria*, vol. 1 (London, 1879), pp. 17–18; William Jesser Coope, *A Prisoner of War in Russia* (London, 1878), p. 182.

9. For a detailed account of these operations, see Yepanchin, *Operations of General Gurko's Advance Guard.*

10. William V. Herbert, *The Defence of Plevna* (London, 1895), p. 131.

11. Greene, *The Russian Army*, pp. 189–92.

12. Ibid., p. 200. Herbert (*The Defence of Plevna*, p. 207) puts Turkish losses at only 2,000.

13. For a detailed discussion of the Romanian army, see Radu Rosetti, "Romania's Share in the War of 1877," *Slavonic Review* 8 (1929): 548–77.

14. For a detailed account, see Alexander Vereshchagin, *At Home and in War 1853–1881* (New York, 1888), pp. 304–26.

15. For details, see Austria, Kriegsarchiv, *Der Russisch–Türkische Krieg 1877–78*, vol. 4, pt. 1 (Vienna, 1911), or John Fife–Cookson, *With the Armies of the Balkans* (London, 1880).

16. Baker (*War in Bulgaria*, p. 245) attributes the relief to an intrigue on the part of Suleiman.

17. Greene, *The Russian Army*, p. 256. Austria, Kriegsarchiv, *Der Russisch–Türkische Krieg*, vol. 5, p. 230, citing Herbert, *The Defence of Plevna*, p. 270, gives Turkish losses as only 5,000 and Russian losses as 20,000. I accept Greene's figures as being more accurate, since if Herbert were correct, Osman, now with numerical parity, could easily have launched an attack on the thinly stretched allies that would have collapsed their position.

18. Rosetti, "Romania's Share," p. 564. Prince Carol was nominally in command.

19. Herbert (*The Defence of Plevna*, pp. 398–99) believed that the breakout would have succeeded had not Osman been wounded in the first attack.

20. Ibid., p. 412. Also see Coope, *A Prisoner of War*, for details on the experiences of a Russian prisoner.

21. Greene, *The Russian Army*, pp. 323–24.

22. Rosetti, "Romania's Share," p. 567.

23. Maurice, *The Russo–Turkish War*, p. 293. L. P. Brockett (*The Conquest of Turkey* [Philadelphia, 1878], p. 663) gives total Turkish losses as 25,000.

24. Herbert, *The Defence of Plevna*, p. 449.

25. It should be noted that the Turkish armed forces had long been employing English and German officers in high command positions.

26. Greene, *The Russian Army*, p. 153.

27. For an account of naval operations in the Black Sea, see Otto Eichelmann, "Der Russische Kriegsbrauch im letzten Krieg mit der Türkei 1877–78," in *Russisch Revue* (St. Petersburg, 1880), pp. 268–69.

28. For details, see Brockett, *The Conquest of Turkey*, pp. 601–8. He gives losses as 1,600 for the Russians and 12,000 for the Turks.

29. McElwee, *The Art of War*, p. 206.

30. This opinion is not universally shared. See Bruce Lincoln, *The Romanovs* (New York, 1976), p. 587.

31. For detailed personal portraits of Nikolay, Gurko, Skobelev, and Radetzky, see Francis Vinton Greene, *Sketches of Army Life in Russia* (New York, 1880), pp. 126–52.

32. The quality of the officer corps did not improve after the war. See John Bushnell, "The Tsarist Officer Corps 1881–1914," *American Historical Review* 86 (1981): 753–81.

33. This may have been due to the fact that while Suleiman was a native Turk, Mehmed Ali was in fact a German whose original name was Karl Detroit.

34. Nicholas Kuropatkin, *Kritische Rückblicke auf den Russisch–Türkischen Krieg 1877–78*, vol. 1 (Berlin, 1889), p. 3.

35. H. Langlois, *Lessons from Two Recent Wars* (London, 1909), pp. 35–36.

# Albania

Strašimir Dimitrov

# THE ALBANIAN NATIONAL MOVEMENT, 1875–78

The years of the Eastern crisis, 1875–78, mark one of the peaks in the development of the Albanian national movement. All of the Balkan nations were involved in the crisis, which, by posing the problem of their present and future, activated all social strata to take a stand on the most important questions of their political and social development.

The political and social situation in Albania during the nineteenth century was certainly extremely complex. For a number of reasons, the Albanians set out on the road of bourgeois-national revival later than the other Balkan nations. Albania was practically the only Balkan country that saw the formation of a feudal class during the years of Ottoman rule. Powerful local rulers, large landlords who to a considerable extent became part of the Ottoman ruling class, arose among the Muslim Albanians. The defeat of Ali Pasha Tepelenë, the Bushatis family in Shkodër, and other local semi-independent feudal landlords did not do away with large landowning aristocrats but only changed their ranks. Families such as the Vrioni, the Toptani, the Vlorë, and the Verlaqi owned tens of thousands of hectares, and the populations of numerous villages were dependent on them. Members of these families held high posts in the Ottoman administration. Men like Suleiman Pasha Toptani, Mustafa Pasha Gjirtli, Abdin Pasha Dino, Ferid Pasha, and others belonged to the Ottoman elite, held ministerial posts, and even served as grand viziers.[1]

In the mountains, feudal landowning coexisted with strong patriarchal traditions. The *fis* (tribe), the *vlaznia* (a large clan), and the neighborhood community persisted there, traditionally enjoying a certain internal autonomy and being ruled by elders, *bayraktars* (standard-bearers), or *voivodes* (chieftains). Even these forms, however, were badly undermined during the nineteenth century by the growth of class inequality as the elders assumed the role of a tribal-clan aristocracy. In some clans and tribal groups, for instance, in the Mirditë clan, the title of chieftain passed from father to son.[2] The tribal-clan character of Albanian society blocked the processes of national consolidation.

Feudal forces maintained a strong grip on the economic and social life of the country. The feudal landlords to a considerable extent inherited the loose autonomy that Ali Pasha Tepelenë and the Bushatis family had once enjoyed. The reforms carried out by the Ottoman authorities during the nineteenth century, aimed at strengthening central authority in the empire, included introducing universal taxation, forcing Muslim Albanians to serve in the administration, and curtailing the semiautonomy of the Ottoman feudal landlords. This of course went against the interests of the peasantry, the town dwellers, and some of the feudal landlords, as well as against those of the ruling clan and tribal elite, and it was the main reason for the appearance of uprisings, rebellions, and general unrest in Albania. The rebellions of the peasantry under the leadership of feudal landowners or clan *bayraktars* not only shook the foundations of Ottoman authority in Albania but also kept the peasantry under the influence of feudal elements and the clan aristocracy.[3] The majority of the artisans in the towns and villages, who increasingly felt the oppression of the bureaucratic Ottoman state, also followed the landlords.

In spite of these difficult conditions, capitalism began to make headway in the country. The populations of cities grew, thus increasing the size of the bourgeoisie. Toward the middle of the nineteenth century Shkodër had 35,000–45,000 inhabitants and contained several thousand workshops and the headquarters of numerous merchant enterprises. During the same period Elbasan and Tiranë already had 20,000 inhabitants. Wealthy merchants with businesses in Constantinople, in Bucharest, and in Italy rose to prominence. The customs policy of the Sublime Porte had a negative effect on the development of local handicrafts. The lack of protectionist duties resulted in hundreds of artisans' being ruined. Many Albanians were forced to emigrate in search of a livelihood to the large towns of the Ottoman Empire or to neighboring countries. Considerable Albanian colonies were established in Constantinople, Bucharest, Cairo, and elsewhere. The consolidation of the economic power of the bourgeoisie and the petty bourgeoisie created the foundation for the growth of the Albanian national movement.[4]

The picture of Albanian society would be incomplete if we were to overlook its cultural and religious fragmentation. During the centuries of Ottoman rule, approximately half of the Albanian population had been converted to Islam. It was converted Albanian landowners considered trustworthy by the Ottoman authorities and the Islamic clergy who rose to high official positions in the empire. A Christian Orthodox population, placed under the Greek Patriarchate after 1767, predominated in southern Albania and Epirus. Wealthy merchants seeking suitable trading conditions beyond the confines of the empire came from the Orthodox community. Roman Catholicism had a solid footing in northern Albania. Each of these religions considered itself the only true religion, had no respect for communities of other denominations, and was actively involved in proselytizing. Each preached admiration for a non-Albanian culture and was the source of penetration of alien cultural and political ideas, at least as far as the top clergy were concerned. The Patriarchate in Constantinople had gradually become a tool of Panhellenic interests. Toward the middle of the nineteenth century Panhellenic writers, assisted by proselytes among the Albanians, were attempting to spread the view that the Albanians were of Hellenic stock, descendants of the ancient Pelasgians, and therefore should aim at joining the Greeks.[5] The Patriarchate and its representatives rejected the teaching of Albanian and its use in the church and promoted the spread of Greek culture and language. On the other hand, the Roman Catholic missionary schools rarely allowed the teaching of Albanian and spread Italian culture and language. Roman Catholicism became a channel for the promotion of Austrian and Italian political and cultural interests.

These conditions explain the delay in the formation of an Albanian national-bourgeois consciousness and hence the lag in the development of a national liberation movement. Even the merchants in the Albanian colonies supported the respective church administrations and made donations to Orthodox or Roman Catholic schools. Nevertheless, it was from these merchant-artisan emigrant communities, who were in close contact with the budding national-bourgeois movements of the other Balkan nations, that the first Albanian leaders advocating cultural and national emancipation emerged. Naum Veqilharxhi created an Albanian alphabet in Bucharest in 1844–47. In his primer *Evetor* he called on "all wealthy and educated Orthodox Albanians" to join the movement for the promotion of their national cultural identity. He castigated those émigrés who had begun "to take pleasure in calling themselves Greeks, Wallachians, and Hellenes" instead of helping in the revival of their people, publishing Albanian textbooks and books, and working toward the establishment of a unified Albanian literary language as a means of saving the Albanians from assimilation.[6]

In the sixties and seventies of the nineteenth century, various strata of Albanian society gradually worked out programs for the resolution of the Albanian question and for the future of Albania. The national-bourgeois movement, which stemmed from the ideas of Naum Veqilharxhi, argued that the Albanians were a nation – that they constituted a single linguistic, territorial, and historical community regardless of their different religions. This view logically led to the demand for national independence. According to its advocates, change in the consciousness and activity of the Albanians was to set in gradually, and Albania would inevitably achieve liberation and become an advanced and educated nation. Among the principal tasks confronting the Albanian national movement were the creation of a common Albanian alphabet, the development of an Albanian literature, and the establishment and consolidation of a common national language. Overcoming the religious fragmentation of the Albanians would mean a gradual shift from a religious consciousness to an essentially new secular national-bourgeois consciousness. This would deprive the feudal-clerical circles of their leading role in the spiritual and political life of the Albanian people, and the leadership of the nation would pass into the hands of the young national bourgeoisie.

The Albanian national movement was formulating its program at a time when the bourgeoisies of the neighboring Balkan countries had consolidated their positions and were openly voicing their intention to take as much territory as they could from the Ottoman Empire and add it to their national territories. A number of Albanian regions were among the disputed territories. Greece claimed southern Albania, and Serbia sought to annex the Kosovo region and northern Albania. The Megali Idea and the dreams of recreating "the Kingdom of Dušan" presented the Albanian leaders with the task not only of finding ways of liberating the Albanians from Ottoman rule but also of preserving their ethnic territory both from the encroachments of the young Balkan bourgeoisie and from the imperialist designs of Austria—Hungary and later Italy. Many Albanian leaders believed that the Albanians would find it difficult to defend their national territory on their own. They saw a possible way out of the situation in administrative and territorial autonomy for Albania within the Ottoman Empire. Within the boundaries protected by the Ottoman army and guaranteed by the Treaty of Paris, they argued, the integrity of the Albanian national territory could be ensured.[7] Since a number of Albanian feudal landowners held high office in the Ottoman administration, it seemed possible for Albania to be ruled by Albanians within the Ottoman Empire. This idea was attractive to the feudal elements connected with the Sublime Porte and to bourgeois landowners as well as to feudal landowners opposed to Ottoman rule and to the young Albanian bourgeoisie.[8]

The autonomist program was not the only program of the Albanian national movement. Eminent émigrés, chiefly from the colonies in Italy, championed the complete separation of Albania from the Ottoman state as soon as possible to open the way for social progress. At the same time, certain Italian Albanians, in cooperation with circles close to the Constantinople Patriarchate, believed that the territorial integrity of Albania could be guaranteed within the framework of a Greco—Albanian dual monarchy. Faced with evidence of Greek aspirations to the possession of Albanian territories, the proponents of this program eventually joined the autonomists.[9] Konstantin Kristoforidhi, Hasan Tahsini, Vasa Pashko, and other representatives of different religious communities undertook a number of attempts to compile a unified Albanian alphabet and establish a Pan-Albanian cultural and educational organization,[10] but they were unable to overcome the resistance of the Ottoman authorities and the Patriarchate. And after the proclamation by Midhat Pasha of the Ottoman constitution of 1876, not even the most ardent believer in Pan-Ottoman constitutionalism hesitated to declare that he was disinclined to allow the Albanian Muslims to establish separate schools.[11] The Albanian national movement was, however, gradually gaining strength, and this became clear during the Eastern crisis.

Unrest broke out in various parts of Albania during the seventies. It began in Shkodër and its vicinity in 1871, provoked by attempts of the authorities to recruit soldiers and impose new taxes in the region. Only a powerful military expedition led by Mehmed Ali Pasha succeeded in crushing the uprising and partially disarming the insurgents.[12] The following year saw a series of campaigns against the Mirditë clan, under its chieftain Preng Bib Doda, which had resisted the attempt of the Ottoman authorities to turn its territory into an ordinary caza administered by a kaimakam appointed by the central government. The Ducagini clan joined this rebellion in 1874 when the Ottoman authorities tried to establish military posts in its territory. When the uprising in Bosnia and Hercegovina broke out, the Ottoman authorities tried to recruit Albanians for action against the insurgents. Not only did no volunteers appear, however, but the government was unable to rally its redif (reservists). The Albanians refused to serve in the army, held back their taxes, hid requisitioned cattle in the forest, and raided Ottoman military posts.[13]

The Albanian national movement increasingly attracted the attention of revolutionary forces in the Balkans, including the Bulgarian national liberation movement. Stoyan Vezenkov and Spiro Djerov had established ties with Albanian leaders as far back as the sixties in planning an uprising in the Kruševo region.[14] During the seventies Bulgarian revolutionaries maintained ties with Albanian leaders through Isaya Mažovsky. In 1874 the latter began negotiations with Gani Bey Toptani of Tiranë and Ali Bey Toska and Sherif Bey of Janina, all of whom were working for the liberation of Albania and the setting up of an independent Albanian state.[15] In 1873 several chieftains of the Mirditë clan went to Cetinje for negotiations with Prince Nicholas.[16] The Ottoman defeats in the fighting with the Montenegrins in 1876 served as a pretext for Preng Bib Doda to begin preparations for a large-scale uprising in northern Albania. Doda sought an alliance with Montenegro provided Prince Nicholas recognized Albanian independence and made no claim on territories inhabited by Albanians. The movement of the insurgents was closely followed and supported in Italy by the League for the Liberation and Fraternization of the People of the Slavic–Greek Peninsula and the Italian–Albanian Committee for the Liberation of the Eastern Albanians, both of which sought to consolidate their influence in Albania.[17]

The decisive phase of the Eastern crisis during the summer and autumn of 1876 posed extremely complex problems for the Albanian national movement. The Constantinople Conference of the ambassadors of the Great Powers gave the question of the improvement of the political and social condition of the subject peoples of the Ottoman Empire great urgency. The likelihood of the breakup of Ottoman rule in the Balkans was increasingly clear. However, the conference gave little attention to the Albanian question, which had not yet become an international issue. It proposed the formation of two autonomous Bulgarian regions, and Korçë and neighboring regions with an Albanian or a mixed Bulgarian–Albanian population were to be included in Western Bulgaria. The claims of Greece to Epirus and of Serbia and Montenegro to Kosovo and other regions inhabited by Albanians were advanced with greater force. Austria–Hungary and Italy clearly expressed their pretentions to hegemony in Albania. The danger of the partitioning of ethnically Albanian territories became very real, while the Ottoman government stubbornly refused to grant the Albanians the right of education in Albanian or to recognize their existence as a nation.

The situation called for action. A group of feudal and wealthy bourgeois landowners from southern Albania met in Janina in 1877 under the leadership of Abdul Frasheri, who had just been elected deputy to the newly established Ottoman parliament. In March 1877, they adopted the so-called Janina Memorandum, which accurately expressed the views of the autonomists at the time. The memorandum proposed the unification of Albanians in an Albanian administrative region including what were then the Shkodër, Kosovo, Bitola, and Janina vilayets. The administration of the newly established vilayet was to be entrusted to an Albanian or an Albanian-speaking Turk. Army recruits were to serve only within the vilayet, and the majority of the revenue from taxation was to be used to meet local needs such as education and public works in the vilayet itself.[18]

The Sublime Porte did not even consider these demands, but the memorandum became an important step toward the working out of a common Albanian program. The establishment of such a vilayet represented the highest hopes of the Albanian bourgeoisie and the feudal elements. Aiming at the preservation of the integrity of areas inhabited by Albanians and opposing the chauvinism of their neighbors' bourgeoisies, the program raised chauvinistic claims in its turn. The four vilayets to be included in the new vilayet contained large areas inhabited by Bulgarians, Greeks, or Serbians and lacking any sizable Albanian population. The demand for the inclusion of these regions in the semiautonomous Albanian vilayet was obviously excessive in its territorial pretentions. The memorandum was presented to the Porte. The Albanian question was presented as an internal matter of Albanian–Ottoman relations.[19] The proposed solution in no way threatened the status quo in the Balkans and did not draw the Albanian problem into the international arena.

The Russo–Turkish War that broke out in April 1877 brought major changes in the situation in the Balkans. True, the stopping of the Russian army north of the Balkan Range, the stabilization of the front at Shipka Pass, the prolonged siege at Plevna, and the deadlock in military action in the Silistra–Ruse–Shumen–Varna Quadrilateral created the impression that the war might never cause serious territorial changes in the Balkans. However, after the fall of Plevna and the rapid advance of the Russian army during the winter of 1877–78 these illusions vanished. Montenegro and Serbia resumed military operations, and the Mirditë insurrection began anew. In January 1878, the Mirditë rebels forced the Ottoman garrison to capitulate, thus overthrowing every form of Ottoman control over their territory. Soon, however, Montenegrin troops entered territories inhabited by Albanians; Prince Nicholas's intention to extend his border to the Drin River was no secret. Serbia began an offensive in Kosovo that was accompanied by a dispersal of the Albanian population. The breaking up of the ethnically Albanian territory had begun.[20] Under the changed conditions, Doda expressed readiness to bring the uprising to an end and begin negotiations with the Sublime Porte.

The crisis accelerated work on the establishment of Albanian organizations for the protection and liberation of the Albanian people. Late in the autumn of 1877 Albanians of various denominations and professions – officials, merchants, intellectuals, interned landowners – living in Constantinople founded a Central Committee for the Protection of the National Rights of the Albanians. It was clear to Abdul Frasheri, his brother Sami Frasheri, Ziya Prishtina, and Vasa Pashko, its founders, that since the Sublime Porte was in no position to protect the Albanian territories the Albanians themselves would have to organize their forces to win autonomy and find allies.

Fearing Russian support for the territorial pretentions of its Slavic allies and under the influence of the so-called Slavic threat, the committee began negotiations with representatives of Greece. The Albanians sought Greek recognition of the territorial integrity of Albania, with the River Kalamas as the border between the two, in exchange for their acceptance of one of the princes of the ruling dynasty in Greece as head of state. However, in 1878 a Greek detachment landed in southern Albania, demonstrating that the Greek bourgeoisie had not given up its intention of occupying as much Albanian territory as possible, and the Albanian national movement had to give up its illusions about the ruling circles in Greece.[21]

The upsurge of the Albanian liberation movement did not go unnoticed by Russian diplomacy. Toward the end of 1877 the former long-standing Russian consul at Bitola, M. A. Hitrovo, then head of the diplomatic chancery of the Russian Danubian army, wrote that "inevitably some kind of independent Albania must be created in the western half of the Balkan Peninsula."[22] This view, however, remained an isolated one. The Treaty of San Stefano envisaged only partial autonomy, comparable to the autonomy enjoyed by Crete since 1868, for Albania. It recognized the independence of the Bulgarian people approximately within their ethnic boundaries, leaving hundreds of thousands of Bulgarians in Thrace under Ottoman rule and at the same time including in Bulgaria regions inhabited by Albanians, for example, the Korçë region. The sanjak of Priština was ceded to Serbia, while some parts of northern Albania were given to Montenegro.[23]

Ceding regions with an Albanian or mixed Albanian–Slavic population to Balkan states provoked a sharp reaction from the Albanians, especially the Constantinople committee. The Sublime Porte and Austria–Hungary used this reaction to turn the Albanian movement into an anti-Russian and anti-Slavic movement and curb its anti-Ottoman character. These attitudes were reinforced by the talks aimed at a revision of the San Stefano Treaty. It cannot be denied that the Ottomans' interest in preserving as much territory in the Balkans as possible and the desire of the Constantinople committee to preserve ethnically Albanian lands led both sides to favor revision of the treaty. Therefore the Porte not only tolerated the committee but assisted it, despite the latter's insistence on administrative autonomy for the Albanian lands. The Porte allowed the Albanians to arm, supplied them with arms, and helped them establish "committees for self-defense." It insisted in its notes to the Great Powers that the Albanian Muslims were Turks and maintained that they opposed any separation from the Ottoman Empire and from the rule of the sultan.[24]

The Central Committee in Constantinople established increasingly closer ties with the committees for self-defense and, with the assistance of the authorities, prepared for the creation of a center for the Albanian movement in Albania itself. Toward the end of May 1878, it was decided to hold a congress in Prizren at which representatives from all the Albanian regions could work out a common political platform. On May 30 the committee issued a proclamation outlining its own program: "We wish to live in peace with our neighbors Montenegro, Greece, Serbia, and Bulgaria. We have no claims against them. However, we are determined to defend all that is ours. Therefore, let the Albanian lands be left to the Albanians!"[25]

In the meantime, the Russian government had appointed Hitrovo civil commissar in Western Bulgaria, with the task of organizing the lands that fell within Bulgaria as the San Stefano Treaty defined it. He won over a circle of Bulgarians and representatives of other nationalities living in these regions, including the Albanian Yusuf Ali Bey.[26] Apparently the anti-Slavic attitudes spread by the Sublime Porte and by the Panhellenic circles had not been adopted by all Albanians. However, there was clearly a separation of the Albanian movement from the mainstream of anti-Ottoman movements.

The Prizren congress opened on June 10, 1878. The Ottoman authorities, assisted by the Albanian feudal elements in Kosovo, had succeeded in getting a number of local feudal landlords, Ottoman officials, and Muslims from Bosnia, Hercegovina, and Bulgaria to attend, and these tended to give the congress a pro-Ottoman character. At the opening of the congress Abdul Frasheri called for the creation of a unified Albanian organization, which, like that of  Skanderbeg (George Kastrioti), would be called the Albanian League. The first decisions of this new Albanian League, however, were far from the national Albanian demands and directly served the interests of the Porte.

The League undertook the creation of an armed force to defend the integrity of the Ottoman Empire. Representatives of any Islamic region (and here the participants had in mind chiefly Bosnia and Hercegovina) could join the League. It declared that it would recognize no authority other than the sultan's.[27] Since the most advanced regions of Albania – southern Albania and the Shkodër region – were poorly represented at the congress, these decisions reflected the views of the predominating pro-Ottoman and Islamic feudal elements. The people of Shkodër refused to recognize them or to join the League unless the sultan's name were omitted. After the arrival of delegates from all regions, the work of the congress took a course closer to the national interests of the Albanians. The League became a centralized organization with a branch in every town. Local committees were obliged to recruit and maintain a certain number of armed men. Its Central Council of Elders had three commissions: Finance, Internal Affairs, and Foreign Affairs, the latter headed by Abdul Frasheri. Generally speaking, the leadership of the League was in the hands of the large landowners and Ottoman officials. Ilias Dibra, whom the Ottoman authorities hoped to use as a tool against territorial claims on the Ottoman Empire, was elected chairman.

The revision of the San Stefano Treaty by the Berlin Congress was carried out in a reactionary spirit. It retained Ottoman domination over most of the Balkan territories of the empire. It gave the Plav and Gusinje regions to Montenegro, while territorial expansion was envisaged for Greece in Epirus and Thessaly. The grounds for conflict of the League with Bulgaria and Serbia no longer existed. Nevertheless, its armed forces were still necessary to the Sublime Porte to block Greek claims to Epirus, the ceding of the Plav and Gusinje regions to Montenegro, and in particular the forthcoming occupation of Bosnia and Hercegovina by Austria–Hungary. The Albanian national leadership would not permit the use of the League's forces in Bosnia, but in spite of this the Porte was in no hurry to break off relations with it.[28]

The Ottoman government refused to cede any territories to Greece, but because it could not completely ignore the decisions of the Berlin Congress it took steps to evacuate the regions given to Montenegro. The League leaders protested, as these were regions inhabited chiefly by Albanians. The Porte sent Mehmed Ali Pasha, "the butcher of Shkodër," to Prizren in August to ensure the transfer of Plav and Gusinje to Montenegro, but Ali Pasha Gusini and others refused to carry out Mehmed Ali Pasha's orders. When the latter attempted to impose his will by force, he was surrounded at Đacovica on September 3, 1878, and killed after a three-day siege.

Essentially this amounted to an open challenge to the Sublime Porte. Some of the functionaries close to the Porte died along with Mehmed Ali Pasha, and thus the prerequisites for overcoming pro-Ottoman illusions were created. The role of national elements in the League grew. This was the background of the extended session of the leadership of the League, which met jointly with representatives of local committees to revise its program. As far back as September the Constantinople committee had begun a campaign for the adoption of a new program closer to national interests of the Albanians, and Sami Frasheri had published a draft of the new program in *Tercuman-i-sark*.

A new program for the League was adopted in Prizren on November 27, 1878, essentially expanding the demands of the Janina Memorandum: (1) All Albanian regions were to be unified in a single Albanian vilayet. (2) A vilayet general assembly, to hold four sessions annually, was to be elected as its supreme authority. (3) The administration of the vilayet was to consist of persons who knew Albanian. (4) Teaching in schools was to be in Albanian. (5) Most of the income from taxation in the vilayet was to be used within the vilayet itself for its benefit.[29]

The new program won the general approval of the Albanians. The local communities were instructed to collect signatures so that this petition could be presented to the Sublime Porte as unanimous. The call for administrative autonomy became the dominant theme in the Albanian national movement, and the League became the organization that sought to implement it. This was a major success of the Albanian liberation movement, a decisive step toward its emancipation from foreign influence.

At the same time, Yusuf Ali Bey and others were advocating an independent Albanian state and complete separation from the Ottoman Empire. Yusuf Ali Bey had long-time friends among the Bulgarian revolutionaries, and during the war he maintained ties with Hitrovo. Although he took part in the formation of the League, its pro-Ottoman orientation did not satisfy him. Early in the autumn of 1878, he approached the Russian commander in chief General E. I. Totleben in Edirne, saying that he had been sent by a "group of unanimous compatriots" who wished "recognition for their independence and their right to establish an independent duchy."[30] Totleben assured him that Russia would favor the establishment of an independent Albanian principality that would live in peace with its Slavic neighbors.

In 1878 Yusuf Ali Bey wrote the pamphlet *Current Conversations Worthy of Notice*, which was translated into Bulgarian by Stoyan Dzhansŭzov and published in Sofia in 1879.[31] In the form of a dialogue with the well-known revolutionary Stoyan Vesenkov, the author discusses the future of Albania and the solution to the Albanian problem. He notes that since the corrupt Ottoman administration could not provide decent living conditions and social progress to the peoples in the Ottoman Empire, the real interests of Albanians required their separation from the Sublime Porte and the creation of an independent Albanian principality. "The oppression in Rumelia will not reach the point of preventing the establishment of Albania as an independent state," wrote the author. "Russia, Italy, Prussia, and the other states have understood this and will support independence."[32]

Yusuf Ali Bey called on "all men known as Albanians, Muslims and Christians alike, and their children" to be ready for sacrifice in the name of Albania. The territorial integrity of Albania could be ensured only through the formation of an independent Albanian state. "If we do not break away from Turkey and win independence soon," he wrote, "on the one hand the Slavic principalities and on the other the Hellenic peoples will assimilate us."[33] His pamphlet contains the thought later formulated better by Sami Frasheri: "The Ottoman Empire is a corpse, and anyone who does not wish to be buried with it should get out of it in time."

The course toward complete political independence pointed out by Yusuf Ali Bey certainly corresponded to the fundamental interests of the Albanian people. However, as long as the League was engaged in an armed struggle with Montenegro and Greece, it could not break with the Porte, especially since it had international support. Therefore European diplomacy in the 1878–79 period still saw the League as a tool in the hands of the Porte.

Toward the end of 1879 a seven-member delegation presented the Porte with the League's new program. It was in no hurry to answer. It did not wish to meet the Albanian demands, but a rebuff would undermine the pro-Ottoman elements in the League. In the meantime, the mass of Albanians undertook the practical rejection of Ottoman rule on the spot. Officials, in particular tax collectors, were driven out, and local authorities were replaced by representatives of the League. The Ottoman courts of law found themselves cut off from the life of the country. Nevertheless, the Porte could not afford to enter into conflict with the League, since it still needed its armed forces to counteract the decisions of the Berlin Congress on the cession of territories to Montenegro and Greece.

The military action that followed against Montenegro and Greece frustrated the decision of the Berlin Congress as to the transfer of Plav and Gusinje to Montenegro and northern Epirus to Greece. Military successes enhanced the prestige of the League and strengthened the position of the autonomists, who believed that the League could rule the Albanian lands.[34] In order to deceive the Albanians, the Porte appointed Albanians governors of the Berat and Gjirokastër sanjaks and placed several Albanians in posts in the central government. The officials won over to the Ottoman party expressed their readiness to support the Porte and even gave up the demand for autonomy.

The further development of the Albanian national movement saw a further divergence of views. The autonomists became increasingly convinced that the Porte had no intention of granting autonomy to Albania. Hence they stepped up their struggle for autonomy, not hesitating to resort to armed resistance. The pro-Ottoman elements withdrew from the struggle, satisfied with the demands for administrative reform recommended by the Berlin Congress for all the Ottoman provinces. The two wings even came to armed clashes. When the territorial questions with Montenegro and Greece were settled, the Porte undertook an offensive against the armed forces of the League's autonomist elements. A large Ottoman force succeeded in destroying the League in 1881 and restoring Ottoman authority over the Albanians.

The Eastern crisis of 1875—79 served as a powerful catalyst to the maturation of the Albanian national movement. Foremost among the movement's political programs was the demand for administrative autonomy. Advocates of autonomy gradually rose to prominence in the movement and made the Albanian League their instrument. A movement supporting the integrity of the Ottoman Empire and limiting its demands to administrative reform also appeared. A demand for Albanian independence and for a complete break with the Ottoman Empire, albeit weak, was also voiced. Thus by 1878 the foundations had been laid for the political programs that vied for priority in the struggle for liberation up to the creation of an independent Albanian state in 1912.

## NOTES

    1. Str. Dimitrov, "Albanskata liga i Iztochnata kriza," *Istoricheski pregled*, 1978, no. 4, pp. 28–29.

2. Iu. A. Ivanova, *Severaia Albaniia v XIX – nachale XX veka: Obshchestvennaia zhizn* (Moscow, 1975), pp. 197 ff.

3. K. Frasheri, *Istoriia Albanii* (Tiranë, 1964), pp. 108–9.

4. St. Pollo and A. Puto, *Histoire de l'Albanie des origines à nos jours* (Roanne, 1974), pp. 125–26.

5. A. Buda, "Données sur le mouvement national albanais en 1859–1861," *Studime historike*, 1965, no. 2, pp. 67–68.

6. P. Pepo and St. Maslev, "Stranitsi iz istoriiata na bŭlgaro–albanskite druzheski otnosheniia prez XIX v," *Istoricheski pregled*, 1960, no. 2, pp. 125–26.

7. A. Buda, "Albanien und die Balkankriese der Jahre 1878–1881," *Actes der Iᵉʳ Congrès Internationale des Études balkaniques et Sud-est Europeénnes*, vol. 4 (Sofia, 1969), pp. 123–24.

8. Ibid., p. 124.

9. Ibid., p. 124–25.

10. *Historia e Shkiperise*, vol. 2 (Tiranë, 1965), pp. 95–97.

11. Pollo and Puto, *Histoire de l'Albanie*, p. 135.

12. I. G. Senkevich, *Albaniia v godi Vostochnogo krizisa (1875–1881)* (Moscow, 1965), p. 59 ff.

13. Ibid., pp. 69–73.

14. D. Doinov, *Natsionalno-revoliutsionnata borba v Iogozapadna Bŭlgariia prez 60-te i 70-te godini na XIX vek* (Sofia, 1976), pp. 67 and 73.

15. *Vŭzpominaniia na Isaiia Radev Mazhovski* (Sofia, 1922), p. 12.

16. Senkevich, *Albaniia v godi Vostochnogo krizisa*, p. 62.

17. Ibid., p. 72 et passim; Buda, *Albanien und die Balkankriese*, p. 126.

18. Pollo and Puto, *Histoire de l'Albanie*, p. 137.

19. Buda, *Albanien und die Balkankriese*, p. 127.

20. Pollo and Puto, *Histoire de l'Albanie*, p. 137.

21. Buda, *Albanien und die Balkankriese*, pp. 126–27.

22. G. L. Arsh, I. G. Senkevich, and N. D. Smirnova, *Kratkaia istoriia Albanii* (Moscow, 1965), p. 99.

23. G. P. Genov, *Mezhdunarodni aktove i dogovori zasiagashti Bŭlgariia* (Sofia, 1940), pp. 255–63.

24. K. Frasheri, *Istoriia Albanii*, p. 118.

25. Buda, *Albanien und die Balkankriese*, p. 127.

26. Doinov, *Natsionalno-revoliutsionnata borba*, pp. 180–81.

27. Senkevich, *Albaniia v godi Vostochnogo krizisa*, pp. 104–5.

28. Ibid., pp. 109–10.

29. Pollo and Puto, *Histoire de l'Albanie*, p. 147; Senkevich, *Albaniia v godi Vostochnogo krizisa*, p. 114.

30. Secret report from General E. Totleben to the Russian representative in Constantinople Lobanov–Rostovski concerning his conversation with Yusuf Ali Bey (Senkevich, *Albaniia v godi Vostochnogo krizisa*, pp. 198 ff.).

31. Only one copy of this book is known. It is in the library of the Bulgarian Academy of Sciences. For this reason it has not been the object of thorough research.

32. Ali Bey Yusuf, *Tekushti razgovori dostoini za vnimanie* Stoian P. Dzhansŭzov trans. (Sofia, 1879), p. 42.

33. Ibid., p. 16.

34. Stavro Skendi, *The Albanian National Awakening, 1878–1912* (Princeton, 1967), p. 97 et passim.

Bulgaria

Vesselin Traikov

# BULGARIAN VOLUNTEERS IN THE SERBO—TURKISH WAR OF 1876

The uprising in Bosnia and Hercegovina in 1875 persuaded the neighboring peoples that only a common struggle could defeat the Sublime Porte. However, since the policies of the Balkan states of the time were associated with the conflicting interests of their bourgeoisies, they reflected many different approaches to the common struggle against the feudal power of the sultan. Together with the influence of the Great Powers, these conflicts of interest were an obstacle to the creation of an all-Balkan revolutionary movement. This was clearly manifested during the uprising in Bosnia and Hercegovina; when Serbia and Montenegro failed to take an active part, the struggle there gradually abated. Similarly, during the April Uprising, the entire force of the Ottoman response fell on the insurgent Bulgarians, and their struggle was drowned in blood. The Russian ambassador in Constantinople, N. P. Ignatyev, had this in mind when he dispatched a message to Tsar Alexander, dated May 19, 1876, which said in part: "All the efforts of the Turks are directed against Bulgaria, which appears to be the empire's basic granary, because the uprising is a blow to the very heart of Ottoman rule in Europe. Troops from all sides are concentrating there en masse."[1] Serbia did not interfere, just as it had not helped its countrymen in Bosnia and Hercegovina in 1875.

The Serbian leaders recognized the necessity of joint action very well, but state policy vacillated, and this had a decisive influence on the events leading to the Serbo—Turkish War in the summer of 1876. Serbia's foreign policy sought to be flexible and to organize the masses for the inevitable military conflict. While its efforts to attract Greece and Romania failed, it did succeed in making contact with the Bulgarian revolutionaries and reaching an agreement, the first of its kind, for coordinated action in the forthcoming war. It undertook to arm four detachments of 1,000 men each that would invade western Bulgaria and touch off an uprising simultaneously with the beginning of the war against Turkey. The exact date for the beginning of military actions was to be decided after additional conversations with the Bulgarian revolutionaries in Bucharest.[2] The premature outbreak of the April Uprising hampered these plans.

Serbia was neither economically nor militarily ready for decisive action in the spring of 1876. Increasing tensions were, however, impelling the country toward war. On June 17, 1876, Serbia signed a treaty with Montenegro, and shortly thereafter troops were mobilized. It had been decided as early as May that Serbia's main military efforts should be directed toward the Morava Valley and the southeast. Mobilization was completed on June 24, 1876, a total of about 120,000 men having been placed on a war footing.[3] On June 27, Prince Milan informed Tsar Alexander II that he was going to declare war and was counting on the massive support of Russia. At last, on June 30, Serbia formally declared war from Deligrad. Two days later, Prince Nicholas of Montenegro also declared war, and military actions began.

The Serbo–Turkish War was waged in an unfavorable international setting. The Great Powers opposed any violation of peace in the Balkans. The only country whose interests coincided with the aspirations for freedom of the nations of Turkey's European provinces was Russia, which actually did not favor a war at the moment because it was not fully prepared to face its complications. Accordingly, St. Petersburg tried to dissuade Serbia and Montenegro from declaring war.[4] Assessing the situation, D. A. Milyutin wrote: "The internal economic rebirth of Russia is in a phase such that any external obstacle may upset the state organism."[5] The Russian leadership was not however, unanimous. An influential group headed by the crown prince, the empress, and Grand Duke Konstantin Nikolayevich was active in support of military action, and it had influential public opinion on its side. This led to irresolution in Russian foreign policy.[6]

The fluctuations in Russian policy were reflected in the moods of the various Bulgarian political factions. The revolutionaries supported active participation with Serbia. Thus, for example, the lead article of *Nova Bŭlgariya* for June 26, 1876, read in part:

> Bulgarian brothers! The time has come for us to stand shoulder to shoulder with our worthy Serbian and Montenegrin brothers, to add their arms to our own, so that we can have a decent place on the Balkan Peninsula, the place history allotted to our forebears, and to proclaim our land free as long as the name "Bulgarians" is heard. Therefore, dear Bulgarian brothers, from the Danube to the Maritsa, from the Vardar to the Morava, from Lake Ohrid to the Black Sea, come and listen to the voice of your brother heroes![7]

The Bulgarians in Russia were of another mind. Together with a group of activists in Romania, they believed that cooperation with Serbia was undesirable. The Bulgarian bourgeoisie, which had a negative attitude toward military action, followed official Russian policy in this respect. The genuine bearers of revolutionary ideas were the toil-worn masses. Thousands of them volunteered during the war against the Ottomans. For example, the numerous Bulgarian emigrants in Serbia at that time were among the first Bulgarian volunteers.

Serbia began preparing to set up volunteer detachments as early as May 1876. On May 1, the government issued an order for the formation of such units. Bulgarians were most numerous in these units; according to information provided by a participant in the war, Glisha Markovich, 1,334 volunteers, of whem 770 were Bulgarians, were recruited up to the declaration of the war on the Timok front alone.[8] Hundreds of young patriots prepared to fight against the Ottoman oppressors set out for Serbia, including not only common soldiers but also Bulgarian officers in the Russian army.[9] The rapidly formed Bulgarian units were divided into detachments and participated actively in the fighting from the first day. On July 2, 1876, the units of Panayot Hitov, Simo Sokolov, Filip Totyo, and Ilyo Markov were in action near Zaječar.[10] Other units were formed under Ivan Vurtopchanina, Hristo Makedonski, Todor Velkov, Lazar Kostov, and others.

At first the military organization of the volunteers was of the haiduk type, but a special "law of the Bulgarian volunteer troops" was worked out and confirmed by General Mikhail G. Chernyayev on July 2. Panayot Hitov was appointed chief. Article 1 defined the Bulgarian action: "The aim of our fighting is to liberate Bulgaria from Ottoman bondage; we will fight until either we win our freedom or we die."[11] Commander-in-chief Chernyayev sent a special message to the Bulgarian people informing them that Russia would help the oppressed peoples and calling on the Bulgarians to organize more units to participate in the struggle.

The original plan of the Serbian high command was for the Bulgarians to cross the border and organize an uprising in Bulgaria. This would facilitate the task of the Serbian army by diverting Ottoman attention. This plan coincided with the aspirations of the Bulgarians. The early movements of the Bulgarian units can be traced in the diary of a member of Hitov's band. On July 3, battles in which bands suffered losses were already being fought near the border at Salaš. On the following day battles were fought on Bulgarian territory near Chuprene, the St. Ivan Monastery, and Gorni Lom. Then, as a result of erroneous information that the uprising was still going on in Bulgaria, the units were ordered to advance eastward. Todor Velkov's band reached Novo Selo in the Vidin district, where the peasants had indeed started an uprising. There, however, they were met by powerful units of the Turkish garrison of Vidin and were scattered. Sider Gruncharov's band advanced eastward along the ridge of the Balkans in an attempt to join the Bulgarian insurgents. Surrounded on all sides by Turkish units, the band was routed near Murgash. The combined bands of Panayot Hitov, Filip Totyo,

Hristo Makedonski, Simo Sokolov, and N. Popninov managed to reach the Chiprovtsi Monastery and the Berkovitsa area. They were sufficiently strong to have penetrated eastward, but on the order of the Serbian high command they withdrew.

Chernyayev had decided to block the Bela Palanka–Niš road and send the troops toward Sofia. In support of this strategy, the Bulgarian units were quickly recalled to Serbia and sent to Bela Palanka. From then on the actions of the Bulgarian units were entirely subordinated to the needs of the front, where the situation was deteriorating. The whole of July was spent in continuous marches and maneuvers undertaken on the order of the Serbian high command. Military considerations required that the insurgent forces and the volunteers have centralized leadership. However, the Serbian commanders organized the units in a way that caused collisions, and a dispute emerged about the formation of independent Bulgarian volunteer bands. Thus the question of the Bulgarian volunteers was continuously under discussion.[12]

The war went poorly for Serbia. The Serbian high command was irresolute, failing to follow up its military successes. For example, the capture of the important strategic point of Babina Glava was not followed by a decisive offensive toward Bela Palanka. Instead, forces were scattered along a very wide front, and this enabled the Turkish high command to take the initiative and recapture Babina Glava. After a three-day battle, the Serbs also had to abandon Knjaževac and Zaječar. Bloody battles followed in which the Turks seized the advantage. Serbian battalions were reduced to slightly more than a hundred men each, without any reserves. On October 23 the Turks were already in Djunis and advancing toward Deligrad. Their offensive could no longer be stopped; the way to Belgrade was open. Chernyayev sent a telegram to Prince Milan insisting on an immediate armistice. The prince and the Serbian government immediately asked the tsar for support. Russia handed Turkey an ultimatum, and the armistice went into effect on November 1, 1876. On the same day Chernyayev handed over his command to Colonel Djura Horvatović and left for Belgrade, afterward returning to Russia. The war was over, even though the peace treaty was not concluded until February 28, 1877.[13]

The struggle of the Serbian people attracted many volunteers from Russia. Nearly 2,000 Russians shed their blood helping the South Slavs to win their freedom. Russian help was particularly valuable in providing command staff. Over 700 officers arrived at a time when Serbia had only about 450.

The inclusion of Bulgarians in the struggle was coordinated by the Bulgarian Central Charitable Society, an organization founded to recruit volunteers, supply them, and send them to Serbia. The Pan-Slavists in Russia who wanted to assist the South Slavs against Turkey were interested in establishing an all-Bulgarian organization to replace the Bulgarian Revolutionary Central Committee. In June they sent Vladimir Semyonovich Yonin, formerly of the Russian Ministry of Foreign Affairs, Anton T. Techarov, a former secretary of the Moscow Slavic Committee, and Peter Enchev, a Bulgarian revolutionary, to Romania. The Moscow and St. Petersburg Slavic Committees asked Yonin to find out whether there was a central organization of Bulgarian émigrés in Romania and, if not, to help establish one.

Conditions in Romania at that time, however, were unfavorable for setting up a revolutionary committee because the country was maintaining strict neutrality. Therefore, on July 10, 1876, the Bulgarian activists founded a new organization that proclaimed only charitable aims. Article 1 of its statute stated: "The aim of the Society is to raise funds in order to help unfortunate, wretched, and needy Bulgarians."[14] Its leadership included an honorary chairman, Vladimir Yonin, a chairman, Kiryak Tsankov, and secretaries P. Enchev and S. Zagorski. This all-national organization tackled the problem of volunteers among the Bulgarians. On the second day of its existence, the Society authorized Yonin and Enchev to enter into negotiations with the Serbian government and others on questions "concerning the political fate of the Bulgarian nation."[15]

The number of Bulgarian volunteers now increased rapidly. They were given the necessary aid by the Society and transported to Kladovo, where all the Bulgarians were to gather. The Society did not, however, possess enough funds to transport all of them. In a letter dated July 30, 1876, Yonin wrote: "At the moment the formation of Bulgarian detachments is taking place mainly in Kladovo, in Serbia, where they are being supplied with weapons and everything necessary. Up to now about 1,500 Bulgarians have gathered in Serbia; this small number is explained by the fact that there are not enough funds to send them, though over 6,000 volunteers await travel expenses."[16] The work of the Society did not go smoothly. The "Elders," who had created their own organization, called the Philanthropic Society, succeeded in influencing some members to withdraw from its board of trustees. A meeting was quickly called, and the board was replenished on August 7, 1876.[17]

The main task was supplying the volunteers. A letter from Kladovo reads,

See that the young men coming over here are at least supplied with clothes and shoes, because many of them arrive practically naked and barefoot: ...If possible, supply each with a revolver and a hundred cartridges, because our detachments here are not given anything but a gun and ammunition... If you do not supply us with the necessary funds, which we need badly, try at least to send us leather for sandals, sackcloth, tins for water, i. e., things that are scarce here. We do not have money to provide them, and therefore we must delay sending the bands to the border.[18]

The Society's board was in constant touch with its branches in the various cities of Romania and elsewhere. Its constant concern was raising funds. About 2,500 volunteers were eventually recruited, not counting the thousands who could not go because funds were lacking. Many quit their jobs and placed themselves at the disposal of the Society, hoping to be sent to Serbia.

In the beginning the Bulgarian volunteers were distributed among the Serbian units. This decision, dictated by the interests of the high command, deprived the Bulgarians of the opportunity they had expected of fighting for the liberation of Bulgaria. A letter from that time reads: "The Bulgarians remained oppressed, scattered everywhere in groups of 200 to 300, deprived of many things and far from being able to realize their purpose."[19] Mounting discontent with the way they were being used led to a demand by the Bulgarian volunteers for the creation of their own independent military unit. General Ivan Kishelski, who went to Serbia to see for himself, wrote: "The Bulgarian volunteers who do not want to pass for native Serbians are still, as before, barefoot and naked, without rucksacks and cartridge belts, and always in the advance guard."[20]

The Society, which was working out plans for a Bulgarian uprising, now insisted on the formation of an independent Bulgarian detachment. Its representative in Serbia was ordered to see that the rifles sent were given to the Bulgarian volunteers for whom they were intended and, "if possible, to gather all the Bulgarians in one detachment under one command as one separate body, whose aim should be to enter Bulgaria."[21] A letter from the Society to the St. Petersburg Slavic Committee, dated August 20, 1876, said:

It is obvious that the Bulgarians now in Serbia are altogether deprived of any proper organization, and their role in the Serbian advance guard is not at all enviable. The Bulgarian Central Charitable Society in Bucharest has decided to do everything possible to gather all the Bulgarian volunteers under one banner and commit their organization to Colonel Alexander Mikhailovich Miloradovich, who is being sent to General Chernyayev on behalf of the Society to negotiate such organization.[22]

Another letter, from the Society in Brăila, pointed out that Yonin had been sent to Chernyayev on a mission to secure the creation of a separate Bulgarian military unit. "Shortly after this we learned that despite all the good promises of General Chernyayev, the Serbian junior officers tried in every way possible to hinder the realization of this desire of ours."[23] Many emigre centers also called for the formation of a separate Bulgarian unit. The newspaper *Vŭzrazhdane*, published in Braila by T. Peev, reported: "The only complete, real, and honorable guarantee for us can be a single Bulgarian army fighting under its own name and banner."[24] The Bulgarians in Galaţi sent the following message to the Society in Bucharest: "We became convinced that not until all the Bulgarians were united under one rule would there be any benefit for us Bulgarians."[25]

Shortly after that, Chernyayev approved the creation of a separate Bulgarian unit. His intention was to have an entire volunteer division of 10,000 men, and therefore he insisted that apart from the 2,500 Bulgarian volunteers already in Serbia, an additional 7,500 should be sent.[26] On September 14, 1876, the Society was informed that the Bulgarian volunteers had been organized into three battalions with Deligrad as their headquarters. These battalions were headed by the Russian officers Count Keler, Colonel Medvedovsky, and Colonel Miloradovich. Simultaneously, steps were taken toward the sending of 7,500 volunteers to form a division, but action was postponed until the situation could be clarified. A Russo–Bulgarian brigade was, however, set up and actively participated in the defense of the Serbian lands. Bulgarian officers educated in Russia participated in the command of the Bulgarian battalions. The second battalion, for example, was entrusted to Captain Raicho Nikolov. The old voivodes were sent to recruit new volunteers. In a letter to Jovan Ristić dated September 19, 1876, the Society welcomed the reorganization: "The Bulgarian Central Charitable Society, founded on July 10 in Bucharest, is gratified by the fact that the organization of separate Bulgarian battalions has begun in Deligrad. The realization of this task, we believe, will smooth out those troubles and bewilderments which regrettably had sprung up between Serbians and Bulgarians at the outset of the war."[27]

The establishment of the Bulgarian unit began very well. In a letter to the Society dated September 5, 1876, Miloradovich wrote: "Your Bulgarian detachment, consisting at the moment of 2,000 men, has achieved a brilliant structure. This [unit] constitutes the Serbian army's Guards, and if you could see it your Bulgarian heart would be overwhelmed with joy."[28] On September 8, the volunteers swore allegiance before the battalion banners. The Russo–Bulgarian brigade carried out feverish preparations until the middle of September and on the 16th took part in a major battle at Krevet Gredetin, a height on the bank of the Morava near Deligrad. The undermanned Serbian army faced 80,000 Turkish troops headed personally by the commander in chief, Abdul Kerim Pasha. The Russo–Bulgarian brigade was ordered to go around the left Turkish flank and attack the Ottoman troops from the rear, and it managed to do this in a fierce hand-to-hand battle. Later in the war the Bulgarian and Russian troops fought valiantly at Djunis.

The unfavorable course of the war caused friction and discontent. In the beginning, the Serbian leadership was counting on a revival of the Bulgarian uprising. As we have seen, it was even thought that the April Uprising was still going on in some parts of Bulgaria. The delay of the declaration of war until the end of June 1876 enabled the Porte to withdraw its troops from the Serbian border and to concentrate them in the insurgent regions. When the war began, the Serbian high command thought that the fires of rebellion would easily flare up again across Bulgaria, but this did not happen. The bands of Bulgarian volunteers that crossed the border at the beginning of July could not make the Bulgarian population rise in arms, especially since after only two days of fighting on Bulgarian territory the bulk of them were withdrawn to reinforce Serbian units along the Timok.

Serbian discontent was reflected in later analyses. Thus, twenty years later, Jovan Ristić wrote:

> The heavy sacrifices Serbia suffered in order to support the Bulgarian refugees and their leaders were fruitless. ...the weapons the Serbian army had given to the Bulgarians on crossing the border were lost: they either threw them away or handed them over to the Turks. ...there were two battalions of Bulgarians in Serbia. Each battalion had about 600 to 800 men well armed with Belgian rifles. In June 1876, they were sent across the border toward Priot and Vidin to awaken the population to rise in arms. Having crossed the border, however, these battalions ended their apostolic mission by either surrendering to the Turkish authorities or throwing away their weapons.[29]

This groundless accusation is reflected even in contemporary historiography. The Serbian historian Petar Opačić of Belgrade maintained at the scholarly conference in Sarajevo marking the hundredth anniversary of the uprising in Bosnia and Hercegovina that "several hundred Bulgarian volunteers who had been transferred from Serbia to Bulgaria at the outset of the war either surrendered to the Turks or returned to Serbia."[30]

Was it possible for the Bulgarians to meet the Serbians' expectation that they would rise in arms? Kishelski accurately analyzed the situation in a note to Milyutin dated October 8, 1876:

> What he [Chernyayev] demanded from the Bulgarians was impossible after the little achieved by Serbia, which for dozens of years had been preparing for a war against not only Turkey but Austria as well and wanted to be the Slavic Piedmont on the Balkan Peninsula: ...It was still more impossible to demand a sudden arming of Bulgaria, which had risen in arms at the initiative of Serbia and afterward remained a terrorized Bulgaria whose every move was closely watched.[31]

Documents dating from that time clearly show the role of the Bulgarians in the war. The Bulgarian volunteers, first as part of the Serbian army and later as separate Russo–Bulgarian brigades, participated in the major battles everywhere. There is ample evidence of their heroism. Horvatović, under whose command they fought, expressed his satisfaction at their valor and success. Later Chernyayev wrote that "the Bulgarians manifested remarkable tenacity."[32] And Miloradovich wrote: "During the general offensive on September 10, I had the honor to command the Bulgarian battalions, and I haven't the least doubt that the future and just military history will pay well-deserved tribute to their valor and manliness."[33] He also wrote on November 26, 1876, to the Moscow Slavic Committee that "the Bulgarians behaved most valiantly and bravely, as befitted real soldiers, under rain and in mud. After a strenuous march on October 6, they again joined the battle and covered the retreat of the troops, holding off the Turkish pressure. The Bulgarians fight as they must, strictly doing their duty."[34] At the end of the war many Bulgarian volunteers were awarded the Serbian Takovski military cross.[35]

Nevertheless, the Serbian leaders were discontented with the Bulgarians. At the same time, many Bulgarian volunteers complained of the way they were treated by the Serbian authorities. Scattered throughout the Serbian units, they were most often in the advance guard and were the first to experience the assaults of the Turkish troops. Of the approximately 4,000 Bulgarian volunteers who went to Serbia, over 1,700 fell dead.[36] Individual volunteers presented their grievances directly to the Society: "The bad attitude of the Serbians toward our Bulgarians up to the last minute, and no less the general circumstances, contributed to the disintegration of the Bulgarian legion in Serbia," said a letter addressed to the Society in Brăila dated November 4, 1876.[37] The Bulgarian volunteers declared that Ristić wanted to use them only to achieve his selfish aims. "Our greatest and sworn enemy," St. Stambolov wrote on August 25, 1876, "is that man in whose hands today is the fate of all of Serbia and maybe of the entire Balkan Peninsula. He heads... the party that wants to make most of our Fatherland Serbian."[38]

The unfavorable course of the war led the Bulgarians to consider how they might continue the struggle. Hopes of working out of Serbia vanished once Ottoman units had gained the upper hand there, threatening the country with a military catastrophe. Bulgarian activists in Romania and Russia began planning new actions, this time from the north through Romania or along the Black Sea. A new uprising was planned in Bulgaria, and steps were taken toward the realization of the plan. Kiryak Tsankov wrote to Pavel Kalyandni in Kishinev on July 30, 1876, that since the Serbians had failed in the war, a new plan including the Greeks, the Romanians, and the rest of the Slavic population was needed. He added: "I think that the wisest thing is for no more Bulgarians to cross over to Serbia, but to go to Dobruja and fight there. We should not be discouraged but should take measures corresponding to the changed military situation."[39]

The Society took other measures. In a letter to the Odessa Slavic Charitable Society dated September 22, 1876, it requested

(1) permission of the Romanian government for the formation of Bulgarian detachments in Romania, with military supplies and weapons to be ferried across the

Danube; (2) strong a detachment organized in South Russia to be shipped across the Black Sea to Bulgaria. It would be sufficient, if this detachment numbered from 1,000 to 2,000, with enough weapons to pass out among the population [so that it could] begin acting in Bulgaria to weaken the Turkish forces, which would then have to be withdrawn from the Serbian borders. This would enable General Chernyayev to change his defensive tactics to offensive ones and to penetrate into Bulgaria.[40]

This assessment of the significance of an assault from Bulgaria was echoed by I. S. Aksakov, who, in a letter to Chernyayev dated September 7, 1876, pointed out that "Bulgaria represents the trunk of European Turkey. The cutting off of the Serbian lands from the Ottoman Empire is like the amputation of an arm or leg. The severing of Bulgaria, however, would be decisive for the Sublime Porte, and because of this the latter will fight most resolutely to retain it."[41] With the significance of intensifying activity on Bulgarian territory in mind, the Society sent to Russia two representatives, the chairman Tsankov and P. Nabotkov, a member of the leadership, to suggest that a special detachment be formed and transported directly to Bulgaria to encourage the population to rise in revolt. No more volunteers were sent to Serbia.[42]

Russia itself was already making other plans. The view that direct action was imperative was gradually getting the upper hand. When Prince Milan declared that without Russian armed intervention Serbia would not be able to resume the war, Tsar Alexander resolutely declared, "No, we ourselves will invade the Balkans."[43] As early as November 11, Aksakov sent a cable to the chairman of the Society in Bucharest: "Circumstances have changed. It is not Serbia but Russia that is organizing Bulgarian detachments on the Romanian border."[44] The Bulgarian volunteers in Serbia gradually began leaving the country for Romania. In the beginning of April of the following year, the last groups of Bulgarians crossed the border and went to Ploieşti, where a Bulgarian volunteer camp was set up. The nucleus of this corps was the volunteers who for several months had fought in Serbia side by side with the Russian volunteers and the Serbian army. The Russo–Turkish War that broke out on April 24, 1877, was for them the continuation of the cause for which so many heroes had shed their blood in Serbia.

The Bulgarian volunteers in the Serbo–Turkish War of 1876 contributed to the gradual unification of Bulgarian society. The movement for the defense of the Bulgarian nation included not only the revolutionary forces but also the activists of the Bulgarian bourgeoisie and persons close to the Bulgarian Exarchate. This process of unification, so eloquently manifested in the Russo–Turkish War of Liberation of 1877–78, was greatly aided by the heroism of the volunteers of 1876.

NOTES

1. *Osvobozhdenie Bolgarii ot turetskogo iga*, vol. 1 (Moscow, 1961), p. 217.

2. Kr. Sharova, "Aprilskoto vŭstanie iozhnoslavianskite narodi," in *Aprilskoto vŭstanie, 1876–1966* (Sofia, 1966), pp. 145–46.

3. Petar Opačić, "Vojne operacije u srpsko–turskom ratu 1876. godine," in *Medjunarodni naučni skup povodom 100-godišnjice ustanka u Bosni i Hercegovini, drugim Balkanskim zemljama i Istočnoj krizi, 1875–1878 godine, Sarajevo, 1–3 oktobra 1975,* vol. 2 (Sarajevo, 1977), pp. 286 ff.

4. A. L. Narochnitskii, "Balkanskii krizis 1875–1878 g. i velikie derzhavi," in *Medjunarodni naučni skup,* vol. 1, pp. 31 ff.; S. I. Bochkareva, "Russko–serbskie otnosheniia v sviazi s serbsko–turetskoi voinoi 1876 goda," in ibid., pp. 351 ff.

5. I. S. Kiniapina, "Osnovni etapi v politikata na Rusiia po vreme na Iztochnata kriza prez 70-te godini na XIX v.," in *Osvobozhdenieto na Bulgariia,* ed. Hristo Hristov et al. (Sofia, 1982), p. 25.

6. *Osvobozhdenie Bolgarii ot turetskogo iga*, vol. 1, pp. 261–62.

7. *Nova Bŭlgariia*, no. 9 (June 26, 1876), pp. 1–2.

8. Tsonko Genov, "Uchastie bolgarskih dobrovoltsev v Serbsko–Turetskoi voine 1876 g.," in *Medjunarodni naučni skup,* vol. 3, p. 278.

9. *Osvobozhdenie Bolgarii ot turetskogo iga*, vol. 1, p. 247.

10. Ivan Kr. Stoichev, *Materiali za deinostta na Panaiot Khitov prez 1876 g. v Sŭrbiia (Neizdadeni dokumenti, pisma, faksimileta i skitsi)* (Sofia, 1939), p. 37.

11. Ibid., p. 48. The original is kept in the Bulgarian Historical Archives of the Cyril and Methodius National Library, Sofia.

12. Kr. Sharova, "Vzaimootnosheniiata mezhdu bŭlgarite i drugite iozhni slaviani po vreme na Iztochnata kriza 1875–1876 g.," in *Medjunarodni naučni skup,* vol. 2, p. 167.

13. Opačić, "Vojne operacije," pp. 281–303.

14. The statute may be found in *Osvobozhdenie Bolgarii ot turetskogo iga*, vol. 1, p. 293–94.

15. Ibid., p. 294.

16. Genov, "Uchastie bolgarskih dobrovoltsev," p. 278.

17. Al. Burmov, *Bŭlgarski revoliutsionen centralen komitet, 1868–1877,* 2d ed. (Sofia, 1950), pp. 157–58.

18. Letter to K. Tsankov in Bucharest, June 30, 1876, *Osvobozhdenie Bolgarii ot turetskogo iga,* vol. 1, p. 271.

19. N. Chekhlarov, *Dokumenti po bŭlgarskoto vŭzrazhdane,* Sbornik narodni umotvoreniia, nauka, i knizhnina 31–33 (Sofia, 1906–7), p. 10.

20. Note to D. A. Milyutin, *Osvobozhdenie Bolgarii ot turetskogo iga,* vol. 1, pp. 446–47.

21. Chekhlarov, *Dokumenti,* p. 5.

22. *Osvobozhdenie Bolgarii ot turetskogo iga*, vol. 1, p. 352.

23. Letter dated September 6/18, 1876, Chekhlarov, *Dokumenti,* pp. 9–10.

24. *Vŭzrazhdane,* no. 13 (September 29, 1876).

25. Letter dated September 17, 1876, Chekhlarov, *Dokumenti,* p. 15.

26. Letter from the Bulgarian Central Charitable Society to the Moscow Slavic Charitable Committee, September 14, 1876, ibid., p. 14.

27. *Osvobozhdenie Bolgarii ot turetskogo iga*, vol. 1, pp. 414–15.

28. Ibid., p. 381.

29. J. Ristić, *Diplomatska istorija Srbije za vreme srpskih ratova za oslobodjenje i nezavisnost, 1875–1878,* vol. 1, *Prvi rat* (Belgrade, 1896), pp. 165 and 168.

30. Opačić, "Vojne operacije," p. 292.

31. *Osvobozhdenie Bolgarii ot turetskogo iga*, vol. 1, p. 446.

32. *Iliostrovannaia khronika voini,* vol. 1 (St. Petersburg, 1877).

33. Tsonko Genov, "90 godini ot sŭzdavaneto i boinite podvizi na rusko–bŭl-

garskata brigada v Sŭrbsko–turskata voina 1876 godina," *Voennoistoricheski sbornik,* 1966, no. 2, p. 16.

34.    Chekhlarov, *Dokumenti,* pp. 43–44.

35.    See, for example, the memoirs of the volunteer participant Lazar Filipov in *Osvobozhdenieto, 1878: Spomeni* (Sofia, 1978) p. 270.

36.    *Osvobozhdenie Bolgarii ot turetskogo iga,* vol. 1, p. 446.

37.    Chekhlarov, *Dokumenti,* p. 28.

38.    *Osvobozhdenie Bolgarii ot turetskogo iga,* vol. 1, p. 358.

39.    *Vŭzpomenatelen sbornik po sluchai stogodishninata ot Osvoboditelnata Rusko–turska voina, 1877–1878 g,* vol. 1, *Dokumentalen sbornik s podbrani materiali ot arkhivite i bulgarskiia vŭzrozhdenski pechat, 1876–1878* (Sofia, 1979). See also Tsonko Genov, "Bŭlgarskata emigratsiia i natsionalno-osvoboditelnoto dvizhenie v navecherieto na Rusko–turskata voina ot 1877–1878 g.," *Istoricheski pregled,* 1968, no. 1, pp. 85–86.

40.    *Osvobozhdenie Bolgarii ot turetskogo iga,* vol. 1, pp. 420–21.

41.    Ibid., p. 387.

42.    Chekhlarov, *Dokumenti,* p. 22.

43.    Bochkareva, "Russko–Serbskie otnosheniia," p. 360.

44.    Cyril and Methodius National Library, Bulgarian Historical Archives, Collection no. 56, File 11–D–1053.

Doino Doinov

# THE PARTICIPATION OF THE BULGARIAN VOLUNTEER FORCE IN THE RUSSO—TURKISH WAR OF 1877—78

Because the Bulgarian volunteer force was one of the most significant manifestations of the Bulgarian national-revolutionary movement and because it was a military unit within the framework of the Russian army and an important part of the history of the traditional Russian—Bulgarian military alliance, it has been the object of special attention in Bulgarian, Russian, and Soviet historiography.[1] To a lesser degree, other historiographies have also discussed it.[2] These studies have produced excellent evaluations of the character, role, and significance of the volunteers, and the most important problems have been relatively precisely and correctly interpreted. Nevertheless, at the risk of some repetition, I want to return to these basic problems with the aim of giving more details and introducing some questions for discussion.

First of all, the volunteer force played an important role in the genesis of the Bulgarian national liberation and revolutionary movement. In the absence of the conditions necessary for an armed national-liberation struggle in Bulgaria, Bulgarians participated, singly or in groups, in the Serbian and Greek uprising, in the uprising of Tudor Vladimirescu, in the Romanian revolution of 1848, in the Cretan Uprising of 1866, and in the Italian national-liberation and unification movement.[3] They also took part in the wars Russia conducted against Turkey in the second half of the eighteenth and in the nineteenth century; there was a well-organized and sizable Bulgarian volunteer detachment, the so-called Bulgarian national *zemska* army, in the war of 1806—12, and volunteer detachments were formed in the wars of 1828—29 and 1853—56.[4]

Of course, the mobilization of volunteers and the creation of special detachments in the struggles of other countries, neighboring or remote, was not solely a Bulgarian phenomenon. Volunteer participation was typical for the second half of the eighteenth century and the whole of the nineteenth.

In some instances it was probably inspired by ideological or humanitarian motives or personality factors. When it was organized on a large scale, however, as was the participation of Bulgarian volunteers in the uprisings and wars just mentioned, it must be considered as a reflection of their aspirations for national liberation. Furthermore, through participation of this kind the volunteers gained social, political, revolutionary, and military experience that enhanced their efforts at liberation.

During the sixties and seventies of the nineteenth century, an organized Bulgarian revolutionary movement based on the new social, economic, and political conditions emerged. Its aim was to prepare and realize a national bourgeois-democratic revolution. In the beginning, in the sixties, this movement was dominated by the idea of setting up volunteer forces in a foreign country (Serbia or Romania) to take advantage of a war between that country and Turkey. This is clear from the plans of Georgi Sava Rakovski and from the participation of the First Bulgarian League in the bombardment of Belgrade in 1862 and the founding of the Second Bulgarian League.[5]

The failure of these attempts and the insignificant results of the military activity of 1867—68 contributed to a radical revision of the Bulgarian national-liberation and revolutionary strategy. Proceeding from these historical lessons and from the necessity for the Bulgarian liberation movement to be independent of the policies of states, Vasil Levski founded the Internal Revolutionary Organization and advanced the thesis that the liberation of the Bulgarian people would be achieved by a popular national revolution. In this approach, the military-revolutionary forces created in the course of the revolution itself assumed a very important role. Help from abroad in the form of detachments of Bulgarian émigrés was not excluded. This strategy was the basis of the Stara Zagora uprising of 1875 and especially of the April Uprising of 1876, both of which ended in failure. The internal revolutionary forces were insufficient to defeat the mighty Ottoman Empire, which had the support of the European powers.[6]

As a result, the Bulgarian revolutionary movement, growing despite the massacre of 1876, once again decided to participate in any anti-Turkish action consistent with the Bulgarian liberation credo. This is evident from the activity of the last Bulgarian Revolutionary Central Committee in Bucharest, the so-called Bulgarian Central Charitable Society, which organized the Bulgarian volunteer detachments that took part in the Serbo—Turkish war of 1867.[7] This was also the premise upon which the Russian suggestion of a Bulgarian volunteer force was accepted unanimously and with enthusiasm.[8] As a form of liberation struggle and as a political strategy, the Bulgarian volunteer force not only accorded with Bulgarian reality but also represented a direct continuation and development of the national-revolutionary movement.

This conclusion is supported by its social and political composition – the participation in it of many members of revolutionary bands, activists in the revolutionary committees, participants in the April Uprising, and former volunteers from the Serbo–Turkish War of 1876. A significant proportion of the volunteers arrived in Romania after the April Uprising, i. e., either had been participants in the uprising or had left their homeland in the difficult situation that followed. We possess only one list of volunteers indicating the dates of their emigration to Romania, but this list of 121 volunteers dispatched from Galaţi in May 1877 shows that 56 had emigrated in 1876 and 14 at the beginning of 1877. Since more than half had emigrated after the April Uprising, they must have carried with them its ideas and spirit.

The organization of so many armed battalions in so short a time was possible largely because of the existence of a central organization. The Bulgarian Central Charitable Society and its branches in Romanian and Russian towns undertook the task of finding, registering, and dispatching groups of volunteers. More came forward than expected, especially compared with the later recruitment of a second set of Bulgarian volunteers. Additional volunteer detachments began to consolidate in the summer and autumn of 1877 in the parts of northern Bulgaria occupied by the Russian army. Although Bulgarians joined the revolutionary battalions, militia, and intelligence service, only about 2,000 men, instead of the authorized strength of 6,000, joined the volunteer detachments numbered 6–12. This was because these detachments were intended for military police activities, not for combat, and their formation was entrusted to village mayors. No organizing center existed to perform the task.[9]

The data analyzed so far show that the volunteer force was a product and expression of the Bulgarian national revolution. However, it needs to be distinguished from the pure formations of the earlier manifestations of the bourgeois-democratic revolution.

The idea of the formation of a Bulgarian military unit under the command of the Russian headquarters had its roots in tradition. It had been suggested by eminent Bulgarian patriots such as Ivan Kishelski and Kiryak Tsankov, but it was the Russian high command that turned the idea into reality. The Russian high command imposed the aims and constraints dictated by tsarist policy and the operation of a regular army. In the minds of the Bulgarian patriots and in the initial plans, the volunteer force was to be a combat unit serving in the advance guard of the Russian army and thus hastening a general uprising in Bulgaria. Originally some Russian military leaders, such as R. A. Fadayev and N. N. Obrutchev, shared this view. In the Statute of the Organization of the Bulgarian Forces, and in other regulations, however, the independence of the Bulgarian volunteer force was restricted. Thus, instead of combat, the volunteer force was assigned security activities. The idea of provoking a general uprising was abandoned. Consequently, the volunteer force lacked some of the features inherent in a national-revolutionary formation because of the class and ideological character of the Russian high command and of tsarism.[10]

Nonetheless, the Bulgarian volunteer force played a more significant role in the course of the war than the one originally assigned to it. First of all, when the volunteer force was formed in Kishinev and Ploieşti, it surpassed all expectations in its numbers and military training. The volunteers showed great endurance, high morale, and a strong will in the difficult march from Kishinev to the Danube and from there to the Balkan and Thracian plain, where it took part in three battles (Stara Zagora, Shipka, and Sheinovo) important for the strategy and tactics of the war. Particularly heroic was the behavior of the volunteers in the battle at Stara Zagora. This baptism by fire showed their military skill and led to a revision of the concept that they should be used only for garrison and guard service. From that point on the Bulgarian volunteer force was used by the Russian high command as a first-class combat unit alongside units of the Russian army.

A supreme manifestation of the fighting skill, patriotic spirit, and readiness for self-sacrifice of the Bulgarian volunteers was the battle in defense of Shipka Pass in August 1877. Shoulder to shoulder with their Russian brothers and suffering many losses, they held the pass. Although a battle of tactical significance, the defense of Shipka had an important strategic consequence as well: the Turkish army was unable to advance into northern Bulgaria and join the army of Osman Pasha at Plevna. The defense of Shipka also had great moral and political significance. It strengthened society's faith in the Bulgarian army and the likelihood of a successful outcome to the war and contributed to an increase in Bulgarian national self-confidence. Doubtless the victory at Shipka had similar significance for Russian society.

The Bulgarian volunteers also participated in the successful battle for the Sheinovo fortifications in January 1878, after which the Russian army victoriously marched toward Edirne and Constantinople. Later the volunteers took part in defeating the bashi-bazouk bands in Kijustendil, Deliormana, and elsewhere, which helped permit the consolidation of the new Bulgarian administration.[11]

The contributions of the volunteer force go beyond these wartime activities. In 1878–79 it became the nucleus of the Bulgarian national army. Thus the volunteer battalions served as a basis for the *zemska* army in the Bulgarian Principality, for the militia, and for the so-called gymnastic associations in Eastern Rumelia. They became the most active element in the movement against the decisions of the Berlin Congress. They were also to be found at the center of the struggle for the unification of the Bulgarian Principality with Eastern Rumelia, a struggle that ended in success in September 1885.[12]

Thus the volunteer force was connected not only with prewar processes but with postwar national development as well. Not merely a phenomenon of the Russo–Turkish War of 1877–78, it was an expression of the Bulgarian national revolution, a means for realizing the most urgent and vital tasks of the nation.

Two questions concerning the history of the Bulgarian volunteer force remain insufficiently researched and even debatable: its social origin and its national composition.

In the literature it has been stated that the volunteer battalions consisted of "the poor and the ruined strata of our people — artisans, peasants, servants, intellectuals, and others."[13] Often cited in support of this view is the testimony of Colonel G. Korsakov that "many paupers participated, and almost all of them were in rags" and that "the majority belong to the peasantry."[14] The composition of the Bulgarian volunteer battalions was in fact mixed, including town dwellers and villagers, craftsmen, tradesmen, teachers, workers, professional revolutionaries, exiles, and former rebels, but a class analysis must take into account other factors as well.

The majority of the Bulgarian volunteers of the so-called first set were emigrants to Romania and Russia. Some were economic migrants — seasonal workers, bricklayers, gardeners, and others. They can be considered wage laborers even though they had left wives, children, and parents behind to cultivate their land and live in their houses. This explains much about the military success of this first set of volunteers. It was the middle-class, closely bound to its hearths, that had largely made up the revolutionary army of the April Uprising, and Ivan Khadzhiisky has said of this sort of fighter that "because of his middle-class origin, he has no fighting strength."[15] By contrast, the prevalence of wage laborers in the volunteer force contributed to its decisiveness, heroism, and continuity. Another large group of participants in the volunteer force was the political émigrés — former teachers, rebels, tradesmen, craftsmen. They had left all their property across the Danube in their enslaved homeland and derived no benefit from it. Although this was only temporary, it placed them in the same situation as the laborers in terms of property. Together these economic and political émigrés constituted the majority of the volunteer force and therefore defined its class character.

Thus it cannot be claimed that the peasantry prevailed in the volunteer force. From the lists of volunteers from Brăila, Galaţi, Slatina, and so on, it is obvious that towns such as Koprivshtitsa, Gabrovo, Sofia, Karlovo, Ohrid, and Ruse are represented by a significant number of volunteers. This is even more the case with the corresponding data on the second set of volunteers. A good illustration is the Tenth Battalion, which numbered 1,137 men. Data on their origins are to be found for only about 305, of whom 180 came from Gabrovo and the rest from Stara Zagora, Drianovo, and so on. Only about 10 percent came from villages and towns of the Gabrovo district.[16]

The Bulgarian volunteer force was formed as a national unit. The notes of General Fadayev and the statutes both called for the formation of battalions of Bulgarian origin to assist the Russian army on Bulgarian territory. In practice, Bulgarian volunteers began arriving in Romania and Russia starting in October and formed first the nucleus of the foot convoy and next the volunteer force. Among the volunteers were a number of Greeks, Serbians (including so-called Old Serbians), Italians, and others. At the beginning some of them were included in the battalions, but by the end of April the question of their participation was under discussion. General Nikolai G. Stoletov requested and received from the high command the following instructions: "According to the commander in chief, the correct organization of the military force of every battalion... depends on the homogeneity of its effectives. That is why he considers that the Bulgarian volunteer force must consist of native Bulgarians only and none from other nations, whether Serbians or other Slavic or non-Slavic emigrants."[17] The chief of the Bulgarian volunteer force accordingly appointed a "special commission" to "investigate the origin of those willing to fight under the banner of the volunteer force."[18] The official data show that the participants in the volunteer force numbered 7,440. The first set consisted of 4,500 men, of whom only 40–50 were of foreign origin; all the rest were Bulgarians from different districts of the country – northern Bulgaria, Dobruja, and Thrace. In later reports A. M. Dondukov wrote that "during the wars up to 1,000 men came from Macedonia alone."[19] The names of 411 volunteers from Macedonia that survived until the liberation of 1878 are known. One-fifth of the force either died in the struggle or did not give their birthplaces in the lists.[20] Built on the national principle under the direct guidance and assistance of the Russian high command, the Bulgarian volunteer force became a link between Bulgarians from different parts of the country, thus uniting the whole Bulgarian nation.

The activities of the Bulgarian volunteer force were a contribution both to the Bulgarian national movement and to the Russian victory in the war of 1877–78. The Bulgarian revolutionary movement had tried before to build up large military and revolutionary formations and to find favorable external political conditions, but either because of its own weaknesses or because of the opposing interests of the Balkan states it had not succeeded. The success of the Bulgarian volunteer force clearly shows the objective coincidence at this moment of the interests of the Bulgarian national-liberation movement and the political aims of Russia. The details of this conjuncture reveal the objectively progressive, liberating character of the

Russo–Turkish War of 1877–78, which provided the opportunity for building national-revolutionary detachments and helped realize the Bulgarian national revolution.

## NOTES

1. At. Benderev, *Istoriia na Bŭlgarskoto opŭlchenie i osvobozhdenieto na Bŭlgariia 1877–1878* (Sofia, 1930); S. I. Kisov, *Bŭlgarskoto opŭlchenie v osvoboditelnata rusko–turska voina 1877–1878: Vŭzspomenaniia* (Sofia, 1902); K. G. Abatszhiev, *Spomeni ot Osvoboditelnata voina v 1877–1878* (Sofia, 1925); L. Filipov, *Vŭzpomenaniia i razkazi za pŭrvoto bŭlgarsko opŭlchenie prez voinata 1877–1878* (Sofia, 1893); R. Dimitriev, *Boevete i operatsiite okolo Shipka vŭv voinata 1877–1878: Voennoistoricheski etiod* (Sofia, 1902); M. Mikhov, ed., *Bŭlgarskoto opŭlchenie: Sbornik dokumenti*, 2 vols. (Sofia, 1956–59); I. Mitev, *Bŭlgarskoto opŭlchenie v Osvoboditelnata voina* (Sofia, 1952); An. Anchev, *Bŭlgarskoto opŭlchenie* (Sofia, 1967); Georgi Vŭlkov, *Bŭlgarskoto opŭlchenie: Formirane, boino izpolzuvane i istoricheska sŭdba* (Sofia, 1983); Khr. Khristov, *Osvobozhdenieto na Bŭlgariia i politikata na zapadnite dŭrzhavi 1876–1878 g.* (Sofia, 1968); Ts. Genov, *Rusko–turskata osvoboditelna voina 1877–1878 g.* (Sofia, 1977); D. T. Anuchin, "K voprosu o bolgarskom opolchenii 1877–1878," *Ruskaia starina* 63 (1889): 195–202; N. P. Ovsianii, *Bolgarskoe opolchenie i zemskoe voisko* (St. Petersburg, 1904); Iv. S. Ivanov, *Bolgarskoe opolchenie i ego sformirovanie v 1875–1879: Zametki i vozspominaniia* (St. Petersburg, 1889); D. V. Konobeev, *Obrazovanie vooruzhenikh sil Bolgarii v period ee Osvobozhdeniia ot turetskaga iga (1876–1879)*, Kratkie soobshchenni Instituta slavianovedeniia ANSSSR 2 (1951); idem, *Rusko–bolgarskoe boevoe sodruzhestvo v Rusko–turetskoi voine 1877–1878* (Moscow, 1953); idem, *Borba bolgarskogo naroda za natsionalnuia nezavisimost v period Russko–turetskoi voini 1877–1878 godov i protiv reshenii Berlinskogo kongresa*, Sbornik Osvobozhdenie Bolgarii ot turetskogo iga (Moscow, 1958); I. K. Fortunatov, *Boevei rusko–bolgarskii soioz v voine 1877–1878 godov*, Sbornik Osvobozhdenie Bolgarii ot turetsko iga (Moscow, 1958); V. I. Kozmenko, *Iz istorii bolgarskoto opolcheniia (1876–1877)*, Slavianskii sbornik (Moscow, 1948); A. A. Ulunian, *Bolgarskii narod i Russko–turetskaia voina 1877–1878* (Moscow, 1971).

2. L. Lamoushe, *La milice bulgare pendant la guerre Turko–Russe* (Paris, 1935); B. H. Sumner, *Russia and the Balkans, 1870–1880* (London, 1962); St. G. Evans, *A Short History of Bulgaria* (London, 1960).

3. N. Todorov and V. Traikov, *Bŭlgari, uchastnitsi v borbite za osvobozhdenie na Gŭrtsiia* (Sofia, 1971); St. Doinov, *Bulgarskoto natsionalnoosvoboditelno dvizhenie 1800–1812* (Sofia, 1979); V. Traikov, "Uchastieto na bŭlgarite v nacionalno-osvoboditelnite borbi na drugi balkanski narodi: Faktor za ukrepvane na nacionalnoto sŭznanie na bŭlgarskiia narod," in the symposium, *Bŭlgarskata natsiia prez Vŭzrazhdaneto* (Sofia, 1980).

4. V. Konobeev, *Russko–bolgarskie otnosheniia v 1806–1812 g. g.: Iz istorii rusko–bolgarskikh otnoshenii* (Moscow, 1958); idem, *Natsionalno-osvoboditelnoe dvizhenie v Bolgarii v 1828–1830 g.*, Uchenie zapiski Instituta Slavianovedeniia ANSSSR 20 (1960).

5. V. Traikov, *G. S. Rakovski, 1821–1867: Biografichen ocherk* (Sofia, 1976); idem, *G. S. Rakovski i balkanskite narodi* (Sofia, 1971).

6. K. Kosev, N. Mechev, and D. Doinov, *Istoriia na Aprilskoto vŭstanie 1876* (Sofia, 1976), pp. 536–58.

7. A. Burmov, "Narastvaneto na revoliutsionniia podem vsred bŭlgarskiia narod prez 1875–78 g.,"*Istoricheski pregled*, 1950, no. 1.

8. Khristov, *Politikata na zapadnite dŭrzhavi*, p. 169; Military Historical Archive, Sofia, f. 1878/910, op. 3, no. 621.

9. Mitev, *Bŭlgarskoto opŭlchenie,* pp. 3–15; D. Doinov, "Bŭlgarskoto opŭl-chenie: Sŭstoianie na prouchvaniiata i niakoi neiziasneni problemi," in the symposium *Osvobozhdenieto na Bŭlgariia,* p. 63.

10. Ibid., pp. 59–60.

11. Vŭlkov, *Bŭlgarskoto opŭlchenie,* pp. 103–234.

12. I. Mitev, *Sŭedinenieto 1885* (Sofia, 1980), pp. 190–91.

13. Mitev, *Bŭlgarskoto opŭlchenie,* p. 43.

14. Ibid.

15. Iv. Khadzhiiski, *Bit i dushevnost na bulgarskiia narod* (Sofia, 1966), pp. 236–37.

16. G. Vulkov and D. Doinov, *Bulgarskoto opaltchenie* (Sofia, 1983), pp. 341–42.

17. *Bŭlgarskoto opŭlchenie,* vol. 1 (Sofia, 1956), pp. 1–10; Tzentralnui Goso-darstucnui Vornnuisturitches Kii Archiv, Moscow, f. VUA, 7783, 1. 16.

18. *Bŭlgarskoto opŭlchenie,* p. 344.

19. K. Tsŭrnushanov, *Okhridskoto sŭzakliatie* (Sofia, 1966), p. 95.

20. D. Doinov, *Natsionalno-revoliutsionnite borbi v Iugozapadna Bŭlgariia prez 60-te 70-te godini na XIX v.* (Sofia, 1976), p. 141.

# Greece

Evangelos Kofos


# GREEK INSURRECTIONARY PREPARATIONS, 1876-78


For the Greeks, the Eastern crisis of 1875–78 broke out at a most inopportune moment.[1] Having experienced destructive setbacks in the fifties (the Crimean War insurrections) and sixties (the Cretan Revolution), they had resolved to pursue a policy of peaceful coexistence with the Ottoman Empire "at least for twenty years."[2] They believed that by then Hellenism, both in the Kingdom and within the empire, would be strong enough to succeed in its national objectives. The events of 1876, particularly the Constantinople Conference, changed this expectation. The Greeks now realized that the nation should be prepared psychologically and militarily, lest Greek interests be completely ignored in the postcrisis settlement. But this was easier said than done. Although certain national societies had made preliminary preparations, the government of Epameinondas Deligeorgis, an Anglophile who still believed that Greek interests could be better served by friendly relations with the Ottoman government, remained cool, if not hostile, to private initiatives for insurrectionary preparations. He continued this line, albeit hesitantly, well into May, a full month after the outbreak of the Russo–Turkish War, when public outcry finally forced the formation of a coalition government – the "ecumenical" cabinet – with the old hero Konstantinos Kanaris as prime minister.

As the Russian armies crossed the Danube and embarked upon the liberation of Bulgaria, government and revolutionary committees began to cooperate closely to prepare or assist insurrectionary movements in the Ottoman provinces. The new government did not exclude the possibility, once the insurrections commenced, of sending the Greek army into Thessaly and Epirus.

Russian reverses at Plevna, however, removed the sense of urgency. Instead, however, of taking advantage of the respite, the Greeks reverted to their old debate: should they or should they not act? Indecisiveness reached the point of paralysis following Kanaris's death in September. The government continued to exist as an "acephalous" cabinet but was unable to take a major decision.

It was only when the Russians reached Edirne that public reaction threw the acephalous government out of office. Alexandros Koumoundouros, a well-known advocate of confrontation with the Turks and cooperation with the Balkan nations, was now entrusted with leading the country into the war. His policy called for the invasion of Thessaly by the Greek army (without an official declaration of war) and for the outbreak of revolts that would support the army. This was a reversal of the role initially assigned to the insurrections. Originally the army was to intervene as a last resort to back up the insurrections. Nevertheless, even this policy was not carried out. Five days after crossing the border, the army was ordered back. The signing of the Edirne armistice had become known, and an attack on the Greek mainland and islands by Ottoman land and naval forces appeared imminent. At the same time, the Great Powers were exerting unbearable pressure on the Greek government to stop the hostilities that threatened to upset the fragile armistice. Koumoundouros complied. He was aware that Greek interests had no chance of being heard, let alone served, at a European peace conference if there had been no armed activity in the subject provinces. Thus, with the recall of the army from Thessaly, he gave the green light for a general outbreak of the long-prepared insurrections in Crete, Epirus, Thessaly, and Macedonia. For a third time, the task assigned to the insurrectionary movement was changed. The subject Greeks — Thessalians, Epirotes, Macedonians, and Cretans — along with volunteers from the Kingdom were asked to rise in revolt not to liberate their land or support the operations of the Greek army but merely to offer Greek diplomacy the arguments it needed to claim whatever it could in what appeared a lost cause.

## Restraining Factors and Insurrectionary Ferment

Probably the most important of the factors that hampered efforts to initiate revolts was the fresh memory of the crushing of the Cretan Revolution. That event had been the last in a long line of similar experiences ever since the establishment of the Greek state. Small- and large-scale uprisings had occurred in the subject Greek provinces and Crete, either as spontaneous, violent reactions of the subject Greeks against their intolerable conditions of servitude or as a premeditated attempt to achieve the objectives of the Megali Idea. In both instances amateurism and romantic delusions had led to disaster. By the mid-seventies the ill-fated experiments of the past had had a sobering influence on the Greek public, which was apprehensive of the consequences of new revolts.

A second restraining factor was doubt whether revolutions and war as substitutes for long-term peaceful coexistence with the Turks really served the interests of Hellenism. To adopt the course of armed confrontation meant falling in with the Russian scheme for the dismemberment of the Ottoman Empire and striking up alliances with the Balkan Slavs. Recalling the emotionally charged feud with the Bulgarians over the establishment of the Exarchate, and suspecting that the Russians had thrown their weight behind Bulgarian claims to the mixed regions of Thrace and Macedonia, many Greeks strongly questioned the wisdom of placing Greek national aspirations under the wing of the tsar of Russia.[3] The Greeks were aware that if they adopted a pro-Russian line they ran the risk of antagonizing the anti-Russian European powers. England and France could easily paralyze Greek military initiatives against Turkey by the mere presence of their naval vessels in Greek waters. The lessons of the Crimean War were not easily forgotten.

Another restraining factor was the debate on the aims of the revolts. Should they be diversionary movements auxiliary to an all-out war effort against Turkey that would involve the regular Greek army? Or should they carry the full responsibility of a liberation struggle and be clandestinely assisted by the Greek state? This debate continued indecisively until the very last moment, to the point that it seriously handicapped the insurrectionary preparations in the critical months of the Russo–Turkish War.

A last factor was the sad state of military preparedness of the Greek Kingdom. After the collapse of the Cretan Revolution, all programs for the development of the Greek army and navy had been drastically curtailed. On the eve of outbreak of the Russo–Turkish War the strength of the Greek army did not exceed 12,500 men, divided as follows: infantry 8,187, artillery 603 (five batteries), cavalry 400 (with 170 horses), engineers 500, medical 172, gendarmerie 2,464. General conscription was seriously undermined by a system of replacements that resulted in de facto exemption of a large number of young men from military service. The professional training of the officers' corps was far below European standards, as the cadres did not profit from observing foreign military exercises or, with very few exceptions, from attending foreign military academies. Worse yet was the quality of senior officers, many of whom had ascended to their rank by dubious means and certainly without any combat experience. No general staff existed to plan or direct large-scale campaigns. Probably the most robust section of the military establishment was the career noncommissioned officers, who had acquired much experience in previous insurrectionary movements, particularly in combating brigandage. Nevertheless, such experience, without proper guidance, could not be sufficient for regular army operations. As for the Greek soldier, various contemporary observers both Greek and foreign agreed that he had remarkable abilities (perseverance, adaptability, intelligence, courage) to sustain difficult military conditions and perform demanding tasks. On the other hand, he was known for his lack of discipline and emotional stability.[4]

Military equipment was in a similar unsatisfactory condition. On the eve of the Eastern crisis a variety of weapons systems were in use, among them the Mylonas rifle, which was locally manufactured, the breech-loading Chassepot, and the old muzzle-loading Remington and Minié carbines. The confusion increased in 1877—78, when the army began to be supplied with new Gras rifles. Worse yet was the situation in the artillery batteries, which were equipped with old-model 12-lb. guns. Only in the beginning of 1878 was the Greek artillery able to form ten new batteries equipped with Krupp guns.[5]

As for the Greek navy, it could hardly be a match for the Ottoman fleet, which was commanded by a British admiral, Hobart Pasha. With the exception of the ironclad *King George* (61 m, 320 hp, 12.5 knots maximum speed), there was no other man-of-war capable of battle duty (with the possible exception of a smaller battleship, the *Queen Olga*). The rest were small vessels useful only for patrol or convoy missions.[6]

As the clouds of war darkened after the failure of the Constantinople Conference, the Greek government initiated a major procurement program and set out to reorganize the army. By the time the decision to invade Thessaly was taken early in 1878, the strength of the army had almost doubled to 25,000 men. General conscription became really compulsory, while the number of replacements and volunteers was sharply reduced.[7]

All these were elements that discouraged plans for initiating revolts. But there were also certain factors that sustained the view that revolts were possible, if not unavoidable.

By the mid-seventies, Greek national ideology had permeated all social strata of the population in the Greek-inhabited provinces of Turkey. In the provinces adjoining the Kingdom, constant movement of people across the borders facilitated the flow of ideas, while frequent uprisings had strengthened the yearning for freedom and unification with the free Greek state. This had been true particularly for Thessaly and southern Epirus. Since the unification of the Ionian islands in 1864, such intercourse extended as far north as Santi Quaranta and Chimara, a few miles from the Greek-held island of Kerkyra. In Macedonia, the rapid spread of Greek education in the southern Greek-speaking and in the central polyglot areas was instrumental in disseminating Greek national ideology irrespective of language differences. In the sixties and up to the commencement of the Eastern crisis of 1875—78 a large percentage of Albanian-speaking Christians in Epirus and Slav- and Vlach-speakers in Macedonia shared the same national sentiments as their Greek-speaking cohabitants. Despite the emergence of Bulgarian nationalism and the clashes between Patriarchists and Exarchists over control of local churches and schools, by the mid-seventies the overwhelming majority of Slav-speakers in the central mixed zone of Macedonia remained loyal to the Ecumenical Patriachate and thence accessible to Greek national ideology.[8] On Crete, Greek national ideology had been cemented among the Christians through a series of national liberation struggles and continuous political activity.

National ideology was hardly sufficient in itself to instigate revolts. What would really tip the scales for the masses was the social and economic conditions in which they lived. Following the military operations of 1875–76 and the outbreak of the Russo–Turkish War the plight of the peasants reached such abysmal depths that a Greek consul reported from Macedonia that the people would welcome not only the Russian army but even "Indo-chinese" bands as long as they promised them deliverance.[9] It was evident that the social causes for revolt were maturing faster than the national ones, at least among the Christian peasantry.

## Revolutionary Kaleidoscope in the Kingdom and the Ottoman Provinces

In the Kingdom the events of 1876 strengthened the ranks of the "activists" among the refugees from the subject provinces, the intelligentsia, including the university students, and the military. Leadership in organizing insurrectionary movements rested with various nationalist societies. By 1875, the most prominent such societies were the Ethniki Amyna, Adelfotis, (which had a clandestine section patterned, more or less, on the Masonic lodge), and Rigas, an antimonarchic as well as nationalist group. In addition, there were minor groupings of a regional character, such as societies of Cretans, Thessalians, Macedonians, and Epirotes, whose leading members could be found in one or another major society.[10]

Until the Constantinople Conference, these societies had not undertaken any significant activity. Thus, early in 1876, when the Serbs approached them with a request to assist in stirring up the subject Greeks to revolt, they demurred, unwilling to act contrary to the government's expressed policy of neutrality. Only a few individuals, such as Leonidas Voulgaris, a well-known revolutionary and supporter of Balkan cooperation, expressed willingness to prepare armed bands to enter Thessaly, Epirus, and Macedonia.[11] Prime Minister Koumoundouros, to whom Voulgaris confided the Serbs' proposals, did not discourage such contacts, although he was careful not to commit his government to any action which would lead to revolt.[12]

Adelfotis concentrated on proselytizing the subject Greeks in order to prepare the ground for armed risings. It appears to have adopted the system of the Philiki Etaireia, which had prepared the Greek War of Independence, in dispatching "apostles" to initiate "brothers" to the "cause." Merchants, professionals, teachers, clergy (including some bishops), community leaders, and even brigand chiefs took the oath to Adelfotis."[13] Ethniki Amyna concentrated on raising funds both in the Kingdom and among the prosperous Greeks of the diaspora and on purchasing arms.[14]

As we have seen, the Constantinople Conference was the signal for adopting a policy of action. The nationalist societies began to alert the subject Greeks to prepare for a general rising. Ethniki Amyna formed a central committee under Konstantinos Paparigopoulos, who was succeeded by Pavlos Kalligas. Later, however, when the "ecumenical" cabinet was formed, Adelfotis and Ethniki Amyna established a joint central committee under Kalligas and took over the direction of the insurrectionary preparations.

On the basis of the hitherto unpublished records of the Central Committee and Kalligas's papers, a fairly accurate picture can be constructed of the way insurrectionary activities were conceived, financed, organized, and brought to their final stage. Consular reports from the provinces and personal archives or published collections of documents of regional societies such as the Cretan and the Macedonian shed additional light on an insufficiently known page of modern Greek history.[15]

## The Central Committee and the Government

Despite the objections of certain minor nationalist or political groupings, among them Rigas, and certain refugee lobbies, Ethniki Amyna and Adelfotis acting jointly proceeded to coordinate their activities with government policy and even to submit themselves to government control and supervision. But they continued to enjoy much freedom of action in planning and organizing the insurrectionary movement, in fund raising and procurement of arms, in expanding their secret network in the Ottoman provinces, and even in selecting cadres for the future armed bands. On matters of general policy, however, such as deciding when to commence large-scale recruitment, dispatch bands across the frontier, or even conduct negotiations with Albanian chiefs for joint action, prior government authorization was necessary.[16]

Since all political leaders were represented in the "ecumenical" cabinet, no political difficulties hindered cooperation between the members of the two societies and the government. Indeed, the government asked to have its own representatives, all military officers, attend the meetings of the Central Committee.[17] Their role was to convey to the committee the government's views, particularly on military issues, and to examine and report to the government the committee's decisions on finances, military operations, recruitment, and arms procurement. On political matters the government authorized two of its members, Foreign Minister Charilaos Trikoupis and Justice Minister Thrasyvoulos Zaimis, to be in charge of all questions connected with the preparation of the insurrectionary movement.[18]

This arrangement continued smoothly until Prime Minister Kanaris's death on September 15. Although Trikoupis and Zaimis retained their mandate, other ministers began to interfere in the committee's work, in order either to encourage the preparations for the revolts (as did Minister of Interior Alexandros Koumoundouros) or to impede them (as did Minister of Finance E. Deligeorgis and Minister of War Charalambos Zymvrakakis). As a result, in the critical closing weeks of the Russo—Turkish War relations between the committee and the government were strained.[19] A major incident that occurred early in January 1878 almost blew the entire effort to pieces. On New Year's Eve, Trikoupis, Zaimis, and Koumoundouros, apparently speaking on behalf of the entire cabinet, gave the committee the go-ahead for bands to be ready to cross the border immediately, signaling the commencement of the revolts. Captain Konstantinos Ischomachos, the committee's military expert, lost no time in rushing to the frontier. Word went out to the committee's agents in the Ottoman provinces to alert the people. A few days later, however, the government went back on its decision, thus placing the committee in a very awkward position and threatening to expose prematurely to the Turks the entire operation.[20]

A new type of government-committee relations emerged when Koumoundouros assumed the premiership on January 23. This shrewd and experienced politician believed that the revolts were much too a delicate and serious matter to be left to private individuals or nationalist societies. For this reason, he decided that the government should take direct, though covert, control of the insurrectionary movement. After some rather harsh exchanges, the new arrangement provided for the Central Committee to continue to exist and, indeed, to appear to be directing the insurrections. In practice, however, it was merely to act as a front for the government, even on minute details.[21] Thus, for all practical purposes, the real headquarters of the insurrectionary movements was transferred to the Ministry of the Interior, where Koumoundouros, in his dual capacity as prime minister and minister of the interior, became the true commander in chief of the revolts that, early in February, began to break out in Thessaly, Epirus, Macedonia, and, naturally, Crete.

As early as July 1877, the government had provided the Central

Committee with a substantial sum of money as well as arms and ammunition from government stores. These, together with the funds raised by the Ethniki Amyna and Adelfotis and the weapons already purchased abroad, formed the material basis for commencing the revolutionary process. Nevertheless, considerable difficulties were raised, particularly by the ministers of war and finance, in forwarding to the committee the funds or supplies already agreed upon by Trikoupis and Zaimis. Thus, whereas in early August the government had endorsed the committee's general plan and budget and had agreed to supply it with 21,000,000 rounds of ammunition, by November the War Ministry had made available only 4,347,100 rounds. Between October and December, i. e., after the Russians had overrun Plevna, government officials not only continued to raise all kinds of trivial obstacles, but on orders from Zymvrakakis even placed entire depots of weapons belonging to the committee under military custody.[22] This situation did not change until Koumoundouros formed his own government and opened the state treasury to finance the armed struggle. According to its records, the Central Committee had administered 1,500,000 drachmas of government funds by May 13 1878, when most of the revolts had ended.[23]

The committee maintained close contacts with select government officials below cabinet level, particularly in the border districts. It was absolutely necessary that such cooperation proceed smoothly in order to maintain the traffic of arms, recruiting of volunteers, and communication across the border. When Koumoudouros took over command of the movement, trusted nomarchs were transferred to border prefectures to coordinate all activities connected with the military operations across the border. Naturally, the provincial committees and special emissaries of the Central Committee continued their work, but they had to clear major decisions with the government's representative.[24]

Most fruitful was the cooperation of the Central Committee with the Greek consuls in the Ottoman regions. As early as July 1877, Trikoupis instructed the consuls to assist the committee's endeavors. The consulates in Macedonia, Thrace, Epirus, and Crete responded with a constant flow of reports, thus furnishing the committee with valuable intelligence on the situation in the provinces, the strength and fortifications of the Ottoman army, and the morale and military potential of the Christians. The consuls also offered valuable advice for strategy and tactics on the regional level. Certain consulates, particularly those of Thessaloniki, under Konstantinos Vatikiotis, Monastir, under Petros Logothetis, and Chania, under Alexandros Logothetis, became real centers, coordinating revolutionary preparations and guiding the political and military leaders and committees.[25]

## Structure

The Central Committee, composed of eight members (four from Ethniki Amyna and four from Adelfotis), was the main coordinating body of the insurrectionary movement.[26] It was assisted by a wide network of local committees and representatives of both societies in the Kingdom, the Ottoman Empire, and the diaspora. The separate councils of the two societies continued to function, giving guidance to their own representatives in the provinces. Wherever the local committee of one society appeared to enjoy better contacts or prestige it assumed leadership. In other instances, impromptu local joint committees came into existence. But no merger developed, as both societies maintained their individuality. This was primarily because of the secret initiation methods and organizational apparatus of Adelfotis. There were, however, instances in which directives from the Central Committee were ignored and local committees, usually of Adelfotis, took risky initiatives by sending weapons or armed guerrillas across the border.[27] Crete was a special case. From the beginning the Cretan representatives and revolutionary chiefs acted through their own channels, bypassing the Central Committee. It is no surprise, therefore, that there was not one Cretan on the Central Committee despite many pleas from Cretans to appoint one, preferably banker Markos Renieris.[28]

Local committees or representatives of the Central Committee could be found in almost all border towns, as well as on the islands near the Turkish coast. They were entrusted not only with arms traffic and recruitment but also with the task of coordinating preparations with the Greeks on the other side of the border. At times they even assumed the delicate mission of conducting secret negotiations with Turkish officials wishing to desert or Albanian chiefs flirting with the idea of a joint Greek—Albanian undertaking.[29] Similar committees in towns in the interior worked mainly at fund raising and recruitment.

Among the Greeks of the diaspora, certain of the old committees established at the time of the Cretan Revolution continued to exist up to the eve of the Eastern crisis. In late 1876, their number rapidly increased as requests from Athens for donations multiplied. In certain countries these committees were authorized to conclude purchases of weapons in the name of the Central Committee, while in other instances they were engaged in propaganda and public relations activities for the Greek cause. In some cases such committees even armed and forwarded to the Kingdom small groups of young and enthusiastic volunteers wishing to enlist in the Greek army or the guerrilla bands.[30] Still, their major preoccupation was fund raising. The records of Ethniki Amyna for the first three months of 1877 provide vivid evidence of the impressive worldwide response of Greek communities. Among the communities listed are those of Calcutta, various towns in the Caucasus, Egypt, England, France, Romania, and the main urban centers of the Otto- man Empire, as well as numerous smaller communities.[31] It should be noted, however, that not all the communities with fund-raising committees necessarily had organizational links with the national societies in the King- dom. Some of their members, however, who had been initiated by these societies acted as liaison for local revolutionaries.

Other groupings continued to function in the Kingdom. As long as the Central Committee monopolized the government's favors, these groups had little to show for their efforts. In the closing months of the war, however, as the government's indecisiveness rendered the Central Committee powerless, some of these groups gained influence, particularly among the anxious subject Greeks. This was particularly true of the Cretans, who as early as 1876 had formed their own "Cretan Center," with Renieris at its head. Cretan chiefs and splinter groups made their own preparations on the side. To avoid confusion, the "ecumenical" government instructed the Central Committee to desist from any initiative concerning Crete. When, early in 1878, the time came for a general revolt on the island, a special Cretan Committee was formed to coordinate all relevant activities in the Kingdom.[32] Similarly, in February and March 1878, Koumoundouros endorsed the setting up of separate Macedonian[33] and Epirote[34] Committees composed of eminent natives of the respective regions. Such an arrangement became easier to handle once the government became the true coordinator of all revolutionary activities.

In the Ottoman provinces, the structure of insurrectionary preparations varied markedly. Because of the conspiratorial nature of the work there is a scarcity of sources on the mechanisms of the insurrectionary movement. Crete is an exception, as the mass character of its revolution and its self- governing administrative system preserved a wealth of material. Consular reports, though valuable in themselves, are not very revealing on this particular subject because of the need for utmost secrecy. Putting together scattered materials, it is possible to conclude that authorized local com- mittees, first of Adelfotis and Ethniki Amyna and later of the Central Com- mittee, had been established in most major urban centers of Macedonia, Epirus, and Thessaly. From the cities a close-knit network of initiated "brothers" or correspondents covered the smaller towns and the coun- tryside. How thorough this organization was is indicated by the fact that when the revolts broke out representatives of almost all the villages in certain localities rushed to participate in the first organizational meetings of the revolutionary political bodies.[35]

The main concern of such committees was of course to prepare the minds of the people for the general rising. Rapid developments in the northern

Balkans and deteriorating conditions locally had rendered their task easier but not without risk, as ultraconservative elements among the Christians were known to object strongly to any confrontation with Ottoman authority.[36] It was also the duty of these committees to solve problems of logistic support for the armed bands, to receive and secure arms supplies, to organize communications, and to alert the local revolutionaries who wished to join the bands of volunteers coming from the Kingdom. The local committees, composed as they were of men of influence, professionals, merchants, and educators, were expected also to shoulder the political work of the revolts. The burden of the actual combat was outside their competence, although when the time came some leaders followed the guerrilla bands, arms in hand.

## Objectives and Military Planning

The strategy of the revolts aimed mainly at three objectives: (a) liberating the Greek-inhabited provinces of the Ottoman Empire and uniting them with the Kingdom; (b) blocking the southern expansion of the Slavs; and (c) if neither was feasible, raising the Greek question at the European peace conference.[37]

From a tactical point of view, the revolts aimed at mass uprisings by the Greeks of Thessaly, Epirus, Macedonia, and Crete and concerted action with the Albanians in Epirus and even farther to the north. From the political as well as the military point of view, the insurgents sought to gain control of entire districts, which they would fortify and secure for a considerable time. "Provisional governments" were to be set up to declare the liberation of each province and its union with the Greek Kingdom.

Having set such ambitious goals, the leaders of the revolutionary committees had to work out detailed operational plans for the entire insurrectionary movement as well as specific plans for each province. In July 1877, Ischomachos submitted his plan, which was endorsed first by the committee and subsequently by the government with only minor changes. Although the actual text has not been found, its contents may be inferred from the committee's records and other documents, as well as from reminiscences of contemporary fighters.[38]

The central concept of this plan was to instigate revolts simultaneously in the three provinces to the north and in Crete. To this end armed bands from the Kingdom would enter not only Thessaly, southern Epirus, and Crete but also Macedonia and northern Epirus, where they would act as nuclei for mass uprisings. As for Macedonia, the plan envisaged the landings of two large armed bands, one on the Gulf of Orfano (Eleftheroupolis) and the other on the Olympus-Pieria coast. The first expeditionary force would aim to stir up the Greeks of Chalkidiki and the Serres sanjak and then move north to establish itself on the Rhodope Mountains, thus drawing the line between the Bulgarian and Greek zones in Macedonia. The other would secure Olympus and the Pieria Mountains, cross the Aliakmon River, and move north to central Macedonia. If everything went according to plan, a splinter group would swing west in the direction of Kozani. Finally, a third armed group, with Ischomachos himself at the head, would move inland, cross Thessaly, and reach Macedonia from the southwest. Its task would be to lead in revolt the population of the Grevena—Kastoria—Florina—Prespa region all the way to the Pelagonian plain. On the Epirus side, a band from Kerkyra would land on the opposing coast in the Santi—Quaranta—Delvine district to start a Greek—Albanian joint rising and thus divert attention from southern Epirus, where incursions were envisaged at many points. In Thessaly, volunteers and local insurgents were expected to establish themselves in almost all the mountain ranges, encircling the Thessalian plain from almost all directions. The focal points would be the Almyros region in the south, the Pilio—Ossa Mountains in the East, and the Pindus Range in the West. On Crete military planning was in the hands of the Cretan chiefs and the elected representatives of the Cretan people. By the end of 1877 many of the chiefs, exiled since 1869, were returning secretly to their island once again to lead an armed clash with the Ottoman occupier. It was expected that the insurrectionary movement would assume massive proportions from one end of the island to the other. If the Turks could not be driven from Crete, they would be restricted to the five or six fortified towns, thus offering the Cretans a valid argument for demanding unification with the Kingdom.

When the plan was conceived it was generally believed that the Russians would continue their victorious march and cross the Balkans without much difficulty. Under the circumstances the Greek revolts would face rather weak resistance from second-rate Ottoman troops, the usual hordes of bashi-bazouks, and Albanian mercenaries. Massive reinforcements from Asia Minor were considered highly unlikely. The regular Greek army would also take the field at the opportune moment. The insurgents were expected to conduct regular offensive operations, seizing and holding large inhabited regions. Although guerrilla-type operations were not excluded, the planners appear to have envisaged regular military tactics even for units operating in regions far from the Greek borders.

## Logistics and Personnel

The logistics of such an enterprise would have been demanding even for a regular military command. In this case, they were shouldered by a committee of eminent scholars, distinguished professionals, successful merchants, and bankers, with only a few professional military in its ranks. Its first priority was to secure the necessary armaments, mostly from abroad. The story of these purchases is an unsung epic involving the voluntary services, fortunes, and personal risks of numerous Greeks in various European, Asiatic, and North African countries before the valuable cargo could be safely unloaded by the committee's agents in Piraeus or some other Greek port.[39] Utilizing the funds collected by the Greek communities of the diaspora, Ethniki Amyna had been able by March 1877 to purchase 45,000 rifles.[40] Eager to get the largest possible number of pieces with the funds available, the committee sought special bargains. As a result, it obtained muzzle-loading Remingtons and Springfields that the European armies were offering for sale at very low prices, as well as small quantities of Chassepots, but no Gras at all. When the time came to use the arms it was found that a great number of them were obsolete. Moreover, the great variety of ordnance created immense problems of ammunition supply that proved fatal to units engaged in a mixture of guerrilla and regular warfare.

The committee seriously discussed the procurement of artillery to support the operations of its armed bands. In the end, this project did not materialize. Another grandiose scheme had a similar fate. The committee's records show that it seriously discussed and partially financed the plans of a certain American by the name of Fachris (?) for the construction of a submarine.[41] Undoubtedly such a formidable weapon in the hands of the Cretan insurgents would have reduced the risks of sea communication between Crete, the Cyclades, and the mainland, but one is bound to question the wisdom of the committee's engaging in such a scheme when the outbreak of the revolts appeared imminent and available resources were meager.

The committee's logistical endeavors were not limited to arming, equipping, and financing the expeditions of armed bands from the Kingdom. A serious problem was how to equip the insurgents in Ottoman regions. From the outset, the committee sought to create secret depots of arms in Thessaly, Epirus, and Macedonia. At tremendous risk, deliveries were made by sea to Crete, Epirus, and Thessaly and to Chalkidiki and Pieria in Macedonia. The bulk of the arms had to be carried by the volunteer bands themselves.[42] Since arms sometimes did not reach their destination overland, it was more convenient to transport them by sea, but the risk of total loss had to be weighed.

The human aspect of the revolutionary preparations was by far the most complex. In the Ottoman provinces as early as the summer of 1876 there were those who were ready for the signal for a new rising. Already two armed bands had infiltrated from the Kingdom and were operating in Thessaly in the old klephtic tradition. By 1877 the subject Greeks in Epirus, Thessaly, and Macedonia expected that hostilities might break out at any moment.

The Ottoman provinces had two types of Greeks as far as their military potential was concerned. The first group was composed of experienced bands of klephts or bandits. In peacetime they were known for their savage treatment of Muslims as well as rich Christians and Jews. In time of war and insurrections they would join the revolutionary bands as freedom fighters, thus serving their nation and themselves. The hope of amnesty shone with equal brilliance in their eyes as that of a liberated Thessaly or Macedonia.[43] In the second group were the thousands of patriots from the villages and even towns who longed to fight the social as well as the national oppressor. Their enthusiasm, however, was inversely proportional to their knowledge of the art of war.

In the Kingdom the assembly of volunteers was more complex. The backbone of the force was comprised of old and new refugees from the Ottoman provinces. They were sincere and enthusiastic in joining the armed bands, but the prospect of liberating their native lands propelled them into pressing for premature and ill-advised initiatives. Next were young men serving in the army, the gendarmerie, and the national guard, who were expected to desert their units to join the revolutionary bands. Certain individuals with knowledge of guerrilla fighting were also on the list: ex-brigands, social outcasts, and even condemned petty criminals who were eager to exchange their remaining sentences for "patriotic" duty. This riff-raff was joined by bona fide patriots, volunteers from the diaspora or from the large Greek centers of the Ottoman Empire, such as Smyrna and Constantinople. A last group of volunteers was the philhellene Europeans. Following a long tradition going back to the War of Independence, such individuals made their appearance in the Kingdom in 1876–78. A number of them joined the bands, offering their valuable military experience to the Greek struggle. The Central Committee's records show that there were proposals for organizing legions of 1,000 Garibaldian Italians and Swiss and as many British.[44] For various reasons, these proposals did not materialize, but they are indicative of the wide appeal the Greek insurrectionary movements enjoyed among a segment of the liberal and adventurous European public.

The problem of leadership was the Achilles' heel of the entire movement. On paper, natives of the respective provinces who enjoyed the confidence of their compatriots were expected to lead the volunteers. But such persons were hard to find. In other cases, the sons of respected old warriors of the War of Independence did not measure up to the standards required. Thus, the leaders who could mobilize a following were absent in the revolutionary movement of 1876–78.[45]

Also absent were coordinated commands. The Central Committee finally chose a system of armed bands operating individually under their own chiefs. Such a system could probably function in an unorthodox type of warfare, but in regular combat this was impossible. The difference in background of the leaders was bound to prove a major handicap. Alongside the army officer accustomed to the tactics taught in a European war academy was a brigand chief familiar only with the old klephtic tricks. In war councils a gendarmerie captain might be seated next to an archbandit, sharing the table with a lawyer and even a priest — a gathering perhaps colorful but hardly conducive to the management of insurrectionary operations. Certainly, such exaggerated conditions were not the rule. As it happened, successful operations were conducted in all three provinces. Battles were won. But the war could not be fought with that type of leadership.

The conduct of the armed revolts which started in February 1878 requires special study. Much had been done in a year and a half to prepare the nation psychologically and materially. The dramatic change of circumstances early in 1878 imperiled the insurrectionary movement but did not kill it. Certain of its more ambitious goals had to be abandoned. Although operations in Epirus, southern Macedonia, and Thessaly lasted for almost two months, they were eventually crushed. Action on Crete, however, lasted until the end of the Congress of Berlin.

Of their three objectives the revolts achieved, in the end, only the third. When in April 1878 the British intervened to obtain a cease-fire, they promised to demand the incorporation of the Greek question into the agenda of the congress as if the revolts were still going on. The promise was kept. The discussion of the Greek question in Berlin opened the way for the liberation of Thessaly and the Arta district in 1881.[46]

## NOTES

1. Standard works on this period are Evangelos Kofos, *Greece and the Eastern Crisis, 1875–1878* (Thessaloniki, 1975); idem, *O Ellinismos stin Periodo 1869–1881; Apo to telos tis Kritikis Epanastaseos stin Prosartisi tis Thessalias,* reprint from *Istoria tou Ellinikou Ethnous,* vol. 13 (Athens, 1981). For older works, consult Stylianos Lascaris, *La politique extérieure de la Grèce avant et après le Congrès de Berlin, 1875–1881* (Paris, 1924); Edouard Driault and Michel Lhéritier, *Histoire diplomatique de la Grèce de 1821 à nos jours,* vol. 3 (Paris, 1925).

2. Great Britain, Public Record Office, Foreign Office Archives 32/467, Stuart to Derby, 301, December 21, 1876.

3. On the mixed reaction of the subject Greeks on this point, see Evangelos Kofos, "The Subject Greeks during the Eastern Crisis of 1875–1878," in *Medjunarodni naučni skup povodom 100-godišnjice ustanaka u Bosni i Hercegovini*, vol. 4 (Sarajevo, 1977), pp. 99–111.

4. Kofos, *O Ellinismos*, pp. 78–79; Miltiadis D. Seïzanis, *I Politiki tis Ellados kai i Epanastasis tou 1878 en Makedonia, Ipeiro kai Thessalia* (Athens, 1878), pp. 29–35; *Megali Elliniki Enkyklopaideia "Pyrsos"* vol. "Ellas," pp. 277–78, and vol. 22, p. 434; P. G. Danglis, *Anamniseis, Engrafa-Allilografia: To Archeion tou*, ed. X. Lefkoparidis, vol. 1 (Athens, 1965), pp. 41–43.

5. Kofos, *O Ellinismos*, p. 79.

6. Ibid., p. 79; *"Pyrsos"*, vol. 10, p. 294.

7. Seïzanis, *I Politiki*, p. 29; Kofos, *O Ellinismos*, p. 80.

8. M. B. Sakellarion, ed., *Makedonia: 4000 Chronia Ellinikis Istorias kai Politismou* (Athens, 1982), p. 460; Evangelos Kofos, "Dilemmas and Orientations of Greek Policy in Macedonia: 1878–1886," *Balkan Studies* 21 (1980): 48–49.

9. Evangelos Kofos, *I Epanastasis tis Makedonias kata to 1878* (Thessaloniki, 1969), p. 171.

10. Kofos, *Greece*, pp. 105–7; idem, *O Ellinismos*, pp. 75–77.

11. Leonidas Voulgaris, *Apokalyfthito i Alithia* (Athens, 1878); also, on Voulgaris, see Kofos, *O Ellinismos*, pp. 53, 62–63; Seïzanis, *I Politiki*, pp. 205–6; Kalligas Papers (in the possession of Marinos Kalligas of Athens; hereafter KP), Kalligas to Voulgaris no. 154, July 19, 1877.

12. Kofos, *Greece*, pp. 47–52.

13. Kofos, *O Ellinismos*, pp. 75–76, quoting relevant sources; Nicholaos, Bishop of Kitros, *Apomnimonev mate tis en Makedonia Epanastaseos* (Memoirs of the Revolution in Macedonia), unpublished papers in Istoriki kai Ethnologiki Etaireia tis Ellados, Athens. Nicholaos gives an account of his initiation into Adelfotis. Also Evangelos Kofos, "O Episkopos Kitrous Nicholaos kai i Epanastasi tou 1878: Ta Anekdota Apomnimonevmata tou," *Makedonika* 20 (1980): 200–201.

14. Correspondence in KP.

15. The minutes of the meetings of the Central Committee of Ethniki Amyna and Adelfotis are deposited in Genika Archeia tou Kratous, Athens, "Tsontos Vardas Archives," File no. 22 (hereafter GAK/IV). On Ethniki Amyna, see KP; on Adelfotis, see Elias Georgiou, *I Politiki tis Gallias kata tas en Thessalia, Ipeiro, Makedonia kai Kriti Epanastaseis tou 1877–1878* (Athens, 1969), quoting from the archives of George Filateros, a leading member of Adelfotis; on the Cretan committees, see Stavros Kelaidis, *O Parthenios G. Kelaidis kai i Proxeniki aftou Allilographia 1854–1904* (Chania, 1930), pp. 37–65; M. Parlama, "Protokollon tou Genikou Archigeiou ton Anatolikon Eparchion tis Kritis kata tin Epanastasin tou 1878," *Kritika Chronika* (Iraklio, 1954), pp. 171–203; Archeia Vivliothikis Voulis ton Ellinon, "Markos Renieris Archives" (for the period 1876–78) (hereafter AVVE/MR); on the Macedonian Committee, see Ioannis Notaris, ed., *Archeion Stefanou Nik. Dragoumi: Anekdota Engrafa gia tin Epanastasi tou 1878 sti Makedonia* (Thessaloniki, 1966); also see E. Kofos, *I Epanastasis*; on Epirus, see D. F. Karatzenis, *Oi Epanastaseis tis Artis tou 1866, 1878* (Athens, 1874), and Danglis, *Anamniseis*.

16. Kofos, *O Ellinismos*, pp. 75–77; idem, *Greece*, pp. 114–15.

17. Initially there were three: Lt. General Artemis N. Michos, and Major Generals Athanasios Valtinos and Alexandros Skarlatos–Soutsos. Valtinos died shortly thereafter, and Soutsos was assigned to a combat post later in the year. (GAK/IV, meeting August 1, 1877, f. A 18, 64 and 68. (*Note:* ff. A 1–71 cover the period from July 12, 1877, to September 23, 1877, while ff. B 1–239 cover the period September 24, 1877 to October 27, 1879.)

18. Kofos, *Greece*, p. 115; KP, Kalligas to Trikoupis, no. 54, October 12, 1877; GAK/IV, ff. A 1–2.

19. GAK/IV, meeting November 11, ff. B 34–38, 57, 78, 86, 89.

20. Strong protest by Kalligas in his letter no. 245, January 22, 1878 (KP); also GAK/IV, ff. B 89 (meeting January 14, 1878), B 94 (meeting January 20).

21. KP, Kalligas to Koumoundouros, nos. 269, February 4, and 278, February 14.

22. KP, Kalligas to Zymvrakakis, no. 48, October 10, and to Trikoupis, no. 54, October 12; also GAK/IV, ff. A 37–38, 49–50, B 24, 34–38, and 45.

23. GAK/IV, meeting June 3, 1878, ff. B. 195–96.

24. Supporting evidence of such cooperation appears in Notaris, *Archeion*; Georgiou, *I Galliki Politiki*; and Danglis, *Anamniseis*; also KP, Kalligas to nomarch K. Evgeniadis (Lamia), February 15, 1878, to nomarch Ilias Pappäiliopoulos (Lamia), no. 433, March 18, 1878, to K. Milionis, no. 368, March 2, 1878, urging him to cooperate with the local nomarch.

25. On the Macedonian consulates, see Kofos, *I Epanastasis* and Notaris, *Archeion*; on consul Vatikiotis, see GAK/IV, ff. A 42, 51, 57–58, 70–71, B 11–12, 25, 33, 39, 44–45, 55, 58, 67, 72, and 73, where the Central Committee specifically acknowledges the General Consulate as the center of the revolt in Macedonia; on the consulate at Chania, see Kofos, *O Ellinismos*, p. 100, and *Greece*, p. 130, n. 4; also many relevant dispatches in Archeio Ypourgeiou Exoterikon (hereafter AYE), File, "Circulars"/1878.

26. The eight members of the joint Central Committee were, from Ethniki Amyna, Pavlos Kalligas, George Vasileiou, Michael Melas, and Stefanos Skouloudis, and from Adelfotis, Nicholaos Damaskinos, Konstantinos Ischomachos, Leonidas Paschalis, and Spyridon Aravantinos (GAK/IV).

27. On an unauthorized dispatch of arms by the Kerkyra Committee, see KP, Kalligas to the Kerkyra Committee of Ethniki Amyna, no. 188, September 29, 1877.

28. Kofos, *O Ellinismos*, pp. 97–100; also GAK/IV, ff. A 11, 20.

29. Seïzanis, *I Politiki*, pp. 129–30; Karatsenis, *Oi Epanastaseis*; GAK/IV, ff. A 2, 7, 8–9, 11–12, 23, 40, 47, 60, B 69, 75.

30. KP, Kalligas to Trikoupis, no. 59, October 16, 1877, reporting collection of 1,000 francs by Bucharest Greeks to finance the dispatch of a detachment of 150 young Greek volunteers.

31. KP, Documents nos. 1–45, letters acknowledging receipt of donations from Greeks of the diaspora.

32. AVVE/MR; also Kofos, *O Ellinismos*, pp. 97–99.

33. Ibid., p. 116; GAK/IV, ff. B 110–11.

34. Ibid., p. 109; KP, Kalligas to Koumoundouros, no. 432, March 16, 1878.

35. Nicholaos, *Apomnimonevmata*. Relevant material is recorded in the works of Notaris, Voulgaris, Georgiou, Seïzanis, and Kofos, *I Epanastasis*, as well as in KP and GAK/IV.

36. Bishop Nicholaos of Kitros was particularly critical of the ecclesiastical establishment.

37. The text that follows is based on materials drawn from KP, GAK/IV, AYE, and books by Kofos (*I Epanastasis* and *O Ellinismos*), Notaris (*Archeion*), Voulgaris (*Apokalifthito*), and Seïzanis (*I Politiki*).

38. On Ischomachos's plan and the government's approval, see GAK/IV, ff. A 2, 4, 5, 9–10, 13–14, 15, 19, 21–22; also Kofos, *O Ellinismos*, pp. 96–121.

39. On a consignment of 10,000 muzzle-loading rifles from St. Petersburg to Trieste and thence to Kerkyra, see Kofos, *Greece*, p. 114, n. 4.

40. Correspondence in KP.

41. GAK/IV, ff. A 51, 53, 55, B 18, 39–40. The first engine-propelled submarine was not constructed until 1886, and even that had a very limited capability to remain underwater.

42. GAK/IV and KP as well as the secondary sources listed in n. 37.

43. An excellent analysis on these armed bandits/guerrillas appears in John Koliopoulos, *Listes* (Athens, 1979).

44. GAK/IV, ff. A 38, B 83–85, 160, 163–64, 167–68, 174, and 182.

45. Seïzanis was particularly critical of this problem (*I Politiki*, pp. 95–96).

46. For a general evaluation, see Evangelos Kofos, "Greece at the Crossroads, 1878–1881: Reappraisal of Priorities in an Evolving Balkan Setting," *Actes, Colloque "La Dernière phase de la Crise Orientale et l'Héllenisme 1878–1881," Volos, Septembre 1981* (Athens, 1983).

Romania

Florin Constantiniu

# MILITARY AND POLITICAL FACTORS IN
# ROMANIA'S WAR OF INDEPENDENCE

Although A. J. P. Taylor's view that Plevna is one the "battles that have changed the course of history" may be considered somewhat extravagant, it is undisputable that the war of 1877–78 was one of the most important chapters in the Eastern Question.[1] Surprisingly, considering the importance of the war, its history is only pallidly reflected in most of the works that have been dedicated to that question, a conclusive example being the treatment of Romania's military contribution to the victory. In so weighty a reference book as *The Encyclopaedia of Military History*, for example, Romania's participation in the war is merely mentioned and nothing is said of the participation of the Romanian army in the development of the military operations.[2] My intention here is not to offer a detailed account of the battles fought by the Romanian army but rather to emphasize two aspects of the Romanian war effort: the role of Romania's military action as a necessary complement to its political efforts at winning independence and the importance of Romania's military contribution.

On the eve of its commitment to the war, the Romanian army, whose revival in modern form was but four decades old, boasted an effective strength of 100,000 men and 1,000 officers, the field army consisting of 58,700 men.[3] The Romanian units were well-equipped. Infantry troops had Peabody and Dreyse rifles and, later on, also Russian-provided Krnkas. The rather heterogeneous artillery comprised, among other things, the 1875-model 87-mm Krupp cannon, the best artillery piece of the time.[4] The comments of foreign observers on the quality of the Romanian army are synthesized in the words of the Austro–Hungarian consul in Bucharest: "The Romanian army has personnel of the highest caliber and in some respects is very well trained, but it lacks any tactical practice whatsoever."[5] In other words, the army that the Romanian state had made such huge efforts to equip had not yet been tested on the battlefield. The Eastern crisis of 1875–78 and the need to ground the political action that led to the proclamation of independence in military strength were to require the participation of the Romanian army in warfare.

Despite its modest size compared with those of the Great Powers, the existence of a Romanian military force that might influence the political-military development of the crisis undoubtedly secured Romania – even before the proclamation of independence – the status of a partner that could not be ignored. After May 9, 1877, it had become more and more obvious that the political decision had to be seconded by military action in order to ensure and consolidate the independence just proclaimed. This idea was clearly set forth in a report sent by the Romanian agent in Vienna, Ioan Bălăceanu, to the then foreign minister Mihail Kogălniceanu: "First, let's fight valiantly, for you cannot imagine what good, from the point of view of morale, the resolute attitude of our small army has done. ...The cannon at Oltenița and Calafat are speaking more eloquently, are pleading our cause better, and are being listened to more than anything our diplomacy and press might produce at present."[6]

The response of the European states to the proclamation of Romania's independence – ranging from indifference through reserve to hostility – made Romania's military commitment a necessity. The Russian decision makers were divided as to Romanian military involvement. The diplomats were hostile to it for political reasons, while the army favored it for pragmatic ones. The conviction that the war would be a triumphal march south of the Danube ensured that the diplomats would prevail: "Russia does not need the cooperation of the Romanian army," a Russian diplomat wrote.[7] The unwillingness of tsarist Russia to accept Romania's offers of cooperation created difficulties for the policy pursued by the government in Bucharest, the aim of which was to consolidate its independence. The political signifi-cance of participation of the Romanian army was pointed to by Kogălniceanu: "Military action by us on the right bank of the Danube is called for to dem-onstrate the impossibility of a return to the status quo ante bellum." The Romanian minister also stressed that Europe, faced with a fait accompli, would be compelled to acknowledge a reality it had thus far refused to sanction: the existence of an independent Romania.[8] The negative attitude of St. Petersburg toward the commitment of the Romanian army to the operations taking place south of the Danube changed with the strengthening of Ottoman resistance and the subsequent failures of the tsar's army. This alteration in the battlefield situation compelled the Russian high command to turn to the Romanian army for cooperation.

As a matter of fact, Romanian military action had begun long before the Russian appeal. Cover of the Danube line by the Romanian army served at the same time as cover for the movement of the Russian troops through

Romanian territory to the theater of war south of the Danube. Turkish artillery fire against Romanian positions on the left bank of the river met with the prompt and efficient response of the Romanian artillery (the first shell was shot at Calafat on April 26/May 8, 1877). The Romanian units repelled the Turkish inroads on the Romanian bank of the river and at the same time carried out reconnaissance missions and destroyed enemy vessels on the right bank. Cooperation with the Russian army had also begun before the conclusion of a formal agreement between the two countries. The Romanian forces provided protection, through brisk artillery fire, for the pontoons of the Russian army and backed with demonstrative fire its crossing of the Danube. They took part in the shelling of Nikopol and occupied the town in order to make it available to the Russian troops.[9]

On July 19/31, the commander in chief of the Russian army, Grand Duke Nikolay, sent a telegram to Prince Carol I asking for the immediate cooperation of the Romanian army in the light of the critical situation his army faced.[10] Though sympathetic to the Russian request because an Ottoman success might have shifted the theater of war onto Romanian territory, Romania's prince and government declined to send Romanian troops into battle unless the Russian high command agreed that they should have their own area of operations and line of communications. This agreement was obtained only after the visit of Carol I to the Russian headquarters on August 17/30, when he was entrusted with the command of the army besieging Plevna.

Strongly fortified and defended by the highly competent commander Osman Pasha, Plevna had become an abscess. The Plevna campaign is too well known to dwell upon, but the important part played by the Romanian army should be pointed out. During the bloody attack on August 30/ September 11, the Romanian troops obtained the only success of the day by carrying the Grivitsa 1 redoubt. Military specialists and war correspondents who were eyewitnesses spoke of the "determined bravery of the Romanians,"[11] emphasizing that the "Romanian army has covered itself with glory."[12]

It has not been sufficiently appreciated that the siege of Plevna foreshadowed in a way some of the characteristics of World War I. At a time when the Prussian army was regarded as a model, the Turks had equipped their infantry with Winchester and Martini—Henry repeating rifles, which had proved their qualities during the American Civil War (1861–65).[13] The association of infantry fire with fortifications and fighting spirit lent great effectiveness to the defense, causing a stalemate on the battlefield that was to be experienced again during the World War I years. At Plevna all the eyewitnesses mentioned the intensity of the fire of the Ottoman defense. The correspondent for the Berne newspaper *Bund* reported "such fire as I saw neither at Solferino nor at Custoza,"[14] while General Franz Totleben, speaking of a "shower of cartridges," wrote that "it seemed as if they were being let fly without respite by a machine."[15] The Romanian and Russian armies were forced to adapt to a hard new reality. The greater, then, is the merit of the young Romanian army that it succeeded in passing such a bloody test.

After a four-month siege, the Turkish garrison reached the end of its endurance. Osman Pasha tried to force an opening in the Russo–Romanian lines but failed in the attempt. Once again, the contribution of the Romanian army — particularly during the battle of Opanez — proved essential in thwarting Ottoman intentions. Osman Pasha in fact surrendered to a Romanian officer, Colonel Mihail Cerchez. An entirely Romanian success, to quote Grand Duke Nikolay, was the occupation of Rahova on November 9/21, an action meant to ensure the right wing both of the troops storming Plevna and of those advancing toward Vidin.[16]

After the fall of Plevna, the center of gravity of Romanian military operations shifted to the area of Vidin, the conquest of which became their main task. Of the battles that preceded the siege of that stronghold, mention should be made of Smîrdan, which once again proved the combat qualities of the Romanian soldier.[17] The shelling of Vidin, which had begun on January 15/27, 1878, was stopped by the conclusion of the Russo–Turkish armistice. The Romanian army occupied Vidin and Belogradchik as security for the peace negotiations. The consistent refusal of St. Petersburg to allow the presence of a Romanian representative at the negotiations opened a new phase in the relations between Romania and tsarist Russia during the Eastern crisis of 1875–78.

Romania's participation in the war and the value of its military contribution made the proclamation of independence irreversible. The events at Grivitsa, Rahova, and Smîrdan turned Romania into an important political and military factor in southeastern Europe. Two foreign observers perfectly grasped the situation. The French consul in Bucharest wrote: "The serious defeats sustained by the Russian army at the beginning of August allowed Romania to make a decent appearance on the stage."[18] And, however paradoxical it may seem, the Russian chancellor A. M. Gorchakov himself, an opponent of Romanian participation in the war who had doubted the capabilities of the Romanian army, wrote: "The Romanians fight well, and this war has the merit of having shown Europe that they deserve to be acknowledged as a nation."[19]

# NOTES

1. A. J. P. Taylor, *The Struggle for Mastery in Europe (1848–1918)* (Oxford, 1957).
2. R. E. Dupuy and T. N. Dupuy, *The Encyclopaedia of Military History* (New York, 1970), pp. 844–46.
3. Cf. Apostol Stan, *Renașterea armatei naționale* (Craiova, 1979).
4. Radu Rosetti, *Partea luată de armata română în războiul din 1877–1878* (Bucharest, 1926), pp. 20–21, 106.
5. Idem, *Un capitol al luptei pentru neatîrnăre, Analele* Academiei Române, Memoriile Secțiunii Istorice, series 3, vol. 26 (Bucharest, 1943–44), pp. 112–13.
6. *Documente privind istoria României: Războiul pentru independentă*, vol. 3 (Bucharest, 1954), pp. 107–8.
7. N. Corivan, *Lupta diplomatică pentru cucerirea independenței României* (Bucharest, 1977), pp. 123–24.
8. Ibid., p. 129.
9. For details on the development of military operations, see *România în războiul de independentă* (Bucharest, 1977), and Constantin Căzănișteanu and Mihail E. Ionescu, *Războiul neatîrnării României (1877–1878):Imprejurari diplomatice si operatii militare* (Bucharest, 1977).
10. For the circumstances in which the telegram was sent, see *România în războiul de independentă*, pp. 159–62.
11. Rosetti, *Partea luată de armata română*, p. 134. See also St. Pascu,ed., *Independența României* (Bucharest, 1977), pp. 250–51.
12. Rosetti, *Partea luată de armata română*, p. 134.
13. Charles Ailleret, *Histoire de l'armement* (Paris, 1948), p. 31.
14. Rosetti, *Partea luată de armata română*, p. 126; cf. Emile Wanty, *L'art de la guerre*, vol. 2 (Verviers, 1967), p. 51.
15. Ion I. Nistor, *Din corespondență lui Totleben de la Plevna*, Analele Academie Române, Memoriile Sectiunii Istorice, series 3, vol. 13, memoir 2 (Bucharest, 1933), p. 256.
16. *România în războiul de independentă*, pp. 236–37.
17. Ibid., pp. 303 ff.
18. Corivan, *Lupta diplomatică*, p. 151.
19. Ibid., p. 146.

Mircea Muşat

# ROMANIAN SOCIETY AND ITS MILITARY POTENTIAL, 1856—79

The Romanian Revolution of 1848 established the achievement of national unity and independence as the fundamental goal of Romanian society. "Having carried out this revolution," wrote the great democratic-revolutionary Nicolae Bălcescu, "we must accomplish two more, a revolution for national unity and later one for national independence, thus ensuring the Romanian nation all its legitimate rights."[1] Bălcescu's prediction was confirmed by subsequent developments, for the struggle for union was carried on in every arena, both within the country and abroad. As the American historian Thad W. Riker concluded, "no people fought more than the Romanians to assert their national aims."[2]

The 1859 union of the principalities of Moldavia and Wallachia, a historic act that laid the foundations of modern Romania, was a decisive step toward the winning of its full independence. Completing what had been begun in 1859, Prince Alexandru Cuza undertook in the 1860s a vast program of reforms that in a short time radically changed the structure of Romanian society. Measures were taken to unify state administration; to replace the obsolete system of weights and measures with a modern one; to set up universities in Iaşi (1860) and Bucharest (1864); to adopt the Napoleonic Code and proclaim equality before the law and equity in taxation; to organize trade, handicrafts, and transportation; to introduce compulsory, general, and free elementary education; and to promote secondary and higher education. The agrarian and electoral reforms and the secularization of monastic holdings harmonized with the needs of Romanian development and contributed to the progress of Romanian society.[3] By establishing a modern organizational framework and introducing reforms, the prince made the Romanian state a strong instrument for achieving complete political unity and independence.

These two major objectives were the main components of Romanian political strategy. Referring to this fact, Austria's consul in Bucharest, Eder, wrote on November 30, 1860: "The Romanians were not thinking only of the fait accompli of Moldavia's union with Wallachia but also of the formation of an independent Dacian–Romanian state which would include all their conationals."[4]

The dethronement of Alexandru Cuza did not change the direction of Romanian policy. Although not everyone agreed on the means or the appropriate moment, independence remained the chief goal of Romanian foreign policy in the decade prior to the 1877 war. On the threshold of the crucial act of proclaiming independence as well as during the national war to ensure it, Romanian society proved completely unified in will and action.

A small country, at that time comprising some 121,000 square kilometers with a population of 5,000,000, Romania succeeded, despite internal and foreign difficulties, in making progress in its development toward capitalism. Against a background of developing productive forces and maturing exchange relations, great social and political changes took place. Agriculture was the main area of improvement in material production. Romania's grain production in 1876 was over eight times what it had been fifty years earlier. The volume of animal products delivered to market was two or three times larger than that recorded at the beginning of the nineteenth century. Industry also recorded progress in the introduction of steam power; the number of the large factories, particularly metallurgical ones, increased, and the oil and salt industries developed. The census of 1860 established that there were 12,867 industrial establishments in Romania, but mostly they were small, employing a total of only 28,867 workers. The census also showed 83,061 craftsmen, including employers.[5] On the whole, the population engaged in extractive processing and industry amounted to at least 120,000 persons, one-third more than in the 1830s.

The development of productive forces was matched by growth in trade. In the 1860s Romania's towns and villages boasted more than 30,000 merchants.[6] A considerable expansion took place also in foreign trade. Exports increased over eleven times and imports nine times in only four decades, remarkable progress that increased Romania's importance in the European economy.

But there were also some negative factors in the decade preceding the proclamation of independence, in particular the maintenance of Ottoman suzerainty. While the tribute itself was not oppressive, by paralyzing the development of the Romanian economy within the international arena the Ottomans had a substantial negative impact on the Romanian economy.

The peasantry continued to be the most numerous class of Romanian society and the main producer of material goods. Industrial development had begun to create a working class, and a town and village bourgeoisie was rapidly developing. Although little affected by the 1864 agrarian reform and increasingly an obstacle to the country's progress, on the whole the landowner class was forced to permit development of the modern Romanian state and to take part in the effort to regain independence. Alongside these classes, Romanian society included other social categories and strata, among them intellectuals and bureaucrats.

In a relatively short time Romanian society recorded remarkable transformations: the peasantry made considerable progress in liberating itself from feudal servitude; the working class showed signs of vitality; the country's economy was growing; the bourgeoisie was asserting itself in all fields; and the landowner class, though still strong, was on the defensive, for the most part obliged to accept the new rules. Within this historical framework, and in the context of Romania's location at the focus of attention of three empires with expansionist tendencies and its need to strengthen the union, the creation of an adequate military instrument became imperative.

The fundamental principles governing Romanian policy in other matters also guided the organization of the army, which had been created exclusively for defense: "The national army will be organized with a view to establishing sufficient power to maintain neutrality, to defend neutrality, and to defend the United Principalities in case of aggression." In the debates of the ad-hoc assemblies it was pointed out that "in any case the armed forces of the United Principalities will be used only for defending their land."[7]

The solution to the important problem of creating a strong instrument of national security was based on the principles of strengthening and developing the standing army and of adopting organizational measures whereby the entire nation would be prepared for the homeland's defense. In 1864 *România militară*, a theoretical military journal, put it as follows: "When the country is in danger, its independence threatened, every citizen able to bear arms has the duty to defend it. Only this support of the population can give an army power and adequate moral strength."[8]

Organizing the national military on the principle of arming the entire people was not only an active concern of military officials, but also broadly discussed in the press. Prominent personalities such as A. C. Rosetti, Cezar Bolliac, Dimitrie Bolintineanu, and many others discussed the matter. The newspaper *Reforma* emphasized that "we do not arm ourselves aiming at winning, we arm ourselves as the Serbs, the Montenegrins, or our forefathers have done, to become stronger, to earn respect, so that the foreigner cannot enter the Romanian countries as into countries of slaves and dead people; so they will see armed breasts and not open arms, step on dead bodies... not on flowers."[9] *Monitorul oastei* stated that "we will not declare war, nor will we attack anyone. [We will fight] only in defense of what man holds most sacred — nationality."[10]

The beginning of the modernization of the Romanian army was welcomed by Romanian public opinion. Addressing the soldiers concentrated in the camp at Floreşti, near Ploieşti, between April and September 1859, a time of international tension that threatened the union, the newspaper *Curierul Principatelor Unite* said: "This first school will prepare you for another, higher one: defenders of the union, be united among yourselves and you will be strong! Let 'Honor and Homeland' be your watchword."[11] In their turn other publications addressed moving appeals to the country's young people, calling on them to spare no effort in preparing to strengthen the country's defense. In *Tribuna României* we find the following call: "A field of arms is opening: rush to it and learn arms, because tomorrow, or maybe the day after tomorrow, this knowledge will be needed; learn beforehand to defend the homeland so that when hard times come we will not find ourselves ignorant and in want of vigor; then regrets and reflections will be of no use."[12] Dimitrie Bolintineanu wrote: "The Romanian people rejoice at the call to arms, [they are] gathered and ready to fight. ..."[13]

In this atmosphere, Cuza skillfully used the international framework created by the Treaty of Paris cautiously but firmly to renew the entire national defense system, focusing on unification and modernization. Starting with the two Romanian armies, he and his associates fused the Moldavian and Wallachian armies into a single body, introduced a new system of recruitment, upgraded the army's equipment and training to the standards of the day, and formed the cadres needed for the military hierarchy. This work had the sympathy of the public.

The bringing together of troops from both Moldavia and Wallachia in the camp at Floreşti in 1859 played an important part in unifying the armed forces. The camp was a school in which the troops, organized in a modern fashion, trained with recently obtained weapons. They received instructions in firing their weapons, carried out combat drills, marches, and various combat deployments, and practiced command unification. The activities ended with maneuvers on August 23, 1859. The experience gained in the camp at Floreşti helped complete the unification of the two armies and produced ideas for the organization of new training camps in the period to come.

Concurrently with the army's standardization, measures were taken to unify the central command by setting up a single Ministry of War and a general staff on November 12, 1859. A joint commission in 1859 established common uniforms and equipment for the two armies and adopted some common regulations for unit training.

Cuza gave considerable attention to the establishment of well-trained cadres capable of carrying out the training and education of the troops. He personally concerned himself with the organization and funding of military education and the schooling of the teaching staff. Beginning with 1859, some officers were systematically sent abroad for study, especially to France. Others were sent to take part in French army maneuvers, while still others were dispatched as observers to countries in which military operations were going on, such as Italy and the United States of America. New regulations were drawn up, and French army regulations regarding internal administration, garrison service, field exercises, battalion training, and administration were translated into Romanian.

Special attention was also given to combat training, including all aspects of tactics and fire. For the first time, instructions for mobilization were drawn up, in order that the "soldier would be prepared at any moment to cope with all contingencies."[14] General military training began to be improved by concentration of troops in camps and by maneuvers. In 1863 over 8,500 troops carried out drills under the direct command of Prince Cuza, who said in his general order on that occasion, "In the camp at Cotroceni, where you have formed a genuine army, you had better learn to appreciate life in union...; do not ever forget the oath you have taken on our banners, and the country that is making such great sacrifices for you will look with pride at the Romanian army's progress."[15]

The reorganization, development, and improvement of the military organism called for equipping it with armament and combat equipment. When Cuza was elected prince, he wrote Napoleon III, the principalities "had only four or five thousand Russian rifles from the time of Empress Catherine and some ten worthless guns of Turkish, Russian, and Austrian origin. Gunpowder, projectiles, and caps came only from Austria, with the result that we could not fire a shot without its permission."[16] On October 1, 1865, we learn in the same letter, Romania had some 70,000 rifles, 25,000 smoothbore muskets, and 72 rifled guns.[17] The financial effort required to achieve these results was supported by subscription by the Romanian public. Simultaneously, action was taken toward developing the capability for manufacturing military equipment. Cuza strengthened the Romanian military partly by including elements of the old autochthonous military organization alongside its modern features. He institutionalized the functional framework to permit the training of many effectives, from young recruits to old reservists, who could be mobilized in the event of aggression.

It goes without saying that this military policy was closely linked to and influenced by reforms achieved in the economic, social, and cultural fields. Of particular importance for the military was the agrarian reform of 1864, because, as Mihail Kogălniceanu put it, "unless the peasants, the bulk of the people, have vital, material interests in defending the land against foreign invaders, we will not have a strong country. Two thousand boyars do not make a nation."[18]

The principles that guided the legislation of Cuza's time were the basis of all subsequent Romanian military structures. In the next stage of development, the organization of the military had as its foundation the provisions of the 1866 Constitution, which proclaimed that "the Romanian United Principalities represent one indivisible state under the name of Romania" whose territory "is inalienable." This principle established the framework of the country's armed forces, in terms of which "every Romanian is a member of the standing army, the militia, or the civil guard in accordance with special laws, ... the army's contingent is determined annually, and... the civil guard created by statute" is organized and mobilized by established regulations.[20] All governments in the subsequent period, irrespective of their political orientation, took care to strengthen the country's defense capacity. Romania's military policy was dominated by the effort to make the military forces as large, well-trained, and well-equipped as possible without consuming more resources than the country could afford while at the same time training as broad a mass of the population as possible.

The "Law on the Organization of the Romanian Army," passed in July 1868, in general implemented these principles, involving all male Romanians in a system of military training for defense of the homeland. The law provided that the military system comprise the standing army with its reserve, the *dorobanţi* corps and the border corps, the militia, the town guard, and the *gloatele*.[21] The standing army was the basic component of the Romanian military. It was made up of infantry, cavalry, engineers, the Danube flotilla, administrative troops, gendarmerie, and firemen. Taking into account the need for laborers in the economy, particularly in agriculture, the term of active military service was set at three years, followed by four years in the reserves. Recruitment was accomplished by lot, as before, all male citizens reaching the age of twenty being obliged to take part in that operation.

As international conditions become more difficult in the first half of the 1870s, the Romanian government decided to enhance the country's defense capacity. A parliamentary resolution of July 1, 1876, said, "We should never forget that the army is one of the conditions of our existence as a state. Consequently it has the right, especially in the present circumstances, to special attention and extraordinary sacrifices."[22] As a result of these measures, by autumn of 1876 Romania had been able to assemble some 37,730 troops, 120 guns, and 7,046 horses. The elements of the Romanian military organism assigned to the protection of the frontiers and garrison service had at their disposal some 10,610 men, 60 guns, and 3,870 horses.

The events of the spring of 1877, especially the proclamation of national independence, provoked an extraordinary ferment throughout the country. Noteworthy, for example, was the petition addressed to the authorities by the inhabitants of Brăila County requesting "weapons and cartridges in order to repel [the enemy] and defend [the country]."[23] The need for uniting in defense was grasped by the entire Romanian people. On May 20, 1877, C. Cezar of Bucharest said: "In the critical circumstances of our days it is the duty of every citizen to come to his country's assistance according to his possibilities."[24] Because of this patriotic enthusiasm, mobilization was carried out in a relatively short time.

This feeling of popular solidarity deeply impressed contemporaries. "Many young men," wrote one of them, "voluntarily enlisted and rushed to the battlefield, while those incapable of fighting freely gave everything they could — horses, oxen, sheep, produce, food, money for the army's equipment. Our wives and daughters were on duty day and night in hospitals."[25] "All the wounds of the war in Bulgaria," said another contemporary, "were endured with stoicism and joy."[26] The most important contribution was made by the peasants. "We note with happiness and pride," wrote the newspaper *Românul* on October 6, 1877, "that the peasant, though the poorest [of us], is always at the head of the line when it is a question of sacrifice for the common good." For the Romanian proletariat, too, the ideal of independence was a constant, and in addition town dwellers, artisans, merchants, officials, those from various private enterprises, the bourgeoisie, and even the local landlord class played an important part. The appeal addressed to Romania's citizens by newspapers evoked a wide echo. "Gather around the homeland's threatened altar," wrote *România Liberă* of August 17, 1877. "Where the Romanian colors are, there is our body and soul. Romanians from far and near, unite under our banner!"

Men of science and culture were also involved. Mihail Eminescu, the Romanians' greatest poet, wrote in the newspaper *Telegraful* for October 5, 1877, that the defense of the forefathers' land had "cost us rivers of blood, centuries of work, our entire past intelligence, all the most sacred feelings of our hearts." Praising the Romanian army's heroism on the battlefield, the same poet, who characterized independence as "the sum of our historical life," wrote in the newspaper *Timpul* for October 8, 1877: "The army, this single representative of the real Romanian people as it is in the plains and fields, still shows the old virtues." Alongside the writers were also men of the theater, musicians, artists. World-renowned Romanian painters such as Nicolae Grigorescu, Sava Henţia, and Carol Popp de Szatmáry went to the front as eyewitnesses to immortalize in their pictures various aspects of the struggle.

The magnitude of the efforts of all these elements of the Romanian people is indicated by the material cost of the struggle, which exceeded 100,000,000 gold lei.[27]

The victories scored by the Romanian army in this war generated great enthusiasm throughout the country. The memoirist C. Bacalbaşa wrote:

During those days I saw unbelievable things. Although the war was yet not entirely over, although its horrible consequences were represented by the lame and one-armed men returning from the battlefield, on the occasion of the annual levy young men crowded as never before to join the army. ...The war, namely, the evidence of the national revival, the confirmed belief that there is indeed a Romanian heroism, awakened the people's consciousness so that young men, their chins up and looking death boldly in the eye, emerged from the poorest huts.[28]

Conscious and mature, wise and resolute, the Romanian nation unanimously consented to the great human, military, and economic demands of the historic moment. "The achievement of state independence by Romania," pointed out Nicolae Ceauşescu, President of the Socialist Republic of Romania, "has thus not been the outcome of accidental circumstances or of a political situation, neither has it been a gift received from abroad; it is the fruit of the fight waged by our forefathers along the centuries, which culminated in the great victory obtained in 1877 on the battlefield against the Ottoman Empire, thus opening a new epoch in our homeland's free and independent development."[29]

## NOTES

1. N. Bălcescu, *Opere*, vol. 4, *Corespondenta: Scrieri, memorii, adrese, documente, note şi materiale* (Bucharest, 1964), pp. 277–78.
2. T. W. Riker, *Cum s-a înfăptuit România* (Bucharest, 1940), p. 61.
3. Mircea Muşat and Ion Ardeleanu, *De la statul geto-dac la statul român unitar* (Bucharest, 1983), p. 221.
4. Biblioteca Academiei Republicii Socialiste România, *Corespondenta consulului austriac din Bucureşti*, Folder 16.
5. *Documente privind istoria României: Războiul pentru independentă*, vol. 1 (pt. 2) (Bucharest, 1954), p. 380.
6. *Analele statistice ale României pe anul 1865* (Bucharest, 1867), p. 42.
7. *Documente privitoare la istoria românilor: Urmare la colectiunea lui Eudoxiu de Hurmuzschi*, suppl. 1, vol. 6 (1895), p. 125.
8. *România militară* 1, no. 1 (January–February 1864): 5.
9. *Reforma*, August 13, 1860.
10. *Monitorul oastei*, 1860, p. 124.
11. *Curierul Principatelor Unite*, no. 2 (May 14, 1859).
12. *Tribuna României*, no. 17 (June 14, 1859).
13. D. Bolintineanu, *Viaţa lui Cuza Vodă: Memoriu istoric* (Bucharest, 1873), pp. 44–45.
14. Vasile Nădejde, *Centenarul renaşterii armatei române (1830–1930)* (Iaşi, 1930), p. 126.
15. *Mesagii, proclamaţii, răspunsuri şi scrisori oficiale ale lui Cuza Vodă* (Vălenii de Munte, 1910), p. 91.
16. Constantin C. Giurescu, *Alexandru Ioan Cuza* (Bucharest, 1973), pp. 103–4.
17. Ibid.
18. A. D. Xenopol, *Domnia lui Cuza Voda*, vol. 1 (Dacia, 1903), p. 183.
19. *România în războiul de independentă (1877–1878)*, (Bucharest, 1977), p. 63.

20.   C. Hamangiu, *Codul general al României: Legi uzuale,* vol. 1, pp. 3–22.
21.   *Monitorul oficial al României,* 1968, pp. 454–55.
22.   *Documente privind istoria României: Războiul pentru independentă,* vol. 1, pt. 2 (Bucharest, 1954), p. 254.
23.   Ibid., vol. 3, p. 186.
24.   Ibid., p. 224.
25.   N. Gane, *Zile trăite* (Iaşi, 1901), p. 212.
26.   C. Becalbaşa, *Bucureştii de altădată, 1871–1884,* vol. 1 (Bucharest, 1927), p. 210.
27.   *România în războiul de independentă (1877–1878)* (Bucharest, 1977), p. 336.
28.   *Adevărul,* January 17, 1899.
29.   Nicolae Ceauşescu, *Romania on the Way of Building up the Multilaterally Developed Socialist Society,* vol. 14 (Bucharest, 1978), p. 302.

Ilie Ceauşescu

# THE ROMANIAN ARMY IN THE WAR OF INDEPENDENCE: ORGANIZATION, COMMAND, STRATEGY

In the long history of the Romanian people's struggle for national survival and independence, the year 1877 is a moment of paramount significance. The winning of independence through victory in war against the Ottoman Empire was one of the great historic achievements of the Romanians' thousand-year existence as a state and a people.

With the emergence of the Eastern crisis of 1875 and the outbreak of the Russo–Turkish War on April 12, 1877, the winning of independence became an urgent necessity.[1] The Romanian public and authorities both focused their efforts on the country's military preparedress, while the government increased its diplomatic activities. One of the most important diplomatic actions was the conclusion of the Russo–Romanian Convention[2] signed on April 4, 1877, according to which Russian armies were permitted to pass through Romania's territory toward the Balkans, the Russian government undertaking to respect the country's territorial integrity and the political rights of the Romanian state. The convention represented a document concluded between sovereign states on the same footing. On April 10, Romania broke off its diplomatic relations with the Porte, and on April 29, as a result of Turkey's bombardment of Romanian towns along the Danube, the Assembly of Deputies passed a motion declaring a state of war with the Ottoman Empire.

Within this framework, on May 9, 1877, Parliament proclaimed the complete independence of Romania. Foreign Minister Mihail Kogălniceanu said, "In a state of war and with relations broken off, what are we? We are independent. We are a free nation."[3] This culminating moment was a huge victory for the masses, a brilliant crowning of the Romanian people's century-old endeavors to realize its enduring desire for freedom and independence. The entire people rejoiced. "From one border to the other," a contemporary wrote, "all hearts are full of an unutterable enthusiasm. The authorities and the established bodies, the towns, the villages, the hamlets, in a word, everyone, young and old, is ready to make any sacrifice to support the homeland's liberty and independence with all the nation's goods, with her gold and her blood."[4]

## Army Organization

In the words of Nicolae Iorga, the Romanian army in 1877 was "not an army in the ordinary sense of the word; it was a national army made up of all social elements."[5] An analysis of the Romanian military structure at the time of the War of Independence supports his conclusion.[6]

The most important element of the armed forces in Romania was the standing army, including infantry, cavalry, and artillery.

The infantry, considered the basic arm, was made up of eight line regiments (two per division) with two battalions each and four mountain battalions (one per division), each with four companies, a total of twenty battalions. The effective strength of an infantry regiment was 34 officers and noncommissioned officers and 740 corporals and soldiers, while mountain battalions had 18 officers and noncommissioned officers and 358 corporals and soldiers.

The cavalry, the second largest service, consisted of two regiments, each with four squadrons. The effective strength of a regiment was 30 officers and noncommissioned officers, 636 corporals and soldiers, and 448 horses.

The artillery was organized in four regiments, each with six batteries (one horse and five fixed artillery). The twenty-four batteries had six guns each; the effective strength of an artillery regiment, according to the 1877 budget, was 28 officers and noncommissioned officers, 499 corporals and soldiers, and 272 horses.

The corps of engineers was made up of a battalion with five companies — four of sappers (each with a telegraph section) and one of pontoniers transferred on January 1, 1877, from the First Artillery Regiment. The effective strength of the engineering battalion was 23 officers and 497 corporals and soldiers.

The Danube flotilla was equipped with four large ships — *Romania, Stephen the Great, Lightning,* and *Swallow* — and numerous smaller ships for observation and patrolling. It had a staff, a floating company, and a harbor company, a total of 20 officers and noncommissioned officers and 186 corporals and sailors.

Logistical corps comprised the administrative officer corps (effective strength 76 administrators and administrative noncommissioned officers), the equipage squadron, for the transport of ammunition and other matériel

(5 officers, 184 corporals and soldiers, 180 horses); the medical company, which was subordinated from 1875 on to the army medical service inspectorate and performed services around military hospitals (3 officers, 278 corporals and soldiers); and the administration labor company of the central equipment depot, which had the mission of providing clothing and food for the troops (7 officers, 356 corporals and soldiers).

The gendarmes were organized in two mounted squadrons and two foot companies with garrisons in Iași and Bucharest. A mounted gendarme squadron comprised 5 officers and 170 corporals and soldiers and a foot company 5 officers and 130 corporals and soldiers.

The firemen served at the same time as the artillery of the territorial troops and were organized, depending on the importance of the town, into divisions, batteries, demibatteries, and sections. At the beginning of 1877 there were two divisions with nine batteries.

The standing army also had a logistics control corps in the Ministry of War to handle the administrative and financial problems of the military system; military courts, organized by territorial division, with a review council whose competence extended to the entire army; and a medical service comprising physicians, pharmacists, and veterinary surgeons who in time of peace served in hospitals and veterinary hospitals and during campaigns worked in coordination with the ambulance service. The term of service in the standing army was seven years, three on active duty and four in the reserves.

The second tier of Romania's armed forces was the territorial troops, made up of infantry (*dorobanți*) and cavalry (*călărași*). Alongside the standing army these constituted the active army of the territorial divisions. Recruited all over the country, these troops were on active duty seven days a month in four monthly territorial shifts. The eight dorobanți regiments set up on July 1, 1872, were doubled on January 1, 1877, to sixteen, each with two battalions. In the 1877 budget they had an effective strength of 426 officers and noncommissioned officers, 1,255 junior cadres (permanent cadres), and 34,314 soldiers per shift. The călărași had been organized since 1872 in eight regiments with four squadrons each. According to the 1877 budget they comprised 145 officers and noncommissioned officers, 573 permanent cadres and 9,216 soldiers per shift. In all the territorial army totaled 45,929 men.

The inactive militia, the third tier of the country's military forces, was organized in battalions (squadrons), regiments, and brigades. They were attached to the territorial troops, which thus supported part of their training and equipping. In 1877 thirty-one militia battalions were mobilized.

The town guard and *gloatele* represented, along with the territorial troops and the militia, the popular elements to which Iorga was referring in the statement quoted above. Made up of legions, battalions, and companies, the guard had the task of ensuring that military orders were carried out in the towns in time of war. The *gloatele,* mobilized only in cases of serious danger, served the militia as auxiliary troops.

The organization and the development of the national military system, its command, guidance, and control, fell upon the Ministry of War and its specialized organisms: the general staff, the staff corps, and the prince's staff.

In spite of the shortcomings inherent in any army that lacked combat experience, Romania's military forces formed a flexible, well-organized body with good training and excellent spirit. These qualities came in for the admiration of the foreign observers, one of whom said that "this army... is very well equipped and has new material of a good quality. The soldiers are well equipped and fed. The cavalry is very good." Another commented, "The active army's soldiers know their job well and will cut a fine figure, I have no doubt, in confrontation with the enemy. ...The corps of the Principality [of Romania] now engaged on the front line are well disciplined, animated by the same positive spirit, and ready to make the greatest sacrifices."[7] Thus endowed, equipped, and trained, the Romanian army contributed outstandingly to the 1877–78 war.[8]

One of its first large-scale actions was providing strategic cover of the Danube.[9] Organized in two corps, it covered the northern bank of the Danube, securing the defense of Romania against a possible Ottoman invasion and at the same time facilitating the concentration of the Russian army. Under the cover provided by the Romanian troops, the Russians began to cross the Prut on the night of April 11–12, 1877. In accordance with the Russo–Romanian Convention, they advanced in four columns to the Danube. At the same time, the Romanian army strengthened and developed the fortifications system in that area while responding to the Ottoman bombardment of Romanian towns on the Danube: Calafat (April 21), Giurgiu (April 27), Olteniţa (April 28), Islaz (May 4), Bechetu (May 11), and Corabia (May 14). Russian or Romanian ships also attacked Ottoman monitors, sinking the *Hivzi–Rahman* with torpedoes in a joint Romanian–Russian action. The Romanian army also contributed to the Russians' successful crossing of the Danube between Brăila and Zimnicea. During the nights of June 14, 15, and 16, 1877, the Romanian troops stationed at the mouth of the Olt River protected transport of the Russian pontoons needed to build the bridge from Zimnicea to Svishtov from the enemy artillery of the fortress of Nikopol. Simultaneously, to distract the enemy's attention from the Russian crossing at Zimnicea, the Romanians simulated the movement of several detachments and fired on enemy columns on the march. Romanian and Russian artillery batteries at Islaz, Flămînda, and Turnu Măgurele contributed to the capture of Nikopol on July 4.

After the defeats suffered by the Russian troops in the two battles of Plevna (July 8–9 and 18), and in response to numerous appeals of the Russian high command, the Romanian command ordered the army to cross the Danube on the improvised bridge at Siliştioara, near Corabia, and proceed toward Plevna. This fortress was strongly fortified and surrounded by the hills of Opanez in the north, Grivitsa in the east, and Radishevo, Brestovets, and Krishin in the south. Romanian troops (the Thirteenth Dorobanţi Regiment) were entrusted with the mission of driving the enemy from the redoubt protecting the Grivitsa fortifications (August 27) and with participating in the general allied attack known as the third battle of Plevna (August 30). After an intense artillery barrage, the Romanian battalions succeeded on August 30 in conquering the Grivitsa 1 redoubt. The victory produced an impressive echo both within the country and internationally. Voicing the feelings of the public, the newspaper *România Liberă* wrote: "The children of the Carpathians fought like lions... . The heroes of Grivitsa have written with their blood a glorious page."[10] Tsar Alexander II of Russia appreciated the Romanian troops' "heroic gallantry, fighting under one of the most crushing of enemy fires."[11] The French colonel L. Gaillard wrote: "The Romanian army covered itself with glory. As a matter of fact, its bravery, its behavior, and the way it served under such new conditions is greatly praised here, as well as the way it was supplied with everything down to the smallest detail."[12]

The actions against Plevna continued, and on October 7 the other Grivitsa redoubt was besieged. Until the final collapse of Plevna, the military actions had two goals: to surround the Turks and to ensure operating space for the forces accomplishing the encirclement. In about forty days (between September 2 and October 12) the Romanian–Russian forces had blocked all communications, thus impeding the flow of supplies to the enemy and closing the ring around Plevna.

Between November 7 and 9 the Romanian troops liberated Rahova, which the Ottomans had made an important point in their military system south of the Danube. Of this feat the Prague newspaper *Politik* wrote: "The Romanian conquest of Rahova was a great deed whose consequences should not be underestimated. Rahova may be a small place, but its capture is very important because it helps close the circle around Plevna... . The Romanian army has undeniably given new evidence of its gallantry."[13] Grand Duke Nikolay, commander of the Russian army in the Balkan Peninsula, wrote the Romanian head of state: "Please allow me to avail myself of this opportunity to repeat that I have always been happy to recognize the bravery and the eminent military qualities of the Romanian army... . The victory scored at Rahova is entirely due to the Romanian army."[14]

The circle around the besieged Plevna gradually closed, subjecting the enemy troops to intense artillery bombardment. The Romanian forces positioned in the inner ring of the blockade totaled forty-one battalions, twenty-eight squadrons, and 112 guns with an effective strength of about 35,000 men.[15] The Ottoman army commanded by Osman Pasha consisted of 10 generals, over 130 superior officers, 2,000 junior officers, and about 40,000 soldiers, of whom 1,200 were horsemen, and disposed of some 77 guns. As a result of vigorous Romanian and Russian assaults, particularly those of November 28, Osman Pasha surrendered, an event with decisive consequences for the whole war. The actions of the Romanian army on November 28 were immediately appreciated. "The Romanians," wrote the newspaper Le Bien Public, "fought bravely; they took part in encircling Plevna and in the final defeat of Osman Pasha, the decisive event of the campaign; they proved in time of war, as in time of peace, their right to exist as an independent nation."[16] "The Romanians," commented Mémorial Diplomatique, "contributed to a great extent to the brilliant action which led to Plevna's conquest. One could say that at a critical moment they saved the day... . The accuracy of the Romanians' fire and the impetuosity of their attack had, in those critical circumstances, a decisive influence."[17]

After the fall of Plevna, Romanian troops took part in the defeat of the Ottoman forces at Vidin and Belogradchik, adding to their contribution to the eventual victory over the Ottoman Empire.

Referring to the participation of the Romanian soldiers in the war of 1877–78, the Soviet historian V. N. Vinogradov has written: "A not very large state laid heavy sacrifices on the altar of its independence: the campaign in Bulgaria involved a field army of 58,000 men, of whom 10,000 lost their lives. In the battles at Rahova, Vidin, and Smirdan [this army] set an example of gallantry and bravery. But it was beneath the walls of Plevna that the chief war operations of the Romanian army, which represented about a third of all the forces there, were carried out. During the second bloody attack on the fortress, as well as in the particularly difficult conditions of the four-month siege of that autumn, in the night struggle of Osman Pasha's last desperate attempt to break out of the blockade circle, the Romanian dorobanţi fought shoulder to shoulder with the Russian soldiers and officers. The latter spoke with high esteem and respect of the military virtues of their allies."[18] The Bulgarian historian Nikolai Ječev, in an lengthy essay devoted to the support given by Romania to the Bulgarians' liberation movement, wrote: "One can say with good reason that in 1877–78 the Romanian people actively and meritoriously contributed to the defeat of the Ottoman Empire and the undermining of the sultan's domination in the Balkans, to the winning of Bulgaria's independence, and to the assertion of their own country's national independence."[19]

The victories scored by the Romanian army in the 1877–78 War of Independence clearly demonstrated the viability of its military system, based on harmonious unity of the basic components of standing and territorial armies, militia, and territorial guards. Thus the principle of the nation in arms found eloquent illustration in the armed forces with which Romania achieved its independence. The vitality of the Romanian military system, the realism of its basic concept, the efficiency of its organizational work, and the success of the financial efforts of the prewar period stand out in bold relief.

## Command

The Romanian general headquarters, the supreme body for the conception and coordination of military operations in the 1877–78 war, had the following structure at the beginning of the hostilities: the general staff (chief colonel Gheorghe Slaniceanu, deputy colonel Constantin Barozzi) had five sections: topographic (one colonel and two majors), operational (one lieutenant colonel and two majors, artillery (one colonel), engineering (one major), logistical, and medical service. The general headquarters also contained the prince's adjutants (one colonel, two lieutenant colonels, two majors, and one captain) and the prince's orderly officers (two captains and one lieutenant).

The headquarters of a division consisted of one division commander, one chief of staff, two officers, one chief physician, and one intendant and *praetor* (military justice). The headquarters of the infantry (line, mountain, and dorobanţi) and cavalry (regular and călăraşi) regiments had a commander and two or three officers for each company or squadron. In all, the Romanian army mobilized on April 6, 1877, had 1,602 officers and noncommissioned officers,[20] a command corps adequate to its structure and operational requirements. According to the army's organizational standards, as we have seen, a line infantry regiment had 34 officers and noncommissioned officers, a mountain battalion 18, a cavalry regiment 30, and an artillery regiment 28. In 1877 the dorobanţi had 426 officers and noncommissioned officers (an average of 26 per regiment) and the călăraşi 145. At an effective strength of 45,929, the territorial army had about 1 officer for every 85 corporals and soldiers.

The basic combat unit was the battalion. Its combat formations were established by the "Regulations on Infantry Exercises and Maneuvers" that went into effect in 1870. On the offensive, the battalion was divided into three echelons: riflemen assigned the mission of covering the front, the support echelon, made up of two companies, which provided reserve riflemen for the first echelon, and the combat corps (the main force). On the defensive, the disposition of the battalion depended on the situation. For repelling a cavalry attack, a square formation was recommended. When exposed for lengthy periods to artillery fire, battalion formations were to be protected by field fortifications designed to take advantage of the terrain. They were also to avoid fire by rapid movements ahead or back.

In the view of Romanian and foreign observers of the time, as well as in retrospect, the attitude of the Romanian high command during the War of Independence must be judged very good. Among the numerous foreign references to this fact, the opinion of the war correspondent of the English newspaper *The Daily News,* appearing on September 27, 1877, is worth quoting:

> It is ceaselessly raining, there is a horrible mud in the trenches and the weather is very cold; the Romanian officers and soldiers are standing motionless at their posts, giving evidence of a courage and a firmness rousing my entire admiration. ...I think that history does not offer another example similar to this splendid army's, one which has met with such tragic occurrences and whose generals have shown such boldness and energy.[21]

The Romanian high command also proved to have a good grasp of all the elements of the military situation, drawing up adequate plans and making correct decisions. On this score a convincing example is offered by the solution submitted by the Romanian general headquarters in the Romanian— Russian joint war council at Radeniţa on August 25, 1877. In contrast to the Russians, who proposed that a new attack on Plevna be launched without delay, the Romanian high command understood that the allied forces were insufficient for another assault. Consequently it proposed to await the reserves coming from Russia, which, together with the Romanian—Russian western army at Plevna, could complete the encirclement. The subsequent development of the military operations south of the Danube confirmed the correctness of this solution.

Romanian officers also showed initiative, firmness, and energy in carrying out tactical orders, thus setting an example for their subordinates. The brilliant successes scored at Plevna, Rahova, Vidin, and Belogradchik were due to the conceptual work and leadership of the Romanian commands at all levels. The small number of losses illustrates this fact. In the first Romanian attack on Plevna, on August 27, losses were 3 officers wounded, 16 soldiers killed and 113 wounded, or 8 percent; in the third battle of Plevna (the conquest of the Grivitsa 1 redoubt) on August 30, losses totaled 19 officers killed and 34 wounded, 2,511 soldiers killed or wounded, about 7 percent of the effectives engaged; in the conquest of Rahova, Romanian losses amounted to 4 officers killed or wounded, 148 soldiers killed or wounded, 6.6 percent of the effectives engaged (3,500 infantrymen, 1,000 cavalrymen, 400 artillerymen, and 150 engineers). The percentage of losses was far below the international standard of that time, demonstrating, given the conditions of harsh conflict with a stubborn and experienced enemy, the remarkable quality of the Romanian high command.

## Strategy

The chief strategic target of the war — the defeat of the enemy in cooperation with the Russian army and the sanctioning of Romania's independence — was established by the highest political organs of the state. Romanian strategy in 1877–78 was subordinated to political imperatives, to the nation's overriding interests. A military understanding with political and strategic overtones materialized in the Russo–Romanian Convention, which clearly stipulated that the tsarist empire was to respect Romania's territorial integrity. The details of the convention referring to the passage of Russian troops through Romania and the relations between the Russian army and local Romanian authorities reveal other evidences of Romanian autonomy in the preliminary stage of the war. Thus, the contact between the Romanian administration and the Russian army was achieved through a representative authorized by the Romanian government, and entry of Russian troops into Bucharest was forbidden in order to ensure freedom of movement for the national government and to prevent any interference in Romanian domestic affairs.

A conclusive demonstration of the subordination of general strategy to the state's fundamental policy is offered by the engagement of the Romanian army in operations south of the Danube. Even before the convention of April 4, 1877, the Russians had asked that the Romanians and Russians cooperate in that campaign, proposing that a joint plan be drawn up for that purpose. Since the bilateral convention had not yet been established and the request came from the tsarist military authorities rather than from the political ones, the proposal was declined. Other proposals of cooperation submitted by the Russian military command were also refused because they would have placed Romanian troops under Russian command.[22] The higher military and political circles in Romania wanted their military participation in the campaign south of the Danube to take place in a way that would preserve the Romanian army's individuality by giving it a distinct area of operations and a single national command. Initially, the Romanian side proposed independent military action in the Vidin area, but subsequently, in response to developments south of the river, it considered a crossing of the Danube at Bechetu in order to carry out actions west of the Iskŭr River.[23]

After the first two Russian battles at Plevna, the frequency of requests by Russian military and political officials for the engagement of the Romanian army south of the Danube considerably increased. They reached a climax in the cable of July 19, 1877, sent to Prince Carol by Grand Duke Nikolay, the Russian commander in chief.[24] Romania's political-military leadership appreciated the new strategic situation: "Now not only are Russian interests involved but Romanian ones as well; the country would be seriously threatened if the victorious Turks were to succeed in driving the Russians back across the Danube."[25] Consequently, the decision was made to allow the Romanian army to cross the Danube and join the Russian army at Plevna. An exchange of letters between Carol and Nikolay at the beginning of August 1877 can be considered the juridical basis of the Romanian army's engagement in the anti-Ottoman campaign south of the Danube. On August 10, 1877, Carol wrote the grand duke: "In its relations with the imperial army, the Romanian army will have to maintain, as Y[our] I[mperial] H[ighness] was willing to recognize in your last letter, its individuality and unity of command, acting of course by the general plan and the orders of Y. I. H."[26]

This attitude has been recognized as wholly justified. According to the official Russian military history of the 1877–78 war, written by members of the imperial general staff between 1898 and 1911,

It is impossible not to recognize that, in particular, the desire of the Romanian command to have its own line of command or, more precisely, of communication was entirely justified by the fact that on the whole it is better for each army to have its own line of command that it can use freely and independently. This fact was the more indispensable to the Romanians in that their army depended entirely on its own means and resources, independent of the Russians.[27]

The policy of preserving the individuality of its army under a single national command guided the officials involved in the negotiations with the allies regarding the command organization of the allied forces at Plevna. The supreme commander of the Romanian army was appointed commander of the Romanian–Russian western army (the chief of staff was a Russian general), and the Romanian field army within its structure was commanded by a Romanian general. All the Romanian units participating in the 1877–78 campaign acted under exclusively Romanian command. The principles laid down at the beginning of Romanian–Russian military relations during the 1877–78 war positively affected the cooperation between the two armies. Under conditions of equality and mutual esteem, the Romanian and Russian armies were able to concentrate their efforts on accomplishing the objectives jointly established by the political and military leaders of the two countries.

At the level of strategy it is appropriate to emphasize the conception and execution of the operation aiming at the covering of the Danube by the

Romanian army in April–August 1877. This operation was conceived and carried out by the Romanian high command to prevent the Turks from crossing the Danube, which would have turned Romanian territory into a theater of war while the Russian forces were on the march to the river. The deployment of the Romanian army during this operation shows that the Romanian high command was seeking to prevent the approach of enemy troops to Bucharest through Vidin (and then Calafat and Craiova), Giurgiu, and Olteniţa. These potential lines of invasion corresponded to the deployment of the bulk of the enemy's forces south of the Danube in the Vidin area and in the Ruse–Silistra–Shumen–Varna Quadrilateral. The strategic covering of the Danube involved a front over 650 km long. Its successful implementation had important strategic consequences: it prevented the turning of Romania into a theater of operations and permitted the Russian forces to pass quickly and without combat to the Danube.[28] Referring to this latter aspect, the London *Times* of May 11, 1877, wrote: "The Romanian troops guarding their own frontier on the Danube did the Russians a great service in impeding the Turks from seizing and strengthening bridge-heads on the northern bank of the Danube."[29] The covering operation continued after the Russian troops had crossed the Danube and advanced into the Balkan Peninsula. Romanian troops concentrated in Olteniţa covered the Russian right flank rear, preventing a possible penetration of the Ottoman forces in Vidin into Romania and the shifting of the entire European Russian front.

Another example of a strategic decision of the Romanian high command that took into account the political and military interests of the country as well as the exigencies of the war was the establishment of military operations subsequent to the fall of Plevna. These moves departed from the strategic principles that the Romanian army should operate independently in a distinct area and that it should not move far from its logistic base north of the Danube. Ottoman troops situated in western Bulgaria threatened the flank of the Russian army in its advance to the south. Therefore the decision was made that the bulk of the Romanian forces south of the Danube would attack the enemy in western Bulgaria. A portion of the troops gathered in the garrisons of Rahova and Nikopol; one division escorted the prisoners to Romania and then covered the Danube between Giurgiu and Călăraşi.[30] This strategic decision was entirely appropriate in the general context of the war, as subsequent developments showed.

On the whole Romanian strategy met the test of the political and military exigencies imposed by the effort at winning independence. It resulted from and was identified with Romania's political interests, both immediate and long-term.

The proclamation and achievement of Romanian independence — the work of the entire nation — was an event of paramount importance in the evolution of modern Romania, an achievement that gave powerful new impetus to the country's economic and social development. "The gaining of State Independence by Romania," says Nicolae Ceauşescu, Secretary General of the Romanian Communist Party and President of the Socialist Republic of Romania, "has thus not been the outcome of accidental circumstances or of a political situation, neither has it been a gift received from abroad; it is the fruit of the fight waged by our forefathers along the centuries, which culminated in the great victory obtained in 1877 on the battlefield against the Ottoman Empire, thus opening a new epoch in our homeland's free and independent development."[31]

The proclamation of independence and its sanctioning on the battlefield, followed by international recognition, eliminated all subordination to the Ottoman Empire. Replacing the status of autonomy with that of full sovereignty gave the Romanian state the opportunity to determine its internal and international policy independently. This created the preconditions for the achievements to come. As Ceauşescu has put it, "Now we can say that without having won independence in 1877, the formation of the national unitary state in 1918 would not have been possible, nor the subsequent developments that ensured the victory of socialism in Romania."[32]

## NOTES

1. N. Ciachir, *România in sud-estul Europei (1848–1886)* (Bucharest, 1968).
2. *Monitorul oficial al României*, 1877, pp. 2671–72.
3. Ibid., no. 118 (May 27, 1877), pp. 3451–53.
4. T. C. Văcărescu, *Luptele românilor în războiul din 1877–1878* (Bucharest, 1887), p. 9.
5. N. Iorga, *Războiul pentru independenţa României: Acţiuni diplomatice şi stari de spirit* (Bucharest, 1927), p. 137.
6. On this problem, see Constantin Olteanu, *Contribuţii la cercetarea conceptului de putere armată la români* (Bucharest, 1979), pp. 205–22; Constantin Căzănişteanu and Mihail E.Ionescu, *Războiul neatîrnării României: Imprejurări diplomatice şi operaţii militare 1877–1878* (Bucharest, 1977), pp. 107–21.
7. Iorga, *Războiul pentru independenţa României*, pp. 102–5.
8. On this problem, see *România în războiul de independenţă 1877–1878* (Bucharest, 1977).
9. See Constantin Olteanu, "Măsurile luate de comandamentul român pentru acoperirea Dunarii în perioada aprilie–august 1877," *Revista de istorie* 30 (1977): 557–68.
10. *România Liberă*, September 3, 1877.
11. *Pagini din lupta poporului român pentru independenţă naţională 1877–1878 (Documente şi texte social-politice)* (Bucharest, 1967), pp. 209–10.
12. Ibid., p. 194.
13. *Românul*, November 16, 1877.
14. Comisiunea istorică a Marelui stat major rus, *Resboiul ruso–turc din 1877–1878 în Peninsula Balcanică*, trans. I. Gărdescu, vol. 5 (Bucharest, 1902), p. 687.

15.  *Istoricul războiului din 1877–1878: Participarea României la acest război* (Bucharest, 1887), pp. 757–58.

16.  *Românul,* February 19, 1878.

17.  Ibid., December 10, 1877.

18.  V. N. Vinogradov, "Voina 1877–1878 gg.: Zaverşaiuşcii stap barbî rumînslogo naroda za nezavisimosti," in *100 let osvobojdeniia balkanskih narodov ot osmanskogo iga* (Moscow, 1979), p. 209.

19.  Nikolai Ječev, "România şi războiul ruso–turc din 1877–1878," *Voenno-istoričeski sbornik,* 1977, no. 2, p. 106.

20.  Radu Rosetti, *Partes luată de armata română în răsboiul din 1877–1878* (Bucharest, 1926), p. 18.

21.  Ion Frunzetti and George Munteanu, coordinators, *Arta şi literatura în slujba independenţei naţionale* (Bucharest, 1977), p. 130.

22.  *Sbornik materialov no russko–turetskoi voine 1877–1878 gg. na Balkanskom poliostrove,* 97 vols. (St. Petersburg, 1898–1911), 3: 899.

23.  Radu Rosetti, *Proiecte de operaţiuni în anii 1876–1878,* Analele Academiei Române, Memoriile Secţiunii Istorice, series 3, vol. 27, memoir 4 (Bucharest, 1945).

24.  *Sbornik,* p. 12.

25.  Rosetti, *Partea luată,* p. 117.

26.  *Memoriile regelui Carol I al României (de un martor ocular),* vol. 10 (Bucharest, n. d.), p. 57.

27.  *Sbornik,* p. 14.

28.  Olteanu, "Măsurile luate," pp. 557–68.

29.  Radu Rosetti, "Cîteva extrase din presa engleză 1877–1878," *Anuarul Institutului de istorie naţională* 4 (1927): 368.

30.  Rosetti, *Partea luată,* p. 84.

31.  Nicolae Ceauşescu, *Romania on the Way of Building up the Multilaterally Developed Socialist Society,* vol. 14 (Bucharest, 1978), p. 302.

32.  Ibid., p. 308.

Mihail E. Ionescu

# THE EQUIPMENT, LOGISTICS, AND PERFORMANCE OF THE ROMANIAN ARMY IN THE WAR OF INDEPENDENCE, 1877—78

An eyewitness to the offensive carried out by the Romanian attack columns against the Grivitsa 1 redoubt during the Romanian—Russian assault on Plevna on August 30—September 11, 1877, wrote:

> Now I could appreciate the bravery of the Romanian soldier. He rushed into the attack with an irresistible impetuosity... . These common Romanian peasants proved that they know to die if they do not win a victory, that the blood of the ancient Dacians flows in their veins. They rushed into this valley of blood with unbelievable gallantry; repelled, crushed, decimated by the shattering fire of a sheltered enemy, they did not retreat a step, did not hesitate for a moment, but unceasingly advanced, resuming the attack without a break and, alas, leaving behind them a great number of dead and dying men.[1]

The English *Daily Telegraph,* commenting on the development of the siege, wrote on October 3, 1877:

> The Romanian troops fought with praiseworthy bravery and delivered the attack repeatedly, having been repelled many times by the dreadful fire of the Turkish infantry. Some soldiers were even killed on the crest of the redoubt escarpment that they had reached by great gallantry and tenacity. In a word, they behaved wonderfully, especially in that this was their first experience and that their attack was directed against a strong fortification and positions defended by a dreaded army. Of their [the Romanians'] artillery even the Russians are speaking with unabashed commendation... . The infantry showed an extraordinary will to fight and a terrible upsurge in circumstances very difficult for young troops.[2]

These two pieces of foreign evidence, chosen from among many others that cannot be accused of subjectivity, bring out in bold relief the Romanian army's qualities in the 1877—78 War of Independence.

What were the sources of this praiseworthy performance on the battlefield? The answer lies in a historical analysis of the chief components of the army at the time of the campaign: its organization, command, equipment, logistics, preparation, training, and moral qualities. The topic of this essay is the relationship to its performance of two of these components — equipment and logistics.

## Equipment

The result of assiduous and laborious activity on the part of the responsible agencies during the preceding decades, Romania's army on the eve of the 1877–78 campaign was a military force that was harmoniously integrated and capable of coping with the multiple demands of the battlefield. Of course, this assessment takes into account both Romania's economic possibilities at that time and its demographic resources. On the whole, the army's equipment was adequate and in some areas even very good, although sufficient quantities were not available for all categories. To bring its equipment up to the level of that of modern European armies, an extended financial effort had been undertaken. The insufficient development of Romanian military industry required emphasis on the purchase of matériel from abroad at the same time as efforts to speed up the multifaceted process of modernization.

This financial effort reached its peak during the development of the Eastern crisis of 1875. In 1875 alone, for example, extraordinary and supplementary credits of 19, 838, 131 lei[3] were allotted for army supplies. To this huge sum was added the 1877 budget of the Ministry of War, about 13,000,000 lei (about 1,000,000 lei of which represented the suspended tribute to the Porte), and the sums received from the Russians for the facilities they used on their passage through Romanian territory on their way to the Balkan theater of operations. In about five months in 1877, the war cost Romania 25,000,000 lei.

Priority was given to the purchase of war matériel from abroad. One should underline that the selection of the various categories of armament, ammunition, equipment, transport means, and medical supplies by the Romanian specialists gave evidence of real technical competence. The most modern materials with the highest technical and tactical parameters available in the international arena were purchased. For instance, in 1877 the country received from French companies 50,000 Peabody rifles, from English firms 5,000,000 metal tubes for Peabody cartridges, and from German companies 5,000 shells and 10,000 shrapnel for the 1868-model 8-cm guns. In the same year Russia delivered 25,000 Krnka rifles, 3,600,000 cartridges, 20 siege guns, 12 mortars, and other weapons.[4] The artillery armament purchased in 1875–77 included 1875-model Krupp guns, with which eight batteries were equipped when the country entered the war.[5] At the same time, important purchases of matériel necessary for the field army were made. On June 3, 1877, delivery was taken of some 5,000 tents;[6] 3,000 camp kettles, 15,300 dixies, and 16,100 canteens,[7] as well as saddles, footwear, cartridge boxes, and ammunition carts, were ordered.

Romanian industry was also involved, within the limits of its productive potential, in equipping the army. The Army Arsenal in Bucharest, the country's main military factory, made and repaired carts for transporting food, ammunition, engineering and medical supplies and equipment, and artillery pieces. The ammunition factories generally satisfied the requirements of some types of weapons. Specialized workshops in different parts of the country produced means of conveyance, pontoons for crossing the Danube, blankets, sheepskins, footwear, and linen.

The basic arms of the Romanian army in the War of Independence were as follows:

Line regiments and mountain battalions and some of the dorobanţi were issued 1868-model Peabody rifles (11.4-mm gauge, 1,000-m range). Most of the dorobanţi were issued 1869-model Krnka rifles (15–24-mm gauge, 500–900-m range), but some of them, along with the militia, received 1862-model Dreyse carbines (11.43-mm gauge, 675-m range). The infantry also had the Linneman spade recently introduced in modern European armies. At least two of the mountain battalions had a Christophe and Matigny machine gun (37 barrels, 11.45-mm gauge).[8] This heterogeneity of weaponry made ammunition supply difficult and hindered the volume of fire in combat. These impediments were, however, not decisive on the battlefield. The Linneman spade allowed the infantry to dig good shelter in the particular terrain and made for the rapid construction of field fortifications, a fact that deeply impressed the military specialists of the time. In a cable of September 5/17, 1877, the Russian commander in chief Grand Duke Nikolay wrote to Romania's prince: "Please give strict orders to the left flank of the Fourth Russian Army Corps and the Second Imeretinski Division to fortify as strongly as your army."[9]

The artillery was equipped with eight 1875-model Krupp (8.7-cm gauge) steel gun batteries, eight 1870-model (7.8-cm gauge) bronze gun batteries, eight 1868-model Krupp (7.8-cm gauge) steel gun batteries, and four 1863-model French (4-cm gauge) bronze gun batteries, the latter being issued to the militia. Additional siege matériel included twenty-six 1863-model bronze guns, eighteen bronze mortars (120-mm), and two bronze gun batteries (152-mm).[10]

The equipment and the training of the Romanian artillery units and their behavior on the battlefield evoked the admiration of eyewitnesses. The Russian allies at Plevna requested that the Romanian high command place at their disposal a section of Romanian guns for ranging fire for their siege batteries,[11] and at the end of the hostilities the Ottoman artillery commander congratulated General Gheorghe Manu, the field army artillery commander, for the effectiveness of its actions.[12] On ammunition consumption we have only scattered data that permit a broad estimate. It is known, for example, that the Third Artillery Regiment used 23,580 projectiles and another battery some 8,243 projectiles. This would indicate an estimated consumption of about 200,000 projectiles by the Romanian artillery as a whole in the course of the war.

The cavalry, both regular and călărașii, was uniformly equipped with saber, revolver, and Dreyse carbine.

The engineers' battalion was equipped with specialized material it needed to accomplish its missions — stringing telegraph wires, building bridges, laying mines, and constructing fortifications.

The medical company had five divisional field hospitals, two army corps field hospitals, a general-headquarters field hospital, and one reserve, all equipped with the necessary medical apparatus. Two field hospitals provided by the Red Cross completed the equipment of the Romanian field army. On June 22, 1877, the correspondent of the London *Times* declared that the organization and the equipment of the Romanian army's medical service were "admirable."[13]

The soldiers were well dressed. Winter clothing, either purchased from the budget of the Ministry of War or donated by the public, reached it in good time.

On the whole, the equipment of the Romanian army in the 1877–78 War of Independence was appropriate to the context of cooperation with the powerful Russian army.


## Logistics

The Romanian army's logistic system during the 1877–78 campaign involved efforts both by specialized military bodies and by the civilian population. The government and the army command organized a system of depots for all the required kinds of supplies. At the same time, depending on the state of military operations, it took over the building and repairing of roads and bridges, the distribution of field hospitals, and the provision of a telegraph communication network between the various components of the field army and between the latter and Romanian towns.

The network of ammunition, food, and fodder depots was organized according to the needs of the battlefield. For ammunition there were the central depot in Bucharest, district depots (one for each division), and smaller depots in each garrison. In urban centers and troop concentration zones near the battlefield, the army command organized food depots (Bucharest, Piteşti, Craiova, Caracal, Turnu Măgurele, Rast, Ciuperceni, Rahova, Lom Palanka), cattle herds (Turnu Măgurele, Caracal, Craiova, Bucharest), bakeries (Bucharest, Turnu Măgurele, Corabia, Caracal, Piteşti, Poiana Mare), and points of assembly for the convoys of carts that were to be sent across the Danube.[14] Troops deployed in Romania supplied themselves by purchasing local goods.

When the army was concentrated at Plevna in the summer of 1877, Olteniţa became the logistic base.[15] This amounted to a change in plans. Initially the Romanian high command had expected the army across the Danube to be fighting west of the Iskŭr River, and now the bridge built in the Bechetu area, at Siliştioara–Măgura, had to be moved to Turnu Măgurele. This took seven days (August 22/September 3 to August 29/September 10) to accomplish, during which time transportation across the Danube could not be ensured and Romanian troops received their food and fodder from the Russians. The logistic base had already been changed once, because in June 1877 the Romanian high command had planned to cross the Danube above Vidin, two ships, six barges, and a steamship having been assembled for the purpose. The repeated shifting of the logistic base involved great difficulties because of the inadequate system of roads (3,300 km in 1874) and railroads (955 km in 1875, with limited rolling stock).

Ammunition and foodstuffs were transported by boxcarts escorted by military detachments. The roads repaired by the engineers' companies needed constant maintenance, becoming impassable because of mud or snow during the rainy autumn of 1877 and the severe winter that followed. From September 24/October 6 to October 7/19, 1877, the regularity of supply suffered while the bridge was out at Nikopol. During this period the troops' food ration was reduced, but this did not dampen their spirits.[16] In order to ensure their provisions, units were compelled to send mounted detachments into the Bulgarian villages near the Balkan Mountains to buy reserves from the natives.[17] In order to prevent a repetition of this situation, at the beginning of 1878 divisional depots were established at Arcer–Palanka, Nazîr Mahala, and elsewhere south of the Danube near the Romanian positions. The heavy snow of December 1877 caused a break in the troops' supply when food and fuel could not get through because the roads were blocked. "The storm and the lack of firewood," wrote the Romanian army supreme commander in his journal on December 8/20, 1877, "has made it impossible to heat the houses. Nor can food be found, and the victuals, especially bread, are nearly at an end; in the headquarters of the Carol front the rations are to be reduced. Toward evening, the snowstorm is growing heavier. ..."[18] According to the same officer, it took three hours to cover the distance covered in an hour at other times, and the temperature was $-22^{\circ}$C. Under these conditions, the troops destined to serve in the Vidin area had to march there from Plevna. Concurrently, the logistic base was moved to the northern bank of the Danube, in the Calafat region. A passage through the snow had to be opened up by ox-driven sledges followed by cavalry squadrons working in fifteen-minutes shifts before the troops could proceed. The flotilla was very helpful in moving the depots. In spite of floating ice on the Danube, it succeeded in ferrying significant amounts of supplies.

The chief means for filling the supply depots with food and fodder was the requisition. In accordance with the "Regulation on the Military Requisition" issued on April 6/18, 1877, "objects and services needed by the army"[19] became liable for requisition. For sixteen months (between April 9/21, 1877, and August 5/17, 1878) the Romanian army was supplied in this way with important quantities of food, fodder, means of conveyance (carts, horses, and carters), and clothing (sheepskins, fur caps, and woolen clothes). The value of the requisitions was about 11,000,000 lei (about 83 percent of the 1877 budget of the Ministry of War), some 1,045,747 working days of conveyance, and 53,676 working days of construction. Peasant carts driven by their owners (264,394 carts and 66,387 draft animals) covered over 26 million km logistically supporting the front.[20] Among the provisions commandeered were 59,238 cattle, 1,386,641 kg of food of various kinds, 1,200 metric tons of cornmeal, 116,199 hectoliters of wheat, 195,485 hectoliters of barley, and over 19,000 metric tons of hay.[21]

The requisitions were supplemented by voluntary contributions. The sum of 1,639,798 lei was gathered by subscriptions and donations for the army's equipment, of which over 1,200,000 lei were used to purchase about 20,000 Peabody rifles. The total value of the donations amounted to over 9,000,000 lei, or about 75 percent of the 1877 budget of the Ministry of War. The rural population voluntarily contributed over 8,000 cattle, about 34 metric tons of corn, 2.5 metric tons of beans and dried vegetables, and some 2,500 sheepskins. All the urban social categories contributed substantial sums of money for armament and medical supplies. The civilian population's feeling of solidarity with the army impressed contemporaries. N. Gane noted some elements of the popular spirit that helped in overcoming the logistic difficulties: "Many young men voluntarily enlisted and rushed to the battlefield, and those incapable of fighting freely gave everything they could – horses, oxen, sheep, produce, food, money for the army's equipment. Our wives and daughters were on duty day and night in hospitals."[22]

The hospital system was well organized, with sufficient capacity for receiving the wounded. These were transported from the battlefield or came by themselves to the divisional field hospitals. Those whose recovery was likely to be prolonged were sent to Mecika, where there was a field hospital.

From here they were evacuated to Turnu Măgurele and thence by oxcart to the railroad, where two hospital trains took them to hospitals in various places. The evacuation normally went smoothly. The wounded arrived at Turnu Măgurele three days after hospitalization in the field.[23] The hospital center in Turnu Măgurele, where Nicolae Kalinderu headed a large team of physicians, had a capacity of 2,000 beds. Dr. Ludovic Fialla, the chief of the temporary hospital service of the Red Cross, who knew the massive efforts of the Romanian medical corps well, wrote in his memoirs: "All the physicians did their job with unfailing scrupulousness. ...All the personnel, students, and nurses followed the example of the physicians, and the level of self-sacrifice was high for all of them. ...The instruments were sufficient and the apparatus plentiful. Thanks to the antiseptics I can say that the treatments were excellent and the healing of the wounds was good... ."[24]

Construction of field telegraph lines was very important for the proper functioning of command communication and of the logistic system. In the Plevna area, specialized subunits of the engineers' battalion strung telegraph lines between Verbiţa and Porodim, Verbiţa, Caciamuniţa,and Nikopol, and Verbiţa and Grivitsa. When the Romanian army moved into the Vidin area, the needed telegraph links were established at once: from Lom Palanka to Arcer Palanca to Nazîr Mahala to Belorada to Rupcea to Smîrdan and from Nazîr Mahala to Tarnek. At the same time the two banks of the Danube were linked by an underwater telegraph cable in the Rast area. These communication links played an important role in overcoming the difficulties that arose in the army's logistic system and were useful in keeping the public informed on the development of military operations.

## Performance

The decisive moment of the entire war was the Romanian army's entrance into the struggle. After the Russian army had passed through Romanian territory, it began to cross the Danube and gradually to move its large units south of the river on the night of June 9/10, 1877. Sixteen days after crossing the Danube, the advanced corps of the central army crossed the Balkan Mountains by surprise and threatened Edirne. The Russians anticipated a very brief and victorious campaign. The Ottoman fortunes took a sudden turn for the better, however, and with the effective defense of Plevna in July 1877 the situation of the Russian troops in the Balkan area became critical. Plevna, a strongly fortified spot with a garrison of over 50,000, represented a serious threat to the Russian southward offensive, thus jeopardizing the stability of the entire Balkan front. This threat to the flank and to the rear was augmented by the equally real danger that the troops at

Plevna commanded by Osman might unite with other Ottoman forces from western Bulgaria and attempt to cross the Danube, thereby cutting the Russians' supply lines. Another possible development was that the Turks might mount a general offensive with the aim of driving the Russian troops back across the Danube before they were able to achieve superiority of forces. (Significant reserves were on their way from Russia.)[25] The official Russian military history points to the paramount importance of Plevna in the general development of military operations: "Indeed, here at Plevna a strategic knot unexpectedly developed that could not be cut except through enormous sacrifices and expenditure of time of which the Turks took advantage."[26] The Russian minister of war General D. A. Milyutin pointed out in a document submitted to the imperial high command that "to remedy a situation as unfavorable and dangerous as ours, there is no alternative but to give up advancing for the time being until more reinforcements arrive, to concentrate our forces, to take up favorable positions, and to build fortifications where they will be of use."[27]

Consideration of the likely evolution of the military situation led the Russian high command to ask the Romanian army to join the Russian forces at Plevna and help annihilate this "Sevastopol" of the 1877–78 campaign. Romania promptly answered this appeal. On July 22/August 3, 1877, Prince Carol wired Grand Duke Nikolay as follows:

> As a result of your telegram of July 19, after great efforts and despite many difficulties I am happy to report that all measures have been taken for concentrating some 30,000 men in order to win Plevna through a common effort with the corps engaged around this position, which is a constant danger to the imperial army. Steps have been taken toward building a bridge as soon as possible between Islaz and Corabia in order to speed the crossing of the Danube and to ensure supply and withdrawal routes.[28]

With this decision, the balance of the military situation south of the Danube again became unfavorable to the Ottoman side. The Romanian army's entry into action had a negative impact on the enemy command. An official Ottoman history written by former superior officers in 1877–78 said: "We were a few steps away from victory when Grand Duke Nikolay was obliged to ask the Romanian army's collaboration in overwhelming the admirable defenders of Plevna."[29] The former members of the Romanian command who in 1887 wrote the official history of the war recognized that this decision to cooperate with the Russian army was needed because "the Russian army, inferior in numbers, was threatened with repulsion on the front line and on both flanks and even with being driven back across the Danube, which would, on the one hand, have prolonged the campaign and, on the other, required the diversion of large elements of the Russian army to Romania, though it was not even a theater of war."[30] The Romanian army's entrance into action took place when the destiny of the war had not yet been decided, when the balance was still unstable. It had as its consequence a shifting of the balance of forces to the disadvantage of the Ottoman Empire, thus shortening the conflict.

The Romanian troops performed well on the battlefield in two special regards. The first was the inexhaustible resources of gallantry and heroism they displayed in the conflict with an experienced and well-fortified enemy. Numerous eyewitnesses recorded with admiration the valor and contempt for death shown by Romanian soldiers and officers during repeated assaults upon the Ottoman redoubts. The Danish Captain Hedeman, attached to the Russian army, wrote in a report to his country's military authorities in September 1877 that the Romanians' attack at Grivitsa was carried out "with great bravery."[31] The correspondent of the Vienna newspaper *Die Presse* wrote:

> The excellent order and cold blood with which the Romanian soldier enters into the attack are proof enough of the troops' morale. I have seen with my own eyes how the Romanian soldier fights, and I can say that he is fearless, brave, and capable in action. The Romanian soldiers display admirable tenacity in the midst of a rain of bullets and both in attack and in defense stand fast in the face of the enemy."[32]

The correspondent of the Swiss newspaper *Bund* reported: "After few moments we met such fire as I saw neither at Solferino nor at Custoza, but the riflemen stood unflinchingly... . I never thought to see such bravery in an army that had never before been under fire."[33]

The second element is the capacity of the Romanian combatants to face the particular difficulties of the 1877–78 campaign. The harshness of this war of position prefigured the conditions of World War I. Passages from the memoirs of two combatants — one on Turkish side and the other a Romanian — emphasize the physical and psychic effort demanded by the Plevna conflict. William V. Herbert:

> The guard service at Bash Tabia [Grivitsa] was most severe and cruel. ... it was so hard that later, the two battalions representing the redoubt guard had to be rotated for rest, each serving for twenty-four hours. No man could stay more than a day in such a situation and under such stress, with the enemy sentinels no more than the width of a road from ours... . The service in Bash Tabia was so dangerous that a man sent here said goodbye to his friends and accepted his destiny. Every hour claimed victims except when the troops concluded an unofficial truce; we could not show even a bit of helmet without inviting a rain of bullets.[34]

Colonel Gh. Slăniceanu:

> We stood day and night in the mud of the trenches without finding so much as a patch of dry land on which to rest a little. ...Many soldiers... were found frozen near their rifles on the edges of the trenches."[35]

The pride of the generation of Romania's War of Independence was the fact that Osman Pasha, the Ottoman commander at Plevna, surrendered to Romanian officers. The official history states that "the important Turkish Generalissimo" declared to the Romanian colonel Mihail Cerchez, the commander of the Second Infantry Division, that "he capitulated with his army," thus recording the definitive end of the Ottoman resistance at Plevna. From Romanian captivity Osman ordered the general capitulation of the Ottoman troops at Plevna (40,000 troops, including 10 pashas, 128 superior officers, and 2,000 junior officers).

The actions carried out by the Romanian army were genuine examples of cohesion, morale, and combat readiness. Whether in the movements to new concentration zones (from Plevna to Vidin and Belogradchik in December 1877) or during the assaults launched in the snow and severe cold of January 1878 against strong enemy fortifications (at Smîrdan and Inova), or in escorting the Turkish prisoners to Romania in the harsh conditions of the 1877–78 winter (during which they showed understanding and kindness to their former enemies), or in their cordial relations of mutual respect and assistance with the local Bulgarian population, or in their spirit of cooperation in struggle with the Russian allies, the Romanian combatants endured with valor and courage the difficulties of a long military campaign against a powerful enemy. The final losses of 10,000 of an effective force of about 100,000 (for the field army the losses amounted to about 20 percent) are an eloquent indicator of the armed effort made for the attainment of independence.

The conclusion is thus clear that the Romanian army in the 1877–78 war was, in its equipment, logistics, and performance, a modern and successful military instrument.

## NOTES

1. Fr. Kohn–Abrest, *Zigzags en Bulgarie* (n. p., 1879) pp. 279–80.
2. Ion Frunzetti and George Munteanu, co-ordinators, *Arta şi literatura în slujba independenţei naţionale* (Bucharest, 1977), p. 131.
3. *Monitorul oastei*, no. 1 (January 12, 1877), pp. 10–13.
4. *România în războiul de independenţă 1877–1878* (Bucharest, 1977), p. 342.
5. *Istoricul războiului din 1877–1878: Participarea României la acest război* (Bucharest, 1887), p. 70.
6. *Documente privind istoria României: Războiul pentru independenţă*, vol. 3 (Bucharest, 1954), p. 518.
7. Ibid., vol. 2, p. 43.
8. Radu Rosetti, *Partea luată de armata română în războiul din 1877–1878* (Bucharest, 1926) p. 106.
9. Ibid., p. 134.

10. Constantin Căzănişteanu and Mihail E. Ionescu, *Războiul neatîrnării României: Imprejurări diplomatice şi operatii militare 1877–1878* (Bucharest, 1977), pp. 116–17.

11. *Istoricul războiului*, p. 426.

12. Rosetti, *Partea luată*, p. 135.

13. Ibid., p. 106.

14. Ibid., p. 123.

15. Ibid., p. 35.

16. Ch. Crăiniceanu, *Impresiuni din război 1877–1878* (Bucharest, n. d.), p. 74.

17. Gheorghe Em. Lupaşcu, *Amintiri din războiul independenţei 1877–1878* (Bucharest, 1927), p. 59.

18. Quoted in Rosetti, *Partea luată*, p. 151.

19. *România în războiul de independenţă*, p. 346.

20. N. Adăniloaie and I. Gh. Cupşa, *Războiul pentru independenţă naţională a României* (Bucharest, 1967), pp. 88 ff.

21. *România în războiul de independenţă*, p. 347.

22. N. Gane, *Zile trăite* (Iaşi, 1901), p. 212.

23. Rosetti, *Partea luată*, p. 128.

24. Ludovic Fialla, *Reminiscente din rezbelul romăno-turc: Anul 1877 şi rolul Societătii Crucea Roşie în timp de pace şi de rezbel* (Bucharest, 1906), p. 72.

25. *Istoricul războiului*, p. 292.

26. Comisiunea istorică a Marelui stat major rus, *Resboiul ruso-turc din 1877–1878 în Peninsula Balcanică*, trans. I. Gardescu, vol. 2 (Bucharest, 1902), p. 188.

27. Colonel Martinov, *Le blocus de Plevna d'après les archives historiques* (Paris, n. d.), pp. 47–48.

28. Quoted in *România în războiul de independenţă*, p. 163.

29. Izzet–Fuad-pacha, *Les occasions perdue...* (Paris, 1900), p. 23.

30. *Istoricul războiului*, p. 292.

31. Radu Rosetti, *Rapoarte daneze asupra războiului din 1877–1878* (Bucharest, 1929), p. 9.

32. Quoted in *România în războiul de independenţă*, p. 224.

33. Rosetti, *Partea luată*, p. 126.

34. William V. Herbert, *The Defence of Plevna 1877, written by One Who Took Part in It* (London, 1895), p. 330.

35. Crăiniceanu, *Impresiuni din război*, p. 59.

36. *Istoricul războiului*, p. 787.

Florian Tucă


# ROMANIA IN THE WAR OF INDEPENDENCE: HELP EXTENDED BY ROMANIANS IN REGIONS UNDER FOREIGN RULE


The political expression of the national will on May 9, 1877, in Bucharest was powerfully echoed in the hearts of the Romanians of regions still under foreign rule. The militant solidarity of the Romanians of Transylvania, Crişana, Maramureş, the Banat, Bukovina, Bessarabia, and Dobruja with their brothers directly engaged in the struggle for independence manifested itself in moral, material, and human assistance to the Romanian state in its efforts in 1877–78.[1]

Participating in Romania's War of Independence

in one form or another, alongside Wallachians, Oltenians, and Moldavians, were also Romanians of the other provinces that were under foreign rule. The inhabitants of Transylvania, Bukovina, the Banat powerfully raised their voice in support of Romania's fight for independence... . In spite of the repressive measures taken by the Austro–Hungarian authorities, relief for soldiers was sent from those provinces, and a large number of young people crossed the mountains and enrolled in the army, shedding their blood in the war for the country's independence – a cherished aspiration of Romanians everywhere.[2]

These feelings of solidarity materialized, first of all, in the full support, openly expressed, for the proclamation of independence and consistently echoed by the Romanian press on the other side of the Carpathians. *Gazeta Transilvaniei* (Braşov), *Telegraful român* (Sibiu), *Familia* (Oradea), *Albina Carpaţilor* (Sibiu), *Gura satului* (Arad), and other newspapers, besides widely and promptly informing their readers on the course of the political and military developments in which Romania was involved (starting with the publication of the text of the Russo–Romanian Convention of April 4, 1877, and the proclamation of independence by Mihail Kogălniceanu on May 9), also reflected in their columns the wishes and hopes of Romanians living under foreign rule.[3] "The most important novelty for us," *Familia* said in its May 15 issue, "can be summed up in the words: 'Romania has proclaimed her independence and, at the same time, has declared war on Turkey.' On May 22, *Telegraful român* answered the skepticism and disparaging comments on the Romanian army carried by some Hungarian newspapers by reproducing the comments of the Austrian newspaper *Neues Wiener Tageblatt*: "The Romanian troops are in the best state of mind and have a determined military carriage, proving in everything they do that they are good troops." "They are well-dressed," *Telegraful român* proudly pointed out, "well-armed, and well-trained." "The cause of the Romanian soldier, *Gazeta Transilvaniei* said in its June 2, 1877, issue, "is a general Romanian cause, his victory is that of an entire nation," adding the wish that the Romanian people might "live that moment when it may be able to celebrate the great festival of its reconstitution, of its unity."

The development of military events south of the Danube was promptly reflected in the columns of the Romanian press beyond the Carpathians through enthusiastic reports on the battles of Grivitsa, Rahova, Plevna, Smîrdan, and Vidin. On November 27 *Familia* wrote: "In the present war the Romanian army has won the esteem and admiration of the entire world. *All Romanians are proudly thinking of it.*" The surrender of the Ottoman army at Plevna was received with joy on the other side of the Carpathians, being commented upon with great satisfaction by all the newspapers in Transylvania and the Banat. "Today," wrote *Gazeta Transilvaniei* on December 1, "Osman Pasha has surrendered" to the Romanian troops; "the Romanians were the first to enter Plevna." As a matter of fact, the fighting around Plevna occasioned in *Gazeta Transilvaniei* on September 8 one of the most inspiring articles on the war:

> The taking of the great redoubt of Grivitsa is due mostly to the admirable heroism of the brave Romanian soldiers, who, defying death, several times rushed upon the formidable fort and, climbing with ladders over the enemy ditches, drove him away from that fortified nest. The victory of Grivitsa restored to our forefathers' sword its old splendour. Today, the entire European press admires the heroic conduct of the Romanian troops in the bloody battle for Plevna.

In addition to press articles and commentaries, the victory at Plevna of November 28, 1877, was also celebrated through numerous street demonstrations and illuminations organized in the towns of Transylvania, the Banat, and Bukovina — Arad, Braşov, Blaj, Beiuş, Sibiu, Gherla, Năsăud, Cîmpulung, Rădăuţi, Suceava, and others.

In Braşov the event was celebrated with almost unmatched enthusiasm. The hills around the city were fairy-like with lights. Flares shot from the heights surrounding the city announced the brilliant victory of the Romanian—Russian troops. At a restaurant significantly called Headquarters of

Grivitsa — as the festive moment is described by *Telegraful român* of December 11 — the intellectuals of the city celebrated the long-awaited news until dawn. On December 2, the news of the victory reached the town of Blaj, and from that moment onwards the watchword was "the fall of Plevna." There, too, in the afternoon — *Gazeta Transilvaniei* of December 8 reported — the intellectuals of Blaj, young and old alike, gathered to celebrate the event.

As was only natural, the inhabitants of the Apuseni Mountains joined in the general enthusiasm. On December 14 and 15, manifestations of sympathy for Romania and its participation in the war for independence took place at Cîmpeni and Sohodol,[4] according to the Hungarian Ministry of Religion and Education, which demanded that the Metropolitan Bishop of Sibiu punish the priest Ioan Pandele, their organizer. Similar manifestations took place elsewhere in Transylvania. At Năsăud, for instance, after the victory of Plevna, clerks, peasants, and students marched in the main street of the town to the firemen's band, singing patriotic songs. Afterward, they gathered at the Hotels Grivitsa and Rahova, where there were fiery speeches by teachers and students. At Gherla, notwithstanding the measures taken by the prefect of Solnoc–Dăbîca County, the students rejoiced at the victories won in the War of Independence.

The course of the military developments at the Balkan front was followed with much interest by the Romanians in Bukovina. At the Austro–Romanian border points, fabulous sums of money were paid for newspapers published in Bucharest and Iaşi carrying news from the front. The victories won by the Romanian troops and the surrender of the Ottoman army at Plevna stirred the Romanians in Bukovina with indescribable enthusiasm. In Suceava, Chernowitz, Cîmpulung, Rădăuţi, and other Bukovinian towns Romanians embraced in the streets, shedding tears of joy.

The moral support for the War of Independence of the Romanians in regions under foreign rule was augmented by an important material contribution. Immediately after the proclamation of independence, committees for the support of wounded Romanian soldiers and the efforts of the Romanian army in general were set up in towns of Transylvania, the Banat, and Bukovina. On May 17, the women of Sibiu, who had formed a support committee chaired by Iudita Măcelariu, had a "Call to All Transylvanian Women" published by *Telegraful român* in which the latter's cooperation and contributions were requested for that lofty patriotic aim. The call was reproduced without delay by *Românul* and *România Liberă* in Bucharest and in other Transylvanian publications such as *Gazeta Transilvaniei* and *Familia*. The appeal of the Sibiu women was much praised, particularly by George Bariţiu in a "Respectful Epistle to the Romanian Women" carried by *Gazeta Transilvaniei*, and therefore found a deep echo in Romanian circles in Transylvania. Among the first to sign the subscription lists were Metropolitan Bishop Miron Romanul, Ilie Măcelariu, former president of the Romanian National Party, Iosif Hodoş, a member of the Romanian Academy, Partenie Cosma, a deputy in the Chamber in Budapest, Visarion Roman, director of the Albina Bank, Paul Dunca, and others. Many artisans and peasants from the villages around Sibiu also subscribed sums of money ranging from 1 to 20 lei.

On May 22, the Committee of the Romanians in Braşov was set up, headed by merchant Manole Diamandi and writers I. Al. Lapedatu and Aron Densuşianu. Its fiery "philanthropic appeal," carried by *Gazeta Transilvaniei* of May 27, garnered 7,540 gold francs in just a few days. "For our brothers over there," the appeal ran, "now faced with the hard need to defend, with weapons in hand, their goods and lives, the voice of charity now comes and asks humanity for help and comfort. The more strongly does this sacred voice look to us for help as it is also the *voice of blood,* as they are *our brothers!"*

Similar committees were set up in Cluj (chairwoman Maria Ilieşu), Oradea (Veturia Roman), and Făgăraş (Anastasia Popescu).

In the city and country of Arad, the support campaign was sustained by the local review *Biserica şi şcoala,* which issued two stirring calls, the first, "A Philanthropic Call to All Romanian Women," on May 24 and the second, "A Philanthropic Note to All Romanian Gentlemen and Scholars," on June 19. The first appeal, signed by Emilia Sturza of Sepreuş, read in part:

> The battle is being fought by Romanians, and we are Romanians too. This relationship brings our hearts close to those of our brothers on the other side of the Carpathians who are fighting and makes us mourn those who will die at enemy hands and wreathe garlands of flowers for those who will bring victory home. This relationship requires that every true Romanian woman make what sacrifices and offers she can afford to help the brave soldiers of Romania.

An initiator of a similar action in Timişoara, Iulia Rotaru, the wife of Pavel Rotaru, a journalist and fighter for the national cause, asserted in *Minte şi inimă* (Arad) on May 22 that "Romanians from everywhere have been working to this human end for a long time now.... therefore, it is impossible this time for the Romanians living in the neighborhood of Timişoara to lag behind, because in all humanitarian, philanthropic, and national matters they have always kept pace with their brothers." In the city of Arad, in addition to the collection initiated by *Gura satului* on May 21, to which the foremost people of the city contributed, another collection was made by George Purcariu, and other subscription lists were opened in the town and villages of the county. At Lipova and Caransebeş several subscription lists were circulated, while in Timişoara, besides Iulia Rotaru's list, there was one initiated by Victoria Maxim, and many others were circulated in the surrounding villages.

Such subscriptions and collections of money and objects were also organized by the Romanian women of Bukovina in the cities of Chernowitz and Suceava. Organized into county committees designed to help wounded Romanian soldiers, they collected money, medicine, dressings, and bandages. These committees were chaired by Eufrosina and Natalia Hurmuzachi, Elena Popovici—Logotheti, Olga Grigorcea, Eufrosina Petrino, Victoria Zotta, Catinca Vasilco, and others.

The activities of the Romanian women's committees in Transylvania and the Banat displeased the Hungarian government (though it itself sponsored Hungarian collections for the Turkish soldiers), and at the end of May it dissolved all such committees, which were violently attacked by such newspapers as *Magyar Polgár, Hon, Hírnök,* and *Kelet,* and forbade the continuation of the collections under way. This arbitrary decision of Count Kálmán Tisza's government, which threatened severe reprisals, only spurred expressions of Romanian solidarity. *Telegraful român* said in its May 22 issue, "We have neither the power nor the desire to oppose the orders of the authorities, but we have a power that no force in this world can ever take away from us, and that is the power of love for humanitarianism, for our *kindred people and sacred religion."* The Sibiu newspaper concluded by saying that, although the committees had been abolished, their activities would be carried on individually, with money and goods being sent directly to the Red Cross in Bucharest.

Under the headline "For the Benefit of the Romanian Wounded," the decision of the Hungarian government was harshly condemned by George Bariţiu in *Gazeta Transilvaniei* of May 22. Romanian women, Bariţiu maintained in his article, were not to "care a bit" about those "fanatical threats" but were to attend above all to the "unbiased, fair judgment of civilized Christian Europe, which would brand us, the Romanians of this empire, as traitors to *our blood* if we did not hasten to the aid of our brothers of *common origin, nation, language, and religion."* For that reason, Bariţiu concluded, the "Romanian women should continue unfalteringly upon the road pointed out by their hearts, the national will, and the example of enlightened Europe, defying the attempts af tyranny and selfishness to kill love for one's homeland."

Following his daring article, Bariţiu was brought to trial in Sibiu, but the women and the other Romanian patriots continued their activities with the same dedication. On June 12, *Gazeta Transilvaniei* issued a new "Appeal to the Romanians," signed on June 9 by fifteen patriots of Braşov along with Archpriest Ioan Petricu, Manole Diamandi, and George Bariţiu, which, as had *Telegraful român,* suggested individual action: "This is an appeal to all Romanians living between the Carpathians and the Tisza, young or old, rich or poor, to contribute to the alleviation of the sufferings of our Romanian brothers wounded in the war." The contribution was asked in the "name of humanitarianism, of *love and blood relationship*... from everyone in whose breast beats a burning *Romanian heart.*"

In this way, activities for the support of wounded Romanian soldiers and their families continued throughout Transylvania and the Banat, with their main centers, in addition to those already mentioned, at Năsăud, Abrud, Orăştie, Haţeg, Oraviţa, Sighişoara, Blaj, Beiuş, Gherla, Baia Mare, Răşinari, Miercurea, Sălişte, Tilişca, Bucium, and elsewhere.[5] In some villages contributions were even made by schoolchildren.

Similar activities were carried on by the Romanian students in Vienna and Budapest. On July 24, the Romanian students in Vienna set up a committee, chaired by Octavian Blasiu, for the organization of collections to which many a member of the Romanian colony in Austria's capital city contributed; a patriotic manifestation to the same end was organized in Budapest on October 20. The money collected by the Romanian students in the two capital cities was sent directly to the Red Cross in Bucharest. The Romanian students in Transylvania voiced their solidarity with Romania's War of Independence in a telegram sent to Prime Minister Ion C. Brătianu, carried by *Gazeta Transilvaniei* of December 11, which ended with the wish: "Let everything lead to the independence of the Romanian homeland and the glory of our people... . Long live the Romanian army and independent Romania!" The money collected as a result of the patriotic activities organized by the Romanians in Transylvania amounted to 124,700 gold francs.[6]

Societies and committees were also set up throughout Bukovina. The members of the Arboroasa Society organized a collection for the arming of students in Bukovina and the Banat who intended to enlist in the Romanian army. An important sum was thus gathered from among students, professors, political figures such as Archimandrite Silvestru Morariu—Andrievici, George Flondor, Nicolae Hurmuzachi, Iancu Zotta, I. Cîntea, and others. Part of the money thus collected was sent to the Romanian students from the valley of the Timok who had taken refuge in Bucharest in order to enlist in the Romanian army.[7] "At the time, there was not a single Romanian in Bukovina," the historian Ion Nistor was to say, "who was not aware of the overwhelming importance of the events taking place south of the Danube, and everyone felt in duty bound to contribute in one way or another to the achievement of the victory everyone so fervently wished for."[8]

However, the most relevant contribution to Romania's efforts during the War of Independence was the enlistment of volunteers from Transylvania, the Banat, and Bukovina in the Romanian army. Their participation "was an impressive expression of national solidarity in implementing one of the most ardent hopes of the people."[9] One never knew the exact number of these volunteers, because the border was crossed illegally in order to avoid any official identification or record, most of the volunteers even changing their names for fear of causing trouble for their families or being condemned as deserters or traitors. For the same reasons, the correspondence between the volunteers and their families was transmitted secretly, signed with pseudonyms or not signed at all, most of the letters being destroyed in order to prevent them from becoming evidence against those to whom they had been addressed. All this notwithstanding, a few names were recorded, and they are enough to show not only the state of mind but also some of the concrete deeds of these volunteers. Most of the names belong to people from southern Transylvania and Bukovina, as they were in closer contact with Romania's frontier regions, population, and even local authorities.

The first group to arrive was from the Făgăraş area, and it was welcomed by the authorities and population of the city of Ploieşti with music, speeches, and flowers. Brothers were coming to join brothers! Both the departure of the group and the reception it was given in Ploieşti alarmed the Hungarian government, causing the Austro–Hungarian foreign minister Gyula Andrássy to lodge an energetic protest with the government in Bucharest demanding the extradition of the refugees. The Romanian government, through Foreign Minister Mihail Kogălniceanu, refused to grant the demanded extradition but assured Andrássy that it would not have the volunteers from Austria–Hungary enlisted in the Romanian army. In the instructions sent on June 13 to the Romanian ambassador in Vienna, Ioan Bălăceanu, the Romanian foreign minister, said, "Vienna will understand that under no pretext whatsoever will we perform the unjust act of delivering to the Austro–Hungarian authorities any innocent Romanian youth from Transylvania who has lately come to our country on one business or another." To this end, he asked Bălăceanu to remind Andrássy of the stand adopted in 1860, when Vienna had demanded the extradition of the Hungarian émigrés in Moldavia who were organizing a legion of volunteers to fight on the side of Piedmont against Austria and the Romanian government had refused to grant it by virtue of the hospitality characteristic of the Romanian people: "Count Andrássy will think the matter over and understand that what was not done in 1860 in the case of persecuted Hungarians cannot be done today, particularly against Romanians."[10]

Yet, the governments in Vienna and Budapest took severe measures to guard the frontier, which, however, did not yield the anticipated results.

Throughout the war, the Romanian army received many such volunters.[11] Research devoted to the matter has so far uncovered the names of Făgăraş volunteers Vincenţiu Grama, a theologian; Nicolae Grancea, a student; Gheorghe Borzea and Ion Dejenar, lawyer's secretaries; Ioan Popovici, a clerk in the prefect's office; Damaschin Radu Popa, an archivist; Nicolae Căluţiu and Petru Drăghici, former students at the secondary school at Blaj; Nicolae Ciuceanu of Orăştie; and Adam Henţiescu of Rîşca. These embodied, together with many others, to quote Nicolae Iorga, the "warm élan of the Transylvanians." The case of the Transylvanian Gheorghe Cîrţan, from Cîrţişoara in Sibiu County, is a telling example of the multilateral efforts made by Romanians of regions under foreign rule in support of the Romanian state in 1877–78. The proclamation of independence found Cîrţan, a shepherd, in Romania, and he donated his flock of 2,000 sheep to the Romanian state and enlisted in the Third Regiment of the line. After the war, "Badea (approximately "brother") Cîrţan" (the appellation by which he would enter the consciousness of his generation and those that followed), a self-educated man and a lover of national history, assumed the difficult task of distributing Romanian books in Transylvanian villages.

On June 13, 1877, Colonel Toma de Gécz, commander of the recruiting center of Sibiu, informed his chiefs that from the military districts of Sălişte and Răşinari some 1,657 recruitable young men might have crossed to Romania, bringing the total number of those who enlisted to 3,843. On June 30, Tisza himself admitted that a "massive desertion" was taking place in Transylvania, demanding that the prefects of the counties of Braşov, Sibiu, Tîrnava Mare, Mureş–Turda, Făgăraş, Trei Scaune, Ciuc, and Bistriţa–Năsăud take strict measures in order to prevent the crossing of the Carpathians.[12]

The same élan was evinced by the young people of Bukovina. On May 7, Partenie Sireteanu, George Săvescu, and Ilie Gherghel, students from the secondary school of Chernowitz, went by way of the Cosmin forest to Romania, while the next day another two students, Alecu Giurgiuveanu and Emilian Hnidei, crossed into Romania at Burdujeni. The two groups joined and were warmly welcomed by the authorities and the inhabitants of the towns of Paşcani and Roman. A similar reception was given them by the students of the University of Bucharest, for the enlistment of Transylvanian and Bukovinian volunteers in the Romanian army was seen as auspicious for the union of all Romanians. In the ensuing days, the frontier was crossed by other young men, such as the veterinarian Dionisie Bucevschi, clerks Emilian Săvescu and Nicolae Bodnărescu, students Ion Fongaci and Constantin A. Popescu of Suceava, and others.

On May 23, 1877, Stefan Wolf, headmaster of the secondary school of Chernowitz, felt compelled to report to the government in Vienna that "several Romanian pupils have fled to Romania." On May 27, Governor Alesany asked the rector of the University of Chernowitz to take energetic measures against those Romanian students who were stirring up national spirit and preparing to leave for Romania. Because the rector answered that the university senate had no police powers, the police intervened and searched the students' houses.

Fighting on the battlefields south of the Danube for independence were many officers from Transylvania and the Banat who had enlisted in the Romanian army after having resigned from the Austro–Hungarian one, whether long before or on the eve of the proclamation of independence. For example, Moise Groza, native of Obreja in Caraş–Severin County, resigned from the Austro–Hungarian army in 1873 and crossed into Romania and to enlist in the Romanian army on July 5 of that year. During the battles of Grivitsa and Plevna he was promoted to major and awarded the Steaua României. In a letter to his wife in Braşov on June 25, 1877, he reminded her that eleven years before he had fought as an Austrian officer. "Today is an important day in my life, because eleven years have passed since the battle of Custoza, where I did my duty without knowing why. *Now I know what I shall be fighting for.*"[13]

That mentality was characteristic of all Romanian officers in the Austro–Hungarian army, and for that reason many Romanian officers from Transylvania and the Banat watched with sympathy the negotiations carried on by the government in Bucharest with the Austro–Hungarian monarchy for the enlistment of a number of Romanian senior officers in the Romanian army. Already at the time when secret preparations were being made for the proclamation of independence, the Romanian government had authorized Vincenţiu Babeş to approach the generals Traian Doda and Nicolae Guran and Colonel David Urs de Marginea. Negotiations with Doda, who was retired and was being offered the office of chief of the general staff of the Romanian army, were carried on through the offices of Eugeniu Carada. Doda did not turn down the offer of the Romanian government but conditioned its acceptance on the approval of Emperor Francis Joseph.[14] From the diplomatic point of view, things were rather complicated. On the one hand, the Hungarian government felt drawn to the Ottoman Empire; on the other, the Austro–Hungarian Empire took a dim view of the struggle for independence of the peoples of southeastern Europe, the more so as it itself dominated a large part of the Romanian people of Transylvania, Crişana, Maramureş, the Banat, and Bukovina. For that reason, Francis Joseph would not consent to Doda's departure, in spite of the repeated intercessions of the Romanian government. Guran was easily forced to renounce the idea of leaving for Romania because he was still on active duty in the Austro–Hungarian army. Besides Moise Groza (later a division general), former officers of the Austro–Hungarian army who fought in the Romanian army included Transylvanians Major Nichita Ignat, from Salva, in Bistriţa–Năsăud County, Constantin Saguna, the grandson of Metropolitan Bishop Andrei Saguna, who was promoted to major on the battlefield; the doctor Captain Ioan Arsene, from Gura Rîului, in Sibiu County; and Second Lieutenant Nicolae Droc–Boreianu, from Răşinari, in Sibiu County. The number of Romanian officers formerly members of the Austro–Hungarian army who enrolled in the Romanian army was certainly even larger than this if one takes into account the effect of the appeal headed "To Arms" carried by *Gazeta Transilvaniei* of May 26, which said that they would be received "with open arms" as volunteers in the Romanian army.

Nicolae Cristea, editor of *Telegraful român*, made a survey of the war in "The Year 1877 Is Drawing to Its End," carried in the December 29, 1877, issue, in which he showed that after the victories won by the Romanian army in the Balkan Peninsula,

> nobody dares separate Romanians from Romanians: wherever he lives, be it Moldavia, Muntenia, Transylvania, the Banat, Hungary, Bessarabia, or Serbia, when it comes to showing that one is a man, the Romanian is as Romanian as all Romanians are. This is what links us to one another, what brings us together and unites us, and this compels the world to acknowledge the fact that we are a people formed of individuals of the same blessed kind.

The awareness of solidarity among the Romanians of all the provinces of former Dacia was stressed by the Banat Deputy Partenie Cosma in the Chamber of Deputies in Budapest on November 25, 1878: "When the hour struck for winning the homeland's independence, the Romanians rushed as one to the impregnable redoubts of the bravest and most terrible enemy... Down there, by the Danube, there is a brave young people that knows its European vocation and is ready to fulfil it, a people anyone would welcome as an ally."[15]

Through the contributions and sacrifices of all Romanians, the national people's war for Romania's independence was thus a telling instance and proof of the unity of the Romanian nation everywhere and a powerful impulse to the accomplishment of Romanian state unity.

Only seven years had passed since the acknowledgment of Romania's independence when Ioan Slavići formulated in *Tribuna* (Sibiu) the phrase that would guide the entire political struggle and cultural activity of the Romanians in Transylvania: "The sun rises in Bucharest for all Romanians!"

Romania's winning of complete state independence had an extraordinary impact upon the Romanians in regions still under foreign rule. In the Banat, for instance, Stefan Nagy, the district judge of Orşova, reported to his superiors that, following the victories of the Romanian troops, the peasants were stubbornly opposing the Austro–Hungarian authorities. In Dubovna, the orders of the district judge were no longer being observed, while in Iabloniţa, Petnic, and other villages troops had to be sent against the discontented peasants. The judge said that the instigator was the Romanian Orthodox priest of Orşova, Mihai Popovici, a close collaborator of Doda.[16]

Pride and hope seized the Transylvanian people, who openly asserted that after the "Balkan Plevna, there will be a Transylvanian Plevna,"[17] meaning that they cherished the hope that the Romanian army would come back to liberate Transylvania. Synthesizing the hopes of Transylvanians, Timotei Cipariu wrote: "The year 1877 is the reassuring halo of a future full of glory."[18] The national movement in Transylvania received a powerful impetus, and the election of 1878 in the Banat and Hungary saw the largest number of Romanian deputies elected to the parliament in Budapest. The great hope that Cipariu referred to and the Romanian people of Transylvania and the Banat cherished — that "Transylvanian Plevna" — was obviously the idea of the impending achievement of national unity. This was demonstrated by the enthusiastic election of General Traian Doda as deputy by the Romanians of the Banat in 1878 and by the resoluteness they showed in supporting their just national claims.

The War of Independence had a powerful effect upon the political struggle of the Romanians in Transylvania and the Banat, stimulating their energies in the defense of their national rights. The successes scored by the Romanian army, the consolidation of Romania's status, and the increase of its prestige in the international arena lent new scope to the national and social movement of the people of Transylvania and the Banat, infusing greater force into anti-Habsburg activities for the achievement of the state unity of the entire Romanian people. Recognizing that Austro—Hungarian rule in Transylvania, the Banat, Crişana, Maramureş, and Bukovina would always be a brake on the self-assertion of Romanian society, people increasingly placed their hopes on Romania, the Motherland, now independent and enjoying a well-defined status in the European arena. Relevant in this respect is the enthusiastic reception extended to Mihail Kogălniceanu in the railway station of Orşova on his way to Berlin to participate in the Congress of June 1878. On that occasion, the choir of Lugoj and the Philharmonic Society of Timişoara came to town to greet the foreign minister, sang beautiful folk songs, and wished him success in his political mission, *Familia* of June 4, 1878, reported.

The impact of Romania's winning of independence upon the Romanians in Transylvania did not go unnoticed by the Austro—Hungarian authorities, which demanded that strict measures be taken against the leaders of the Romanian national movement. By an order of March 12, 1878, the Ministry of the Interior in Budapest called upon the prefects of Transylvania to take appropriate steps:

After the war — which can be considered as over now — according to the information received from various regions, anti-state nationalistic activities are continuing with increased intensity, while in some places overt manifestations have been singled out. Nationalist agitators are holding meetings and making plans for the organization of an anti-state movement and for misleading the lower strata of the people, who are inadequately informed.[19]

The Austrian authorities of Bukovina kept a close watch on the state of mind of its Romanian population, which openly expressed its hope of uniting with Romania. In the autumn of 1877, reprisals against Romanians came one after another. Police reports informed the higher authorities that the "peasants are openly declaring that they have agreed with the Romanian priests and boyars to snatch Bukovina away from Austria and unite her with Romania." Many Romanian priests and peasants were arrested and expelled from Bukovina on the charge of being agitators hostile to the Austrian state. Among them were Ion Vasiliu of Verpolea, Vasile Paznic of Volcivet, Nicolae Cozmei of Serbăuţi, and others.

During the Balkan crisis and the war for Romania's independence, the attention of the leaders of the Romanian national movement of Transylvania and the Banat turned to supporting their brothers fighting for freedom from Ottoman domination and the sanctioning of their full independence. That broad solidarity movement contributed to the strengthening of relations between various centers of the Romanian national movement, laying the groundwork for future cooperation with the Romanian National Party. The enthusiasm generated by the War of Independence among the people of Transylvania and the Banat demonstrated to their leaders that the peasantry, capable of supporting and sustaining the national movement, should necessarily form its social basis. As a result, the progressive Transylvanian and Banat intelligentsia moved closer to the village world, and the results were not late in appearing. The activities carried on throughout Transylvania and the Banat in 1877–78 testified once more to the development of national consciousness, which after the winning of Romania's independence acquired increasingly clearer contours for the millions of Romanians living outside the frontiers of the Romanian state. It had become obvious to everyone that for Romanians there was but one goal left, namely, a unitary national state.[20]

To political activists, the stand unequivocally expressed by the entire Romanian population of Transylvania and the Banat during the War of Independence was conclusive proof that political cooperation with the governing parties was unpopular and would not enjoy the support of the Romanian peasantry. George Bariţiu rightly believed that the year 1877 had marked a turning point in the life of the Romanians of Transylvania: "The Romanians from Braşov, Sibiu, and other so-called activists have awakened out of their sleep; and having seen that more than a hundred Hungarian newspapers as one opposed the independence of the Romanian state, they have awakened indeed."[21] The change in attitude of the activists created the preconditions for the unification of the Romanian national movements of Transylvania and the Banat.

Speaking of the influence of Romania's War of Independence upon the Romanian subjects of the Austro–Hungarian monarchy, Valeriu Branişte wrote that the winning of national independence in 1877 "has electrified the entire Romanian world. The national consciousness, torpid until yesterday, has acquired gigantic dimensions. One witnesses the beneficent influence of this spiritual revival in all fields of our public life... The psychological embryos of the revival now felt in all the domains of public and private life must be traced to this great moment in our history."[22]

The proclamation of Romania's independence and its sanctioning on the battlefields of all Romanians' national people's war of 1877–78 had as a consequence of utmost importance the political unification of the Romanian national movements in the Austro–Hungarian empire through the fusion of the two Romanian national parties – the National Party of the Romanians in the Banat and Hungary and the National Party of the Romanians in Transylvania – during the conference held in Sibiu in 1881, on the anniversary of the day the independence of their brothers in Romania had been proclaimed.

Written on the banners of one generation after another and sanctioned by the blood shed by the Romanian army on the battlefield, the winning of Romania's full state independence was strong new proof of the Romanian nation's unswerving determination to be united and strengthened its hope of accomplishing state unity, being in fact its prelude and prerequisite.

## NOTES

1. See *România în războiul de independenţă, 1877–1878* (Bucharest, 1977), pp. 355–65; *Independenţa României* (Bucharest, 1977), pp. 204–8, 225–27, 239–42; *Independenţa: Lupta milenară a poporului român* (Iaşi, 1977), pp. 65–66, 70–72; Gheorghe D. Stoean and Ion Gh. Pană, *Epopeea independenţei României, 1877–1878* (Cluj–Napoca, 1977), pp. 98–99, 104–5, 107–12, 114–20; Constantin Olteanu, *Masele populare şi războiul de independenţă* (Bucharest, 1977), pp. 140–49; *Masele populare în războiul pentru cucerirea independenţei absoulte a României, 1877–1878* (Bucharest, 1979), pp. 249–95.

2. Nicolae Ceauşescu, *Romania on the Way of Building up the Multilaterally Developed Socialist Society*, vol. 14 (Bucharest, 1978), pp. 298–99.

3. See Cătălina Crisiarcu, "Publicistica," in *Arta şi literatura in slujba independenţei nationale*, coord. Ion Frunzetti and George Munteanu (Bucharest, 1977), pp. 103–8; Constantin Avram, *Lauda vitejiei româneşti (Eroismul ostaşilor români în războiul pentru independenţă oglindit în publicistica vremii)* (Bucharest, 1977); *De lîngă Plevna: Războiul de independenţă in presa transilvană*, ed. Titus Moraru and Ovidiu Mureşan (Cluj–Napoca, 1977); Stelian Vasilescu, *Familia: Corespondenţe de la Plevna*, ed. Vicul Faur (Timişoara, 1977).

252 FLORIAN TUCĂ

4. Paul Abrudan, "Un document inedit privind demonstrația de la Cîmpeni și Sohodol cu prilejul capitulării Plevnei," *Studii și comunicări* 19 (1975): 263.

5. See Valeriu I. Bologa, "Ajutorul românilor ardeleni pentru răniții războiului independenței," *Transilvania*, 1941, no. 5–6; Paul Abrudan, "Ajutorul bănesc și material al transilvănenilor în sprijinul războiului pentru cucerirea independenței de stat a României," *Revista de istorie* 30 (1977): 23–46, 279–300; I. D. Suciu, "Solidarizarea românilor bănățeni cu războiul de independență," *Revista de istorie* 30 (1977): 397–412.

6. Vasile Netea, "Războiul pentru independență: Manifestare a unității și solidarității tuturor românilor," *Revista de istorie* 30 (1977): 805.

7. Octav Monoranu and Ion Cocuz, "Ecouri ale războiului de independență în Bucovina," in *Almanah "Tribuna"* (1976), p. 84.

8. I. Nistor, "Consecințele războiului de neatîrnare asupra românilor din Bucovina și Basarabia," in *Războiul neatîrnării, 1877–1878* (Bucharest, 1927), p. 175.

9. Nicolae Ceaușescu, *Romania on the Road of Completing Socialist Construction*, vol. 3 (Bucharest, 1969), p. 650.

10. *Documente privind istoria României: Războiul pentru independență*, vol. 3, (Bucharest, 1953), pp. 1230–31.

11. Sextil Pușcariu, "Răsunetul războiului de independență în Ardeal," in *Războiul neatîrnării, 1877–1878* (Bucharest, 1927); Nistor, "Consecințele războiului;" Bologa, "Ajutorol românilor"; Ioan Lupaș, *Istoria românilor*, vol. 4 (Sibiu, 1944), pp. 469–70; Stefan Pascu, *Istoria Transilvaniei* (Sibiu, 1945), pp. 235–36; I. Luncan, W. Marian, and Gh. Oancea, *Independența României: Participări bănățene* (Timișoara, 1977).

12. Liviu Maior, *Transilvania și războiul pentru independență, 1877–1878* (Bucharest, 1977) p. 31.

13. Sextil Pușcariu, "Douăzeci de scrisori ale lui Moise Groza din războiul de la 1877," *Anuarul Institutului de istorie națională* 4 (1926–27): 232.

14. Suciu, "Solidarizarea românilor," p. 405; Maior, op. cit. pp. 28–30.

15. I. V. Păcățian, *Cartea de aur sau luptele politice naționale ale Românilor de sub coroana ungară*, vol. 6 (Sibiu, 1910), p. 680.

16. Suciu, "Solidarizarea românilor," p. 408; Aurora Dolgu, "Ecoul războiului de independență din 1877–1878 în Banat," *Studia Universitatis Babeș Bolyai*, Historia, fasc. 1 (1968): 93; *Lupta românilor din Transilvania pentru libertate națională (1848–1849)*. (Bucharest, 1974), pp. 410–11.

17. Ștefan Pascu, *Marea Adunare Națională de la Alba Iulia* (Cluj, 1968), p. 143.

18. Quoted in V. Netea, *Lupta românilor din Transilvania pentru libertate națională (1848–1849)* (Bucharest, 1974), pp. 410–11.

19. Paul Abrudan, "Documente inedite privind solidaritatea românilor transilvăneni cu România în războiul de independență," *Studii și comunicări* 19 (1975): 271.

20. Maior, op. cit., p. 54.

21. G. Barițiu, *Părți alese din istoria Transilvaniei pe două sute de ani în urmă*, vol. 4 (Sibiu, 1891), p. 490.

22. Valeriu Braniște, *Societatea teatrală G. A. Petoulescu* (Brașov, 1902), p. 21, cited in Suciu, "Solidarizarea românilor," p. 411.

Constantin Căsănişteanu

# ROMANIA BETWEEN SAN STEFANO AND BERLIN

The war of 1877—78 ended with the treaty initialed at San Stefano on February 19, 1878. The treaty acknowledged the independence of Romania, Montenegro, and Serbia and extended the territory of each; it also acknowledged Romania's right to Dobruja (Articles 1—5). Bulgaria was declared an autonomous principality to be ruled by an elected prince under Ottoman suzerainty; the new state extended from the Danube to the Aegean and from Lake Ohrid to the Black Sea (Articles 6—7). While a Bulgarian national army was being organized, Russian troops were to remain south of the Danube for another two years with a view to maintaining order; communications for the Russian contingent were to pass through Romania and the ports of Varna and Burgas (Article 8). Bosnia and Hercegovina received autonomy within the Ottoman Empire (Article 14). Epirus, Thessaly, and Albania were granted self-administration on the model of the regime introduced in Crete in 1868 (Article 15). Administrative reforms were introduced in Armenia, while in the Caucasus Russia received Batum, Ardahan, Kars, and Bayazid, as well as the territory up to Soganli-dag.

The signing of the Treaty of San Stefano marked the culmination of the tsarist policy of expansion and domination in southeastern Europe. When military operations had finally opened the way for the Russian army to enter Constantinople, Britain had reacted by sending a squadron to the straits. There were two major reasons for the British decision. On the one hand, the consolidation of Russian influence in the Balkan Peninsula violated the balance of power, a traditional principle of British foreign policy; on the other hand, as a guardian of the Ottoman Empire, Britain could not let the "sick man of Europe" die. British intransigence threatened to turn into war. Russia, its forces exhausted by the Balkan campaign, was unable to cope with another war. Further discussion of the terms of the San Stefano Treaty within the framework of a European forum appeared the only way to avoid a military confrontation.

When the European chancelleries had been informed of the stipulations of the treaty, the conflict of British and Russian interests on the Eastern Question took the form of a formal disagreement. Britain demanded that all the terms of the Treaty of San Stefano be submitted to a European congress, whereas Russia, while agreeing that a conference be convened, insisted that it concentrate only on those issues in the peace treaty that were of interest to the European powers, and not on those pertaining to Russo–Ottoman relations. Because the disagreement actually masked the endeavors of Britain to maintain its position in the Near East and the eastern Mediterranean and Russia's wish to ensure at any cost its domination of the Balkan Peninsula, which the Treaty of San Stefano had sanctioned, it had the potential of escalating into a conflict that might engulf the entire continent.

It was in this tense atmosphere that the Romanian government learned of the text of the Treaty of San Stefano in early March. From the very first moment, Prime Minister Ion C. Brătianu and Foreign Minister Mihail Kogălniceanu declared that Romania must protest most vehemently against the treaty, which stipulated, among other things, that in exchange for Dobruja Romania must cede three counties in southern Bessarabia (retroceded in 1856) that had been Romanian territory from time immemorial. Because Romania's participation in the envisaged congress was doubtful, its independence not having been acknowledged by the powers, Kogălniceanu asked Virnav Liteanu, the Romanian diplomatic agent in Berlin, to point out that in pursuance of the Treaty of Paris of 1856 Romania had the right to declare war and make peace and that consequently its presence at the congress was not in any way dependent on the acknowledgment of its independence. The aim of Romania's presence at the congress, Kogălniceanu wrote, was to protest the Treaty of San Stefano, the stipulations of which were seriously prejudicial to its national interest.

The tension in Bucharest increased on March 15 when in the Chamber of Deputies Deputy Protopopescu-Pache called on the government to state its position with regard to the treaty. Kogălniceanu declared that the government would be "unable" to prevent the Russian troops on their way to Bulgaria from crossing Romanian territory. As far as Romania's exclusion from the peace negotiations was concerned, the government could only voice a protest. Kogălniceanu refused to comment on the territorial changes. Discontented deputies and senators suggested creating a joint commission of the two chambers to draw up a protest against the treaty.

In a circular note sent to the Romanian diplomatic agents for submission to the governments to which they were accredited, the Romanian foreign minister pointed out once more the unacceptability of the treaty's terms pertaining to Romania and declared that his country considered itself in no way bound by a document it had not initialed. The same day it was decided that Brătianu should go to Vienna and Berlin to explain Romania's stand.

On March 21 Russia's reaction to the position adopted by Romania led to a crisis in the relations between the two governments. Chancellor Gorchakov summoned General I. Ghica, Romania's diplomatic agent in St. Petersburg, and asked if Romania intended to protest Article 8 of the Treaty of San Stefano, which stipulated the right of the Russian troops to pass through Romania on their way to Bulgaria. The Russian chancellor told Ghica that if that intention materialized the tsar would order the Russian army to occupy Romania and disarm its military. In response, Ghica pointed out that the article in question was highly prejudicial to Romania's interests and dignity and that the Russian government should discuss the matter with the Romanian authorities. Prince Carol firmly rejected the threats of the chancellor on the same day: "An army that fought in front of Tsar Alexander II at Plevna may fight until annihilated, but it will never be forced to lay down its arms."[1] On March 23, in an audience with Baron Stuart, the Russian representative in Bucharest, the prince pointed out that the tsar could not disarm an army that had demonstrated its bravery in his very presence and to which he himself had awarded hundreds of decorations. He concluded by expressing Romania's wish to maintain the best relations possible with its former wartime ally.

The increase of tension in Romanian–Russian relations took place in an international framework foreshadowing war. Rumors that Britain would eventually resort to arms because of the Russian intransigence were both alarming and persistent. The Russian imperial cabinet feared that in the event of an Anglo–Russian war, a hostile Romania might go so far as to cut off Russia's communications with its troops in Bulgaria. If this were to happen, the contingent south of the Danube would be isolated and in danger.

On March 24 Kogălniceanu sent another circular note to Romanian diplomatic agents abroad in which he once again stressed Romania's protest of the Treaty of San Stefano. After a detailed analysis of the way the treaty prejudiced Romanian interests, he pointed to the special iniquity of Article 8. In April 1877, when Romania was not yet independent, Russia had concluded a convention with Romania securing the right to move its troops through Romanian territory. Now that Romania was independent, Russia no longer discussed the issue of the passage of its troops through Romanian territory with the Romanian government but settled the question in a treaty with Turkey from which Romania had been excluded. Kogălniceanu concluded that the bilateral agreement at San Stefano was a "denial of our sovereignty and a danger to the moral and material interests of the Romanian nation."[2]

Meanwhile, through an indiscretion Gorchakov's declarations to Ghica became public, causing a storm in the two Romanian chambers and lively agitation in Europe. Faced with the European leaning toward Romania and the firm stand of the Romanian authorities, St. Petersburg started to show a more flexible attitude. On March 26 Baron Stuart told Carol at a reception that St. Petersburg had noticed the conciliatory note of his message. The very next day Carol received an extremely warm letter from Alexander thanking the Romanian prince for the congratulations conveyed to him on February 21, 1878.

Nonetheless, St. Petersburg did not cease to apply pressure. Even in his otherwise friendly letter, Alexander disassociated the actions of the Romanian government from the attitude of the prince, a tactical device allowing him to criticize Carol indirectly. He expressed his regret at the behavior of the Romanian ministers, who, he said, had created tension in Romanian–Russian relations that was harmful to Romanian interests. The same evening, alarming news was received in Bucharest. The Russian Eleventh Infantry Division had occupied the town of Giurgiu and had set up its headquarters between the Neajlov and the Sabar Rivers. In the light of the new circumstances, Kogăl-niceanu advised Carol to concentrate the Romanian army in Olteniţa to be prepared for any contingency. Carol hesitated to take any step that might justify Russian military action against the Romanian army. On the one hand, he still hoped that the movements of the Russian army were not aimed against Romania; on the other hand, informed that Gorchakov himself had disavowed the conversation with Ghica, he believed, with good reason, that the Russian government was beating a retreat. Deciding not to let the troop movements pass without response, Kogălniceanu sent Baron Stuart a note in which he protested them, the more so as on March 31 two regiments of Cossacks had bivouacked at Băneasa, on the outskirts of Bucharest, without asking permission of the Romanian authorities.

On April 1 the Russian General A. Drentlen came to Carol with apologies for the unusual presence of the Cossack units. Carol suggested setting up a line of demarcation from Giurgiu to Bucharest to Ploieşti, west of which any advance of the Russian troops was forbidden. In the ensuing days the idea grew that the government and the prince should move to Craiova in order to maintain their freedom of action.

On April 17, the tension between St. Petersburg and Bucharest further increased as a result of a letter received from Alexander in which he said that he had to make the Romanian ministers "foresee the possible steps their conduct might force me to take."[3] He concluded by expressing his hope that an agreement would be reached and insisting upon his need to ensure communications with his troops in Bulgaria. On the same day Kogăl-niceanu sent a circular letter to the Romanian diplomats letting them know that the country was actually occupied by the Russian army; he also called Ghica back from St. Petersburg for consultations.

At this point, Britain, unwilling to accept the advantages gained by Russia following its victory over Turkey, moved a fleet toward the mouth of the Danube. The Romanian–Russian conflict about the circumstances in which the Treaty of San Stefano had been concluded aroused great discontent causing the Russian imperial government to contemplate the possibility that communications with its troops might be cut off. Therefore, Romania's military action was meant, first and foremost, against Britain and Austria–Hungary. On April 20, the Council of Ministers met in Bucharest and decided that the Romanian army should take up positions on the line connecting Piteşti, Cîmpulung, and Tîrgovişte, while cavalry was deployed along the Argeş River as far as Găesti and Titu. It was also decided that Prince Carol should move to Olteniţa. On April 29 Carol left Bucharest, but not before receiving the Prussian consul, who had agreed with the decision.

The journey to Olteniţa and then northern Muntenia lasted until May 15, by which time international developments had led to a new turn in Romanian–Russian relations. The energetic stand of Britain, which was in favor of either war or a congress that would redefine the terms of the Russo–Turkish peace, finally ended in the convening of that European forum in Berlin. With the decision to submit the Treaty of San Stefano to a congress, Romania turned its attention to obtaining admittance to the congress for its representatives. All the demarches of the Romanian government to make itself heard in Berlin failed. Consequently, the government sent the congress a memorial in which it demanded (1) a guarantee of Romania's territorial integrity; (2) prohibition of the passage of foreign troops through Romanian territory; (3) restoration of the Danube delta and Snake Island; (4) war reparations proportional to Romania's military contribution; and (5) acknowledgment of Romania's independence and neutrality.

On June 20 the Romanian delegates, Ion Brătianu and Mihail Kogălniceanu, were allowed to present the Romanian point of view to the congress, but, as in the case of Greece a few days before, Romania was heard but not listened to. The attitude of the congress was to be perfectly summed up by Benjamin Disraeli, the British prime minister, who, after listening silently to the Romanian representatives, told them laconically, "In politics ingratitude is often the reward for the highest sacrifices."[4]

Despite Disraeli's cynicism, the congress acknowledged Romania's independence, but final acknowledgment was conditioned on the granting of Romanian citizenship to its Jewish inhabitants. Dobruja, an ancient Romanian territory the great majority of whose inhabitants were Romanians, was once again within the borders of the young state. Southern Bessarabia was incorporated into Russia; Romania became a member of the Danubian Commission, and its neutrality was unanimously challenged by the participants in the congress.

The Congress of Berlin lent new shape to the political and strategic map of southeastern Europe, at the same time sanctioning Romania's independence and entry with full rights into the Concert of Europe.

## NOTES

1. General R. Rosetti, *Corespondenţa generalului Iancu Ghica, 2 aprilie 1877–8 aprilie 1878* (Bucharest, 1930), pp. 179–80.
2. N. Iorga, *Correspondance diplomatique roumaine sous le roi Charles I<sup>er</sup>* *(1866–1880)* (Bucharest, 1938), p. 342.
3. *Memoriile regelui Carol I al României (de un martoc ocular)* (Bucharest, n. d.), p. 90.
4. Ibid., p. 44.

Serbia

Gale Stokes

# SERBIAN MILITARY DOCTRINE AND THE CRISIS OF 1875—78*

The internal development of Balkan states after the crisis of 1875—78 has never been a major theme of historical research. Historians who can recite all the international implications of the crisis usually limit themselves to mentioning the achievement of independence or the acquisition of territory as the main internal consequences. Yet, by permitting the creation of dependent states that took on all the trappings of independence, the crisis created, or at least strengthened, a dichotomy between the nominal political framework — which consisted of a constitutional state with political parties, a bureaucracy, and an army — and the actual social situation, which remained essentially peasant. This contradictory situation formed the structural basis of the political options Balkan peoples eventually faced.[1]

Perhaps the least studied of the institutional components of this structure has been the army. In the case of Serbia, at least, this is curious, because the army played an obvious and integral role in politics, particularly after the turn of the twentieth century. Mere mention of the name Dragutin Dimitrijević, or Apis, is enough to indicate the need to understand the position of the army in Serbian public life. Apis's professional army was created as a reaction to the failures of the Serbian national militia in 1875—78. Nineteenth-century Serbian military doctrine held that spontaneous peasant uprisings supported by the direct military intervention of a national militia could achieve independence for Serbia and the rest of the Balkans if the Great Powers could be persuaded not to intervene. Serbs had faith in the ability of the peasant as a natural warrior and believed implicitly that as soon as these warriors were mobilized and led into battle, uprisings would erupt throughout the Balkans.

---

* I would like to thank John Boles and Ira Gruber, my colleagues at Rice University, and David MacKenzie of the University of North Carolina at Greensboro for their helpful comments on this article.

The combination of a Serbian peasant army and spontaneous peasant revolt would overwhelm the Turks and push them out of the Balkans. Para-doxically, the series of events that actually achieved Serbia's independence, the wars of 1876 and 1877–78, completely discredited this doctrine. By 1883 the Serbs had abandoned their national militia and romantic ideas of peasant revolt and begun building a professional army.[2]

Naive as early Serbian doctrine may seem in hindsight, it was based on what Serbs believed was a strong martial tradition of spontaneous peasant military exploits.[3] During the First Serbian Uprising from 1803 to 1813, Serbs who had learned something of military methods through their service in the Austrian *Freikorps* led an untrained and occasionally unwilling peasantry to significant victories over janissary forces and the sultan's armies. These semiskilled military leaders were assisted by self-taught but naturally able leaders whose experience as bandits, or haiduks, made them rough-and-ready military commanders. The eventual failure of the uprising did not detract from its many military successes, the memory of which was kept fresh by a cycle of epic oral poetry that glorified the actions of the natural leaders and their equally natural troops.

During the Second Serbian Uprising from 1815 onward, Miloš Obrenović did not attempt to build a national army, and in fact spontaneous peasant outbursts during his reign were usually directed against his despotic rule. Instead he introduced Serbia's first permanent military force. During the 1830s he created a group of about 2,000 men under the direction of a hand-ful of young officers trained with the Russian army in Wallachia and Bessarabia. In 1839 Serbia's first army law authorized a strength of about 4,000 men led by 63 officers. At any given time about one-quarter of this modest force was on border duty, while others performed ordinary police functions. The whole "army" got together for practice at most only one month a year. The troops received arms, but for a uniform the state provided only a cap.[4]

The era of the Constitution Defenders, with its weak prince and enormous internal controversies, was not conducive to reform, although in 1854 a proposal for a national militia was drafted. In 1860, when Prince Michael Obrenović came to power, he immediately began to strengthen Serbia militarily. Michael's long-range goal, at least until the last year of his reign, was for the Balkan peoples, led by a resurgent Serbia, to drive the Turks from the Balkans. By allying Serbia with the Greeks, Romanians, Monte-negrins, and Bulgars he believed he could create a force strong enough to defeat the Turks without having to rely on the Great Powers, whose involve-ment he hoped to avert. His first step was to create an army. Serbian tradi-tion, as well as the poverty and low educational level of the population, made the formation of a national militia (*narodna vojska*) organized around territorial units the most feasible solution.[5] In 1861 Michael decreed the creation of a militia of seventeen regiments (*pukovi*), one for each of the seventeen okrugs, or counties. Each srez (a subunit of the okrug) contributed one battalion (*bataljon*) to the regiment, and each opština (the smallest local unit) contributed companies (*rote*) on the basis of population. Each okrug was also to have a cavalry unit and a unit of engineers, while citizens of Kragujevac and Belgrade were to create six artillery battalions.

The original law setting out this organization decreed a very optimistic training schedule. The companies were to train on Sundays and holidays, the battalions once every two weeks for two days, and the regiments once a year for two weeks. As in the First Serbian Uprising sixty years before, each soldier had to provide his own clothing, food, and weapons, which were to include a rifle and bayonet or, in the absence of the latter, a yataghan (a long curved knife), and sixty rounds of ammunition.[6] Every male in full possession of his faculties between the ages of twenty and fifty was liable for service. Those to age thirty-five were placed in Category 1, troops "ready for movement." The rest formed Category 2, reserves. It was calculated that the militia "ready for movement" would number about 50,000 soldiers.[7]

The newly created officer corps of the militia was also nonprofessional, particularly at the noncommissioned and company grades, appointments to which could be made by the administrator of an okrug. Commandants of battalions were appointed by the minister of war, also a new post, and the prince himself appointed regimental commanders. At first the lower and middle ranks of the national militia were filled by local leaders with martial reputations, but when this led to conflicts between these leaders and the state bureaucracy it became more and more common to combine the functions of civil chief of a district with command rank in the national militia. This removed the possibility of civil/military conflict, but it also lessened the interest of the peasant in the militia, which he came to see as just another bureaucratic imposition.[8]

To regularize command of the army and militia, in 1862 Michael removed the army administration from the Ministry of Interior and established an independent Ministry of War, which by 1865 had a staff of four sections: general military affairs, supply, accounting and control, and engineering. The standing army continued to exist at the same level of strength as provided by the law of 1839 in four services: infantry, cavalry, artillery, and gendarmes. Unlike the national militia, the standing army was paid and trained regularly.[9]

Michael's general policy of organizing the Balkan Christians to eject the Turks depended also on the second tenet of Serbian military doctrine, the readiness of the Balkan peasantry to revolt. This was an old idea. As early as 1597 a certain Father Athanasius claimed in a request to the Roman curia that 200,000 Christian warriors were waiting in the mountains for his signal to march on Constantinople, and recently Stephen Fischer—Galati and Dimitrije Djordjević have claimed that the entire history of the Ottoman period in the Balkans is marked by the tradition of the revolutionary peasant.[10] In fact, rarely did jacqueries in the Balkans become widespread (exceptions include the Croatian Peasant Uprising of 1573), but the First Serbian Uprising was one of those occasions, and it inspired the Serbs. Michael's plan, actually conceived and administered by his foreign minister, Ilija Garašanin, was to foment an uprising in Bosnia through a network of agents, to encourage the Bulgars by training a Bulgarian legion, and to link all the Balkan peoples in a web of alliances. Michael planned the main uprising for 1867, but when preparations lagged the uprising was postponed, and in the fall of 1867 Michael drastically changed his policy, turning toward Hungary for diplomatic support to construct a railroad and perhaps obtain Bosnia by diplomatic means.[11]

Serbia entered the war of 1876 with Prince Michael's national militia as its main fighting force and with faith in the revolutionary élan of the peasantry unshaken, even though the network of agents in Bosnia had been permitted to collapse.[12] Clear-headed analysis of the results of Serbia's policy in eastern Bosnia after the spontaneous uprisings in Hercegovina and north-western Bosnia in 1875 might have indicated that this reliance on mass revolutionary uprisings was a vain hope. In August and September 1876 the Serbian government sent armed bands into southeastern Bosnia and the Sanjak of Novi Pazar, which were relatively peaceful, to foment uprisings there. Not only did the untrained leaders of these bands prove as inept militarily as they were adept at plundering, but the peasants had to be forced to rise. As one historian put it, "many peasants were driven into revolt because, like Karadjordjević in the First Uprising, the bands [sent by the Serbian government] burnt their homes."[13]

Nonetheless, ferment in Bosnia and Hercegovina unleashed an enormous outpouring of enthusiasm in Serbia, at least among the educated. By the spring of 1876 the liberals, under the leadership of Jevrem Grujić and Jovan Ristić, had become convinced that it was time to turn loose the great liberating power lurking in the peasantry. With Bosnia and Hercegovina still unpacified and Bulgaria in turmoil from its April Uprising, it seemed that thousands of South Slavic peasants stood ready to respond to the sound of the Serbian tocsin. These romantic ideas, not to call them a military doctrine, eventually overcame the rational objections expressed by conservatives such as Jovan Marinović and the diplomatic caution that Jovan Ristić himself momentarily displayed when he returned to power in April 1876.

The most important single factor in the war set off by these enthusiasms was the dominant role played in Serbian strategy and command by Russian officers, especially General Mikhail Grigorevich Chernyayev. Serbia went to war in 1876 without having prepared itself diplomatically. Without support from any Great Power, its only ally was Montenegro. But throughout the critical period the Russians had spoken with two voices, the official voice of the Foreign Ministry, which advised caution and peace, and the unofficial voice of the Pan-Slavists, which advised war and aggression. The Serbs chose to listen to the unofficial voice. When Chernyayev arrived "privately" in Belgrade late in April 1876 it was taken as a sign that official Russian help was not far behind.

Chernyayev was accepted so readily (he received Serbian citizenship almost immediately and was placed in command of the main Serbian army) not only because of his reputation as the "Lion of Tashkent" but because the Serbs had very few officers of their own. Even so, officer education in Serbia was very good, at least as rigorous as training in the Velika škola and substantially better than the arrogant Russians thought.[14] Since its formation in 1850 in conjunction with the opening of the Kragujevac munitions factory, the Artillery School in Belgrade, which was actually a military academy, had produced six to ten well-trained officers a year. The rigorous five-year curriculum completed by these graduates included not only military subjects but general history, Serbian history, French, German, Turkish, hygiene, and dancing, as well as physics, chemistry, mathematics, and other subjects. Even the sclerotic Russian Colonel N. I. Bobrikov was impressed in 1877 with the "excellent capacities and military knowledge of the Serbian officers, who would do any Great Power proud."[15] By the time of the first Turkish war 186 officers had completed training at the artillery school, and a high percentage of them remained in service.[16]

Still, the Serbs had no actual command experience and no general officers. The 300 to 400 Serbian officers were woefully inadequate for an army that some estimates place at a peak size of about 130,000 men. Eventually, approximately 700 Russian officers came to Serbia to participate in what the Slavic Benevolent Committees hoped would be the great war of liberation. The first deleterious effect of this influx was on the war plan. Serbs had been making war plans since Michael's day, usually concerned with how to take best advantage of an uprising in Bosnia. At the key moment, however, in the spring of 1876, two alternative strategies presented themselves. The first proposed fighting a defensive war on Serbia's southeastern frontier facing Niş and attacking across Serbia's southwestern frontier into Novi Pazar toward Montenegro. The idea was to hold off the main Turkish military force, which was in Bulgaria, while linking up with the Montenegrins and giving maximum assistance to the Bosnian and Hercegovinian rebels. This strategy had the advantage of striking toward Serbia's main political objective, Bosnia. The second strategic proposal was to establish defensive positions on all borders except the one facing Niš and attack the most important Turkish force there with the main Serbian force. A virtue of this idea was that it conformed to a central tenet of European military thinking: attack the enemy's main force and destroy it, and the war is won. It had a second advantage for Chernyayev. It sent Serbia's army away from Bosnia, which the Russians were in the process of promising to Austria–Hungary, and toward Bulgaria, which the Russians were determined to liberate. When Chernyayev chose the second strategy, the question was decided.

In order to fight the war the entire national militia, both Category 1 and Category 2, was mobilized into four armies. Toward the southwest and Bosnia the Ibar army of 11,500 men, under the command of General Frantisek Zach, was to attack Zenica. This mistake, which was not Chernyayev's fault, tried with too few troops to achieve the goal of the rejected strategic plan without providing any of its support. A second army, consisting of 20,000 men, was posted to the Drina under the command of General Ranko Alimpić with the assignment of defending against the strong Turkish forces in Bosnia. General Milojko Lešjanin commanded the Timok army of 25,000 men, which was to contain any Turkish threat from the direction of Vidin. Finally, the main force of 68,000 men, under Chernyayev, was to cross the border to the southeast and attack Niš. As a whole, the army consisted of 158 infantry battalions, 18 field batteries, 5 mountain batteries, 3 siege artillery batteries, 18 horse artillery batteries, 18 squadrons of cavalry, 6 battalions of engineers, and 6 squads of medics.

Until the eruption of the crisis of 1875, Serbia had made little effort to supply its forces. Each militia unit was to assign one out of every ten soldiers to take care of supply, usually by finding ways to transport needed foodstuffs and fodder from the home regions of the troops. During the months preceding the outbreak of war heroic efforts were made, but they fell far short.[17] Serbia's medical corps was equally unprepared. The Serbs entered the war with nineteen doctors, five doctor's assistants, one pharmacist, and four pharmacist's aides. Each battalion was supposed to assign eight persons to serve as medics and carriers of the wounded, but until the war started no other provision was made. During the war help from Russia and England filled this gap somewhat.

The unpreparedness of the Serbian militia in terms of supply and medical services was matched by a lack of weapons. Almost immediately after the passage of the national militia law of 1861, Prince Michael had realized that it was impossible to expect an army, even a militia, to arm itself, despite the provisions of the law requiring each soldier to provide his own weapons. With only 7,000 rifles on hand in 1863, Michael obtained a promise from the Russians for 70,000 more, but because of diplomatic and other problems only about 31,000 were received. These smooth-bore muzzle-loaders were retrofitted by the Kragujevac Munitions works into breech-loading weapons with rifled bores. After 1866, when Austria permitted further importation of arms, some 55,000 Peabody rifles were distributed to Category 1 troops, and the Kragujevac plant produced even more under license. Category 2 of the militia was armed with Green rifles, which had a tendency to foul after only seven to eight rounds.[18] The failure of this rifle was a partial cause of the rout of the Serbian militia in the 1876 war.

The one area in which Serbian provisions were adequate, although still inferior to the Turks,' was artillery. The munitions works at Kragujevac had been producing muzzle-loading guns since 1852, although they were not up to the range or accuracy of the breech-loading Krupp guns possessed by the Turks. Serbia produced shells for both its guns and its rifles but did not possess the reserves of lead and saltpeter to sustain other than a very short war.[19]

On July 2, 1876, the eighth anniversary of Milan Obrenović's accession to power, the young prince sent his troops across the borders, having declared his intention to "assure the tranquillity and integrity of Turkey" in his declaration of war two days earlier.[20] Milan's armies faced a total Turkish force of approximately 126,000 trained troops and 20,000 irregulars (bashi-bazouks) organized into 137 infantry battalions, with 192 guns, 62 squadrons of cavalry, and 12 squads of engineers. Of these, more than 5,000 regular troops (nizam) and 24,000 experienced reserves (redif) defended Niš, backed up by a reserve of approximately 2,500 regulars and 10,400 reserves in southern Bulgaria.[21] In Vidin and northern Bulgaria over 10,000 regular troops and almost 20,000 trained reserves faced Lešjanin's force of 25,000.[22]

Despite what appears to be numerical equality or even superiority, the Serbian armies were inferior to the Turks in several ways. First, the Turkish army consisted of trained troops; only the bashi-bazouks were irregulars. Second, Turkish infantry were armed with Martini—Henry rifles and the Turkish cavalry with Winchester rifles, both of which had greater accuracy, range, and rate of fire than the Serbian Peabodies and Greens.[23] Turkish artillery was similarly superior. Third, the Turks held fortified positions, whereas the Serbs had only begun to fortify their side of the border before the war started, leaving them open to potential disaster in the event of a retreat.[24] Finally, the Serbs were at a disadvantage because they intended to take the offensive. By the mid-nineteenth century improvements in both rifles and guns had made the task faced by offensive operations very difficult.[25] Commanders of even well-trained armies had not yet achieved the discipline necessary to mount the dispersed and varied attack that was needed against moderately well-defended positions. And the Serbian army was not well trained. To have succeeded in a major offensive operation, the Serbs needed better weapons and better training, not to mention better leadership. Lacking all three, it is no wonder that after one or two minor successes the Serbs were pushed back on all fronts within a week of the start of hostilities.

The war, which lasted until the Russians imposed a truce on the Turks on October 30, completely exhausted Serbia.[26] Unprepared diplomatically and militarily, it had been unprepared financially as well. Until 1875 Serbia had been able to maintain a balanced budget, even though expenditures slightly outran income, by using income from the holdings of Prince Michael that had reverted to the state on his assassination. By early 1876 Serbia had about 900,000 dinars on hand.[27] When the uprisings in Bosnia and Hercegovina broke out, the parliament authorized the government to seek a loan of 24,000,000 dinars. But even with this approved it proved impossible to secure foreign loans, and a voluntary bond sales campaign within the country generated only about 5 percent of the needed amount (ca. 1,225,000 dinars). The next step was to conduct a forced loan in which the necessary amounts were assigned to each region, but even this raised only about another 10 percent of the authorized amount (ca. 2,750,000 dinars). After the war started, the Slavic Committees in Russia agreed to sponsor a loan of approximately 12,000,000 dinars; eventually about 6,800,000 dinars was received. All of these efforts fell far short of the need. In order to entice Montenegro into the war, the government paid a 520,000 dinar subsidy to the Montenegrins and then quickly spent the rest of its assets, including not only all its capital but an additional 2,500,000 dinars held by the government in trust funds (e. g., the Widow's and Orphan's Fund). Other steps included simply not paying bills and lowering the salaries of all government employees to a maximum of 1,200 dinars a month. Finally, the most important step, and the one with the deepest social consequences, was the requisitioning of goods. This raised the equivalent of almost 8,000,000 dinars, but it also meant that the countryside was stripped bare to outfit the army. By the time the war was over the ability of the peasantry to sustain more requisitions was exhausted.

All of the problems mentioned so far provide adequate reasons for Serbia's failure in this first war. Lack of preparation in all aspects made the struggle with the huge Ottoman Empire a mismatch. But perhaps Serbia's most serious deficiency was in generalship. Whereas one of the best Turkish generals, Osman Pasha, later the defender of Plevna, led a major Turkish force, the Serbs were led by Chernyayev and his Russian officers, who held many of the major posts in the Morava army. Chernyayev's tactics emphasized the weaknesses of Serbia's militia. Massive frontal assaults simply could not work with such poorly trained troops. Although he did not lack bravado, Chernyayev did not have the nerve of command. With each defeat he sank into despair; with each success he concluded that the war was about to be won. Furthermore, he did not balance his initial strategic mistake of attacking the main Turkish force with tactical ability. Even when he did correctly analyze a situation, as when at the battle of Veliki Izvor he promised Colonel Djura Horvatović badly needed help on his flank, he could not muster the energy or decisiveness to deliver. Finally, he was unable to discipline his Serbian subordinates, who fought constantly among themselves and sometimes simply did not follow the Russians' orders even when they could understand Russian, which was not always the case. And of course, as one might imagine, the vain Chernyayev became incensed when anyone questioned his authority.

Chernyayev was particularly dissatisfied with his Serbian troops. It is true that the militia was hard to manage, and, particularly in the early days of the war, whole units simply went home.[28] But when they were well led the Serbian troops fought effectively, especially in defensive battles and increasingly as they gained experience later in the war. At least two Serbian commanders distinguished themselves, the brutal disciplinarian Horvatović and Prince Milan's adjutant Kosta Protić. The type of weapons held by the Serbs was also a factor in their fighting success. On the offensive they could not approach the Turkish positions without taking murderous fire, but on the defensive they could and did hold their fire until they could mass it and repulse the attacking Turks. This result was normal in the nineteenth century. The fact that the Serbs could sustain defensive operations when adequately led shows that the Serbian troops were not as bad as Chernyayev constantly claimed. Poorly led, very poorly clothed and fed, provided with little training, and equipped with outmoded weapons, the Serbian soldier fought better than he has been given credit for, despite the negative outcome of the war.

The peace treaty adopted in February 1877 technically restored the status quo ante, but only technically. In fact, Serbia's geopolitical situation had changed completely. Early in the 1876 war the liberal General Ranko Alimpić had reminded Prince Milan that "Bosnia is our primary objective," but by the turn of 1877 it was clear that Bosnia was lost.[29] In good measure because of Serbia's actions, Russia and Austria–Hungary had agreed on a division of spoils that gave Bosnia and Hercegovina to Austria–Hungary. Aware of this, if not privy to every detail of the bargain, the Serbian government had to abandon its long-held hope of obtaining Bosnia. Also abandoned was the faith in a Balkan uprising. One of the reasons the main offensive had been taken in the direction of Niš was the expectation the Bulgars would rise, and advance guards had been sent into Bulgaria to distribute weapons. But the Bulgars did not rise. In fact, when they did not refuse the Serbian weapons entirely, some Bulgarians actually turned them over to the Turks.[30] "It is especially disconcerting to our troops that there is no uprising in

Bulgaria," the minister of war reported on August 18, 1876, "and even more that the Serbs in Turkey have not risen in arms."[31] "The participation of the Christians, particularly of the Bulgarians, failed in a manner which amazed everyone," said Jovan Ristić.[32] Badly shaken by these failures, romantic faith in peasant revolution began to drop out of Serbian military doctrine.

The second tenet of Serbian military doctrine, the notion of a national militia, suffered as well. Whatever positive assessments might be salvaged, the brute fact was that the national militia had failed in 1876. Before the loss of faith this failure engendered could be turned into military reform, however, Serbia had to face a second war. Russia finally declared war on Turkey in April 1877. Since they expected victory, since they did not respect Serbian arms, and since they had agreed with the Austrians not to enter Serbia, the Russians at first showed little interest in Serbian participation. But when the Russian army was stopped at Plevna, even the small extra pressure the Serbs could place on the Turks began to seem important. In November the Serbian government received what amounted to a personal request from the tsar to attack the Turks, and on December 14, 1877, two days after the fall of Plevna, the Serbs entered the war.

Serbia was just as unprepared diplomatically and financially for this war as it had been for the first one. Ristić was able to conclude no advance political agreement with Russia, and only under the greatest pressure and at the last minute did the Russians agree to a stipend of 500 dinars a day for every 1,000 troops the Serbs put across the Turkish border. Militarily, however, the Serbs were much better prepared. In the midst of the first war Minister of War Tihomilj Nikolić, having incurred Chernyayev's wrath by expressing outrage at the misconduct of Russian officers and volunteers in Serbia, had had to resign. He was replaced by Sava Grujić. A radical who had fought in the Polish Insurrection of 1863 and who had been removed from duty as late as 1874 for political activity, Grujić was perhaps nineteenth-century Serbia's best military mind. Immediately he began reorganizing the army, providing a commissariat and medical services, and preparing for a second war. Grujić restored an adequately armed militia of close to 80,000 men, divided into five corps. The Drina and Javor corps, consisting of 19,000 and 15,000 troops respectively, were to guard the borders against Bosnia and Novi Pazar.[33] The Timok–Zaječar corps had 8,800 troops with which to guard the border toward Vidin. The main force consisted of the Šumadija corps, which had 16,000 troops and 42 guns, and the Morava corps, which consisted of 18,000 troops and 46 guns.

One of the advantages of the new army was its purely Serbian leadership. Prince Milan remained the commander in chief, but now the relatively able Stojan Protić acted as his chief of staff and the very able Grujić as his minister of war. The field commanders proved to be quite good also. Horvatović aggressively led his Timok–Zaječar corps in an offensive thrust toward Kula, while Lešjanin and Jovan Belimarković gave competent leadership to the Morava and Šumadija corps. Although relatively inexperienced, these commanders had the advantage over their Russian predecessors of knowing their troops and being able to encourage them. Despite personal conflicts over precedence and credit, Serbia's military leadership during the second war, even down to the company level, was considerably superior to that of the first war.

Leadership was, of course, not the whole story in Serbia's better showing in the second war. The main reason for that success was the depletion of the Turkish forces, which were considerably inferior to those of the first war. The Turks held the line in the Balkan Mountains against the Russian invaders for some time, but it took all their strength. Furthermore, only two days before the Serbs entered the war, the Russians broke through at Plevna and soon thereafter started streaming into southern Bulgaria. When the Serbs started their advance on December 14 they faced only the remnants of the Turkish army, mostly Asiatic and Albanian irregulars fortified by a stiffening force of regular Turkish troops. For example, at the first battle of Kuršumlija, six Serbian battalions of approximately 4,800 men faced a Turkish contingent of 400 regular soldiers and 2,000 irregulars. At Niš, the greatest Serbian prize, about 15,000 Serbian troops faced a garrison of approximately 5,000.[34] The only instance in which the Serbian army was stopped in this six-weeks' war was at the fortress of Samokov, near Kuršumlija, where it encountered fierce resistance from Albanian troops defending the route to Priština.[35]

The combination of better leadership, weaker resistance, and improved organization led to important Serbian successes, and, after the well-known machinations of San Stefano and Berlin, to the accession to Serbia of some 11,100 square kilometers of territory.[36] But the successes of the second war did not change the views of Milan and his generals about the need to get rid of the national militia. Milan came to power in 1868 not because he was elected by a great national parliament (which he was) but because Colonel Milivoje Blaznavac swore the small units of the standing army in Belgrade to Milan's support, thus deciding the issue before any of the political mechanisms could get into motion following Michael's assassination. Milan never lost his interest in retaining the loyalty of the army. In 1873, when he appointed his first government after Blaznavac's death, he insisted that the minister of war "be as little responsible to the ministry as possible and work mainly in agreement with me."[37] Milan vigorously defended his officers. In 1874 he rescued Belimarković from justified claims of corruption, for example, even though Belimarković was a liberal and therefore not politically close to him.

As did many nineteenth-century rulers, Milan used his standing army as an internal security force.[38] During the crisis years of 1875–78 two major incidents of resistance to his rule demonstrated its efficacy. In the first, units of the standing army quickly restored order in Kragujevac early in 1875 when the radical victors in a local election broke out the red flag and purportedly shouted "Long Live the Republic." In the second, the standing army responded loyally when in November 1877, just days before the start of the second war, a militia unit near Kragujevac rebelled during its mobilization and seized the town of Topola for four days on behalf of Peter Karadjordjević, the pretender to the throne. Standing army units from Belgrade quickly crushed the revolt. Milan used this rebellion to solidify his hold over the officer corps by executing Major Jevrem Marković, a war hero but also, as brother to the famous socialist Svetozar Marković, a long-standing opponent. In both wars the regular units of the standing army were used only sparingly against the Turks. Milan wanted them closer to home for more important duty – keeping him on the throne.

For all these reasons, then, the military doctrine of the Serbs changed at the end of the Turkish wars. In 1881 the general staff placed an order with a German manufacturer to supply the Serbian army with Mauser rifles, and in 1883 the Progressive government introduced a completely new army law providing for universal conscription and the creation of a conscript army in line with the best European military thinking. Reliance on a peasant army providing its own weapons, led by untrained elders, and helped by spontaneous revolts beyond the Serbian borders was replaced by a system of universal training in regular army barracks, arms depots, and professional cadres. This change from the romantic vision of a revolutionary peasantry to the modern ideal of the nation in arms, with its impact on the peasantry through the educative effects of military training and on politics through the creation of a professional officer corps, must surely be counted as one of the most important and least remarked consequences of the crisis of 1875–78.

## NOTES

1.   For a fuller discussion of this point, see Gale Stokes, "Dependency and the Rise of Nationalism in Southeast Europe," *International Journal of Turkish Studies* 1 (1980): 54–67.

2.   The best work on the Serbian army in the period 1875–78 is Milorad Ekmečić, "Srpska vojska u nacionalnim ratovima od 1876 do 1878," *Balcanica* 9 (1978): 97–129, an English-language adaptation of which appears as the next article in this volume. For the Yugoslav historiography of the period see idem, "Rezultati jugoslovenske istoriografije o istočnom pitanju 1875–1878. godine," *Jugoslovenski istorijski časopis* 16 (1977): 55–74, and Jelena Maksin and Anica Lolić, *Bibliografija jugoslo-*

*venske literature o velikoj istočnoj krizi, 1875–1878*, Istorijski institut, Gradja, 20 (Belgrade, 1979), which lists 836 titles. Other sources used for this article include Slobodan Jovanović, *Vlada Milana Obrenovića*, vol. 2 (Belgrade, 1934); David MacKenzie, *The Serbs and Russian Pan-Slavism 1875–78* (Ithaca, N. Y., 1967); idem, *The Lion of Tashkent: The Career of General M. G. Cherniaev* (Athens, Ga., 1974); Sava Grujić, *Vojna organizacija Srbije* (Kragujevac, 1874); Jevrem Grujić, *Zapisi*, vol. 3 (Belgrade, 1923); and Nikola P. Škerović, ed., *Zapisnici sednica ministarskog saveta Srbije 1862–1898* (Belgrade, 1952).

3.    On this tradition, see Wayne Vucinich, "Serbian Military Tradition," in *War and Society in East Central Europe*, ed. Béla Király and Gunther E. Rothenberg, vol. 1 (New York, 1979), pp. 285–324. For a superb critique of the romantic tradition, see Fikret Adanir, "Heiduckentum und osmanische Herrschaft," *Südost-Forschungen* 41 (1982): 43–116.

4.    Grujić, *Vojna organizacija Srbije*, pp. 66–67.

5.    "National militia" seems to me to render the flavor of the Serbian term best in English, but other translations, such as "popular army," would be equally correct.

6.    Gavro Škrivanić, "The Armed Forces in Karadjordje's Serbia," in *The First Serbian Uprising 1804–1815*, ed. Wayne Vucinich (New York, 1982), p. 309.

7.    Milo Djurdjevac, "Narodna vojska u Srbiji 1861–83 godine," *Vojno-istorijski glasnik* 20, no. 4 (1959): 78–93.

8.    See "Srbija," in *Vojna enciklopedija* (Belgrade, n. d.).

9.    See "Vojska," in *Narodna enciklopedija Srpsko–hrvatsko–slovenačka*, ed. Stanoje Stanojević (Zagreb, n. d.).

10.    Adanir, "Heiduckentum," p. 57; Stephen Fischer–Galati and Dimitrije Djordjević, *The Balkan Revolutionary Tradition* (New York, 1981).

11.    Gale Stokes, *Legitimacy through Liberalism: Vladimir Jovanović and the Transformation of Serbian Politics* (Seattle, 1975), pp. 113–20.

12.    Milorad Ekmečić, *Ustanak u Bosni 1875–78* (Sarajevo, 1973), pp. 52–53 and 105–9.

13.    Vukoman Šalipurović, *Ustanak u zapadnom delu stare Srbije 1875–1878* (Titovo Užice, 1968), p. 79.

14.    It should be recalled that except in Prussia, military education in Europe was not conducted to a very high standard. Michael Howard reports that "the standard of teaching at great military colleges [of France], at St. Cyr, Metz and Saumur, was deplorable, and the intellectual calibre of the senior officers in no way corresponded to their panache. ...In 1870 the Germans were to be astounded at the illiteracy of the officers who fell into their hands" (Michael Howard, *The Franco–Prussian War* [New York, 1962], p. 16).

15.    Quoted by Draga Vuksanović–Anić, "Uloga Vojske u kulturnom životu Srbije i ratovi 1876–1878 godine" *Srbija u završnoj fazi velike istočne krize*, ed. Danica Milić, Istorijski institut, Zbornih radova, 2 (Belgrade, 1980), p. 318.

16.    See "Topolivnica" and "Vojna akademija," in *Narodna enciklopedija*.

17.    For a thorough review of the desperate efforts to make up for years of neglect in a few months, see Petar Milosavljević, "Pripreme Srbije za rat sa Turskom 1876. godine," *Balcanica* 9 (1978): 131–57.

18.    Ekmečić, "Srpska vojska," p. 108.

19.    Neutral Romania hindered Serbia's war effort by imposing a prohibition on the transshipment of lead and by seizing supplies already in transit from Russia (Škerović, *Zapisnici saveta*, p. 196).

20.    MacKenzie, *Serbs and Russian Pan-Slavism*, p. 100.

21.    Nizam troops were Muslim recruits that served four-year terms. They constituted the standing army of the Ottoman Empire. Categories 1 and 2 of the redif troops served in this reserve force for eight years (four years in each category) after completing their nizam service. Only after the war with Serbia had begun did the Ottoman government start to call up Categories 3 and 4 of the redif, which consisted of

those who had avoided conscription for some reason. Therefore, the redif forces the Serbs faced were experienced members of Category 1 and 2 (F. Maurice, *The Russo–Turkish War 1877* [London, 1905], pp. 15–26).

22. These figures were thoughtfully provided the Serbian government by Russia's ambassador in Istanbul, General N. P. Ignatyev (J. Grujić, *Zapisi*, p. 186).

23. Breech-loading rifles came into common use in the 1860s, although they were known in the first half of the century. One of the most popular systems, which was used both for retrofitting muzzle-loaders and for constructing new rifles, was invented by Henry O. Peabody of Boston and was called the "falling block." Peabody rifles were adopted by Bavaria and Mexico, as well as by Serbia, and the falling-block idea became the principle on which the Martini–Henry rifle used by the Turks (so-called because Friedrich von Martini, an Austrian lace manufacturer, invented the breech mechanism and Alexander Henry, an Edinburgh gunmaker, the barrel) was constructed. The English adopted this weapon in 1871 and armed the Turks with it in time for the Eastern crisis. The Turks were among the first to use the Winchester repeating rifle, the only weapon of its kind in actual use in the 1870s, devastating the Russians at Plevna with their superior firepower. See Harold L. Peterson, ed., *Encyclopedia of Firearms* (New York, 1964), articles on "Breechloaders," "Berdan," "Martini–Henry," and "Winchester"; and W. W. Greener, *The Gun and Its Development*, 9th ed. (London, 1910), pp. 701–75.

24. In May the government dispatched Category 1 of the national militia from the Belgrade area to Deligrad to construct fortifications, which later proved valuable. Other than this, however, preparations were nil (Škerović, *Zapisnici saveta*, p. 161).

25. Howard, *Franco–Prussian War*, pp. 6–7.

26. Petar Opačić has written several summaries of the military aspects of the war. Typical is "Vojne operacije u srpsko–turskom ratu 1876. godine," in *Naučni skup: Otpor austro–ugarskoj okupaciji 1878. g.*, ed. Milorad Ekmečić, Akademija nauka i umetnosti Bosne i Hercegovine, Posebna izdanja, 30, Odjeljenje društvenih nauka, 4 (Sarajevo, 1979), pp. 281–304.

27. Serbia did not have its own currency until after the Congress of Berlin, but for ease of comparison the various values indicated in the sources have been translated to approximate dinar equivalents using the offical exchange rates shown in *Zbornik zakona i uredaba Srbije* 20 (1867): 36–42, and 34 (1879): 211–14.

28. Commanders despaired that the peasant simply did not want the war, and Prince Milan admitted that if all the deserters were shot, "we would have to shoot half the army" (J. Grujić, *Zapisi*, p. 195).

29. MacKenzie, *Serbs and Russian Pan-Slavism*, p. 103.

30. J. Grujić, *Zapisi*, p. 194. A force of some 3,000 Bulgarian volunteers did fight with the Serbian army, however.

31. Ibid., p. 208. In 1875 some Serbs living in the area between Višegrad and Novi Pazar revolted, and a volunteer corps from these rebels was formed for use on the Ibar front in 1876, but the movement was so small and disorganized that it had little effect. See Šalipurović, *Ustanak u zapadnom delu stare Srbije*.

32. MacKenzie, *Serbs and Russian Pan-Slavism*, p. 102.

33. Since the Serbs had no intention of angering Austria by invading these areas and the Turkish forces there were much too weak to consider invading Serbia, this was probably an overexpenditure of strength.

34. Generalstab der fürstlich serbischen Armee, *Der Serbisch–Türkische Krieg von 1877–78* (Belgrade, 1879), pp. 27 and 65.

35. Savo Skoko has written several summaries of the military aspects of the war. Typical is "Pregled Operacija Srpske vojske u srpsko–turskom ratu 1877–1878," in *Naučni skup: Otpor austrougarskoj okupaciji*, ed. Ekmečić, pp. 281–304.

36. Henryk Batowski, "Die territorialen Bestimmungen von San Stefano und Berlin," in *Der Berliner Kongress von 1878*, ed. Ralph Melville and Hans-Jürgen Schröder (Wiesbaden, 1982), p. 60.

37. Živan Živanović, *Politička istorija Srbije,* vol. 1 (Belgrade, 1923), p. 275.
38. Howard, *Franco—Prussian War,* pp. 10–12.

Milorad Ekmečić

# THE SERBIAN ARMY IN THE WARS OF 1876–78:
# NATIONAL LIABILITY OR NATIONAL ASSET?*

The army played a dual role in national liberation wars, directly as a military force and indirectly as a social factor shaping the long-term integration of the nation. While the Serbian army had its greatest impact in both these roles between the revolution of 1848 and the Berlin Congress of 1878, the concept of an army was an important part of the initial idea of national struggle. Dositej Obradović instructed the rebellious Serbs as early as 1806 that an army was "the first and most important thing," the basis "upon which the whole undertaking must be erected."[1] Later Stojan Novaković considered the army the most illustrious facet of Serbian national life. "When you have seen the army of a nation," he said, "you have seen that nation in its most beautiful and most manly form."[2] "Many favorable circumstances helped the Serbian people achieve its political center and build a durable pivot of national existence," Novaković said, "but in the efforts of the Serbian people to create Serbia, one of the most important tasks was carried out by soldiers and by the waging of war."[3]

Since Serbia acquired a professional army only after the wars of 1876–78, before that time having had only a poorly organized and neglected militia that became important at all only with its reorganization in 1861, Novaković's view may seem erroneous. The purpose of this study is therefore not only to describe the organization and military effect of the Serbian army prior to and during the wars of 1876–78 but to appraise the army's larger importance in the historical rise of the Serbian people.

The year 1878 was a turning point in the history of the Serbian army. From then until 1883, programs for reorganizing the regular standing army

* This paper was originally presented at the conference on Society in Change held at Brooklyn College and the Graduate School and University Center of the City University of New York on March 14, 1978.

were put into effect. The speed with which new models of military organization were accepted obscures the fact that the idea of change had been germinating for a long time. Although units of a standing army had been created as early as 1808, they had had only minor importance in the struggle for independence, wasting their energies in serving the prince at court and in border protection. Barely visible, they had had mainly symbolic significance for Serbian foreign policy. The small regular force had lasted until 1876, when it had been absorbed by the poorly managed militia. The whole burden of the wars of 1876–78 was carried by the militia alone.

The story of the national army (*narodna vojska*, the official title of the popular militia) was quite different. Scholars differ as to the historical origins of the national army. Some have considered it inspired by the combination of Serbian historical tradition and the success of the Garibaldian volunteers, which had demonstrated the practical advantage of popular forces in the unification of Italy.[4] Others have suggested that the national army was "a completely new institution" when it was established in 1861.[5] In fact, at the time no one believed that the national army represented anything new. It was regarded as a living remnant of the historical life of the nation and thus valid for the future. "Our real national development," it was said in 1866, "will begin only when our institutions are [established] on a Serbian national foundation."[6] It was believed that the national army should not be merely a copy of a foreign system and would come alive only when the common villager accepted the rifle in the same way he did the plow and the bucket.[7]

Serbian planners calculated that the national army would be ten times cheaper than a regular standing army of 20,000 men.[8] This was extremely important because of Serbia's poverty. As Prince Miloš said to a French representative in 1860, "one does not do great things with small means, and we have only small means."[9] The Swiss model, which also served as inspiration, was seen as "better suited to any rather small country that needs a large army but disposes of weak finances."[10] A final argument that tipped the scale toward the creation of a national army was undoubtedly the Montenegrin victory at Grahovo in 1858, which seemed to demonstrate the efficacy of militia-style organization.

Actually, only intellectuals and that portion of public opinion that read newspapers debated military reorganization in any way. No theoretical justification was needed to introduce a system that most felt had been more or less in existence since 1815. The ideal of a national militia was already established in the folk consciousness at the time of the First Serbian Uprising. Karadjordjević's military organization on the basis of territorial division was basically the same as the one used during the reign of King Milutin (1282–1321).[11] The trend continued in the Second Uprising. As Miloš put it, "The

whole Serbian people is under arms and a soldier."[12] Miloš believed that
with this dictum he could raise fifty to seventy thousand soldiers from a
country of only six to seven hundred thousand inhabitants. But this force
was anything but well-disciplined. The peasant militiamen were not easy to
command; Miloš himself had to cut his own hair short to persuade his small
cadre of riflemen to do the same.[13]

Organization into a militia was a natural outgrowth of a culture in which
the entire population was permanently armed. For men, wearing weapons
was an essential part of the folk culture. Up until 1848 no noticeable
difference existed in this regard between the Serbs of the principality and
those still living under Turkish rule. Even in 1851 the villagers in Bosanska
Krajina were permanently under arms. Not only "the Muslims but even the
rayas wear arms at their belts. They used to travel with rifles even to till
their fields."[14] After 1848, as the principality began its modernization, the
custom there began to decline. By 1876, Milan Dj. Milićević could complain
that the Serbian peasant had lost the ability to wear his dramatic old national
dress. "Earlier a peasant, well-dressed, armed, riding upon horseback with
a long rifle over his shoulder, a pistol at his belt, and a pair of embroidered
gloves over the saddle was a real delight to the eye."[15] Thus, just as a territorially organized militia in which all males theoretically served was being
established by law, the folk custom of wearing arms was withering away.
We may suppose that the two events were not unrelated.

During the rule of the Constitution Defenders (1842–58), the casual
system of general recruiting in case of emergency was not changed and,
indeed, was considered more than adequate. In September 1848, Ilija Garašanin claimed to a visiting French envoy that Serbia "was able to gather in
a moment 150,000 good soldiers, and in need, the nation could be called to
arms thus forming an army of 200,000."[16] Not until 1853, under the pressure of the possibility of a Russo–Turkish war, did the government establish
more definite rules. In 1854 it promulgated a thirty-six-point "Regulation
for Training and Organization of the National Army."[17]

Under these rules the army was divided into infantry, artillery, and cavalry
composed of companies (rote), batteries, and cavalry troops (escadroni).
The territorial principle was used. "Companies are to be formed," the regulation stated, "by soldiers from neighboring villages so that it will be easier to
gather them for training."[18] Every local community (opština) provided a
company and every county (srez) a battalion. Soldiers supposedly were to
be called for training three times a week for three hours in the morning.
The administrator of a region (okrug) was in charge of coordinating the
companies in his region; no higher commands were specified. No new officers
were created, but noncommissioned officers retired from the regular army
were to make up the training cadre.[19]

This system created a solid foundation on which the reform of 1861 could be based. Although the reform of 1861 was cast in a somewhat more offensive spirit than that of 1854, the two reforms shared the emphasis on tradition, the territorial principle of recruitment, and the avoidance of a large officer corps by using prominent citizens as officers. As early as the deliberations of the national parliament of 1859, which was actually an extension of the liberal St. Andrew's Parliament of 1858, it was proposed that Serbia "undertake as soon as possible a reform of the national army that would correspond to the needs of our country and the progress of the times."[20] Major Jovan Belimarković "presented the bases on which it would be possible to do this consistently with our situation and by only a minor increase in the military budget."[21]

The new military organization had two separate entities: a regular standing army, which was an expansion of the tiny force that had been in existence for some time, and the newly established national militia, which had formerly existed only as a nonobligatory national tradition. The regular standing army, organized as garrison soldiers, immediately underwent a limited reorganization. A main army command was established under the direct command of the prince (earlier it had been a part of the general police forces). Service in its ranks was shortened from four to three years, and its numbers were significantly increased, although with some 3,600 recruits it was still only large enough to serve for sentinal duty, honor guards, and occasionally putting down minor unrest. The regular army consisted of four battalions of infantry, two troops of cavalry, two batteries of artillery, and a unit of engineers.

For the larger objectives of liberating the Serbian nation and achieving the purposes of the First Balkan Alliance, a more powerful military force capable of waging large-scale war with Turkey was needed. Such a force was created by the law of August 30, 1861, entitled "Organization of the National Army."[22] With modifications, this is the law that created the army that went to war in 1876. "All Serbs without distinction" from age twenty through age fifty were considered potential soldiers. In the first class were included those from twenty to thirty-five years of age, who were expected "to be ready for immediate marching." Those from thirty-five to fifty formed the second class, who were to be ready for marching "only later." If the country were in extreme jeopardy, a third class could be raised. "Only clergymen and those acknowledged as physically disabled for ordinary service are excluded from the obligation to defend the country."[23]

The national army had four services: infantry, cavalry, artillery, and engineers. The addition of an engineering corps is what gives the reform of 1861 its more offensive character. The most important roles were given to artillery and infantry, the first for its administrative cadre, emphasis on technological improvement, and a theoretical presupposition that the artillery would be the most important element in the entire force, the second for its numbers. The cavalry was very small (2,500 cavalrymen versus 46,000 infantrymen). As a nation of peasant smallholders, Serbia was simply unable to remove from production the number of horses a large cavalry would require. As in 1854, the national army was organized on the territorial principle, with a company from every opština, a battalion from every srez, and a regiment from every okrug. The cavalry was composed of srez companies and okrug squadrons, while engineering battalions were organized by okrug. Only the cities of Belgrade and Kragujevac were privileged to form artillery units. It was estimated that the total number of soldiers in the army would not exceed 50,500.[24] Five higher territorial commands arranged by river systems managed the army: the Drina—Sava, Southern Morava, Timok, Eastern-, and Western Morava commands. The prince was the commander in chief, but a new Ministry of War was established as well, headed at first by a French military engineer. A general staff was not introduced until January 1876. Its absence was felt, but all earlier efforts to institute one failed.

Lack of officers was the persistent weakness of the national army. Educated soldiers were scarce, and there was little desire to create a professional officer corps. It was believed that the most prominent citizens would provide a reliable substitute and serve as a symbol of the democratic orientation of the national community as well. The yearly output of the Artillery School (the formal name of the military academy) established in 1850 never exceeded about ten graduates, with the result that the military list of 1874 showed only 317 officers of all ranks, including only 5 colonels and 20 majors. Still, many a politician considered this figure larger than necessary. By 1876 the number of officers had risen to 460, but the fact that almost 700 Russian volunteer officers had to be added to the army in 1876 shows that the native Serbian officer corps was inadequate.[25] During the war some battalions did not have even one active officer. The most senior officer was Frantisek Zach, the youngest Milivoje Blaznavac.[26] A law of 1867 permitted foreigners to be officers in the Serbian army, but their participation was rare and usually limited to the higher ranks. Furthermore, they did not command the same respect as did the native officers, even when they were Serbs from north of the Sava. Michael Obrenović did not have more than 200 educated officers at his disposal, and in the period 1855 to 1866 only 77 officers graduated from the Artillery School.[27] These were employed mostly in the five major commands, as specialists and staff officers, rather in the field commands. There, noncommissioned officers and officers to the rank of captain were appointed by the administrators of the okrugs. Battalion commanders and cavalry commanders were appointed by the Ministry of War and colonels by the prince.

In 1863 the Serbian government invited a Russian military commission to investigate the army's preparedness, equipment, and organization. The commission, led by a Colonel Leer, pinpointed inadequate training and ill-prepared personnel as the most glaring of many weaknesses. Soldiers in training were not taught to accept the basic rule of any army: obeying a command.[28] A Prussian visitor in 1867 reported the same thing, pointing out that "because of a complete absence of genuine officers and adequate equipment, [the Serbian army] seems ill prepared." Even the prince himself shared the common view that some staff officers should be brought into the Serbian army "from a country well disposed toward Serbia, but first of all from Prussia."[29] This idea was almost a constant, although it was clear that only Russia was ready for such a commitment.

To the common soldier the situation did not seem much better. When called for training, villagers had to bring their own equipment, including arms. According to the law, training was permitted only on Sundays and holidays.[30] Larger maneuvers were to occur in the autumn after the crops were in. Despite the existence of such rules since 1854, mobilization for large-scale training was rare and became a social event of the first order, remembered with emotions similar to those associated with war itself. Not until 1866 was a large maneuver, involving nine battalions of infantry, four troops of cavalry, and a battery of cannon, conducted.

In such a military organization, changes were needed and often made, but in the absence of radical reform any change, no matter how small, was regarded as a change for the worse.[31] In time the staffs of the higher commands were abandoned, and military administrations were created at the okrug level, which permitted local civil administrators to take on the duties of military command. Such a reorganization was suitable for meeting only the routine needs of administration. Lacunae in the organizational structure were not filled by a systematic chain of command, and the leadership of the country acted as if it did not really believe its own claims that in the long run war was inevitable. In all likelihood, the leadership found inculcating the desire for war useful but feared the actuality of one.

At first, by the law of March 1862, all members of the national army, but particularly those in the first class, had to equip themselves with clothing, weapons, and even a horse it they were in the infantry.[32] The government did not organize quartermaster services. The peasant soldier had to supply his own food and fodder for his horse. This is one reason maneuvers and practice sessions were kept so short, since otherwise serious problems of supply and transportation quickly arose. Regulations concerning uniforms existed from the beginning, but at first they only stated what sort of cloth the peasant should make his uniform from and how it should be tailored. The first class of recruits was uniformed only after a general surtax was introduced in 1864. The recruit was obliged to wear the uniform only for training, parades, church holidays, "and, in case of marriage, for his own wedding party."[33] This made it a sort of formal dress for festive occasions and was an important reason for change in the male national costume of the Serbian village at about this time. The more expensive old costume began to be abandoned and a cheaper, ready-made uniform, the first to appear in Serbian history, became accepted. The state still did not care about footwear; each soldier brought his own. For the second class, the state provided only a military overcoat and even left the headgear to the peasant's ingenuity, permitting him to cut it out of black lamb's wool "in the shape of a national fur cap." This is one of the reasons the traditional fez, along with the white trousers and long jacket, disappeared from the Serbian village. A contributing reason was the adoption of the fez as standard wear by the Turkish army, which led the Serbian villagers to exclude it from their folk costumes in favor of a forage cap.

The main problem was weaponry. As an agricultural country whose border trade was closely monitored by the Austrians, Serbia found it difficult both to produce and to import arms. In the beginning, every infantryman was to arm himself with a long rifle and bayonet (or yataghan), as well as a pistol and sixty cartridges of ammunition. This was an onerous expense for the peasant, especially since the custom of wearing arms was declining and weapons were hard to find in the modest domestic markets. Even when there were weapons, they were of varied and doubtful quality. Still, in 1862 only about half the soldiers called up were without rifles, but the number available from government souces did not exceed 7,000. In 1863 the government succeeded in getting a commitment of 70,000 rifles from Russia, of which about half (along with 3,000 sabers) finally arrived. However, all these rifles were smooth-bore muzzle-loaders that had to be retrofitted to modern standards. The state-owned armory in Kragujevac was modernized to do this and brought its production up to 500 new rifles and 5,000 retrofits a month, as well as one six-piece battery of cannon.[34] By 1866 new machinery had raised the artillery production to five batteries a month.[35] Given Balkan conditions and the technology of the time, the Kragujevac factory was relatively well equipped and managed. A visiting Italian consul in 1863 found it "in better condition than ours in Turin in 1848,"[36] which may say more about the problems of the Italian plant than about the virtues of the Serbian one. Of four steam engines at the factory in 1863, only one was as strong as 30 horsepower. One-sixth of the plant's labor force of 1,500 was foreign. Working conditions were poorly regulated, making it no wonder that it was at this factory that modern social unrest associated with industrial labor first appeared. A vocational training school was established near the factory. Its copper came from the mines at Majdanpek, which supplied Kragujevac and had a small amount left over for sale.[37] Coal was also available locally, so that the infant arms industry represented a closed-ended interdependent system, the first proving ground of industrialization in Serbia. Even after unification in 1918 almost all industrial enterprises could claim at least one aging skilled craftsman who had apprenticed his trade in the factories of Kragujevac.

The licensed rifle produced at Kragujevac was the Peabody, praised in Serbia as the best choice for the time, although later it became apparent that it was inferior to the Martini–Henry rifle used by the Turks.[38] Only the first class was supplied with this weapon. The second class received Green rifles, probably the worst of the Serbian weapons. The "Greenovača," as the privates nicknamed it, was the source of steady complaints as well as of defeats in 1876. After seven or eight shots the barrel tended to foul with soot and scum.[39] More than once it was the cause of panicky flight on the part of troops effectively disarmed by jams in their rifles.

Although Serbia found in its Kragujevac plant a way of satisfying its basic weapons requirements, it took a long time to manufacture the arms necessary for a war with Turkey. Only by 1867 did it seem possible to equip an army of 100,000 soldiers, provided that not all were combat troops and that several shortcomings were overlooked.[40] Transport, despite some early efforts in 1864, remained inadequate, as did medical services, whose bare beginnings can be traced to 1865.[41] Transport, of course, continued to rely on oxen, since horses were in short supply.

In spite of advances in comparison with the situation in 1860, Serbia was still not in a position to confront the reformed Turkish army. The military in Turkey was organized according to sophisticated European standards and had more financial resources and better-educated personnel than the Serbian army. On the other hand, Turkey faced the prospect of long-term social unrest in the empire, since the Christian population was far from docile. Among the least so were the Serbs, whom Turkey had always regarded as its main military enemy in the Balkans, although since the Ottoman army was always superior to the Serbian it did not fear a one-on-one war with Serbia. As early as 1827 the grand vizier estimated that the Muslim population of European Turkey alone could maintain 300,000 soldiers under arms, on the basis of one soldier per fifteen inhabitants.[42] A later military reform obliged all Muslims in the empire from age twenty through age twenty-nine to join the ranks. Christians were freed of this obligation on payment of a fixed tax. On the eve of the 1876 war, the Turkish army was divided into three parts: the regular army (nizam), the reserves (redif), and the volunteers (mustafiz). The nizam consisted of 210,000 soldiers, 150,000 of them in regular service; the redif consisted of 192,000 troops, and the volunteer task forces for rear guard and so forth numbered 300,000.[43] Serbs estimated in 1867 that the Albanians alone, using their traditional methods of recruiting volunteers, could raise a force of 150,000.[44] To all of these could be added a police force (*zapti*) of 14,000. These figures indicate why Serbia could not dare to consider open war, even as part of a local alliance.

The Turks were also well armed. New-model rifles were introduced in 1866, when the cavalry received the Winchester. By the war of 1876 approximately 39,000 of these weapons were in use. With a rate of fire of eighteen shots per minute, it was considered the best rifle in the world at that time. The Winchester's rate of fire was more than twice that of the standard Serbian weapons, even better when one took into account the sloppy retrofits of the Kragujevac munitions plant (done "in the Turkish style," as one Italian general paradoxically put it). For cannon, the Turks had breech-loading Krupp guns, 504 pieces in all.[47] All Serbian artillery was muzzle-loaded. As an additional advantage, the Turkish military academy, established in 1830 on the model of St. Cyr, was more modern and better designed than the Serbian one. One hundred new officers graduated from it each year.[48]

Repeated minor changes attempted to make the Serbian national army approximate the regular army in uniforms and armament. The same drill for both armies was introduced in 1876, and it was claimed that "as of now no difference between national and regular armies exists, either in their regulations or in the confidence of the ruler."[49] Reorganization of the commands and staffs of both armies in 1874 improved the chain of command, and commands for all units in the main groups were formed. But in terms of fighting spirit, attitude toward obligations and duties, discipline, and ability to undertake coordinated action, the national army remained a mass of hastily assembled peasants led by unsophisticated administrative officials.

Discipline remained a serious problem. The peasant was not in the habit of blindly obeying authorities, civil or military. The main way of obtaining obedience was beating, which was one of the three punishments authorized for soldiers, although it was limited to thirty strokes.[50] Beating was abolished in 1873 but remained in common use in the military. It was reintroduced officially in 1877.[51] Disobedience and desertion were endemic, challenging the basic operation of the military mechanisms. Corruption at the higher levels was also common and led the parliament in 1874 to investigate the financial dealings of the minister of war.[52]

With the standards of its army not yet perfected, it was clear that an offensive war with Turkey was beyond Serbia's capacities. It had only reached the point at which it might undertake a defensive guerrilla war in the event of an invasion or perhaps turn a war between Turkey and another Great Power to its advantage. The gap between the hopes of fulfilling Serbia's historical task and the practical reality led to disputes among both political and military theoreticians. Sava Grujić attempted to demonstrate the advantages of the militia system in his 1874 book *Military Organization in Serbia.*[53] Paja Putnik answered Grujić in 1875 with a book entitled *Thoughts on the Military Organization of Serbia.*[54]

Putnik believed the Prussian model better suited to Serbia's coming tasks and preferred infantry to artillery. He believed the territorial system of recuitment was suitable only for primitive communities, and in his opinion Serbia was "far from primitive." Instead of a militia, Serbia needed a regular standing army based on conscription that was larger than the current standing army, staffed by competent officers, and trained for larger tactical assignments. He also urged distinguishing between guerrilla warfare and "mountain warfare."[55] The validity of his analysis was confirmed by the experience of the wars of 1876 and 1877–78 and the changes in Serbian military organization that followed.

It is impossible to say whether the war of 1876 came too early or too late for Serbia. Militarily and diplomatically it was not at all ready for such a war. The Balkan alliance on which so much energy had been expended in the previous decade did not exist. Nor had any preparations been made with the Great Powers, with the result that Austria–Hungary and Russia stepped in to assume direction of the outcome. Instead of well-prepared and timely insurrections in Turkish territories, a chain of unconnected agrarian rebellions broke out spontaneously and set in motion an Eastern crisis. Consequently, Serbia did not govern events but was governed by them.

The first insurrections were in Hercegovina and Bosnia; Bulgaria remained calm for almost a year. Fearing Serbian activity in the direction of Bulgaria, the Turks concentrated 65,000 regular troops along the frontier from Vidin to Novi Pazar, backing them up with a reserve force of 50,000.[56]

Serbia's single ally was Montenegro, with which a treaty of military and political cooperation was signed in Venice on June 4, 1876. By this agreement Serbia was obligated to mobilize 120,000 soldiers, including reserves. It was taken for granted that the two sides would cooperate, which meant that the Montenegrin prince was to conduct his operations in concert with the Serbian war plan and that the main battlefield was to be south of Serbia.[57] When the fighting actually started, however, these agreements remained an empty shell. Instead of one national war, two different wars were conducted by two partners associated more by mutual rivalry than by common military objectives. Prince Milan complained that "Montenegro is playing a game with the Turks. They stroll into Hercegovina, where there aren't any Turks, instead of marching with their army into the valley of the Lim and Drina to Foča, where they might be conducting action jointly with Serbia."[58]

Serbia entered the war under the pressure of events that seemed about to push Russia into an active campaign. The Russian ambassador in Constantinople, Ignatyev, followed by many other Pan-Slavists, did his best to provoke Russian intervention. He even hinted that this was the secret desire of the tsar himself. "What would you like, that the sovereign openly express his secret wish? Of course he cannot do that. But I keep repeating to you: as soon as you declare war, Russia will follow immediately."[59] Official Russia, on the other hand, while doing nothing to encourage the Serbs, did take the precaution of speaking with the Austrians about the fate of Bosnia and Hercegovina. Even in advance, Serbia was facing a serious sacrifice of its interests.

Even the Slavic Committees were not actually in favor of Serbia's war aims, despite the number of Russian volunteers they sent to Serbia. They had their own ideas about "the war of a foreign country, without official government help and outside any organization of the state." By the end of the 1876 war, they were greatly disappointed with the Serbs, especially with their interest in allying themselves with the Roman Catholics in Bosnia. "The failure of the war," the president of the Moscow Slavic Committee wrote in December 1876, "was linked to its objective of unifying the South Slavs by seizing southern Serbia and Bosnia instead of aiming simply at overthrowing Ottoman sovereignty – in a word, it was linked to empty phraseology and lies." Therefore, he argued, Russia should abandon Serbia and cleave to Bulgaria. "For us and for the Slavic future, Bulgaria is more important than Serbia." Only a minor diplomatic presence would be needed in Serbia, he continued. It would be enough to leave one agent responsible for spreading the knowledge of the Russian language and literature. The main center of Slavic activity should be in Bulgaria.[60]

Still, some 3,000 Russian volunteers appeared on Serbian battlefields.[61] Russian volunteers filled the vacant places in the senior officer corps as well as serving in junior positions. Some military commands ended up completely in Russian hands, while others were jointly commanded or contained officers from other countries. One came across such exotic combinations as a Russian commander with a Serbian staff and an English aide-de-camp.

The Serbian war council, established in April 1876, was headed by the former director of the Artillery School, František Zach, a Czech national and a former Polish political conspirator. In 1875 he was promoted to general, the first in Serbia to achieve this rank.[62] It soon became apparent, however, that his promotion was due to theoretical work and long service rather than practical ability in the field, and the prince himself often presided over council meetings. Because political figures were members also, political analysis usually took precedence over military decisions.

The official objective of the war Serbia declared on Turkey on June 30,

1876, was the liberation of the provinces in which Serbs lived, thus completing national unification and creating the basis of an independent state. Bosnia, Hercegovina, and Old Serbia were the provinces the Serbs had in mind. Their objectives with regard to Albania and Macedonia remained unstated. Still, the offensive operations of the war were directed toward the south, into the Niš area. The strategic presumption was that the other areas would fall by themselves once victory was won on the main battlefield. The Serbs knew that their army was smaller in general than the Turkish army, but they hoped to be able to muster numerical superiority in the important places and the crucial battles. To do this, they had to retain the initiative.

The plan of the Serbian army was to fork at Niš, one column proceeding to Sofia and the other to Macedonia and Kosovo. The ethnic character of these territories was not really clear at this time, while the border between Serbs and Bulgars was relatively well accepted. Macedonia was considered Serbian territory only by a handful of Serbian intellectuals led by former students of Russian schools and universities. The strategic design of the war rested on the vague presumption, prompted by earlier contacts between Bulgarian and Serbian politicians in the 1860s, that a Bulgarian uprising organized under Serbian control would create an atmosphere of cooperation between the two peoples. The Serbs considered the Bulgarian national goal consistent with Serbian interests. The presumption never had a chance to be tested, however, and the final division of territory was conducted not through mutual understanding but by the Great Powers.

In Bosnia and Hercegovina, the military convention with Montenegro drew a clear line between Serbian and Montenegrin spheres running along the Neretva River to the town of Knjic in the north. The clarity of the division in Montenegro contrasted with its vagueness in the south, with the result that when Serbia's main offensive was directed southward it was cut off from its main political objectives, Bosnia and Hercegovina. Instead, Serbia found itself fighting in a territory in which the expected popular uprising did not occur and in which Russia kept a vigilant eye on developments. From the very start, therefore, Serbia was destined to lose in the west and not gain in the east. This strategic shortcoming determined the fate of both the war and the national movement.

Financially, Serbia was unable to cover the expenses of so large an endeavor. It paid for the war by punitive taxes, a compulsory internal loan, exhausting requisitions in the villages, lower government salaries, postponement of all cash payments, and a 5,000,000-dinar loan from Russia. By the time of the settlement of 1878, the Serbian debt had reached 27,000,000 dinars, much of which was in the form of requisitions from citizens.

During the 1876 war Serbia raised an army of 220,000, taking all forces into account, including about 180,000 fighters. Of these, 21,500 were killed, injured, or missing. Of 325 officers engaged in the war, 79 were lost.[63]

Immediately after the outbreak of the war, Turkey raised an army of 494,397 soldiers, including 186,000 in Bulgaria and 107,000 in Bosnia, Hercegovina, and northern Albania.[64] Since these figures include reserves and some units were divided, they are not completely accurate. It should also be remembered that many of these troops were stationed to guard against any possible Russian entry into the war. In Serbia the initial mobilization put 124,000 men under arms (this did not include the third class), with 22,000 horses and 6,000 oxen. This was an extremely large number for a country of only 1,300,000 inhabitants.

Overall, army units were divided into offensive and defensive units, the former for active detachments and the latter for reserves. The reserve had twenty-eight battalions. A new unit, the corps, was introduced. Members of the regular standing army were dispersed among units of the national army (a process that was not repeated in the second war of 1877–78, when the regular army retained its separate identity). All told, six divisions (thirty-six brigades and eighteen battalions were raised. To these were added some thousands of foreign volunteers, some fighting separately and others with Serbian units. Mostly these were Russians and Bulgarians. About forty Italians were stationed along the Drina.

The front was split into four parts, two offensive and two defensive. Along the main offensive line facing Niš were 68,000 troops (the Morava army), to which the independent Knjaževac detachment added 7,000 men. On the second offensive front, the Ibar River army consisted of 12,500 troops under the initial command of Zach. The first objective of the Morava River army was to attack toward Niš and take the important citadel there. Following this first victory, enemy forces were to be pursued and defeated in a second crucial battle somewhere in the south ("without any doubt on Kosovo Plain").[65] This great victory would provide a proper time and place for a solemn proclamation of Prince Milan king of Serbia and the unification of the surrounding provinces (Kosovo, Bosnia, Hercegovina) with Serbia in an integral national state.

The two remaining fronts were to be defensive. The eastern army, on the Timok River, had 25,000 soldiers, and the western army, on the Drina, had 20,000. These two formations were to protect the flanks of the two main offensive operations and to organize a rebellion in eastern Bosnia. Helped by detachments of volunteers, the western army was to advance toward Sarajevo and create the necessary atmosphere for the expected proclamation of union between Serbia and Bosnia.

In practice some of these dispositions were altered and some even abandoned. First, the plan did not concentrate a Serbian force that was numerically superior to the Turks' along the critical Niš front. Instead of two-thirds, only 53 percent of the army was concentrated there. Even that small number was reduced on the eve of the opening of hostilities, when an entire division was withdrawn. Stringing forces out along a 100-kilometer front had a similar weakening effect, a mistake "which in itself held the germ of failure."[66] Politicians in the war council did not have much confidence in the offensive capabilities of the national army, and this had its negative consequences both for strategic planning and for the conduct of the war.

The Turkish army was numerically stronger, even though it was split into even more groupings than the Serbian. Along the main front at Niš the Turks concentrated 35,000 soldiers backed up by 25,000 reserves stretched out from Sofia to Thrace. The total force on all fronts was 133,000 soldiers and 20,000 bashi-bazouks (Circassians, Albanians, and local Muslims). The Turkish army at Niš even boasted a small unit of Jewish volunteers.[67] As early as August 1875, the Serbian envoy in Constantinople reported that Turkey was concentrating some 160,000 soldiers along the Serbian frontiers.[68]

As a whole the Turkish army in this war was better organized, better equipped, and better led than the Serbian army. It shared a deeper military tradition, was more sophisticated than its opponents, and exhibited more fighting spirit. "The Turks are fanaticized," said Zach.[69] The Russian anarchist Sergey Kravchinsky–Stepnyak was amazed to find that even in Hercegovina the insurgents were conducting their war "without either love or hatred."[70] The British press reported that during assaults "Russian officers drove the Serbs into battle at pistol point."[71] Fear of the Turks' superior weapons and especially fear of falling into Turkish captivity drove the Serbian soldiers into mass flights. "What is worse than anything," said Jevrem Grujić, "is that the soldiers flee before the enemy. There were cases where entire battalions fled before thirty or forty Turks or Circassians."[72] As a result, the numbers of some units dropped considerably. Omer Pasha Latas's prediction, having observed the Serbian national army on maneuvers, that in war this peasant mass would immediately take to its heels came true.[73] If an uninformed witness on the battlefields of 1876 had been asked which army was inspired by the revolutionary spirit of national liberation, he would without doubt have pointed to the Turkish, not the Serbian, side.

In addition, the Serbs faced other shortcomings. Supply and transport were extremely sluggish. Serbia had no railroads. Drawings from the period show cannon being hauled by oxen behind wagons full of hay. Organized withdrawals in case of failure were not anticipated, and this led to panic after unexpected defeats. Often, too, the Turks attacked along lines that the Serbs had considered naturally so well protected that they had not bothered to fortify them.[74]

Serbian command personnel were insufficiently experienced. Promotions had been passed out on the basis of seniority, political devotion to the ruling dynasty, and time spent in office. Therefore the burden of command fell on the shoulders of the Russian volunteers, and from the beginning of the war they had a great deal of influence in shaping Serbia's war program in accordance with Pan-Slavist political objectives. This participation of the Pan-Slavists helped the Russian government by freeing it of the necessity for taking responsibility for the consequences of the war. Official Russia could view its interventions to bring about an armistice and conclude a peace treaty as favors to the Serbian government while at the same time conducting negotiations with Austria–Hungary concerning Bosnia and Hercegovina that were inimical to Serbian interests. Having Russian officers in command also caused serious communications problems. Some Serbian officers were sufficiently well educated to understand the Russian officers, but a great many middle-ranking officers who received written commands in Russian simply could not read them. The magnitude of the problem is indicated from the datum that during the short war some 116,000 written messages were delivered.

The best-known and most influential Russian officer in Serbia was General Mikhail Grigorevich Chernyayev. As a colonel Chernyayev had commanded the Russian detachment that first entered Tashkent. Miffed at not having been promoted to general for that exploit, he entered into a controversy with the Ministry of War that led to his retirement. Receiving a courtesy appointment as general upon retirement, Chernyayev became "opposition-minded" and took up the editorship of *Russki mir.*[75] After the uprising in Bosnia it became the only paper in Russia to urge the government not to limit its aid to Serbia to financial help.[76] Earlier, in 1867, he was regarded as having been "one of the greatest friends Serbia had in Russia."[77] Chernyayev's bearing was decidedly unmilitary, and only his saber, belt, and pointed moustache suggested the military man.

In 1875 the Pan-Slavists decided to send Chernyayev to Serbia "to pressure Russia to go to war against the Turks for the purpose of protecting the Bulgars."[78] After the war the Serbs bitterly complained that Chernyayev had been sent with the "unbrotherly mission . . . to pester our politicians to enter the war against Turkey."[79] Although in the beginning it was not clear what he was up to, the Serbian government decided on May 24, 1876, "to take former Russian General Chernyayev under its protection, and then to grant him citizenship and employ him in the government's service with the rank of general. All this to be completed tomorrow."[80] Of course, the government did not take this step merely because it was ill informed. The unpopular and inept government had no alternative. When the insurrections broke out in Hercegovina and soon thereafter in Bosnia, national public opinion became extremely agitated, and the government found itself facing a possible national revolution. Fearing such a possibility and lulled by assurances that it had little to lose, it chose to trust in a Russian intervention against Turkey.

In his casual way, Chernyayev believed that fomenting a rebellion in Bulgaria and broadening the one in Bosnia and Hercegovina would be an easy task. He also hoped to be able to bring in official Russian support. But Alexander II did not approve of his promotion to Serbian general. Sava Grujić was present when Chernyayev received a message from the tsar to that effect and found him "very confused" but in hope that "after the first successes the tsar would approve and even send him medals."[82] When told that the Serbian army was incapable of taking the offensive, he shrugged it off:

> Nonsense. You yourselves don't know yet what you have. Only a few hundred more Russian officers and doctors, which you will get as soon as war is declared, and your army will be quite complete. I hope in the name of God to create an example as yet unheard of and unseen in this world; with Serbian peasants I will grind the rotten Turkish empire, the very same empire that once inspired fear and trembling in all of Europe, into dust and ashes.[83]

Those who attributed to him the idea that he could conquer Constantinople in only fifteen days, since he was still uninformed of the real distance from the Serbian border to Sofia, may be exaggerating, but there is no doubt that Chernyayev was overconfident before the war began.

Chernyayev established a personal staff of about sixty officers, all but seven or eight of whom were Russians.[84] His officers' mess was "like a fair," with about thirty people always present at the table, often "not two of them acquainted with each other."[85] Serbian officers, who behaved clumsily in the presence of ladies from Russia, secretly cut off small pieces of wallpaper in the dining room for souvenirs, while those near Chernyayev said that personally he displayed "unparalleled boorishness." He also established a Slavic Guard to stand vigil in front of his headquarters. Each member of the guard, dressed in his national costume, represented a Slavic nation, among which Chernyayev unaccountably included Albania.[86] Still, it would be an injustice to deny that Chernyayev was regarded as, and probably was, the ablest officer in Serbia at the time. Although "he was much given to dreams and optimism, still he surpassed all the officers, both Serbian and Russian, in his military training and experience."[87] Consequently, in 1876 Chernyayev was more than just the first soldier in Serbia. He was, in the opinion of some, almost a "temporary dictator."[88]

Chernyayev was part of the second wave of Russian volunteers that shoved aside those who had come with the outbreak of rebellion in 1875. The political views of this second wave differed from those of the first volunteers, who had come to the Balkans "to acquaint themselves with the guerrilla warfare necessary for an uprising in Russia."[89] The Pan-Slavists who came in 1876 with Chernyayev brought a different, aristocratic spirit to Serbia that was alien to the mood of the peasant soldier. Their headquarters became noblemen's retreats of a kind at which peasant soldiers had to serve by waving branches over the dinner tables to keep away the flies. Many of the officers were not at all qualified for command. An English visitor was right when he said that some of them "in other countries would consider themselves fortunate if they found positions as managers and markers in a billiard saloon."[90]

Fearing that Chernyayev's departure would leave the Serbian militia leaderless, the government yielded to the Russian general in everything, even to the extent of replacing ministers who had offended him. It seemed that Serbia was a "region ceded to Chernyayev."[91] He believed that the main objective of Serbia's war was to keep the front open until Russia joined in the struggle against Turkey, thus taking the cause of the Balkan Slavs in its own mighty hands. Serbia's entire war effort was designed as an aspect of the policy of a Great Power that officially did not approve of it. Thus the national struggle became an instrument of world diplomacy and not a genuine national enterprise.

The main criticism of Chernyayev's military qualifications came from the Russian officers themselves, some of whom regarded him as suitable to command a division at most.[92] Some who fell into Turkish captivity accused him of mechanically applying Moltke's strategy at Metz and Paris in 1870—71 to the Serbian meadows in 1876.[93] In any event, it is certainly true that in preparing his war plans, he did not take into account the possibility of retreat.[94] Some of his most vigorous opponents mocked him as a newspaper editor rather than a soldier. Colonel of the Imperial Guard Mileta Despotović, a Serbian national, "told him off to his face in front of the members of the high command, saying that with his lack of knowledge and disorderliness he would kill off Serbia at the outset."[95]

The exact number of volunteers that came to Serbia is uncertain. In October 1876 the Serbian government estimated that there were "only 3,000," including about 2,400 soldiers and 600 officers in all units.[96] In his autobiography Chernyayev counted 2,645 men with him in Serbia, although in October 1876 he reported 2,844, including 644 officers.[97] General Sava Grujić, claiming to be in possession of an exact list, said that there were no more than 2,400 volunteers, while in other estimates the number, including two Russian battalions and two Bulgarian, has been pared as low as 2,000.[98]

The Bulgarian unit was established by the Russian government as "the first unit of the new Bulgarian army."[99] In Serbia these volunteers were first classified as Russian, with the result that many went to Romania to be organized into new detachments.[100] I. S. Ivanov, a Bulgarian in Russian service in Kishinev, was in charge of recruiting the Bulgarian volunteers. He later asserted that he organized as many as 5,000 in Serbia, a figure which cannot be confirmed from the Serbian side.[101]

The Russian officers were unable to escape the defeatist spirit of the national army. In the overall disintegration of the moral fiber of the army their own morale corroded as well, and a dark mood of early escape from the war began to overtake them, sometimes leading to desertion on the battlefield, running away "at once and without delay, since the Serbs were neither fighting nor showing any desire to fight."[102] From the Serbian point of view, it was estimated that some two hundred of the Russians were "pure idealists," about five hundred "useful," and the rest a disinterested and sometimes disillusioned mass.[103] Among the last named were ones so unfamiliar with Serbia's geographical location that they confused it with Persia. Military failure increased the mutual mistrust between the Serbs and the Russians. A contemporary parody had the Serbian prince address the Russian volunteers as follows: "Brother Russians, we love you, but I still beg of you to go home by ceremonial parade. Straight to Russia!"[105]

At the very beginning of the actual military operations, Chernyayev and the Serbs made a major tactical mistake. Following an unconfirmed report of Turkish troop movements, the main Serbian force was directed to attack Niš in two columns, thereby preventing them "from going into action as an organic whole."[106] Only when the Turks forced the Serbs back on the defensive did the army regain its unity. This mistake permitted the Turks "to break through the Serbian front at will wherever they wanted, and they did so wherever they attacked with a significant force."[107] For this reason the attack toward Niš and Pirot had to be abandoned.

Other mistakes abounded. Units were replaced just as dispositions were taking place, causing confusion. The column sent in the direction of Niš was split into four elements.[108] This mistake was compounded by an effort to regroup divisions into corps, which made them less maneuverable in mountainous terrain.[109] The four attack columns actually caught a glimpse of Niš but on the same day retreated to their initial positions. Also, no advantage was taken of the quick victory of the Knjaževac detachment at Babina Glava. Instead, the Turks attacked Zaječar, and the Serbian advance toward Bela Palanka was ruined. The Timok army retreated, leaving Veliki Izvor in Turkish hands. When efforts to repulse the Turkish attack on the left wing failed, the army had to undertake an overall defensive posture. Feeling confident that there would be no renewal of insurrection in Bulgaria, the Turks poured all their reserves from Thrace into the Morava Valley, quickly seizing Zaječar and Knjaževac. After about two weeks, they changed their direction of attack toward Aleksinac. Serbian resistance was fierce, but the national army's lack of confidence prevented it from profiting from its victory at Šumatovac. The Turks took advantage of the breakdown to launch a new offensive in September that would surely have achieved great victories if the Serbian government had not meanwhile succeeded in persuading the Great Powers to enforce a truce. The armistice was declared on September 15.

Just at this moment, Chernyayev decided to attempt to save the situation by declaring Prince Milan king of Serbia, but Milan himself refused to countenance the offer. After this comedic interlude, the truce expired, and on October 19 the Turks broke though following a victory at Šiljegovac. Ten days later came the successful assault on Djunis, at which only the Russian volunteers provided substantial resistance. The Serbian army reacted to this final defeat with headlong flight. Chernyayev himself reported that all the Russians were dead and the Serbs were fleeing. Following an ultimatum from Russia, the Turks agreed to accept a two-month truce on October 31. This truce was prolonged until February 18, 1877, when the peace was signed returning to the status quo ante bellum.

A similar situation obtained on the other Serbian fronts. In the east the army retreated after an ill-conceived attack.[110] Along the Timok a defensive front of minor importance was maintained. In the west, after a brief advance into Bosnia, the Serbian army, helped by a handful of Italian Garibaldians, withdrew in haste and disorder. Commanding General Ranko Alimpić was reported as saying "he did not place enough confidence in his troops."[111] A similar advance toward Sjenica broke down immediately, General Zach showing himself in this effort as unfit for the strains of command.[112]

These initial operations showed that the national army was incapable of conducting a serious war against Turkey by itself. It had suffered extremely heavy losses. In some cases battalions had been reduced to company strength by the time of the armistice. Such losses crushed what little morale the rank and file had managed to maintain. "It has already penetrated to the troops that we are alone in our struggle against the Turks. It especially affects our men that there is no uprising in Bulgaria, and that even the Serbs in Turkey have not risen in arms."[113] A few Serbs even joined Turkish units. Among the 2,215 Turkish prisoners of war taken in the 1878 war, more than 20 had Serbian names.[114]

The very roar of the modern Turkish guns led to mass retreats ("by their sound, by their long range, and by their accuracy [the Turkish guns] were superior to all other weapons").[115] Any sort of marching, especially withdrawals through hilly and overgrown territory, usually resulted in waves of desertions. Even self-mutilation in order to avoid heavy assaults was frequent. But worst was the lack of trust and confidence between the Russian officers and the Serbian peasant army. In 1876 Russians constituted two-thirds of the officer corps. The order given by Chernyayev after Djunis that the Russians should withdraw from the front lines was considered treason by the Serbs.[116] Chernyayev claimed that the war would not have been lost had "Russia responded in a timely manner with a sufficient intervention."[117] In other words, he suggested that the war had been lost because his own strategy of provoking Russian intervention had failed.

But this was not the whole truth. The principal reason the war was lost was the immaturity of the Serbian national army. The reason for the defeat was indeed political, but not in the sense Chernyayev meant. The mistake was entering a war without the strength to endure. It was the shortcomings of the entire military system created after 1861, not a temporary and casual failure of command, that were responsible. Reliance on foreign officers to conduct the war was a fatal error. Neither the Russian participation at Niš nor the Garibaldian on the Drina could achieve anything lasting.[118] The moments of token tenacity shown by the more sophisticated European revolutionaries were rare enough, and in any event these persons were conducting their own politics, for example, opening a Masonic Lodge in Belgrade. "The commander in chief at the front wanted one thing, the chief of staff ordered something else, and the spongers did something else."[119]

When a new program of reform was considered, the first thing discarded was the national army system. In place of the militia, the very word for which became distasteful, a conscript army led by professional and educated personnel was proposed as the salvation of Serbia. The militia system, which at one time was praised as the symbol of democracy in Serbian society, was discarded as the scapegoat for the lost war. The bloody experience of 1876 seemed to permit no argument of this decision.

The second war against Turkey in 1877–78 proved to be a more fortunate enterprise than the first, although it was strategically and tactically conceived almost identically.[120] Serbia was better prepared for this war. Politically it did not rush headlong into it, and militarily it did not permit foreign volunteers to provide the core of army leadership. It sought specific guarantees, but political agreements between Russia and Austria–Hungary, although not really known to the Serbs, precluded making Bosnia and Hercegovina the main strategic objectives. Although warned bluntly by the Austro–Hungarian envoy that any action toward Bosnia and Hercegovina, including fomenting clandestine activity, would be regarded in Vienna as injurious to Austrian interests, the Belgrade government decided "not to give any promises that could be undertrstood as a renunciation of Bosnia or as ceding it" to the Dual Monarchy.[121] Already in November 1876 it was clear in Belgrade that Serbia could reenter the war only if Russia declared war and if the annexation of Bosnia (with Hercegovina to Montenegro) and Old Serbia was promised. In that case, it was estimated that Serbia could raise fifty battalions of infantry and twenty-five batteries of "good artillery."[122] But since it had to be assumed that Serbia no longer had any chance of obtaining Bosnia, all the government could do was maintain silence. The avoidance by Russian envoys and diplomats of any promises regarding Bosnia was extremely disappointing to the Serbs, and an Austrian warning not to intervene in the Novi Pazar area hinted at Vienna's long-term policy of preventing a geographical linking with Montenegro. The dream of integrating the Serbian nation proved divorced from the harsh realities of 1877.

From the military point of view, an attack on the weakened Turkish flank was consistent with Serbia's real strength. Even though the Serbian army was weak, the Turks continued to fear its intervention. At the outset of the conflict with Russia, the sultan is reported to have remarked that "the appearance of an enemy at Sofia from the Serbian side, from which Lord save us, would be a great danger and would open us to conquest."[123] This was perhaps the only time the Turks admitted that the Serbian army was not just a mass of "naked sons," but after all a *cin asker, asli asker*, a good army. In the event, the Serbs intervened in 1877 exactly where the Turks feared they would. Engaged in large-scale battles with the Russians, the Turks were forced "to reduce their force in the Niš citadel to an impossible minimum" while trying to compensate for their loss by increasing the fortifications.[124]

Russia entered the war on April 24, 1877, but unable to achieve a timely victory at Plevna it was eventually forced to request Serbia to join in the struggle. Serbia's reluctance and the fact that it did not enter the war until December 15, two days after the fall of Plevna, left it in poor political standing in St. Petersburg. The delay, which resulted from certain internal developments, was the principal reason the Serbian army failed to liberate Skopje and the Kosovo region.

In preparation for the second war, Serbia had reorganized its army units and filled the vacant posts. The officer corps was replenished by lowering eligibility requirements. These changes enabled Serbia to muster 82,000 troops in December 1877 (124 battalions, 24 cavalry troops, and 232 cannons).[125] Financially the country was exhausted, having been forced to pay some 12 to 15 million ducats for the restoration of the areas devastated in the first war and to support some 200,000 people made homeless by Turkish depradations.[126] Serbia conducted some twenty-two battles in the second war, losing 5,410 men, including 510 officers.[127] The regions of Niš, Pirot, and Vranje, which had fallen to the Turks 502 years earlier, were quickly liberated. The army even debouched into "the bloody Kosovo region" that every soldier knew from the epic songs.[128] The writer Miloš Milojević and Archimandrite Nikifor Dučić led bands of volunteers that also liberated parts of the Sanjak of Novi Pazar.[129]

The end of the war on January 31, 1877, virtually obligated Serbia too to seek a truce and draw a demarcation line. Russia was clearly going to control the outcome of the prospective peace settlement. As soon as the Russians showed their cards in 1878, the Serbian people "found themselves crowded, confined, as if the Serbian nation had somehow fallen," as Mihailo Polit Desančić put it.[130] The disappintment was all the worse because it was felt that Serbia's only success in the first war had been drawing the Russians in. Their favoring Bulgaria was taken as a national punishment of Serbia, which had undertaken so many sacrifices only to suffer a historic defeat.

The military performance of the Serbian army in the second war was greatly affected by the fact that it was closer to its own society than most armies of the time. An army in the Balkans differed from the peasantry only in the bearing of arms. "Only the piles of crossed rifles, the gravity of the sooty cannons, and the presence of some companies of the regular army" gave a military bearing to a crowd that resembled a tribe from the period of the migration of nations.[131] The national army, both in peace and war, was a sensitive barometer of the national social situation. The question in every mobilization right up to 1914 was whether the peasants would leave their fields. And once in uniform, the peasant did not want to remain idle. He wanted a quick battle and a quick resolution. Practice the peasant considered idleness, even though it took all his free time. "Every day from dawn until noon [we drill], and in the afternoon we practice marksmanship and listen to theoretical discussions and the like," complained one soldier in his diary.[132] Usually soldiers drilled five to twelve hours a day, but unless they saw the Turks beyond their own trenches they did not feel they were accomplishing the great purpose of the war. Whatever that purpose was, it was not connected with creating a Great Bulgaria, although a national revival on the ruins of Kosovo would not have seemed foreign. Because of the national epics, no one had to be educated to that goal. It was in an effort to give the common soldier something to fight for that Chernyayev floated his short-lived attempt to make Milan king in 1876.[133]

On the other hand, almost the entire intelligentsia was possessed by the democratic ideal of autonomy. Demonstrations with the "Red Banner" in Kragujevac in 1876 were just one episode in their struggle. There was, therefore, an important cleavage of purpose between the intelligentsia and the leadership of the army. "All those noble ones," complained Andra Knićanin, "get themselves assigned to kitchens and supply depots. That intelligentsia, the ones who complain about the officers and the army, those scribomaniacs, those gossips and sidetrackers who find their way to greasy salaries, that highly educated band who are thinking only of their ministerial chairs [do not go to the front]."[134] The most popular Serbian poet, Jovan Jovanović—Zmaj, left Serbia because of a dispute over his officer's rank, and Djura

Jakšić also got into trouble. It was said that there were not five intellectuals at the front. Nor did the soldiers have a positive view of life in the rear, of the parties and balls in Belgrade.[135] It took years for these feelings to abate, and as late as 1881 a satirical poem implying that officers in the last war were cowards created a scandal.[136] There were even a number of people in Serbia who did not want any sort of war for unification of the Serbian people: "We don't need the Hercegovinian karst or the naked rocks of Bosnia for which our poor here in Serbia would be impoverished and devastated."[137] A French envoy reported meeting Serbian officers who supported the idea of a trialist reform in the Habsburg Empire in which Serbia would be included.[138]

The war greatly affected the political development of Serbia because it showed that the country was operating at the level of a semidespotic government that undertook reforms not because real democratic attitudes underlay society, but only to appease public opinion. "If reforms are begun from below," said Jovan Ristić, minister of foreign affairs and de facto head of the government, "they very easily can turn into disorder and call forth disturbances the result of which no one can predict."[139] Ilija Garašanin, one of the early builders of the Serbian political system, believed that internal tranquility was the precondition for an active foreign policy, since the destructive tendencies in the Serbian people made them "very spoiled children." A war against Turkey could be victorious only if tight internal discipline was imposed, "because we will not be able to make Englishmen out of our people for a long time."[140]

Similar attitudes at times afflicted the army too. On the eve of the second war, on December 8, 1877, a military mutiny broke out on the Stanović Plain, just outside of Kragujevac. The assembled soldiers of the Lepenica battalion rejected their swearing in and fled to Topola, the site of Karadjordjević's citadel and the capital of Serbia during the First Serbian Uprising.[141] Martial law was imposed on several districts, and after the rebellion had been quickly put down the local citizens were forced to raze Karadjordjević's citadel to the ground.[142] Investigations supposedly showed that the rebellion was incited by intellectuals, and some prominent among them, such as Aćim Čumić and Jevrem Marković, were indicted for high treason.[143] Several persons, including Marković, were executed, while others, including Čumić, were sentenced to long prison terms. In fact, the links between the political opposition and the rebellion have never been proven, but the rebellion did delay Serbia's entry into the war, thus hindering efforts to seize Macedonia. The rebellion was, however, symbolic of the alienation of the peasant masses from the political leadership.

Later military theorists drew constructive lessons from the bleak experiences of 1876–78, although they were reluctant to allege inadequate political management. Their work was valuable in the theoretical preparations for victory in the Balkan Wars of 1912–13. In fact, the main critical work on the war of 1876 appeared in the year 1912.[144] The motto that "after the war all generals are brilliant" led the author of that work to be milder in his criticism than he could have been. In his list of twenty key lessons of the war, he found that only the organization of the rear provided any experience useful for the future. The cavalry, in particular, "was unfit for any independent and decisive military action."[145] Artillery and engineering units seem to have performed better, perhaps because of the larger percentage of educated persons in those units. The panicky flights were attributed both to the army's organization and to the government's policy. During the second war, when the peasant did not feel he was alone in a devastating struggle, "there was only one case of panic in the whole course of the war."[146]

Without question, the wars of 1876–78 played a fateful role in the history of the Serbian nation. Beside the revolutions of 1804 and 1815, no other event engaged the nation on such a large scale or for such important ends. At the same time, it was the only national war in nineteenth-century Europe not led by the intelligentsia. Alienated from the decision to go to war, they left a gap that the Pan-Slavists filled. They also left the political field to the politicians alone. The clear result was a diminished degree of South Slavism in the events of 1876–78.

These were typical bourgeois wars. The basic thing peasants were striving for in Bosnia and Hercegovina was the settlement of the agrarian question, but from the outset of the uprisings the Serbian government promised the Muslim aristocracy in those regions that their property rights would be protected. In the negotiations between General Alimpić and Prince Nicholas of Montenegro concerning an alliance it was even suggested that the Muslim nobility of Bosnia might propose its own candidate for the South Slavic throne in the event of a dynastic crisis.[147] The massive participation of the Pan-Slavists in the first war poisoned the possibility that the national army could be a constructive instrument in the Serbian national movement by opening a gulf between the upper and lower strata of society. No European risorgimento could hope for success in the nineteenth century without the participation of the intelligentsia and the peasantry. It was very risky to enter into any partnership with the Great Powers with an instrument as shaky as the national army. With such an army Serbia would have achieved better results if it had pursued the Pan-Slavists' policy of conducting a war, without the state's participation, on someone else's territory with the help of volunteers and popular uprisings. Fewer military feats on the open front and more guerrilla activity in Bosnia and Bulgaria would have produced a greater impact on the outcome than the course actually chosen.

The defeats of 1876–78 had constructive consequences. By disclosing both the political and the military weaknesses of the society, they helped the country to mature and adopt more modern European models. A negative heritage of the wars, however, was the greater role of the army in national life. Acting as the guardian of the established political and social order, the army influenced politics, industrialization, and even the way people dressed. For this reason, Stojan Novaković's view that the military played a positive role in building a modern Serbian society should be replaced by Vuk Karadžić's advice to Prince Miloš in 1832: a ruler who keeps an army only to protect himself and his administration is lost.[148]

## NOTES

1. Nikola Radojčić, "Dositejevo pismo o uredjenju i prosvećenju Srbije," *Letopis Matice Srpske,* no. 300 (1914–1921), p. 24.
2. Stojan Novaković, *Stara srpska vojska: Istorijske skice iz dela "Narod i zemlja u staroj srpskoj državi"* (Belgrade, 1893), p. 5.
3. Ibid., p. 3.
4. Grugur Jakšić and Vojislav Vučković, *Spoljna politika Srbije za vlade kneza Mihaila: Prvi Balkanski savez* (Belgrade, 1963), p. 50.
5. Slobodan Jovanović, *Druga vlada Miloša i Mihajla* (Belgrade, 1933), pp. 280–81.
6. Dragašević, "Misli o srpskoj narodnoj vojsci," in *Vojin: List za vojne nauke, veštine i novosti, 1866,* vol. 2 (Belgrade, 1867), p. 40.
7. Ibid., vol. 3, p. 69.
8. Ibid., p. 71.
9. T. W. Riker, "Michael of Serbia and the Turkish Occupation," *Slavonic and East European Review* 12: 138.
10. Sava Grujić, *Vojna organizacija Srbije s kratkim pregledom vojne organizacije starih i novih naroda* (Kragujevac, 1874), p. 61.
11. Stojan Novaković, *Stara srpska vojska,* p. 69.
12. Radosav Marković, *Vojska i naoružanje Srbije kneza Miloša* (Belgrade, 1957), p. 165.
13. P. B[orisavljevic], "Kratki pregled organizacije naše vojske," *Ratnik,* 1887, no. 1, p. 44.
14. Toma Kovačević, *Opis Bosne i Hercegovine* (Belgrade, 1879), p. 68.
15. M. Dj. Milićević, *Kneževina Srbija,* vol. 2 (Belgrade, 1876), p. 117.
16. Ilija Garašanin to Prince Alexander Karadjordjević, September 21, 1848, Državna Arhiva Srbije.
17. Published in March 1854 with the signatures of Herkalović and Nenadović.
18. Ibid., Point 6.
19. Ibid., Point 33.
20. Živ. Živanovic, *Politička istorija Srbije u drugoj polovici devetnaestoga veka, 1858–1875,* vol. 1 (Belgrade, 1923), p. 53.
21. Ibid.
22. Milutin Stepanović, *Registar sviju zakona, ukaza, raspisa, rešenja, objašnjenja i t. d., koja su štampana u vojnim zbornicima i službenim vojnim listovima od 1858 pa do 1882 god. zaključno, a imaju trajne ili istorijske važnosti za vojsku* (Belgrade, 1883), p. 75.
23. Ibid. (Article 2 of the Law on the Organization of the National Army).

24. Živanović, *Politička istorija Srbije,* p. 76.
25. Slobodan Jovanović, *Vlada Milana Obrenovića,* 2 vols. (Belgrade, 1934), 2: 69.
26. Václav Žáček, *František A. Zach* (Prague, 1977), p. 236.
27. Novica B. Rakočević, *Ratni planovi Srbije protiv Turske od Vožda Karadjordja do Kralja Petra* (Belgrade, 1933), p. 75.
28. Sava Grujić, *Operacije Timočko–Moravske vojske,* 4 vols. (Belgrade, 1904), 1: 6–7.
29. J. Albrecht von Reiswitz, *Belgrad–Berlin, Berlin–Belgrad, 1866–1871* (Munich, 1936), pp. 85–86.
30. Stepanović, *Registar,* p. 81 (Article 33 of the Law).
31. Jovanović, *Vlada Milana Obrenovića,* 2: 281.
32. Stepanović, *Registar,* p. 130 (Article 37 of the Regulation on the Organization of the Main Staffs of the National Army and their Duties).
33. Stepanović, *Registar,* p. 234 (The Rules on the Distribution, Use, Preservation, and Maintenance of Uniforms in the National Army).
34. Jakšić and Vučković, *Spoljna politika Srbije,* p. 188.
35. Ibid.
36. Rade Petrović, "Saradnja Kragujevca i Torina," *Ital–Jug* (Rome) 7, no. 2 (1977): 23.
37. Report of Minister for Military Affairs Blaznavac to the Assembly, October 16, 1867, in *Protokoli redovne narodne skupšine držane o Mioljudne 1867. godineu Kragujevcu* (Belgrade, 1868), p. 243.
38. Jovan Ristić, *Jedno Namesništvo 1868–1872* (Belgrade, 1894), p. 25, says that the Peabody rifle is "among the most advanced in Europe."
39. Mita Petrović, *Ratne beleške 1876, 1877 i 1878,* vol. 1 (Čačak, 1955), p. 227.
40. Nil Popov, *Srbija i Turska od godine 1861. do 1867. godine* (Belgrade, 1879), p. 118.
41. Vladan Djordjević, *Istorija srpskog vojnog saniteta,* vol. 1 (Belgrade, 1879), p. 205.
42. F. E. Bailey, *British Policy and the Turkish Reform Movement: A Study in Anglo–Turkish Relations 1826–1853* (Cambridge, 1942), p. 7. Jovan Petrov, *Zbornik razni poleznih predmeta* (Belgrade, 1843), says that Turkey had 180,000 soldiers in its army at that time.
43. I. I. Rostunova, ed., *Russko–Tureckaja vojna 1877–1878,* (Moscow, 1977), p. 49.
44. Jakšić and Vučković, *Spoljna politika Srbije,* p. 341.
45. Rakočević, *Ratni planovi,* p. 95.
46. Ahmed-Midhat Efendi, *Sbornik tureckix' dokumentov' o poslednej vojne* (St. Petersburg, 1879), p. 11.
47. Rakočević, *Ratni planovi,* p. 113.
48. M. A. Ubicini, *Lettres sur la Turquie...,* vol. 1 (Paris, 1853), p. 470.
49. *Protokoli redovne narodne skupštine,* p. 242.
50. Stepanović, *Registar,* p. 176 (The Law on Military Discipline: The General Foundations of Subordination, November 16, 1862). This was endorsed by a ministerial order of March 27, 1864 (ibid., p. 227).
51. *Zbornik zakona i uredaba izdanih u knjažestvu Srbiji,* vol. 29, pp. 634–43; vol. 32, p. 144.
52. *Protokoli vanredne narodne skupštine koja je držana u Kragujevcu 1874* (Belgrade, 1874).
53. Sava Grujić, *Vojna organizacija Srbije* (Kragujevac, 1874). On the same topic, see Četnik Siniša (pseudonym of Bogdanović Simeun), *Vojena snaga Turske, Srbije i Crne Gore* (Novi Sad, 1872).
54. Paja Putnik, *Misli o vojenoj organizaciji Srbije* (Pančevo, 1875).
55. Ibid., pp. 5, 54.

# 302 MILORAD EKMEČIĆ

56. Vlad. J. Belić, *Ratovi srpskog naroda u XIX veku (1785–1918)* (Belgrade, n. d.), p. 75.

57. See Article 11 of the agreement of October 5, 1866 (Jakšić and Vučković, *Spoljna politika Srbije*, p. 488).

58. Jevrem Grujić, *Zapisi: Druga vlada Obrenovića i Turski ratovi*, vol. 3 (Belgrade, 1923), p. 195.

59. V. M. N. Pokrovskij, *Diplomatija i vojni carskoj Rossii v XIX stoletii* (Moscow, 1924), p. 259. Pokrovskij quotes the diary of General Gasenkampf.

60. "Nakanune našej poslednej vojni," *Russkij Arxiv* 35 (1897): 259.

61. Vasilj Popović, "Berlinski kongres," *Bratstvo* 22 (1928): 7.

62. J. Z. R. Žuborić, *General Frant. A. Zach: Životopisný nástin* (Prague, 1898), p. 36.

63. A. J. M. Kratak, "Pregled svih bojeva u drugom ratu 1877/78 god." *Uzdanica: Vojnički list za pouku, negovanje vojničkih vrlina i vitešku zabavu* 4, no. 4 (October 1902): 315.

64. Ahmed-Midhat Efendi, p. 11.

65. Rakočević, *Ratni planovi*, p. 118. On the Ibar army, see Stevan Ignjić, *Užice i okolina 1862–1914* (Užice, 1967), pp. 37–49.

66. Rakočević, *Ratni planovi*, p. 128.

67. Sava Grujić, *Bitka na Djunisu: IX prilog za istoriju srpsko–turskog rata 1876 godine* (Belgrade, 1898), p. 21.

68. Jovanović, *Vlada Milana Obrenovića*, 1: 443.

69. Žáček, *František A. Zach*, p. 253.

70. Jovan Jovanović, "Sergej Mihajlović Kravčinskij–Stepnjak: Učesnik u Hercegovačkom ustanku 1875 godine," *Godišnjak Društva istoričara BiH* 19 (1973): 273.

71. Dorothy Anderson, *The Balkan Volunteers* (London, 1968), p. 24.

72. Grujić, *Zapisi*, p. 194.

73. Jovanović, *Druga vlada Miloša i Mihajla*, p. 287.

74. Grujić, *Operacije*, p. 2.

75. A. N. Hvostov, *Russkie i Serbii v' vojnu 1876 goda za nezavisimost xristiane: Obščij kritičeskij obzor'* (St. Petersburg, 1877), p. 25.

76. S. A. Nikitin, *Slavjanskie komiteti v Rossii* (Moscow, 1960), p. 273.

77. Vladan Djordjević, *Srpsko–Turski rat: Uspomene i beleške iz 1876, 1877 i 1878 godine*, vol. 1 (Belgrade, 1907), pp. 2–3.

78. Svetozar Magdalenić, *Slike iz naših ratova sa Turcima i Bugarima 1876, 1877– 1878 i 1885–1886 godine*, vol. 2 (Belgrade, 1910), p. 28. On the arrival of Chernyayev and the Russo–Bulgarian volunteers, see also Grujić, *Operacije Timočko–Moravske vojske*, 4: 148–73. Officially, the Russian government was not advising Serbia to declare war on Turkey; see S. I. Bočarova, "Russko–serbskiie otnošenija v svjazi s Serbsko–Tureckoj vojnoj 1876 goda," in *Medjunarodni naučni skup povodom 100-godišnjice ustanka u Bosni i Hercegovini*, vol. 1 (Sarajevo, 1977), p. 355. Russian official policy was divided on this issue; see Barbara Jelavich, *The Ottoman Empire, the Great Powers, and the Strait Question 1870–1887* (Bloomington, 1973), p. 90. Yet the government secretly gave money to Kartsov, as is apparent from the above-quoted letter from the chairman of the Moscow Slavic Committee. See also T. G. Svjatko, "Iz istorii narodnogo dviženija v Rossii v poderžku borby južnix Slavjan za svoju nezavisimost' v' 1875–76," in *Obščestvenno-političeskie i kulturnie svjazi narodov SSSR i Jugoslavii* (Moscow, 1957), p. 27.

79. Magdalenić, *Slike*, p. 29.

80. Nikola Škerović, *Zapisnici sednica Ministarskog saveta Srbije 1862–1898* (Belgrade, 1952), p. 174.

81. Hvostov, p. 27.

82. Sava Grujić, *Bugarski dobrovoljci u srpsko–turskom ratu 1876 godine* (Belgrade, 1892), p. 10.

83. Magdalenić, *Slike*, pp. 31–32.

84. Ibid., p. 62.
85. Ibid., p. 103.
86. Djordjević, *Srpsko–turski rat,* p. 464.
87. Jovan Ristić, *Diplomatska istorija Srbije za vreme srpsko–turskih ratova za oslobodjenje i nezavismost 1875–1878,*vol. 1 (Belgrade, 1896), p. 147.
88. Jovanović, *Vlada Milana Obrenovića,* 2: 71.
89. V. M. Xevrolina, "Revolucionnoe narodničest'o i nacional'no-osvoboditelnoe dviženie na Balkanax' 1875–1877 gg.," in *Slavjanskoe vozroždenie* (Moscow, 1966), p. 67.
90. Anderson, *The Balkan Volunteers,* p. 30.
91. Jovanović, *Vlada Milana Obrenovića,* 2: 73.
92. Rakočević, *Ratni planovi,* p. 114.
93. Grujić, *Bitka na Djunisu,* p. 8.
94. Grujić, *Borbe za odbranu istočne granice 1876 godine: V prilog za istoriju srpsko–turskog rata te godine* (Belgrade, 1898), p. 23.
95. Ibid., p. 12.
96. Škerović, *Zapisnici,* p. 323.
97. Nikitin, *Slavjanskie komiteti v Rossii,* p. 319; idem, "Russkoe obščestvo i nacional'no osvoboditel'naja borba južnix Slavjan v 1875–76 g.," in *Obščestvenno-političeskie i kulturnie svjazi,* p. 65. In October 1876, General R. A. Fadayev ordered the recruitment of 15,000 Bulgarian and 5,000 Russian volunteers; see I. V. Koz'menko, "Iz istorii bolgarskogo opolčenija (1876–1877)," in *Slavjanskij sbornik: Slavjanskij vopros i russkoe obščestvo v 1867–1878 godax* (Moscow, 1948), p. 121.
98. Grujić, *Operacije Timočko–Moravske vojske,* 4: 85.
99. A. A. Ulunjan, "Učastie bolgarskogo naroda v Russko–Tureckoj vojne 1877–1878 gg.," in *Slavjanskoe vozroždenie* (Moscow, 1966), p. 222.
100. Georgi Jazarov, "Formirane na b'lgarskoto opolčenie," in *Russko–Turskata osvoboditelna vojna 1877–1878* (Sofia, 1977), p. 69.
101. Grujić, *Bugarski dobrovoljci,* p. 32.
102. Hvostov, p. 8.
103. Magdalenić, *Slike,* p. 3.
104. Hvostov, pp. 9, 10.
105. Andra S. Knićanin, *Ratni dnevnik,* vol. 1 (Belgrade, 1881), p. 168.
106. Sava Grujić, *Naša ofanziva 1876 godine: IV prilog za istoriju srpsko–turskog rata te godine* (Belgrade, 1898), p. 10.
107. "Gradja za istoriju srpsko–turskog rata 1876 godine," in *Ratnik: List za vojne nauke, novosti i književnost* 33, no. 3 (March 1895): 348–49.
108. Petar Opačić, "Vojne operacije u srpsko–turskom ratu 1876 godine," in *Medjunarodni naučni skup povodom 100-godišnjice ustanka u Bosni i Hercegovini,* vol. 2, p. 288.
109. Petar Pešić, *Naš rat sa Turskom 1876/77 godine: Kritička studija 1912 godine* (Belgrade, 1925), pp. 184–85.
110. Ibid., p. 22.
111. E. d'Ormessony, *Vingt deux jours en charette à travers la Serbie,* entry on December 2, 1877, quoted by Draga Vuksanović–Anić, "Dnevnik francuskog vojnog izaslanika iz 1877," *Politika* (Belgrade), June 29, 1977. Stevan Ignjić, "Dogadjaji na Drini 1876 godine," *Vojnoistorijski glasnik,* 1973, no. 2–3; Mileva Alimpić, *Zivot i rad generala Ranka Alimpića u svezi sa dogadjajima iz najnovije srpske istorije* (Belgrade, 1892).
112. Žáček, *František A. Zach.*
113. Škerović, *Zapisnici,* p. 211, conference of August 19, 1876.
114. Supreme Command of the Serbian Army, *Rat Srbije sa Turskom za oslobodjenje i nezavisnost 1877–1878 godine* (Belgrade, 1879), pp. 271–308.
115. Ibid., p. 73.
116. Petar Pesić, *Naš rat sa Turskom,* p. 177.

117. Grujić, *Operacije Timočko–Moravske vojske*, 4: 172.

118. The exact number of the Garibaldian volunteers in Serbia in 1876 has not yet been established. It has been estimated at no more than forty persons, at least during August 1876. See Nikša Stipčević, "Marko Antonio Kanini i Srbija," *Jugoslovenski istorijski časopis* 3–4 (1976): 132; Djuzepe Barbanti Brodano, *Garibaldinci na Drini 1876* (Belgrade, 1958).

119. St. Binički, *Odlomci iz ratnih beležaka 1876 g.* (Belgrade, 1891), p. 4.

120. M. M. Magdalenić, *Gradja za istoriju rata Srbije sa Turskom za oslobodjenje i nezavisnost 1877–78 godine* (Belgrade, 1894), p. 2.

121. Škerović, *Zapisnici*, p. 325.

122. Ibid., p. 237, conference of November 5, 1877.

123. Ahmed-Midhat Efendi, p. 38.

124. Magdalenić, *Gradja za istoriju*, p. 30.

125. Belić, *Ratovi srpskog naroda*, p. 86.

126. Škerović, *Zapisnici*, pp. 238, 241.

127. A. J. M. Kratki, "Pregled svih bojeva u drugom ratu"; idem, *Brojni pregled gubitaka srpske vojske u ratu 1877 i 1878 po korovima*.

128. Magdalenić, *Gradja za istoriju*, p. 119.

129. Živanović, *Politička istorija Srbije*, p. 380.

130. Polit Desančić, *Političke besede*, pt. 1 (Novi Sad, n. d.) p. 378.

131. Jovanović, *Vlada Milana Obrenovića*, 2: 39, quoting the diary of Pera Todorović.

132. Knićanin, *Ratni dnevnik*, p. 12.

133. "Gradja za istoriju srpsko–turskog rata 1876 godine," *Ratnik* 33 (1895): 485.

134. Knićanin, *U odbranu naših oficira* (Belgrade, 1881), p. 6.

135. Knićanin, *Ratni dnevnik*, p. 159.

136. Poem with the title "To the Heroes" punned into "To the Bullocks" in the satirical magazine *Cosa za šalu i zbilju: Suvremenli slikar našeg javnog života* 1, no. 22 (1881).

137. Alimpić, *Život i rad generala Ranka Alimpića*, pp. 523, 524.

138. Vuksanović–Anić, "Dnevnik," *Politika* (Belgrade), July 8, 1977.

139. Branko Petrović, *Jovan Ristić: Biografske i memoarske beleške* (Belgrade, 1912), p. 36.

140. Jakšić and Vučković, *Spoljna politika Srbije*, p. 212.

141. Živanović, *Politička istorija Srbije*, p. 363.

142. "Rešenje Knjaza Milana," *Zbornik zakona i uredaba izdanih u knjažestvu Srbiji* 32 (Belgrade, 1878): 124–30.

143. Živanović, *Politička istorija Srbije*.

144. Pešić, *Naš rat sa Turskom*, pp. 183–94.

145. Jevrem Marković, *Uput za taktičku upotrebu konjice u ratu* (1877); Vuksanović–Anić, "Dnevnik," *Politika* (Belgrade), July 14, 1977.

146. Savo Skoko, "Pregled operacija srpske vojske u Srpsko–Turskom ratu 1877–1878," *Medjunarodni naučni skup*, 2: 277; Nikola Ilić, *Oslobodjenje Južne Srbije 1877–1878* (Belgrade, 1977).

147. Alimpić, *Živat i rad generala Ranka Alimpića*, p. 532.

148. *Vuk Karadžić o unutrašnjoj politici Kneza Miloša: Njegova pismo knezu od 12. aprila 1832,* ed. Ljuba Stojanović (Belgrade, 1923), p. 23.

Dimitrije Djordjevic

# THE SERBIAN PEASANT IN THE 1876 WAR

The 1875—78 Eastern crisis began with a peasant rebellion in 1875 in Herce-govina and Bosnia and the April 1876 uprising in western Bulgaria. In June 1876 Serbia and Montenegro declared war on the Ottoman Empire, and this in turn involved Russia in the armed conflict in April 1877. Thus a local rebellion developed into a Balkan and European crisis. The peasant move-ment was an expression of dissatisfaction with the domestic Ottoman authori-ties. Serbia and Montenegro tried to impose their own solution to the Balkan problem, and their failure provoked Russia into facing Europe with a fait accompli in the Eastern Question.

The peasant upheavals in Bosnia and Bulgaria followed the traditional pattern of Balkan agrarian-national movements. Serbia and Montenegro, later joined by Romania and Greece, resorted for the first time to regular war rather than agrarian revolution as an instrument of their national policy. They were inspired by the examples offered by Italy and Germany in their struggles for unification during the 1860s and by the economic and political development of the Balkan states themselves. However, the Balkan armies assigned the task of liberation were still in a formative stage, organized more as popular militias than as modern standing armies.[1] They reflected the peasant concept of the nation in arms shaped in the course of centuries of confrontation with Ottoman rule. Their structure was imposed by the limited financial resources of Balkan states and the lack of time to prepare and train a modern army. The 1876 war surprised Serbia in the midst of the transition from agrarian revolutions to modern warfare. The performance of the peasant soldier in the face of the requirements of modern warfare proved decisive in its outcome.

The Law on the Organization of the National Army of 1861 introduced conscription for all Serbs aged twenty to fifty years. The army was based on the Swiss model. Units were organized on the territorial principle: the conscripts of a village formed a company, the companies of a district made up a battalion, and counties organized regiments. Officers were recruited among state officials, village elders, and veterans of the small standing army.[2] Suddenly, in the early 1860s, Serbia was able, at least in theory, to raise some 50,000 men, and that number was augmented over the years. At the beginning of the 1876 war Serbia mobilized 124,000 soldiers organized in six divisions, with thirty-six brigades and eighteen battalions, not counting several thousand volunteers from neighboring Balkan regions and elsewhere in Europe.[3] They were armed with rifles either obtained from Russia or manufactured in the arsenal at Kragujevac. In the middle of the 1870s the artillery had about two hundred old-model pieces.[4]

This type of military organization had both advantages and disadvantages. It suited the peasant's traditional affiliation with the village. Family and neighborhood ties contributed to a feeling of unity and esprit de corps. However, familiarity interfered with discipline: emotions prevailed over duty. The peasant was proud to carry the gun and wear the uniform but resented the time spent in training, which he would rather have spent in the field. An army of this kind was more a group of armed peasants than a modern military organization; it offered numbers rather than quality. In the 1876 war the Serbian militia was to confront the reorganized Ottoman army, some 130,000 regular troops (nizam) and 20,000 to 30,000 irregulars or bashi-bazouks, mostly Circassians and Albanians, equipped with modern Winchester rifles and 504 cannons purchased from Krupp.[5]

Until the very beginning of the war, the Serbian political leadership was confused about whether to enter the war and risk the extinction of Serbia or to let the opportunity to accomplish its national goals slip away. The prince and the government were under tremendous pressure from nationalist circles. The rebellion in Bosnia pointed to a forthcoming general Balkan uprising.[6] The Bulgarian uprising echoed the cry: our brothers are screaming for help! On June 4 the Serbian general staff obtained information about a new uprising in Varna. General Chernyayev, who had joined the Serbian army in May, warned on June 6 that without support the Bulgarian movement would collapse.[7] The Serbian decision to enter the war on June 20 was based on three assumptions: the expected general Balkan uprising, the weakness of the Ottoman army, and immediate support from Russia.[8] All of them proved to be wrong. The war council in Belgrade was contemplating two strategic alternatives, the Serbian and the Balkan. The first required an offensive in the direction of Bosnia, the second an attack toward Bulgaria. Hoping to launch a Balkan upheaval, the Serbian offensive was directed toward the city of Niš and a front on the River Morava.[9] Serbia entered the war militarily, economically, and diplomatically unprepared.

From the very beginning, a striking discrepancy between the nationalist urban population, especially the intelligentsia, and the village was apparent. In the 1870s, ideas of modern nationalism were rooted in the city. The uprising in Bosnia and Hercegovina and the Serbo–Turkish War were the consequence of the joint activity of the nationalist revolutionary organizations of the 1860s, the United Serbian Youth (Omladina), liberals, socialists, Orthodox priests, Pan-Slavists, and refugees from Ottoman territories. The organization of underground revolutionary committees and bands of irregulars, the supplying of arms to the insurgents across the border, and the spreading of propaganda manifested the fervor of the nationalistic public.[10] It suited the era of romanticism: youngsters, eager to join the war, acquired uniforms and bid farewell to their girlfriends, "going to die on the battlefield."[11] Wealthy citizens purchased horses to join the cavalry.[12] A young lieutenant in the reserves carried a tent and a bed he had brought from Paris with him to the front.[13] Professional soldiers in the small standing army enthusiastically greeted the war. In 1876 Serbia had only 460 career officers, but they were joined in the war by 700 Russian officers recruited among volunteers.[14] Many of the young cadets from the Artillery School, future commanders in the wars of the twentieth century, distinguished themselves in the 1876 campaign.[15]

Contrary to the bellicose atmosphere prevailing in the city, the village remained, if not reluctant, at least passive toward the war. The Russian general Chernyayev, who assumed command of the Serbian army, recalled: "I had been struck by the popular apathy to the imminent war. I had not noticed even the slightest enthusiasm among the mustered militia."[16] The Italian volunteer and member of the Garibaldian detachment on the Drina Giuseppe Barbanti–Brodano got the same impression about the peasant "who left his family behind not knowing whether he can feed them next year."[17]

An important factor in this attitude was the fact that the war started in June, in the midst of the summer work in the fields, but there were more decisive factors. The behavior of the peasant in moments of crisis can be taken as a barometer of his general socioeconomic situation and the political climate in the country. During the nineteenth century and after the liberation from the direct Ottoman rule, the Serbian peasant went through a painful adaptation to modernization that involved the penetration of new capitalist economies and the development of institutions of the state and called for a reevaluation of his traditional values and ways of living. Accustomed for centuries of foreign rule to challenging state authority, the peasant now needed to espouse the idea of his own national state. The incorporation of the peasant into the new social, economic, and political environment was a slow and gradual process marked by village-state and village-city confrontations. The extended peasant family (the *zadruga*) was disintegrating under the pressure of the money economy. The state introduced urban bureaucracy, higher taxation, and conscription into the village. The city became the main beneficiary of modernization. Its life-style and its exploitation of the countryside alienated the village. The peasant was left at the bottom of the social ladder, in poverty and with an illiteracy rate of 98 percent in the 1870s. He played the role of an object in urban politics.[18] No one consulted the peasant when war was declared, but he was asked to assume the main burden of it and to sacrifice his life and property. Facing death and war destruction, the peasant asked, "Where are the ones who were the loudest in pushing us into war?"[19]

The village was the peasant's state, the family his nation. His nationalism was instinctive and religious, but poor education and lack of knowledge of geography kept him from going very far beyond the village and county limits. One peasant deputy said in Parliament: "If we wrench [sic] Bosnia, my own field will not become any larger."[20] Another soldier expressed his feelings in the following way: "Imagine a man who owns a house and a fireplace, who earns his crust of bread, and who now has to leave his wife and children and die for the freedom of some Bosnians and Hercegovinians whom he has never seen before."[21] Leaving his village for the first time to enter Bosnia or the Sanjak of Novi Pazar, the peasant felt that he was moving into foreign territory. Looking at the canyons of Javor Mountain, a peasant from Mačva thought aloud: "Why does our prince need these rugged and deserted rocks? He would do better to give them to the Turks and settle their population on the rich plain of Mačva."[22] The peasant understood the war and the need to fight in terms of defending his own home and village. After an unsuccessful charge on Javor Mountain at the beginning of the war, a group of soldiers were leaving their company. Stopped by an officer, they replied: "When the Turk comes to our home, we'll know how to defend it."[23] Another soldier said: "I would know how to fight on the Drina and to die if necessary, but I don't know what kind of country this is. Even their homes are different from ours."[24] The historian Vladan Djordjević once reproached a group of soldiers for not joining their comrades in the ongoing battle. "Let them fight," they answered. "Everyone is protecting his own home. Why should we do it for them?"[25] When fighting for his village, the peasant became a reputable warrior. Živojin Mišić, who participated in the 1876 war as a cadet, described the struggle of soldiers from Šiljegovac who refused to obey the order to retreat and defended their village house by house.[26]

Insufficient training prior to the war created a serious problem during the 1876 campaign. The peasant was trained in the vicinity of his village twenty-five days per year, on Sundays and holidays, with an extra five days usually thrown in after the harvest.[27] Initially the soldier had to provide himself with food and clothing. Later the state provided uniforms, allowing peasants to wear them not only during exercises and parades but also on religious holidays and at soldiers' weddings. Milorad Ekmečić correctly points out the influence of the uniform on the traditional peasant national costume.[28] The Balkan peasant had long known how to handle a musket, but modern warfare required more than that. In the 1876 war the peasant was reluctant to fight in trenches and fortifications and preferred to ambush the enemy rather than charge in frontal assaults. When forced to fight in an open field, peasants stuck together like a herd, which increased the casualties. Indeed, they fought as if it were a revolution rather than a conventional war.[29]

Thousands of volunteers from Russia, Bulgaria, and Europe came to Serbia to join in the fighting. The Serbian command expected a great deal of them. A proclamation was issued on June 18 calling on "our brave Montenegrins, our Hercegovinian heroes and numerous suffering Bulgarians as well as the glorious offspring of Themistocles and Botzares" to join together with the Serbs.[30] Six weeks before the beginning of hostilities, the Ministry of War in Belgrade ordered the recruitment of volunteers and the organization of bands along the Serbian borders on the Drina, the Ibar, the Morava, and the Timok. A special Montenegrin delegate at Serbian headquarters was appointed for this purpose.[31]

Of the volunteers who came to fight in Serbia, with the exception of the Bulgarians only a few were peasants. Pan-Slavist committees organized throughout Russia dispatched mostly officers, physicians, and nurses to Serbia. Only twenty to thirty among them were ordinary soldiers. The committees in Europe sent intellectuals, revolutionaries, and physicians.[32] These volunteers were of three kinds: (1) Pan-Slavists, idealists, revolutionaries, republicans, socialists, and fighters for freedom, who were not professional soldiers, knew little about war, and were ready, like desperados, to fight and die for their ideas; (2) army officers seasoned in previous wars in Russia or Italy, who joined the new war expecting promotions, medals, and glory on the battlefield; and (3) adventurers, social outcasts, drunkards, and troublemakers who expected a good time in Serbia.[33] They made a colorful combination of Don Quixotes and Garibaldis, Parisian students and Russian Cossacks, brigands and brawlers. Some sought death in suicidal charges, some came not knowing whether Serbia was a Persian province or not, some drank themselves into madness.[34] General Chernyayev, an idealist and a careerist, hoped to enter Constantinople in fifteen days and become the Serbian George Washington.[35]

The Serbian peasant admired the courage of some of the volunteers and expected more of them than they could offer, but he was also afraid of the excesses of some among them. The foreign military men did not understand the peasant mentality. The Russian volunteers brought with them the spirit of aristocratic Russia. Professional officers looked upon the soldier as an object of war. Chernyayev brought his cook and his coachman with him from Russia. Champagne and caviar were served in his headquarters, while the peasant-soldier had to chase flies during his meals.[36] The parade of Russian volunteers on the occasion of the consecration of a flag sent from Moscow left the population of Belgrade cool, half impressed and half afraid of the foreign soldiers.[37] The peasants experienced similar feelings while attending the solemn formation of the Otrjad Plostunov, called the Death Legion, whose banner had a skull and crossbones embroidered on it.[38] In the volunteer detachment on the Drina organized by the Garibaldian Chelso Cherutti, Italians, Belgians, Frenchmen, Germans, Czechs, and a Norwegian were enrolled. They spoke, cursed, and sang in eleven languages. Professor Keller from Leipzig conversed with Barbanti–Brodano from Bologna in Latin, and Sergeant Fagioli tried to communicate with Serbian peasants in Italian.[39] While the Serbians had never heard of Mazzini, the Italians discovered the "Serbian trinity": *objava* (permit), without which nothing could be done; *sutra* (tomorrow), when something would be done; and *paprika* (red pepper), which hurt their stomachs more than Turkish bullets.[40] Of all these people, the physicians and nurses enjoyed the highest esteem of the population.[41]

The peasant population along the frontier, fearful of Ottoman reprisals and uncertain about the outcome of the war, was cautious and reserved toward the Serbian troops during the opening offensive. Balkan volunteers were recruited among students, workers, former haiduks, and refugees from Ottoman territory. In addition to the many Bulgarians who came to Serbia from Romania and southern Russia, a good number of them happened to be in Serbia at the beginning of the war, working as seasonal workers, gardeners, brickmakers, and carpenters. The Serbian command mobilized the poor, uneducated peasants, in shabby clothes, untrained and unwilling to fight. In July 520 of these peasants openly declared their reluctance to be sent to the front, and they were left in the countryside to build roads and work in the fields.[42] Other Bulgarian detachments under the command of Russian officers and their own leaders took an active part in the war. Romanian peasants in eastern Serbia were included in the Romanian battalion under the command of Colonel Catargi.[43]

The reponse to the call for volunteers from South Slavic regions was less than expected. The anticipated thousands of volunteers from Vojvodina, where the nationalistic public was very vocal in favor of the war, never arrived. Those who crossed the frontier were disappointed by the shortage of equipment and uniforms.[44] The Serbian Committee in Zagreb recruited some three hundred students, who joined the Serbian army on the Drina.[45] The company of volunteers on the Drina recruited "various elements," mostly former haiduks, who had to be kept under strict control. They were joined by students from the Belgrade seminary.[46] The group of seven hundred volunteers at the front on Javor Mountain looked more like a band of haiduks than an army unit.[47] The Princess Natalia Battalion was recruited among Belgrade servants, artisans, and apprentices and lacked military training.[48] All these volunteer units were commanded by amateurs, including the professor Miloš Milojević, the archimandrite Nikifor Dučić, a certain priest Žarko, and the leaders of a number of former haiduk bands.[49] The commander in chief of all the volunteers on the western front, Lieutenant Colonel Gruja Mišković, had only a primary education and had obtained his only military experience during the 1848–49 campaign in southern Hungary.[50] Units very much resembled the Turkish bashi-bazouks: a colorful mob in varied clothing, with European hats, caps, and Turkish fezzes. Later they were given soldier's caps (šajkača) and uniforms to "hide their rags."[51] Volunteers were supposed to get a small allowance (four grosh per day), but it was delivered irregularly, which once caused a mutiny. At the end of the war the government paid each of them 30 grosh and issued passports so that they could leave the country.[52]

The peasant expected his officer to charge ahead of him. When the officer was killed or wounded, the company was likely to disintegrate. Officers of the militia, recruited among nonprofessionals, often issued contradictory orders and did more yelling than commanding.[53] Russian military reports stated that the peasant-soldier did not follow commands and lacked military discipline.[54] The war was mainly fought on the southeastern front. In the west, where the army was on the defensive and only sporadic fighting occurred, the war was conducted in a bizarre way. After occasional encounters, units returned to regular bivouacking. Officers issued daily orders and "paternal instructions" to the soldiers the way peasants would organize work in their fields. In the morning officers enjoyed coffee and plum brandy. They dined together and exchanged visits with neighboring bivouacs to talk about ongoing events or to sing and drink.[55] There was something patriarchal in such behavior, as if the country were not at war. One gets the impression that the rain was more resented, because of the lack of tents, than the war itself.

This kind of life, in spite of occasional attacks and retreats, could not contribute much to the fighting spirit of the soldier. Officers who had defected to Serbia from the Military Frontier brought with them ideas about warfare acquired in the Habsburg army. "The soldier had only to know," wrote one of them, "how to quell a mutiny or rebellion, whether it be *uzbuna* (alarm), *pobuna* (mutiny), or *buna* (rebellion). If he joined one or instigated one, he would be shot."[56] Punishment for defection and desertion was cruel: beating or execution by shooting. At the beginning of the war some three hundred deserters were caught and sentenced to death by court-martial. Some were pardoned by the prince; the rest were executed in front of their comrades.[57] Colonel Djura Horvatović, commander in eastern Serbia, authorized officers to execute deserters without court-martialing them.[58] On one occasion a soldier ordered to carry out an execution asked to be replaced, the condemned being his brother. His request was refused, and he was threatened with the same sentence if he disobeyed.[59] On another occasion General Chernyayev met a group of alleged deserters. Enraged, he cried to their guards: "They ought to be shot!" The guards took his angry remark literally and immediately acted on it.[60] In less serious cases, soldiers were given fifty or more strokes. Once a group of two hundred soldiers, among them some older men, heads of families, and village mayors, were forced to undergo this ordeal for panicking during a false alarm.[61] These drastic measures were used to improve discipline, especially during the first phase of the war.

The peasant army continued to operate according to old customs. The peasant was taken from his home but kept close contact with his family. Vladan Djordjević, who participated in the war as a physician, gave a lively description of this attitude:

> From the first battle to the last, from the Drina to the Timok, from Javor to Aleksinac, the same phenomenon could be seen. The moment the battle was over and the troops returned to their bivouacs, women, children, fathers, mothers, uncles, aunts, all sorts of relatives rushed from all sides to visit their Peter or Paul, even if he had only been away from home for three days. The camp looked like a country fair. A bunch of women and children, talking and eating, were sitting around each soldier as if they were attending a village fair instead of within reach of enemy guns. The only difference from a village festival was that the *kolo* was not danced. From daybreak until late evening, caravans of old people, women, and children on horses and oxcarts passed by our headquarters — no power in this world could stop them.[62]

The worst came when the Ottoman army launched a counteroffensive and invaded Serbian territory. The population of the invaded territories, frightened to death, joined the army in retreat, contributing to the confusion and panic. "A crowd of women, children, and old people were escaping in carts loaded with their household belongings," wrote Dr. Djordjević. "The entire load was not worth a single *dukat,* consisting of torn blankets, straw pillows, broken kettles. Small children unable to walk were sitting on the top of all this. Cattle, poultry, goats, and sheep accompanied the crowd. Old men were cursing, women were weeping, children crying — it was total chaos."[63] Uprooted people looked back at clouds of smoke pouring from the houses and fields that the invading bashi-bazouks had set afire. "The entire Morava Valley was in flames," wrote one witness. "Thick smoke from the earth mixed with the clouds in the sky. It was frightening just to look at it."[64] The cold and rain of autumn only made things worse.

In such an atmosphere, it was easy to panic. False alarms were frequent and usually created confusion. Entire units, fearing encirclement and capture, deserted the front.[65] During the fighting the soldier was constantly curious about what was happening in his neighborhood, which brigade was fighting on either side of him, and whose cavalry was charging.[66] An old peasant proverb says that grief comes before revenge. If a brother or father were wounded no one could prevent the soldier from leaving his post to carry him off the battlefield.[67] The peasant had good reason to be worried: he knew that the enemy was better armed and organized. He was especially afraid of the bashi-bazouks, who traditionally undressed corpses and left them naked on the battlefield. The medical service in the Serbian army was insufficient. There were not enough attendants to carry the wounded, and the worst fear among soldiers was to be caught alive. The Turks rarely took wounded as prisoners of war. Usually the Circassians executed them, sometimes chopping their heads off. The wounded hid in the bushes or the woods and then took advantage of the darkness to crawl back to their lines. There were cases in which they stayed hidden for five days before joining their comrades.[68] In the immediate vicinity of the front, women waited to bring food and brandy to their relatives. After the battle, many sought their loved ones among the dead, often close to the Turkish lines.[69]

In the face of atrocities, the soldier was constantly thinking about his home and family. He collected and carried in his field pack anything he thought might be useful once he returned home: tin containers, nails, rope. One soldier carried a 5=1b. wolf trap that he had discovered in an abandoned house.[70] Every army unit had its mascot — a goat, sheep, a fox, even a wolf — that the soldiers fed and cared for.[71] The peasant had an instinctive compassion for the enemy dead. "Poor guys, who knows where they had to come from!" said one of them, looking at dead Turks. When the war prisoners were escorted through the city of Jagodina, some older men insulted and attacked them. The guards protected the prisoners, saying to the offenders, "Where were you when they were armed?"[72] During the autumn truce, spontaneous contact between soldiers of the two sides was established. Having promised not to harm each other, they put their rifles away and exchanged horses for tobacco, which the Turks lacked.[73] The officers intervened to prevent fraternization, dangerous for fighting morale.

The 1876 war had three stages. The first consisted of an offensive strategy emphasizing a war on Ottoman territory. The failure of this strategy and the first setbacks surprised the soldier and shook his morale. The second phase was defensive — preventing the invasion of the country. Seasoned by the first battles and engaged in protecting his village, the peasant fought better and was successful in the battles of Šumatovac and Bobovište. The third phase, however, brought defeat to the exhausted popular army. Serbia was isolated in the war and unprepared to face the power of the entire Ottoman army. Russia, Romania, and Greece stayed out of the war, and the expected Bulgarian uprising never occurred. Serbia suffered 5,000 dead and 9,500 wounded. The entire eastern and southern parts of the country were devastated and some 200,000 people left homeless.[74] In the 1876 war the Serbian soldier manifested characteristics of the entire Balkan peasantry at the same stage of development: acceptance of sacrifice, fear of enemy reprisals, and the stubborn will to survive. Under the more favorable circumstances created by the internationalization of the Eastern crisis, the reorganized Serbian army was to do better in 1877–78.

## NOTES

1. Dimitrije Djordjevic, "The Role of the Military in the Balkans in the Nineteenth Century," in *Der Berliner Congress von 1878* (Wiesbaden, 1981), pp. 317–47.

2. Sava Grujić, *Vojna organizacija Srbije s kratkim pregledom vojne organizacije starih i novih naroda* (Kragujevac, 1874); Paja Putnik, *Misli o vojenoj organizaciji Srbije* (Pančevo, 1875), pp. 5, 54, 158; Milorad Ekmečić, "Srpska vojska u nacionalnim ratovima od 1876 do 1878," *Balcanica* 9 (1978): 101; Michael Boro Petrovich, *A History of Modern Serbia*, vol. 1 (New York, 1976), pp. 312–16; Slobodan Jovanović, *Druga vlada Miloša i Mihaila* (Belgrade, 1933), pp. 178–85; idem, *Vlada Milana Obrenovića*, vol. 2 (Belgrade, 1933), pp. 39–41; Živan Živanović, *Politička istorija Srbije u drugoj polovini XIX veka*, vol. 2 (Belgrade, 1923), pp. 75–76.

3. Ekmečić, *Srpska vojska*, pp. 113–14. Exact figures are difficult to establish. Putnik, referring to the middle of the 1870s, says 5,622 regular troops, 68,364 troops of the first line, and 41,400 reserve troops, with an additional 14,000 men in supply units. Sava Grujić offers for first-line troops 99,000 and reserve troops 84,000, a total of 183,000 (Putnik, *Misli o vojenoj organizaciji*, p. 4). See also Vladimir Belić, *Ratovi srpskog naroda u XX veku* (Belgrade, n. d.), pp. 106–7.

4. Putnik, *Misli o vojenoj organizaciji*, p. 45; Ekmečić, *Srpska vojska*, pp. 106–7.

5. Ekmečić, *Srpska vojska*, pp. 108–9; Belić, *Ratovi srpskog naroda*, p. 77. The Ottomans concentrated against Serbia in 1876 fifteen battalions in Bosnia, forty-six battalions in Hercegovina, forty-five battalions in Niš, and thirty-two battalions in Vidin.

6. Stevan Ignjić, "Dogadjaji na Drini 1875–1876," *Vojno-istorijski glasnik*, 1973, nos. 2–3, p. 233.

7. Sava Grujić, *Bugarski dobrovoljci u srpsko–turskom ratu 1876* (Belgrade, 1892), pp. 17–19.

8. Jovanović, *Vlada Milana Obrenovića*, p. 9.

9. Vrhovna komanda srpske vojske, ed., *Rat Srbije sa Turskom za oslobodjenje i nezavisnost 1877–1878* (Belgrade, 1879); Petar Pešić, *Naš rat s Turskom 1876–77* (Belgrade, 1925); Sava Grujić, *Operacije Timočko–Moravske vojske*, vol. 1 (Belgrade, n. d.); idem, *Bitka na Djunisu: XI Prilog za istoriju srpsko–turskog rata 1876* (Belgrade,

1898); idem, *Borba za odbranu istočne granice: V Prilog za istoriju srpsko–turskog rata te godine* (Belgrade, 1898); I. I. Rostunov, *Russko–Tureckaia voina 1877–1878* (Moscow, 1898); Belić, *Ratovi srpskog naroda,* p. 76; Petar Opačić, "Vojne operacije u srpsko–turskom ratu 1876," in *Medjunarodni naučni skup povodom 100-godišnjice ustanka u Bosni i Hercegovini,* vol. 2 (Sarajevo, 1977).

10. Dimitrije Djordjevic, *Revolutions nationales des peuples balcaniques 1804–1914* (Belgrade, 1962), pp. 120–32.

11. Andra Knićanin, *Ratni dnevnik,* vol. 1 (Belgrade, 1881), pp. 1–2, 7.

12. Putnik, *Misli o vojenoj organizaciji,* p. 41.

13. Mita Petrović, *Ratne beleške 1876, 1877 i 1878* (Čačak, 1955), p. 55.

14. On the Serbian officer corps, see Putnik, *Misli o vojenoj organizaciji,* pp. 25, 27, 30, 34; Ekmečić, *Srpska vojska,* pp. 103–4.

15. Savo Skoko and Petar Opačić, *Vojvoda Stepa Stepanović u ratovima Srbije 1876–1918,* 4th ed. (Belgrade, 1981), pp. 37, 40, 47, 53, 59–60; Živojin Mišić, *Moje uspomene,* 3d ed. (Belgrade, 1981), pp. 31–79.

16. David MacKenzie, *The Lion of Tashkent: The Career of General M. G. Cherniaev* (Athens, 1974), p. 126.

17. Djuzepe Barbanti–Brodano, *Garibaldinci na Drini 1876* (Belgrade, 1958), p. 204.

18. Vladimir Karić, *Srbija, opis zemlje, naroda i države* (Belgrade, 1887), pp. 216–18, 253, 615–16.

19. Milutin Spasić, *Srpsko–turski rat: Ratne beleške* (Novi Sad, 1877), p. 23.

20. Karić, *Srbija,* p. 218.

21. Spasić, *Ratne beleške,* p. 23.

22. Petrović, *Ratne beleške,* p. 72.

23. Idem, p. 66.

24. Idem, p. 73.

25. Vladan Djordjević, *Srpsko–turski rat: Uspomene i beleške iz 1876, 1877 i 1878 godine,* vol. 2 (Belgrade, 1907), pp. 159–60.

26. Mišić, *Moje uspomene,* p. 70.

27. Putnik, *Misli o vojenoj organizaciji,* p. 14.

28. Ekmečić, *Srpska vojska,* pp. 105–6.

29. Barbanti–Brodano, *Garibaldinci,* p. 204; Mišić, *Moje uspomene,* p. 68; Putnik, *Misli o vojenoj organizaciji,* p. 113.

30. Živanović, *Politička istorija Srbije,* p. 339. In July Chernyayev issued a special proclamation to the Bulgarians calling them "to stand up and throw off the evils of oppression" (Grujić, *Bugarski dobrovoljci,* p. 35).

31. Grujić, *Bugarski dobrovoljci,* pp. 19, 23.

32. The participation of volunteers in the 1876 war is treated in other papers in this volume.

33. Svetozar Magdalenić, *Slike iz naših ratova sa Turcima i Bugarima 1876, 1877–1878 i 1885–1886 godine,* vol. 1 (Belgrade, 1910), pp. 1–3; Barbanti–Brodano, *Garibaldinci,* pp. 203–4.

34. Magdalenić describes a Russian volunteer who rushed toward the Turkish lines, rolling up his sleeves and yelling: "I shall strangle them all, like dogs, with my bare hands!" (*Slike iz naših ratova,* p. 14). See also Ekmečić, *Srpska vojska,* p. 120."

35. Magdalenić, *Slike iz naših ratova,* p. 39; MacKenzie, *The Lion of Tashkent,* pp. 124, 127. For a description of the various types of volunteers, see Djordjević, *Srpsko–turski rat,* p. 175; Knićanin, *Dnevnik,* pp. 165–66, 189–91.

36. Ekmečić, *Srpska vojska,* p. 119.

37. Barbanti–Brodano, *Garibaldinci,* pp. 146–47.

38. Pera Todorović, *Dnevnik jednog dobrovoljca* (Belgrade, 1964), p. 149.

39. Barbanti–Brodano, *Garibaldinci,* pp. 212–13, 207, 219–20.

40. Idem, pp. 109–10.

41. Dorothy Anderson, *The Balkan Volunteers* (London, 1968), pp. 13–41.

Most of these women were dedicated, patient, and liberal-minded. From Russia came some fifty to sixty young women, among them the niece of Bakunin, to serve in hospitals. An interesting personality was Jelena Markusova, from Holland, who joined the volunteers on the River Drina and smoked, drank, and fought with them on horseback with saber and revolver in hand. The Serbian poet Djura Jakšić compared her to Joan of Arc in one of his poems. Later accused by Russian intelligence of being an Austrian (or British? ) spy, she had to leave Serbia (Spasić, *Ratne beleške*, pp. 37–38; Knićanin, *Dnevnik*, p. 44).

42. Grujić, *Bugarski dobrovoljci*, pp. 33–34; Todorović, *Dnevnik jednog dobrovoljca*, p. 59.

43. Djordjević, *Srpsko–turski rat*, pp. 457–60.

44. Spasić, *Ratne beleške*, pp. 6–7.

45. Ignjić, "Dogadjaji na Drini," p. 240.

46. Djordjević, *Srpsko–turski rat*, pp. 118–19.

47. Spasić, *Ratne beleške*, p. 12.

48. Todorović, *Dnevnik jednog dobrovoljca*, p. 63.

49. Grujić, *Bugarski dobrovoljci*, p. 19.

50. Honest and courageous, he knew only two commands: "Charge" and "Don't retreat" (Knićanin, *Dnevnik*, pp. 74–75).

51. Spasić, *Ratne beleške*, p. 36.

52. Idem, pp. 19, 47–48; MacKenzie, *The Lion of Tashkent*, p. 142.

53. Stanislav Binički, *Odlomci iz ratnih beležaka 1876 godine* (Belgrade, 1891), p. 4; also Petrović, *Ratne beleške*, p. 66; Mišić, *Moje uspomene*, p. 69.

54. Ekmečić, *Srpska vojska*, p. 104.

55. Knićanin, *Dnevnik*, pp. 24–25, 27–28, 47.

56. Putnik, *Misli o vojenoj organizaciji*, p. 17.

57. Djordjević describes the terrible scene of the execution (*Srpsko–turski rat*, pp. 68–71).

58. Mišić, *Moje uspomene*, p. 69.

59. Petrović, *Ratne beleške*, p. 71.

60. Todorović, *Dnevnik jednog dobrovoljca*, p. 81.

61. Petrović, *Ratne beleške*, pp. 155–57.

62. Djordjević, *Srpsko–turski rat*, p. 124.

63. Idem, p. 56.

64. Binički, *Odlomci iz ratnih beležaka*, pp. 32, 34.

65. Spasić, *Ratne beleške*, pp. 16, 18; Jevrem Grujić, *Zapisi: Druga vlada Obrenovića i turski ratovi*, vol. 3 (Belgrade, 1923), p. 287; Petrović, *Ratne beleške*, pp. 52, 145–48.

66. Mišić, *Moje uspomene*, p. 68.

67. Putnik, *Misli o vojenoj organizaciji*, p. 5.

68. Petrović, *Ratne beleške*, pp. 51, 63; Todorović, *Dnevnik jednog dobrovoljca*, p. 67.

69. Petrović, *Ratne beleške*, pp. 52, 79.

70. Mišić, *Moje uspomene*, pp. 55–56.

71. Idem, pp. 114–15.

72. Idem, pp. 88–89, 103.

73. Spasić, *Ratne beleške*, pp. 45–46.

74. Jovanović, *Vlada Milana Obrenovića*, p. 91.

# IV
# Peacemaking

Vladien N. Vinogradov

# THE BERLIN CONGRESS OF 1878 AND THE HISTORY OF THE BALKANS

The Berlin Congress epitomized the rivalry, more than a century in duration, between the Great Powers in the Balkans. Two courses clashed at Berlin: that of Russia, which sought to undermine the domination of the Porte on the peninsula, and that of Britain, supported by Austria–Hungary, whose efforts were aimed at preserving the status quo in southeastern Europe, in other words, perpetuating Ottoman power there in a slightly modified and modernized form. As Kh. Khristov has written, "The Anglo–Russian contradictions in the Balkans and the Near East were the main axis on which the policy of the Great Powers revolved."[1] Nonetheless, we cannot view the Balkans of the time merely as the scene of a squabble among the great vultures. Congress participants could not ignore the powerful impact of the liberation movements of the Balkan peoples themselves.

The judgment passed on the Congress by contemporaries was unanimous: Russia had suffered its bitterest defeat, and British policy had won the day. Naturally, Bulgaria was deep in grief, but the disappointed Russian public went into mourning too, its government everywhere scathingly criticized for having lost the fruits of its victory. At student gatherings and in artistocratic salons, among enraged Pan-Slavists and discontented officers, the public found its scapegoat in the unlucky diplomats. In Britain, on the other hand, Parliament, the court, and the press appraised the treaty signed in Berlin as their triumph. Prime Minister Benjamin Disraeli and Foreign Minister Robert Salisbury received the Order of the Garter for their success.

But is the judgment of history the same as the often hasty and shortsighted judgment of contemporaries? On the basis of the study of documents and archival materials, by comparing the results of the Congress with the decades of previous history and placing these events in historical perspective, Soviet historiography has come to the conclusion that in this case the contemporaries were wrong.

In their penetrating analyses of the Eastern Question, Marx, Engels, and Lenin invariably stressed the selfish aims of all the powers in the Balkans, each seeking to turn the region into its own sphere of influence. This characterization applied to the policies of all the Great Powers without exception. There are no grounds whatever for depicting the rivalry in the Balkans exclusively as the "defense" of the Western powers, in the first place Britain, against tsarism or as defense of the imperial lifelines. Tsarist policy was dictated by the possibilities open to it and guided by political and military-strategic considerations. The question of territorial expansion in the Balkans had already been removed from the agenda before the Russo—Turkish War of 1828—29. During his well-known visit to St. Petersburg in the spring of 1826, the Duke of Wellington requested and received confirmation of the abandonment of all tsarist territorial claims in the Balkans. On four occasions this policy was recorded in official acts: the Anglo—Russian St. Petersburg Protocol (April 1826); the Treaty of London (July 1827); the so-called Impartiality Protocol (December 1827); and the Tsar's Manifesto on the Declaration of War (April 1828). The Treaty of Adrianople did not contravene these obligations. For tsarist Russia the question was one of political influence, not territorial expansion.

Soviet historians draw a hard-and-fast distinction between the undoubtedly selfish plans and designs of tsarism — its desire to establish its predoninance in the region — and the objective results of Russia's policy. A monument to the role played by Russia in the Balkans is the consolidation and international recognition of first autonomous and then independent states of Serbia, Greece, Romania, and Bulgaria achieved through the liberation movements of these peoples and the Russo—Turkish Wars. Here is the authoritative commentary of William Ewart Gladstone: "Unquestionably, Russia is the protector of the Slavs.... To all appearances she has offered them a service as splendid and durable as ever was conferred by a great state on an oppressed and unhappy people."[2] Some English scholars take this position also; according to the historian Robert Seton—Watson,

> Today it is no longer possible to deny that the Russian advance ended a corrupt and altogether effete regime and, by letting air and light into regions that had been hermetically sealed for centuries, was a real gain for civilization. ...The undoubted advantage of Russia... rested on ties of blood and religion, strengthened by the fact that despite many faults and ambitions, she had repeatedly made sacrifices for the Christians of the East such as no other Power had made and was therefore regarded as their natural champion and liberator.[3]

Britain's policy of maintaining the status quo in southeastern Europe discounted the interests of the minority peoples. This was most evident during the preparations for and in the course of the Crimean War of 1853—56. On the eve of that war Lord John Russell, one of the leading members of the British cabinet, proposed extracting the eyeteeth of the bear by destroying the Russian fleet and arsenal on the Black Sea, even though in 1841 Russia had signed a convention on the straits that prohibited the passage of war vessels. Locked in the Black Sea, its fleet did not present any danger to Istanbul or to British communications in the Mediterranean. As a result of the war, Russia's sovereign right to protect the shores of the Black Sea, which are not British but Russian, Bulgarian, and Romanian, was violated.

Another aspect of the activity of the Anglo–French coalition in 1853–56 was the suppression of the liberation movement in the Balkans. In their treaty of alliance with Turkey, London and Paris declared: "The existence of the Ottoman Empire in its present limits is essential to the maintenance of the balance of power among the states of Europe."[4] The peoples subject to the Porte were sacrificed for the sake of the "balance of power" (and, in fact, the goal of Anglo–French hegemony). The outcome of the war meant the prolongation of the direct Ottoman domination over Bulgarians, Bosnians, Hercegovinians, and a sizable portion of the Serbians and Greeks. The movement for reunification with kindred lands that began in the Greek kingdom was put down by Anglo–French occupation (General Forait's division and the British Forty-seventh Infantry Regiment).

According to the English historian R. T. Shannon, "after 1856 the Foreign Office expended immense energy and ingenuity in ignoring obstinately the mounting evidence that its Eastern policy was getting increasingly out of touch with reality."[5] Indeed, the system established at Paris tried to preserve a structure whose day had passed: the domination of the Ottoman Empire over much of southeastern Europe, the detachment of southern Bessarabia from Russia, and the prohibition of a Russian fleet on the Black Sea. This system was being eroded on two sides: on the one side, by the liberation movements of the oppressed peoples and, on the other, by Russia's vigorous diplomatic activity. The best proof of its lack of viability and its imminent doom was the crisis that broke out shortly after the signing of the Paris Treaty of 1856. In 1859 its architects were forced to sanction the unification of the Danubian principalities and the creation of a new state, Romania. In 1866 the uprising on Crete almost effected the island's separation from the sultan's possessions. In 1870 Russia's Chancellor A. M. Gorchakov undertook a resolute and successful diplomatic action: he declared that Russia would no longer accept the prohibition of a Russian fleet on the Black Sea. The London Conference of 1871 formally acknowledged the accomplished fact. Unrest and uprisings continued in the Balkans, culminating in the 1875 uprising in Bosnia and Hercegovina and the April 1876 uprising in Bulgaria.

The St. Petersburg court anxiously watched the drama unfolding in southeastern Europe. To the end of their days, the generation of diplomats of the Gorchakov school never forgot the lessons of the Crimean War and were afraid of rousing "all Europe" against Russia by intervening in the conflict. Gorchakov's famous statement after the conclusion of the Paris Treaty — "Russia is not pouting but rallying itself" — meant that in the Balkan theater tsarism went over to protracted defense. Diplomatic isolation (despite the Three Emperors' League), the tense situation within the country, the unceasing struggle against the revolutionary movement, extreme depletion of finances, and the incomplete state of the military reform all dictated extreme caution. In reality this was impossible, all the more so since, with the uprisings in Bosnia, Hercegovina, and Bulgaria and the entry of Serbia and Montenegro into a war with the Ottoman Empire, a wave of sympathy for the South Slavs, active and effective, swept over Russia. "Fortunately," wrote A. I. Herzen, "the Winter Palace is not the whole of Russia and even not the whole of St. Petersburg. ...The other Russia is hailing you and extending her hand to you."[6] Volunteers went to the Balkans, funds were raised, and, most important, the government came under strong pressure to provide military aid to the insurgents, the only measure that could save the situation.[7] Serbia's defeat in the war and the crushing of the heroic April Uprising showed that the forces within the Balkans were inadequate to throw off the yoke of the Porte.

For two years tsarism tried to induce the Concert of Europe and the Ottoman Empire to resolve the question by introducing comparatively broad reforms in the Balkans and failed completely. The diplomatic sounding undertaken in Vienna had a sobering effect. The desire to prevent Austria–Hungary's active interference impelled St. Petersburg to make considerable concessions. Under the Budapest Convention (January 1877) it agreed to the Austrian occupation of Bosnia and Hercegovina. The tsarist government knew how painfully this news would be received in Russia. In the course of the negotiations it also discarded the possibility of establishing a large Slavic state. Since the possible achievements of a war had been reduced to the minimum in advance, the convention was not conducive to the fanning of warlike sentiments among the initiated few. Lastly, both the court and the ministry realized that the most dangerous foreign enemy was Britain, which was prepared at any propitious moment and by any means, whether political pressure, financial pressure, the threat of forming a coalition, or the declaration of war, to deprive Russia and the Balkan peoples of the fruits of their victories.

Official Russian policy veered between two poles — the pressure of the public, which insisted on a liberation campaign in the Balkans, and the numerous apprehensions caused by the hostility of Britain and Austria–Hungary, the fear, that is, of repeating the "Crimean situation" with its attendant internal complications. It is extremely important, however, that in the end the proclaimed main aim of the war was the liberation of the Balkan peoples, clearly demonstrating that the pressure exerted by public opinion on the ruling circles was highly successful. It is important also that from the very start St. Petersburg declared unambiguously that neither the occupation of Constantinople nor the possession of the straits was a part of its plans. Gorchakov asserted in his announcement of May 18/30, 1877, that "without being able to determine in advance the development and course of the war, the imperial cabinet nonetheless reiterates that the occupation of this capital is not in the plans" and that "to preserve peace and general calm," the question of the Black Sea Straits would have to be settled "with general consent on just and truly all-European principles." Thus, in advance the tsarist government left two important problems of continental importance to the judgment of the powers, being perfectly well aware that it would not be supported by the majority of them. Gorchakov also wrote about the deep sympathy of the Russian people for the "miserable plight of the Christians" in the Balkans, linked as they were with the Russians by ties of "faith and race." He justly pointed out that the discontinuation of the "intolerable abuses" of the Ottoman administration "does not contradict any European interests."[8]

Initially, the peace program formulated by the moderate party headed by Gorchakov called for a "small war" with an offensive pressed up to the Balkan Range but not crossing it. Provisions were made for the formation of an autonomous Bulgaria to the north of the Balkans, the introduction of a "regular" administration (this formulation was Alexander II's) in its southern part, expansion of Serbia and Montenegro, the restitution to Russia of southern Bessarabia, which had been wrested from it in 1856, and the transfer of part of Dobruja to Romania. Austria–Hungary was offered "compensation in Bosnia and, partly, in Hercegovina"[9] (but not annexation of these regions as a whole).

These initial comparatively modest intentions soon changed. Contacts with representatives of the Bulgarian public and the enthusiasm with which Bulgarians joined volunteer units convinced the Russian government that this integral country could not be divided. On May 30/June 11 and June 1/13 Gorchakov sent telegrams to Ambassador P. A. Shuvalov in London containing important changes in the Russian peace program on the key Bulgarian question. Gorchakov informed his ambassador that it would be impossible to leave under the Ottoman yoke that part of the country that had "suffered most severely from Turkish massacres" and that was inhabited by "the most numerous, industrious, and developed population." Bulgaria "must be integral and autonomous," he concluded.[10]

The truly national character of the struggle in the Balkans, the universal support for the Russian army, and the magnificent victories of the Russian and allied warriors led to the collapse of the moderate peace program. Policy was now shaped not by the cautious Gorchakov but by a group headed by War Minister D. A. Milyutin and former Ambassador to Constantinople N. P. Ignatyev. The viewpoint of this circle was incorporated into the San Stefano preliminary peace treaty.

The war cost Russia dearly. The figure of 200,000 dead and wounded speaks for itself. But the human resources of the country were not, of course, depleted. By great financial exertions the armed forces were kept at the level of 1,800,000 men. It was not the losses but the fear of an assault by Austria—Hungary that compelled the withdrawal of troops from the Balkan army beginning in March 1878. The experience of the Crimean War had shown that the British navy could strike at Russian shores in the Black Sea, the Baltic, and the Pacific. This was a compelling motive for the dispersion of the Russian forces. It was fear of encirclement, of a coalition of powers, not the impossibility of continuing the war, that compelled tsarism to make concessions and to agree to the British demand that "any treaty between the government of Russia and the Porte affecting the treaties of 1856 and 1871 must have an all-European character."[11] The outcome of this was the agreement between Shuvalov and Salisbury and the Berlin Treaty of 1878, revising, to the detriment of Russia and the Balkan peoples, the conditions of the San Stefano peace.

The question arises whether this result was a compromise or a Russian surrender. In Russia, recognition was universal that it did grave and ruinous damage to the Balkan peoples, first and foremost to the Bulgarians, and that new obstacles had been erected to their complete liberation. Even official circles close to the court and far from progressive realized that an unnatural dissection of a nation had been conducted in Berlin. The hope was expressed, however, that the situation would not persist for long. The perspicacious Milyutin was confident that "no matter what limitations are now placed by European diplomacy on the independence of southern Bulgaria, no matter how restrictive the frontiers fixed for it, . . . the small autonomous Bulgaria now being formed in the northern Balkans will serve as a core for a future aggregation of the Bulgarian people in one independent state."[12] In the same vein were statements made by N. K. Giers, then assistant foreign minister. The Russian authorities took steps to encourage this view. Consuls were instructed "to apply all efforts to maintaining . . . ties between the two halves of Bulgaria and countering all influences directed to disuniting them."[13] Milyutin called for moving quickly to form a Bulgarian army from inhabitants of both sides of the Balkan Range as a real guarantee of the existence of the new state and a precondition for its unification.[14]

Indeed, only a few years passed before the artificial dismemberment of

Bulgaria imposed by the Berlin Congress collapsed. True, the Berlin retreat caused many difficulties for tsarism within the country. Except for a few liberals, the public, which had hailed the San Stefano treaty and had no idea of the Reichstadt talks or the Budapest Cenvention, not to mention the Shuvalov–Salisbury understanding, revolted at the decisions of the Congress. The hopes of the Russian court for the consolidation of its position and an increase in its prestige in the country were dashed. The career of Shuvalov, the main Russian negotiator in Berlin (though ranked as the second delegate), was in shambles, and Gorchakov's star went into decline.

But the judgment of history and the judgments of historians must be passed not on the spur of the moment or under the influence of momentary feelings. On the strength of documents, on the basis of a sober and rounded analysis of the situation, the Berlin Treaty was a significant step forward in the liberation of the Balkans.

The crisis of 1875–78 was precipitated by the Balkan peoples and reached its culmination in the Russo–Turkish War. The combat strength of the Russian army was 554,000 men. Operations against Turkey were conducted by Romanian, Montenegrin, and Serbian men and officers and by the Bulgarian militia. Khristov rightly says that "the liberation of Bulgaria was achieved by Russia's material and military forces with the direct and active participation of the Bulgarian people."[15]

Lenin wrote that the war of 1877 consisted of "bourgeois-national movements or 'convulsions' of bourgeois society freeing itself from various forms of feudalism."[16] He saw the most vital "interest of the people" in "powerful bourgeois-progressive national movements involving millions."[17]

The sequel of 1875–78 was magnificent for the Balkans in the most crucial meaning of the word: the revival of the Bulgarian state after five hundred years under the Ottoman yoke and international recognition of the independence and territorial expansion of Serbia, Montenegro, and Romania. These epoch-making events speak for themselves. In the course of the Balkan crisis and the Russo–Turkish War, important social changes also took place in southeastern Europe. A bourgeois-democratic revolution was accomplished in Bulgaria. The process of bourgeois development, progressive at that time, and the parallel process of the formation of capitalism's concomitant and gravedigger, the proletariat, developed with growing force here and in other Balkan states. The domestic market expanded, closer links were established with the foreign market, the socialist movement struck roots, and Marxism began to spread in its ranks.

All this happened despite the terms of the Berlin Treaty, which in a number of cases inhibited the national and social development of the Balkan peoples. This is why Soviet historical scholarship as a whole shares the conclusion of A. L. Narochnitsky that "the Western powers could only weaken but not eradicate the results of the Russo—Turkish War and the liberation movement of the Balkan peoples."[18]

The Anglo—Austrian policy of preserving the status quo in southeastern Europe collapsed. Comparison of the British program and the Berlin results makes clear their incongruity. Lord Derby, reputedly the most moderate of British ministers, had rejected the very idea of forming even a small Bulgaria, seeing in it a forerunner of the ruin of the Ottoman Empire. His successor Salisbury, in the memorandum of April 1, 1878, that was the basic programmatic document of British policy, opposed an outlet to the Black Sea for Bulgaria, the return of southern Bessarabia to Russia, and the incorporation into Russia of Batum and some Armenian regions. All this was now consigned to oblivion. Most important, the Berlin Congress put paid to the status quo policy that for three-quarters of a century had obstructed the processes of national liberation and recognized the failure of attempts to preserve the Porte's domination over a greater part of the peninsula. All this crumbled under the pressure of the Balkan peoples and as a result of the Russo—Turkish War. There are therefore no grounds whatever for regarding the Congress as a sort of diplomatic Cannae at which Disraeli routed and put to flight his opponents.

British plans with regard to the Ottoman Empire now became more modest. It was decided to press only for the integrity of the Ottoman possessions in Asia — that part of it, of course, which adjoined Russia. Hence the guarantee of the Turkish possessions in Asia, which did not prevent the direct imperialist seizure of Cyprus, supposedly to strengthen the Turkish "defense." Lord Salisbury, the main architect of the British plans, admitted the utter failure of the old principles (true, not in an official declaration but in a letter to Laird, his ambassador in Constantinople): "The time has passed for talking about 'independence and integrity.' It was something of a sham in 1856, as events have proved. But it would be a mockery now. The Porte must recognize that it needs protection."[19] This "protection" meant the further subordination of the Porte to British policy.

There was, of course, another and more gloomy tendency in the decisions of the Berlin Congress shaped by the position of Britain and the countries supporting it. In leaving a considerable part of the South Slavic lands under the Porte's authority and placing Bosnia and Hercegovina under Austro—Hungarian occupation, the Congress sowed the seeds of the numerous conflicts and military clashes which provided the grounds for calling the Balkans "the powder keg of Europe." The contribution of the Anglo—Austrian "peacemakers" in the persons of Disraeli, Salisbury, and Andrássy to this part of the Congress's decisions was decisive.

It is worthwhile dwelling on one more problem connected with the Berlin Congress: tsarism and the Balkans. To quote V. M. Khvostov, "In its actual results, the Russo—Turkish War fell far short of what the tsarist government that declared it had sought to achieve. It did not strengthen but weakened tsarism's influence on the world scene."[20] This comment reflects the general consensus of Soviet historiography. The point is proved by the disagreements between the ruling circles of Bulgaria and Russia in the 1880s. At times attention is drawn to the quarrel between Alexander III and Prince Alexander of Battenberg, which, of course, contributed its bit to the deterioration of relations between the two countries. But this dispute developed in the framework of the general relationship of tsarism to the Balkans. Frederick Engels wrote on this score, "It is known that a strong anti-Russian party was formed in every state that arose on Turkish territory and attained full or partial independence. And if this was so at a time when Russia's aid was the only refuge from the Turkish yoke, what can we expect when the fear of this oppression disappears?"[21]

The overthrow or weakening of Ottoman power in one region or another, achieved with the help of Russian troops and diplomacy, gave impulse to economic and social processes that brought to social life new strata with the young Balkan bourgeoisie at their head. The progressive circles positively disposed toward a forward-looking Russia hated tsarism. The bourgeois strata, with their craving for business activity, turned their gaze not to the backward state in the East but to the West, seeking economic and political cooperation. Russia's successes in southeastern Europe led in the long run not to the strengthening but to the weakening of tsarism's positions there. In the 1830s Greece, liberated with considerable help from Russia, came into the sphere of influence of the West; in the 1850s the Danubian principalities and in the 1860s Serbia became part of the Austrian orbit.

To some extent tsarist diplomats recognized the sad circumstance that Russia's successes abroad did not benefit it. In a note of March 28/April 9, 1878, Gorchakov asserted that the exclusive aim of the temporary administrative measures in Bulgaria "is to contribute to national development and make possible the convocation of the first Bulgarian assembly for finalizing the organization of the principality." And he added, "If Moldavia—Wallachia, which owed its existence to Russia and is its neighbor, became totally independent of it, there is all the more reason to anticipate the same result in relation to Bulgaria, territorially separated from Russia."[22]

The historical significance of the Russo—Balkan ties lies in the fact that Russia contributed — in wartime by military operations and in peacetime, despite all the zigzags and retreats in tsarist policy, by other means — to the undermining of Ottoman domination in the region, thereby bringing nearer the decade, the year, the day of liberation. As D. Kosev has put it, "every educated person knows full well that in the long run, after nearly a century of struggle, the Balkan peoples, always linked in decisive moments with

Russia and Russo–Turkish wars, achieved emancipation, although not complete, and created independent Balkan states, while Russia did not get even a patch of land on the Balkan Peninsula."[23]

## NOTES

1.  Kh. Khristov, *Osvobozjzdenieto na Bolgaria i politika ta na zapadnite derczavi* *(The Liberation of Bulgaria and the Policy of the Western Powers)* (Sofia, 1968), p. 171.
2.  *Parliamentary Debates*, 3d ser., vol. 237, p. 1367.
3.  R. W. Seton–Watson, *Disraeli, Gladstone, and the Eastern Question* (London, 1935), pp. 4, 20.
4.  J. C. Hurewitz, *Diplomacy in the Middle East* (New York, 1972), p. 144.
5.  R. T. Shannon, *Gladstone and the Bulgarian Agitation* (London, 1963), p. 16.
6.  A. I. Herzen, *Poln. sobr. soch... (Complete Works)*, vol. 10 (St. Petersburg, 1919), p. 437.
7.  Some of the latest works on this subject are: *Russko–turetzkaia vojna 1877–1878. (Russo–Turkish War of 1877–1878)* (Moscow, 1977); *Russko–turetzkaia vojna 1877–1878 i Balkani (Russo–Turkish War of 1877–1878 and the Balkans)* (Moscow, 1978); *Stoletie osvobojzdenia Bolgarii ot osmanskogo iga. (The Centenary of Bulgaria's Liberation from the Ottoman Yoke)* (Moscow, 1978); *Rossija i natzionalno-osvoboditelnaja vojna na Balkanah (Russia and the National-Liberation War in the Balkans)* (Moscow, 1978); *Stoletie osvobojzdenija balkanakih narodov ot osmanskogo iga. (The Centenary of the Liberation of the Balkan Peoples from the Ottoman Yoke)* (Moscow, 1979); A. L. Narochnitsky, "Balkanskij krizis 1875–1878 i velikie derjzavi" (The Balkan Crisis of 1875–1878 and the Great Powers), *Voprosy istorii*, no. 11, 1976 and "Berlinskij kongress, Rossija i jujznie slavjane" (Berlin Congress, Russia, and the South Slavs), *Novaya i noveishaya istoriya*, no. 2, 1979; V. N. Vinogradov, *Russko-turetzkaja vojna 1877–1878 i osvobejzdenie Bolgarii (The Russo–Turkish War of 1877–1878 and the Liberation of Bulgaria)* (Moscow, 1978); K. B. Vinogradov, "Nakanune russko–turetzkoj vojni 1877–1878." (On the Eve of the Russo–Turkish War of 1877), *Istoriya SSSR*, no. 1, 1978; A. A. Ulunyan, *Aprolskoje vosstanie 1876 v Bolgarii i Rossija (The April Rising of 1876 in Bulgaria and Russia)* (Moscow, 1978); L. I. Narochnitskaya, *Rossija i natzionalno-osvoboditelnoje dvijzonie na Balkanah v 1875–1878 (Russia and the National-Liberation Movement in the Balkans in 1875–1878)* (Moscow, 1979); V. P. Chorniy, *Geroicheskaja epopeia bolgarskogo naroda (The Heroic Epic of the Bulgarian People)* (L'vov, 1976).
8.  *Osvobojzdenie Bolgarii et turetzkogo iga (The Liberation of Bulgaria from the Turkish Yoke)*, vol. 2 (Moscow, 1964), pp. 80–82.
9.  S. L. Chernov, "Osnovnie etapi razvitija russkoj ofitzialnoj programmi reshenija Vostochnogo voprosa v vojne s Turtziej (1877–1878)," *Russko–turetzkaja vojna 1877–1878 i Balkani (The Russo–Turkish War of 1877–1878 and the Balkans)* (Moscow, 1978), p. 29.
10.  *Osvobojzdenie Bolgarii et Turetzkogo iga (The Liberation of Bulgaria from Turkish Yoke)*, vol. 2, pp. 107–8.
11.  AVRP (Archive of Russia's Foreign Policy), Chancellery Fund, 1878, Case 58, Sheet 37.
12.  D. A. Milyutin, *Dnevnik*, vol. 3 (Moscow, 1950), pp. 69–70.
13.  *Osvobojzdenie Bolgarii ot turetzkogo iga (The Liberation of Bulgaria from the Turkish Yoke)*, vol. 3, p. 207.
14.  Ibid., p. 160.
15.  Khristov, *Osvobojzdenieto na Bolgarija*, p. 12.
16.  V. I. Lenin, *Complete Works* (in Russian), vol. 26, p. 144.

17. V. I. Lenin, *Complete Works* (in Russian), vol. 2, p. 101.
18. "Berlin Congress," p. 83.
19. Seton–Watson, *Disraeli, Gladstone, and the Eastern Question,* p. 426.
20. *The History of Diplomacy,* vol. 2 (Moscow, 1963), p. 133.
21. K. Marx and F. Engels, *Works* (in Russian), vol. 9, p. 32.
22. AVRP, Chancellery Fund, 1878, Case 58, Sheet 286–288.
23. *Novaya i noveishaya istoriya,* no. 5, 1979, pp. 36–37.

Hristo Hristov

# RETROSPECT AND ANALYSIS OF THE SAN STEFANO TREATY

The Treaty of San Stefano was the result of Russia's victorious war against the Ottoman Empire in 1877–78. At the cost of great material losses and casualties in a war that lasted nearly a year, the forces of the Ottoman state were routed and the Sublime Porte was compelled to seek an armistice and peace. A large number of Bulgarian volunteer detachments — combat, reconnaissance, transport, and supply units — were active during the war in support of the Russian army. This represented the continuation of the Bulgarian national liberation struggle and its amalgamation with the military operations of the Russian army. The participation on the Russian side of Romanian, Serbian, and Montenegrin troops also contributed to the Russian victory.

The Bulgarian national liberation struggle was an important factor in the victory and hence in Bulgaria's liberation not only because of the Bulgarians' direct participation in the war but because of the role of their struggle in creating the prerequisites for its declaration, conduct, and outcome. Without it the Bulgarian national question would not have been raised before the public and the governments of the major European states, the Constantinople Conference would not have been convened, and the Russo–Turkish War would not have been declared.

Another significance of the Bulgarian national liberation struggle was that in the course of it the Bulgarian nation was consolidated, its self-awareness strengthened, and its differentiation from the other Balkan nations effected. National self-awareness contributed to the determination of the territorial scope of the nation. It played an essential role in the discussions of the Bulgarian question and the working out of proposals for its solution by international diplomatic conferences and meetings.

The goal of Bulgarian national self-determination was important in defining the boundaries of the Bulgarian state during the drafting of the Treaty of San Stefano. It is true that the treaty was the work of Russian diplomacy, imposed after a prolonged and blood-drenched war to satisfy the interests of the Russian state in resolving the complex and tangled Eastern Question. As regards the restoration of the Bulgarian state, however, the Treaty of San Stefano conformed to an objective process, confirming the boundaries of the Bulgarian nation that it had itself determined during the national-revival period. These boundaries had been recognized by the Ottoman authorities in 1870 by the issuance of a *ferman* establishing the Bulgarian Exarchate.

The diocese of the Bulgarian Exarchate comprised modern northern and southern Bulgaria, Dobruja, the upper reaches of the Morava River, and a considerable part of Macedonia. The *ferman* of 1870 provided for the inclusion in the Exarchate of new territories in the event that the Orthodox population, or two-thirds of it in a particular area, sought through a referendum to come under its jurisdiction. Such referenda were held under the control of the Ottoman authorities in many areas of Macedonia, and thus practically all of Macedonia was included in the diocese. The boundaries of the Bulgarian principality envisaged by the Treaty of San Stefano in general corresponded to those of the Bulgarian Exarchate. Obviously this was not accidental. In working out the treaty, Russian diplomacy took into consideration which territories were inhabited by a predominantly Bulgarian population.

The self-determination of the Bulgarian nation was expressed not only in the establishment of the Exarchate but in many other events in the course of the struggle for liberation. Even when the idea of creating a Balkan or South Slavic federation was discussed, the leaders of the Bulgarian liberation movement included in the Bulgarian state all the areas in which the population defined itself as Bulgarian, including Moesia, Thrace, and Macedonia. Such a formulation was, for instance, embodied in the draft protocol prepared by the Slavic Benevolent Society for the establishment of a joint South Slavic state by Bulgaria and Serbia.

Demands for national self-determination and delineation of the boundaries of the Bulgarian nation were included in many documents of the Bulgarian revolutionary movement after the Crimean War. In numerous articles published in the Bulgarian national-revival press and in their personal correspondence, all the major figures of the revolutionary movement, such as Georgi Rakovski, Vasil Levski, Lyuben Karavelov, Hristo Botev, and many others, declared themselves in favor of national self-determination and unification of the regions in which the majority of the population was Bulgarian.

The events which developed in the Balkans in the nineteenth century in connection with the liberation struggles of the Serbs, Greeks, and Bulgarians were closely watched by the Western European states, Austria—Hungary, and

Russia. Under the pressure of these struggles and the accelerated disintegration of the ruling feudal system, the Ottoman Empire moved toward its decline. The question arose who would be its heir in the Balkans and who would take possession of Constantinople and the straits. Russia and the Habsburg Empire confronted each other in the Balkans, while Britain and Russia were the chief rivals for Constantinople and the straits.

There is no question that Russia, Austria–Hungary, and the Western European states had the same objective in the Balkans: the extraction of maximum territorial and other gains from the decaying Ottoman Empire. There were differences, however, in the implementation and results of this policy. Russia was working toward the destruction of the empire by assisting the liberation struggles of the peoples enslaved by it. The Western states, in contrast, sought to preserve the empire so that they might subject it to their political and economic interests, and for this reason they essentially opposed the liberation struggles of the Balkan peoples or made insignificant concessions when things reached the point of unrest, uprisings, and mutinies.

The Balkan peoples saw in Russia an ally and protector. This was especially true of the Bulgarians. Some of the most eminent figures of the Bulgarian national revival had studied in Russia. The new Bulgarian educational system had been developed with its assistance. Its diplomacy had helped in the solution of the Bulgarian church problem. At international conferences and meetings after the Crimean War, Russia's diplomacy had raised the question of administrative self-rule for the Bulgarians and the other peoples enslaved by the Turks.

After the outbreak of the Eastern crisis of 1875 (the uprisings in Bosnia, Hercegovina, and Bulgaria), the two states most interested in the events in the Balkans — Russia and Austria–Hungary — tried to coordinate their policies toward the Ottoman Empire. The following year led to a new complication in the situation; the April Uprising broke out in Bulgaria and the Serbo–Turkish War was declared. This made the Russian and Austro–Hungarian diplomacies still more active. In June 1876, these two states signed the Reichstadt agreement. In content and formulation the two parties' records of the agreement differ. The record of the Russian side says that Russia and Austria–Hungary were to act in coordination to regulate the consequences of the Serbo–Turkish War. They were not to render assistance to the formation of a major Slavic state in the Balkans or the expansion of Montenegro and Serbia at the expense of Turkey. Austria–Hungary was to acquire the right to annex so-called Turkish Croatia and some parts of Bosnia bordering on it, while Russia was to get back Bessarabia, of which it had been deprived by the Paris Treaty of 1856. The record of the Russian side also says that if, as a result of the success of the Christians, the Ottoman Empire were defeated, "in Bulgaria and Rumelia independent principalities could be set up within their national boundaries. Epirus and Thessaly could be attached to Greece, and Constantinople could become a free city."[1] In the Austro—Hungarian version, approximately the same thing is said about Montenegro and Serbia. "Bosnia, Rumelia, and Albania," the record continnes, "may become autonomous states. Thessaly and the island of Crete should be annexed to Greece. Constantinople and its suburbs, the territory of which is subject to determination, would become a free city."

After the bloody suppression of the April Uprising and the temporary discontinuation of the military operations in the Serbo—Turkish War on the initiative of Russia, an ambassadorial conference was convened in Constantinople. Representatives of Russia, Britain, France, Germany, Austria—Hungary, Italy, and the Ottoman Empire took part. In personal meetings before the opening of the conference, the Russian ambassador in Constantinople, N. P. Ignatyev, acquainted the first British delegate, the Marquess of Salisbury, with the proposal prepared by Prince Tseretelev and the secretary of the American Mission in Constantinople, E. Schuyler, for reforms in the Ottoman state. This proposal provided for the establishment of a united Bulgarian autonomous region.[2]

On his arrival in Constantinople, Salisbury received extensive information on the Bulgarian national question from members of the staff of the British embassy and from a number of Bulgarian public organizations and private persons. He agreed in principle to the introduction of reforms in the Ottoman Empire but raised objections to the program proposed by Ignatyev. The most important objection concerned the establishment of a united Bulgarian autonomous region. Salisbury was of the opinion that if such a region were created it would be too large and strong. It would disturb the internal equilibrium of the Ottoman Empire and threaten its unity and power. In response to Ignatyev's program Salisbury proposed "pacification" of the regions in revolt in European Turkey through limited reforms or ordinary administrative measures.[3] Meanwhile, however, a change in Salisbury's stand was brought about by receipt of fuller information on the question and by vacillation in the British cabinet on Balkan and Near Eastern policy. The change in his attitude became noticeable during the preliminary meetings of the conference.

By reciprocal concessions between Ignatyev and Salisbury, agreement was reached on submitting a common program to the conference for the restoration of peace between Turkey and Montenegro and Serbia and for reforms in Bosnia, Hercegovina, and Bulgaria. The proposal was subjected to prolonged discussion, and a comprehensive and detailed program was drafted. Under its terms Montenegro was to acquire part of southern Hercegovina and northern Albania and the right of free navigation on the Bojana River; Serbia was to retain its prewar frontiers with a certain correction along the Drina River; Bosnia and the rest of Hercegovina were to be merged into one region under the rule of a governor-general approved by the sultan.[4]

Owing to the resistance chiefly of the British and Austro–Hungarian delegates, Ignatyev's proposal of the establishment of a united autonomous Bulgaria was rejected. It was decided that Bulgaria should be divided into two provinces – an eastern one, with Turnovo as its principal city, and a western one, with Sofia as its principal city. The eastern province was to include the sanjaks of Turnovo, Ruse, Tulcea, Varna, Sliven, and Plovdiv (except for the cazas of Sultan Eğri, and Ahi Celebi in the Rhodope Mountains) and the cazas of Kirkklise (Lozengrad), Mustafapasa (Svilengrad), and Kizilagac (Elhovo). The western province was to incorporate the sanjaks of Sofia, Vidin, Niš, Skopje, and Bitola (except for its two southern cazas), along with the three northern cazas of the sanjak of Serres and the cazas of Strumitsa, Veles, Tikveš, and Kostur. Each of these provinces was to have as governor a Christian Turkish subject or a foreigner appointed by the sultan with the consent of the Great Powers. There were provisions for each province to have an elected legislative assembly and an administrative commission with executive functions. A militia made up of Christians and Muslims and a gendarmerie exercising police power were also planned.[5] This proposal, though radical, maintained the sultan's sovereignty over the two Bulgarian regions and the unity of the empire. While dividing the Bulgarian area into two provinces, to a large extent it conformed to the ethnogeographic boundaries of the Bulgarian nation, essentially the boundaries of the Bulgarian Exarchate.

The news of the calling of the Constantinople Conference spread quickly in the Bulgarian areas under Turkish rule and among the émigrés abroad, causing a great ideological stir. Everywhere south and north of the Danube Bulgarian patriots sat down to work out programs for reform in the Ottoman Empire envisaging broad autonomy or complete political freedom for the Bulgarians. In this respect, of particular importance were two documents drafted by the Constantinople Bulgarians, "The Wishes of the Bulgarians" and "The Wishes of the Bulgarian Nation," which advocated autonomy for the Bulgarians in a united region whose boundaries coincided with those of the Exarchate.[6] Of even greater importance, because it was more radical, was a third document, approved by the Bulgarian People's Convention held in Bucharest November 18–24, 1876. Entitled "Political Program," it said that in order to establish peace in the Ottoman state the Turks must discontinue their "incessant atrocities" and fulfill the just demands of the Bulgarian people for political freedom. This would happen when European states stopped supporting Turkey and insisted on the unification of the Bulgarian people within the boundaries of a single state. This and other documents prepared by Bulgarians were submitted to the Constantinople

Conference, but it apparently ignored the demands they put forward for the establishment of an independent and united Bulgarian state.[7]

In the course of the preliminary meetings of the conference, the Turkish authorities were kept informed of the differences between the delegations and of the determination of the London government to defend the integrity of the Ottoman Empire by military force. Under these circumstances the Turkish delegate Safvet Pasha declared in the opening session of the conference that the Sublime Porte would not accept the proposed reforms. During his statement, cannon fire was heard announcing the introduction in the empire of a constitution granted by the sultan. In fact, this was only a political ploy, since the constitution neither guaranteed the interests of the Christian population nor secured real political and civil rights for the ordinary Turkish and other Muslim populations.

The rejection of the program worked out by the Constantinople Conference exacerbated the Eastern crisis. The Russian government faced the dilemma whether to insist that the Sublime Porte accept the proposals of the conference or reconcile itself to its refusal. The first choice ran the risk of war, for which Russia was unprepared because of financial difficulties and the as yet incomplete reorganization and rearmament of the army. It was also clear from the conference that in the event of war it would have to act alone. However, no other way of resolving the conflict and preserving Russia's influence in the Balkans seemed possible. In his speech before the Moscow nobility on November 9, 1876 (old style), the tsar had declared that if the forthcoming conference of the powers could reach no general agreement, he had the "firm intention" of acting alone. The time had come for him to do so.

Availing itself of its alliance with Germany and Austria–Hungary (the Dreikaiserbund), Russia took steps to coordinate its policy with that of the Vienna government. On January 3/15, 1877, the two states signed a secret convention in Vienna, Article 1 of which read in part: "Owing to the fact that conditions in Bulgaria favor the operation of autonomous institutions, they [the two governments] shall take upon themselves the obligation to demand at the Conference broader autonomy, accompanied by guarantees, for this province."[8] From the text of the convention it is clear that at the end of the Constantinople Conference the Russian government was preparing to insist on broader autonomy for Bulgaria. Turkish resistance to this policy led to the sharpening of the conflict and hence to war. The Austro–Hungarian government agreed to Russian policy with respect to Bulgaria but raised the demand of occupying Bosnia and Hercegovina. In accordance with Article 7 of the convention, the Austro–Hungarian emperor acquired the right to choose the moment and mode of occupying these provinces with his troops. This act did not signify solidarity with the occupation of Bulgaria by Russian troops, but it certainly was not hostility to Russia either. This diplomatic quibbling meant that in the event of war Austria–Hungary would observe neutrality in exchange for the rich booty of Bosnia–Hercegovina.[9]

The secret convention shows that in order to secure Austria–Hungary's neutrality the Russian government agreed to the occupation of two Slavic provinces by the Danubian Monarchy. This was eventually to undermine Russia's prestige as a defender of the Balkan Slavs, and it was obviously done only out of utter necessity in view of the impending war with Turkey. A product of this necessity was the inclusion in a supplementary convention to this act, adopted later by the two governments, of a text to the effect that the contracting parties excluded the establishment of a large Slavic or other state in the Balkans. With this Russia shut the door not only on the formation of a greater Serbia or Montenegro but also on the national unification of the Bulgarian people.[10]

Preparing for war with Turkey, the Russian government made a fresh attempt at a collective resolution of the Eastern Question by signing the London Protocol of January 19/31, 1877. It did not contain any specific threat to Turkey for its refusal to accept the reforms proposed at the Constantinople Conference. It only directed a warning to the Sublime Porte to introduce reforms in the empire and to pacify its European possessions. In practice this encouraged it to resist Russian pressure.[11]

These events led, step by step, to the declaration of the Russo–Turkish War on April 12/14, 1877. Having numerical superiority over the forces of the Ottoman Empire on both the Balkan and Anatolian fronts in the first months of the war, the Russian army at first met with considerable success. Soon, however, it was forced onto the defensive. The Balkan front was the decisive one, since through it Constantinople could be quickly threatened. In July the Russian troops crossed the Stara Planina Mountains and invaded northern Thrace. There they threatened Edirne and Turkish communications in the valley of the Maritsa River. Before long, however, they were compelled to withdraw under the pressure of Turkish troops transported by British ships from the Montenegrin front. In their rear in northern Bulgaria, a large Turkish army made its way to the east and consolidated itself in the town of Plevna. This turn in the course of the war calmed the British, who had been alarmed by the successes of the Russian army in Thrace and had entered, in the summer of 1877, into secret negotiations with regard to common action with Austria–Hungary against Russia.

The course of the war was reversed again by the successful defense of Shipka Pass by Russian troops and Bulgarian volunteers and by the taking of the fortress of Plevna. Under harsh winter conditions, the Russians crossed the Stara Planina Mountains for the second time and rapidly advanced on Stara Zagora, Plovdiv, and Edirne. This compelled the government of the sultan to sue for an armistice. While the negotiations were in progress, the Russians captured Edirne, reached the shores of the Aegean and the Sea of Marmara, and drew near Constantinople. The military aid promised by Britain was never delivered, and the government of the sultan had to agree to the terms laid down by the Russians for the discontinuation of military operations. These included the "Fundamentals of Peace" worked out in St. Petersburg.

The signing of the armistice and the acceptance of the "Fundamentals of Peace" took place in Edirne on January 19/31, 1878. The agreement contained the following basic principles: (1) Bulgaria, within the boundaries defined by a Bulgarian majority and by no means any smaller than indicated by the Constantinople Conference, was to become an autonomous tributary principality with a Christian national government and a popular army. (2) The independence of Montenegro was to be recognized and its territory increased with the lands it had occupied during the war. (3) The independence of Romania and Serbia was to be recognized. The former was to be given sufficient territorial compensation, and the borders of the latter were to be modified in its favor. (4) Bosnia and Hercegovina were to be granted autonomy with adequate guarantees, and similar transformations were to be introduced in the other Christian provinces of Turkey. (5) The Sublime Porte was to pay indemnity to Russia for its military expenses and losses during the war and to conclude an agreement with Russia on shipping through the Bosporus and the Dardanelles and on the withdrawal of the Turkish garrisons from the Danubian towns.[12]

The cease-fire did not end the diplomatic war. Even prior to the signing of the armistice, the British ambassador in Constantinople had alarmed his government with his report on the "Fundamentals of Peace." The war party in the government pressed for decisive action to stop the Russian march to the Dardanelles and Constantinople. For this purpose, Parliament was convened on January 17, 1878, and voted extra war credits. Fresh demarches were made for an alliance with Austria–Hungary, whose interests had not been taken into consideration in preparing the "Fundamentals of Peace." The Vienna government hesitated to take an openly anti-Russian position, but the talks with London did not remain secret, and this encouraged the Sublime Porte to put up resistance to the implementation of the peace treaty.

The peace negotiations were further hampered by the promise given in advance by the tsar that the powers that had signed the Paris Treaty of 1856 would jointly discuss the questions of Constantinople and the straits. Another hindrance was the fact that Russian troops had not occupied all the areas envisaged as included in the Bulgarian principality. After the armistice the Turkish command began to build up its troops there and to prepare for the resumption of military operations, particularly after the passage of a detachment of British naval vessels into the Sea of Marmara.

In this situation the Russian government decided to turn for assistance to its allies, Germany and Austria–Hungary, although the latter was inclined toward rapprochement with Britain. Germany was trying to appear unconcerned with the resolution of the Eastern Question by declaring its loyalty to the Dreikaiserbund. At the same time, it did not want to alienate Austria–Hungary, which was dissatisfied with the "Fundamentals of Peace." Nevertheless, at the invitations of St. Petersburg and Berlin the Vienna government consented to holding a tripartite conference in Vienna in February 1878 to discuss the peace terms. There it declared itself against the inclusion of the lands south of the Stara Planina Mountains in the Bulgarian principality and other clauses in the draft peace treaty proposed by Russia.[13]

It became clear at the tripartite conference that Russia had no other way of crushing Turkey's resistance and achieving a peace treaty than to resume military operations and threaten the seizure of Constantinople. This was achieved by a military demonstration by the Russian army corps deployed in the proximimity of Constantinople. It was then that the Sublime Porte capitulated. The negotiations, started in Edirne, were concluded in San Stefano (modern Yeşilköy), where the Treaty of San Stefano was signed on February 19/March 3, 1878.[14]

Between the preliminary accords of Russia with Austria–Hungary and the reform proposals prepared by the Constantinople Conference, on the one hand, and the Treaty of San Stefano, on the other, there were both similarities and considerable differences. The Russian stand on the peace terms evolved in the course of the war. The most essential changes were those concerning the statuses of Bulgaria, Bosnia, and Hercegovina.

With respect to Bulgaria, Article 6 of the treaty stipulated that it was to become an autonomous tributary principality with a Christian government and a national army. Its boundaries were to coincide, by and large, with the boundaries of the Bulgarian Exarchate and the two regions mentioned in the program of the Constantinople Conference, with three essential differences: Northern Dobruja was to be ceded to Romania and the Morava area to Serbia; Bulgaria's outlet to the Aegean, between the mouths of the Rivers Mesta and Struma, was not included in the diocese of the Exarchate and did not figure in the conference proposals.

The most important provision in the Treaty of San Stefano with respect to Bulgaria, along with its boundaries, was that it envisaged the creation of a tributary Bulgarian principality. This marked an advance toward the realization of the cherished goal of the Bulgarians, full political independence.

Instead of providing for two autonomous provinces, the treaty set up a united Bulgarian state including almost all the areas in which, during the national revival, the majority of the population had asserted its Bulgarian nationality. Even so, not all Bulgarians would have been included in the new state. Remaining outside the boundaries of the principality were considerable western Bulgarian areas in the valleys of the Rivers Morava and Nišava, several areas inhabited by Bulgarians in the Central Rhodope Mountains, and, as we have seen, northern Dobruja.

Besides Article 6, Bulgaria's position was affected by Articles 7–12. Article 7 determined the way of electing a Bulgarian prince and the working out of a constitution by an assembly of Bulgarian notables. Article 8 prohibited Turkish troops from remaining in the Bulgarian principality. This and the following articles provided for the destruction of the Turkish fortresses on the southern bank of the Danube, determined the size of the tribute to be paid to the Sublime Porte, and regulated the disposition of the real property of Muslims who chose to emigrate from Bulgaria.

Article 14 regulated the position of Bosnia and Hercegovina. It stipulated that in these two regions the reforms proposed by the Constantinople Conference were to be introduced. According to the preliminary accords between the Russian and Austro–Hungarian governments, the two provinces had been destined to be occupied by Austria–Hungary. In the drawing up of the program of reforms by the Constantinople Conference, the Porte obviously failed to impose its claims concerning these two Slavic regions. The Russian government probably had this in mind in formulating Article 14. It is also possible that the reaction of public opinion in Russia, which was resolutely opposed to the cession of South Slavic lands to Austria–Hungary, was also taken into consideration.

Articles 1 and 2 concerned Montenegro. They recognized its independence and incorporated considerable territory within its new boundaries. The next two articles regulated the position of Serbia, which also won national independence and considerable expansion of its frontiers to the east and south in the valleys of the Morava and Nišava Rivers and in Old Serbia. A joint Serbo–Turkish commission, with the aid of a Russian commissioner and the participation of a Bulgarian representative, was to draw Serbia's borders with Bulgaria and Turkey. Serbia was obliged to withdraw its troops from the western Bulgarian lands occupied in the course of the war.

The position of Romania was dealt with in Articles 5 and 19a. Article 5 recognized its independence, and Article 19a arranged the ceding to it of northern Dobruja, including the sanjak of Tulcea, which included the cazas of Kiliya, Sulina, Mahmudia, Isaccea, Tulcea, Măcin, Babadag, Hirşova, Constanţa, and Medgidia, as well as the islands in the Danube delta and Snake Island. "Not wishing to annex this territory and the islands in the delta," it stipulated, "Russia shall retain the right to exchange them for the part of Bessarabia separated by the Paris Treaty of 1856 and delineated in the south by the Kiliya branch and the mouth of Stari Stambul."

Article 15 provided for the introduction of the Constitution of 1868 on the island of Crete. Article 16 obliged the Porte to implement the reforms required by local needs in the regions inhabited by Armenians and ensure their security against the Kurds and Circassians. Article 17 granted full and general amnesty to all Ottoman subjects detained or exiled for their opposition to the authorities Article 18 delineated the Turco–Persian frontier. The next article concerned the payment of 1,410,000,000 rubles in war indemnities to Russia. Of these, 100,000,000 were considered the money equivalent of the lands ceded to Russia in the Balkans and Asia Minor (northern Dobruja, the land around the towns of Ardahan, Kars, Batum, and Bayazid, and the territory up to Zoganlug). The payment of the balance of the indemnities minus 10,000,000 rubles for Russian interests and institutions in Turkey was to be settled by mutual agreement between the two governments.

Several articles settled the property matters of Muslims emigrating or intending to emigrate from the territories ceded to Russia and the protection of Russian monks and other clergymen residing or traveling in Turkey. Article 24, dealing with shipping through the Bosporus and the Dardanelles, was important. Both passages were to remain open in war and peace to the merchant ships of neutral countries sailing from or to Russian ports. Articles 25–28 settled the withdrawal of the Russian troops from the territories in which Turkish rule was restored and the reciprocal exchange of prisoners of war. The last article, 29, stipulated when and how the ratification of the treaty was to be effected.

The view that Ignatyev was the creator of the Treaty of San Stefano has gained ground in the historical literature, largely because he was the author of the original draft. With the assistance of Nelidov, he conducted the negotiations with the Turkish delegates, and he completed the working out and signing of the treaty. It is necessary to point out, however, that Ignatyev's activity expressed the political efforts of Russia to preserve and consolidate its influence among the South Slavs and particularly among the Bulgarians, at that time considered its most reliable ally in the pursuit of its Near Eastern policy. A desire to satisfy the national demands of the Armenians and the Greeks was also noticeable. As an ambassador of long standing in Constantinople, Ignatyev was thoroughly familiar with the state of the Ottoman Empire and the development of the national liberation struggles. Thus the strivings of the enslaved peoples to gain political freedom and to do away with the decayed Ottoman feudal socioeconomic system also found expression in the treaty.

The Treaty of San Stefano had a national- and social (antifeudal)-liberation character to varying degrees for the various Balkan peoples and for the Armenians in Asia Minor. It set up a tributary Bulgarian principality, implemented reforms in Bosnia and Hercegovina in the spirit of the proposals of the Constantinople Conference, applied the Constitution of 1868 to Crete, and carried out reforms in Epirus, Thessaly, and other parts of European Turkey and Asia Minor, among other things for the protection of the Armenians. For these reasons, and also because not only was Turkish political domination abolished but the feudal system, or a transitional socioeconomic one with many feudal remnants in force, was also destroyed, the Treaty of San Stefano and the Russo—Turkish War of 1877—78 contributed to national and social liberation. They constituted a major step forward in the centuries-long struggle of the Balkan peoples and the Armenians for freedom. This was true in largest measure for the Bulgarians, whose life under Ottoman domination was characterized by the hardest conditions of national and social oppression.

The Treaty of San Stefano was an important step toward solving the complicated and multifaceted national problem in the Balkans. Because of the counteraction of Britain, Austria—Hungary, and the other Great Powers, Russia decided that in the war against Turkey only the Bulgarian national question could be resolved in a radical manner. This decision corresponded to Russia's opportunities and interests at the time and to the existing balance of power in the Balkans and in Europe. A radical solution to the Bulgarian national problem did not, however, mean harming the national interests of the other Balkan peoples. The boundaries of San Stefano Bulgaria were not arbitrarily invented by Russian diplomacy. They corresponded to the real territorial position of the Bulgarian nation, sanctioned by so important an international forum as the Constantinople Conference and recognized by scores of the most eminent European and American scholars, diplomats, and travelers. It is to be regretted that the same Great Powers whose representatives had participated in the Constantinople Conference rejected the Treaty of San Stefano at the Congress of Berlin and thus inflicted a blow not only on Bulgarian national liberation but also on the national liberation movements of the other peoples enslaved by Ottoman rule. This policy of the Great Powers can only be considered an antipopular and reactionary one, one that held back the development of the Bulgarians and other Balkan peoples and of the Armenians in Asia Minor.

## NOTES

1.  S. Stefanov, *Mezhdunarodni aktove i dogovori,* (Sofia, 1958), p. 137.
2.  I. V. Kozmenko, *Ruskata diplomatsiya i formiraneto na bulgarskata durzhavnost sled Osvobozhdenieto,* (Sofia, 1982), p. 31.

3. *Osvobozhdenie Bolgarii ot turetskogo iga,* vol. 1 (Moscow, 1961), p. 546.

4. G. E. Noradounghian, *Recueil d'actes internationaux de l'Empire Ottoman,* vol. 3 (Paris, 1902), pp. 409–11.

5. Ibid.

6. H. Hristov, "Dva proekta za durzhavno ustroistvo na Bulgaria ot 1876," *Izv. na Inst. za istoriya pri BAN,* 16–17: p. 479.

7. N. Chehlarov, *Dokumenti za bulgarskoto vuzrazhdane,* Sb. NUNK, kn. XXII i XXIII, dyal istoriko-filologichen i folkloren (Sofia, 1906–1907), pp. 40–45.

8. S. Stefanov, Op. cit., p. 138.

9. Ibid.

10. Ibid., p. 140.

11. Ibid.

12. S. S. Tatishchev, *Imperator Aleksandr II, ego zhizn i tsarstvovanie,* vol. 2 (Moscow, 1911), pp. 438–39.

13. H. Hristov, *Osvobozhdenieto na Bulgaria i politikata na zapadnite durzhavi* (Sofia, 1968), p. 144; About Germany's policy see K. Kosev, *Bismarck, Iztochniyat vupros i Bulgarskoto osvobozhdenie, 1856–1878* (Sofia, 1978), p. 272 et seq.

14. G. P. Genov, "Mezhdunarodni aktove i dogovori zasyagashti Bulgaria," *GSU, yuridicheski fakultet,* 34, no. 1 (1938–39), p. 241 et seq.

Imanuel Geiss


# THE CONGRESS OF BERLIN, 1878: AN ASSESSMENT
# OF ITS PLACE IN HISTORY


The Congress of Berlin in 1878 was a key factor in issues of war and peace in southeastern Europe during the late nineteenth century. A product of Great Power politics, it nonetheless had a tremendous impact on the lives of the various peoples in the Balkans who had become the objects of Great Power decisions. The historical constellation of 1878 is comparable to that of the next great international conference in Berlin, the West Africa or Congo Conference of 1884–85. The parallels and differences between the two events are obvious enough and need not detain us long – the Balkan peoples emerging from the rule of two decaying dynastic empires but remaining under the direct and indirect influence of the European Great Powers in the first instance, the peoples of Africa falling under the emerging rule of the European colonial powers, large and small, in the second. The dissolution of the Ottoman Empire and the Dual Monarchy by 1918 and the end of colonial empires after World War II bred tensions between rival Great Powers and conflicts among successor states. The "Balkanization" of southeastern Europe followed World War I, while on a larger scale the "Balkanization" of Africa through the emergence of former colonial administrative units as new national states followed World War II. Many of the new states are struggling with the same kind of problems the dynastic empires faced before 1918, only now on a smaller scale. We can see many of our present problems already in the making around the time of the Congress of Berlin and in fact even affected by it in one way or another.

Such a historical constellation is liable to produce misunderstanding and resentment through the Great Power chauvinism of historians representing those powers. Most of these (unless they are specialists in a given region) are wont to view the histories of the "smaller" or ex-colonial powers as marginal or as only a function of their own "Great Power" history, granting them at best a kind of benevolent condescension. Correspondingly, more often than not there is resentment among the members of the "smaller" nations against the Great Powers that lorded it over them in the past and against the historians who continue to do so in their modern writing. At the same time, the "smaller" nations are prone to touchiness on national questions and may become unjust to minorities in their own new national states, aggressive toward fellow (and rival) successor states in their region, or prickly toward Great Powers (past or present).

For a citizen of a former Great Power — in fact, the one that was host to the Congress of Berlin and that twice had such a devastating impact on southeastern Europe but that now, as a divided nation, has no direct political interest in the region (similarly to the situation of 1878) — it may be hazardous to comment on the Congress of Berlin and its influence on southeastern Europe a century ago. The risk is the greater in that I cannot boast of any expert knowledge of the languages or history of southeastern Europe. My contribution can be only a modest one — trying to place the Congress of Berlin in historical perspective, fitting it into the framework of our general subject of Balkan societies in war and revolutions during the 1870s.

The relevance of my subject is obvious enough, because the Congress of Berlin concluded the great Eastern crisis of 1875—78 and the eighth Russo—Turkish War of 1877—78. But the congress was the product of several major factors in modern European, indeed world, history that I would like to assemble and analyze by what I like to call the macro-historic approach. A broad synthesis of well-known facts may make for a better understanding of a very complex historical process.

Placed chronologically about halfway between the Congress of Vienna in 1815 and the outbreak of World War I in 1914, the Congress of Berlin was perhaps the single most important event between 1815 and 1914 in the field of European international relations.[1] It is rivaled only by its immediate predecessor, the Congress of Paris of 1856, which ended the Crimean War and the seventh Russo—Turkish War.[2] Thanks to its centenary in 1978, the Congress of Berlin has gotten the scholarly attention it deserves,[3] even though it was, seen superficially, only a case of that sort of traditional diplomatic history that has recently fallen into such disrepute among "progressive" historians. Actually, explaining the true historical importance of the Congress of Berlin can become a fascinating exercise in combining "traditional" diplomatic and political history with social and economic history — always, of course, with a broad brush.[4]

The Congress of Berlin has to be seen against the historical background of events immediately preceding it — the Eastern crisis (1875—78), the eighth Russo—Turkish War (1877—78), and the Treaty of San Stefano (1878) — and in the context of more long-term historical factors that conditioned its outcome, such as the Eastern Question,[5] of which the crisis of 1875–78[6] was but one important segment; the South Slavic Question, one of the major corollaries of the general Eastern Question;[7] and the traditional rivalries of the European Great Powers. Historically, the oldest and most powerful factor was the dynamics of Russia's century-old expansion, which threatened both the Ottoman Empire and Austria–Hungary. England's attempt at sustaining the Ottoman Empire as long as possible against Russia was fairly recent. Finally, Germany was the new rising star but still waiting in the wings.

The raw materials for conflict were provided by the tensions arising from the decline of the Ottoman Empire since its failure before Vienna in 1683. The Treaty of Küçük Kaynarca in 1774 had inaugurated, formally as it were, the long-drawn agony of the Ottoman Empire and the Eastern Question. The decline of Ottoman power made for a vast power vacuum, which, as usual in history, other powers tried to fill — Russia, on the one hand, and the rising national movements of the Greeks and the South Slavs, on the other. Since Austria had refused aid to the Serbian and Greek uprisings of 1804 and 1821, Russia, the Great Power closest at hand, became the great ally of the national movements in southeastern Europe: Russian Pan-Slavism and South Slavic nationalism became wedded, mutually strenthening each other, while the tsarist government tried to take a middle course, calculating the potential of the rival Great Powers, Austria–Hungary and England. The tsar and his government also came under pressure from public opinion set in motion by liberal reforms after the Crimean War.[8]

In part because England tried to prop up the Ottoman Empire in an effort to keep Russia out of the Mediterranean, the primary conflict in Europe during most of the nineteenth century was between England and Russia. It extended to Central Asia and the Far East, where Russian and British expansions clashed as well. Britain, then the greatest sea power, tried to hold back Russia, the greatest land power. These chronic tensions led to one major war between England and Russia, the Crimean War, and several times both powers came to the brink of war elsewhere, above all in the wake of Russian victories in the eighth Russo–Turkish War, when early in 1878 Russian troops stood before Constantinople and the British fleet had entered the Bosporus. Only in 1907 was the traditional confrontation between Britain and Russia pushed into the background in the face of the new challenge of Germany's *Weltpolitik*.

Austria's hostile neutrality in the Crimean War created a secondary front of conflict in the region between Austria–Hungary and Russia, both originally defenders of the ancien régime and united to restrain a divided Poland. But in 1878 the great European war did not take place because Britain and Austria–Hungary shrank from its costs and because Russia was too exposed strategically and too weakened by an upsurge of revolutionary and terrorist activities. The terrorist wing of the suppressed Narodniki[9] led Bismarck and Salisbury, the new British foreign secretary, for the first time to detect the force of revolution at work behind the apparently imposing facade of tsarist autocracy.[10] Bismarck even made the distinction between social revolution and a more general Pan-Slavist revolution but saw them as intending to bring down tsarism and threatening the balance of power in Europe by seeking expansion. The Congress of Berlin derived its particular place in these wider developments by inhibiting both Pan-Slavist expansion and the threat of social revolution.

The Greater Bulgaria of the San Stefano Treaty proved unacceptable to the powers because they feared it would establish Russian hegemony in the Balkans. Led by England and Austria—Hungary, the powers insisted on revising that treaty on the basis of the Treaty of Paris of 1856, which had made the Ottoman Empire a member of the Concert of Europe and guaranteed its territorial integrity. The logical consequence was that all changes in the territorial status of the Ottoman Empire had to be approved by all the other powers. Because Bismarck, the "honest broker," became a partner in thwarting Russia after its victories over the Ottoman Empire, Russian anger turned against the German Empire.

Prussia had been almost a Russian satellite state, given its rescue by Russia at the end of the Seven Years' War in 1762, the Russo—Prussian Alliance of 1764, and its part in the partitions of Poland. Prussia had been saved twice more by Russia, in 1807 and 1812—13, and again in the European Revolution of 1848—49 when Russia forced it to suppress the uprisings of 1849 in defense of the Frankfurt Constitution. No wonder that for Marx and Engels Prussia was "Russia's jackal." The new German Empire, however, was only superficially a successor state to Prussia in foreign policy. The momentum of German unification and of industrialization had rapidly changed the old weak Germany into a powerful empire in its own right, which a generation later even developed its own expansive aims.[11]

When Bismarck, almost a year after the Congress of Berlin, learned of Tsar Alexander II's angry complaint about Emperor Wilhelm I, Germany's new strength enabled him to rush into an alliance with Austria—Hungary within two months. Bismarck had wished to keep his options open as long as possible. He wished to preserve the stability Europe had enjoyed after the Treaty of Paris of 1856, since which time no Great Power had been allied to another (except Italy with France and Prussia in 1859 and 1866). But by not supporting Russia at the Congress of Berlin Germany provoked Russian resentment the more bitter because of the great expectations nourished by public opinion in Russia during the war against Turkey.[12] Thus the Congress of Berlin, with its inevitable disappointment for Russian hopes, inaugurated an estrangement between Germany and Russia that ran counter to a political tradition of more than a century's standing.[13] This new confrontation between Germany and Russia became one of the major factors accounting for the outbreak of World War I, when Russia threw its weight behind Serbia and Germany behind Austria–Hungary.

At the same time, Germany and Austria–Hungary tried to contain social revolution wherever possible. The national revolutionary character of the South Slavic movement, which was linked to Russian Pan-Slavism, threatened dynastic monarchies such as Austria–Hungary. Early in the Eastern crisis, General Bluhm, the German military attaché in Constantinople, had drawn the chancellor's attention to the consequences of a belt of South Slavic states reaching from the Adriatic to the Aegean that would bar the Central European powers from future access to the Ottoman Empire.[14] And when Austro–Hungarian troops invaded Bosnia–Hercegovina in August 1878, the German consul at Sarajevo, Frommelt, explicitly drew the parallel between resistance to the occupation and the Paris Commune.[15] One of Bismarck's strongest arguments when pleading with an unwilling Emperor Wilhelm I for the Dual Alliance was that, in contrast to revolution-ridden Russia, Austria–Hungary was a solidly conservative and reliable partner.[16]

For Austria–Hungary as well, the Congress of Berlin was a turning point. Since Hungary's collapse under the onslaught of Ottoman expansion in 1526, the Roman Catholic South Slavs had been content under Habsburg rule as long as it meant protection against Ottoman conquest. With the decline of Ottoman power new considerations came into play: the idea of nationalism radiated from the French Revolution; industrialization began; Serbia rose as a spearhead of South Slavic nationalism against the Ottoman Empire and then against Austria–Hungary; and, finally, the Compromise of 1867 created the Dual Monarchy.[17] Hungarian nationalism was confronted by the nationalism of Hungary's minorities, in particular, that of the South Slavs and the Romanians.[18] In fifty years, the Dual Monarchy had been destroyed.[19]

At the same time, Austria–Hungary had plunged into a policy of limited expansion in the Balkans at the expense of both the decaying Ottoman Empire and the emerging South Slavic movement. Even before the actual outbreak of the revolts in Hercegovina and Bosnia in 1875, the leaders of the Dual Monarchy had earmarked those provinces for incorporation into Austria–Hungary.[20] Vienna's motives were manifold: strategic defense of the Dalmatian coast, acquired in 1815; compensation for losses in Italy and Germany in 1859 and 1866; and a kind of advance defense against the dreaded rise of South Slavic nationalism. Ever since the Serbian uprising of 1804, Austrian statecraft had tried to prevent the creation of a unified state of all or most South Slavs. Acquiring Bosnia and Hercegovina would withhold those provinces from Serbia, the main champion of the South Slavic national movement.

The occupation and administration of Bosnia and Hercegovina by Austria–Hungary, formally decided by the Congress on June 28, the anniversary of the Battle of Kosovo (1389), was only a compromise. Austria–Hungary annexed the provinces only thirty years later in the wake of the Young Turk Revolution. In the interim the two provinces were treated as though they were already integral parts of the Dual Monarchy, although with a special status. But as early as summer 1878 a German paper, the *Augsburger Allgemeine Zeitung*,[21] warned of the dire consequences the forced occupation of Bosnia and Hercegovina against the wishes of most of the population would have on Austria–Hungary. In fact, the Dual Monarchy incorporated into itself in 1878 the critical additional explosive matter that was to rend it at the end of World War I. The mutinous tradition in both provinces turned against the new hegemonic power, for the first time in the very hour of occupation in summer 1878 and then in another uprising in 1881–82. It was in that rebellious tradition that the first generation of Serbian intelligentsia grew up in the last years before World War I. The frustration of the young South Slavic nationalists crystallized in the "Young Bosnia" movement and then in the outrage of Sarajevo.[22] The structural deficiencies of dualism and South Slavophobia were thus exacerbated by the acquisition of Bosnia and Hercegovina.

For the Ottoman Empire the Congress of Berlin brought another forty years of precarious existence. The powers succeeded in preventing the destruction of it that had been threatened by the Treaty of San Stefano by cutting down the size of Russian-dominated Bulgaria, creating Eastern Rumelia, and restoring Macedonia and Albania to the Ottoman Empire. In 1876 the empire's chronic internal crisis had provoked the Constitution of 1876 and a liberal interlude that ended when the Russian army stood before Constantinople in early 1878. The Ottoman delegate in Berlin, Carathéodory Pasha, represented both the old tradition of Phanariot service to the sultan and the brief interlude of modern liberalism, but the latter was already an anachronism by the time of the congress. The end of the Ottoman Empire had been sealed by the eighth Russo–Turkish War. Western ideas of nationalism had corroded the millet system, that unique structure that had given religious and social autonomy to three major non-Muslim minorities (Orthodox, Armenians, and Jews, Islam being the fourth millet). The effects of industrialization, pressure for reform along Western lines, and demands for territorial autonomy also undermined the empire. But the millet system had also ossified from within into ruling oligarchies of religious and aristocratic leaders, provoking unrest among the lower classes within the non-Muslim millets.[23] Nor did the millet of Islam give sufficient scope to the awakening aspirations of non-Turkish Muslims. At the end of the Crimean War the sultan abolished the millet system with the second great reform decree, the Hatt-i-Hümayun of 1856, just in time to impress the Congress of Paris with his reforming zeal.

The breakdown of the millet system reactivated old differences. One of the first indications of this was the mutual slaughter of Christians, Druzes, and (Sunnite) Muslims in Lebanon and Damascus in 1860,[24] the forerunner of the present civil war in Lebanon. In the Balkans the millet system was replaced by ferment within the Orthodox Christian community. In 1870, under Russian and Bulgarian pressure, the Ottoman government created the Bulgarian Exarchate, an Orthodox church structure independent of the Patriarch at Constantinople, who was Greek. Two years later the Patriarch declared the Exarchate schismatic. These tensions over ecclesiastical matters between the Greeks and the Bulgars within the empire foreshadowed later national conflicts.

During the Eastern crisis the hatred accumulated since the end of the millet system exploded into orgies of mutual massacre in the Balkans. The centuries-old peaceful coexistence between Muslims and Christians in the villages and towns of the Balkans broke down. Muslims massacred Christians in putting down the Bulgarian uprising of 1876 in the "Bulgarian Horrors," and Christians responded during the eighth Russo–Turkish War with no less bloody massacres of Muslim populations. The waves of dispossessed and distracted Muslim refugees that converged on Constantinople created serious additional problems on top of the normal confusion reigning in times of serious defeat.[25] Parallels may be found in the mutual massacres during the Greek War of Independence about fifty years before, the Lebanese massacres of 1860, and, on an even greater scale, the wholesale mutual slaughter of Hindus and Muslims when, almost seventy years after the Congress of Berlin, British rule in India was withdrawn and chaos broke out in the sudden power vacuum of the Indian subcontinent. That these massacres have little to do with mere religious "fanaticism" can best be shown by the massacres that took place within the Muslim populations themselves when Pakistan broke up in the violent secession of Bangladesh a generation later.

One of the consequences of the nightmarish experience was the emergence of a Turkish nationalism that tried to square the preservation of imperial rule for the Turks with modern Western ideas such as constitutionalism and representative democracy. The upshot was a drive for enforced assimilation that had disastrous results. Violent opposition broke out among suppressed national minorities, first of all among the Armenians in 1895. This provoked the first of the terrible massacres of them, to be followed by the genocide-type massacres of 1915–16 for which Armenian terrorist commandos are still demanding revenge from Turkish officials. On the Turkish side, the myth of the Turkish *nation une et indivisible* persists today, denying the very existence of Armenians and Kurds as national minorities to the point that it is dangerous even to mention their names.

The Ottoman Empire, although apparently saved for another forty years by the Congress of Berlin, in reality never recovered from the blows it suffered during the Eastern crisis and the eighth Russo–Turkish War. The long-term effects, which may still be seen in the contemporary Republic of Turkey, were probably more telling than the losses in territory and population that reduced the republic to about one-fifth of the Ottoman Empire (including the former vassal states that became independent in 1878).

While the Ottoman Empire at the Congress of Berlin was in the ambivalent position of being both object of the manipulations of the Great Powers and a formal member of the Concert of Europe, the South Slavs clearly were only objects of the congress, although by their uprisings and wars against the empire they had initiated and escalated the crisis, provoked Russian intervention, and contributed to Russia's victories in 1878. For the three new successor states of Greece, Romania, and Serbia and also for Montenegro, the Congress of Berlin brought gratifications of varying sorts. The powers granted Greece in principle its first major territorial expansion since independence. A convention between Greece and the Ottoman Empire ceded Thessaly and most of the Epirus to Greece in 1881 but still withheld Crete. Montenegro's independence, which the Montenegrins had proclaimed earlier but which the Ottomans had never conceded, was formally and unequivocally recognized, and it received some territorial gains. Serbia and Romania advanced from their status of broad autonomy under the suzerainty of the sultan to full sovereighty and even some territorial gains.

But in their hour of apparent triumph, rifts among the emerging national movements began to appear. Clashing territorial claims, in particular in Macedonia, based on different periods of quasi-imperial Bulgarian and Serbian rule over Macedonia in the Middle Ages, provoked serious rivalries after 1878. Because the new states were not represented at the congress itself, Russia took care of Bulgarian interests and Austria–Hungary took care of Serbian ones. By giving Macedonia back to the Ottoman Empire, the Congress of Berlin only postponed the Macedonian question that has poisoned international relations in the Balkans ever since. Similar rivalries were building up between the Romanians and the Bulgarians over Dobruja. Further, the congress forced Romania to cede southern Bessarabia to Russia despite Russia's promise of territorial integrity to Romania when it allowed Russian armies free passage through its territory. This was the beginning of Romanian national resentment against Russian expansion. Serbia's ambition for Old Serbia, which since the Battles of Kosovo in 1389 and 1448 has been largely occupied by Albanians, was only partially fulfilled, but this laid the groundwork for the future clash of Yugoslav and Albanian nationalism in what is now a chronic problem.[26]

For Bulgaria, of course, the Congress of Berlin was a national catastrophe that turned the Treaty of San Stefano from a reality into a blueprint for the future. The division of the country into Bulgaria and Eastern Rumelia lasted only until 1885, but all aspirations to a restoration of San Stefano Bulgaria produced clashes. At the same time, Bulgaria came into the orbit of Russia for the first time, although it later turned to Austria–Hungary and Germany until World War II.[27] As for Serbia, after the Congress of Berlin it came into the orbit of Austria–Hungary, thus forgoing until 1903 its historic role as spearhead of the South Slavic national movement.

The Congress of Berlin ratified the principles prepared by the clandestine diplomatic agreement of Reichstadt (1876) and the Budapest Convention (1877). It divided the Balkans into spheres of influence in order to regulate the expansive rivalries in the region. In the long run the Austrian and Russian policy failed, partly because of the inner dynamics of political developments that reversed the direction of allegiances. Bulgaria drifted into the "Germanic" camp and Serbia joined the Russians after 1903. The increased momentum of the South Slavic national movement after 1903 disrupted the precarious balance of powers in the Balkans and threatened the existence of one of them, Austria–Hungary.

Three more incipient national questions were ignored by the Congress of Berlin in the interest of Great Power politics – the Albanian, the Armenian, and the Jewish. Predominantly Muslim Albanians, who had formulated their national aspirations for the first time in 1878 with the Albanian League of Prizren, were pushed back into the Ottoman Empire. Their situation was complicated by Serbian demands for Old Serbia, including the by now largely Albanian Kosovo region. The Armenians had hoped to be given the predominantly Armenian regions of eastern Anatolia as a basis for a national state of their own, but their hopes were disappointed, and the ground for future conflicts and massacres was unwittingly prepared.

The Jewish question was barely scratched at the Congress of Berlin, but even then its two most important aspects were apparent – discrimination against Jews with the rise of modern anti-Semitism (the word being coined a year after the congress in Germany) and the first timid request for a Jewish national state in Palestine, a few years before the emergence of organized Zionism.[28] In the debate on the conditions for granting or recognizing the independence of Romania, Serbia, and Montenegro, the powers demanded full equality for all their citizens. Serbia and later also Romania had to abolish their discriminatory laws against Jews. In the eighth session of June 28, which also stipulated the occupation and administration of Bosnia and Hercegovina by Austria–Hungary, Russian Chancellor Gorchakov explicitly defended Russian special legislation against Jews,[29] thus announcing Russian official anti-Semitism three years before the murder of Alexander II and the following first wave of pogroms.

One of the many petitions to the congress that were studiously ignored by the Great Powers was by a group of German Jews from Breslau asking for a Jewish state in Palestine under the suzerainty of the sultan. Nothing came of the initiative, which foreshadowed the emergence of Zionism. Nevertheless, that modest petition pointed ominously to our present Middle East conflict. Geographically the conflict in Lebanon and elsewhere may still be thought of as lying within the orbit of an Eastern Question. Because of the rivalries of the world powers of our own day, the raw materials for possible world conflict have shifted from the Balkans to the Middle East.

Here, then, is the place to discuss the relevance of the Congress of Berlin to general questions of war and peace. The secretary-general of the congress, the German diplomat Joseph Maria von Radowitz, claimed in a private analysis of its results that it had achieved at least five years without a general war between the powers:

> For five years at least, I believe the newly created situation will be able to last. Then the Greeks perhaps may render necessary another conference. But now we have saved Europe from war and shown how to reach agreement in future without conflicts. This is the gain of the congress: For the first time such an achievement has succeeded in preventing a great war. The other congresses came about only when the powers had already severely damaged each other, and from them new European conflict arose.[30]

Peace among the Great Powers was preserved, in fact, much longer than just five years. Yet the solutions of the Congress of Berlin were only interim solutions. Some of them, such as the ban on uniting Bulgaria or the establishment of Batum as a free port, lasted only a few years. Others, above all the occupation of Bosnia and Hercegovina, which led, under the conditions created by the Compromise of 1867, to the outrage of Sarajevo via the annexation of 1908, were linked directly to the outbreak of World War I.

It is easy today, with the knowledge of historical hindsight, to sneer at the shortsightedness of the statesmen who were making decisions in 1878. The results of the Congress of Berlin were a complex set of compromises that satisfied hardly anyone at the time. Among the Great Powers, Russia felt aggrieved, but only because of its exaggerated hopes of aggrandizement. Fulfilling Russian hopes would have meant general war in Europe comparable to that of 1914, even without the system of alliances that emerged gradually after the Congress of Berlin. This was the kind of "great war" that Radowitz and many of his contemporaries in responsible positions must have seen the Congress of Berlin as preventing.

But even the new or emerging Balkan states would not have avoided conflict much longer, because in spite of the ideal of South Slavic solidarity their clashing claims and counterclaims blocked any clear-cut solutions and, indeed, heralded even more violent conflicts for the future. Simply following the principle of national self-determination as an alternative to the egotism of the Great Powers was certain to fail in the maze of Balkan complexities. Here the tides of expansion and decline of several imperial structures since the days of the Macedonian–Greek Empire under Alexander the Great had thrown the ethnic, religious, and cultural patterns of heterogeneous populations into a confusion that defied any simplistic solutions, such as, for example, centralizing and culturally assimilating nationalism. Every possible drawing of boundaries always left embarrassingly large numbers of national or religious minorities on both sides of new "national" frontiers. These minorities could be accommodated only by honestly applying the principles of equality, tolerance, and autonomy, thus blurring the concept of national democracy *une et indivisible,* or by federalism. The many compromises of the Congress of Berlin could only postpone the conflicts among the new national democracies in the Balkans because the underlying problems were far too complex to be solved in any high-handed manner from above without wounding the pride of one or another of the emerging nations. The bloody conflicts these perceived slights created were sad but perhaps not abnormal or even excessive for the collective conduct of humanity when compared with the terrible conflicts arising from the decay and downfall of other great imperial structures.

In any case, the Congress of Berlin highlighted once more the explosive consequences of the vast power vacuum generated by the Eastern Question. Since the Greek War of Independence had first disrupted the Holy Alliance, the slipping of southeastern Europe from the grip of decaying Ottoman power caused serious confrontations among the Great Powers. The Crimean War was the first war among them since Napoleon, but it did not become a general conflagration because, among other issues, the Italian question and the German question were still hanging in the balance. After 1871, when Italy and Germany had been reorganized and united into viable national states, the situation was profoundly changed, because the two new powers emerging from the Italian and the German power vacuum were now able to act autonomously. The War-in-Sight crisis of spring 1875 demonstrated that rivalry between Germany and France in the West could escalate into a great war at any time even in the absence of an alliance system. Soon after, the Eastern crisis of 1875–78 demonstrated that the same mechanism was at work in the East or, rather, the Southeast. Tensions among Russia, Austria–Hungary, and Germany could at any time be turned into armed conflict by local or regional conflicts in the Balkans. These first two great crises of post-1871 Europe pointed to the potential for conflict on both fronts of the future World War I, the Western and the Eastern/Southeastern, pinpointing their geographical locations and the mechanisms for setting off

the war. If both fronts should be activated at the same time, a great conflagration was sure to result, as it actually did in 1914.

The Congress of Berlin, while neutralizing some of the regional conflicts
in the Balkans for a time, helped to link the two fronts in Europe by indirectly ushering in the European alliance system. The Dual Alliance of 1879
was a direct consequence of the setback the Congress of Berlin had inflicted
on Russia in order to preserve peace among the Great Powers. Failure to have
done this, which was a distinct possibility on at least one occasion, would
have plunged Europe into a great war even in 1878. When the European
alliance system was completed by the Anglo–Russian Convention of 1907,
it ensured that the two fronts would be almost automatically ignited once
the material available for compromise had been consumed by further international crises and once one of the Great Powers became engaged against
another. Thus, the Congress of Berlin, fascinating in itself, becomes important
also for understanding the origins of the great war that it succeeded in
postponing for thirty-six years.

For yet another reason the Congress of Berlin may give us food for
thought in our troubled present. One of the immediate short-term causes
of the Eastern crisis was the world economic crisis of 1873 that ushered in
the Great Depression. The crisis of 1873 hastened the bankruptcy of the
Ottoman Empire, which tried to save itself by more rigorously taxing its
non-Muslim subjects, thus provoking the first uprisings in Hercegovina and
Bosnia in 1875. The economic depression also hastened Russia's decision to
go to war against the Ottoman Empire in 1877.[31] While the Congress of
Berlin succeeded in finding provisional compromise political solutions, the
structural problems raised by the economic crisis of 1873 and the Great
Depression remained. A year after the Congress, the Dual Alliance between
Germany and Austria–Hungary against Russia was matched by the introduction of protective tariffs to help German agriculture and industry. The
agrarian protective tariff brought into the open the incipient structural
divergence between imperial Germany and tsarist Russia, while the industrial
protective tariff was the beginning of "the rise of Anglo–German
antagonism."[32] The German protective tariffs had the long-term effect of
two economic declarations of war that, as so often in history, preceded the
actual military conflict. At the same time, protective tariffs pushed Germany,
probably against the wishes of their first exponents, into a policy of
economic imperialism, expansion overseas, and domination on the European
continent.[33] Just as the first world economic crisis of 1857 was the economic
backbone of Napoleon II's Second Empire and drove him into a series of
increasingly less successful foreign adventures, the world crisis of 1873, in
a much more devious and complicated way, made for revolts and wars in
1875–78 and helped to prepare the conditions for World War I. Even that

war engulfed the first symptoms of economic crisis just beginning to be felt early in 1914. The effect of the world economic crisis of 1929 is simple and well known: political crisis almost everywhere, leading in Germany to the rise of Nazism and to World War II.

Today we can appreciate such ghastly mechanisms more fully in that we are again in the grip of a world economic crisis that has been creeping along since 1973 and that is producing crises and unrest all over the world, in West and East alike. In such a situation we can only hope that falling back into policies of "protecting" national economies will not lead again to economic as a prelude to actual warfare.

Seen in such perspectives, the Congress of Berlin becomes an example of early regional crisis management by the Great Powers of the time. We can better understand now the conditions of its temporary success and the limits of its possibilities without removal of the underlying causes of conflict. The rivalry of world powers for world domination of their particular system and the striving for hegemony in the long run can only provoke opposition, conflict, and disaster.

## NOTES

1.  William N. Medlicott, *The Congress of Berlin and After: A Diplomatic History of the Near Eastern Settlement, 1878–1880* (London, 1938); also Karl Otmar Frhr. von Aretin, ed., *Bismarcks Aussenpolitik und der Berliner Kongress* (Wiesbaden, 1978); I. Geiss, ed. *Der Berliner Kongress 1878: Protokolle und Materialien* (Boppard/Rhein, 1979); Ralph Melville and Hans-Jürgen Schröder, eds., *Der Berliner Kongress von 1878: Die Politik der Grossmächte und die Probleme der Modernisierung von Südosteuropa in der zweiten Hälfte des 19. Jahrhunderts* (Wiesbaden, 1982).

2.  Winfried Baumgart, *Der Friede von Paris 1856: Studien zum Verhältnis von Kriegsführung, Politik und Friedensbewahrung* (Munich, 1972).

3.  See von Aretin, *Bismarcks Aussenpolitik und der Berliner Kongress*; Geiss, *Der Berliner Kongress 1878*; Melville and Schröder, *Der Berliner Kongress von 1878*.

4.  Dietrich Geyer, *Der russische Imperialismus: Studien über den Zusammenhang von innerer und auswärtiger Politik 1860–1914* (Göttingen, 1977); also Barbara Jelavich, *A Century of Russian Foreign Policy, 1814–1914* (Philadelphia, 1964); Paul Kennedy, *The Rise of the Anglo–German Antagonism 1860–1914* (London, 1980); I. Geiss, *German Foreign Policy 1871–1914* (London, 1976).

5.  M. S. Anderson, *The Eastern Question 1774–1923* (London, 1966).

6.  Mihailo D. Stojanović, *The Great Powers and the Balkans 1875–78* (Stanford, 1969).

7.  Dimitrije Djordjević, *Révolutions nationales des peuples balkaniques 1804–1914* (Belgrade, 1965).

8.  Geyer, *Der russische Imperialismus*.

9.  Ronald S. Seth, *The Russian Terrorists: The Story of the Narodniki* (London, 1966).

10.  On Bismarck, see his memoranda to Emperor Wilhelm I pleading for the conclusion of an alliance with Austria–Hungary, especially that of September 7, 1879, published in *Grosse Politik*, no. 461, and in Geiss, *German Foreign Policy*, pp. 183–86.

On Salisbury, see Richard Milman, *Britain and the Eastern Question 1875–1878* (Oxford, 1979).

11.   For more detail based on recent research, see I. Geiss, *Europe and the Origins of the First World War: Towards Overcoming the Concept of "War Guilt"* (Sydney, forthcoming).

12.   Geyer, *Der russische Imperialismus*, pp. 64–69.

13.   Bruce Waller, *Bismarck at the Crossroads: The Reorientation of German Foreign Policy after the Congress of Berlin 1878–1880* (London, 1974).

14.   I. Geiss, "Die deutsche Reichspolitik gegenüber der Aufstandsbewegung in der Herzegovina und in Bosnien, 1875–1878," in *Deutschland und die Vorgeschichte des Ersten Weltkriegs* (Munich, 1978), pp. 76–107, esp. 103–6.

15.   Ibid., p. 86; also Robert Kann, *The Multinational Empire: Nationalism and National Reform in the Habsburg Monarchy, 1848–1918*, 2 vols. (New York, 1964).

16.   See note 10.

17.   Peter Berger, ed., *Der österreich–ungarische Ausgleich von 1867* (Vienna and Munich, 1967).

18.   Kann, *The Multinational Empire*.

19.   This explains why Luigi Albertini started his study of the origins of World War I with the inception of the Compromise of 1867; see L. Albertini, *Origins of the War of 1914*, 3 vols. (London, 1952–57).

20.   Stojanović, *Great Powers*, p. 32.

21.   Quoted in *Schulthess' Europäischer Geschichtskalender* 19 (1878): 108–9, my translation: "Whether the Porte will resist the Austrian invasion cannot be said for sure. But this much is certain: the Bosnian Muslims are all in arms and hardly inclined to throw down their weapons before the approaching Austrian troops. If the Muslims in Bosnia were to form a regular national militia and confront the Bosnian Christians with the alternative of death or a common stand in armed resistance, the occupation of Bosnia would become a rather bloody piece of work, and many thousand Austrian soldiers could perish in it. Once the job has been done Austria will have an additional province, with heaps of rubble rather than places, wastes rather than roads, a province that will for decades be a heavy burden on the Austrian treasury that cannot be relieved without most severely damaging the Hereditary Provinces [*Erblande*]. In every future war Austria wages at any frontier she will have to station a considerable number of troops to protect her southern frontiers. Serbia, Bulgaria, and Montenegro will not stop demanding the independence of Bosnia and its admission to the federation of South Slavic states; thus, Austria will have to reckon in earnest with those states. Nor should anyone harbor illusions about the difficulties which the occupation as such will have to overcome. The Austrian troops will have to advance as though in hostile country and to secure every stage of their advance – which will certainly take months, considering how poor roads are in Bosnia. The 60 million granted by the imperial delegations will hardly cover that difficult labor. The Bosnian fruit, it is to be feared, appeared sweet only as long as it was hanging in the tree; as soon as the first bite is taken it will be noticed how sour it really is. Even Count Andrássy will have to learn that forbidden fruits are not always sweet and that expanding an empire may not always strengthen it."

22.   Vladimir Dedijer, *The Road to Sarajevo* (London and New York, 1966), chaps. 10–15.

23.   Kemal H. Karpat, "The Social and Political Foundations of Nationalism in South East Europe after 1878: A Reinterpretation," in *Der Berliner Kongress von 1878*, ed. Melville and Schröder, pp. 385–410.

24.   Karpat, "Social and Political Foundations", also Stanford J. Shaw, *History of the Ottoman Empire and Modern Turkey*, 2 vols. (Cambridge, 1977–78), 2: 142–43.

25.   Karpat, "Social and Political Foundations," pp. 397 ff.

26.   Peter Bartl, *Die albanischen Muslime zur Zeit der nationalen Unabhängigkeitsbewegung (1878–1912)* (Wiesbaden, 1968).

27.   Charles Jelavich, *Tsarist Russia and Balkan Nationalism: Russian Influence*

*in the Internal Affairs of Bulgaria and Serbia, 1879–1886* (Berkeley, 1958).

28. For more detail and the relevant literature, see I. Geiss, "Die jüdische Frage auf dem Berliner Kongress 1878," *Jahrbuch des Instituts für Deutsche Geschichte* 10 (1981): 412–22.

29. Geiss, *Der Berliner Kongress 1878,* pp. 84–85, 252–53.

30. Joseph Maria von Radowitz, *Aufzeichnungen und Erinnerungen aus dem Leben des Botschafters Joseph Maria von Radowitz,* ed. Hajo Holborn (Stuttgart, 1925), p. 58, my translation.

31. Dietrich Beyrau, "Depression und Kriegsentscheidung: Russlands Weg in den Balkankrieg 1876/77," in *Stadtverfassung, Verfassungsstaat, Pressepolitik: Festschrift für E. Nanjoks,* ed. F. Quartal and W. Setzler (Sigmaringen, 1980), pp. 217–29.

32. Kennedy, *The Rise of the Anglo–German Antagonism.*

33. David Calleo, *The German Problem Reconsidered: Germany and the World Order, 1870 to the Present* (Cambridge, 1978), pp. 16–18.

# V
## Repercussions of the Insurrections and Wars on Armed Forces

Ilia Iliev and Momtchil Ionov

# THE INFLUENCE OF THE RUSSO–TURKISH WAR OF 1877–78 ON BALKAN ARMIES

The Russo–Turkish War of 1877–78 was progressive. It was a just war, a war of liberation. As what amounted to a bourgeois-democratic revolution against Ottoman feudalism, it played a decisive role in the social, economic, and political development of the Balkan states and, to some degree, the development of their armed forces. It has therefore received special attention in both bourgeois and Marxist historiography. There are still, however, many problems that, if properly studied, could throw light on specific aspects of the war and its results. One of these is the impact of the war on the status and development of Balkan armies. While this problem has been touched upon or directly examined in many publications with differing aims, characters, and methodologies, there is no study that deals with Balkan armies as a whole. An investigation of this kind offers an opportunity for the drawing of objective, realistic, and general conclusions by means of comparative analysis and synthesis. In the following presentation we have used the available published sources on the theme as well as archival documents and other materials.

The defeat of the Ottoman Empire in the war of 1877–78 contributed to its disintegration and revealed the backwardness of the Turkish army in organization, recruiting, training, mobilization, and command. Nonetheless, for decades after the war the Turks made no substantial changes indicating that they had learned anything from the experience. They continued to overlook the increased role of mass armies and the changes in the scope and character of military operations that the course of the war had confirmed. Only after the Young Turks' coup d'état in 1908 did the empire undertake a basic restructuring of its army.

The war of 1877–78 laid the foundations for the development of the Bulgarian army with the direct assistance of the Russian army stationed on

Bulgarian territory. It constituted a continuation of the Bulgarian national liberation movement. Besides the 3,000 Bulgarians who served in the Romanian army, many Bulgarian revolutionary bands and battalions joined the struggle, and individual informants and interpreters were part of Russian staffs and army units.[1] In order to aid the offensive of the Russian army across the Danube, a Bulgarian volunteer force joined its ranks. Its history has been comparatively well analyzed.[2] The latest research shows that it involved 12,822 men.[3]

The San Stefano Treaty was the culmination of Russia's liberation campaign. The restoration of the Bulgarian state made it necessary to form an army, one of the most important social institutions and an integral part of the bourgeois state. The creation of a Bulgarian army was made easier by the presence of trained military personnel who had participated in the war and the assistance of the Russian army. The well-armed and trained volunteer corps, with its matériel and combat experience also helped.[4] A difficulty for the army was the complicated European political situation, in which the growing appetites of the Western countries led to interference in the relationships among the Balkan states. Another problem was that the Balkan countries had no general staffs or experience of their own in the conduct of war.[5]

The San Stefano Treaty provided for the formation of a Bulgarian army and granted Russia the right to deploy six infantry and two cavalry divisions on Bulgarian territory.[6] The onerous task of organizing the Bulgarian army was assigned to the tsar's commissioner in Bulgaria, Adjutant-General A. M. Dondukov–Korsakov. The plan for the formation of the Bulgarian Territorial Troops, issued in April 1878, characterized it as a militia, and it was based on the experience of the Bulgarian volunteer force. A territorial principle was employed; companies and cavalry squadrons were to be turned into battalions or even brigades or divisions when necessary. The army consisted of 236 infantry companies, 65 cavalry squadrons, and 64 artillery companies, a total of 84,750 men (a considerable number for that time).[7] Impelled by their own interests in the Balkans, the Western powers initiated the Berlin Congress, held in July 1878. The congress cancelled the provisions of the San Stefano Treaty and divided Bulgaria into three parts, one of them being the self-governing Bulgarian Principality. The Berlin Treaty, described by the French historians Lavisse and Rambould as "a monument of selfishness, an act of envy, an act immoral and low,"[8] created extremely difficult conditions for the development of the Bulgarian army. The initial Russian intention to structure it in terms of a territorial principle was hindered by the partition of Bulgaria and could be realized only in regions where there were Russian troops.

Twelve volunteer battalions established during the war constituted the nucleus of the army. Their reorganization had begun in April and was completed in July 1878.[9] In spite of the Berlin Treaty, Russia continued to build up the Bulgarian army, which retained a unified structure for both parts of Bulgaria — the Principality and Eastern Rumelia — even though the latter remained under the suzerainty of the sultan. The army consisted of thirty infantry battalions, eight batteries, six cavalry squadrons, two companies of field engineers, and a company of siege artillery, a total of 31,400 troops.[10] This was far below the number initially planned because of the territorial and manpower limitations created by the Berlin Congress. Russia's disregard of the stipulations of the treaty aroused protest from the Western powers and Turkey, as a result of which five infantry battalions, two cavalry squadrons, and two batteries were removed from the army. Thereafter the armed forces of the Bulgarian Principality and Eastern Rumelia developed separately up to their union in 1885.[11] The political division of Bulgaria created a special mission for the new army — the uniting of the Bulgarian nation.

The Berlin Treaty gave the Bulgarian Principality the right to maintain a national militia but obliged it to destroy its existing border fortifications without building new ones. Turkey was granted the right to station troops and gendarmerie in Eastern Rumelia. Since the Western powers continued to tolerate the Ottoman Empire, Russia remained the only patron of the Christians on both sides of the Balkan Range.[12]

The Russian administration and army left Bulgaria in the spring of 1879. A temporary regulation issued the same year gave the Bulgarian Territorial Troops a new name, the Bulgarian Army. This was a regular army and included (together with the new Sofia military district) the existing twenty-three infantry battalions, four cavalry squadrons, eight batteries (six infantry, one mountain, and one mounted), one and a half engineer companies, and the logistical command of the local ordnance depot, a total of 16,240 enlisted men.[13]

In 1880 the necessity of creating an armed force to work toward the union of Eastern Rumelia and the Principality led to the formation of the National Volunteer Corps, a relatively independent organization under the command of the Council of Ministers. The volunteer corps recruited men who had been discharged from the regular army after ten years of service. It consisted of infantry and cavalry units numbering from one to two hundred men, to be consolidated into battalions when necessary. The latest research indicates that it numbered about 100,000 men.[14]

The tendency of armed struggle to expand to large-scale warfare that the 1877—78 war had confirmed called for the formation of higher-level military units consisting of different services. The organizers of the Bulgarian army were well aware of this need but unable to meet it immediately after the war.

Regimental organization was introduced in 1880 with the formation of an artillery and a cavalry regiment. General P. D. Parensov's concept of brigade structure was not adopted until 1883. At that time the three regional military commands were disbanded and replaced by four brigades of infantry consisting of six battalions each. A cavalry brigade was also formed consisting of the First and Second Cavalry Regiments. The artillery was reorganized into two regiments consisting of three batteries each. The next year regimental organization was extended to the infantry. Eight infantry regiments consisting of three battalions and an auxiliary company each were formed, with the provision that the second battalion would be augmented as an independent regiment in wartime. This kind of organization allowed for a peacetime strength of 1,793 per regiment and a wartime strength of 3,951.[15]

The Eastern Rumelian militia was established by law as an independent army. Initially, there were two provincial district commands – Plovdiv and Sliven – with two brigades each, a total of nine infantry battalions. By July 1879, the number of battalions had been increased to twelve, and the brigade commands were disbanded. Two years later the province was divided into twelve recruiting commands. The evolution of the Eastern Rumelian militia into a regular army was difficult. After the elimination of the provisional Russian government, the militia did not undergo any organizational change; it continued to consist of twelve infantry battalions and a depot. Its numbers increased from 3,503 in 1875 to 7,500 in 1879.[16]

In August 1879, a Danube fleet was formed from the Russian ships given to Bulgaria and ships captured from the Turks, a total of twelve vessels.

The war of 1877–78 also had a substantial impact on the structure of the Greek army. The two divisions of four brigades each that had been formed at the beginning of the war were replaced in January 1878 by four military commands, one of which was disbanded by the end of the year. In the same year four new infantry battalions were formed, the infantry thus amounting to twenty battalions in all, and the engineers reached eight companies, in two battalions, while the evzones, cavalry, and artillery remained almost unchanged. Thus the peacetime strength of the Greek army totaled 16,021 and its wartime strength 31,926. In April 1880, the military commands were disbanded. The term of active service in the standing army was set at three years, followed by six years in the reserves and a further ten in the National Guards. Two years later a law was passed regulating the size of the army: twenty-seven infantry battalions and seven detached evzone battalions for the land forces, four divisions of four squadrons each for the cavalry, five detached battalions for artillery, and three battalions for the engineers, a total peacetime strength of 24,505.[17]

Regimental structure was adopted by the Greek army almost four years after its introduction into the Bulgarian, beginning in 1884 and being completed in the fall of the following year. According to the supplementary regulations of 1885, which provided for the introduction of brigade and divisional structure, the infantry was to consist of ten regiments and eight detached evzone battalions, the cavalry and artillery of three regiments each, and the engineers of one regiment. Thus the peacetime strength of the army was greatly increased, as can be seen from the following table:

| Year | Personnel | Volunteers SUBJECT TO MOBILIZATION | Total |
|------|-----------|-------------------|-------|
| 1882 . . . . . . . . . . | 29,534 | 1,500 | 31,034 |
| 1883 . . . . . . . . . . | 29,500 | 2,800 | 32,300 |
| 1884 . . . . . . . . . | 30,692 | 3,500 | 34,192 |
| 1885 . . . . . . . . . | 30,652 | 3,500 | 34,152 |

The Law of 1878, its correction of 1882, and the regulations of 1884 stated that men who had served a year in the regular army were to be enlisted in the reserve for ten years; those with active service of two years were enrolled in the reserve for nine years and those exempt from military service for eleven years. Service in the National Guards was set at eight years. The Russo—Turkish War of 1877—78 had a definite impact on the Greek army. In contrast to the situation in Bulgaria, where Russian influence was very strong and the armed forces had been set up with the direct assistance of the Russian army, French influence was much more important in Greece, largely because of the presence there from 1882 through to December of 1887 of a special French military mission.

Serbia laid the foundations of its military reorganization in November 1878. The brigade and corps organization was rather poorly set up because of the short time available for its introduction and the shortcomings of the administrative system in the newly annexed territories. The standing army included an infantry brigade composed of two regiments, a cavalry brigade of four regiments, and a regiment of engineers and cavalry. The national militia's first and second levies comprised troops organized by districts. In all the Serbian army consisted of four corps with two infantry divisions, an artillery and a cavalry regiment, and other units. In 1883 the Serbian government began a reform of its army under the impetus of the accumulation of territorial and manpower resources, the lessons of the war, and the observation of Western armies. The militia system was liquidated and replaced by conscription. In peacetime the standing army, which comprised the first levy of soldiers on two-year tours of active duty and reservists up to the age of thirty, consisted of five infantry regiments, a cavalry regiment, seven artillery regiments, and a battalion of garrison artillery. In wartime, mobilization brought the army to five infantry divisions with three regiments, a cavalry and an artillery regiment, and a company of engineers, a total strength of 111,493. The reserve army was made up of the second levy and consisted of five divisions with artillery, cavalry, and transport regiments and a company of engineers, a total strength of 54,044. The third levy had sixty infantry battalions. Thus in theory the Serbian army had a total strength of 221,177.[19]

The Russo–Turkish War of 1877–78 had a direct impact on the Romanian army as well. The territorial redistribution assigning southern Dobruja to Romania led to the setting up in 1878 of a military council for the region. In the spring of 1880 a special division was formed which was later reorganized and renamed the Fifth Territorial Division.[20] A special supreme council was established with the task of solving the problems uncovered in the course of the war and drawing up a program for the reorganization of the Romanian army. The new structure reflected the results and lessons of the war as well as the modern trends in military science in the Balkans and in Europe. According to the territorial structure adopted, the Romanian army comprised a regular army (eight infantry regiments, four artillery and two cavalry regiments, two battalions of engineers, and one railway squadron) and a territorial army (thirty-four artillery detachments, thirty infantry regiments, and twelve cavalry regiments). In 1880 the infantry units were increased from sixteen to thirty and the cavalry regiments from eight to twelve. The next year thirty more reserve regiments of infantry were organized. In wartime the standing army and the territorial army were combined to form operational groups of variable structure. Conscription was introduced for men between the ages of twenty-one and forty-six. The term of service was four years in the regular army and four in the reserves; for the territorial infantry the terms were six and two years respectively and for the territorial cavalry five and three years. The reorganization of Romania's armed forces was rather ineffective, increasing the size of the army only from 67,121 to 100,361 men by 1880.[21]

A tendency toward the employment of conscription can be observed in the armies of all the Balkan states. This was a logical result of the social, economic, and political developments of the period. Rearrangements in the Bulgarian army were carried out with the aid and direct supervision of the Russian command. The shift to conscription was made difficult there by the conditions created by the Berlin Congress. The general staff and the foreign officers serving in the militia and gendarmerie in Eastern Rumelia had to reject almost 20,000 young men of each levy because the total number was more than the treaty allowed. Some of these men were selected for active service by drawing lots, and the rest were directly enrolled in the volunteer corps.[22]

Initially the command of the Bulgarian army consisted only of Russian commissioned officers. The lack of officers made the establishment of a military school a necessity as early as the beginning of 1878. The military training and curriculum followed the Russian pattern. By September 1885, 450 officers had graduated from it, but that was not enough to satisfy the needs of the army. Ninety-two more young men were sent to Russian military schools, and many of the Sofia military school's graduates trained in Russian army units. The shortage of noncommissioned officers, who had proved to be of great importance during the war, was compensated for by volunteer corps personnel and by the staff of the Russian army. In 1883 special detachments were formed to train specialized personnel. Nevertheless, by September 1885 there was still a shortfall of 266 noncommissioned officers.[23]

The Russian commanders' stay in the Bulgarian Principality and Eastern Rumelia was an education for the officers and men of the Bulgarian army. In the other Balkan states, many officers had taken part in the war or trained in Russian military schools, where the wartime experience was passed on. Commanders of the Romanian, Serbian, and Greek armies who had been trained in Austro—Hungarian, French, and German military schools were less able to benefit from that experience.[24]

The war demonstrated the advantages of rifled infantry and artillery weapons and had a direct impact on the organization of matériel support, particularly in the new Bulgarian army. To meet the needs of the Bulgarian Territorial Troops, the Russian army donated 36,000 rifles of various models (5,000 of which were trophy Turkish Martini—Henry rifles), 90,000,000 cartridges, 236 guns, 167,086 artillery rounds, 2,223 horses, 54,000 uniforms, and 15,000 haversacks. For the equipment of the Eastern Rumalian militia the Russian command donated rifles with cartridges, 27,000 revolvers, and 6,400 swords. The rearmament of the new Greek, Serbian, and Romanian armies after the war forced each country to allot large credits for the purpose. For example, in the period 1879—85 Romania allocated over 25 percent and Greece almost 50 percent of its budget to the army, a substantial part of which went for armament.[26]

The war also influenced the training, instruction, and education of Balkan armies. In the Bulgarian army the Russian commanders directly or indirectly introduced Russian doctrine, ideology, and principles. The attempts of Prince Alexander of Battenberg and other Western officers to impose the Prussian system of training and education proved fruitless. In Bulgaria particular attention was paid in training to inculcating love for the newly liberated homeland and for the army as a symbol of the people's independence and will. A main aim of the Russian and the Bulgarian commanders was to instill martial virtues in their men. Great attention was paid also to the training of noncommissioned and commissioned officers. Class orientation was an inevitable element of this education and training. Organized training of commissioned officers began with the establishment of the Sofia military school immediately after the war, and the training of Bulgarian noncommissioned officers began in 1883. Training there and in Russia was in the spirit of the Russian school. Enlisted men were also trained according to Russian regulations. In this way, the ideas of A. Suvorov, M. Dragomirov, S. Makarov, and others spread throughout the Bulgarian army. Attention was paid to offensive maneuvers; defense was regarded as a temporary form of warfare to be replaced by offense whenever conditions warranted. Proof of the strong Russian influence on the training of the Bulgarian army is the preservation of Russian terms in Bulgarian military terminology today.[27]

The impact of the war on the other Balkan armies is indisputable, but the influence of Russia and the war of 1877–78 on them was gradually transformed and reduced by the pro-Western political orientation of their countries. Thus, for example, with the increase in German and French influence in Romania, priority was given to defensive tactics. The Turkish commanders' attention to defense, especially in fortifications, in 1877–78 caused the Russians to engage considerable forces in sieges. The idea of building a strong defensive system dominated postwar Romanian military doctrine, and this is why in March 1883 only 15,000,000 lei were allocated to the military. This tendency persisted until the beginning of World War I, despite the direct participation of the Romanian army in the capture of Plevna during the Russo–Turkish War.[28]

The state of affairs was similar in Greece. The specially invited French military delegation mentioned above was assigned the task of "supervising the training of the Greek army and examining some of the fortifications."[29] The orientation of Serbia to Austria–Hungary affected the degree of influence that the war of 1877–78 had upon the training of its army. This influence was comparatively greater among the postwar graduates of the Serbian military school, since they were taught by officers who had participated in it.[30] That the training of Serbian officers and men was unsatisfactory is indicated by their defeat in the war with Bulgaria in 1885.

During the war, staffs began to play an increasingly inportant role in planning, preparation, and management, and this led to improvement in the structure and functions of the Balkan army staffs. In the postwar period the staffs of the various national armies were reformed according to concepts specific to each.[31] In Bulgaria this process was difficult because of the separation of the armies of the Bulgarian Principality and Eastern Rumelia. However, with the earnest assistance of the Russian civil administration and its military department, the difficulties were relatively rapidly overcome. Posts that did not exist in the Russian army were created to take into consideration the special Bulgarian conditions.[32]

The creation of mass armies called for an increase in the quantities of matériel and manpower required. The fierceness of the hostilities entailed enormous losses that the imperfect system of mobilization employed in Russia in 1870 could not compensate for. After the war greater attention was paid to mobilization problems. One of these measures taken was to reduce the term of active duty and prolong the term of service in the reserve in order to increase the number of the trained men. In the first years of the postwar period there were no offices in the Balkan ministries of war that dealt with mobilization problems. In Greece a special office called "Military Districts and Mobilization" was established only after the reorganization of the Ministry of War in 1884. In Bulgaria in 1885 one of the three duty officers in the cabinet of the defense minister was put in charge of mobilization problems. The situation was no better in the other Balkan countries.

Until 1884—85 the main authorities for performing a mobilization were the military and the recruitment commands, districts, and regions. Their borders coincided with national administrative units. No plans or regulations defined the character, volume, and terms of their activities. Mobilization arrangements during that period consisted in drawing up wartime vacancies and lists of the reserves subject to mobilization, as well as making mobilization checks. The mobilization capabilities of the Balkan countries were affected by the shortage of matériel. After the war, several small military equipment factories were built, but they could not satisfy the growing needs of the armies. Capitalist ownership of the means of production was a disadvantage in that it prevented a quick transition of private industry and agriculture to military production. This became evident during the wars of 1885, 1912—13, and even 1914—18.[33] Until 1885 the system of mobilization was one of the weakest aspects of of the Balkan armies, one that neglected the experience gained during the war of 1877—78.

The war had a strong impact upon the art of war in the Balkans in 1885, 1912—13, and 1914—18. In 1877—78 a considerable number of Bulgarian revolutionary units were incorporated into the Russian army for purposes of sabotage, reconnaissance, and other missions. For example, fifty men were included in the Fourth Uhlan Regiment, one cavalry squadron in the Third Infantry Narva Regiment, and thirty men in the Seventh Kinbur Regiment.[34] Before and during the Balkan War of 1912—13, which in character and aims was a continuation of the war of 1877—78, the Bulgarian command used the experience of the Russian forces in forming more than a hundred volunteer units from the population of newly liberated Thrace and Macedonia. These units acted in the enemy's rear and aided the offensive of the Bulgarian and allied armies. They supplied information about the structure, concentration, and deployment of the Turkish forces, carried out sabotage missions that demoralized the enemy army and the civilian population, and protected the Christian population from the outrages of the Turks. Furthermore, as a result of the experience of the war of 1877–78, on the eve of the Balkan War a special volunteer force, the Macedonian–Edirne Volunteer Corps, was formed from among emigrants from Thrace and Macedonia as part of the Bulgarian army. Numbering 14,640 men, it had as its prototype the Bulgarian volunteer force. The Macedonian–Edirne volunteer corps took an active part in the hostilities and showed great bravery in repelling the Turkish landing at Bulair and Sarköy in the beginning of 1913.[35]

The secret strategic deployment of the main Russian forces in the direction of Svishtov, Veliko Turnovo, and Stara Zagora in the 1877–78 war served as a model for planning operations of the Bulgarian army in the Thracian theater during the Balkan War, for example, the concentration and the deployment of the Bulgarian First and Third Armies. The secret deployment of a whole army, the Third, led to success in the battle of Lozengrad, in which the army covered a distance of more than 120 kilometers in six days, a comparatively rapid pace for the time.[36]

The secret night crossing of the Danube by the Russian army in 1877, with full sound and light camouflage and special group distribution, was emulated by the Bulgarian army in World War I. The Romanian forces that crossed the Danube near the village of Riahovo were repelled and forced to withdraw because of unsatisfactory preliminary preaparation, organization, and interaction. At the end of November 1916, the Bulgarian army, having learned from the Russian experience of 1877 and from the Romanian failure, succeeded in crossing the Danube near Svishtov and Somovit and capturing Bucharest.[37]

Using the experience of the active defensive tactics and withdrawals of the Russian army and the Bulgarian volunteer corps near Nova Zagora and Stara Zagora in June–July 1877, the Bulgarian command carried out defensive actions in the early stages of the war with Serbia in 1885. It employed small covering detachments in different directions against numerically superior Serbian forces to provide time for concentration of the Bulgarian forces toward the Serbian border. The realization of the Bulgarian strategy was made possible by the high morale of the Bulgarian soldiers and their commanders. Those qualities had been developed under the influence of the Russian army in the postwar period from 1878 to 1885. The Balkan Wars confirmed that rapid maneuvers were becoming more significant.

Under extremely difficult conditions of weather and terrain, two battalions of the First Sofia Infantry Regiment covered a distance of 86 kilometers in 36 hours while the Eighth Infantry Regiment covered 95 kilometers.

The special deffensive features of the 1877–78 war were developed further during the Serbo—Bulgarian War of 1885, when the defenses near the town of Slivnitsa, including redoubts, lunettes, and trenches, were built on the model of the Russian fortifications of 1877–78. The skirmishing line won recognition as an element of the infantry order of battle. The increased necessity for interaction between the infantry and the artillery was confirmed.[38] The creative use of the experiences and lessons of 1877–78 brought victory to the Bulgarians in 1885. In the words of Friedrich Engels, "the Bulgarians, who amounted to one-third of the Serbian army (not counting the Russian officers), defeated them all down the line and won the respect and the admiration of all of Europe."[39]

The Russian siege of Plevna in 1877 was studied by the Bulgarian command and the experience creatively applied both in the peacetime training of the Bulgarian army and during its wars. Examples include the maneuvers near Shumen on the eve of the Balkan War and the siege and the capture in March 1913 of the Edirne fortress, one of the strongest in southeastern Europe. Over 33,000 men were taken captive in Edirne, along with 413 guns, 12,236 rifles, 46 machine-guns, and more than 10,000,000 cartridges. A French specialist called this "one of the most glorious feats of arms in the military history of all peoples."[40] Another example was the capture in September 1916 of the equally important Tutrakan fortress, where 28,500 soldiers and officers were taken captive, along with enormous quantities of weapons and ammunition. In the Edirne operation the following lessons of 1877–78 found full expression: close interaction among the infantry, artillery, engineers, and cavalry, concentration of the main forces in the area of the main assault, and correct and timely maneuvers.[41]

During the Balkan Wars, one Bulgarian concept was to mount offensives in several directions by means of large advance detachments. For example, the Rhodopa, Haskovo, and Kurdjali detachments liberated tens of Bulgarian towns and villages in Thrace and Macedonia. The brave actions of the Kurdjali detachment and the Macedonian—Edirne volunteer corps resulted in the capture of the entire corps of Javer Pasha, 9,500 men, over 9,000 rifles, and 8 guns.[42]

In the course of the war of 1877–78, the Russian army established military administration and a local militia in the newly liberated towns. The Bulgarians used this experience in the Balkan Wars (1912–13) by forming in the liberated lands of Thrace and Macedonia provinces under the rule of a military governor whose functions resembled those of the Russian authorities during the war of liberation. New local administrative bodies were established, as well as local militias for the preservation of law and order, the supply of food and fodder, and the formation of volunteer forces.[43]

It is evident that the war of 1877–78 played a decisive role in the postwar development of the armies of the Balkan countries. The influence of Russia and the war of 1877–78 were most evident in Bulgaria. The foundations of the Bulgarian army were laid in the course of the war itself (the Bulgarian volunteer force), and it developed under the control and with the direct assistance of the Russian army. The influence of the war on the armies of the other Balkan countries was weaker in direct relationship to their foreign policies and military orientation toward France, Germany, and Austria–Hungary.

The impact of the war was clearest in the peacetime development of the armies of the Balkan countries in the period 1878–85. The influence of the war on military strategy and tactics was demonstrated during the wars of 1885, 1912–13, and 1914–18.

## NOTES

1. Atanas Benderev, *Istoria na bulgarskoto opaltchenie i osvobozdenieto na Bulgaria 1877–78* (Sofia, 1930), p. 65; S. I. Kisov, *Bulgarskoto opaltchenie v osvoboditelnata rusko–turska vojna 1877–78 g.: Dejstvieto na 3-ta druzina ot bulgarskoto opaltchenie* (Sofia, 1897), p. 22; Akop A. Ulunjan, *Bulgarskiat narod v rusko–turskata vojna 1877–1878 g.* (Sofia, 1972); Stefan Dojnov, "Utchastieto na bulgarskia narod vav vojnata," in *Rusko–turskata osvoboditelna vojna 1877–1878* (Sofia, 1977), pp. 279–319.

2. Benderev, *Istoria na bulgarskoto opaltchenie*; idem, *Bulgarskoto opaltchenie*, 2 vols. (Sofia, 1956–59); Atas Venedikov, *Istoria na bulgarskoto opaltchenie i osvobozdenieto na Bulgaria 1877–1878* (Sofia, 1930); N. P. Ovsiannii, *Bolgarskoe opoltchenie i zemskoe vojsko: K istorii grazdanskogo upravlenia i okkupacii v Bolgarii v 1877–1879 g.* (St. Petersburg, 1904); Stoyan Penkov, *Boen primer i bratska pomosht* (Sofia, 1974); Yono Mitev, *Bulgarskoto opaltchenie v osvoboditelnata vojna*, 2d ed. (Sofia, 1955); Georgi Vulkov, *Bulgarskoto opaltchenie: Formirane, bojno ispolzuvane i istoritcheska sadba* (Sofia, 1983).

3. Rumen Rumenin, *Bulgarskoto opaltchenie 1877–1878 g.: Litchen sastav, po dokumenti na CVA Veliko Turnovo* (Sofia, 1978), p. 14; Mitev, *Bulgarskoto opaltchenie*, p. 47.

4. CVA, f. 42-k, op. 1, a. e. 12, l. 2–60; a. e. 57, l. 28–29; Georgi Vulkov, *Ruskite utchiteli na bulgarskoto vojnstvo* (Sofia, 1977), pp. 9–26, 89–214; N. R. Ovsiannii, *Russkoe upravlenie v Bolgarii v 1877–1879 gg.: Rossiiskii imperatorskii komissar v Bolgarii general-adjutant knjaz A. M. Dondukov–Korsakov*, vol. 2 (St. Petersburg, 1906), pp. 43–46.

5. K. Iretchek, *Bulgarski dnevnik (1879–1889)* (Plovdiv–Sofia, 1930), p. 159; *Kratak obzor na bojnia sastav, organizatziata, popalvaneto i mobilizatziata na bulgarskata armia ot 1878 do 1944 g.* (Sofia, 1961), p. 13; *Mezdunarodni aktove i dogovori (1648–1918)* comp. Slava Stefanova, ed. Petar Petrov (Sofia, 1958), pp. 15–54.

6. *Mezdunarodni aktove i dogovori*, pp. 148–51.

7. *Bulgarskata zemska vojska 1878–1879 g.: Sasdavane na bulgarskata vojska sled osvoboditelnata rusko–turska vojna*, Sbornik ot dokumenti i materiali (Sofia, 1959), pp. 119, 120, 125–40; *Osvobozdenie Bolgarii ot turetzkogo iga, dokumenti:*

*Borba za sosdanie bolgarskogo gosudarstva 1878–1879*, vol. 2 (Moscow, 1967), p. 153; *Sbornik materialov po grazdanskomu upravleniu i okkupatzii v Bolgarii 1877–1879 g. g*, vol. 4 (St. Petersburg, 1905), pp. 288–97.

8.   Er. Lavisse and Al. Rambould, *Histoire générale du IV siècle à nos jours*, vol. 12, *Le monde contemporain 1870–1900* (Paris, 1939), pp. 477–78.

9.   CVA, f. 42-k, op. 1, a. e. 12, l. 2–60.

10.   *Bulgarskata zemska vojska*, pp. 107–9.

11.   Goran Todorov, *Vremennoto rusko upravlenie prez 1878–79 g*. (Sofia, 1958), pp. 100, 292–93; *Bulgarskata zemska vojska*, pp. 101–3.

12.   Muratov, *Dokumenti za dejnostta na rusite po uredbata na grazdanskoto upravlenie v Bulgaria ot 1877–1879 g*. (Sofia, 1905), p. 302; P. D. Parensov, *Iz proshlogo: Iz bospomenania ofitzera Generalnogo shtaba*, vol. 4, *V Bolgarii, tcherez 30 let* (St. Petersburg, 1908), p. 123; *Mezdunarodni aktove i dogovori*, pp. 148–51.

13.   *Sistematitcheski sbornik na zakonite, ukazite, zapovedite i tzirkularite po voennoto vedomstvo ot 1877–1878 g. do 1 januari 1901 g*. (Sofia, 1901), pp. 153–57; CVA, f. 1, op. 5, a. e. 49, l. 1–11.

14.   I. Panajotov, "Opit za saedinenieto na Knjazestvo Bulgaria s Istotchna Rumelia pres 1880 g.," *Izvestia na bulgarskoto istoritchesko druzestvo* 22–24 (1848): 17–41; *Darzaven vestnik* (Sofia), December 10, 1880; *Istoria na srubsko–bulgarskata vojna 1885 g*. (Sofia, 1925), p. 45.

15.   CVA, f. 1, op. 1, a. e. 9, l. 3; f. 1, op. 5, a. e. 58, l. 101, and op. 5, a. e. 57, l. 116, 522; *Istoria na srubsko–bulgarskata vojna*, pp. 87–88; Benderev, *Istoria na bulgarskoto opaltchenie*, p. 382.

16.   CVA, f. 42-p, op. 1, a. e. 37, l. 65; a. e. 39, l. 40; a. e. 41, l. 271; *Bulgarskata zemska vojska*, p. 229; "Materiali za istoriata na Iztotchnorumeliiskata militzia i zandarmeria 1879–1885 g.," *Voennoistoritcheski sbornik* 4 (1930): 137, 139, 140; *Istoria na srubsko–bulgarskata vojna 1885 g*. (Sofia, 1971), p. 99.

17.   *Istoria tis organoseos tu eliniku statu 1821–1954* (Athens, 1957), pp. 50–60.

18.   *Istoria tis organoseos*, pp. 59–62.

19.   Tchervenakov, *Ustroistvo na vaoruzenite sili na Surbia ot 1827 do 1885 g.,* CVA, inv. N 3552, l. 17–19; *Documente privind României: Documente privind Războiul pentru independenţă, Evenimente militare premergataare anului 1877*, vol. 1 (Bucharest, 1959), pp. 64, 67, 667–69; *Documente privind istoria militara poporului Român: iulie 1878–novembre 1882* (Bucharest, 1974), p. 206.

20.   *Documente privind istoria*, pp. 23, 26, 33, 45, 54, 88–89, 140, 167–68, 203.

21.   *Documente privind istoria*, pp. vii–viii, 22, 23, 34, 51, 55–56, 95–96, 131, 201–10, 226, 228–30.

22.   Georgi Vulkov, "Izgrazdane na bulgarskata armia sled osvobzdenieto," in *Rusko–turskata osvoboditelna vojna 1877–1878* (Sofia, 1977), pp. 339–40.

23.   Vulkov, "Izgrazdane na bulgarskata armia," p. 342; CVA, f. 42-l. op. 1, a. e. 1, l. 1–4.

24.   *Istoria na srubsko–bulgarskata vojna*, p. 121; *Documente privind istoria*, pp. 173–74; *Istoria tis organoseos*, p. 64; Vl. Jorjevitch, *Istoria srpsko–bugarskog rata 1885 g.,* vol. 1 (Belgrade, 1908), pp. 14–15.

25.   CVA, f. 42-p, op. 1, a. e. 37, l. 65; a. e. 39, l. 40; a. e. 41, l. 271; "Materiali za istoriata na Iztotchnorumeliiskata militzia," pp. 137, 139–40; *Bulgarskata zemska vojska*, p. 229; *Isotriatis organoseos*, p. 59; *Istoria na srubsko–bulgarskata vojna*, pp. 98–102; *Istoria na srubsko–bulgarskata vojna* (Sofia, 1971), pp. 83–88, 99–100.

26.   Vulkov, *Ruskite utchiteli*, Table No. 1; *Istoria tis organoseos*, pp. 59, 64; *Documente privind istoria*, pp. 79–82, 203.

27.   *Sistematitcheski sbornik*, pp. 1, 806, 807, 1154, 1208, 1210, 1244; *Bulgarskata zemska vojska*, pp. 615, 619, 806; *Darzaven vestnik* (Sofia), April 1880; *Istoria na srubsko–bulgarskata vojna* (Sofia, 1971), pp. 77, 89; CVA, f. 42-k, op. 1, a. e. 43, l. 13, 27 and a. e. 48, l. 228.

28.   R. Atanasov, *Srubsko–bulgarskata vojna 1885 g*. (Veliko Turnovo, 1926), p.

21; V. Tcholpanov, "Vlianie na ruskoto i savetskoto voenno izkustvo varhu bulgarskoto voenno izkustvo," *Izvestia na voennoistoritcheskoto nautchno druzestvo* 2 (1966): 50.

29. *Istoria tis organoseos,* p. 63.

30. *Istoria na srubsko—bulgarskata vojna* (Sofia, 1971), p. 135.

31. *Istoria tis organoseos,* pp. 52—65; *Documente privind istoria,* pp. 33, 370; Vulkov, "Izgrazdane na bulgarskata armia," pp. 349—51.

32. Vulkov, "Izgrazdane na bulgarskata armia," pp. 349—51.

33. *Istoria na srubsko—bulgarskata vojna* (Sofia, 1971), pp. 76—82, 97—99, 107—13, 126—29, 140—41; Benderev, *Istoria na bulgarskoto opaltchenie,* pp. 7—8; *Istoria tis organoseos,* pp. 53—54, 59, 62; *Documente privind istoria,* pp. 147—51.

34. *Osvobozdenie Bolgarii ot turetzkogo iga,* pp. 304, 336—37, 449.

35. Petar Darvingov, *Istoria na Makedono—Odrinskoto opaltchenie,* 2 vols. (Sofia, 1919—25); *Balkanskata vojna 1912—1913 g.* (Sofia, 1961), pp. 176—83, 383, 389—401.

36. Radko Dimitriev, *Treta armia v Balkansk ta vojna* (Sofia, 1922), pp. 104—21; Abdullah Pasha, *Spomeni ot vojnata protiv Bulgaria 1912 g.* (Sofia, 1929), p. 108; *Balkanskata vojna,* pp. 109—228.

37. Tshte Atasov, D. Christov, and B. Tcholpanov, *Bulgarskoto voenno izkustvo prez kapitalizma* (Sofia, 1959), pp. 288—89; A. Christov, *Istoritcheski pregled na Obshtoevropejaskata vojna i utchastieto na Bulgaria v nea* (Sofia, 1925), pp. 343—47, 382—83.

38. Blenkner, *Voennoistoritchesko znatchenie na srubsko—bulgarskata vojna* (Sofia, 1900), p. 100; *Istoria na srubsko—bulgarskata vojna* (Sofia, 1971), pp. 165—223, 226.

39. K. Marx and F. Engels, *Sotchinenia,* 2d ed., vol. 36 (Moscow, 1965), p. 473.

40. Cited in A. Peicher, *Primosat na blgarskiat narod za razvitieto na voennoto izkustvo* (Sofia, 1972), p. 19.

41. Atanas Peytchev, *Prinosat na bulgarskia narod za pazvitieto na voennoto izkustvo* (Sofia, 1972), p. 19; *Balkanskata vojna,* pp. 383—446; *Bulgarskata armia v svetovnata vojna 1914—1918 g.*, Vojnata sreshtu Rumania prez 1916 godina, Podgotovka na vojnata i Tutrakanskata opertzia, vol. 8 (Sofia, 1939), pp. 243—679; *Kratka voenna istoria na Bulgaria 681—1945* (Sofia, 1977), pp. 300—301; *Odrin 1912—1913: Spomeni,* comp. Momtchil P. Yonov (Sofia, 1983).

42. *Balkanskata vojna,* pp. 287—309.

43. Vladimir Karamanov, "Niakolko dami za sazdadenia ot voennite vlasti Strumishki okrag v natchaloto na balkanskata vojna pres 1912 godina," *Voennoistoritcheski sbornik* 8, no. 18 (1934): 58—94.

Robert J. Donia

# THE HABSBURG IMPERIAL ARMY IN THE OCCUPATION OF BOSNIA AND HERCEGOVINA

In late July 1878 several columns of the Habsburg imperial army crossed the border into the Ottoman provinces of Bosnia and Hercegovina, inaugurating a period of Austro—Hungarian rule that was to last until the monarchy's dissolution in 1918. The Dual Monarchy was acting in accord with a mandate from the Great Powers in the Treaty of Berlin to "occupy and administer" Bosnia and Hercegovina.[1] The Habsburg authorities approached their challenge with the enthusiasm and self-assurance typical of nineteenth-century European colonial conquerors in non-Western lands. But neither occupying nor administering these volatile Balkan provinces proved to be an easy task: strife in these lands contributed mightily to the great conflagration that broke out in 1914 and ultimately destroyed the monarchy.

To occupy and pacify Bosnia and Hercegovina, imperial authorities employed three types of military organizations, each targeted against a particular type of violent threat to public order. Regular imperial army units were given the mission of initially conquering the provinces and defeating large-scale resistance to the monarchy's authority. A gendarmerie was created to establish and maintain local security. The "Streifcorps," a special auxiliary arm of the gendarmerie, was designed to eliminate persistent brigandage in the mountainous hinterlands of Bosnia and Hercegovina. In this article, I shall describe the deployment of these three organizations and assess their impact on the occupied provinces during the first decade of Habsburg rule.

Ironically, in accomplishing their primary missions, all three military organizations also inadvertently contributed to the imbroglio of ethnic and social conflict in the occupied lands. The armed forces brought about major changes in Bosnia and Hercegovina but not always in the manner desired or expected by imperial officials. While they disarmed most groups and persons with violent intent and insured that large-scale violence was no longer a viable means for Bosnians to achieve political aims, in so doing they often aroused the antagonism of the local population. Because all military groups were made up primarily of soldiers from the monarchy proper rather than from the occupied lands, this rancor was often translated into resentment of the Dual Monarchy as a whole. Thus much contention was merely rechanneled rather than eliminated, and many of the issues came to be fought out in the political arena rather than by paramilitary forces.

## Bosnia and Hercegovina before Habsburg Occupation

In the latter half of the fifteenth century the Ottoman Turks conquered Bosnia and Hercegovina. Their rule was at first relatively tolerable for the Slavic population. Many Slavs voluntarily accepted Islam, adding a third religion to the Catholic and Orthodox faiths.[2] In subsequent centuries religion became an increasingly important marker of ethnicity: Orthodox Slavs were Serbs, Catholic Slavs were Croats, and Muslim Slavs constituted an ethnic group known as the Bosnian Muslims.

When Ottoman administration began to weaken in the seventeenth and eighteenth centuries, strife between the three major ethnic groups intensified. Many Muslim landlords usurped the right to own land rather than simply administer it on behalf of the sultan, with the result that many Croatian and Serbian peasants were enserfed. Muslim landlords frequently abused their peasants, and local pashas arbitrarily taxed the population. Peasant uprisings increased and were frequently occasions of interethnic acrimony. Despite the Ottoman "reform" movement of the nineteenth century, Constantinople's control over Bosnia and Hercegovina was sporadic and incomplete for many decades prior to 1878.[3]

As Ottoman control deteriorated and landlord abuses increased, brigandage came to be a way of life for many lower-class Bosnians and Hercegovinians. Brigand bands were normally made up of members of a single ethnic group. In addition to retaliating against their oppressors, the brigands sought to conduct economic activities free from the bounds of control by the state or their landlords. They smuggled salt and tobacco (two state monopolies), rustled cattle, and maintained caches of arms. Brigands were most secure in the mountain retreats in eastern Hercegovina. They could strike quickly, then retreat into the mountains or simply melt back into the villages whence they came. At times it was difficult to distinguish between bandits, shepherds, and national heroes. Shepherds tended their flocks and occasionally staged bandit raids; brigands attracted hundreds of followers and gave stirring orations to villagers at times of rebellion against Ottoman authority. All Bosnian ethnic groups cherished (and still cherish) the memory of brigands, regarding them as champions of group resistance to oppressive rule and foreign domination.

In 1875, Ottoman administrative abuses collided with the growing resentment and aspirations of the Christian population. Christian (mainly Serbian) peasants launched a full-scale rebellion against their Turkish overlords, and the resulting upheaval created general instability in southeastern Europe.[4] Serbia and Montenegro declared war on the Ottoman Empire in 1876 in defense of their Serbian brethren in neighboring Bosnia and Hercegovina. Russia entered the fray by declaring war on the Ottomans in 1877. In the spring of 1878 the Russians delivered a heavy blow to the Ottomans by nearly conquering Constantinople. The Ottomans, forced to sue for peace, found their authority in Bosnia and Hercegovina severely debilitated.

The unrest of 1875–78 exacerbated the tendency of all ethnic groups in Bosnia and Hercegovina to organize armed bands. Serbs and Muslims had the largest paramilitary groups. Serbian insurgents organized pandour corps, militia-like groups that fought against Ottoman regulars and other Muslim forces. Ottoman gendarmes, known as *zaptieh*, were almost all Bosnian Muslims; they fought Christian rebels during the 1875–78 period and often went on freebooting expeditions to terrorize Christian peasants. Deserters from regular Ottoman army units wandered the countryside, looting and plundering. The well-armed population came to view any government as an unwelcome intruder. Bosnians associated "government" more with capricious rule and arbitrary taxation than with orderly civil administration.

Much as Serbian brigands formed the nucleus of the rebellion against Ottoman rule in 1875, renegade Ottoman forces posed a considerable potential threat to any Habsburg occupation. By the spring of 1878 the deterioration of Ottoman authority in the countryside was virtually complete. The Turkish regime was no longer able to feed and clothe its own soldiers, nor could it curb the excesses of the deserters who roamed the countryside. When the Porte attempted to draft more soldiers from the Muslim population in 1878, conscription could be carried out only in towns and garrisons, and some confrontations took place between Ottoman authorities and Bosnian Muslims.[5] The loyalty of many Ottoman regulars was suspect. Of twenty-three Ottoman battalions stationed in Bosnia and Hercegovina, nineteen were made up entirely of Bosnian Muslim conscripts, and almost all battalions were stationed in the conscripts' home towns.[6] Turkey's defeat at the hands of Russia in March 1878 exposed to all the hopeless weakness of the Ottoman state and raised the possibility of another power's occupying Bosnia. Many Bosnian Muslims, determined to resist occupation by any Christian power, made plans to defend Bosnia on their own.

The issue of a possible Habsburg occupation put the Ottoman authorities on the spot. Most Ottoman officials were Muslims and not naturally sympathetic to the notion of Habsburg occupation, but neither could they sanction a popular resistance movement. Tensions rose between Bosnian

Muslims and the Ottoman authorities, particularly in the major cities of Bosnia and Hercegovina. In May 1878 the lower- and middle-class Muslim elements in Sarajevo began to pressure the Ottoman authorities to resist any foreign occupation. Bosnian Muslim landlords worked to avoid an open revolt, and on June 5, 1878, prominent Muslim landlords in Sarajevo formed the National Council, a group that met with the blessing of the Ottoman governor and yet satisfied for a time the demands of the lower- and middle-class artisans. On July 3, word arrived in Sarajevo that the Dual Monarchy had been awarded Bosnia and Hercegovina by the Great Powers meeting in Berlin. Lower-class Bosnian Muslims, faced with the imminent prospect of a Christian power governing their land, forced a membership change in the National Council and ousted many moderate landlords. After July 6 the council was dominated by lower-class Muslims committed to armed resistance against Habsburg occupation of Bosnia and Hercegovina.[7]

Throughout July 1878 the Council coexisted uncomfortably with the remnants of Ottoman authority in Sarajevo. Even though his authority was weakened, the Ottoman governor retained the loyalty of many Bosnians and control of munitions critical to any armed resistance to Austro–Hungarian occupation. On July 12, a new Ottoman military commander for Bosnia arrived from Constantinople with a battalion of troops, temporarily strengthening the governor's hand. But the new troops were reluctant to fire on their fellow Muslims. On July 28, Bosnian Muslim irregulars attacked the fortress where the Ottoman troops were quartered, and the newly arrived soldiers refused to fire on their attackers. Bosnian Muslims stormed the fortress and seized the munitions depot. These events doomed the Ottoman military commander and the governor. The National Council met, formed a provisional government, and arrested the Ottoman commander. The Council immediately became the focal point of planning for massive armed resistance to Habsburg occupation.

In a sense, the Bosnian Muslim radicals staged one of the most futile revolutions in history: they overthrew the Ottoman government on its last day in power before Habsburg troops invaded Bosnia. Some historians even suspect that the Ottoman authorities abetted the Muslim resistance movement, although Rade Petrović has recently concluded that Ottoman officials worked diligently to maintain peace and discourage Bosnian Muslim resistance.[8] Nevertheless, the Bosnian Muslims were quickly able to assemble an impressive coalition of forces to fight Austro–Hungarian troops. Leading figures in the movement included the colorful Muslim bandit Hadži Loja and the Mufti of Pljevlja, Mehmed Vehbi Šemsekadić. Joining the resistance were many Muslim zaptieh, entire units of Ottoman regulars that defected to fight the Habsburgs, Bosnian Muslim bandits, Serbian brigands, and a few Croats and Jews. From August until October of 1878, these forces fought valiantly to drive the modern, well-equipped Habsburg troops from their native land.

## Imperial Army Troops: Initial Deployment

In late July the Habsburg army began its entry into Bosnia and Hercegovina in a spirit of blithe optimism, even frivolity. Count Gyula Andrássy, foreign minister at the time of the occupation, anticipated that a demonstrative entry into Bosnia with token imperial forces ("a squadron of hussars and a regimental band") would suffice to win the loyalty of the population for Austria–Hungary.[9] Andrássy's high hopes echoed those of other imperial authorities, who were ecstatic that Habsburg territorial gains were again proceeding at the expense of the enfeebled Ottoman Empire. Imperial officials were eager to show that they could bring security and progress to the chaotic provinces through education and superior administrative practices.

For a time these high expectations seemed justified: the first few days of the invasion resembled a military parade. On Bosnia's northern boundary, three divisions making up the Thirteenth Corps under the command of Feldzeugmeister Joseph Freiherr von Filipović crossed the Sava River on July 29. The Sixth Division crossed at Brod, the Seventh Division at Gradiška, and the Twentieth Division at Šamac, each to begin a drive toward Sarajevo along different communication arteries.[10] Local Ottoman garrison commanders and civilian officials greeted the Habsburg troops, and the imperial commanders left most of them in their positions under new supervision. Simultaneously units of the Eighteenth Division under the command of Feldmarschall Leutnant Stefan Jovanović moved north into Hercegovina from Austrian Dalmatia.

The ebullience and tranquility were short-lived. Within a few days the advancing imperial army units encountered resistance from local Muslims and from units dispatched by the National Council in Sarajevo. In early August the Sixth Division fought major encounters at Maglaj and Žepče, the Seventh Division met strong resistance at Jajce and Banjaluka, and the Twentieth Division was temporarily driven back from Donja Tuzla. The opposition came not from well-organized, unified fighting forces but from bands of Muslim and Serbian brigands, Ottoman army deserters who were native Bosnians, former Ottoman gendarmes, and others recruited by opponents of Habsburg occupation. These motley soldiers conducted hit-and-run guerrilla raids in the forested, mountainous terrain, and they succeeded in arresting the advance of the imperial regulars, with their disciplined formations and heavy loads of supplies and munitions.

The upsurge of resistance startled the monarchy's military commanders.

Filipović, advancing from the north, ordered his troops to secure the major communication arteries to the interior and to drive toward Sarajevo; pacification of the countryside could wait until later. Jovanović, moving north and east into Hercegovina from Dalmatia, sought to take Mostar as quickly as possible and secure his major communications with Dalmatia. Mostar was taken by units of the Eighteenth Division on August 5. The battle for Sarajevo lasted much longer, since the Sixth, Seventh, and Twentieth Divisions had to overcome resistance and make a long drive to the interior. After extensive house-to-house fighting, Sarajevo was taken by Filipović's men on August 19. The imperial troops had faced opposition units as large as several thousand men.

From the military standpoint, the conquest of Sarajevo and Mostar was only the first step in securing the provinces. Muslim-led forces melted away in the face of superior Austro–Hungarian firepower, but they quickly regrouped after the imperial army had passed. Even before Sarajevo was taken on August 19, the general staff mobilized the First, Fourth, and Thirty-sixth Divisions and the Twentieth Infantry Brigade to secure Filipović's rear communication lines. After Sarajevo was conquered, Filipović requested further reinforcements, and the Thirteenth, Fourteenth, Thirty-first, and Thirty-third Divisions and the Fourteenth Cavalry Brigade were mobilized.[11] The resulting total force of about 250,000 men, making up the Second Army, was able to move beyond securing the two major cities and conduct search-and-destroy operations.

Beginning in late August, the imperial forces aggressively pursued concentrations of opposition forces and secured all communication lines. Large battles were fought in northeastern Bosnia, where the Mufti of Pljevlja had sizable units under his command. To the east of Sarajevo, Habsburg units took towns one by one until they had secured the area to the Drina River. In northwestern Bosnia heavy fighting took place at Ključ and Bihać before the imperial army conquered the area. Habsburg commanders quickly adjusted to fighting in the mountains of Bosnia by sending advance scouting parties into higher terrain to avoid ambushes.[12] Eventually, with the advantage of greater numbers and superior firepower, the emperor's army succeeded in dislodging the resistance forces from their trenches and fortifications. Although the fighting lasted into October 1878, the imperial forces crushed the large-scale resistance movement and disarmed opposition forces. The cost was much higher than anticipated. The Second Army's 250,000 men, about one-third of the imperial army's entire war strength, suffered over 5,000 casualties, including over 800 men killed.

The primary losers in the battles of 1878 were the Bosnian Muslims, who had frequently used violence with success to resist effective rule from Constantinople and to retain their privileged position as the dominant ethnic group in Bosnia and Hercegovina. Ottoman military forces had frequently been poorly disciplined and unreliable instruments of central government control. Many units stationed in Bosnia were made up largely of Bosnian Muslim conscripts, and those dispatched from Constantinople (such as the battalion that arrived in Sarajevo in July 1878) were also subject to impulses of independent behavior when faced with local turmoil or disorders. Their leaders could easily be enticed or coerced into taking sides in local political quarrels, especially when communications with Constantinople were poor. Members of the Bosnian Muslim local elites were thus able to conclude informal alliances with Ottoman military commanders or undermine their authority by appeals to Constantinople. Such tactical victories often served to increase the prerogatives of Bosnian Muslim landlords in dealing with Christian peasants as they chose.

The Habsburg imperial victory in 1878 meant that the Bosnian Muslims could no longer influence government policies by resort to paramilitary activities. The zaptieh and brigand bands were mostly destroyed, disarmed, or disbanded in the fighting that lasted from August to October of 1878. Having lost an important political tool that they had systematically used in Ottoman times, thousands of Bosnian Muslims – peasants, landlords, and artisans alike – emigrated to Constantinople and elsewhere in the Ottoman Empire rather than remain in Bosnia under a Christian occupier.[13] Those who remained gradually turned to less violent forms of protest such as petitions and audiences with imperial authorities. In the first years of the occupation, some Muslims protested, occasionally successfully, against the forcible quartering of Austro–Hungarian troops in Bosnian homes.[14] With the exception of the uprising of 1881–82 (to be discussed below), the interests of the Bosnian Muslims were advocated by means strikingly peaceful when compared with the violence so often employed by Muslim bandits and gendarmes during the Ottoman years and in 1878. Around the turn of the century, for example, Muslim political activists launched a province-wide campaign for educational, cultural, and religious autonomy.[15] These peaceful activities went on even though the imperial army's presence, as a rule, rendered archaic the kind of informal agreements with which Bosnian Muslim local leaders had achieved many of their aims under Ottoman rule.

From the monarchy's standpoint, the imperial army accomplished its primary mission in 1878. But military leaders were unable definitively to secure the two provinces and wipe out brigandage in mountainous areas. They faced serious political constraints. The expenses of the occupation had been met out of special allocations voted by the Delegations, but political opposition to further expenditures in Bosnia and Hercegovina was particularly strong in the Hungarian half of the monarchy. Imperial authorities could not retain troop strengths at desired levels; as will be seen below, they were even forced to settle for a gendarmerie well below authorized strength. Furthermore, they wished to avoid any embarrassing armed confrontations that might call into question Austria—Hungary's ability to administer its newly acquired Balkan colony. From the very outset of the occupation, Vienna urged its officers in the field to compromise whenever possible to avoid bloodshed.[16] Consequently imperial authorities frequently vacillated and negotiated in an effort to stave off undesired confrontations with the local population. The new regime retained most existing village and community leaders regardless of their attitudes toward Austria—Hungary, thus postponing definitive control in many rural areas.

## Creation of the Gendarmerie

Even as the Muslim-led resistance movement of 1878 was being suppressed by main units of the imperial army, Austro—Hungarian authorities moved to organize a permanent gendarmerie so that some regular troops could be withdrawn. On September 11, 1878, Filipović ordered the creation of a gendarmerie corps to establish order and to maintain local security in the occupied provinces.[17]

Filipović's directive envisioned a new Habsburg gendarmerie corps that embodied organizational principles of the defunct Ottoman-era zaptieh units but was led by well-trained cadres from the Dual Monarchy. In line with plans for civil administration in the provinces, Filipović adopted Ottoman territorial boundaries as the basis for deploying the gendarmes. His directive called for a force of 3,091 men, the strength attributed on paper to the defunct zaptieh units. Because of budgetary limitations, a force of this size was never achieved, but Filipović began by ordering that 200 gendarmes be brought from the monarchy to provide the leadership cadres of the new force. He expected other gendarmes to be recruited from the Christian and Muslim population within Bosnia. He especially hoped to bring many former zaptieh members (all Muslims) into the ranks.

In October 1878 Hauptmann Emanuel Cvjetićanin was appointed commander of the new corps. Under his command, cadres assembled in Sarajevo in late October to form the core of the new gendarmerie. They came from several different Habsburg military units: gendarmes from Croatia—Slavonia and from the Austrian half of the monarchy, *serežani* from the Croatian Military Frontier, and noncommissioned officers from the imperial army. In November Cvjetićanin formed seven "wings" of the corps and dispatched five, one to each of the regions of Bosnia: Travnik, Tuzla, Bihać, Banjaluka, and Sarajevo. Each wing was headquartered in the regional capital (each region bore the name of its capital city), with posts established in district capitals and other towns where appropriate. Fifty-four posts were initially established in late 1878 and manned by about 1,200 gendarmes; by the end of 1881, 142 posts had been established and the corps had grown to 1,900 men.

The two remaining wings were designated for service in Hercegovina, but cadres for these two units were held in Sarajevo until January 1879. Jovanović elected to put existing armed groups under the Habsburg imperial banner rather than organize a new gendarmerie built around cadres from the monarchy. Muslims were allowed to retain their zaptieh units under the command of a Muslim major, Mehmed Rašidović. The armed Serbian insurgents who had led the rebellion against Ottoman rule from 1875 to 1878 were also given the status of Habsburg gendarmes. Both outfits retained their old uniforms and their own weapons; the only outward symbol of their new status as imperial gendarmes was a yellow armband worn on the left arm. The situation was depicted aptly in the words of Fernand Braudel (who was speaking of an earlier era in this same region): "The brigand became the gendarmes' auxiliary."[18]

Jovanović's decision to temporize with the Serbian insurgents, even though it was overruled in a few months by higher authorities, had disastrous consequences for the monarchy. The Serbian forces had close ties to the local population in eastern Hercegovina, and they were well-armed, experienced mountain fighters with a strong tradition of independence. In bestowing upon them the mantle of imperial approval, Jovanović hoped to win their support for Austria–Hungary's new administration. This effort failed. The loyalty of the pandours was dubious, and the units remained for several years an obstacle to effective Habsburg control in eastern Hercegovina.

In late December 1878, the joint ministers of the monarchy ordered the consolidation of all gendarmes into a unified corps for Bosnia and Hercegovina, and several organizational changes followed. In January 1879 Oberst-Leutnant Josef Adžia was made the new commander of the corps, and three "inspection commanders," each with responsibility for two or more wings of the corps, were appointed. Hauptmann Paul Lukić was sent to Mostar to reorganize the gendarmerie in Hercegovina, and on January 15 the cadres of Wings 6 and 7 (sixty-five men in all) were dispatched from Sarajevo to Mostar and Trebinje to rebuild the gendarmerie on the Bosnian model. Lukić soon established twenty-five posts in Hercegovina.

The authorities concluded that it was politically unwise to dissolve the Serbian pandour corps in Hercegovina. They created the core of the new gendarmerie and hoped that the Serbian pandours would leave their own units and join the new force. But few did so, fearing the prospect of serving under commanders from the monarchy or under Muslim zaptieh commanders, who frequently received more favorable treatment. The pandour units thus existed in organizational limbo; they retained their leaders and their weapons but were neither recognized nor supported by the imperial authorities.

Although the deployment of cadres from the monarchy was virtually complete by the spring of 1879, the imperial authorities still faced a host of problems in building an effective, unified gendarmerie corps that was genuinely Bosnian in composition. The first units were truly ragtag bunches of soldiers. A single post was normally led by four or five experienced gendarmes from the monarchy, augmented by two or three noncommissioned officers from the imperial army. Other personnel usually included Muslim ex-zaptiehs, new Muslim recruits, and Christian recruits of Orthodox and Catholic faith. Cadres from the monarchy wore the uniforms of their units, the zaptiehs had their own uniforms, and other recruits wore civilian clothes. In 1879 corps commanders made mandatory a red cap for Christian recruits and a fez without a tassle for Muslims, thus further contributing to the heterogeneity of the gendarme units. As many as five different weapons systems were found at a single post in 1880, making it nearly impossible for the unit to bring effective firepower to bear on an opponent.

Makeshift uniforms and the shortage of weapons were symptoms of the malady of inadequate financial support for the gendarmes. The reasons for this failure were political. As mentioned previously, the initial expenses of the occupation had been met with the approval of the Delegations, but the authorities could not count on any further authorizations from those bodies. Since the resistance of 1878 had required greater expenditures than the army had anticipated, funds for further security operations were difficult to justify. Military leaders could not retain troop strength of the imperial army at desired levels, and authorities were forced to settle for a gendarmerie of about 2,000 men rather than Filipović's original goal of 3,091. Despite a number of reforms and adjustments, the gendarmes were for many years inadequately paid and poorly equipped. Little wonder that native Bosnians did not exactly rush to join the ranks of the fledgling organization.

The tangled web of interethnic relations further complicated the task of building a reliable corps. The Ottoman-era zaptieh units had been entirely Muslim in composition and had frequently helped Muslim landlords collect dues from their Christian peasants at the point of a gun. Many former zaptiehs at first joined the Habsburg gendarmes; over one thousand reported for duty in the first few months of the occupation. But few remained in the ranks for long. Since only cadres from the monarchy were permitted to command units and lead patrols, the former zaptiehs were relegated to an inferior status which they naturally resented. Furthermore, the monarchy's officials wanted the new corps to enforce the payment of peasant dues only when other legal avenues had been exhausted. This transformation of the role of the gendarmerie caused many Muslims to abandon the new units. Despite their predominance in the pool of desired recruits, Muslims were badly underrepresented in the ranks of the gendarmes. A survey from 1897 showed only 67 Muslims out of a total 2,310 men in the corps.[19]

Recruiting native gendarmes, regardless of their ethnic affiliation, proved to be much more difficult than the authorities had imagined. The conflicts mirror the contrasting expectations held by leaders of a disciplined military organization and by members of a society accustomed to sporadic voluntary service in locally organized bands. Former zaptieh and pandour unit members were accustomed neither to regular pay nor to day-to-day service in their units. They frequently spent their paychecks in one wild, drunken evening, then departed for several days as they normally had done under Ottoman rule. Recruits also expected to be stationed in their home towns as they had been in Ottoman times. They often simply walked away when told that they would need to attend a training camp that lasted two weeks. Some Bosnians refused to undress for the physical examination required of new recruits. The authorities often waived the examination rather than lose the service of volunteers, so disease and ill health persisted in the corps.

Bosnians found few incentives to join the imperial gendarmerie. They were not permitted to lead patrols, and they could not expect favorable treatment at the hands of commanders from the monarchy or local superiors of a different ethnic group. When the gendarme cadres were first dispatched, commanders in Mostar, Trebinje, Travnik, and Donja Tuzla undertook enforced recruitment, alienating the population and other potential recruits in those areas. (The recruits were released after a storm of protest.) The pay and benefits were far below those available to gendarmes in the monarchy proper, and compensation for Bosnian recruits was less than for soldiers drawn from the monarchy.

Because financial incentives were inadequate, most native recruits came from the lower classes, including many former serfs and urban vagabonds who had grievances against Muslim landlords. Some of the new recruits used their newly acquired status and weapons to intimidate their former oppressors. After some of the monarchy's original cadres had completed their tour in 1880, leadership in some units fell to Bosnian commanders. Complaints of unjust arrests and mistreatment increased, and Muslim landlords were especially vocal. Muslim landowners found it particularly galling to be abused by former serfs, whom they considered socially and religiously inferior. The gendarmes thus often contributed to ethnic and social conflict rather than reducing it, and the status of the imperial gendarmerie suffered accordingly.

The Habsburg gendarmerie in the occupied provinces never attracted a substantial percentage of native recruits. Figures from 1897 show that only 394 of 2,310 gendarmes (17 percent) were natives of Bosnia and Hercegovina. Over one third — 827 — came from Croatia and Slavonia, and men from these areas held many positions of command. Over half the corps was Roman Catholic. The figures show that Croats from the monarchy dominated the gendarmerie at least until the end of the nineteenth century. Their dominance in the gendarmes paralleled their leading role in civil administration. Many Croats were politically sympathetic to the occupation and had served in the imperial bureaucracy. And because they already knew the language, Croats were naturally attracted to service in the civil service and gendarmerie of Bosnia and Hercegovina.

The failure to develop an indigenous, multiethnic gendarmerie in Bosnia and Hercegovina must be judged one of the failures of Habsburg policy in its newly acquired colony. The gendarmerie remained an alien tool of imperial policy rather than becoming a self-policing force of local citizens.

## The Gendarmerie and the Uprising of 1881—82

The gendarmerie's primary mission was to end brigandage. Imperial army units had subdued major centers of resistance by the autumn of 1878, but armed bands still controlled many rural areas.[21] Brigandage constituted a threat to everyday security and a barrier to definitive government control. Undermanned and poorly equipped, the gendarmes had their work cut out for them.

In late 1878 the most conspicuous threat was in the Bihać region in northwestern Bosnia, close to the Bosnian border with the monarchy itself. Prior to the occupation, armed bands in that area had raided Habsburg outposts, rustled cattle from grazing areas near the border, and generally harassed communities in the Habsburg Military Frontier. After the occupation began, imperial forces could pursue these bandits into the Bosnian hills. Robbed of their safe haven, the brigands were subdued in 1879 by the gendarmes, and a number of bandit leaders were shot or captured.

Eastern Hercegovina posed another problem entirely. Serbian brigands in this area could strike with impunity and flee into the mountainous hinterlands or into Montenegro. By 1878 the Serbian pandours had nearly complete control of some areas and functioned almost as a civil administration. Furthermore, the government was concerned with thousands of predominantly Serbian refugees who had fled from eastern Hercegovina into Montenegro and Serbia during the unrest of 1875—78. Habsburg officials encouraged the refugees to return to eastern Hercegovina to prevent dangerous émigré communities from forming in neighboring lands. Faced with a stringent budget and a strong desire to avoid further armed conflict, Habsburg authorities elected to befriend the pandour leaders and leave them in place. In the fall of 1878, as we have seen, the government allowed Serbian pandours to form their own gendarmerie units under recognized resistance leaders.[22] Those who joined were put on Austrian state salary. When this decision was rescinded in early 1879 with the creation of a unified gendarmerie corps, officials took no steps to dissolve existing pandour units. Firmly committed to persuasion rather than coercion, Habsburg officials gave both salaries and sanction to Serbian leaders who were strident opponents of imperial rule.

From 1878 to 1881, the government continued to temporize in eastern Hercegovina. Hoping to calm peasant discontent, the government reduced some agrarian dues in the Gacko area from the conventional one-fifth to one-seventh or one-eighth of the crop.[23] Still, many peasants refused to pay any dues to their landlords in the early years of imperial rule. Serbian brigands terrorized Muslim landlords or their agents who ventured into the countryside to collect agrarian dues. In 1879, Serbian pandours participated in resistance to Austro–Hungarian census taking,[24] and over the next two years they refused to support government tax collection activities. Happy as they were to accept salaries from Habsburg officials, they continued their active resistance to any extension of new governmental functions in eastern Hercegovina.

Erratic resistance turned to full-scale rebellion in November 1881, when the government published a new army law that required military service by all males in the occupied provinces.[25] The law was intended both for the occupied lands and for the Dalmatian province of Krivošije, where Habsburg authorities had tried to implement conscription in 1869 but had been forced to back down because of a rebellion by the Serbian population. To pacify the Bosnian Muslims, the law included a provision that their religion and customs would be respected in the imperial armed forces. Nevertheless, rumors abounded in Hercegovina that Muslims would be forced to change their religion. Conscription was not completely new in Bosnia and Hercegovina; the Ottomans had introduced a measure in 1868 to compel service by all Muslim males. But it had never before been applied on a wide scale to the Christian population, and it aroused great hostility among the Serbs. Furthermore, it gave Serbs and Muslims a common cause against the Habsburg authorities, as both groups understood its importance as a symbol of the monarchy's permanent control over the occupied lands.

The army law, coming as it did at a time of weak Habsburg administrative control and an undermanned gendarmerie corps, caused the smoldering resentment to burst into the open. Serbian pandours massacred a gendarme patrol in early January 1882, and subsequently most Serbian pandours went into open rebellion. On January 10, the gendarme post at Ulog was surrounded and eventually captured by the Serbs.[26] In the next few days several other posts were overrun, and ambushes of gendarme patrols became a regular event into early February. Faced with a rebellion in Hercegovina and in neighboring Krivošije, the government mobilized a total of six divisions. In Hercegovina, the First, Eighteenth, and Forty-fourth Divisions were used in February and March to put down the rebellion. The imperial army units used local gendarmes as guides, and about 400 recruits were drawn from the Catholic population of Mostar and Stolac to aid in putting down the Serb and Muslim rebels. By May of 1882 the resistance had been put down by the army's regulars, although the problem of brigandage remained as before. In September of 1882 occupation forces were reduced to fifteen battalions, and the problem of controlling brigandage was once again left to the gendarmes.

After the rebellion of 1881–82, imperial officials reorganized the gendarmerie corps in 1883 and somewhat changed its mission.[27] Leadership was given over to the civilian district authorities rather than to the post commander, making the gendarmes more of an extension of local police authority than a subordinate organ of the imperial army. The reform called for the release of any pandour and zaptieh members not qualified for the gendarmes. Recruits to the gendarmerie had to meet with the approval of civilian district officials. But since the gendarmes functioned after 1883 mainly to soften potentially volatile collisions between rival ethnic groups they continued to be perceived as the military arm of Habsburg administrative control.

## Brigandage and the Streifcorps

The uprising of 1881–82 caused officials to make a firm commitment to eliminating brigandage. The conventional gendarmerie units were seen as too closely tied to their posts and dependent upon regular supplies to undertake major offensives against brigand bands. In November 1882 imperial authorities created a special branch of the gendarmerie called the Streifcorps, designed to provide a mobile rapid response capability.[28] The Streifcorps was a small elite group consisting of only 4 officers and 307 men drawn principally from volunteer noncommissioned officers and soldiers of the occupation forces. The troops were equipped with light weapons, commanded not to wear sabers, and trained for survival in the mountains of eastern Hercegovina. On November 28, 1882, the three Streifcorps "wings" began operations, one each in Bileća, Gacko, and Nevesinje.

To assist the Streifcorps, a string of thirty-seven gendarmerie posts was established to seal the border between Hercegovina and Montenegro. At first the Streifcorps had little success in locating brigands, but in April they chased down and shot a number of pandours carrying Austro–Hungarian arms. In March 1884 three more wings were added, doubling the size of the force. The Streifcorps' successes increased as they patrolled higher into the mountains, and in 1884 they occupied a number of outposts in the high grazing meadows of the mountains adjacent to Montenegro. In late 1883 and 1884 the Streifcorps reported a number of successful operations, and the threat of brigandage began to subside.

In March 1891 the Streifcorps was formally dissolved, its mission largely accomplished. From the monarchy's standpoint, the Streifcorps was a great success. Because of the Streifcorps operations, thousands of refugees returned from Montenegro to their homes in eastern Hercegovina in the years after 1882.

## Conclusion

Each of the three major Habsburg military units in Bosnia and Hercegovina accomplished its mission in the first decade of imperial occupation, although occasionally with more difficulty than had been originally anticipated. Main units of the imperial army destroyed the resistance movement of 1878 and put down the rebellion of 1881–82. The gendarmerie, with the aid of the Streifcorps auxiliary units, succeeded in eliminating brigandage by about 1890. In both instances the field commanders displayed flexibility and determination in making the necessary adjustments to fighting irregular guerrilla forces in mountainous terrain. We may conclude that the imperial military forces were successful in reducing the level of violent confrontation and making the occupied provinces secure for civil administration.

Why did the Bosnian resistance groups fail? Two reasons are apparent. First, the occupation denied brigands and rebels the haven of safety that they needed to regroup and rearm. Northwestern Bosnia offered no refuge for bandits, for they were surrounded on all sides by Habsburg-occupied territory. After 1882 both Serbia and Montenegro, traditional havens for Serbian rebels in the east, were forced by Austro–Hungarian diplomacy to abandon overt support for Serbian insurgents.[29] But second, and doubtless more important, was the localized nature of resistance to imperial rule. Insurgent forces, both in 1878 and in 1882, lacked a central organization to coordinate their actions and never had a cohesive plan for victory. Without a central leadership and a plan of action, Bosnian resistance leaders were too easily isolated and ultimately destroyed by the well-equipped, centrally led imperial forces.

Despite its military victories, the imperial army could not overcome the underlying antagonism between the Habsburg occupiers and the population of Bosnia and Hercegovina. Political opposition was not eliminated; rather, it was rechanneled from violent confrontation into nonviolent protest, from rural rebellion into urban-based political movements. The fundamental conflicts between occupied and occupier remained, symbolized by the persistent inability of the authorities to attract local recruits into the gendarmerie. By the early twentieth century the interests of Bosnian ethnic groups were represented not by brigand bands but by ethnic political leaders who presented their extensive demands to high imperial authorities.

## NOTES

1.    Leopold Neumann and Adalphe Plason, eds., *Recueil des traités et conventions conclus par l'Autriche avec les puissances étrangères* (Vienna, 1883), p. 778.

2.    A discussion of these conversions is found in John V. A. Fine, Jr., *The Bosnian Church: A New Interpretation* (Boulder, Colo, 1975), pp. 381–87.

3.    An overview of the deterioration of Ottoman authority is provided in Avdo Sućeska, "The Position of the Bosnian Moslems in the Ottoman State," *International Journal of Turkish Studies* 1, no. 2 (1980): 1–24.

4.    The classic work on the rebellion of 1875–78 is Milorad Ekmečić, *Ustanak u Bosni 1875–1878*, 2d ed. (Sarajevo, 1973).

5.    Berislav Gavranović, ed., *Bosna i Hercegovina u doba austrougarske okupacije 1878. godine* (Sarajevo, 1973), p. 78, Vasić to Andrássy, Sarajevo, February 15, 1878. The reports of the Austro–Hungarian consul in Sarajevo, Konrad Vasić, vividly portray the chaotic situation in 1878.

6.    Ibid., pp. 203–4, Vasić to Andrássy, July 15, 1878.

7.    For a history of the events in the summer of 1878, see Hamdija Kreševljaković, *Sarajevo u doba okupacije Bosne 1878.* (Sarajevo, 1937), pp. 3–60.

8.    Rade Petrović, "Pokret otpora protiv austrougarske okupacije 1878. godine u Bosni i Hercegovini," *Posebna izdanja akademija nauka i umjetnosti Bosne i Hercegovine* 43 (1979): 47–60. This volume is a collection of papers delivered at a conference in Sarajevo in October 1978 on the 100th anniversary of the Austro–Hungarian occupation.

9.    Eduard von Wertheimer, *Graf Julius Andrássy, sein Leben und seine Zeit*, vol. 3 (Stuttgart, 1910), p. 153.

10.    Vinzenz von Haardt, *Die Occupation Bosniens und der Hercegovina* (Vienna, 1878), pp. 20–26. My account of the military operations of 1878 is based on this work and on Alfons Falkner von Sonnenburg, *Über Operationen im Gebirgsland* (Munich, 1885).

11.    Mehmedalija Bojić, "Svrgavanje turske vlasti i odbrambeni rat Bosne i Hercegovine protiv austrougarske invazije 1878. godine," *Posebna izdanja akademija nauka i umjetnosti Bosne i Hercegovine* 43 (1979): 81–86.

12.    Robert Donia, "The Battle for Bosnia: Habsburg Military Strategy in 1878," *Posebna izdanja akademija nauka i umjetnosti Bosne i Hercegovine* 43 (1979):109–20. In this article I have summarized the operational adjustments made by imperial commanders. Further discussion of the invasion of 1878 may be found in Gunther Rothenberg, *The Army of Francis Joseph* (West Lafayette, Ind., 1976), pp. 101–2.

13.    Mustafa Imamović, *Pravni položaj i unutrašnjo-politički razvitak Bosne i Hercegovine od 1878. do 1914.* (Sarajevo, 1976), pp. 108–13.

14.    For example, Arhiv Bosne i Hercegovine, Sarajevo, Yugoslavia. 1087/Präsidial Register Bosnien und der Hercegovina, 1881, "Gesuch der Mohammedanern aus Sarajevo," October 18, 1881.

15.    See Robert Donia, *Islam under the Double Eagle: The Muslims of Bosnia and Hercegovina, 1878–1914* (Boulder, Colo., 1981), pp. 128–80.

16. Hamdija Kapidžic, *Hercegovački ustanak 1882. godine* (Sarajevo, 1973), pp. 10–11.

17. Bosnia and Hercegovina, Landesregierung, *Geschichte der Sicherheitstruppen und der öffentlichen Sicherheit in Bosnien und der Hercegovina 1878–1898* (Vienna, 1898), p. 5. This work is a thorough and remarkably critical history of the gendarmerie and Streifcorps. I have relied on it extensively in the account that follows.

18. Fernand Braudel, *The Mediterranean and the Mediterranean World in the Age of Philip II*, vol. 1, trans. Sian Reynolds (New York, 1966), p. 57.

19. Bosnia and Hercegovina, Landesregierung, *Geschichte der Sicherheitstruppen*, appendix A.

20. Ibid.

21. Ibid., pp. 22–25.

22. Kapidžic, *Hercegovački ustanak*, pp. 29–31.

23. Ibid., p. 34.

24. Ibid., pp. 50–51.

25. The rebellion of 1881–82 is best treated in Kapidžic, *Hercegovački ustanak*. For discussion of the military operations, see Rothenberg, *The Army of Francis Joseph*, pp. 103–4. Diplomatic developments are discussed in Charles Jelavich, "The Revolt in Bosnia–Hercegovina, 1881–2," *Slavonic and East European Review* 31 (1953): 420–36.

26. Bosnia and Hercegovina, Landesregierung, *Geschichte der Sicherheitstruppen*, p. 54.

27. Ibid., pp. 69–74.

28. Ibid., pp. 61–65.

29. L. S. Stavrianos, *The Balkans since 1453* (New York, 1965), pp. 515–16.

# VI
## Conclusions

Stephen Fischer—Galati

# POLITICAL, ECONOMIC, AND SOCIAL REPERCUSSIONS OF WARS AND REVOLUTIONS ON BALKAN SOCIETIES

Appraisals of the significance and repercussions of revolutions and wars of national liberation vary. They are a function of ideological positions and prejudices, of perceptions of the ultimate significance of the events.[1] In the case of the wars and revolutions of 1875–78 in the Balkans, the stress has been placed on the heroic efforts of the peoples of southeastern Europe in seeking and securing national independence, consolidating previous gains, or paving the way for the struggle for their full historic rights as nations and peoples. The wars and revolutions of 1875–78, according to this interpretation, secured the national independence of Serbia, Montenegro, and Romania, the autonomy of Bulgaria, as a prelude to the gaining of total independence, and the eventual restoration to Greece, Serbia, Bulgaria, and Romania of historic lands held or controlled by foreign powers. Thus, in the broadest sense, 1878 was only a stepping stone — albeit a crucial one — in the historic struggle of the peoples of southeastern Europe for total national liberation, integration, and independence.

In line with this argumentation, the emphasis of historians and other interpreters of the Balkan crisis of 1875–78 — and, for that matter, all the Balkan crises previous and subsequent to the Congress of Berlin — has been primarily on its political aspects. Indeed, the image of the Balkans as a powder keg, as the focus of political instability caused primarily by the insatiable and irrational ambitions of leaders committed to utopian nationalist goals, has been promoted by most interpreters of the history of southeastern Europe and of Europe in general.

While in most interpretations the problems attributed to Balkan nationalism are intertwined with those related to imperialism, imperialism itself has generally been regarded as a political phenomenon connected expressly with the concerns and destinies of the historic Eastern European empires of the Habsburgs, Romanovs, and Ottoman Turks. Moreover, the actions and policies of modern empires, such as the German, British, and French, related to the affairs of southeastern Europe in the years immediately preceding and, especially, following the events of 1875–78 have also been regarded primarily as manifestations of political imperialism. In short, the historical interpretations of the significance and repercussions of the wars and revolutions of that period have been largely political and, as such, rather simplistic.[2]

There are, of course, good reasons for emphasizing political factors, since wars of national liberation presuppose a total commitment of nations and their leaders to the attainment of the political goal of nationhood. Moreover, wars of national liberation are internally generated and must ultimately be realized by the efforts of the peoples involved. External factors must be regarded as auxiliary to the triumph of the nation. Nationalism is thus an irresistible, deep-rooted, historical force that must and will triumph despite all obstacles. External factors may influence the course of events but cannot determine the outcome of the historic struggle.

There are few variants of this script according to which the unification of the nation and the securing of independence have always been the primary historic goal of the peoples of southeastern Europe. That goal, moreover, cannot be divorced from the fulfillment of the corollary need for rewarding the victorious people and their leaders. An equitable distribution of the nation's wealth, a "democratic" resolution of the centuries-long struggles, is mandatory after liberation. Thus, there is nothing irrational or irresponsible in the efforts of the brave and determined leaders and masses of southeastern Europe first in assuming the risks and responsibilities inherent in the wars and revolutions of the years 1875–78 and second in furthering national goals after the successes recorded by their own efforts and sacrifices during those years.

There is some merit in this reading of the historical process, as nobody can deny the depth of the commitment of the peoples of southeastern Europe to the struggle for national liberation during those memorable years. The national cause was embraced by the overwhelming majority of the peoples and their leaders, and their sacrifices and determination played a major though not decisive role in the outcome and resolution of the conflict. Realistically, neither the bravery nor the determination of the peoples of the Balkans could ensure victory over the armed forces of the Ottoman Empire. External assistance was imperative and decisive, and the price of that assistance was high if for no other reason than that the assisting power itself had to make compromises with other powers fearful of possible changes that would affect their own interests in Eastern Europe. And since the assisting power also had interests of its own, which did not necessarily coincide with the interests of the fighters for national liberation, the fighters had to accept compromises and solutions that were not necessarily compatible with their own aspirations. In other words, neither the provisions of the Treaty of San Stefano nor the decisions of the Congress of Berlin fulfilled the aspirations of the peoples of southeastern Europe. The decisions were made by the Great Powers – granted, with some regard for the sacrifices of the Balkan peoples, but ultimately in terms of their own goals, concerns, and interests.

It may be argued that everybody, including the leaders of the peoples of the Balkans, was playing the game of *reculer pour mieux sauter* and that alterations in the decisions of the Congress of Berlin were both inevitable and even envisaged, if not actually promoted, by the main protagonists. But what matters in the last instance is that the agreement of Berlin took into account factors significantly different from those considered in previous resolutions of Balkan crises, whereas the goals of the revolutions and wars of liberation in the Balkans remained essentially uniform throughout the nineteenth century. In other words, the resolutions adopted at Berlin reflected the interests of both developed powers and less developed ones and incorporated the basic elements of both the old political and the new economic imperialism, and the underdeveloped nations of southeastern Europe generally failed to understand this fully. It seems fair to say that the Balkan peoples and their leaders had understanding of and experience with the political imperialism of the traditional historic empires – the Habsburg, the Russian, and the Ottoman – but were only marginally aware of the nature and dynamics of the imperialism of the advanced industrial powers in a rapidly changing outside world and, as a result, were unable to envisage fully or to cope with the repercussions – political, social, and economic – of the decisions reached at Berlin.

Transition from servitude to autonomy and from autonomy to independence poses problems for both leaders and subjects under the best of circumstances. Under the circumstances prevailing in 1878, such transitions were even more difficult and complex. Newly independent states such as Serbia and Romania had during the long years of autonomy developed mechanisms for the conduct of political affairs and had been able to prepare themselves for independence through both internal measures and external ties. They knew "how to play the game," but only to the extent allowable by their status as vassals of the Porte and their dependence on external assistance for the attainment of their ultimate political goal. Problems raised by the development of state bureaucracies and of military establishments, by agrarian reform, by incipient industrialization were coped with – if not necessarily resolved to the satisfaction of the masses – within the body politic of essentially underdeveloped agrarian societies and states. Political parties, reflecting the interests of the bureaucracies and of the landowning or commercial classes, existed and functioned primarily to secure their own interests. After the gaining of independence by Serbia and Romania, the basic patterns of governance and of sociopolitical organization remained essentially unchanged except for adaptations required by the growing economic penetration of forces identified with the interests of the new imperialism. The same was true of independent Greece. In Bulgaria, however, the problems related to autonomy were more complex largely because of the circumstances and the timing of its attainment.

Bulgaria did not enjoy a protracted period of adjustment to statehood as had its Balkan neighbors. If anything, it regressed from de facto independence to limited autonomy because of political considerations beyond the Bulgarians' control and therefore became the focal point of complex international rivalries. Autonomous Bulgaria had to grow up fast at a time when the simpler solutions of the preimperialist age were no longer fully applicable. And yet the Bulgarian leaders and people were endowed with an uncommon level of political and social idealism, with a genuine belief that they could enjoy the fruits of victory and set up a democratic society and soon-to-be independent state that would function well in the late 1870s and beyond. Democracy and independence proved, however, to be largely illusory, for adjustments imposed by *Realpolitik* became imperative shortly after the euphoria of success had died down. It is not that the Turnovo Constitution was ignored; rather, it had to be interpreted and applied in a manner contrary to the expectations, or at least hopes, of the Bulgarians. The bureaucratic state, with its military requirements, and problems of adjustment to the change in status from that of an Ottoman possession to that of an area coveted by European powers for economic and/or political reasons precluded the implementation of the romantic democratic notions embodied in the constitution. The realities of the developing state disappointed many and exacerbated tensions which had been sublimated by the common goal of national liberation from the Ottoman Empire.

Most of the tensions evident in Bulgaria, and for that matter also in Romania, Serbia, and Greece, were related to or caused by the changing economic, and corollary social, problems connected with imperialism and modernization.[3]

Investment and speculation by foreign capitalists in the Balkans antedated the crisis of 1875—78. Railroad construction was symbolic of the new economic imperialism, and it entailed significant loans from foreign banking houses and speculators. The exporting of agricultural products from the Balkans to foreign markets also gained momentum in the pre-1878 period, with resultant dislocation of landholding patterns and concentration of land in the hands of landlords and agricultural entrepreneurs to the detriment of the peasants' interests and well-being. However, these trends became universal and devastating to the interests of the masses only after the Congress of Berlin. Rapid railway building, the principal means of Western capitalist penetration into the Balkans, entailed ever greter indebtedness of Balkan governments to foreign capitalists. Similarly, the constant growth of agricultural exports changed the pattern from subsistence farming to commercial farming in most of the peninsula and from pastoral economies to agricultural economies everywhere. Furthermore, the development of a money economy, overpopulation, migration from village to town, dependence on usurious loans, and all the other accoutrements of modernization precipitated if not entirely caused by economic imperialism and related economic factors proved extremely unsettling for the peasantry and exacerbated internal social conflicts between the masses and the landowning classes, between town and village, between governments and subjects.[4]

The complexity and social and economic consequences of imperialism, industrialization, and modernization were perceived, and gradually at that, only by government leaders, individual entrepreneurs, landlords, merchants, bankers, and intellectuals in the years following the crisis of 1875–78. In general, the rulers chose to exploit the opportunities created by the changes that occurred after 1878 for the benefit of themselves and their supporters. The panacea for internal unrest and discord was the promotion of nationalist causes. The attainment of the seemingly utopian goal of total independence for all conationals within the borders of the enlarged national state became the rallying point of Balkan political leaders.[5]

The attainment of that goal, however, depended on external support, on exploitation of Great Power rivalries and imperialistic conflicts for the ostensible benefit of the nation. The array of international alliances and alignments affecting the Balkan states in the years immediately following the crisis of 1875–78 is well-known. But it is worth noting that even the pursuit of nationalist goals could not be divorced from changing economic and social realities, that the relatively simple and rudimentary exploitation of Great Power rivalries of earlier years became more and more intertwined with economic considerations, and that dependency on foreign allies and supporters became more extensive and affected all levels of society. The problems of underdeveloped independent states in the modern age were only vaguely understood in 1878 by the rulers of the Balkan peoples, but within less than a decade after the Congress of Berlin their understanding had improved markedly. And yet because their solutions invariably reverted to the utilization of the simple common denominator of nationalism, which could not in fact provide answers to the real problems of the imperialists or of those used by or connected with the power brokers of the post-Berlin era, the Balkan states were in constant turmoil as the nineteenth century progressed.

Thus, if the gaining of national independence, or autonomy, in 1878 represented a major victory for the Balkan nations, the consequences and repercussions of victory did not prove to be as beneficial as the Balkan peoples and leaders had envisaged. The rising expectations of nations were largely frustrated by the inevitable political, social, and economic problems that faced the rulers and subjects of the newly established states. Yet these problems were largely caused, and certainly aggravated, by the changing conditions of the industrial world and the corollary new imperialism and by the confrontation of the new imperialism and the historic imperialism of the Eastern European empires. The Balkan states were inevitably engulfed in the new problems and conflicting interests of the European powers and either perfected their techniques of adaptation or learned them in the years following the crisis of 1875–78. And this was done at the high cost of political and socioeconomic instability in the Balkans.

Whether the price was worth paying, whether payments were inevitable under the circumstances prevailing in the world in the second half of the nineteenth century, whether alternative solutions to those adopted in the Balkan states could have been perceived and applied are questions eliciting complex and controversial answers. In fact, we know the answers, and in all probability, none of the factors which led to the Balkan crisis of 1875–78, to the resolution of that crisis in 1878, and to the events of the years immediately following that resolution could have been altered by reasonable historical inquiry and analysis. What both poses problems and provides answers is the *raison d'état*.

## NOTES

1. An interesting and important interpretation of and commentary on these issues is contained in Viorica Moisuc and Ion Calafeteanu, *Afirmarea statelor naționale independențe unitare din centrul și sud-estul Europei, 1821–1923* (Bucharest, 1979).

2. A critical analysis of these issues is contained in Dimitrije Djordjevic and Stephen Fischer–Galati, *The Balkan Revolutionary Tradition* (New York, 1981), pp. xi–xv, 227–36.

3. Valuable data and interpretations are contained in John R. Lampe and Marvin R. Jackson, *Balkan Economic History, 1550–1950: From Imperial Borderlands to Developing Nations* (Bloomington, 1983), pp. 21–322.

4. In addition to the work by Lampe and Jackson, see the case study by Daniel Chirot, *Social Change in a Peripheral Society: The Creation of a Balkan Colony* (New York, 1976), pp. 89–137.

5. Standard arguments and new interpretations are to be found in Peter F. Sugar and Ivo J. Lederer, eds., *Nationalism in Eastern Europe* (Seattle, 1969).

# Biographical Index

Abbott
: German consul in Thessaloniki, killed in 1876.

Abdülaziz (1830–76)
: Sultan of the Ottoman Empire 1861–76.

Abdülhamid II (1842–1918)
: Sultan of the Ottoman Empire 1876–1907.

Abdul Kerim Pasha (1811–85)
: Commander in chief of the Turkish troops that defeated the Serbian army at Djunis.

Acton, John Emerick Edward Dalber, First Baron (1834–1902)
: British historian.

Aksakov, Ivan Sergeyevich (1823–86)
: Russian public figure and Slavophile, one of the founders and leaders of the Slavic Charitable Committee in Moscow.

Alesany
: Habsburg governor of Bukovina during the 1877–78 Russo–Turkish War.

Albrecht, Archduke (1817–95)
: Grandson of the Emperor Leopold II, inspector general of the imperial and royal army 1869–95.

Alexander II (1818–81)
: Russian tsar 1855–81.

Alexander III (1845–94)
: Russian tsar 1881–94.

Ali Pasha (c. 1741–1822)
: Turkish governor of Janina.

Alimpić, Ranko (1820–82)
: Serbian general, commander of Drina forces in both Turkish wars.

Allard
: French trader killed by bashi-bazouks in the Rhodopes in 1876.

Andrássy von Csík-Szentkirály und Kraszna Horka, Count Gyula (1823–90)
: Hungarian prime minister 1867–71, imperial and royal minister of foreign affairs 1871–79.

Antim I (Athanas Mihailov Chalakov) (1816–88)
: Bulgarian cleric, politician, and public figure; first exarch of the independent Bulgarian church 1872.

Bismarck, Otto von (1815–98)
> German politician, chancellor of Prussia and Germany 1862–90.

Blasiu, Octavian
> Romanian student at University of Vienna, chairman of the committee to support the Romanian cause in the 1877–78 Russo–Turkish War.

Blaznavac, Milivoje (1824–73)
> Serbian general, regent 1868–72, prime minister 1873.

Bobrikov, Nikolay Ivanovich (1839–1904)
> Colonel in 1877–78 Russo–Turkish War, later commander of St. Petersburg Guards Regiments and governor general of Finland.

Bodnărescu, Nicolae
> Romanian native of Bukovina, volunteer in the Plevna battles of the 1877–78 Russo–Turkish War.

Boerescu, Vasile (1830–83)
> Romanian jurist and political figure, minister of foreign affairs 1871–75, 1879–81.

Bolintineanu, Dimitrie (1819–72)
> Romanian writer, participant in the 1848 Revolution, minister during the reign of Prince Alexandru Ioan Cuza.

Bolliac, Cezar (1817–81)
> Romanian writer and publicist, participant in the 1848 Revolution and militant for the 1859 union of the principalities.

Borzea, Gheorghe (1851–91)
> Romanian native of Făgăraş, volunteer in the Romanian army in the 1877–78 Russo–Turkish War.

Botev, Hristo (1848–76)
> Bulgarian national revolutionary, revolutionary democrat, poet, and publicist.

Botzares, Markos (1778–1823)
> Suliote captain and fighter for the liberation and independence of Greece in 1821.

Branişte, Valeriu (1869–1928)
> Romanian publicist and political figure, fighter for political unity of the Romanian people.

Brătianu, Ion I. C. (1821–91)
> Romanian statesman, prime minister 1876–88.

Bucevschi, Dionisie
> Romanian veterinary surgeon, volunteer in the Romanian army in the 1877–78 Russo–Turkish War.

Bushati, Mehmed bey
> Albanian feudal ruler of the independent Shkodër pashalik 1757–75, whose heirs governed the region until 1832.

Căluţiu, Nicolae
  Transylvanian Romanian, volunteer in the Romanian army in the 1877—78 Russo—Turkish War.

Cantea, Ion
  Romanian from Bukovina, supporter of the Romanian cause in the 1877—78 Russo—Turkish War.

Carada, Eugeniu (1836—1910)
  Romanian economist and publicist, first director of Romania's National Bank.

Carlyle, Thomas (1805—81)
  British essayist, historian, and philosopher.

Carnavon, Henry Howard Molyneux Herbert, Fourth Earl of (1831—90)
  British statesman.

Carol I (1839—1914)
  Prince 1866—81, then king 1881—1914 of Romania, commander of the western army (Romanian and Russian) during the 1877—78 Russo—Turkish War.

Cartan, Gheorghe (1849—1911)
  Self-educated Romanian peasant from Transylvania, fighter for Romanian national liberation, volunteer in the Romanian army in the 1877—78 Russo—Turkish War.

Catargi, Colonel
  Volunteer in 1876 and commander of the Romanian detachment in Serbian service.

Catherine II (the Great) (1729—96)
  Russian empress from 1762, promoter of foreign policy of expansion.

Ceauşescu, Nicolae (b. 1918)
  General secretary of the Romanian Communist party 1965, president of the Socialist Republic of Romania 1974, commander in chief of the armed forces.

Cerchez, Mihail (1839—84)
  Colonel, later brigadier general, commander of the Romanian 2nd Infantry Division during the 1877—78 Russo—Turkish War.

Cezar, Constantin
  Inhabitant of Bucharest during the 1877—78 Russo—Turkish War.

Chernyayev, Mikhail Grigorevich (1828—98)
  Russian general, commander of Serbian armies in 1876.

Cherutti, Chelso (1845—?)
  Garibaldian who fought in Italy 1859—62, Spain 1873, and Hercegovina 1875—76, volunteer in the Serbian army in 1876.

Cîrţan, Gheorghe
  Transylvanian Romanian, volunteer in the Romanian army in the 1877—78 Russo—Turkish War.

Ciuceanu, Nicolae (1856–1937?)
Transylvanian Romanian volunteer in the Romanian army in the 1877–78 Russo–Turkish War.

Cosma, Partenie
Romanian political figure, deputy of Bihor County in the Budapest Chamber of Deputies.

Cozmei, Nicolae
Romanian priest in Bukovina, fighter for Romanian national liberation.

Cristea, Nicolae
Publisher of the newspaper *Telegraful român* during the 1877–78 Russo–Turkish War.

Cuza, Alexandru Ioan (1820–73)
Prince of the United Principalities of Moldavia and Wallachia 1859–66.

Damaskinos, Nicholaos (1834–1910)
Law professor and rector of Athens University.

Decazes, Charles Elie Louis, Duke of Glücksburg (1819–86)
French foreign minister.

de Gécz, Toma
Colonel in the Austrian army, commander of the recruiting center in Sibiu in 1877.

Dejenar, Ion
Transylvanian Romanian, volunteer in the Romanian army in the 1877–78 Russo–Turkish War.

Deligeorgis, Epameinondas (1829–79)
Greek politician and prime minister.

Densuşianu, Aron (1837–1900)
Romanian poet and literary critic.

Derby, Edward Henry Stanley, Fourteenth Earl of (1799–1869)
British prime minister 1858, 1866–68.

Derby, Maria Catharine, daughter of the Fifth Earl de la Warr (?)
Wife of the Fourteenth Earl of Derby.

Diamandi, Manole (1839–99)
Romanian merchant in Transylvania, chairman of Braşov committee to support the Romanian cause in the 1877–78 Russo–Turkish War.

Dibra, Ilias Pasha
Albanian landowner, Ottoman dignitary; president of the Central Council of the Albanian League 1878–81.

Dino, Abedin Pasha
Albanian landowner, Ottoman dignitary; one of the leaders of the Albanian League; minister of foreign affairs of the Ottoman Empire 1880.

Elliott, Sir Henry George (1817–1907)
    British diplomat.
Eminescu, Mihail (1850–89)
    Romanian poet, contributor to the Bucharest newspaper *Timpul*, activist for Romanian independence.
Enchev, Peter
    Bulgarian revolutionary, representative of the Bulgarian Central Charitable Society to the Serbian government.
Engels, Friedrich (1820–95)
    Political philosopher and military expert, served in the artillery brigade in Berlin in 1841; associate of Karl Marx and one of the founders of Marxism.
Eötvös, Károly (1842–1916)
    Hungarian politician and writer.
Fadayev, Rostislav Andreyevich (1824–83)
    Russian major general, military writer, and publicist.
Ferid Pasha
    Albanian, Ottoman dignitary, grand vizier 1904–8.
Fialla, Ludovic (1832–1911)
    Romanian surgeon, director of the Red Cross hospitals and of the "Independence" hospital in Turnu Măgurele during the 1877–78 Russo–Turkish War.
Filaretos, George (1843–1929)
    Greek journalist, politician, and democrat.
Flondor, George
    Romanian political figure in Bukovina.
Florescu, Ion Emanoil (1819–93)
    Romanian general and statesman.
Fongaci, Ion
    Native of Bukovina, volunteer in the Romanian army in the 1877–78 Russo–Turkish War.
Frasheri, Abdul (1839–92)
    Albanian deputy to the Ottoman parliament, leader of the Albanian League 1878–81.
Frasheri, Sami (1850–1904)
    Albanian scientist, writer, Ottoman civil servant, ideologist of the Albanian national-liberation movement.
Freeman, Edward Augustus (1823–92)
    British historian.
Froude, James Anthony (1818–94)
    British historian.

Fuad Pasha
  Commander of Turkish rearguard during Suleiman's attempted retreat to Philippopolis.
Gaillard de Ferry
  French vice-consul in Plovdiv 1868–75.
Garašanin, Ilija (1812–74)
  Serbian politician of the Constitution Defender era and foreign minister.
Garibaldi, Giuseppe (1807–98)
  Guerrilla general, fighter for the unification and independence of Italy and other states.
George I (Christian William Ferdinand Adolphus George) (1845–1913)
  Prince of Denmark to 1863, then king of Greece.
Gherghel, Ilie
  Native of Bukovina, volunteer in the Romanian army in the 1877–78 Russo–Turkish War.
Ghica, Ioan Gr. (1829–91)
  Romanian general and political figure, diplomatic agent at Constantinople and then at St. Petersburg 1878–81.
Giurgiuveanu, Alecu (1857–?)
  Native of Bukovina, volunteer in the Romanian army in the 1877–78 Russo–Turkish War.
Gjiritli, Mustapha Pasha (?–1891)
  Albanian, Ottoman dignitary, consecutively governor of the eyalets of Shkodër, Janina, Bosnia, Tripoli, Yemen, Baghdad, etc.
Gladstone, William Edward (1809–98)
  British statesman, prime minister 1868–74, 1880–85, 1886, 1892–94.
Gorchakov, Prince Aleksandr Mikhailovich (1798–1883)
  Russian political figure; minister of foreign affairs 1856–82, chancellor 1866–82.
Gouzon
  French trader killed by bashi-bazouks in the Rhodopes in 1876.
Grama, Vincenţiu (1852–1920)
  Transylvanian volunteer in the Romanian army in the 1877–78 Russo–Turkish War.
Grancea, Nicolae (1851–91)
  Transylvanian volunteer in the Romanian army in the 1877–78 Russo–Turkish War.
Green, John Richard (1837–83)
  British historian.
Grigorcea, Olga
  Romanian native of Bukovina, supporter of the Romanian cause in the 1877–78 Russo–Turkish War.

Grigorescu, Nicolae (1837–1907)

Romanian painter, produced numerous sketches during the 1877–78 War of Independence.

Groza, Moise (1844–1919)

Captain on the staff of the Romanian 14th Infantry Division in the 1877–78 Russo–Turkish War.

Grujić, Jevrem (1827–95)

Serbian politician, leader of the "1858 liberals."

Grujić, Sava (1840–1913)

Serbian minister of war 1876–78, later several times prime minister of Serbia.

Gruncharov, Sider Kostadinov (1839–76)

Leader of a detachment of Bulgarian volunteers; perished in battle near Sofia during the Serbo–Turkish War.

Guran, Nicolae A. (1824–88)

Austrian lieutenant field marshal of Romanian origin, supporter of the struggle for Romanian liberation from Habsburg domination.

Gurko, Count Ossip Vladimirovich (1828–1901)

Russian general; commander of advance guard June–July 1877, commander of Imperial Guard and Ninth Corps December 1877–January 1878.

Gusini, Ali Pasha

Albanian landowner, member of the leadership of the Albanian League 1878–81.

Hedeman

Danish army captain, joined the Russian field army on the Balkan front during the 1877–78 Russo–Turkish War.

Henţia, Sava (1848–1904)

Romanian painter who accompanied Romanian troops in the 1877–78 Russo–Turkish War and produced numerous paintings with scenes from the front.

Henţiescu, Adam (1856–1925)

Transylvanian volunteer, corporal in the Romanian army in the 1877–78 Russo–Turkish War.

Herbert, William V.

German-born British historian, volunteer officer in the Ottoman army during the 1877–78 Russo–Turkish War.

Hitov, Panayot Ivanov (1830–1918)

Head of a large volunteer band in the Serbo–Turkish War of 1876; national representative in liberated Bulgaria after 1878.

Hitrovo, M. A.
> Russian diplomat, chief of the diplomatic service of the Danubian army 1878–79.

Hnidei, Emilian
> Native of Bukovina, volunteer in the Romanian army in the 1877–78 Russo–Turkish War.

Hobart Pasha (Augustus Charles Hobart Hampden) (1822–86)
> English captain and Turkish admiral, commander of the Ottoman fleet.

Hodoş, Iosif (1830–80)
> Romanian writer and political figure in Transylvania, one of the founders of the Romanian Academy in 1866.

Horvatović, Djura (1835–95)
> Army officer, trained in Habsburg army, later joined Serbian military; colonel, later general, commander in eastern Serbia in 1876; Serbian representative in St. Petersburg 1885, minister of war 1886–87.

Hurmuzachi, Eufrosina
> Romanian native of Bukovina, one of the founders of district committees to aid wounded Romanian soldiers in the 1877–78 Russo–Turkish War.

Hurmuzachi, Natalia
> Romanian native of Bukovina, one of the founders of district committees to aid wounded Romanian soldiers in the 1877–78 Russo–Turkish War.

Hurmuzachi, Nicolae (1826–1909)
> Romanian writer, native of Bukovina.

Ignat, Nichita (1829–99)
> Major in the Austrian army until 1866; from 1868 on in the Romanian army; staff officer in the 1877–78 Russo–Turkish War.

Ignatyev, Count Nikolay Pavlovich (1832–1908)
> Pan-Slavist, Russian ambassador to the Sublime Porte 1864–77.

Ilieşu, Maria
> Romanian native of Transylvania, chairwoman of Cluj committee to support the Romanian cause in the 1877–78 Russo–Turkish War.

Iorga, Nicolae (1871–1940)
> Romanian historian, writer, publicist, and political figure.

Ischomachos, Konstantinos
> Macedonian officer of the Greek army, chief military commander in the revolts of 1878.

Isidor
> Metropolitan of St. Petersburg.

Lapedatu, I. Al. (1844–78)
>Romanian writer and fighter for Romanian rights in Transylvania.

Layard, Sir Austen Henry (1817–94)
>British author and diplomat, ambassador in Constantinople 1877–80.

Le Gay, Leandre (1833–87)
>French diplomat, vice-consul in Sofia 1874–77.

Lešjanin, Milojko (1830–96)
>Serbian general, commander of the Timok army in both Turkish wars.

Levski, Vasil Ivanov (1837–73)
>Bulgarian nationalist revolutionary and revolutionary democrat.

Logothetis, Alexandros
>Greek diplomat, consul general at Chania during the revolt of 1878.

Logothetis, Petros
>Greek diplomat, consul at Monastir during the events of 1877–78, subsequently at Thessaloniki.

Măcelariu, Ilie (1822–91)
>Romanian political figure in Transylvania, fighter for Romanian national liberty, and supporter of Romanian cause in the 1877–78 Russo–Turkish War.

Măcelariu, Iudita
>Romanian fighter for independence, native of Transylvania, chairman of the Sibiu committee to aid wounded Romanian soldiers in the 1877–78 Russo–Turkish War.

Makarov, Stepan Ossipovitch (1848–1904)
>Russian naval officer, later vice-admiral; commander of the Russian 1st Squadron in the Pacific 1904, died at Port Arthur.

Makedonski, Hristo Nikolov
>Bulgarian revolutionary, former haiduk, and author of interesting memoirs.

Marcus, Jelena
>Volunteer in western Serbia 1876.

Marinović, Jovan (1821–93)
>Serbian prime minister 1873–74, leader of conservatives.

Markov, Ilyo (1805–98)
>Bulgarian fighter for national freedom, leader of a detachment.

Markovich, Glisha
>Participant in the military actions of 1876 and author of valuable memoirs of the Serbo–Turkish War.

Marković, Jevrem (?–1878)
>Serbian officer, hero of 1877–78 Russo–Turkish War, shot as conspirator in Topola uprising; brother of Svetozar.

Marković, Svetozar (1846–75)
> Serbian socialist.

Maxim, Victoria
> Romanian native of the Banat, supporter of the Romanian cause in the 1877–78 Russo–Turkish War.

Mazovsky, Isaya
> Bulgarian revolutionary, champion of a united front of Bulgarians and Albanians against Ottoman domination 1876–88.

Medvedovsky, Colonel
> Russian colonel commanding volunteer detachments during the war.

Mehmed Ali Pasha (Karl Detroit) (1827–78)
> Ottoman field marshal, delegate to the Berlin Congress in 1878; commander of abortive Plevna relief expedition 1878; assassinated by Albanians.

Melas, Michael (1833–97)
> Influential Greek businessman of Epirote descent, member of the Greek Central Committee in 1877–78.

Michael the Brave (1558–1601)
> Prince of Wallachia 1593–1601, of Transylvania 1599–1600, and of Moldavia 1600; first ruler of the united Romanian principalities.

Michos, Artemis N. (1803–77)
> Greek lieutenant general.

Midhat Pasha (1822–84)
> Turkish statesman and reformer.

Milojević, Miloš (1840–1902)
> Serbian history professor and writer, ardent nationalist, commander of a volunteer unit 1876.

Miloradovich, Aleksandr Mikhailovich
> Russian officer of Serbian origin, commander of volunteer units.

Milyutin, Count Dimitry Alekseyevich (1816–1912)
> Russian general, minister of war, and army reformer.

Mirsky, Prince
> Russian general, commander of assault column at battle of Shipka Pass, January 1878.

Mišić, Živojin (1855–1921)
> Serbian army officer, later general and voivode, deputy chief of the general staff of the Serbian army in 1914.

Mišković, Gruja (1825–80)
> Serbian lieutenant colonel, commander of volunteers on the western front 1876.

Mollinary von Monte Pastello, Baron Anton (1820–1904)
> Austro–Hungarian field marshal.

Morariu, Andrievici Silvestru (1818–95)
   Vicar general 1877–79 and metropolitan bishop of Bukovina's Metropolitan church, material supporter of the Romanian cause in the 1877–78 Russo–Turkish War.
Moulin
   French consul in Thessaloniki, killed in 1876.
Nabotkov, P.
   Member of the leadership of the Bulgarian Central Charitable Society.
Nagy, Stefan
   Judge in Orşova in 1877.
Napoleon III (Louis-Napoléon) (1808–73)
   Emperor of the French 1852–71.
Nedim Pasha, Mahmud
   Ottoman grand vizier 1875–76.
Nelidov, Aleksander Ivanovich (1835–1910)
   Russian diplomat.
Nicholaos (1840–82)
   Bishop of Kitros, revolutionary leader in the Pieria region of Macedonia.
Nicholas (1841–1921)
   Prince 1860–1910, then king 1910–19 of Montenegro.
Nikolay Nikolayevich (1856–1929)
   Russian grand duke, brother of the tsar and commander in chief of the Russian armies in the 1877–78 Russo–Turkish War.
Nikolić, Tihomilj (1882–1936)
   Serbian minister of war 1876.
Nikolov, Raicho (1840–85)
   Bulgarian revolutionary, later an officer in the Bulgarian army; killed in the unification of the Bulgarian principality with Eastern Rumelia.
Novikov, Eugen Petrovich (1826–1903)
   Russian ambassador in Vienna 1870–80.
Obrenović, Michael (1823–68)
   Prince of Serbia 1839–42, 1860–68.
Obrenović, Milan (1854–1901)
   Prince of Serbia 1868–89.
Obrenović, Miloš (1780–1860)
   Prince of Serbia 1815–39, 1858–60.
Obrenović, Natalija, née Keško (1859–1941)
   Princess and queen of Serbia 1875–89.
Obruchev, Nikolay Nikolayevich (1830–1904)
   Russian general, assistant to Dimitry Milyutin, author of Russia's 1877 war plan.

Osman Nuri Pasha (1832?/1837–1900)
Turkish marshal, commander of Vidin army 1876, leader of defense of Plevna 1877.

Palmerston, Henry John Temple, Third Viscount (1784–1865)
British statesman and prime minister 1855–58.

Pandele, Ioan
Transylvanian Romanian, supporter of Romanian cause in 1877–78 Russo–Turkish War.

Pangalos, Nikolas
Greek revolutionary.

Paparigopoulos, Konstantinos (1815–91)
Athens University professor, author of the monumental six-volume history of the Greek nation, president of Central Committee of Greek revolutionary organization Ethniki Amyna.

Parensov, Pyotr Dimitryevich (1843–1914)
Russian army officer; major general 1878, general minister of war of Bulgaria May 20, 1878–March 22, 1880.

Paschalis, Leonidas
Macedonian Greek patriot, lawyer, member of the Central Committee of the Greek revolutionary organization 1877–78.

Pashko, Vasa
Albanian Christian politician and writer; Ottoman dignitary, governor of Lebanon.

Pavlović, Alexander Nikolaević
Bulgarian revolutionary.

Paznic, Vasile
Romanian patriot, native of Bukovina, supporter of Bukovinan union with Romania.

Pazvanoglu, Osman (1758–1807)
Pasha of Vidin.

Peev, Todor Stoianov (1842–1904)
Bulgarian revolutionary, member of the Bulgarian Revolutionary Central Committee in Bucharest, member of the Bulgarian Academy of Sciences.

Petricu, Ioan
Romanian patriot from Transylvania, supporter of the Romanian cause in the 1877–78 Russo–Turkish War.

Petrino, Eufrosina
Romanian native of Bukovina, supporter of the Romanian cause in the 1877–78 Russo–Turkish War.

Radetzky, Joseph (1766–1858)

Austrian field marshal, hero in 1848–49 and governor of Lombardy 1849–57.

Rakovski, Georgi Sava (1821–67)

Bulgarian nationalist, revolutionary, democrat, writer, publicist, historian, and ethnographer.

Reitern, Count Mikhail Kristoforovich (1820–90)

Russian statesman, minister of financial affairs 1862–78.

Renieris, Markos (1815–97)

Governor of the National Bank of Greece, professor of law, revolutionary, Supreme Court justice.

Ristić, Jovan (1831–99)

Serbian foreign minister and prime minister 1875–80, leader of "1869 liberals."

Roman, Veturia

Chairwoman of the Oradea committee to support the Romanian cause in the 1877–78 Russo–Turkish War.

Roman, Visarion (?–1885)

Romanian economist and editor in Transylvania, director of the Albina Bank, active supporter of the Romanian cause during the 1877–78 Russo–Turkish War.

Rosetti, A. Constantin (1816–85)

Romanian publicist and political figure, participant in the 1848 Romanian Revolution and fighter for the union of the principalities in 1859 and the attainment of Romanian independence in 1877–78.

Rotaru, Iulia (1848–1907)

Romanian native of the Banat, supporter of the Romanian cause 1877–78 Russo–Turkish War.

Rotaru, Pavel

Transylvanian newspaperman, active supporter of the Romanian cause in the 1877–78 Russo–Turkish War.

Safvet Pasha, Mehmed (1815–83)

Turkish statesman, minister for foreign affairs 1876–77.

Saguna, Andrei (1809–73)

Orthodox bishop of the Romanians in Transylvania and Hungary, one of the leaders of the Transylvanian Romanians' fight for national liberation.

Salisbury, Robert Arthur Talbot Gascoyne-Cecil, Third Marquess of (1830–1903)

British statesman, prime minister 1885–86, 1886–92, 1895–1902.

Săvescu, Emilian
   Romanian native of Bukovina, volunteer in the Romanian army in the 1877—78 Russo—Turkish War.
Săvescu, George
   Romanian native of Bukovina, volunteer in the Romanian army in the 1877—78 Russo—Turkish War.
Schönfeld, Baron Anton von (1827—98)
   Austro—Hungarian general staff officer.
Schuyler, Eugene (1840—90)
   American political figure, consul in Constantinople 1875—76.
Sherif Bey
   Albanian politician 1875—81.
Shuvalov, Count Peter Andreyevich (1827—89)
   Russian diplomat.
Sireteanu, Partenie
   Romanian native of Bukovina, volunteer in the Romanian army in the 1877—78 Russo—Turkish War.
Skanderbeg (George Kastrioti) (1405—68)
   Albanian national hero, leader of the Albanian struggle against the Ottoman invaders.
Skouloudis, Stefanos (1838—1928)
   Greek politician of Cretan origin, prime minister 1915.
Slăniceanu, Gheorghe (1835—85)
   Romanian general, war minister, chief of staff of the Romanian army of operations before Plevna, commander of detachment during the siege of Rahova in the 1877—78 Russo—Turkish War.
Slavići, Ioan (1848—1925)
   Romanian writer, native of the Banat, supporter of the liberty of Transylvanian Romanians.
Sly
   French citizen killed by bashi-bazouks in the Rhodopes in 1876.
Sokolov, Simo (1848—1918)
   Bulgarian revolutionary, participant in the Serbo—Turkish War.
Soutsos, Alexandros Skarlatos (1808—87)
   Greek major general.
Stambolov, Stefan Nikolov (1854—95)
   Bulgarian revolutionary and political activist, prime minister 1887—94.
Stuart, Baron Dimitry Fedorovich
   Russian diplomat, consul general at Bucharest, signer of the Russo—Romanian Convention of April 16, 1877.
Stubbs, William (1825—1901)
   British historian and bishop of Oxford.

Sturza, Emilia
Romanian native of the Banat, supporter of the Romanian cause in the 1877—78 Russo—Turkish War.
Suvorov,Aleksandr Vasilyevich, Prince (1730—1800)
General of the Russian army.
Széll, Kálmán (1845—1915)
Austro—Hungarian finance minister 1875—78, prime minister 1899—1903.
Tahsini, Hasan (1832—84)
Albanian scientist, rector of the first Ottoman university, activist of the Albanian national movement.
Techarov, Anton T.
Secretary to the Moscow Slavic Committee.
Tegetthoff, Baron Wilhelm (1827—71)
Austrian naval officer, commander of fleet in 1866, subsequently commander in chief.
Tisza von Borosjenő und Szeged,Kálmán (1830—1902)
Revolutionary in 1848—49, later leader of the Hungarian Liberal party and prime minister 1875—90.
Toptani, Gani Bey
Albanian politician 1875—78.
Toptani, Suleiman Pasha
Albanian landowner, Ottoman dignitary 1878—81.
Toshka, Ali Bey
Albanian politician 1878—81.
Totleben, Franz Ivanovich (1818—84)
Russian general who engineered defense of Sebastopol 1854—56, commander of Russian army in the Balkans 1877—78.
Totyo, Filip (1830—1907)
Bulgarian revolutionary and leader of revolutionary detachments; headed a volunteer detachment during the Serbo—Turkish War of 1876.
Trikoupis, Charilaos (1832—96)
Greek politician, many times prime minister.
Tsankov, Dragan Kiryakov (1828—1911)
Bulgarian statesman, leader of the Liberal party, prime minister 1880 and 1883—84.
Tsankov, Kiryak Antonov (1847—1903)
Bulgarian revolutionary, president of the Bulgarian Central Charitable Society.
Tseretelev, Prince Alexey Nikolayevich (1848—83)
Russian diplomat and military writer.

Wolf, Stefan
> Headmaster of the secondary school in Chernowitz in 1877.

Yonin, Vladimir Semyonovich (1837–?)
> Russian Slavophile who assisted in the creation of the Bulgarian Central Charitable Society.

Yusuf Ali Bey
> Albanian publicist and politician 1878–81.

Zach, František Aleksandar (1807–92)
> Czech general in Serbian service 1850–78.

Zagorski, S.
> Member of the leadership of the Bulgarian Central Charitable Society.

Zaimis, Thrasyvoulos (1825–80)
> Greek politician and prime minister.

Zhivkov, Georgi Atanasov (1844–99)
> Bulgarian minister of education 1887–94.

Zotta, Iancu (1840–96)
> Romanian political figure in Bukovina.

Zotta, Victoria
> Romanian native of Bukovina, supporter of the Romanian cause in the 1877–78 Russo–Turkish War.

Zymvrakakis, Charalambos (1812–80)
> Greek army officer of Cretan origin, minister of war 1877.